Physical Education Handbook

Life is a series of games—games of finding answers, finding amusement, persuading people, winning friends, raising families, and performing rituals. Some persons relish the game of life and enjoy all the sub-games to the hilt. Others play them grimly, with their eyes fixed on the scoreboard, too much concerned with staying ahead to enjoy the game.

Don Robinson (Phi Delta Kappan)

DON CASH SEATON
*Former Chairman, Department of Health,
Physical Education, and Recreation, University of Kentucky*

IRENE A. CLAYTON
*Former Director of Physical Education,
Bryn Mawr College*

HOWARD C. LEIBEE
*Professor of Physical Education for Men,
The University of Michigan*

LLOYD L. MESSERSMITH
*Chairman, Health and Physical Education Department,
Southern Methodist University*

FIFTH EDITION

Physical
Education
Handbook

Prentice-Hall, Inc., Englewood Cliffs, New Jersey

In play there are two pleasures for your choosing,
The one is winning, the other losing.

Byron

Seaton, Clayton, Leibee, and Messersmith

PHYSICAL EDUCATION HANDBOOK
Fifth Edition

© 1951, 1954, 1959, 1965, 1969 by PRENTICE-HALL, INC., Englewood Cliffs, N.J.

C—13—667469—0, P—13—667451—8

LIBRARY OF CONGRESS CATALOG CARD NUMBER: 78–76298

Printed in the United States of America
Current printing (last digit):
15 14 13 12 11 10 9 8 7 6 5 4 3 2 1

PRENTICE-HALL INTERNATIONAL, INC., *London*
PRENTICE-HALL OF AUSTRALIA, PTY. LTD., *Sydney*
PRENTICE-HALL OF CANADA, LTD., *Toronto*
PRENTICE-HALL OF INDIA PRIVATE LTD., *New Delhi*
PRENTICE-HALL OF JAPAN, INC., *Tokyo*

Preface

FIRST EDITION

This *Handbook* was prepared and published in 1951, the first textbook in the field designed especially for students in service (required) programs of physical education. The authors believed that there was a need for a basic text for beginners which would include a large variety of sports expertly described. Most sports and activities found in modern programs were selected. A brief history, nature of the game, selection and care of equipment, basic rules, techniques and fundamentals, strategy, safety hints, playing courtesies, terminology, and selected references were included for each sport and activity.

The authors also felt that far too many students completed their requirement in physical education without an appreciation for and an understanding of the cultural, healthful, and recreational values of the program. The first three chapters were presented to help the student develop this understanding and an accepted philosophy of physical education and recreation.

It was most gratifying to find that the *Handbook* was also used extensively by physical education majors, classroom teachers, high school students, and youngsters who wish to learn "on their own."

SECOND EDITION

The second edition was based upon a thorough survey of the opinions of approximately 315 instructors (representing 63 institutions) who had used the *Handbook*. As a result of this survey, a chapter on fundamental activities was included, and the following sports added: lacrosse (for men), shuffleboard, skiing, and table tennis. All the chapters were revised, new illustrations added, and a new sample test for each sport provided in the appendix.

THIRD EDITION

In the third edition, the authors revised several chapters, especially those in which changes in the rules or accepted techniques had taken place. The basketball chapter was divided into men's and women's sections, and horsemanship, spincasting, and skin and scuba diving were added. The selected references were revised, and many playing courtesies, hints, and safety suggestions added. A glossary of terms was included for each sport and the tests in the appendix rewritten. An effort was made to include more helpful illustrations and to make the material in general more attractive and useful to the student.

The authors agreed that, in addition to promoting physical fitness and sports efficiency, physical education has academic and cultural values because of the emphasis that physical education places upon the basic responsibility of the individual.

FOURTH EDITION

The unprecedented success of the *Handbook* has made it necessary to revise and expand its content for the fourth time. Recent emphasis upon physical fitness has prompted the adding of Chapter 5, "Physical Fitness and Appraisal," which should serve all students who wish to improve their fitness. The popular form of exercises called isometrics is included in this chapter.

The popularity of squash racquets prompted the addition of this sport. Skish was added to the angling chapter and ballroom dance to the dance chapter. Women's gymnastics was added to the chapter on gymnastics. The chapter on track and field was expanded to include relays, while the Dolphin Stroke was added to the swimming chapter.

All the other chapters have been revised in response to the many users who were kind enough to send us their criticisms and suggestions.

The questions in the appendix were dropped because most instructors would rather have them carried in the *Teacher's Guide*. They are revised and published there, and it is hoped that all instructors using the *Handbook* will secure a copy.

Again, the rules have been brought up to date; new, more helpful illustrations added; and sports skills elucidated when found necessary.

The authors trust that all users will find this edition even more helpful than those of the past and that its use will make physical education courses more purposeful, give incentive to the students, and add to the academic respectability of physical education.

FIFTH EDITION

The continued success of the *Handbook* prompted the fifth edition. Included in the edition are many suggestions made by users of the fourth edition, and for these the authors are most grateful. The contents of each chapter have been expanded by the addition of materials pertinent to the history, nature of the activity, techniques and fundamentals, equipment, safety, helpful hints, and strategy of the various sports. The rules have been brought up to date and the officials necessary for each sport are now included. In addition, new illustrations have replaced many of those used in the fourth edition and more illustrations have been included in an effort to make the contents more meaningful.

Considerable revision has been made in the first three chapters, and the chapter on physical fitness has been completely revised to make it more individualistic and valuable. The rapid growth and popularity of judo prompted a new chapter devoted to this phase of the combative sports. Additional new materials include charts of competitive diving scoring, artificial respiration, first aid, the conducting of tournaments, weight training systems, and programs for participants in athletics; also included are new court and field diagrams.

Teachers and physical education majors will be pleased to learn that the *Teacher's Guide* has been completely revised to adjust to this edition. In the guide they will find valuable teaching plans, visual aids, and testing materials for all chapters.

Acknowledgments

The authors wish to acknowledge their indebtedness to those who gave freely of their time and generously shared their knowledge in the writing of this textbook.

The chapter on physical fitness, appraisal and programming, was completely revised by Dr. Donald C. Stolberg, a professor and assistant division director at the University of Toledo.

Dr. Dennis Lambert of the University of Vermont completely revised the skiing chapter.

The new chapter on judo was prepared by Dr. John Nicholas Pyecha, instructor in judo at the University of North Carolina, and research director of the Armed Forces Judo Association.

Don Cash Seaton wishes to express appreciation to:

Dr. Milo G. Karsner, associate professor of physical education, Western Kentucky University, formerly of the University of Kentucky, for preparing the original materials from which the archery, badminton, and volleyball chapters were adapted.

Miss Geraldine Polvino, assistant professor at Eastern Kentucky University, for reviewing the chapter on volleyball and making many pertinent suggestions.

Dr. Warren Boring, professor, California State College at Long Beach, for revising and updating the chapter on wrestling which was originally prepared by the late Henry A. Stone of the University of California.

Scott D. Breckinridge, Jr., for preparing the original fencing material which Abdelmonem Rizk, University of Kentucky, who learned to fence in Egypt and competed throughout Europe, revised for the fifth edition.

The late H. H. Thompson from the Agricultural Extension Division, University of Kentucky, for preparing the original angling material which has been ably revised by Dr. John Payne, associate professor, Virginia Polytechnic Institute. Dr. Payne also revised the chapter on archery.

Irene A. Clayton wishes to express her appreciation to:

Miss Suzanne R. Cross, former president of the United States Field Hockey Association and former member of several United States touring teams, as well as United States teams and reserve, for her excellent presentation of the materials on field hockey. Miss Cross was also helpful in solving the problems involved in photographing subjects portraying skills for women. In addition, she has compiled the material on riding. Miss Julie Baird and Mr. Kob Ryen, assistant professor of animal husbandry, University of Kentucky, made helpful suggestions for the horsemanship chapter.

Acknowledgment is made to Mrs. Ann Carter Mason for her reorganization of the material on modern dance and to Miss Gloria K. Schmidt for her contributions to the revision of the section on relaxation.

To Miss Sharon Ann Plowman for the up-dated material on volleyball for women, and Miss Janet Yeager for her assistance with the chapter on field hockey, the author indeed expresses her appreciation. All are members of the Department of Physical Education, Bryn Mawr College. Likewise she wishes to thank Miss Grace Kenney, chairman, Department of Physical Education, Gettysburg College, for her contribution to the volleyball material for women, and Mrs. Gail Strathdee Harwi, former Bryn Mawr College faculty member, for the reorganization and presentation of the chapter on women's basketball.

Harold C. Leibee is indebted to the following present and former staff members of the University of Michigan for their assistance in the preparation of material either generally or in their fields of specialization:

Patric Cavanaugh; Stephen Galetti, for new materials in basketball; George Greey; William Helms; Albert Katzenmeyer, golf coach, who posed for the golf photos and gave valuable suggestions for the chapter; Newton Loken, gymnastics coach; Andrew Kozar; Dennis Rigan, golf; Kenneth Simmons, who provided the material for the weight training systems and programs for sports and also gave valuable suggestions for the exercises; William Murphy, tennis coach, for his contributions to the revision of the chapter on tennis and for his valuable suggestions for the teaching of tennis. Irv Schloss, member of the Professional Golfers Association of America, and Tom Helm made valuable suggestions and criticisms on the golf chapter.

The author is also indebted to graduate assistants Jack Barclay, golf; George Vanis, men's and women's gymnastics; and Robert Richards, weight training; and Gary McCabe and Kenneth Stokes who posed for the photos in weight training, and to Sue Brown and Arno Lascari for posing for the photos in gymnastics.

Lloyd L. Messersmith wishes to express his appreciation to:

Mike Muckleroy who assisted in preparing the chapter on skin and scuba diving, and Paul Hook who assisted with the soccer chapter; A. R. Barr for helping him in writing and revising the chapter on swimming and diving; the following for posing for pictures: Paul Hook, George McMillion, Linda Parchman, Martha C. Wood, Mary Philbrick, Ann Smith, Kay Collins, Charles Hill, Lindsay Smith, and James Martin.

Contents

Appendixes

Introduction:
THE REQUIRED PHYSICAL EDUCATION PROGRAM

The principal aim of gym-nastics is the education of all youth and not simply the minority of people highly favored by nature.

ARISTOTLE

That phase of education concerned with the teaching of skills, knowledge, and attitudes in activities concerned primarily with body movement is called physical education. Most schools, colleges, and universities recognize the importance of this form of education, whose goals serve those of all education, by requiring physical education of all students.

The program provides each student with an opportunity to assess his fitness, and to develop skill and understanding that will enable him to enjoy a productive stay in college and a more meaningful existence after college. In a broad view of education, physical education has unique opportunities for developing desirable character and social traits as well as defined responsibilities toward the physical development of the individual.

Objectives of increased strength and endurance, better motor skills, and improved health practices are not only ends in themselves but are means to better adjustment to society. In this respect, physical education is an aspect of education that may be appropriately described as *education through the physical*.

College programs of physical education are based upon a thorough analysis of the student's health, fitness status, and recreational needs. Utilizing these data, the student and his instructor should cooperate in planning a program that will best meet the needs of the individual student.

In some schools the program will begin with an orientation class that exposes the students to the why, when, and how of physical education, and then acquaints them with a wide variety of activities in an effort to determine those for which they have the most talent and greatest need.

In other schools the first semester or year is devoted to scientific study of the factors affecting health and fitness, emphasizing those associated with cardiovascular diseases. Actual experiments are carried on in the laboratories in which the student hopefully convinces himself of the benefits of and needs for a sound program of physical fitness and recreational skills.

Still another system, found most often in private colleges and in states with good high school programs of physical education, is one that stresses a physical fitness program followed by a selection of sports, dance, and aquatic activities.

In general, freshmen are not allowed complete freedom in the selection of other subjects. Prerequi-

sites are necessary before electives may be chosen. So it is with physical education. The privilege of selection usually follows the completion of certain groundwork in the areas of knowledge and physical abilities. In some situations, students may take fitness and/or skill tests to obtain advanced standing and thus bypass certain basic requirements. Students who must be restricted in their activity are enrolled in the remedial or adaptive program, while those allowed no activity are assigned to classes in personal health and sports appreciation.[1]

Why require physical education?

In a purely voluntary program, it has been discovered that those who most need physical education do not elect to take it. The obese, the frail, and the unskilled find it most difficult to enroll because they are ashamed of their physiques, afraid of being injured, or so unskilled that they do not have the courage to enroll. Then, too, as Walt Whitman declared, "there are simpletons who mistake neglect of the body for culture of the mind."

From the institutions' standpoint the requirement makes for maximum utilization of facilities because students can be assigned to regular classes throughout the school day and reserve the late afternoon and evening hours for intramurals and recreation.

The aim of education is to make it *interest-compelling* and *self-motivating*. To that end, compulsion is viewed as merely a temporary expedient

[1] Also known as sports orientation, sports understanding, and sports survey courses.

to introduce the student to opportunities that are offered him and to give a groundwork in the tools that will be needed later for self-direction. Once sufficiently acquainted with these opportunities, the student is encouraged to exercise his own choice in the follow-up process. In other words, within the general requirement, generous leeway for individual option is offered.

Students are encouraged to maintain a balance between team and individual sports in their selections. Both have their values. In favor of individual sports is the fact that most persons are physically unable to participate in vigorous team sports for a very prolonged period in adult life. Also, it is easier after school days to pick up one or two opponents for a friendly match than it is to get two teams together. On the other hand, freshmen students should not overlook the benefits to be derived from team sports. Being members of a team assists them in making new friends and in developing sociability. They learn to cooperate with other individuals and identify themselves as a part of a group with a common cause.

Intramurals

Learning sports and gaining proficiency in competition is enhanced through participation in the intramural sports program for both men and women. This is a voluntary free-time program in sports that provides an avenue for competition among various campus groups. On college campuses the sources for recruitment of teams for participation in the intramural sports program include fraternities, sororities, classes, housing units, and clubs of various kinds. This program provides students not on varsity teams with an opportunity to implement in a competitive situation the knowledge and skill they have acquired in the instructional phase of physical education. This experience tends to enhance the values inherent in competitive sports, including the development of organic vigor, team play, sportsmanship, group loyalties, and the refinement of sport skills.

NATURE OF PHYSICAL EDUCATION

The great Greek philosopher and scientist, Aristotle, once said, "He who thus considers things in their first growth and origin, whether a state or anything else, will obtain the clearer view of them." Let us review briefly, then, the historical concepts of physical education.

First, it is well to point out the fact that a routine, highly systematized type of education is basically a product of the modern historical era. So also is the present system of physical education. *Second,* throughout the history of mankind, just as concepts and practices in education have changed, so have they changed in physical education. *Third,* although exercise is fundamentally a large part of physical education, a close examination of the lives of previous societies of men reveals that exercise alone is not a true representation of physical education. Man has always had a propensity or natural bent for physical activity, and this natural urge has always carried educational or learning implications with it.

The dichotomy of mind and body has been replaced by a psychosomatic view of man in which the individual is viewed as a total entity. This view is expressed by Julian Huxley when he states: "Mind is not an entity in its own right, and our minds are not little separate creatures inhabiting our skulls. . . . For the biologist much the easiest way is to think of mind and matter as two aspects of a single, underlying reality." [2]

Primitive peoples

In primitive times, the different types or categories of physical activity we know today were all in evidence. They have been present in all subsequent societies, although the emphasis has fluctuated, depending on the kind of society and culture prevailing. Primitive man received most of his exercise

[2] Julian Huxley, *Evolution in Action* (New York: Harper & Row, 1953; Signet Science Library Edition), pp. 76–77.

through the ordinary daily pursuits that were necessary for him to earn a livelihood. The play of children was in large part an imitation of those adult activities. The primitives, however, did not limit their play and exercise to labors alone, or to the imitative, spontaneous, and often creative play of children. They engaged in activities of a warlike nature, and in times of peace practiced these skills as recreational pastimes.

The one activity that held first place among the primitives, both in esteem and in practice, was the dance. The dance was interwoven with all phases of the primitive's life. It was used to placate the gods in propitiation for wrongs done and in thanksgiving for divine assistance. The dancers imitated in pantomime fashion not only their own pursuits, such as the hunt or chase and war, but also the animals and forces of nature, such as the bear, buffalo, snake, rain, and fire. Most of these dances were religious ceremonies in origin, as were many of the primitive's games. Other games and sports were at one time useful and practical pursuits. No longer possessing utilitarian value, they have survived as vestigial activities to be engaged in for recreation.

The ancient Greeks

Without a doubt, the ancient Greeks placed more emphasis on the educational side of exercise than any society previous to them. At the height of Greek civilization, we find two basic types of physical education—one exemplified by the Athenians, the other by the Spartans. Although both Athenians and Spartans engaged in many of the same activities and accepted the educational importance of exercise, there were radical differences in emphasis.

The Athenian ideal was one of harmony. The Athenians attempted to blend all aspects of life into a harmonious whole. The central theme in art, sculpture, religion, music, dance, sports, and so on, was the harmonious mean. Moderation in all things characterized their philosophy. The aim of education was to develop the mental, aesthetic, moral, and physical abilities of man to enable him to better serve the state. No one aspect was emphasized to the exclusion of another. The idea of individual freedom encouraged each one to achieve individual excellence. Physical education ("gymnastics") enjoyed a favored place in Athenian education. There were special teachers of gymnastics, and each of the gymnasiums had a supervising official called a "gymnasiarch." The Athenians exercised and played for the sheer enjoyment it afforded them. They admired the body beautiful, and actively strove to cultivate it.

The Spartans were motivated and conditioned

by a strong spirit of militarism. Every phase of the Spartan's life was geared to the fulfillment of this purpose. The state exercised dictatorial control over the lives of the people. The physical exercises were all designed to develop strong, sturdy bodies capable of withstanding the rigors of military life. Every boy went through vigorous foraging and woodcraft training, living in barracks and undergoing tremendous physical hardships. Each was compelled to spend the greatest part of his young life preparing for the army; once he attained manhood, he served in the army as long as he could be of value, and he was always subject to call to duty.

To the Greeks we owe a debt of gratitude for the idea and ideals of the Olympic Games. They originated the ancient Olympics in 776 B.C. and sponsored them every four years until they were discontinued in A.D. 394 by Emperor Theodosius because professionalism and corrupt practices tended to dominate the attitude of the participants and spectators. The modern games were revived in 1896 under the leadership of Baron Pierre de Coubertin (1863–1937), and it was fitting that the first of the modern games were staged in Athens, Greece, with 285 competing athletes from 13 different nations in attendance. The Games proved to be an important factor in Greek culture and were a gigantic spectacle then, even as they are now.

The Romans

The Romans were greatly influenced by much of the Greek culture, but they never completely accepted the ideals of Greek physical education. Like the Spartans, the Romans were principally a militaristic nation. Military games and exercises took precedence over the development of the well-rounded man. Whereas the Greeks were a nation of participants, the Romans were a nation of spectators. Gladiatorial games and professional exhibitions occupied a prominent place, to the exclusion of other sporting contests.

The Middle Ages

As the Roman Empire began its decline, there arose the Christian concept of life that was to dominate Western civilization for many centuries. Roman physical education activities had become so prostituted and debased that the early Christian Fathers could see no recourse except to abolish and suspend them.

The Roman world eventually fell prey in A.D. 476 to invading barbarians from the North who had a low standard of culture. Many centuries were required to overcome the disastrous consequences of these invasions. Education and learning received a severe setback, and only the prodigious efforts of the medieval monks preserved what little knowledge was saved. If education was retarded during the early medieval period, the development of physical education was far more effectively delayed. Men everywhere looked for solace and comfort in things of the spirit. The philosophy of asceticism, debasement of the body for elevation of the soul, developed during the Dark Ages because people saw no hope for personal comfort or satisfaction in the rugged struggle for existence, so looked to life after death for attainment of these goals. Obviously, such a view detracted from the development of physical education.

Recreational or play activities approved by the Church were impregnated with a strong religious motive and included such items as appreciation of sacred art, architecture, and music. Religious festivals, especially those occurring on the great feast days of the Church, were often elaborate affairs, and welded the entire population into a uniform attitude of prayer and reverence. They also offered the people a certain amount of recreation.

Toward the close of medieval times, the practice of chivalry provided the nobility with a system of education that included a period of vigorous physical training. The aim of chivalric education was to train the youths to be strong in character and in body in order to defend their holy religion. Jousts and tournaments, which were individual and group contests between the knights, were gala affairs and approached modern sporting spectacles in glamour and magnitude. As the medieval era drew to a close, the invention of more modern weapons and methods of warfare rendered further development of education for knighthood ineffectual. The jousts and tournaments remained for a time, but eventually their brutal and bloody features were no longer endorsed by the populace.

Modern nations

The rise of modern nationalism presaged great things for physical education. Individual nations had to be strong in order to protect and defend their national boundaries. The need for strong, sturdy soldiers necessitated the institution and development of an effective system of physical education. Man's increasing fund of knowledge, in the sciences in particular, also helped promote physical education.

In more recent times, the emancipation of the masses from heavy toil through the inventions of modern technology has been a contributing factor in widening the scope and practice of physical education. Changing currents in educational thought have given physical education an increasingly wider place in the modern educational program.

EUROPEAN PROGRAMS. Germany was the pioneer country of modern times to develop a system of physical education. An early leader of this period was Friedrich Ludwig Jahn (1778–1852), known as the Father of German Gymnastics, who was motivated by patriotism and wanted to develop a strong Germany in order to avenge his country's defeat at the hands of France.

Other countries soon followed Germany's example. In Denmark, Sweden, and Finland, in particular, there emerged special systems of physical education. While the programs of these countries differed, they resembled one another in the fact that there was little provision for free play. They were principally gymnastic programs, with everybody performing the same thing in formation and in unison to a routine cadence or sequence. Switzerland uses gymnastic exercises also, but emphasizes rhythm in connection with them; this gives a strong beat or accent to one exercise of a series. In late years, Germany has been strongly influenced by this Swiss innovation.

The programs of these countries are substantially the same today, although additions and improvements have been made. These countries have no school and college competition in sports as we have in this country. Athletic competition for amateurs is sponsored mainly by athletic clubs similar to the New York Athletic Club or Los Angeles Athletic Club. Recently, however, some efforts were instituted to bring sports into the school curriculum.

Certain features that stand out in the programs of the different European countries have to a degree been incorporated into our own physical education programs. The German program was built around heavy gymnastic apparatus, such as the high bar, parallel bars, rings, and horses, which are still today a prominent part of gymnastics.

Sweden emphasized the medical side of gymnastics and subsequently developed a system of corrective exercises, noted especially for the held or fixed positions at various stages throughout the exercise. The leader in the development of this program was Per Henrik Ling (1776–1839), who promoted a program of activities which he called medical gymnastics. The same type of exercises have been used with great success in treating wounded soldiers.

Finland utilizes the conditioning exercises of its neighbors but also incorporates so-called mimetic drills into its program. Students simulate throwing javelins or weights without actually using any implements or equipment. This idea is now used in programs in this country to teach mass groups the proper techniques in such sports as bowling, golf, swimming, tennis, handball, and basketball.

Denmark developed a system of gymnastics particularly suited to the needs of its predominantly agricultural population. It is called "fundamental gymnastics." Examples of this type of activity may be found in the conditioning or warming up exercises, sometimes called "grass drills," used for football and other vigorous sports. Franz Nachtegall (1777–1847) provided early leadership for this program in Denmark. Others included Niels Bukh (1880–1950), who promoted a program called "primitive gymnastics," patterned somewhat after Ling's system in Sweden but differing from it in that activities were conducted in a continuous rhythmic fashion in lieu of the fixed and held positions of the Ling system. Bukh toured the United States in the early 1920's with a group of Danish gymnasts, and since then several gymnastic groups have visited this country from Denmark and Sweden.

England has long been a nation noted for its predilection to sports. Numerous English sports and the sporting tradition of England were transplanted to the American continent by the early colonists. To England goes the credit for developing the groundwork and enthusiasm for sports so common to its colonists and to countries all over the globe. The American people, in particular, have inherited and built on this special liking for sports.

EARLY PROGRAMS IN THE UNITED STATES. Physical education, as we know it today, was not introduced into the schools of this country until about the time of the Civil War. The early settlers had little time for frivolity or entertainment. Play was for very small children. Recreation and sports were chiefly the property of the wealthy.

The first school programs of physical education were introduced by European immigrants who came to this country during the last century. These programs, reflecting the nationalistic ideals of their native homelands, were very formal in nature and restricted in content. Academic-minded educators reluctantly but gradually accepted these formal types of programs. The chief argument used in favor of physical exercise was that city boys no longer had chores or physical work to do while away at school. It was reasoned that physical education would counteract this deficiency. At about the same time, owing to the changing structure of our society, an increase in the leisure time of the common man afforded him opportunity for wider participation in athletic sports and recreational activities.

Early efforts to introduce athletics into the school program were rejected by school men. Students, however, persisted in promoting athletics under their own direction. As a result of increasing abuses associated with their promotion and also of changes in educational philosophy, educators, sensing the potential educational features of athletics, decided to take over control of school athletic programs. Some contended that athletics afforded students a way to relieve surplus energy or blow off steam, and to them athletics were a good means of keeping the boys busy and out of mischief. In most cases the administration and promotion of athletics and physical education were separately maintained. Thus there arose an artificial division of two naturally associated movements.

INFLUENCE OF THE SCIENCES.   Since the turn of the present century, several factors have contributed toward bringing athletic sports and physical education into an organic union. Most notable influences perhaps have been in the biological sciences and in the newer sciences of psychology and sociology, which in turn have considerably altered educational thought and practice.

Biology's chief contribution to education has been the principle of growth, which is closely akin to the idea of development so emphasized in education today. Other biological sciences, such as anatomy, physiology, chemistry, and nutrition, have provided vast quantities of knowledge that have served to broaden the scope of physical education.

Modern psychology has advanced the thesis that man is an organic unity. All aspects of a person's makeup have a bearing on the final product. Education is no longer concerned merely with imparting knowledge to improve the intellect alone. Just as the ancient Athenians emphasized the mental, moral, aesthetic, and physical aspects of man's life, so also does modern education in the United States today. Another feature has been added, however—the social. The impetus in this area has been supplied by sociology. Man must learn to get along with his neighbor. Group adjustments must be made if an individual is to live a full life and contribute his fair share to the common good.

Psychology has also been responsible for advancing principles concerning the processes of learning and for improving techniques and methods of instruction. Mental hygiene, which is an offspring of psychology and psychiatry, has contributed new ideas on the emotional aspects of man's life.

All of the above ideas have played their part in shaping modern educational practices. A person must be well-instructed in all of the above aspects or fall short of achieving a well-rounded and balanced personality that can be readily adapted to meet rapidly changing conditions of present-day society.

PRESENT-DAY PHYSICAL EDUCATION.   A wide and varied number of subjects in the school curriculum are necessary to meet the needs of students and to assist them in achieving an all-around, balanced education. Physical education is only one of many school subjects, yet it plays a very important part in contributing to the full development of the student's personality.

Today, physical education programs bear little resemblance to the earlier formal gymnastic-type program. They are now largely composed of sports with a wide variety of activities designed to meet the varying needs of all students. Gymnastics is only one activity on the long list of sports in the modern program. To name only a few, there are such popular team sports as basketball, field hockey, soccer, softball, speedball, touch football, track and field activities, and volley ball; such body conditioning activities as gymnastics, tumbling, wrestling, and weight lifting; such recreational sports as angling, archery, badminton, bowling, fencing, golf, handball, swimming, and tennis; and the dance, which has creative as well as developmental and recreational values. To a greater or lesser degree, the American college program of physical education includes the above activities, with the opportunity for the student to receive instruction and to participate in them. Riding, where stables are available, additional racquet sports, where facilities permit, and skating and skiing in winter, can be added.

Interscholastic and intercollegiate sports are closely associated with physical education, and in most cases are handled by the same personnel. Intramural sports provide a broad base for releasing the competitive urge of the student body. The required or service programs attempt to reach all students with a program that is basically instructional in content and purpose.

Programs of physical education are becoming more flexible than ever before to take care of the individual's own needs and interests. On the college and university level, more academic content is included to give an appreciation of health, safety, and sports in one's personal life and in our American culture. The participants enjoy having a knowledge of the background of the rules, techniques, and strategy of various activities. All colleges and universities are now giving examinations on these points in their required courses, whereas previously the students only had to participate in exercise. The emphasis is not so much on exercise for the sake of exercise as it is on having the student acquire skills and understandings that will stay with him as a permanent part of his life interests.

PROFESSIONAL NEEDS.   While still only on the horizon, there are evidences of courses being designed to tie in with professional needs. The forester or engineer can well utilize information on handling canoes, life saving, first aid, and survival knowledge for life in the open; the future journalist who plans to write about or broadcast sports events can use some courses in the technique of sports; the artist or illustrator needs to know correct form in sports along with his knowledge of anatomy; the architect can well utilize information on the construction of sports buildings, playgrounds, and apartment recreational provisions. So, too, the student of municipal government should know about recreation commissions and about governmental taxes on sports; the student of music about the various forms of the dance and the musical accompaniments for them, the place of music in community recreation centers and in camps, and the marching formations for school bands; the student of education about games the classroom teacher teaches and supervises in the elementary grades, about handling children's holiday or birthday parties, and about handling social recreation get-togethers for adults.

A great deal of time and effort is now going into scientific laboratory research in physical education, particularly in the fields of physiology and psychology as they affect the teaching and learning of elementary neuromuscular and sport skills. Testing is being used as never before. An individual becomes interested when he can visualize and follow his own improvement and relate it to that of other individuals on a comparable basis.

In summary, physical education is more than exercise. It is more than a muscle builder or a circulation quickener. It is more than aimless and frivolous play, or having fun. It is more than athletic competition. Physical education also has health knowledge to impart, group experiences to offer, the joy of effort and achievement to give, the teaching of skills in lasting recreative interests as its responsibility; it must develop appreciations from the standpoint of a spectator and reader of sports, as well as a participant in them. Physical education is education. It must always be in step with the current practices and procedures in education. It must always contribute to the all-around development and education of students.

OBJECTIVES OF PHYSICAL EDUCATION

Many college students who are required to elect a course in physical education frequently raise questions like the following: "What good will physical education do me?"; "Just what am I supposed to get out of physical education?"; "Why can't I use that time to better advantage in learning more about my own special field?" Too often no attempt is made to answer these well-intentioned queries. Conse-quently, many students flounder around somewhat aimlessly in their physical education classes. They are never introduced to the educational reasons as to why they are there or what they are supposed to accomplish; or, what is far worse, they receive an erroneous or one-sided view of physical education.

An educational program of physical education can make contributions to all the phases of individual development, although it contributes much more to certain aspects than to others. Objectives will be considered under five categories: *physical fitness, motor skills, knowledge, social objectives,* and *aesthetic* (or *appreciation*) *objectives.*

An objective is hardly worthwhile if the student receives no benefit or value on attaining it. The benefits or values one may receive from physical education are closely associated with the objectives. Consequently, the discussion that follows includes both the objectives and values of physical education.

Physical fitness objectives

By its very nature, physical education's chief contribution to the education of an individual is in the area of the physical. Foremost among these objectives is the attainment of a measure of *physical fitness.* Physical fitness must not be confused with merely avoiding being confined to a sick bed. There should be a sparkle and buoyance to living as well. Physical fitness means the ability to carry one's work load without staggering, to participate in recreation with ease and enjoyment, and withal to have a reservoir of endurance to meet the emergencies of life. In any occupation or profession, there are many crises that demand extra effort and there should be adequate physical endowment to meet them.

Properly directed physical activity helps maintain the body in *good health.* While exercise is not a means of preventing or curing disease, it is a well-known medical fact that a person in run-down physical condition is susceptible to illness and has a slow recovery or convalescence once taken ill. Exercise, used wisely, helps keep the body from getting into this state of lowered resistance. It builds up the muscles and vital organs of the body so they are capable of taking more strain, and consequently are kept at a higher level of efficiency.

Health is more than freedom from physical disease or disability, however. It includes that very important but complicated quality, *mental health.* One of physical education's greatest contributions to health is in this area. Participation in a sport or game takes one's thoughts away from oneself. Life's troubles and problems are forgotten for the moment, and the participant emerges from the games tired in body but refreshed in spirit. Although it is difficult to measure the effectiveness of exercise in preventing mental illness, most authorities agree it can be very helpful. It is true, too, that sports and games are widely used in treating certain types of mental illness.

Motor skills objectives

In order to enjoy any pursuit, a person must achieve a certain amount of proficiency in it. Thus a primary objective of physical education is the learning of the *skills* necessary for participation in sports and other recreational activities. The road to learning skills can be shortened with the help of guidance and instruction. Faulty habits are very apt to be acquired if one starts out learning a sport skill on his own. An individual need not acquire the finesse or polish of an expert to enjoy the satisfaction that comes from a successfully executed performance.

In addition to learning skills that are necessary for the playing of sports, students in physical education should strive to acquire certain *safety skills* vitally important to modern-day society. Many times one's very life will depend upon whether or not one possesses a certain ability. The skills of swimming, lifesaving, protecting the body in falling, peripheral vision, coordination of mind with body, and many others, can be developed to varying degrees through the physical education program.

Knowledge objectives

At first glance, it may seem that there is little mental content in physical education. Quite the contrary is the truth, however. Before one can learn to play a game, he must learn the *rules*. Once he knows the rules and has achieved a certain proficiency in the activity, he will be interested in acquiring knowledge of the *strategy* of the game. In game situations, a mastery of strategy or finesse greatly facilitates the making of split-second decisions that occur with clock-like regularity. Such training provides good preparation for the actualities of life.

Not to be overlooked are the facts one should learn about *health precautions of exercise*. This information is so important that a separate chapter (Chapter 3) is devoted to it. The values of activity or exercise are closely associated and will be discussed in more detail in the same chapter.

Social objectives

The newer emphasis in education has been in the direction of improving the ability of students to get along together. Educators call it *socialization of the individual*. In this age of social conflict, this objective looms rather large.

A physical education program offers unlimited opportunities for fulfilling the broad social objectives of democratic education. There is no more swift, no more lasting leveler or common denominator of interest than sports. The sports page, radio, television, and conversation are evidence of the universal interest taken in sports by old and young, by business man and housewife, by all—by *all,* without distinction of age, sex, race, nationality, wealth, or creed. In sports, the participants may learn valuable lessons in getting along with people that carry over into their everyday life. In real life, not all gain first place, not all win first prize, not all receive the acclaim and renown of the hero. So it is that sports are an ideal laboratory for education for living.

In sports a person must learn to exhibit the same qualities that are necessary for a successful and happy life in a democratic society. He must acquire attitudes and habits of *loyalty, cooperation, initiative, self-control,* and *courtesy.* He has experience in being a *leader* and also a *follower.* He learns to adapt himself to constantly changing conditions of the game, just as he must in the game of life.

In an educational sports program, an individual will learn to give credit where credit is due. He learns to give recognition to a well-executed performance. He learns how to take the hard knocks, as well as victories, and how to react properly. He learns to subdue his emotional outbursts for the good of the common cause. The majority of educators are agreed that an educationally sound program of physical education has as significant a contribution to make in this area as any other school subject. One has but to notice the sociability and good-natured rivalry that takes place in a game of softball, basketball, bowling, golf, horseshoes, handball, or tennis, to see evidence of the changes that occur in the social conduct of the players as the result of their participation in physical education activities.

The social objectives in education are also concerned with teaching habits and attitudes concerning *standards of right ideals and of human conduct.* They are principally standards or ethics that an individual should follow in order to get along better with his neighbor. Thus, it can be seen that they are closely related and sometimes identified with the social objectives of education.

In sports activities, the citizenship objectives may be summed up in one ideal, namely, *sportsmanship.* Basically, sportsmanship means being humble in victory and gracious in defeat. Gradually, however, it has come to mean much more than that. Its meaning today closely approaches the idea of the Golden Rule in action. A true sportsman becomes instilled with a sense of justice and fair play. He does not try to hedge or slide by the rule. Most sport competition is carried on without the benefit of officials or impartial judges of the play. The participants themselves make the decisions. An individual who continually abuses this privilege will soon find himself an outcast. He must learn to play the game according to the rules and the spirit of fair play if he wishes to retain his self-respect and his status among his fellow men.

To be successful in sports and to enjoy them, one must learn the lesson of *self-discipline*. A person cannot live riotously and play sports with impunity. A certain amount of training and conditioning of the body is required.

Aesthetic (or appreciation) objectives

Not all of us can learn to be expert musicians, artists, composers, dancers, engineers, scientists, and so forth. Many of us are unable even to be amateurs in the multitude of specialties that are a product of present-day society. It is the concern of education, though, to teach us to appreciate the finer contributions of these professions.

In the field of physical education, the aesthetic objectives may be confined to three general areas: (1) appreciation of exercise and its aesthetic effect on the body, (2) appreciation of sports, and (3) appreciation of the wise use of leisure.

Everybody admires a person who walks with grace and ease, moves effortlessly, and maintains a youthful figure. The individual who holds his head high, talks with forcefulness, possesses rhythmical muscular coordination, agility, and skill, is indeed one to be envied. Yet these qualities are available to all of us to a certain degree by regular and systematic participation in sports and physical activities.

It is not to be denied that an appreciation of one of the most important of our social and cultural institutions will broaden a person's understanding of his society. Certainly to appreciate the full value or worth of sports in our society requires a certain amount of knowledge about sports. A cursory knowledge will not suffice; neither, on the other hand, is an exhaustive or professional study of sports needed. But, certainly, some knowledge of the rules, strategy, and terminology of sports is necessary. There is also a wealth of educational material in the social and cultural aspects of sports. (This will be discussed in more detail in Chapter 2.)

To appreciate the importance of leisure, it is first necessary to understand the tremendous impact of modern technology on modern society. Mankind has been liberated from the drudgery of work and toil that was formerly its lot. Instead of being a slave whose labor assures the leisure of the elite, man now has the machine, which gives him a leisure comparable to that of a privileged ruling class of former centuries.

It can easily be discerned that men can use their leisure either constructively or destructively, wisely or unwisely. A primary objective of physical education is to impart to the students a philosophy, buttressed by facts, of the *wise use of leisure time*. Students must be made aware of the vital part that wholesome recreation can play in the enjoyment of a full life, and especially the role of sports in this respect. It is the purpose of physical education to teach students sports skills and sports interests that will become a permanent part of their everyday adult life.

Individual check list of objectives

Earlier in this chapter it was mentioned that quite often college students in the required physical education program have little idea of what they should accomplish as a result of their participation in the physical education program. The following list of concrete objectives is included for the convenience of such students. It is merely to serve as a guide and may be modified to suit individual needs.

A student should acquire proficiency in as many of the following items as is possible.

I. *Activities*
   A. Swim 50 yards
   B. Team sports (successful participation in two)
   C. Recreational and individual sports (successful participation in five)
   D. Elementary marching tactics
   E. Proper lifting techniques and principles
   F. Principles of aesthetic posture
   G. Satisfactory score on a physical fitness test
   H. Satisfactory score on a motor skills test
   I. Rhythmical activities, i.e., social dancing and folk dancing (men and women), modern dance (women)
   J. Correct techniques in fundamental skills, i.e., running, jumping, throwing, and climbing
   K. Selection of proper clothing for sports activities
   L. Proper selection and care of equipment

II. Health and hygiene understandings

A. Influence of fatigue on personal health
   1. Relations of over-fatigue to exercise values
   2. Effects of physical condition on fatigue
B. Foot care
   1. Selection of shoes for proper foot care
   2. Blisters and how to avoid them
   3. Athlete's foot
   4. Clean and properly fitting socks
C. Bath after exercise
   1. Health reasons
   2. Social reasons
   3. Relation to the cooling-off period
D. Restricting activity after illness
E. Restrictions due to defects (remediable and non-remediable)
   1. Heart defects
   2. Muscle and bone defects (sprains, strains, breaks, atrophy, etc.)
   3. Blindness, partial sight, and other eye defects
   4. Excessive weight deviations (under- and over-weight
F. How to maintain physical fitness
G. Importance of early treatment of remediaable defects
H. Importance of warm-up and cooling-off periods
I. How to warm up
J. Selection of proper dress for sports activities
K. Importance of diet, sleep or rest, and personal hygiene
L. First aid

III. Knowledge of sports

A. Appreciation of sports as a spectator
   1. Skills
   2. Strategy and rules
   3. Team play
   4. Role of officials
   5. Sportsmanship
B. Courtesy and sportsmanship as a player
C. Place of sports in American life
   1. Historical
   2. Peacetime
   3. War periods
   4. Depressions

IV. Sports participation in later years (after school)

A. Classification of sports activities for participation at various age levels
B. Corecreational sports
C. Values of different sports
   1. Physical
   2. Social
   3. Mental
   4. Relationship to various professions
D. How to enjoy life in the open
   1. Camping
   2. Hiking
   3. Safety
E. Citizen's role in the promotion of sports and recreation
   1. Personal support
   2. Group activity
F. Finding recreation in a new community
   1. Organizations—YMCA, YWCA, CYO, YMHA, American Legion, Junior Chamber of Commerce, Hot Stove League, etc.
   2. Public Recreation—Schools, Parks, Recreation Department, Community Centers
   3. Churches
   4. Industrial programs

SELECTED REFERENCES

Bucher, Charles, *Foundations of Physical Education* (4th ed.). St. Louis: The C. V. Mosby Co., 1964.

Cowell, Charles, and Wellman L. France, *Philosophy and Principles of Physical Education.* Englewood Cliffs, N. J.: Prentice-Hall, Inc., 1963.

Cratty, Bryant J., *Psychology and Physical Activity.* Englewood Cliffs, N. J.: Prentice-Hall, Inc., 1968.

Davis, Elwood C., and Donna Mae Miller, *The Philosophic Process in Physical Education* (2nd ed.). Philadelphia: Lea & Febiger, 1967.

Duncan, Ray O., and Helen Watson, *Introduction to Physical Education.* New York: The Ronald Press Co., 1960.

Hackensmith, C. W., *History of Physical Education.* New York: Harper & Row, 1966.

Huxley, Julian, *Evolution in Action.* New York: Harper & Row (Signet Science Library Book), 1953.

Menke, Frank G., *The New Encyclopedia of Sports.* New York: A. S. Barnes & Co., 1960.

Patterson, Ann, and Edmond C. Hallberg, *Background Readings for Physical Education.* New York: Holt, Rinehart & Winston, 1965.

Rice, Emmet A., John Hutchinson, and Mabel Lee, *A Brief History of Physical Education* (4th ed.). New York: The Ronald Press Co., 1958.

Van Dalen, D. B., E. D. Mitchell, and B. L. Bennett, *A World History of Physical Education.* Englewood Cliffs, N. J.: Prentice-Hall, Inc., 1953.

Voltmer, Edward F., and Arthur Esslinger, *The Organization and Administration of Physical Education* (4th ed.). New York: Appleton-Century-Crofts, 1967.

Weston, Arthur, *The Making of American Physical Education.* New York: Appleton-Century-Crofts, 1962.

Williams, Jesse F., *The Principles of Physical Education* (8th ed.). Philadelphia: W. B. Saunders Co., 1964.

Zeigler, Earle F., *Philosophical Foundations for Physical, Health and Recreation Education.* Englewood Cliffs, N. J.: Prentice-Hall, Inc., 1964.

Cultural Aspects of Sports

He that will make a good use of any part of his life must allow a large part of it to recreation.

JOHN LOCKE

It is becoming more and more evident that to obtain a comprehensive all-around knowledge and understanding of any society, one must study its cultural patterns and institutions.

Sports and the related activities that comprise the program of physical education and recreation are merely one of the many cultural patterns prevalent in any society. The form that this pattern takes depends on such factors as geography, historical traditions, religion, economic, political, and social institutions, and education. Limitations of space preclude a comprehensive detailed presentation of the cultural aspects of all types of sports. This book will suggest a few of the many areas in which the student may pursue further study on his own initiative. A knowledge of all the factors that influence sports and peoples' attitudes toward sports is vital for an understanding of the people and the society in which we live. With the increasing emphasis on the cultural aspects of sports comes an added richness that improves and embellishes the educational stature and the contributions of physical education to the well-rounded education of students.

Leisure and culture

Before we consider the purposes of recreation in relation to the increasing amount of leisure time, let us look at its implications, so prophetically described by Sir Bertrand Russell a number of years ago.

Thirty years ago, the case for leisure for the common man was summarized by Bertrand Russell in an essay entitled *In Praise Of Idleness*. Russell asserted that there is far too much work done in the world, that immense harm is caused by the belief that work is virtuous, and that what needs to be preached in modern industrial countries is quite different from what had always been preached. From the beginning of civilization until the Industrial Revolution, he said, a man could as a rule produce by hard work little more than was required for the subsistence of himself and his family, although his wife worked at least as hard as he did, and his children added their labor as soon as they were old enough to do so. Modern technique, he foresaw, would make an end to a time in which leisure was the prerogative of a

12

small privileged class. Leisure would become a right evenly distributed throughout the community. The morality of work, he wrote, is the morality of slaves, and the modern world has no need for slavery. Athenian slave owners, he pointed out, employed part of their leisure in making a permanent contribution to civilization which would have been impossible under just economic systems. Leisure for the few was only rendered possible by the labors of the many. But their labors were valuable, not because work is good, but because leisure is good.

In America, Russell observed, men often work long hours even when they are already well off; in fact, some of them dislike leisure not only for themselves but also for their sons. Oddly enough, they do not mind their wives and daughters having no work at all. The snobbish admiration of uselessness which in an aristocratic society once extended to both sexes is, under a plutocracy, confined to women; this, however, does not make it more in agreement with common sense.

The wise use of leisure is a product of civilization and education. A man who has worked long hours all his life is likely to feel bored if he suddenly becomes idle. But without a considerable amount of leisure a man is cut off from many of the best things. For thousands of years, the rich have preached the dignity of labor while taking care themselves to remain undignified in this respect. The notion that the desirable activities are only those that bring a profit has made everything topsy-turvy. We think too much of production and too little of consumption.

Russell recommended that education should provide tastes which would enable a man to use leisure intelligently.[1]

Physical education, especially sports and dance participation, can and does make a great contribution to this wise use of leisure. Jokl also claims that, "Like art, sport washes away from the soul the dust of everyday life." [2]

Increased leisure

America has changed from a largely rural agricultural society to an urban, industrialized society. We live in smaller houses, we depend on others for at least part of our existence. Our society has changed markedly and the tempo of change is continually increasing with the age of automation.

[1] Ernst Jokl, *Sport and Culture* (New York: Pergamon Press, 1964), p. 3.
[2] *Ibid.*, p. 3.

As predicted by Russell, the increase in leisure time has posed for present-day society serious social and economic problems which have not been satisfactorily resolved. In addition, the pace of living has speeded up with the industrial and machine age. Man's work in most cases has become a monotonous routine. There is little opportunity for expressing individuality. Native impulses are thwarted. The nervous tension is all-pervading. We are approaching an era in which the push-button type of work is not uncommon, and so a person has few challenges to his ingenuity, few chances to satisfy his basic psychological needs and desires. People are being forced to look elsewhere than their work to satisfy these fundamental drives. Leisure time can be used to enrich life, to offset the routine of everyday living, to compensate for the one-sidedness of our work. It is in this sense that recreation can make its greatest contribution to our society.

Purpose of recreation

Physiologists tell us that when we are completely tired we need rest or sleep, but that when we are only partially tired we can get relaxation and even recuperation by doing something different from the thing we have been doing. The musician does not keep the strings of his instrument taut all the time; the drummer has learned to loosen the calf-skin head of his drum when it is not being beaten; the athlete knows better than to try continuously to break his record. And so in the same sense none of us can work all the time at sustained pressure. Recreation offers a variety of activities that in turn offer change. And in change there is relaxation. Recreation is meant to uplift and uphold, not to tear down and destroy. Recreation cheers the human spirit; it is a *re-creative* tonic for a tired body and weary soul. More than that, it is an avenue for self-expression—an outlet for eager muscles and eager impulses. Recreation helps us to relax from the constant tension of attending to our work. Thus refreshed, we find the mental stability so needed in these days of a highly complex and complicated society.

Classification of recreations

Recreation need not be elaborate or expensive. Many simple forms of recreation are available that are fully as satisfying as the more expensive kind. The two basic types of recreation are the *spectator,* or passive, and the *participating,* or active. For most people, the spectator type is just as popu-

FIGURE 2-1. The Cotton Bowl, where nearly 80,000 persons gather to see Southern Methodist University play football. Courtesy S. M. U. Department of Athletics.

lar as their purses will allow. There is catharsis and empathy value in attending the spectator sports. They imbue us with holiday spirit; they allow us to jump up and down, cheer and shout, and relieve pent-up emotions in many ways. Such enthusiasm, however ethnocentric, is most stimulating.

There are other *spectator* forms of entertainment, such as dramatic and musical events, records, radio, television, movies, and reading. We hold a brief for this passive and vicarious recreation. Books and movies help satisfy the wish for new experience; the onlooker can identify himself with the athlete, the actor, the artist, or the hero in the book. There is satisfaction in being able to appreciate a high level of performance.

Despite its usefulness in appreciation, vicarious experience can never give the complete joy of actual participation. It is incomplete if not accompanied by the satisfaction of direct experience in some form of recreational activity. This accounts for

the facts that intramural sports are everywhere on the increase and that the camping and outing movement is growing so rapidly. This observation is not limited to the physical forms of recreation alone. It is true of the other types as well. During recent years there has been a marked increase in dramatics, music, and arts and crafts and social recreations.

Agencies for recreation

Students usually are provided with a tailor-made recreational program that is easily available. After they leave school, however, they have no clear-cut program or else they are not familiar with the organizations that sponsor recreational activities.

Agencies promoting recreation are those operated by federal, state, and local branches of government. On a national level, the National Park Service has developed parks close to the large industrial areas. These parks and their facilities are open to the public. The U.S. Forest Service and many State Forests permit the public to use the vast expanse of forests and recently developed lands for outdoor recreational purposes, for camping, hunting, fishing, and other outdoor sports.

On the local level, many organizations, civic and semi-public, offer recreational programs. Public schools frequently are open to year-round recreational programs, financed by the municipal budget. Organizations such as YWCA, YMCA, CYO, and Boys Clubs all offer broad programs for a wide age range at a nominal fee. Commercial teams and recreational programs sponsored by industries are not unusual.

Sports and economics

The present century has witnessed a remarkable increase in the expenditures for recreational goods and services. This has been made possible not only as a result of an increase in leisure time, but also because of a marked rise in the standard of living and an increase in the purchasing power of the average consumer. It has been estimated recently that Americans as a whole spend more than $45 billion annually for recreation. This amount exceeds the total value of farm output in the United States in a given year. The boat manufacturing industry alone has produced nearly ten million power boats. Recreation has become the biggest industry in many of our states. In addition, federal, state, and local governments are spending tens of millions of dollars each year for recreational purposes.

Records indicate that sports are engaged in by the more affluent families in the U.S. Eighty per cent of sporting goods equipment is purchased by families with an income of $8000 or more, and these ten million families reside largely in the metropolitan areas. This indicates that the buyers of sports equipment are limited to members of families with an income above the average for the population generally. The rapid increase of expenditure for sports equipment is indicated by the fact that only 754 million dollars were spent for this equipment in 1946 while the figure for 1970 is expected to reach 2.5 billion dollars.

Many recreational goods carry a high federal tax and provide the federal government with a considerable source of revenue. The federal admissions tax on athletic contests has been a substantial source of revenue. Other types of activities, one of which is horse racing, are taxed by state and local governments. Over fifty million fishing and hunting licenses also provide tax income.

The recreation industry provides thousands of people with employment. Many are working in the amusement industry, others in making recreation goods, and still others in maintaining federal, state, and local recreation programs.

Sports and professions

Several scientific studies and surveys have been made that seem to indicate a very decided relationship between vocational and recreational interests. Studies of successful professional people and of outstanding students preparing for the professions indicate that people in different professions follow certain patterns in their choice of recreational activities. Only the most significant of these patterns will be mentioned here.

The recreational choices of certain professions, for example, architecture, insurance, and real estate, are influenced by the valuable business and social contacts they make in their spare time activities. The architect is very exclusive in his recreations, putting all his recreational eggs in one basket. He usually belongs to the most exclusive and expensive club in the community, such as the country club, a city club, or a yacht club. He is most interested in making contacts with a privileged clientele who can afford to put his professional talents to use.

Insurance salesmen and real estate men are the most avid joiners of all. They belong to as many clubs and lodges as possible, because the more contacts they make, the better their business will be. They are very interested in sports like golf that give them opportunities for increasing social contacts.

The physicians are at the top of the list in the individual sports like fishing and hunting. They must get away into the wide open spaces or isolated locations in order not to be interrupted or called back to the office for emergencies. They also pursue such hobbies as collecting that can be quickly put aside when there is an emergency call. Specialists, who have regular office hours, are more likely to join clubs and fraternal organizations or play golf.

Civil engineers and foresters rank high among enthusiasts of fishing, hunting, and other outdoor recreations. Engineers who work in the city (mechanical, chemical, and electrical) are more interested in sports like golf and tennis.

Bankers and lawyers frequently belong to civic clubs and fraternal organizations. The banker occupies a place of prominence in the community and is expected to participate in its social and civic life. Lawyers, in the main, have practically no interest in hunting, fishing, or swimming, but they do play golf and tennis in a leisurely manner. Their competitive life is largely expressed through their legal experiences.

Teachers and clergymen are apt to select the inexpensive recreations. They are especially interested in hiking, gardening, reading, writing, and travel.

College students in pre-professional courses have a marked liking for certain sports. The students in forestry, journalism, physical education, law, and the literary courses show the greatest variety of interests and most versatility of choice. Students in the sciences, architecture, and general education have the fewest interests. This narrowed range of interests is due in part to their intensive pursuit of the things they do enjoy.

Sports and hobbies

A hobby is something that is intermediate between work and play. It results in something useful or tangible after you are through with it. For example, gardening would be a hobby because it produces flowers and vegetables; so would photography, which results in pictures. There are any number of collecting hobbies, experimental hobbies, and hobbies of raising flowers, plants, and different kinds of animals.

In general, all sports afford hobby interest in offering instruction to younger pupils and in promoting sports programs. Some sports are more adaptable for hobby purposes than others. A few examples serve to point out the numerous possibilities for tieing up sports interests with hobbies.

Archery is well-suited to tie up with craftwork, as you can make your own bows and arrows, or collect ancient weapons. Canoeing and fishing may be associated with photography and ichthyology. Folk dancing often leads to an interest in folk lore. Some people make a hobby of studying the dances of the pioneers, those of different regions and different countries. This type of hobby involves an interest in ethnology and anthropology. Golf may be tied up with the study of plants and trees, and with nature appreciation. The sport of hunting goes well with the collection of guns and mounted specimens of game. Sailing may evolve an interest in the collecting of ship models or in naval architecture. Walking and hiking may be associated with travel, photography, bird watching, collecting, and writing.

An association of hobby with one's favorite sport provides unlimited opportunity for broadening one's horizon of activities, and this in turn leads to greater enjoyment in particular recreational interests.

Sportsmanship

Courtesy is the true mark of every sportsman. Certain sports like tennis, golf, bowling, and bad- minton have built up over the years a code of ethics that all experienced players follow. These courtesies are unwritten rules. However, in a friendly, sociable game in which no penalties are prescribed for unsportsmanlike acts, as they are in team sports, the traditional courtesies serve to keep the game on an honorable plane and help minimize the absence of impartial officials. Every sports enthusiast, especially the novice or beginning player, should acquaint himself with the courtesies that the participants are expected to follow in the sport of his choice.

Sportsmanship is more than friendly rivalry on the part of the participants. It extends to include all those who make a habit of witnessing sporting spectacles. Spectators have a part in shaping the attitude of people in general toward sports. In order to do their full share, spectators must have a knowledge and understanding of the rules of the game and the techniques of play. They must learn to appreciate an artistically executed performance. They must realize that the officials are impartial judges of the play; while they do their best to be neutral, they sometimes make mistakes because they are human.

Schools and colleges are doing a great deal toward making it possible for spectators to be better informed about the finer points of the different sports. Courses in sports appreciation are being added to an increasing number of college curricula. Demonstrations and clinics are being held before contests for the benefit of the spectators.

Corecreational sports

A rather recent trend in sports is the promotion of corecreational sports. It has been found that certain social values can be gained when a mixed group plays together in a leisurely, friendly manner. Some sports lend themselves to this type of play, while others do not. The individual sports in which doubles matches can be played are ideally suited for corecreational purposes, for example, tennis and badminton. Archery, bowling, and table tennis also lend themselves to successful play by mixed groups. Purely recreational sports in which there is very little or no competition are also popular in a corecreational program—that is, sports like swimming, riding, hiking, bicycling, skating, skiing, boating, and dancing. In the congenial atmosphere of sociability found in sporting activities, the timid, backward individuals often become more sure of themselves and adjust more readily with persons of the opposite sex.

Sports and discrimination

As do music and the arts, sports and athletic participation transcend race, creed, and nationality.

They have been one of the most potent forces for integration in this country. No longer does the sponsor, the coach, or the fan take cognizance of the player's color, religion, or social status; they ask only, "Is he the best player, is he a winner, does he fit into the team, and can he produce?"

Relatively few activities are so free from discrimination as are school, college, and professional athletics. Similarly, most recreation areas on national, state, and local levels are open to all regardless of color, social status, or religious beliefs. Thus sports have become one of our nation's best vehicles for social justice.

Many Negroes have become national heroes in such sports as football, basketball, track, and baseball, and have become some of the highest paid players in professional sports of all times. Although Negroes represent only 11 per cent of the population of the United States, black United States athletes have assembled more than three times the number of Olympic successes they were expected to gather in terms of their proportional representation. Many of these fine young athletes, traveling as they do to foreign countries, are becoming some of our finest good-will ambassadors.

A recent survey by the United States Department of Health, Education and Welfare disclosed that of the 10,698 athletic scholarships granted by the 59 colleges studied, 638, or about 6 per cent, went to Negroes, while only 1.5 per cent of the 796,709 students enrolled were black.

Sports over the world

We may commonly think of sports only as they are found in our own country, the *United States*. But countries all over the world are gradually acquiring a sports consciousness, although to date it has been those of Anglo-Saxon origin that have led the way. In our neighbor country *Canada* the sports of ice hockey and lacrosse are national favorites along with their own version of rugby football and American baseball and basketball. In *Great Britain* cricket, soccer, and rugby football are well established. In the northern countries of *Europe* the winter sports of skiing and skating are popular, both in non-competitive and competitive form, along with wrestling, mountain climbing, and various forms of gymnastics. Soccer is a favorite in the *South American* countries, along with polo and a game of Spanish origin called pelota. In *Oriental* countries English soccer is well known, but the more newly introduced American games such as baseball, basketball, and volley ball are rapidly taking hold. The *Chinese* are especially skillful in the latter sport.

For many years *Japan* has practiced a special form of wrestling called jujitsu, with its common forms of judo and karate. Lately that country has produced champion baseball players, gymnasts, girl volley ball players, and swimmers. The *Latins of Europe* are devotees of soccer, tennis, and fencing, although they are beginning to experiment also with American games. *Italy* also has boccie, an outdoor form of bowling. In *Germany* and *Denmark* an outdoor game called "handball" is common. The *Hungarians* and *Czechs* excel in gymnastics, water polo, and table tennis. The *Irish* play indoor handball as known to the United States. In this panorama of sports it must be remembered that certain sports like track and field events, boxing, wrestling, and swimming go back to ancient times and are found in practically all countries, although in different forms that are indigenous to the culture of the country in question.

Since about 1950, the *Russians* have taken a governmental approach to the promotion of sports participation for all, and, as a result, challenge the United States and the rest of the world for dominance. Soviet athletes today figure in the top ranks of half the world's games, being especially strong in ice hockey, judo, rowing, ice skating, track and field, volley ball, water polo, weightlifting, and wrestling.

When *Sports Illustrated* ranked world strengths in 20 sports (counting first three places), the United States barely nosed out the USSR 69 to 67, but both outstripped their closest rivals, Italy and Germany, three to one. However, if the ratings were made on the basis of population, Australia, Denmark, Hungary, Southern Rhodesia, Belgium, New Zealand, Canada, Austria, Sweden, and Italy would rank as the top ten.

No less than 25,000 athletes from nearly every nation of the world will compete this year in international games.

THE OLYMPIC GAMES. An important factor in universalizing sports is the Olympic Games held every four years. Here the picked amateur athletes of the various countries compete under standardized rules.

The founder and father of the modern Olympics (revived in Athens, 1896) was the Baron Pierre de Coubertin, a French rower who conceived of them as an instrument for peace. In their very origin (*ca.* 776 B.C.) the Olympic Games were a celebration of peace, the peace of Zeus. Coubertin believed that a better world or a better nation could be brought about only by better individuals, and that the spirit of fair play promoted by international competition, free from political entanglements and honoring the individuals, was the key to success. He very wisely insisted that no official team or nation scores be kept.

The Olympic Games are not solely a sporting spectacle, however. There are competitions in architecture, town planning, painting, sculpture, crafts, graphic art, literature, dramatic works, music, and musical composition. In addition, the pageantry of the Games is grandiose. There is a wealth of material on the cultural and social significance of the Games and of the customs of different nations. This includes the meaning of the Olympic flag, the flags of different countries, and the dress of the different peoples; the reasons for the release of homing pigeons, the Torch Relay Race, and the international twenty-one-gun salute. The significance of these and many other items furnishes material of interest to all students.

More recently, the Pan-American Games have served to bring about a better understanding of our Latin American neighbors. Athletes of the United States meet with athletes of these countries on the friendly field of athletic competition and thereby have an opportunity to gain a deeper insight into the manners and customs of other peoples. Operations like these cannot help but broaden a person's outlook on life and afford him an opportunity for a much more rounded type of education.

SELECTED REFERENCES

American Association for Health, Physical Education, and Recreation, 1201 Sixteenth Street, N.W., Washington, D.C., 20036:

> *Recreation Research*, 1966. 256 pp.
> *Spectator Sportsmanship*, 1961. 80 pp.
> *Values in Sports*, 1963. 136 pp.

Brightbill, Charles K., *Man and Leisure*. Englewood Cliffs, N.J.: Prentice-Hall, Inc., 1961.

Camping the National Forests—America's Playground. Forest Service, U.S. Department of Agriculture. Washington, D.C.: U.S. Government Printing Office, 1962.

Corbin, H.D., *Recreation Leadership* (2nd ed.). Englewood Cliffs, N.J.: Prentice-Hall, Inc., 1959.

Jokl, Ernst, *et al.*, *Sports in the Cultural Pattern of the World*. Helsinki, Finland: Institute of Occupational Health, 1956.

Kaplan, Max, *Leisure in America: A Social Inquiry*. New York: John Wiley and Sons, Inc., 1960.

Menninger, W.C., "Recreation and Mental Health," *Recreation*, XLII (1948), 340.

Meyer, Harold D., and Charles K. Brightbill, *Community Recreation* (3rd ed.). Englewood Cliffs, N.J.: Prentice-Hall, Inc., 1964.

————, *Recreation Administration: Text and Readings*. Englewood Cliffs, N.J.: Prentice-Hall, Inc., 1956.

Neumeyer, Martin, and Esther S. Neumeyer, *Leisure and Recreation*. New York: The Ronald Press Co., 1958.

Pieper, Josef, *Leisure, the Basis of Culture*. New York: Pantheon Books: Random House, Inc., 1964.

President's Council on Youth Fitness, *Physical Fitness Elements in Recreation*. Washington: The Council, October, 1962.

Smith, Hope M., "Creative Expression in Physical Education," *J. Health, Physical Education, and Recreation*, 33, pp. 38, 39 (1962).

Yukic, Thomas S., *Fundamentals of Recreation*. New York: Harper & Row, 1963.

Desirable Health Practices in Exercise

In nothing do men more nearly approach the gods than in giving health to men.

CICERO

The purpose of this chapter is twofold: (1) to present elementary facts concerning the benefits of exercise, and (2) to discuss helpful hints and precautions for individuals who engage in physical exercise. The first item should help in increasing one's knowledge and understanding of how the body operates. The second is of utmost importance for the preservation of the safety and well-being of the individual, particularly the adult not in the best of physical condition. For the average student such information is not readily available. Not only will an habitual use of these hints make exercise more healthful, but it also will serve to make physical recreations in adult life more enjoyable.

VALUES OF EXERCISE

Life is activity. The basis of even so-called inert organic materials is activity. Movement is characteristic of all types of life. Once movement ceases, so does life.

Compare the body to a machine. One that lies idle will wear out or rust far more quickly than one used regularly. A house not lived in will soon deteriorate and fall apart. A rubber tire stored away eventually crumbles and rots away through disuse.

While the above examples are extremes, they vividly illustrate what would happen to the human body if a person remained at complete rest for a prolonged period of time. In times past, exercise was a part of one's work, but today we have to seek it; we have to cultivate it.

The consensus of scientific opinion today is that exercise is of value to most individuals. It is further agreed that exercise, to be effective, should meet certain fundamental requirements. It must be *regular, enjoyable, vigorous,* and *suited to the individual.*

Young children require four to six hours of physical activity daily; adolescents, two to four hours; and adults, from one to two hours, although the exercise may be partly obtained in one's work. It is impossible to set aside that much time during the school day for physical education classes for each child. The schools do the best they can in the limited time allotted to them. In physical education classes the students are taught skills and activities that serve to make their daily play activities more meaningful and enjoyable.

Physiologically speaking, a person can meet

his daily requirements for physical activity in a variety of ways. He may do it through physical labor such as walking, mowing, gardening; through body-building activities such as calisthenics, push-ups, or setting-up exercises; through recreational sports and games. The important thing is that the more enjoyable one's exercise, the more beneficial it usually is. Most of the experts in the fields of education, mental hygiene, sociology, psychology, and related areas concur in the opinion that exercise obtained through recreational sports or games is usually of more all-around benefit to individuals than other forms of exercise.

For conditioning purposes, vigorous activity engaged in for a short period of time is of more physical benefit than a less vigorous one followed for a longer period. For most people, violent exercise is neither necessary nor advisable. In your exercise, though, you should use the large muscle groups of the arms, legs, trunk, and back as much as possible. Of course, individual differences exist and no hard and fast rules should be adhered to on this point. Naturally the older a person, the less vigorous his activity should be.

Not all people have the same general abilities or capacities. Neither can everybody engage in the same sports or recreations. A person should select those activities best suited to his needs and individual preference.

Physiological values

One common benefit of exercise is the improvement of efficiency in function of the vital organs and the muscular system. The physically trained person will, in his everyday pursuits, expend proportionately less energy and put less strain on his body than the sedentary or physically untrained individual. Another general effect of regular exercise is that it helps promote the growth and development of different body parts. There are many other physiological benefits of regular exercise that will be discussed briefly.

IMPROVED CIRCULATION. Exercise serves to promote better circulation throughout the entire body. This results in part from the fact that the heart pumps out a *greater volume* of blood with *fewer strokes* per minute. For example, the pulse or rate of heart beat for the normal individual under ordinary circumstances is between 70 and 80. For the trained athlete a pulse in the low 60's is not uncommon; in many cases it may be in the 50's, and in rare instances in the low 40's. Training in the endurance type of activities usually results in a lower pulse rate than training in speed or strength

type of activities. For example, in a study of track and field champions it was found that marathon runners on the average had a pulse rate of 59, long distance men of 61, middle distance runners of 63, and dash men or sprinters of 66. A national bicycle champion is reported to have had a pulse rate of 42. Activities that develop muscular strength, like weightlifting or apparatus work, do not have such a remarkable effect on the circulatory system as the above type of activities, and therefore should be accompanied by some form of endurance exercise such as running.

How is it possible to lower the pulse rate through exercise? The explanation is surprisingly simple. The heart is a muscle and, like any other muscle, will increase in size and power when called upon to extend itself regularly. Many raise the question, "Might not 'athlete's heart' result?" The answer is NO. Medical science today recognizes this as a myth. The evidence available indicates that the normal or organically sound heart of a person under 30 *cannot* be permanently injured by exercise.[1] Without compulsion, the individual will cease his effort before the danger point. The real danger all too often is the "loafer's heart," which results from insufficient exercise.

The middle-aged heart, however, has lost its resiliency, and needs to be retrained carefully before engaging in sudden efforts of strength or speed. Where death has resulted because of a failure in the circulatory system of an individual while he was exercising strenuously, it has been observed that his heart or circulatory system had been damaged by disease at some previous date. Injury, however, from exercise *may* result when too severe a strain is placed on the heart by someone who is not in adequate physical condition for the demands of the activity; and, in particular, injury is likely to occur from severe exercise if the heart has been weakened by illness or by infectious disease.

Exercise promotes improved circulation by aiding the "peripheral heart" action. This means that the movement of muscles and body organs assists in returning the blood to the heart. This is especially important in the extremities of the body. If one is forced to stand still a long time, twitching of the toes and leg muscles aids peripheral circulation and helps avoid fainting.

Improved circulation assures improvement in the heat-regulating mechanism of the body. Exercise warms the body when it is cold, while on hot days mild exercise has a cooling effect on the body. Ex-

---

[1] Some physiologists include no age limitation in this assertion.

ercise not only speeds up circulation but also assures the different body muscles of their share of the blood supply. It accelerates blood to the legs and arms and increases evaporation, which cools the body.

IMPROVED RESPIRATION. Respiration, or breathing, is the means by which oxygen is taken into the body and the waste products of oxidation carried off. During exercise, the rate of respiration increases. The trained person will have a slower and deeper respiration than one who is out of condition, and will meet the demands placed on his respiratory system with less effort and more efficiency.

IMPROVED DIGESTION. Exercise aids digestion in two ways: (1) it increases the appetite because of the consequent increased demand or need for food by the body, and (2) the movement of the digestive organs speeds up the peristaltic action that moves the digested food along more rapidly and easily.

IMPROVED ELIMINATION. Elimination is greatly aided and constipation prevented by exercise. The peristaltic action increases, and therefore the processes of excretion are more efficiently regulated. Physically active persons are much less apt to be afflicted with kidney stones and similar ailments than sedentary people.

Many waste products are removed through the sweat glands in the skin. This process is speeded up during vigorous exercise. The perspiration also has a cleansing effect on the skin.

IMPROVED MUSCULATURE. The muscles become stronger through use. Also, the general muscle tone of the body is improved through exercise. The

special value of calisthenic and body-conditioning exercises lies in the fact that especially weak muscle groups can be singled out for developmental attention. Posture can be improved by developing the elastic muscles of the back. Strong abdominal muscles assist in preventing a flabby, sagging abdomen, and also prevent the pooling of blood in the lower abdomen, thus reducing faintness or vertigo.

OTHER VALUES. Another value of exercise is the increase in production of red blood cells in the bone marrow. The hemoglobin count of the blood also is raised through activity. Exercise can help in keeping blood pressure from becoming too high.

Regular exercise improves and maintains the general all-around fitness of the individual. For instance, it increases strength, endurance, agility, and coordination. It retards the onset of fatigue. Mild fatigue resulting from exercise is a good preventative of insomnia; however, overexercise and lameness of muscles will have a contrary effect and should be avoided.

Exercise is effective in reducing neuro-muscular tension. Muscular relaxation is basic to mental relaxation. Tension in either the mind or muscles sets up nerve impulses that travel between the two. This makes it impossible to have complete relaxation in one without relaxation in the other. (See Chapter 5.)

Longevity

Americans today live more than three times as long as the citizens of Rome did during Julius

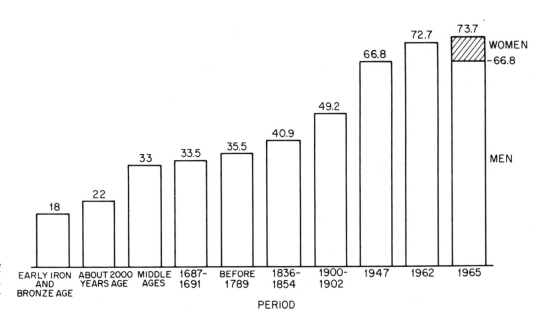

FIGURE 3-1. The increase of longevity (Adapted by E. Jokl from Louis Dublin, Metropolitan Co.)

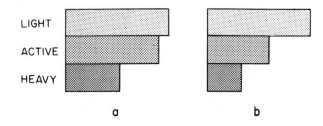

FIGURE 3-2. Ratios of death from coronary heart disease (a); and incidence of degenerated cardiac changes found post mortem (b) in 5000 males, age 45–70, whose vocational occupations involve light, active, and heavy physical work. The comparatively favorable status of the most active group is apparent. (From Prof. J. N. Morris, ET AL.)

Caesar's time and twice as long as they did during the Revolutionary War. The total length of life is greatest among industrial nations. This remarkable extension of life expectancy through the ages is shown in the accompanying chart. (See Fig. 3-1.)

This increase in longevity has been due to three principal factors: (1) drastic reduction of the rate of infant mortality, (2) improvement in nutrition, and (3) conquest of infectious diseases by medical science.

The age-old enigma of whether or not strenuous exercise lengthens life is still debatable. Recent studies, however, have shown that persons who are active *throughout* their lives have superior longevity records. (See Fig. 3-2.) Morris has drawn attention to the startling differences between London bus driv-

ers who sit practically all day and the active conductors who must collect fares on the double-deck vehicles. Similarly, Karvonen, in Finland, found that former skiing champions lived about seven years longer than inactive subjects. (See Fig. 3-3.)

Longevity does not depend upon the strength of muscles but upon the absence of organic disease and the capacity of the cardiovascular systems to withstand the day's stresses. It has been noted by most studies throughout the years that former athletes in general do not live longer than non-athletes of similar station in life. This may be due in part to the fact that athletes tend to die by violent means (by accident and in war) more often than non-athletes, and that relatively few continue a physically active life after the age of thirty.

Jokl concludes, "That in technological societies such as the United States where the degenerative cardiovascular diseases are the leading cause of death, a sustained exercise regime is likely to prolong the span of life by several years, probably as much as a decade. . . . However, the short intensive physical training adopted by the majority of outstanding athletes in the United States today between ages 16 to 26 *does not* lengthen the span of life." [2]

[2] Ernst Jokl, "Effect of Sports on the Cardiovascular System," *Encyclopedia of the Cardiovascular System*, Chapter 25 (New York: McGraw-Hill Book Company, Inc., 1961).

FIGURE 3-3. (*Left*) Percentage of survival of Finnish champion skiers as compared with that of the general male population. At the 50 per cent level, the difference is approximately seven years in favor of the skiers. (*Right*) Corresponding data for the students of Cambridge University, England. (By M. J. Karvonen, Finland.)

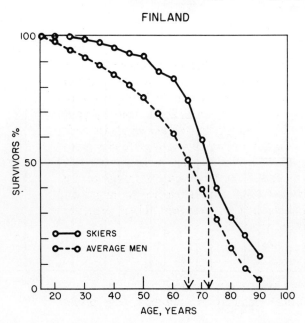

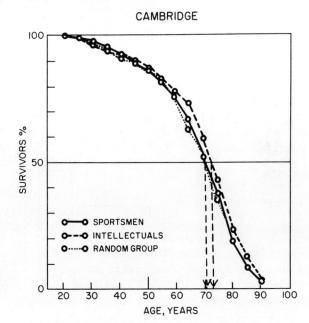

Psychological values

Exercise is relaxing to the mind. It improves the mental tone of an individual. It assists in maintaining mental health. An interesting game takes the mind off oneself and concentrates it on outward interests. For this reason a healthful game or hobby is more valuable than walking. Exercise also permits release of pent-up emotions through socially approved channels. It provides for self-expression. It is a means of satisfying primitive urges and wishes for new experience, security, response, recognition, and participation. It is a means of developing confidence and of obtaining the joys and satisfactions that come from a successfully completed task. Many sports contain self-testing values by means of which a player can compete against his own performance, for example, golf and bowling. Exercise may be done alone or with others.

Sociological values

Man is strongly motivated by the social instinct of gregariousness. He desires to be with and mingle with his fellow men. This instinct or desire may be satisfied through sport. In sports, other social values such as teamwork, loyalty, and sportsmanship may also be achieved. The congenial atmosphere of sports offers opportunity to develop fellowship and friendships. Sports have corecreational values also.

HINTS AND PRECAUTIONS FOR EXERCISE

Certain things must be kept in mind if exercise is to be beneficial, if the participant wishes to avoid strains and pains, if he desires not to harm his health, and if he wants his exercise to be thoroughly enjoyable. There are principles that, if followed, will increase and improve the rate of learning and consequently the participant's level of achievement. A more efficient performance in turn leads to greater thrills and joys for the individual player.

Regular physical check-up

The importance of a periodic physical examination by a physician cannot be overemphasized for every individual. The necessity for this increases as one grows older. It is of fundamental importance for people who participate in physical recreations.

Serious damage to one's health may easily result from the failure to find out first what activities your body is capable of undertaking.

Training regimen

Follow a regular training routine. Get in condition for your favorite sport. It is foolish to go all out in any activity before your body is in condition for it. Adults must train more slowly than younger people. Avoid the athletic "binge" on a weekend. Be regular in exercise habits and prevent sore, stiffened muscles.

One advantage of being in good physical condition is that this condition will continue for two or three months in spite of a curtailment of exercise. After this time, however, continued inactivity will cause well-trained individuals to retrogress markedly. After adequate condition is achieved it may be maintained with a smaller amount of training. People often ask, "Is physical conditioning for one sport carried over to conditioning for other sports?" Yes, there is an organic carry-over; but the use of different muscles and different coordinations causes temporary muscular lameness and fatigue. Also, rushing from training and participation in one sport to another demanding severe training often causes "staleness."

Another question frequently asked concerning physical conditioning is, "Is it harmful to stop exercise suddenly after being accustomed to a vigorous exercise program?" It is not harmful, but if one is used to being in condition, he does not feel as well when he stops exercising, and a state of lassitude follows prolonged inactivity. Waste products accumulate and are not carried off as rapidly as when he was active.

Warm-up

Limber up muscles before subjecting them to vigorous effort. You do not race the motor of an automobile on a cold winter morning without warming it up, neither should you race the motor of your body without preparing it for the increased demands for vigorous activity. Warming up the muscles gradually increases their elasticity and makes them ready for greater efforts. The large muscle groups of the arms, legs, and trunk should receive the major attention in limbering up exercises. These exercises should not be too violent.

Tapering-off

Permit your physiological mechanisms to return to normal gradually. An abrupt change places a greater burden on your body, causing discomfort. Immediately after violent exercise, move about moderately rather than sit still. If one "stops slower" after exercise, his breathing and heart rate will recover much more quickly and his temperature is equalized more rapidly. If one keeps moving about after vigorous exertion a breeze is created around him that also helps to cool him off more quickly; however, avoid cooling off too rapidly after heavy perspiration.

Flopping down on the ground after hard competitive exercise is an undesirable practice. Acids and other waste products produced by exercising muscles cause capillaries to open wide, thus getting more blood to the needy muscles. So, if a person relaxes suddenly after hard competitive exercise, the increased flow of blood will stagnate in the open capillaries. Only the contractions of the muscles of the arm, leg, trunk, and internal organs can drive blood back to the heart. Therefore, sudden relaxation after vigorous exertion may cause dizziness, nausea, or even fainting.

Muscular stiffness and soreness

If only slightly muscularly lame, one should employ moderate exercise for recovery rather than remain inactive. Moderate exercise helps the pumping action of the heart that is necessary to bring new blood to body parts. A moderate walk on Sunday will help one limber up the stiffness from Saturday more effectively than complete rest. The new blood carries away waste products and thereby reduces muscle lameness more quickly.

Avoid drafts or sleeping in rooms that are too cold. Avoid sudden movements when leaning over, as in reaching for a golf bag, and you will lessen troubles arising from a lame back.

Moderation

Observe moderation in your sports, especially as you grow older. Avoid overdoing and overstrain. Unless you show resiliency, you are overdoing. Emotional stresses in sports can be as serious as overexertion. Certain individuals need to be careful about attending exciting athletic spectacles. Be careful when breathless. Take your time. Use many short rest periods, particularly if gardening or shoveling snow or carrying loads you're not accustomed to. Be careful about overenthusiasm for exercising outdoors in early spring and late fall. This is an easy time to chill. Consequently, if perspiring, it is a wise precaution to take a bath and change your clothes. In the summer do not try to get a tan in one day. Tanning

may be harmful, especially when it is attained the "blistering way." Most physicians warn about the dangers of overexposure to the sun.

Diet

In general, people who participate in sports require more food than those who lead sedentary lives. Activity requires energy, and food is the source of energy. Maintain a balanced diet. You should avoid eating a heavy meal immediately prior to participating in a strenuous activity of a competitive nature where the emotional stress is apt to be high. However, light or moderate activity may be safely pursued shortly after eating. If you intend to engage in a recreational sport shortly after a meal, eat moderately and without haste. Eating rapidly or when emotionally upset may lead to "indigestion." Do not overeat when tired. It is better to wait until your physiological processes have readjusted themselves. Eat a very light meal or wait a while before eating a heavy meal after vigorous exercise. When exhausted, you can get a quick lift from a small amount of food like a candy bar or a soft drink. This is because sugar is quickly and easily digested and reaches the blood stream in a comparatively short time.

The basic principle in weight control is simple. If one eats more calories than the body uses, the surplus is stored as fat. A person wishing to reduce must cut down on the number of calories eaten. He should not indulge in bizarre diets or crash programs, but seek the guidance of a physician.

Fitness and fatness

The mortality rates of overweight persons between the ages of 20 and 65 exceed those of normal weight by 15 per cent. Obese people are more apt to develop high blood pressure, heart disease, and diabetes, are poorer surgical risks, and have less resistance to infection. It should be kept in mind that every pound of fat requires 4500 feet of blood vessels and expansion of capillaries. This places a tremendous work load on the heart.

It is difficult to determine one's proper weight because body structures are so varied. The accompanying chart prepared by Dorothy W. Sargent lists weights in six different categories. A person is underweight if he is more than 15 per cent under the average weight; slender, 7.5 to 15 per cent under average; stocky, 7.5 to 15 per cent over; overweight, 15 to 30 per cent over; obese, 30 per cent over average weight. (See Fig. 3-4.)

Exercise is a controlling factor in maintaining body weight. Diet used wisely will help. Overweight individuals may reduce by long continued periods of strenuous exercises—not to be followed by overeating. With underweight individuals, appetite is stimulated and poundage may be added if care is taken not to overdo.

The role of exercise in overweight has taken on greater significance during recent years. Bruch found that most fat children are physically less active than lean children; that *inactivity* is the chief cause of obesity; and that inhibition of activity represents a more fundamental disturbance of metabolism than overeating. Jokl has presented evidence

FIGURE 3-4. Average weights for men, 21 to 29 years old, and women, 17 to 29 years old. Weight is in pounds, and is based on height. (From Dorothy W. Sargent, M.S., "Weight-height Relationship of Young Men and Women," *American Journal of Clinical Nutrition*, November, 1963.)

YOUNG MEN

HEIGHT (IN.)	UNDER-WEIGHT	SLENDER	NOR-MAL	STOCKY	OVER-WEIGHT	OBESE
63	111	121	131	141	151	170
64	114	124	134	144	155	175
65	117	128	138	148	159	179
66	120	131	141	152	163	184
67	123	134	145	156	167	188
68	126	138	149	160	171	193
69	130	141	152	164	175	198
70	133	145	156	168	180	203
71	136	148	160	172	184	209
72	140	152	165	177	189	214
73	143	156	169	181	194	219
74	147	160	173	186	199	225
75	151	164	178	191	204	231
76	155	168	182	196	209	237
77	159	173	187	201	215	243
78	163	177	192	206	220	249

YOUNG WOMEN

HEIGHT (IN.)	UNDER-WEIGHT	SLENDER	NOR-MAL	STOCKY	OVER-WEIGHT	OBESE
58	88	95	103	111	119	134
59	90	98	106	114	122	138
60	93	101	109	117	125	142
61	95	104	112	120	129	146
62	98	106	115	124	132	150
63	101	109	118	127	136	154
64	103	112	122	131	140	158
65	106	116	125	134	144	162
66	109	119	128	138	148	167
67	112	122	132	142	152	172
68	115	126	136	146	156	176
69	119	129	140	150	160	181
70	122	133	143	154	165	186
71	125	136	147	158	170	192
72	129	140	152	163	174	197
73	132	144	156	167	179	202
74	136	148	160	172	184	208

to the effect that a sustained regime of intensive physical training may change physique and *character* of obese children. He further explains that the reduction of excess fat, as a result of long-term adjustments to physical training, is invariably accompanied by a gain in lean tissue.

It must be concluded that a combination of the correct amount of exercise and diet is the most effective method of controlling weight. See Figure 3-5 for calorie energy expenditures for various activities.

Clothing

Cleanliness is the first rule in regard to clothing to be worn in playing sports. This is important not only for the purpose of minimizing skin infections, but also for aesthetic values. Dress comfortably. Avoid clothing that fits too tightly. Care should be given to select properly fitting shoes and socks. Wool or part-wool socks are better than cotton ones. Two pairs are better than one. They help prevent blisters on the soles and heels of the feet. Wear clean socks without holes that might cause blisters.

Dress warmly when necessary. If possible, do not expose yourself to inclement weather; when exposed, follow all possible safeguards. If caught in the rain, take as hot a bath as possible to induce perspiration. Avoid sitting around in wet clothes after exercise as this causes chill.

Rest

Adequate rest is necessary for health. The average individual requires eight or nine hours of sleep each night. A growing boy or girl needs more than a mature man or woman. Exhausting exercise or work necessitates additional rest. Get your rest regularly if you exercise; otherwise, exercise may tear you down rather than build you up.

Shower

A daily bath or shower is an accepted practice in modern society. A shower should always be taken after exercise for both hygienic and social reasons. Such a shower cleanses the skin, reduces chances of skin infections and rashes, and removes unpleasant body odors. Do not go out into the cold immediately after a hot shower. Follow a hot shower by a short, cool one, particularly if going outdoors at once. Never take a cold shower just before going to bed or immediately after exercise. The warm shower will cause relaxation. Avoid plunging into a cold shower after perspiring very freely. This brings about a reaction that causes one to perspire again. There are individual differences to be consid-

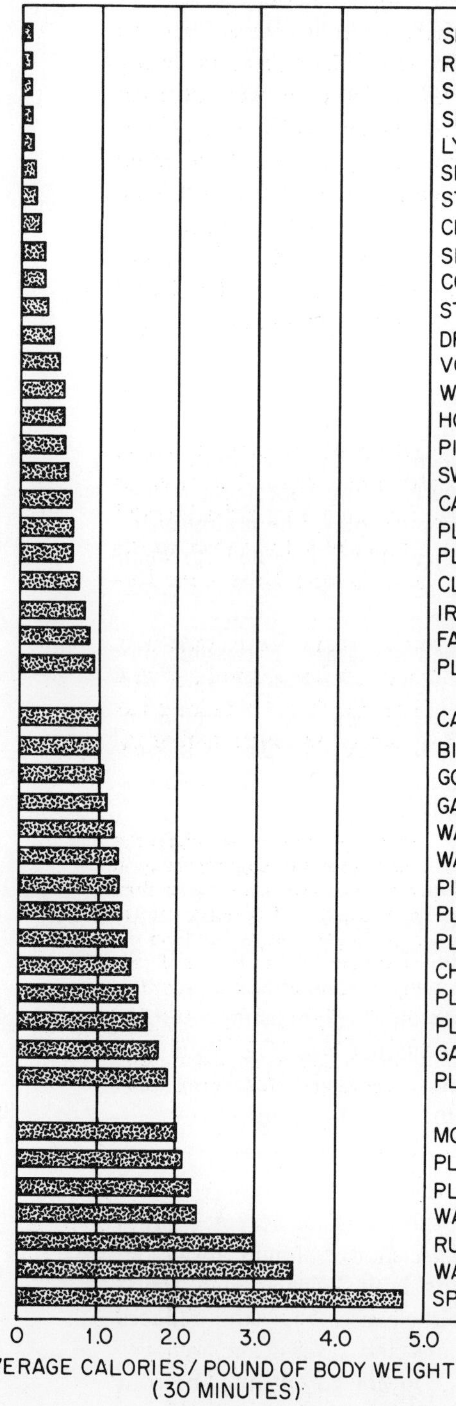

Activity	120 #♀	160 #♂
SLEEPING	28	38
RESTING IN BED	28	38
SITTING NORMALLY	29	38
SITTING READING	29	38
LYING QUIETLY	32	43
SITTING EATING	33	44
STANDING NORMALLY	34	45
CLASSWORK, LECTURE	40	53
SITTING, WRITING	44	59
CONVERSING	44	59
STANDING, LIGHT ACTIVITY	58	78
DRIVING A CAR	72	96
VOLLEYBALL	83	110
WALKING ON LEVEL (2.27 MPH)	84	112
HOUSE PAINTING	—	112
PITCHING HORSESHOES	85	113
SWEEPING FLOORS	88	—
CARPENTRY	—	123
PLAYING PING-PONG	93	124
PLEASURE SWIMMING (BACK STROKE, 25 YD/MIN)	93	124
CLEANING WINDOWS	99	—
IRONING CLOTHES	103	—
FARMING, PLANTING, HOEING, RAKING	—	150
PLEASURE SWIMMING (BREAST STROKE, 20 YD/MIN)	115	154
CALISTHENICS	120	160
BICYCLING ON LEVEL ROADS	120	160
GOLFING	130	173
GARDENING, WEEDING	141	188
WALKING ON LEVEL (4.47 MPH)	159	212
WALKING DOWNSTAIRS	160	213
PICK-AND-SHOVEL WORK	—	214
PLAYING TENNIS	166	221
PLAYING BASKETBALL	169	225
CHOPPING WOOD	—	240
PLEASURE SWIMMING (BACK STROKE, 40 YD/MIN)	200	267
PLEASURE SWIMMING (CRAWL, 45 YD/MIN)	209	284
GARDENING, DIGGING	—	298
PLEASURE SWIMMING (BREAST STROKE, 40 YD/MIN)	231	306
MOUNTAIN CLIMBING	241	321
PLAYING SQUASH	—	332
PLEASURE SWIMMING (CRAWL, 55 YD/MIN)	255	340
WALKING ON LEVEL (5.80 MPH)	273	364
RUNNING, LONG DISTANCE	361	481
WALKING UPSTAIRS	416	555
SPRINTING	561	748

AVERAGE CALORIES / POUND OF BODY WEIGHT (30 MINUTES)

AVERAGE CALORIES (30 MINUTES)

FIGURE 3-5. Approximate energy expenditure in various physical activities and "inactivities." Comparison-ranking in calories per pound per 30 minutes and examples calculated for a 120-pound and a 160-pound person. Data from a summary by C. F. Consolazio, R. E. Johnson, and L. J. Pecora, *Physiological Measurements of Metabolic Functions in Man.* New York: McGraw-Hill Book Company, 1963, pp. 330–32. (Figure adapted from Perry B. Johnson, *et al., Physical Education: A Problem Solving Approach to Health and Fitness.* New York: Holt, Rinehart & Winston, Inc., 1966, p. 215. Reprinted by permission.)

ered; if a person reacts violently to an extremely cold shower, he should avoid this extreme. Allow the body to cool off gradually. After the shower, dry the body briskly and thoroughly, especially the feet. Dust powder between the toes.

If no hot showers are available after exercise, a brisk rubdown with a towel is preferable to jumping into a cold shower. Drying the body briskly helps one cool off. It also serves as a gentle massage that relaxes muscles, helps remove waste products, and reduces lameness in muscles more quickly because of the increased circulation following it. For the same reasons an alcohol rubdown after exercise reduces lameness.

Illness

Be especially moderate in exercise following colds, influenza, and infectious diseases. If there is any doubt about how much you can do, see your physician first, or get advice from a health service.

Injuries

Too much care or caution cannot be used when dealing with injuries received in exercise. Even the slightest cut or scratch, if neglected, may lead to serious complications. There have been instances where floor burns received from a fall on a gymnasium floor have resulted in leg amputations. Similar results have been known to occur from scratches received in playing tennis. Prompt and immediate first aid should be administered in case of all injuries, however slight they may be. After first aid, the safe procedure is to consult a physician. If you receive an injury in your physical education class, ask your instructor what should be done. If there is the slightest sign of an infection developing from an injury, go to the health service or a physician without delay.

Exercise and competition harmful for females?

For many years there has been an unsubstantiated belief that strenuous exercise, especially athletics, is detrimental to the health of the female. This generally accepted concept has been based upon such vague assumptions that athletic women become mannish and have difficulty bearing children, that activities which require jumping may cause damage to healthy pelvic organs, and that girls should participate only in expressive, artistic, and rhythmical forms of exercise.

These imagined physiological calamities have

been gradually disproved by the research of physiologists and the general observation of experts in the field. Studies of female athletes have shown rather conclusively that child-bearing is "easier," of shorter delivery duration, and fertility ratios were found to be no different than for non-athletic females. Many women have been found to improve their physical efficiency during early pregnancy and following childbirth. The normal menstrual period is not disturbed by exercise, even in its competitive forms, and often a girl's best performance is recorded during this period. It is recommended that a girl carry on her regular physical education activity during this period unless advised otherwise by her physician.

Smoking is harmful

Smoking stands condemned for those who are concerned for their health and physical fitness. It has long been recognized that smoking is detrimental to athletic performances, especially for those sports that require endurance, and has therefore been forbidden by most coaches.

Studies during recent years have shown a strong statistical association between smoking and coronary heart disease. (See Fig. 3-6.) Smoking has been accused of causing cancer by such authorita-

FIGURE 3-6. Mortality ratios by number of cigarettes smoked per day. The death rate of men smoking regularly at a rate of less than ½ pack per day is 34 per cent higher than the death rate of men who never smoked. The death rate of men smoking 1–2 packs a day is 96 per cent higher than the death rate of men who never smoked. The death rate of men smoking 2 packs or more a day is 123 per cent higher than the death rate of men who never smoked. (Adapted from C. Cuyler Hammond and Daniel Horn, *Smoking in Relation to Death Rates,* from a report to the annual meeting of the American Medical Association, New York, June 1957.)

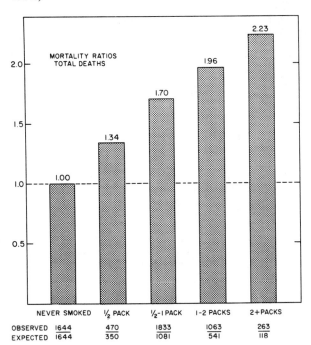

tive bodies as the World Health Organization, the United States Public Health Service, the Royal College of Physicians of London, and the American Cancer Association. The Royal College of Physicians in its report to the government states, "Cigarette smoking is a cause of lung cancer and bronchitis and probably contributes to the development of coronary heart disease and various less common diseases . . . and that heavy cigarette smokers may have thirty times the death rate of non-smokers." (See Figs. 3-7 and 3-8.)

With this weight of evidence against smoking, it is estimated that one million students now in school will die prematurely of cancer before they are 70 years of age.

Drugs and the athlete

Athletes have always hoped for a miracle potion (or drug) that would improve their abilities. However, medical science does not know of any such ergogenic aid and a trained athlete's performance cannot be improved pharmacologically. The most consistent claims for such powers have been ascribed to amphetamine, but no scientific investi-

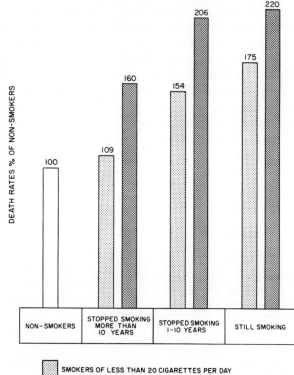

DEATH RATES FROM CORONARY HEART DISEASE
AMERICAN MEN AGED 50-70

FIGURE 3-7. The relationship between numbers of cigarettes smoked per day and lung cancer death rates in three prospective studies. The figure shows how much the risk of getting lung cancer is multiplied in those who smoke various numbers of cigarettes per day compared with the risk of non-smokers. The first horizontal line in the figure indicates ten times the risk of non-smokers, and so on.

The similarity of the steady increase in lung cancer risk with increasing cigarette smoking found by these three independent studies is impressive. The higher British rates may be due to the British habit of smoking cigarettes to a shorter stub length than the Americans and to the greater exposure of British men to air polluted by domestic and industrial smoke.

FIGURE 3-8. The relationship of death rates from coronary heart disease to smoking habits. These figures are taken from the American prospective study by Hammond and Horn. The death rate of heavy smokers was twice that of non-smokers, and even after they had given up cigarettes for more than ten years the rate was still half as much again as for non-smokers. In the lighter smokers the excess was still considerable, but those who had given up for more than ten years had a death rate nearly the same as that of non-smokers.

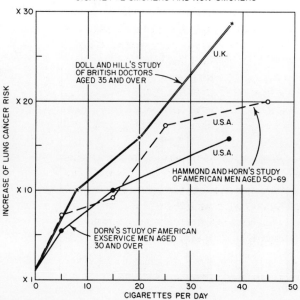

RATIOS OF LUNG CANCER MORTALITY BETWEEN
CIGARETTE SMOKERS AND NON-SMOKERS

gator has ever shown that this stimulant (commonly known as "bennies") will improve an athlete's performance. A number of studies have shown an opposite effect—that its use causes a significant impairment of efficiency.

While it is not possible to improve one's physical ability, it is quite easy to impede ability. The use of narcotics such as morphine, codeine, and heroin will adversely affect one's ability to perform. Although narcotics play a necessary role in the treatment of severe pain, there is always a chance of addiction and the recovery from drug addiction is pitifully small—less than 10 per cent make a complete recovery.

Among other drugs that not only affect one's physical performance but may be harmful to his mental balance are the depressants, hallucinogens, and solvents. The depressants are barbiturate drugs and tranquilizers used as sedatives. The hallucinogens, including LSD, DMT, peyote, mescaline, and also marijuana, have received an inordinate amount of publicity. None has any established medical value. Inhalation of solvents (glue is one) resembles alcohol intoxication, and one of its greatest dangers is suffocation. The use of hallucinogens may develop strong psychological dependence and may ruin an athlete's career. Most young people who use such hallucinogens (including marijuana, "pot") do not have stable central nervous systems and for this reason they are particularly dangerous for them.

Safety

Everybody interested in sports is vitally concerned with making the playing of a game as safe as possible. The equipment, rules, and courtesies are all designed to protect the players insofar as is humanly possible. The ultimate responsibility for the participants' safety, however, rests in large measure on the players themselves. A participant should keep in mind not only his own welfare, but that of the other players as well. Each sport has its own safety code and each of the chapters on the different sports in this book contains a section devoted to the safety precautions for that particular sport. Follow these precautions. Protect yourself, your teammate, and your opponent.

Time to exercise

Students enrolled in physical education often do not have a choice of time to participate; however, the last part of the afternoon is accepted as the best time for recreational exercise. There is plenty of time for showering and dressing. And having no full, busy day ahead makes people more ready psychologically for a good work-out. They do not have to face a day's work tired out from exercise. This is true for mental workers as well, because if one is tired out bodily, it is hard to concentrate on study. Also, exercise in the late afternoon helps to remove many of the waste products that have resulted from the day's work. Avoid the heat of the day if possible; if exercising, keep moving, and loiter in the shade whenever possible.

The time least suited for exercise is immediately after a meal, just after getting up in the morning or before going to bed at night, and when ill or injured. Early in the morning, metabolism is low and heavy exercising is like racing a cold motor. If you exercise at this time of the day, your exercise should not be violent but should be of a warming up nature. Vigorous exercise before sleep is detrimental because it increases circulation, and, if of a competitive nature, it causes excitement, all of which makes for wakefulness. Exercising when you are ill or injured or just after an illness may result in irreparable harm to your health, because the body is in a lowered state of resistance at this time.

From the mental standpoint, the time to exercise is when you think you are too busy to do so because then you are probably working so hard you are most in need of relaxation. A sign of overwork is the inability to detach oneself from one's work. Yet this is the sign that a change is needed. A quotation is used to illustrate this point. Malcolm Bingay, the columnist, writing in the *Detroit Free Press,* spoke of his friendship with Henry Ford as follows: "By having many other interests," he (Ford) said, "that is the way to keep the mind open and happy. Have hobbies, have other interests than your own business. Never get into a rut. . . . If I cannot solve some problem concerning the Ford Motor Co. and it looks as though we were up against a stone wall, I forget all about it. Just drop it! I come out here to the fields and watch the birds and the flowers, or I devote my time to research on soy beans. Or I mend watches or dance or go to a show. Anything that happens to appeal to me as long as it has nothing to do with business. Then, after I am rested from these activities, I return to the problem that had me stopped. Invariably I have found a solution by this time. Or, rather, I have not actually found it; it has found me."

Choice of exercise

Find recreations that compensate for the excessive demands of your occupation, for example, to offset continuous standing, sitting, or use of eyes. Barbers and dentists are prone to varicose veins and flat feet. Exercise tends to equalize circulation and is very beneficial to men in those occupations requiring long hours of standing. The desk worker gets relaxation from a change of activity. As his work tires only his nervous system, his muscles are still fresh and ready for physical activity after a day's work. Chronic fatigue, which is very apt to plague the sedentary worker, can often be prevented by regular amounts of physical activity. Recreational exercise for the desk worker, however, should not be too strenuous.

Have more than one favorite sport so that more muscles are used and certain muscles are not overworked. Select sports that can be geared to your abilities and endurance rather than ones that set the pace for you. In later life, recreational exercise differs greatly from that of youth. It is largely an individual matter to be worked out by each person in accordance with his preference, his physical capacity, and his leisure. No rigid criteria can be established to determine at what age an individual should stop playing a particular sport. For this reason, each individual should be the best judge of what he is capable of undertaking, that is, provided he has the assurance of a physician as to the status of his health. A word of caution is advisable. The 60-year-old can probably participate in most activities if he plays at a pace suited to the physical capacity of a 60-year-old. He should not attempt to keep up with a 20- or a 30-year-old. He must play at a slower pace, use more frequent rest periods, pause when out of breath, and not push himself to the point of exhaustion. Remember, though, that the person who continually plays his favorite sport, other things being equal, can probably continue to play it at an older age than a person who has not played regularly. Above all, as you grow older, be philosophical about decreasing ability. Gear yourself to a less strenuous pace. Play doubles instead of singles whenever possible.

Speed and endurance

Speed is an attribute of youth. The average age of champions in the 100- and 200-yard dashes is between 18 and 22. On the other hand, strength and endurance reach a peak at a much later age. For example, most marathon champions average between 35 and 45 years of age. Once speed is lost, it cannot be regained. The older an adult becomes, the less he should subject himself to activities in which speed or sudden starts and stops are fundamental factors in playing the game. It is important to remember that strength and endurance have to be continually maintained. They cannot be acquired by piecemeal methods. If an older person has long neglected conditioning, he should begin gradually with mild exercises. If he keeps up his physical conditioning, he can undertake endurance tasks along with the younger person. Witness the seemingly tireless efforts of seasoned guides, hunters, and trappers who tire out their younger but less experienced companions.

Learning skills

There are no short cuts to learning a motor skill. There are, however, certain fundamental principles which, if followed, will serve to make the learning process more enjoyable and consequently increase the satisfactions to be derived from sports participation.

Skill is learned once in a lifetime, whereas strength and endurance must be regained many times. A player who has once been an expert in a certain sport will always demonstrate "the motions" of proper form even though they may not be executed well. The skill in the form of execution is retained even though at first there is not the old success in obtaining results. This emphasizes the importance of learning carry-over skills that can be maintained beyond school days and throughout life. In sports such as archery, swimming, bowling, tennis, badminton, and golf, a person gains skills that do not decline too noticeably; and, in these, he can also regulate the pace of competition so that he does not overdo. Handicapping devices also make it possible to compete against better players.

The ideal time to learn sports skills is now—while you are in school. An individual's motor skill and his ability to master fine neuro-muscular coordinations pass their peaks somewhere between the ages of 25 and 30. Thereafter, a gradual decline sets in, continuing to the later years of life. It is encouraging to note that regular practice of a motor skill retards this decline markedly. In fact, a person who practices a motor skill regularly will barely recognize any loss of his ability, the decrease will be so slight. Skills may be learned no matter how old a person may be, but it takes a little more time, more effort, and more persistence on the part of the older player. His learning rate is slowed in part because he may not have the same enthusiasm as a youth and there may also be conflicting responsibilities. But if an older person makes up his mind to learn some new sport skill and sticks to it, he can achieve a great deal.

The most important advice to offer anyone starting to learn a new sport is to start out under the guidance of an expert instructor. In this way the learning of faulty habits and incorrect techniques will be held to a minimum. Such bad habits retard the rate of learning and require endless relearning practice if they are to be overcome.

Certain things assist in the learning process, while others slow down or retard the rate of learning. Regular practice is a *must*. Short and frequent practice periods are better than longer and fewer ones. A person should learn the proper form first. He should try to get the kinesthetic feel and a mental picture of the correct movement before attempting to go "all out." Interest in the activity will promote faster and more efficient learning.

Fatigue slows down the learning rate, since it not only causes discomfort for the performer, but also increases the frequency of faulty habits and mistakes. "Staleness" is a form of fatigue. A good remedy for staleness is rest or a complete cessation of participation in that activity where staleness has set in. Sometimes a change to another kind of activity will cure staleness.

Summary

Once the student has finished the required physical education classes, his exercise becomes a matter of individual choice. The more enjoyable and satisfying an individual's exercise, the more likely he will be to continue it. The enjoyments of exercise cannot be had by piecemeal methods. Exercise must be a habit. It must be cultivated to be enjoyed. The discussion in this chapter has presented suggestions that should help the performer to keep his exercise on a sane and even keel. They are important enough to be mentioned again in outline form.

1. Have a periodic physical check-up by a physician.
2. Follow a regular training regimen.
3. Be regular in exercise habits.
4. Limber up muscles before engaging in vigorous activity.
5. Practice moderation in your sports; avoid overdoing and overstrain.
6. After vigorous exercise, move about rather than sit still; cool off gradually.
7. Eat a nourishing and well-balanced diet, but avoid a heavy meal immediately preceding or following exercise.
8. Wear clean, warm, comfortable clothing; avoid too tight clothing; wear two pairs of socks.
9. Get your rest regularly.
10. Take a warm shower after exercise; follow it by a short cool one; dry thoroughly.
11. Be cautious in exercise following illness.
12. Give immediate first aid for all injuries, however slight.
13. Follow the safety precautions, including rules and courtesies of the sport.
14. Time your exercise to fit your pattern of living; avoid heat of day if possible, being cautious not to get an overdose of sunburn.
15. Select sports suited to your interests, needs, and abilities.
16. Secure guidance of an expert instructor when learning new sports.
17. Use short and frequent practice periods.
18. The time to exercise is when you think you are too busy to do so.

SELECTED REFERENCES

American Association for Health, Physical Education, and Recreation, 1201 Sixteenth Street, N.W., Washington, D.C., 20036:
   Drug Abuse: Escape to Nowhere, 1967. 104 pp.
   Exercise and Fitness, 1964. 24 pp.
   Fit for College, 1959. 12 pp.
   Why Physical Education? (College).
   Why Physical Education? (High School).
   This is Physical Education, 1965. 24 pp.

Hickman, C.P., *Health for College Students.* Englewood Cliffs, N.J.: Prentice-Hall, Inc., 1963.

Johns, Edward B., W.C. Sutton, and L.E. Webster, *Health for Effective Living* (3rd ed.). New York: McGraw-Hill Book Co., Inc., 1962.

Johnson, Perry B., *et al., Physical Education—A Problem Solving Approach to Health and Fitness.* New York: Holt, Rinehart & Winston, Inc., 1966.

Johnson, Warren R., ed., *Science and Medicine of Exercise and Sports.* New York: Harper & Row, 1960.

Jokl, Ernst, "Athletic Status of Women," *British J. Phys. Med.,* XX (1957), 247.

————, "Fitness and Fatness," and "Physical Activity and Body Composition," *Proceedings Conference on Body Composition.* New York: Academy of Sciences, January, 1963.

Karpovich, P.D., *Physiology of Muscular Activity* (6th ed.). Philadelphia: W.B. Saunders Co., 1965.

Mayer, J., and B. Bullen, "Nutrition and Athletic Performance," in *Exercise and Fitness.* Chicago: The Athletic Institute, 1960.

Montoye, H.J., "Sports and Length of Life," *Science and Medicine of Exercise and Sports,* ed. W.R. Johnson. New York: Harper & Row, 1960.

Spain, D.M., and D.J. Mathan, "Smoking Habits and Atherosclerotic Heart Disease," *J. American Medical Association,* CLXXVII (1961), 683.

Steinhaus, Arthur H., *Toward an Understanding of Health and Physical Education.* Dubuque, Iowa: Wm. C. Brown Co., 1963.

Taylor, H.J., "The Mortality and Morbidity of Coronary Heart Disease of Men in Sedentary and Physically Active Occupations," in *Exercise and Fitness.* Chicago: The Athletic Institute, 1960.

Physical Fitness:
APPRAISAL
AND PROGRAMMING

There is a danger at the present time in the enthusiasm for cramming of the brains of our young people with facts, scientific or otherwise, that there will be inadequate time for the establishment and perpetuation of physical fitness, which should never stop.

PAUL DUDLEY WHITE, M.D. (1960)

The leaders of men in all periods of history, in practically every field of endeavor, have been those who possess strong and active bodies as well as fertile and imaginative minds. Biblical leaders, characterized by Moses, David, and Paul, were men of strength as well as character. In ancient and medieval history Socrates, Plato, Aristotle, Hannibal, Mark Antony, Alexander the Great, Richard the Lionhearted, and William the Conqueror stood out among men because of their fitness and courage as well as for their intellect.

Modern history is replete with such men. Many of our presidents, beginning with George Washington, were men of this calibre. It is claimed that Washington defeated Nathan Hale in broad jumping with a leap of over 23 feet. Abraham Lincoln, revered throughout the world as our greatest president and humanitarian, was an unusually strong man. His feats of strength during his pioneer days at New Salem, Illinois, led to the acceptance of his leadership in that community and thence to the legislature. During his campaign for the presidency he was called the "Illinois Rail-splitter," and many anecdotes of his prowess were well-known.

Theodore Roosevelt was probably America's greatest exponent of physical fitness. Every school boy is aware of his inspiring story of overcoming his sickly youth to become a rugged outdoor enthusiast, legendary hero of the Rough Riders and then the president who "carried a big stick." His distant cousin, Franklin Roosevelt, was also a great believer in fitness, but unfortunately was struck down by polio before he became president.

According to the United Press, most of the world leaders of today are symbols of fitness.

Today's Americans, however, are less fit than their fathers or their grandfathers, and, in increasing numbers, less fit for military service. American children cannot match their European counterparts on simple physical fitness tests. In fact, English girls, ages 10–12, show superiority to American boys of the same ages in such tests as sit-ups, standing broad jump, and the 600 yard walk-run.

Fitness

Physical fitness, according to the President's Council on Fitness, is a broad quality involving medical and dental supervision and care, immunization and other protection against disease, proper nutrition, adequate rest, relaxation, good health practices, sanitation, and other aspects of healthful living. It further states that exercise is an essential element to achieving and maintaining physical fitness. Strength, speed, endurance (cardiovascular capacity), and other desirable physical qualities can only be developed through vigorous activity, but complete fitness is achieved through a sensible balance of all these provisions adapted to age, maturity, and capability of the individual.

The late President Kennedy, an exponent of the strenuous life, went a step further and said:

> For Physical Fitness is not only one of the most important keys to a healthy body, it is the basis of dynamic and creative intellectual activity. The relationship of the body and the activities of the mind is subtle and complex. Much is not yet understood, but we do know what the Greeks knew: that intelligence and skill can only function at the peak of their capacity when the body is healthy and strong; that hardy spirits and tough minds usually inhabit sound bodies.

> In this sense, physical fitness is the basis of all the activities of our society. And if the body grows soft and inactive, if we fail to encourage physical development and prowess, we will undermine our capacity for thought, for work, and for the use of those skills vital to an expanding and complex America. Thus, the physical fitness of our citizens is a vital prerequisite to America's realization of its full potential as a nation, and to the opportunity of each individual citizen to make full and fruitful use of his capabilities.

Fit for college

The present emphasis upon scholarship in our schools and colleges throughout the nation tends to overshadow the student's judgment regarding the need for physical fitness. All too often he feels that he cannot afford to devote the time necessary to attain and retain a state of fitness through participation in physical education, athletics, and intramural sports. This chapter is presented for the use of this type of student as well as those enrolled in physical fitness classes. The programs of exercise included herein are all time savers and have a special value for use throughout life.

The American Association for Health, Physical Education, and Recreation defines the college student's responsibility as follows:

> American college students have their work cut out for them. The demands made upon their strength and intelligence are heavy, real, and constant. In the unending struggle to preserve our culture against those forces which would destroy it, col-

lege students of today will become leaders who must guide the way.

> The responsibility and the opportunity are personal. Not only must college students become technically, philosophically, and artistically prepared as productive citizens, but they must also live in such a manner as to preserve and develop their own heritage of health so necessary for their survival in this scientific but sedentary age.

> For such tasks as the college student faces today, there is no substitute for a personal fitness and a competence which will see him through. At every stage from freshman year through post-graduate study, success—full creative success—depends upon the way the student uses his personal resources, the way he develops his talents. It becomes clearly a personal responsibility to maintain a type of life which will enable him to rise to the heights which will be required of him.

Student weaknesses

The noted physiologist, Dr. Arthur H. Steinhaus,[1] reminds us that we moderns are physically weak in three muscle areas:

> *First,* many men and most women are weaklings in hands, arms, shoulders, and upper trunk muscles. Consequently their chins protrude and shoulders sag.

> *Second,* weak abdominal muscles accented by a layer of fat allow the pelvis to sag. This tips the spine forward in the lower back, and the resulting sway back invites the low back pain.

> *Third,* many people have weak, aching, and deformed feet so they cannot enjoy movement of any kind. Instead of walking with every foot muscle and pressing the tips of five toes to the ground with every step, they just stump along. With their feet encased in poorly fitting shoes they seem to walk over their feet as over solid clods on the ends of stilts—and high heels don't help matters.

This chapter will be concerned with developing the entire body, placing special emphasis upon these weak areas. It will also be concerned with an evaluation and progress of each person's fitness.

FITNESS APPRAISAL

Essentially, everyone knows when he is overweight, out of condition, or lacking in strength and

[1] Arthur H. Steinhaus, *How to Keep Fit and Like It* (Chicago: The Dartnell Corporation, 1957).

SUBJECT: _____   Age: _____   _____

Weight: _____   _____

Height: _____   _____

I. GENERAL FITNESS:

    A. Physical Fitness Index:

        1. Lung Capacity _____   _____

        2. Back Strength _____   _____

        3. Leg Strength _____   _____

        4. Right Grip Strength _____   _____

        5. Left Grip Strength _____   _____

        6. Push-ups _____   _____

        7. Pull-ups _____   _____

        8. Arm Strength _____   _____

        Obtained Strength _____   _____

        Normal Strength Index _____   _____

        Physical Fitness Index _____   _____

    B. Cardiovascular Fitness:

        (Harvard Step Test - short form)

        Index _____   _____

    C. Nutritional Status:

        Wetzel Grid _____

    D. Biceps Girth:

        Right _____   _____

        Left _____   _____

    E. Blood Pressure:

        Systolic _____   _____

        Diastolic _____   _____

    F. Chest:

        Relaxed _____   _____

        Inspiration _____   _____

    G. Mechanical Symmetry:

    H. General Coordination:

    I. Motor Fitness:

        1. Explosive Power _____   _____

        2. Two-minute Sit-ups _____   _____

        3. Burpee (30 sec.) _____   _____

        4. Pull-ups _____   _____

        5. Dips _____   _____

FIGURE 4-1. Record for refined evaluation of general fitness (From Donald K. Mathews, *Measurement in Physical Education*. Philadelphia: W. B. Saunders Co., 1968, p. 350.)

endurance. Innumerable subjective cues suggest the onset of these conditions long before they become serious health problems. Unfortunately, the process of rationalization enables one to ignore the cues. And often one's self-image is not honest or realistic. A physical fitness test, with its clear-cut criteria of status based on statistical norms, makes rationalization and disregard of the personal status more difficult.

All students should take time to measure and analyze their physical fitness and to ask themselves the following questions:

1. What is my present status?

2. What is my physical fitness (performance) age?
3. What is the image I present to others?
4. How can I improve my physical fitness?
5. Can I increase my ability to work and study better?

The *first* step in any fitness appraisal is a thorough health examination. If your school has not provided this examination you should secure one before proceeding with this class.

The *second* step is an appraisal of your physical fitness. Many schools have developed their own tests, the results of which may be recorded on the accompanying form. (Fig. 4-1.)

The *third* step is programming and scheduling. If the previous two steps were intelligently followed, they should form a sound basis for guidance in selecting the most needed physical activities.

The *fourth* step is to re-evaluate. After a number of weeks or at the end of the course one's fitness should be re-evaluated to measure progress.

Basic components identified

The four components described below represent physical capacities that are needed and have a direct relationship to a person's ability to function as a physically effective person.

1. CARDIO-RESPIRATORY CAPACITY. Cardio-respiratory capacity is the ability to persist in strenuous tasks. It reflects the capacity of the cardiovascular and respiratory systems to supply the working muscles with oxygen. This is the key to the most desirable component of fitness—endurance, the ability to work and play without undue fatigue. It involves the most important muscle of the body, the heart.

2. MUSCULAR ENDURANCE. Muscular endurance is the ability to persist in localized muscular effort. The limiting nature of the individual muscle or muscle group to continue contracting under load results in cessation of work. The more movement demanded, the greater the contribution to endurance.

The following components are aimed almost entirely at developing the skeletal muscles and, because they do not demand much oxygen, they do not qualify as cardio-respiratory components.

3. MUSCULAR STRENGTH. Muscular strength is the maximum amount of force or strength that a muscle or muscle group can exert in a single effort. The effort can be isometric or isotonic in nature. Isometric strength (static strength) implies a muscular contraction against resistance without movement. The muscle contracts; work is performed; but the joint remains fixed as the force is applied against an immovable object or surface. (See Figs. 4-10 to 4-15.) Isotonic strength (dynamic strength) represents the more typical strength form. The muscle contracts, shortens, and the joint moves against the resistance through a range of motion. In this case, the resistance is moved or portions of the body move in relation to a surface.

4. FLEXIBILITY. Flexibility represents the functional capacity of the joints to move through a normal range of motion.

Some promoters of physical fitness also include power, balance, agility, and speed as basic components of physical fitness. These parameters reflect aspects of physical fitness as well as aspects of motor ability or motor fitness. The physical coordination component intrinsic to these parameters does not readily permit uncoordinated persons to make reasonable improvements through practice, especially when comparisons are made within groups. Therefore, their close association with the basic components listed is appreciated, but their inclusion leads to confusion and discouragement among the physically unsophisticated and the uncoordinated.

Basic components evaluated

It is essential to consider physical fitness from a personal point of view. Each person has a performance background, a personally estimated physical capacity, and an operating motivational framework. It is more advisable to relate to personal achievement than to relate to group standards or personal expectations within a peer group. In other words, a person should be competitive with himself.

PHYSICAL FITNESS TESTS

There are a great variety of tests that purport to measure physical fitness. Some measure only two or three components of fitness and others claim total measurement. For this reason we are presenting a variety of tests from which to choose.

Cardio-respiratory tests

RUNNING TESTS. The time required to run a prescribed distance provides a reasonably effective technique for estimating cardio-respiratory capacity. The distances generally used range from one-half mile to two miles. These tests are limited, however, because of the difficulty in controlling the running rate and evaluating the mechanical efficiency advantage that some performers possess.

FIGURE 4-2. Twelve Minute Run-Walk Test of Cardiovascular Efficiency

DISTANCE COVERED	FITNESS CATEGORY
Less than one mile	I. Very poor
1 to 1¼ miles	II. Poor
1¼ to 1½ miles	III. Fair
1½ to 1¾ miles	IV. Good
1¾ or more	V. Excellent

If you score in the first three categories you fail the test.

One of the most recent run-walk tests was devised by Dr. Kenneth H. Cooper [2] for the United States Air Force. The object is to run-walk as far as possible in 12 minutes. Your score is determined by the accompanying table. (See Fig. 4-2.)

STEPPING TESTS. Stepping up and down on a 16- to 20-inch bench and measuring pre-exercise and post-exercise heart rates results in a more effective technique for estimating cardio-respiratory capacity. The principle being applied in these tests is that after a standardized work task (steps per minute for regulated time) more fit performers are able to return recovery heart rates to resting values more quickly.

Harvard step test (short form)

This test is a simple method of measuring the ability of one's circulatory system to recover from exercise of an endurance nature. It is prescribed for young men.

Subject steps up and down a 20-inch bench 30 times a minute for five minutes (or less if he cannot maintain the pace). Subject's pulse is counted at one minute to one minute and thirty seconds after exercise.

FIGURE 4-3. Scoring the Harvard step test (From Peter V. Karpovich, *Physiology of Muscular Activity*, 5th ed. [Philadelphia: W. B. Saunders Co., 1959], p. 286.)

DURATION OF EFFORT	HEART BEATS FROM 1 MINUTE TO 1½ MINUTES IN RECOVERY										
	40–44	45–49	50–54	55–59	60–64	65–69	70–74	75–79	80–84	85–89	90–OVER
0 – 29″	5	5	5	5	5	5	5	5	5	5	5
0′30″–0′59″	20	15	15	15	15	10	10	10	10	10	10
1′ 0″–1′29″	30	30	25	25	20	20	20	20	15	15	15
1′30″–1′59″	45	40	40	35	30	30	25	25	25	20	20
2′ 0″–2′29″	60	50	45	45	40	35	35	30	30	30	25
2′30″–2′59″	70	65	60	55	50	45	40	40	35	35	35
3′ 0″–3′29″	85	75	70	60	55	55	50	45	45	40	40
3′30″–3′59″	100	85	80	70	65	60	55	55	50	45	45
4′ 0″–4′29″	110	100	90	80	75	70	65	60	55	55	50
4′30″–4′59″	125	110	100	90	85	75	70	65	60	60	55
5′	130	115	105	95	90	80	75	70	65	65	60

[2] Kenneth H. Cooper, M.D., and Kevin Brown, *Aerobics* (New York: M. Evans and Company, Inc., and Bantam Books, 1968). Copyright © 1968 by Kenneth H. Cooper, M.D., and Kevin Brown. Reprinted by permission of the publishers, M. Evans and Company, Inc.

$$\text{Index} = \frac{\text{Duration of exercise in seconds} \times 100}{5.5 \times \text{(pulse count)}}$$

Below 50 = poor
50-80 = average
Above 80 = good

Fig. 4-3 may be used to facilitate scoring. Instructions: (1) Find the appropriate line for duration of effort, (2) then find the appropriate column for the pulse count, (3) read off the score where the line and column intersect, and (4) interpret according to the scale for the short form.

Modified step test for girls and women (college age)

Subject steps up and down on an 18-inch bench 24 times per minute for three minutes. When

FIGURE 4-4. Cardiovascular efficiency of college women.[3] Table for conversion of pulse rates to cardiovascular efficiency scores for those completing the three-minute step test

STANDARD	NAT'L SCORE	30-SEC. PULSE
Excellent	96 and above	32 and below
	91–95	34– 35
	86–90	36– 37
	81–85	38– 39
	76–80	40– 42
	71–75	43– 45
Very Good	66–70	46– 49
	60–65	50– 54
Good	55–59	55– 58
	49–54	59– 66
Fair	44–48	67– 73
	39–43	74– 83
Poor	33–38	84– 98
	28–32	99–116
Very Poor	0–27	117–120

Note: In considering the use of the cardiovascular efficiency test, it should be noted that although the test has been shown to be both valid and reliable as a means of differentiating among groups of subjects in various states of cardiovascular efficiency, there is some overlapping of categories. Thus, each score cannot indicate a precise state of fitness and it is suggested that the ratings here be used primarily for purposes of general classification.

[3] *Research Quarterly*, American Association for Health, Physical Education and Recreation, Washington, D.C., XXXIV, No. 4 (Dec. 1963), 461.

stepping has been completed, subject sits down and rests. At end of one minute of rest, the operator takes the subject's pulse for 30 seconds.

Equipment:

1. Eighteen-inch bench or chair of sturdy construction.
2. Clock with sweep second hand and/or one stop watch for each test administrator.
3. Metronome (set at 96 beats per minute).
4. Pencil and data sheet.

Subjects who are *unable* to complete three minutes of stepping may determine their scores by using the following formula:

$$\text{Score} = \frac{\text{Number of seconds completed} \times 100}{\text{30-second pulse} \times 5.6}$$

The following items may be of interest:

1. Mean score = 48.9; pulse range 25–120; stan-

dard deviation 10.4; standard error of the mean = .214

Total number of subjects = 2362 (usable scores)

2. The number of subjects unable to complete the test was 316 or 13.3 per cent. (In the Eastern district all but 4.2 per cent completed three minutes of stepping.)

3. Thirty competitive swimmers, at the height of their training season when they swam three to five hours daily, had a mean score of 67.

GENERAL FITNESS TESTS

AAHPER test

This test for girls was devised by the National Section of Women's Athletics of the American Association for Health, Physical Education and Recreation. The tests should be administered only to girls

FIGURE 4-5. Scoring table for short battery performance levels

SCALE SCORE	ST.BD.J.	BASKETBALL THROW	POTATO RACE	OR SQUAT-THRUSTS	SIT-UPS	PUSH-UPS OR	PULL-UPS
100	7'9"	78'	8.4	9–1	65	61	47
95	–7"	75'	.6	9	61	58	45
90	–4"	72'	.8	8–3	57	54	42
85	–2"	68'	9.0	8–1	54	51	39
80	6'11"	65'	.4	8	50	47	37
75	–9"	62'	.6	7–3	46	43	34
70	–7"	59'	10.0	7–1	43	39	32
65	–4"	56'	.2	7	39	36	29
60	–2"	53'	.4	6–2	36	32	26
55	–0"	50'	.6	6–1	33	28	24
50	5'9"	46'	11.0	6	29	25	21
45	–7"	43'	.2	5–2	25	21	18
40	–5"	40'	.6	5–1	22	17	16
35	–2"	37'	.8	4–3	18	13	13
30	–0"	34'	12.0	4–2	15	10	10
25	4'9"	31'	.4	4	11	6	8
20	–7"	27'	.6	3–3	7	2	5
15	–4"	24'	13.0	3–2	3	1	3
10	–2"	21'	.2	3	1	0	1
5	–0"	18'	.4	2–3	0	0	0
0	3'9"	15'	.6	2–2	0	0	0
Your Score 1st							
Your Score 2nd							

who have been approved for strenuous exercise and only two tests per day should be given. (See Fig. 4-5.)

How to take tests

STANDING BROAD JUMP. Stand, toes touching line, extend arms over head, squat, bringing arms backward, spring forward, bring arms forward, throw feet out as far as possible to land. Score best out of two jumps. (See Chapter 5.)

POTATO RACE. Start behind one line, run to the opposite line 30 feet away, pick up block, and return it to first line; repeat for second block. Two trials and score the best time.

SIT-UPS. Lie on back with partner holding ankles, sit up as many times as possible, not bending knees. Score the number.

PUSH-UPS. Lie on floor face down with knees bent straight up. Push up with arms until straight, let down touching chest to floor, repeat, keeping body straight.

SQUAT-THRUSTS. Standing, do a deep knee bend placing hands in front of feet, jump, extending legs backward full length, with weight resting on hands and toes in a front leaning position. Return to squat. Repeat and score as many as completed in ten seconds.

The tests should be given again at the end of the course and the improvement noted by the scale (Fig. 4-6).

FIGURE 4-6. Amount of improvement expected in one semester (using 1954 revision of scoring table)

Improvement (Final Score Minus Initial Score)

INITIAL SCORE	AVERAGE	GOOD	SUPERIOR
90–99	–7 to 1	2 to 6	7 or more
80–89	–4 to 5	6 to 10	11 or more
70–79	–1 to 8	9 to 13	14 or more
60–69	2 to 11	12 to 16	17 or more
50–59	5 to 13	14 to 18	19 or more
40–49	6 to 15	16 to 20	21 or more
30–39	8 to 17	18 to 22	23 or more
20–29	11 to 20	21 to 25	26 or more
10–19	15 to 25	26 to 30	31 or more
0–9	22 to 32	33 to 37	38 or more

FOUR TESTS OF FITNESS

Dr. Arthur H. Steinhaus in his pamphlet, *How to Keep Fit and Like It,* recommends these four tests of fitness.

1. **The Burpee Test (for agility and heart response)**

   (a) Determine normal standing pulse rate. Count by 15-second periods until two consecutive periods give the same count.

   (b) Practice the squat-thrust, i.e., squat with hands on floor between the knees, thrust feet back to straight support; return to squat, then to stand.
   Do this squat-thrust four times, as fast as possible under a stop watch. Time to the second and allow no short-cuts. This is a test of agility.

   (c) At the finish of the four squat-thrusts the assistant again counts the pulse rate in 15-second periods. When the rate is back to normal after two consecutive identical readings stop counting. The elapsed time in quarter-minutes is convertible into the heart response score. (If the heart response score is higher than the agility score, the exercises were probably done too slowly.)

2. **The Curl (for abdominal strength)**

   (a) Lie flat on back. Raise head, shoulders, and upper trunk, slide fingers on thighs until they touch the kneecaps. Return.

   (b) Count the number of times performed.

3. **Pull-ups (for arm and shoulder strength)**

   Men (a) Hang from horizontal bar, feet off floor, with any grip. Pull up until chin is over the bar without kicking.

   (b) Let down to full arm hang, repeat as many times as possible.

   Women (a) Hang from the same support in the same way.

   (b) Clock the number of seconds able to hang.

4. **Sargent Jump**

   (a) Stand beside a wall, heels together. Reach as high as possible with inside arm, marking with chalk.

   (b) Then jump as high as possible marking with the chalk again.

   (c) Measure the number of inches between the two marks. Note: Most schools have a regular jump board that can be adjusted to the standing height, with inches marked on board.

FIGURE 4-7. Scoring tables (Adapted from Arthur H. Steinhaus, *How to Keep Fit and Like It*. Chicago: The Dartnell Corp., 1957.)

MEN 15–25

SCORE	BURPEE AGILITY (TIME IN SECONDS)	HEART RESPONSE	PULL-UPS (NO.)	ABDOMINAL CURLS (NO.)	SARGENT CHALK JUMP (INCHES)
100	5.5	30	18.5	104	26.5
			18	100	26
90					
	6		17	95	25
80		45	16	90	
			15	85	24
				80	
70	7		14	75	23
		60	13	70	22
			12	65	
60			11	55	21
	8	75	10	50	20
			9	45	19
50		90	8	40	18
	9		7	35	17
		105		30	15
40			6		14
	10		5	25	12
		120		20	11
30			4		10
	11		3	15	8
		135			7
20			2	10	6
	12				5
		150	1	5	4
10					3
	13			1	2
					1
0		165	0	0	0

WOMEN 15–25

SCORE	BURPEE AGILITY (TIME IN SECONDS)	HEART RESPONSE	HANGING	ABDOMINAL CURLS (NO.)	SARGENT CHALK JUMP (INCHES)
100	7	30	109	45	18
			105	43	
90					
			100	40	17
80					
	8	45	90	35	16
70			80		15
	9	60	70	30	14
			60	25	
60					
	10	75	50	20	13
		90	40		12
50					
	11	105		15	10
40			30		8
	12	120	20	10	6
30					
	14	135	15		4
	15		10	5	3
20				3	2
	16	150	5	2	1
			3		
10				1	
			1		
0	17	165	0	0	0

MEASURE YOUR OWN PHYSICAL FITNESS

Your Showing

PASS   FAIL

Balance

1. Hold diver's stance (on toes, arms outstretched, eyes closed) for 20 seconds.   ____ ____

2. Squat and balance on hands for ten seconds, toes off ground, knees outside elbows.   ____ ____

3. With one finger on floor, take ten turns around finger, then walk a ten-foot line in five seconds.   ____ ____

Flexibility

4. Bend at waist and touch floor, keeping knees stiff. (Women touch palms.)   ____ ____

5. From sitting position with knees held down, bend forward slowly until forehead is eight inches from floor.   ____ ____

6. Lie face downward, with back held down and hands behind neck; raise chin 18 inches from floor.   ____ ____

Agility

7. Kneel so that insteps are flat on floor; spring to feet and balance three seconds.   ____ ____

8. Spring up from floor and touch hands to toes while in air. Do five times.   ____ ____

9. Squat; extend legs backward (hands to floor); extend legs forward; turn over; return to squat; stand. Do this six times in 20 seconds. (Women squat, extend legs backward, return to squat, stand six times in ten seconds.)   ____ ____

Strength

10. Pick up partner your own weight and place on shoulders in ten seconds.   ____ ____

Your Showing

PASS   FAIL

11. With heels on floor, head on partner's knees and hands on hips, hold body rigid for 30 seconds.   ____ ____

12. Lie face downward. With arms extended, and without using elbows, press up until body balances on hands and toes. (Women do forearm press-ups and hold for 20 seconds.)   ____ ____

Power

13. Do standing broad jump, the distance of your height plus one foot.   ____ ____

Endurance

14. Do 15 full-length push-ups from floor. (Women do 30 from knees.)   ____ ____

15. Lie on floor, straddled by standing partner. Grab his hands and pull yourself up until your chest strikes his legs, 20 times. (Women do ten.)   ____ ____

16. Sit in V-position with legs and back off floor. Hold for 60 seconds.   ____ ____

17. Run in place for two minutes at 180 steps per minute. Then hold breath for 30 seconds.   ____ ____

18. In succession, do 200 two-footed hops, 200 straddle jumps (jumps from I to inverted-Y position), 200 alternate-stride hops, 50 hops on each foot, and as many squat-jumps as possible.   ____ ____

Totals   ____ ____

To help you judge your own performance, here's what happens to the majority of normal young adults who take these tests at the University of Illinois' Physical Fitness Research Center:

Men: 1-pass; 2-fail; 3-fail; 4-pass; 5-pass; 6-fail; 7-pass; 8-fail; 9-fail; 10-pass; 11-pass; 12-fail; 13-pass; 14-pass; 15-pass; 16-pass; 17-fail; 18-fail.

Women: 1-pass; 2-fail; 3-pass; 4-pass; 5-pass; 6-fail; 7-pass; 8-pass; 9-pass; 10-pass; 11-fail; 12-pass; 13-fail; 14-pass; 15-fail; 16-fail; 17-fail; 18-fail.

PRE-PROGRAM CONSIDERATIONS

After physical fitness testing, it is essential for a person to reflect on the results of the various tests in relation to his needs and to begin a reasonable program to correct his deficiencies or to generally improve basic fitness level.

Interpretation of basic physical capacity

Physical capacity should be related to the demands of a person's life and to his ability to meet its challenges. An individual should be strong enough to have muscle control and a reasonable strength potential. However, since urban living restricts human movement, it would appear that the cardiorespiratory component should require the most attention. Flexibility must be considered with special attention, since many sports activities do not provide flexibility opportunities. Flexibility deficiencies can lead to low back pain. This condition can strike with amazing swiftness and the typical response to daily activity does not usually give any indication that rigidity and minimum functioning is at the danger-point.

Interpretation of motor abilities

An individual who is highly proficient in motor skills (sports participation) must evaluate the cardio-respiratory value of his sport or sports, and, if deficient, plan to supplement his exercise program with those activities requiring more endurance. Likewise, those who score high in muscular strength, flexibility, and balance should assess their cardio-respiratory value and make adjustments. All persons should also select and learn sports and exercises that will contribute to their well-being throughout life.

Principles governing performance

There are many qualifying principles which govern the individual's level of performance. The United States Office of Education, Committee on Wartime Physical Fitness for Colleges and Universities, listed several important principles underlying the development of physical performance as a guide for an individual in planning his own program:

1. *The principle of use*—That which is used, within reason, develops.
2. *The principle of reach*—The individual must push himself gradually to new levels of effort (the overload principle).
3. *The principle of time*—It takes continuous effort, extended over protracted periods of time, to develop strength, skill, and endurance.
4. *The principle of rhythm*—Rest must alternate with exertion.
5. *The principle of urge*—The individual must want to achieve; there must be incentive.
6. *The principle of normal risk*—In any worthwhile endeavor, risks must be taken.

Of all the principles listed above, the "principle of urge" is most important. The individual must have the will to increase his performance level and to keep it on a high plane.

Rate of improvement and adaptation

When one is not accustomed to strenuous exercise, soreness, stiff muscles, and fatigue result. This is a natural reaction that all persons experience and it should not be considered serious or dangerous to one's health. The period of adjustment usually lasts for a week or two and is the critical time when many beginners are tempted to quit. By "sticking to it" and continuing a correctly prescribed increase in exercises one soon overcomes his soreness and becomes adjusted to the routine.

He then experiences a period of improvement in performance, muscle tone, and cardiovascular adjustment until he reaches his maximum level of fitness. This may take a number of weeks for those who began in the poorest of condition, and only three or four weeks for those who started on a higher level.

Following this, one can usually maintain a high level of fitness or condition by less strenuous but regular and faithful adherence to exercise and desirable health practices of rest and proper nutrition. (See Chapter 3.)

SPECIALIZED PHYSICAL FITNESS PROGRAMS

Sports participation produces physical fitness to varying degrees. The vigorous and endurance types of sport such as running, cycling, rowing, swimming, soccer, handball, wrestling, and squash are excellent cardiovascular developers, but such recreational activities as golf, volleyball, fishing, hunting, bowling, baseball, softball, and table tennis contribute very little to one's cardio-respiratory improvement. (See Fig. 4-8.)

FIGURE 4-8. Rating of sports (From Arthur H. Steinhaus, *How to Keep Fit and Like It.* Chicago: The Dartnell Corp., 1957, p. 70.)

SPORT	ENDUR-ANCE	AGILITY	STRENGTH LEG	ABDO-MEN	ARM AND SHOULDER	AGE RANGE RECOMMENDED
Archery	L	L	L	M	H	All ages
Badminton						
Singles-Doubles	H—M	H	H	M	M	Singles under 50
Basketball	H	H	H	L	L	Under 30
Baseball (hard)	M	H	H	M	M	Under 45
Bicycling	M	L	H	L	L	All ages
Bowling	L	L	M	L	M	All ages
Boxing	H	H	H	H	H	Not recommended *
Canoeing and Rowing						
Recreational	M	L	M	M	H	All ages
Competitive	H	L	H	M	H	Under 30
Field Hockey	H	H	H	M	M	Under 30
Football	H	H	H	H	H	Under 30
Golf	L	L	M	L	L	All ages
Handball						
Singles-Doubles	H—M	H	H	M	H	Singles under 45
Heavy Apparatus						
Tumbling	L	H	H—M	H	H	Under 45
Hiking	M	L	H	L	L	All ages
Horseshoes	L	L	L	L	M	All ages
Judo	H	H	H	H	H	Under 30
Lifesaving	H	M	H	H	H	Under 45
Skating						
Speed	H	M	H	M	L	Under 45
Figure	M	H	H	L	L	All ages
Skiing	H	H	H	M	M	Under 45
Soccer	H	H	H	M	L	Under 45
Softball	L	H	M	M	M	Under 50
Swimming						
Recreational	M	L	M	L	M	All ages
Competitive	H	M	H	M	H	Under 30
Table Tennis	L	M	M	L	L	All ages
Tennis						
Singles-Doubles	H—M	H	H	M	M	Singles under 45
Touch Football	H	H	H	M	M	Under 30
Track						
Distance	H	L	H	M	M	Under 45
Jumps	L	H	H	H	M	Under 45
Sprints	M	M	H	M	M	Under 45
Weights	L	M	H	M	H	Under 45
Volleyball	L	M	M	L	M	All ages
Wrestling	H	H	H	H	H	Under 30

* H—high; M—medium; L—low (referring to contribution to fitness items)

If one participates in the latter type of recreational activities, he must choose a more strenuous endurance type if he wishes to attain a high level of fitness.

Cooper [4] claims that a person must exercise vigorously enough to produce a sustained heart rate of at least 150 beats per minute for five minutes if the activity is to be sufficient to improve cardio-respiratory function. The benefit begins after five minutes of exercise, and, if it doesn't, the exercise must be continued considerably longer.

Cardio-respiratory emphasis

JOGGING. Jogging means running at a pace not much faster than walking, interspaced with breath catching walking segments. It incorporates all

[4] Cooper, *op. cit.,* p. 23.

CATEGORY			DISTANCE	TIME	TIMES	POINTS
I	II	III	(miles)	(mins.)	a week	a week
WEEKS						
1 ST	1 ST	· · ·	1	13:30	5	10
2 ND	· · ·	· · ·	1	13	5	10
3 RD	2 ND	1 ST	1	12:45	5	10
4 TH	3 RD	· · ·	1	11:45	5	15
5 TH	4 TH	2 ND	1	11	5	15
6 TH	5 TH	3 RD	1	10:30	5	15
7 TH	6 TH	· · ·	1	9:45	5	20
8 TH	· · ·	4 TH	1	9:30	5	20
9 TH	7 TH	5 TH	1	9:15	5	20
10 TH	8 TH	· · ·	{ 1, 1 1/2	9 16	3 2 }	21
11 TH	9 TH	6 TH	{ 1, 1 1/2	8:45 15	3 2 }	21
12 TH	· · ·	7 TH	{ 1, 1 1/2	8:30 14	3 2 }	24
13 TH	10 TH	· · ·	{ 1, 1 1/2	8:15 13:30	3 2 }	24
14 TH	11 TH	8 TH	{ 1, 1 1/2	7:55 13	3 2 }	27
15 TH	12 TH	9 TH	{ 1 1/2, 2	7:45 12:30 18	2 2 1 }	30
16 TH	13 TH	10 TH	{ 1 1/2, 2	11:55 17	2 2 }	31

NOTE: START PROGRAM BY WALKING. THEN WALK/RUN, OR RUN, AS NECESSARY, TO MEET THE CHANGING TIME GOALS.

TO MAINTAIN FITNESS AFTER COMPLETION OF CONDITIONING PROGRAM, FOLLOW ANY ONE OF THESE ALTERNATIVES:	1	8	6	30
	1	6:30	5	30
	1 1/2	12	4	30
	2	16	3	30

FIGURE 4-9. "Aerobics Running Program"

former adapts to the work by adjusting the exercise time and/or the rest time.

CIRCUIT TRAINING. Circuit training attempts to improve as many components of physical fitness as it can, by incorporating them into a continuous series of exercises. The exercises, which challenge the performer at a level below his maximum potential, are grouped into stations and spaced apart. Generally, eight to twelve stations are selected. The training load at each station is varied with each individual to about 50 per cent of his maximum capacity. The selection of the position of the activities within a lap of the circuit is made with consideration for a desirable or practical sequence considering the continuous nature of the performance. Some circuits require one lap with continuous running from one-half to two miles added at the end, while others stress running as a part of each lap of the circuit and repeating the cycle up to three consecutive times. There should be a pre-test to establish the load for each individual. Total time then becomes the quantitative measure. The performer is re-tested after a period of time and the circuit loads can be adjusted.

Strength emphasis

All forms of isometric (see Figs. 4-10 to 4-15) or isotonic strength development programs, including calisthenic-type activities, are examples of specialized strength fitness activities. The generalized category is called weight training or progressive resistance weight conditioning. (See Chapter 32.) Most of the gymnastics apparatus activities, other than trampolining or vaulting, also provide a basis for sound strength development. (See Chapter 15.)

Coordination emphasis

All forms of rhythmical calisthenics promote varied fitness results depending on the intensity and duration of the activity. They are also used as warm-up activities preceding more specialized work. Gymnastic tumbling and free exercise provide these advantages also. Modern dance programs stress coordination and aesthetic involvement while producing excellent fitness results.

Rhythmical calisthenics, tumbling, free exercise, and dance all stress flexibility as a major component in their basic skill progression development.

Calisthenics

1. Stand with arms raised sideward, palms down; pull arms backward, turning palms up. Chest up, chin in. Repeat.

the advantages of distance running without the pressures of competition. It is the poor man's cross country program where finishing the distance is the objective. Group or pack running is recommended, although certain strong-willed individuals can push on by themselves. It is important to schedule the running course and to drive forward as confidence dictates. The slow trot can be increased as physical conditioning permits, along with the total distance to be covered. (See Fig. 4-9.)

INTERVAL TRAINING. Interval training programs are developed around a preset progression using cycles of regulated exercise and rest. Initially, a distance base is set up. The performer attempts to cover the distance in a prescribed time, which challenges him but is below his best. After the distance is covered, the performer observes his time and rests for a prescribed time segment. The cycle is then repeated again and again for the desired number of repetitions. Modifications are introduced as the per-

FIGURE 4-10. Military press

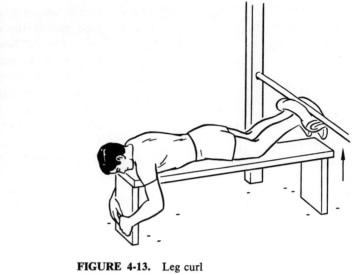

FIGURE 4-13. Leg curl

FIGURE 4-11. Dead lift

FIGURE 4-14. Leg press

FIGURE 4-12. Toe riser or shoulder lift

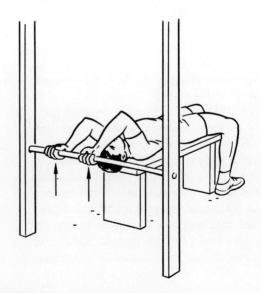

FIGURE 4-15. Triceps developer

2. Stand erect, hands at side. Jump to feet apart, clap hands over head. Repeat.

3. Stand feet apart, arms sideward shoulder level. Bend forward, touch left toe with right hand. Return, repeat to opposite side.

4. Lie on back, hands behind head (men, knees straight; women, bent), curl to sitting position touching right elbow to left knee. Return, repeat, opposite elbow to knee.

5. Lie on back, hands at side on floor, raise legs (straight) six inches off floor, hold, raise to perpendicular. Lower to six inches, then to floor. Repeat.

6. Stand feet apart, hands behind the head. Bend trunk forward at waist. Swing trunk to left, rear, right, and back to front. Repeat.

7. Fold arms across chest, squat, placing one foot to front, leg straight. Change position of feet. (Russian dance.)

8. Lie prone, hands behind head. Lift chin off the floor as high as possible and hold. Return to prone and repeat.

9. Lie prone, arch back with arms at side. Bend knees and try to touch buttocks with heels or grasp toes with hands and hold. Return and repeat.

10. Run in place, lift knees high, increase tempo until tired.

Repeat each exercise rapidly, as many times as possible.

Isometric exercises

Isometric contraction exercises have become very popular in recent years, especially for athletes wishing to augment their training programs and among business men who feel that they cannot "waste" the time exercising.

It is the type of exercise in which neither the person nor the object moves. In this type of contraction there is no change in the length of muscle. (When a muscle increases or decreases its length it is called isotonic contraction.) This may be one of the best methods of developing muscle strength and explosive power available today.

The advantages of isometrics are that they take very little time (not more than ten minutes) and very little fatigue results. On the other hand, they do *not* provide a "work-out" by themselves, they do not develop endurance, and they do not give one the feeling of accomplishment during the first few days.

Instruction:

1. Warm up before beginning the isometric workout. Remember that for complete development, it is necessary to include flexibility, agility, and endurance exercises before or after the isometrics.

2. One all-out effort per day on each exercise is sufficient to develop the muscle to its maximum. No more than ten different exercises are necessary each day.

3. Begin the exercise gradually, take three or four seconds to reach maximum effort, then sustain the effort for six seconds the first four weeks, then increase to eight seconds, and after eight weeks one may be able to hold maximum tension for 12 seconds.

4. During this period one's mental concentration must increase and thereby the effort of the muscle is increased. Complete concentration is essential on every exercise.

5. It is recommended that weightlifting be included once a week in the program. This furnishes a good method of measuring improvement in strength.

6. Breathe naturally, or employ force-breathing; do not hold breath for a long period of time because intra-thoracic pressure decreases circulation to the brain and fainting may result.

All exercises are designed for an adjustable horizontal bar.

1. *Shoulder shrug*—Stand erect, bar at height of hands, arms fully extended downward. Grip bar, shoulder width, and shrug shoulders upward as hard as possible.

2. *Military press*—Set bar two inches above head, stand directly under grasp bar, look straight ahead, tighten leg, hip, and back muscles, and push as hard as possible. (See Fig. 4-10.)

3. *Dead lift*—Place bar two inches below knees, feet shoulder width, toes out, back and arms straight, and buttocks low. Lift with full effort. (See Fig. 4-11.)

4. *Toe riser*—Place bar back of neck (use pad), feet 12 inches apart, toes straight ahead, knees locked, and body erect. Rise on toes with maximum effort. (See Fig. 4-12.)

5. *Leg curl*—Lie on stomach with knees slightly bent under bar, hook heels under bar, press upward, trying to bend knees. (See Fig. 4-13.)

6. *Leg press*—Lie on back, hips directly under bar, bend knees to 150° angle, and place feet under bar. Keep pelvis flat, head up, and push upward with maximum strength. (See Fig. 4-14.)

7. *Bench press*—Sit on bench under bar two inches above chest, grasp shoulder width, keep feet on floor, and press upward as hard as you can. Move bar up three inches and press again.

8. *Explosive start*—Assume a three-point football charging position with legs against one post and shoulders against another. Exert maximum pressure with shoulder and legs.

9. *Knee lifter*—Adjust bar slightly higher than the knees. Lift knee under the bar with all your strength. Alternate.

10. *Triceps developer*—Lie on back on bench about 18 inches from the bar at face level, grasp with hands and lift. (See Fig. 4-15.)

Self-resistive exercises

Hold maximum tension for three to six seconds. (See Fig. 4-16.)

1. Sitting, lace hands behind head. Try to force head backward resisting with arms.

2. Sitting, place hands on forehead. Try to push head forward, resisting with arms.

3. Sitting, place one hand on side of head, with other grasp the seat of the chair. Try to push head sideward.

4. Sitting, interlock hands in front of chest, pull. Same position, push.

5. Sitting, clasp hands behind back, force shoulders back.

6. Sitting, clasp hands under knees. Pull up with arms, resist with legs.

7. Sitting, place hands on top of knees. Push down with arms and hands.

8. Standing, arms at side. Grip fists as hard as possible.

9. Lie on back, hands clasped behind head. Raise trunk to three-quarter sitting position, try to force head forward.

10. Lie on back, hands under head, palms down. Arch back to bridge and hold.

11. Standing, lunge right foot sideward, right hand on thigh. Push with arm and hand.

12. Standing, arms forward. Raise left leg straight and half-squat on right leg. Hold.

13. Standing with one foot under table or bar. Try to lift with hands and arms.

14. Lying on back, legs up and spread. Place hands inside of knees and try to force knees outward. Place hands outside of knees and try to force knees inward.

A rope, towel or strap can be used for these exercises and others devised for their use.

HOW TO KEEP FIT AFTER COLLEGE

There is a tendency for too many students to stop vigorous exercises after completing their physical education requirement, especially after they have graduated. The many complexities of life, establishing a home, and earning a living, occupy so much of the young graduate's time and effort that he often neglects his physical fitness. A casual round of golf or a night of bowling will simply not do the job of maintaining fitness. And the occasional weekend at the beach with the usual overexposure to the sun may even be harmful.

Neither is there an easy way. Business men often mistakenly place their faith in the values of the vibrator, the massage, or the steam bath. Vigorous exercise is the answer, and vigorous exercise takes will power, time, and effort.

Most of the exercises described in the preceding pages can be used all through life, with many adaptable to the "desk job." The so-called isometric exercises (also called tension or static exercises) are particularly well-suited for the business man's routine. In addition to these are many common sense activities that can be practiced daily which will contribute to one's fitness.

Everyday fitness tricks

1. Walk briskly to and/or from work. Or get out of the bus or car a few blocks early and walk through the park. Walk fast enough that abdominal muscles contract.

2. Walk briskly around the block several times after evening meal. Time yourself for a mile—reduce time each week until you can walk it in 15 minutes, or run it in 12 minutes.

3. Try to run a short distance every day of your life.

4. Buy a bicycle and use it daily.

5. Participate in at least one sport at least twice weekly.

6. Take "setting-up" exercises, prescribed previously, every day.

7. Go hunting, fishing, camping, or picnicking occasionally.

8. Romp or wrestle with your children.

9. Dance occasionally.

10. Swim as often as you can.

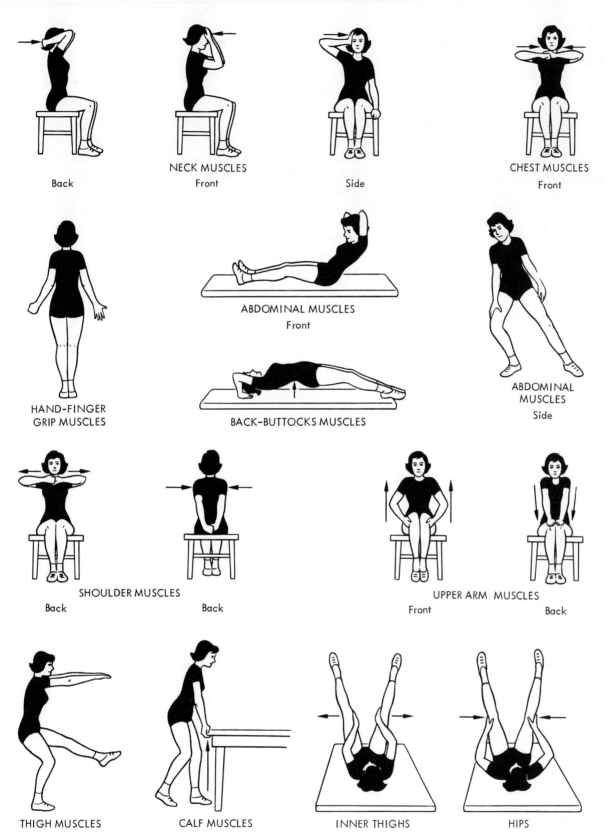

Back   NECK MUSCLES   CHEST MUSCLES

Front   Side   Front

ABDOMINAL MUSCLES
Front

HAND-FINGER
GRIP MUSCLES

BACK-BUTTOCKS MUSCLES

ABDOMINAL
MUSCLES
Side

SHOULDER MUSCLES   UPPER ARM MUSCLES

Back   Back   Front   Back

THIGH MUSCLES   CALF MUSCLES   INNER THIGHS   HIPS

FIGURE 4-16. Tension exercises employing maximum (isometric) tension, held for six seconds three times, once per day. Contract muscles to hold a body region in a set position while you apply force with another set of muscles or by a partner. The muscles exert the tension to resist the force. The arrow indicates the direction of the pulling or pushing force by your partner or by your own muscles. (From Janet Wessel, *Movement Fundamentals,* Englewood Cliffs, N.J.: Prentice-Hall, Inc., p. 127.)

At the office

1. Walk around the room occasionally; open windows and breathe deeply.
2. Do your chair exercises as described in these pages.
3. Tighten your stomach muscles every time the phone rings.
4. Walk up or down to the next floor or two.
5. Hand wrestling is fun and vigorous.

At home

1. Women—scrub, sweep and clean vigorously and with good posture.
2. Men—repair, mow, and work vigorously and with good posture.
3. Set up a backyard gymnasium and sports area including basketball goals, handball court, ropes from trees, and so on.
4. Follow the keep-fit programs on radio and television.
5. Lift properly for safety: bend knees, abdomen in, get close to the object and lift, keeping back straight.

You are on your own

The loss of one's physical fitness usually lowers a person in the eyes of his associates. People who are physically fit are usually more confident and determined, are happier, and often have the ability to adjust more easily to diverse and stressful conditions.

Ernst Jokl, M.D., emphasizes the preventative value of regular exercise, stating, "Those who maintain activity have better performance records, less degenerative diseases, and probably longer life expectancy than the general population . . . there is little doubt that physical activity as a part of life can significantly delay the aging process."

Now it is up to you. Do you want to become a "fat boy" or a "flabby girl" with chronic below-par feelings, or a trim person who seems to be a master of his own destiny? You are establishing the pattern while in school and the chances are that you will follow that pattern throughout life.

SELECTED REFERENCES

American Association for Health, Physical Education and Recreation, 1201 Sixteenth Street, N.W., Washington, D.C., 20036:
    Fit for College. 1959.
    Fitness for Secondary Youth. 1956.
    Weight Training in Sports and Physical Education. 1962.

Bowerman, William J., and W. E. Harris, *Jogging.* New York: Grosset and Dunlap, Inc., 1967.

Brouha, Lucien, "The Step Test, A Simple Method of Measuring Physical Fitness for Muscular Work in Young Men," *Research Quarterly,* XIV, No. 1 (March, 1943).

Casady, Donald R., *et al., Handbook of Physical Fitness Activities.* New York: The Macmillan Company, 1965.

Cureton, T. K., *Physical Fitness Appraisal and Guidance.* St. Louis: The C. V. Mosby Co., 1947.

Golding, Lawrence A., and Ronald R. Bos, *Scientific Foundations of Physical Fitness Programs.* Minneapolis, Minn.: Burgess Publishing Co., 1967.

Hooks, Gene, *Application of Weight Training to Athletics.* Englewood Cliffs, N.J.: Prentice-Hall, Inc., 1962.

Johnson, Perry B., *et al., Physical Education—A Problem Solving Approach to Health and Fitness.* New York: Holt, Rinehart & Winston, Inc., 1966.

Karpovich, Peter, *Physiology of Muscular Activity* (6th ed.). Philadelphia: W. B. Saunders Co., 1965.

Larson, Leonard A., and Racheal D. Yocom, *Measurement and Evaluation in Physical Health and Recreation Education.* Englewood Cliffs, N.J.: Prentice-Hall, Inc., 1962.

Massey, Benjamin H., *et al., The Kinesiology of Weight Lifting.* Dubuque, Iowa: William C. Brown Company, Publishers, 1959.

Mathews, Donald K., *Measurement in Physical Education* (3rd ed.). Philadelphia: W. B. Saunders Co., 1968.

Morehouse, Laurence, and Philip Rasch, *Scientific Basis of Athletic Training.* Philadelphia: W. B. Saunders Co., 1958.

Morehouse, Laurence E., "Physiological Basis of Strength Development." *Exercise and Fitness.* Chicago: Athletic Institute, 1959.

President's Council on Adult Fitness, *Adult Physical Fitness.* Washington, D.C.: The Council, 1963.

President's Council on Youth Fitness, *Physical Fitness Elements in Recreation.* Washington, D.C.: The Council, 1962.

Royal Canadian Air Force, *Exercise Plans for Physical Fitness* (XBX for women, 5BX for men). Ottawa, Ontario, Canada: Queen's Printer and Controller of Stationery, 1962.

Scott, M. Gladys, and Esther French, *Measurement and Evaluation in Physical Education.* Dubuque, Iowa: William C. Brown Company, Publishers, 1959.

Steinhaus, Arthur H., *How to Keep Fit and Like It.* Chicago: The Dartnell Corp., 1957.

————, *Toward an Understanding of Health and Physical Education.* Dubuque, Iowa: William C. Brown Company, Publishers, 1963.

Van Huss, Wayne, *et al., Physical Activity in Modern Living.* Englewood Cliffs, N.J.: Prentice-Hall, Inc., 1960.

Wessel, Janet, *Movement Fundamentals, Figure, Form, Fun* (2nd ed.). Englewood Cliffs, N.J.: Prentice-Hall, Inc., 1961.

Fundamental Activities

For some time the term fundamental, or basic, activities was used interchangeably with the terms body mechanics and body movement. Although the courses in instruction for these activities were similar in content, there was also considerable differentiation in content, purpose, and method of instruction. Recent thinking, however, has brought about more distinction in the use of these terms and somewhat general acceptance of a specific definition for each term.[1] This chapter on fundamentals will deal with a study of selected movements fundamental to activities of common usage in everyday living. Thus consideration will be given to performance in standing, sitting, walking; running, jumping, throwing,

and catching; lifting, carrying, pulling, and pushing. Let it be understood that such a list could be increased by many activities, but it is purposely limited because of the usual time allotment for the course and the advantage to be gained by concentration on a few basic movements.[2] Although relaxation is not essentially an activity, the knowledge of principles needed toward accomplishment of relaxation is essential to living, especially in periods of tensions, excitement, and increasing demands on one's time and energy.

A course of this kind has as its purpose the development of each individual to his highest level of performance through understanding of fundamental principles, and the opportunity to apply in practice with instruction such factors as: balance, alignment and weight distribution, basic rhythmic responses, and relaxation. A student interested in further analysis than that herein presented should have a knowledge of anatomy, kinesiology, compo-

---

[1] The National Association for Physical Education of College Women—Workshop Meeting—1956:

Body mechanics—The application of physical laws to the human body at rest or in motion. This term does not denote any specific set of activities or course content.

Basic movement—Movement carried on for its own sake, for increased understanding, or for awareness of the movement possibilities available to the human body.

Basic or fundamental activities—Motor skill patterns that form the foundation for the specific skills required in daily life, work, sports, dance—standing, walking, running, jumping, pushing, lifting, throwing, etc.

[2] The basic rhythmic fundamentals and steps are believed an essential part of such a course and are included in the chapter on the dance.

nents and application of force, leverage, gravity, resistance, and the interrelationships of all these in regard to the moving human body.

STANDING—SITTING—WALKING

The average college individual is awake at least 16 hours of the 24-hour day. Because most of these 16 hours are spent in activities of standing, sitting, and walking, it seems within reason that one perform these activities with a minimum amount of strain, yet in a manner that is socially acceptable. Postural habits, by the college age, have been fairly well established, but are not without the possibility of modification, adjustment, or new coordinations in movement. These changes cannot always be accomplished quickly, but understanding of fundamental principles and *willingness* to practice and persevere will produce gratifying results to the individual.

Standing

Standing posture varies with individuals and is affected by such factors as health (including mental attitude), body build, and occupation. Although one cannot use a single description of good posture as that which everyone should attain, he can recognize as essential elements of good posture such factors as proper body alignment and weight distribution, position of the feet, and good muscle tonus.

BODY ALIGNMENT AND WEIGHT DISTRIBUTION.[3] Were a plumb line dropped from the ear lobe of a person in good standing position, it would fall through the shoulder joint, very slightly behind the hip joint, very slightly in front of the knee joint, and through the prominence on the outside of the ankle bone. Viewing the body laterally, this line can be considered the edge of a plane dividing the body into a front and back section. Viewing the body from the anterior, a second plane passing through the body would divide it into a right and left half. The place or line of intersection of these two planes is called the *gravital* or *weight line*. At about hip level, a third plane could be passed which would divide the body into upper and lower sections. At the place the third plane intersects the gravital line

would be found the *center of gravity,*[4] a place around which the body balances in every direction.[5] Because the body is not one solid mass but is composed of segments, the closer each segment approaches the weight line, the more *stable* will be the entire body. Other factors concerned with stability are: (1) broad base, (2) low center of gravity, and (3) the proximity of the weight line to the center of the supporting base. The body weight falls about halfway between the heels and the balls of the feet.

POSITION OF THE FEET. The feet, in good standing position, are usually placed four to six inches apart and in a parallel position. Although some authorities consider a toeing-out position as normal, those who advocate the parallel position would appear to have the sounder reasons. In this latter position, the base is firm in both forward-backward and lateral directions as compared with the weaker triangular foot position (smaller base) resulting from the toeing-out position. The parallel foot position also places less strain on the leg muscles, and the body weight can be transferred along the entire longitudinal arch of the foot.[6]

TONUS. Good muscle tonus, a state of firm muscle structure and readiness for action, is essential to maintaining good posture.

TOTAL PICTURE. The total picture of the best standard in standing posture is one of shallow curves of the upper and lower back, a slight tilt forward-upward of the pelvis to help decrease the curve of the lower back, the head back and the chin comfortably down [7] (thus reducing the curve in the neck and upper back region), the abdominal wall flattened, the chest lifted, and the shoulders relaxed and back. This position can approximate good body mechanics in standing.

Common postural faults or departures from accepted form

LORDOSIS. An increased curve in the lower back frequently caused by a forward-downward tilt of the pelvic girdle.

---

[3] Body alignment—the position of the weight-bearing parts of the body, the head, neck, trunk, legs, and feet, in relation to one another. In good alignment, each part gives support to the part above, thus the feet and legs to the pelvis, the pelvis to the trunk and spinal column, and so on.

[4] The center of gravity of all objects is determined by locating a point about which the object balances in all directions.

[5] Balance is important in maintaining good posture.

[6] The *longitudinal* arch extends across the entire foot, from heel to toe in direction. The *transverse* arch is formed by the shafts of the metatarsal bones and extends from side to side of the foot. Symptoms of low arches are pain in the feet or legs, callouses on the balls of the feet, and depression of the upper side of the foot above the ball.

[7] To find this position, try the two extremes of chin well up, then chin well down, and be certain the head is back.

KYPHOSIS. An increased curve, usually in the upper back, although it can extend along the entire back.

SCOLIOSIS. A condition in which the vertebrae of the spinal column deviate from the normally straight mid-line down the back. *Functional scoliosis,* usually called lateral curvature of the spine (C curve), is the result of deviation of all the vertebrae to right or left, and in its early stages of development is accompanied by more or less of a twisting of each individual vertebra toward the concave side. This type of curvature is commonly caused by poor standing or sitting habits. *Structural scoliosis* frequently follows the functional type. The C curve develops into an S curve, with accompanying rotation of the vertebrae and ribs, resulting in depression of one side of the front chest and fullness of the back of that same side.

FORWARD HEAD. Head not carried in proper alignment above supporting neck.

ROUND SHOULDERS. Usually associated with flat, sunken, or hollow chest position.

PROTRUDING ABDOMEN. Relaxed abdominal muscles; sometimes caused by exaggerated curve of the lower back (lordosis).

KNOCK-KNEES. Can be determined by standing in normal position and noting if knees touch when ankles are more than two inches apart.

BOWLEGS. Sometimes caused by hyperextension of the knees, and in such cases correctible.

PRONATION. A position of the feet in which the standing weight is borne on the inner border of the foot.

CLUBFOOT. Extreme position of the foot in which the standing weight is borne on the outer border of the foot.

Typical exercises for correction of common postural faults

FOR CORRECTION OF FORWARD HEAD. Sitting, with legs crossed, elbows bent and at shoulder level, place fingertips lightly at base of neck. Push the head against the fingers, keeping chin down. As exercise is repeated, increase the resistance offered by the fingers against the base of the head. (See Fig. 5-1.)

ROUND SHOULDERS. Standing, preferably at a corner of two walls, at slightly more than extended arm's length from the wall, place palms of hands on wall at shoulder level, with fingers of each hand pointing toward the opposite hand. Keeping the feet (and heels) on the floor, knees straight (trunk maintaining the same alignment with the pelvis as in good standing), attempt to bring the

FIGURE 5-1. Starting position of exercise for forward head

chest toward the wall (corner) by bending elbows out and stretching at the shoulders. The hands remain in place throughout.

WEAK ABDOMINAL MUSCLES. Lying flat on the floor, arms extended and placed on the thighs, start curling the body by bringing the head, then shoulders and upper back, forward off the floor. The arms will slide along the thighs, and feet will remain on the floor. (See Figs. 5-2 and 5-3.)

FIGURES 5-2, 5-3. Exercise for weak abdominal muscles. (Upper figure) Starting position. (Lower figure) Head, shoulders, and upper back curving forward.

LORDOSIS. Position is on floor and on back, with knees bent enough to permit feet to be on the floor, arms at side. If one hand can be passed between the floor and the lower back, try to flatten the back against the hand by shifting the pelvic position down in back and up in front. When this is mastered, straighten the knees somewhat and try to maintain a flat lower back position. Always start with the knees bent and extend them gradually until they are nearly, but not entirely, straight.

FLEXIBILITY. Stand with feet apart, trunk bent forward-downward, and relaxed, with arms dangling. Bob easily up and down for three counts, then circle the trunk; arms start left and continue up into complete extension, over to the right, and return to the

FIGURES 5-4 through 5-7. Exercise for flexibility. (*Far left*) Starting position. (*Left center*) Trunk circle starting left. (*Right center*) Trunk circling continuing to full extension. (*Far right*) Trunk circling continuing to right.

forward bend position. Repeat bobbing and circle to the right. (See Figs. 5-4, 5-5, 5-6, and 5-7.)

FOOT AND ARCH EXERCISES. (a) Sitting so that legs can swing freely, extend legs somewhat forward, feet in line with legs (toes straight ahead). With foot and toes placed forward, start to circle the feet so that soles face one another, then bring the foot up toward the leg, continue to circle it around until the toes are directly in line with the legs. From this position, the circling movement stops and the feet are again stretched forward and downward. Each foot has described a semicircle. (b) Sit on a chair so that feet can be placed on the floor but not bearing entire body weight. Keeping foot in this position, curl the toes forcibly under as though picking up marbles or ruffling up a rug or towel with the toes. The toes are then relaxed and the exercise repeated several times in succession.

Typical exercises for dysmenorrhea

As pointed out in Chapter 3, females should carry on a regular exercise program during their menstrual period unless advised otherwise by a physician. Relief from pain can often be obtained through exercise at this time if circulation in the abdominal area is increased.

Billig developed an exercise for the prevention of dysmenorrhea which has proved successful in many instances (see Fig. 5-8). He instructs the girl to stand side to wall. She then places her near elbow, forearm, and palm on the wall with her elbow

in line with her shoulders. The outer hand should be placed slightly behind and low on her outer hip. She should contract her abdominal and hip muscles to flatten her lower back and tip her pelvis up in front, then shift her hips slightly forward and in toward the wall as far as possible, giving an extra stretch from her outer hand. It is desirable to hold as much stretch as possible even if painful. This exercise should be repeated three times a day for at least two months for best results.

FIGURE 5-8. Billig's exercise for dysmenorrhea (From Wessel, *Movement Fundamentals*, p. 159.)

The American College of Obstetricians and Gynecologists [8] recommends the following exercises:

EXERCISE I. Ten times, alternate. Starting position: side stride, stand with arms raised sideward at shoulder height, palms up.

Turn the trunk to the left. Keeping the knees straight, bend the trunk and touch the left foot with the right hand. Each time the exercise is done, an attempt should be made to reach around the outer side of the opposite foot until the pupil can touch the heel of that foot.

The exercise is practiced four times to the left side and four times to the right side during the first week. The exercise is increased two times to each side each week until a total of ten times to each side has been reached.

The exercise is to be practiced three times a day at regular intervals.

EXERCISE II. Ten times, alternate. Starting position: correct standing position with the arms at the sides, feet parallel and a few inches apart.

Swing the arms forward-upward and the left leg backward simultaneously. Return to position. Repeat same to the right. The exercise must be practiced vigorously to be effective.

The exercise is practiced four times to the left side and four times to the right side during the first week. The exercise is increased two times to each side each week until a total of ten times to each side has been reached.

The exercise is to be practiced three times a day at regular intervals.

Sitting

SITTING DOWN AND GETTING UP. It is important to realize that the base of support is to be shifted from the feet to the chair. Thus one must know the location of the body in relation to the new base (the chair).

SITTING DOWN. In preparing to sit down, stand near and in front of the chair with the calf of one leg next to it. This is necessary so that when sitting, the body will move in an almost erect position, with the leg muscles controlling the action. When sitting on a straight chair, full use should be made of the chair seat and lower back of the body for support. Sit with the buttocks well back on the chair, with the body against the back of the chair. The upper trunk can rest slightly against the upper

[8] Published by Paul B. Hoeber, Inc., Medical Division of Harper & Row. Copyright 1960 by American College of Obstetricians and Gynecologists, Vol. 16, No. 4, October, 1960.

back of the chair. Legs may be crossed gracefully at the knee or at the ankle, or feet may be placed on the floor, one slightly ahead of the other. Chairs constructed for secretarial workers give support to the upper back.

GETTING UP. With both knees flexed, one leg forward, the other back, and feet on the floor, push with the back leg, lifting body weight and transferring it to the forward foot. (If a deep lounge chair is used, it will be necessary to slide back into it after sitting down, or slide forward before attempting to rise.)

Walking

Walking is the process of locomotion in which the body weight is transferred from one forward-swinging leg and foot to the other. It differs from running in that at no time is there lack of contact with the floor. The outstanding characteristic of the walk is the period of double support. For clarity of description, the walk will be discussed in terms of leg action, foot action, arm swing, and hip and shoulder girdle action.

LEG ACTION. Starting with a forward stride position, the body weight is over the forward foot and the other leg is fully extended backward, ready to start a forward swing. As this action occurs, the knee and hip are flexed slightly at first as the thigh is brought forward. The leg is describing somewhat of an arc.[9] When approximately the mid-point of this arc is reached, there is more flexion to permit clearance from the ground or floor. The power leg is extended, the heel contacts the floor. As the heel of the swinging leg touches the floor, the supporting leg has become extended, after which the body weight

FIGURES 5-9 through 5-11. Walking. (*Left*) Foot position, weight on forward foot, other foot about to start forward swing. (*Center*) Foot position, forward swing has been completed; the heel transfers the weight through to the forepart of the foot. (*Right*) Foot position, weight transferred to forward swinging foot after it has contacted ground; cycle about to start again.

[9] The foot describes the arc, with the hip joint as the center.

shifts forward and the cycle is repeated. (See Figs. 5-9, 5-10, and 5-11.)

FOOT ACTION. The heel receives the weight, which is immediately transferred through to the ball of the foot as the leg prepares to swing forward and renew the cycle. The outside border of the foot may strike the floor before the rest of the foot, due to its fleshy character. Foot placement is considered best when the inner border of each foot falls closely along an imaginary line, with care being taken not to cross this line in a weaving motion.

ARM SWING. The arms hang relaxed and tend to move forward and backward, sometimes slightly toward the center of the body, with a flexed elbow at the end of the forward swing. The arm then swings back, slightly past the body, but not crossing it, and the elbow again may be slightly bent. The arms move in opposition to the legs—thus right leg, left arm swing forward.

HIP AND SHOULDER GIRDLE ACTION. As legs and arms swing forward and backward, there is an accompanying movement of the hip and shoulder girdles on the same side and in the same direction as the moving segments (right leg-right hip, left arm-left shoulder). The result is an easy movement without loss of balance.

NATURAL WALK. A natural walk is one in which the arms and legs swing easily, although the length of the stride and the number of steps taken will vary with individuals. The essential factor causing this variation is the height of the individual, particularly in terms of length of legs. There should be little up and down movement of the body. As the speed of the walk is increased, it is accompanied by increased body inclination. Movement is facilitated by this inclined position because, for one thing, the body is more in line with the driving leg. There is also an increase in the length of the stride until the speed of the walk is greatly accelerated, at which time the length of the stride is shortened, permitting the faster movement of the legs to drive more continuously. There is an accompanying acceleration of arm movement, necessitating a shorter arm swing; thus the elbow is bent more than in the natural walk.

Other related facts

1. Individuals develop a characteristic rhythm to their stride. These characteristics are due to length of legs and feet, natural position of the legs, a forced lengthened or decreased size of step, or personality factors. One's own normal rate of walking is usually most economical in terms of energy requirements. This rate may be increased somewhat without additional expenditure of energy. Saunter-

ing requires more energy than the normal walking rate. Approximately two and one-quarter miles an hour is the average rate for women; for men it is approximately three and one-half miles an hour.

2. Climbing necessitates more forward inclination of the body than does walking on level ground.

3. Side to side sway of the body (hips) in walking is commonly caused by (a) allowing the weight to be borne totally on one foot with a side-sway transfer, rather than a forward transfer of weight, and (b) improper arm swing in relation to hip action (exaggerated or decreased arm swing).

4. The position of the foot when wearing high heels is similar to that found in fast running when the heel does not touch the ground. There is a tendency to toe in. The body is thrown forward and the knees tend to lock. The usual result is that of a hollow lower back (lordosis) and prominent hips. For proper balance, the entire body from the feet up should be shifted back. A shortened stride will help maintain balance.

RUNNING, JUMPING, THROWING, AND CATCHING

Because many studies give strong indications that the ability to run, jump, throw, and catch have an important relationship to skill in participation in sports, these fundamentals will be valuable to an acceptable and/or improved skill, and enjoyment of sport performances.

Running

The run is a result of walking speed increased until the driving leg pushes the body off the floor, although continuing to move in its original direction. There is a short period of suspension when there is no contact with the floor. In the run, the stride is lengthened and there is some body lean. The ball of the foot makes the first contact, the heel coming down later—although sometimes not at all. Another characteristic of the run as contrasted with the walk is the somewhat flexed position of the knee, resulting in the back lift of the heel, and the more flexed elbow, both positions thus permitting a more rapid swing of the parts. The arm swings vigorously and on the forward swing, the hand sometimes crosses the front of the body. As in the walk, the arms and legs swing in opposition. In high speed running, the reaching leg tends to reach down for contact almost directly under the body; it is inadvisable to swing the arms forward beyond the mid-line of the body.

Jumping

In the standing broad jump, the essential factors are: (1) the take-off, (2) the arm swing, (3) the leg tuck, and (4) the position of the trunk. (See Figs. 5-12, 5-13, 5-14, and 5-15.)

FIGURES 5-12 through 5-14. Standing broad jump. (*Right*) Preliminary backswing. (*Center*) Moment of take-off. (*Left*) Immediately following take-off; arms still lifting body.

A standing broad jump necessitates a strong two-footed take-off with the body at an angle of about 45 degrees. At the take-off and throughout the jump, the trunk is inclined well forward so that the body weight will not drop behind the feet which, in landing, would shorten the jump. At the time of

FIGURE 5-15. Position of body in phases of standing broad jump

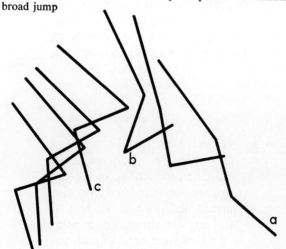

take-off, the legs are extended, the toes leaving the ground last, and the arms are swung upward to help lift the body and pull it forward. As the body approaches the mid-point of the arc through which it is moving in its flight, the knees are flexed and the arms push down and back to thrust the body forward. The legs are extended and, as the feet make contact, the arms are flung forward to help carry the body. For the varying positions of the trunk, see Fig. 5-15. At the moment of landing there is a slight ankle, knee, and hip flexion to avoid jarring the body.

Throwing (overhand)

PRELIMINARY MOVEMENT. The right-handed thrower will grasp the ball with the fingers slightly spread (see Fig. 5-16); the right elbow is bent and raised almost to shoulder level. As the elbow is drawn back, the hand reaches the shoulder, the elbow is straightened, the trunk is rotated slightly to the right and back, and also inclined sideward so that the right shoulder is lower than the left. The weight is on the right foot. The left arm is extended for balance. The left leg is also extended, the foot just touching. This back swing or preliminary movement is necessary to the throw proper. (See Figs. 5-17 and 5-18.)

THE THROW. The throw is accomplished by bringing the right arm forward with the elbow leading at shoulder height for a short time. The arm is then extended and the hand whips through rapidly. This arm action is accompanied by a rotation of the trunk to the left. When the ball is released with a snap of the wrist, the hand is in front of the shoulder, the trunk is forward, and the weight has been transferred to the forward (left) foot. (See Fig. 5-19.)

FOLLOW-THROUGH. The follow-through is essential to completion of the action. The right arm becomes fully extended, the trunk continues its rotation to the left with the left arm swinging backward, and frequently the weight of the body falls forward, resulting in a step on the right foot.

Factors essential to the throw are: speed, distance, and direction. Speed and distance of the throw are related to the force exerted. A long back-swing and good body rotation in the preliminary part of the swing will increase the speed of the ball. The distance the ball will travel is dependent also upon the angle at which it is released and the speed at which it travels. If one is throwing for distance, therefore, the ball must be released at an angle, but no greater than 45 degrees with the horizontal.

FIGURES 5-16 through 5-19. Overhand throw. (*Far left*) Holding the ball, fingers grasped around it. (*Left center*) The backswing. (*Right center*) Probable completion of backswing. (*Far right*) The ball has already been released. This is not the follow-through.

Factors such as pull of gravity, wind and air resistance, and the size, weight, direction and spin of the ball, all affect the distance a ball travels. Direction of the throw depends upon the spin of the ball, the wind resistance, and, quite obviously, the direction at the point of release.

Catching

The essentials necessary to good catching are: (1) to keep the eyes on the ball so that its position is known, (2) to contact the ball with the hands, and (3) to hold on to the ball. For balls that are to be caught above waist level, the thumbs of both hands are together, or nearly so, and the fingers pointed up (see Fig. 5-20); for balls to be caught

FIGURE 5-20. Catching a ball thrown above waist height. Eyes on ball, hands with thumbs together.

below waist level, the little fingers of both hands are together, or nearly so, and fingers pointed down. In order to hold on to the ball after contact is made, the fingers cup the ball, and hands, arms, and sometimes the body must "give" with the ball, or move in the direction in which the ball is traveling. This action can and should become a preliminary swing to the throw that is to follow. Thus the catch and throw become continuous in movement.

LIFTING—CARRYING—PUSHING AND PULLING

It is to be remembered that—as was true in standing, so in all activities—the principle to be observed is that of keeping all parts of the body over the base of support. When one is carrying an object it is to be considered a part of the body. When the body is moving, the new base of support must be anticipated and the body aligned accordingly.

Lifting

Whenever an object is lifted from below, stand close to it, place one foot slightly in advance of the other, keep the back straight, the ankles, knees, and hips flexed. In this position the entire body remains over the base of support and close to its line of gravity. To straighten up, the strong leg muscles (not the muscles of the back) are used to push the body and object lifted to the erect position.

FIGURES 5-21, 5-22. (*Left*) Carrying a very heavy load. Body shifts from ankles to the load side. Arm used for balance. (*Right*) Pushing object end-over-end. Hands placed above center of gravity of object.

When an object is lifted up high, the base of support must be very stable because the center of gravity is raised. (See page 51 on stability.) Therefore, the feet should be apart in a forward-backward stride position.

Carrying

A weight carried on one side should be carried close to the body, with the body line shifted from the feet up to the opposite side of the body. If the weight must be carried away from the body or is very heavy, raising the arm on the opposite side will help compensate for the load. Carrying a tray on one shoulder necessitates adjusting the body to include the tray within the base of support. This can best be done by a slight shift of the body to the opposite side (not a shift from the waist alone). A weight carried in front of the body again necessitates a slight shift of the body, this time backward from the ankles. The shift should be only enough to include the load with the body, so that both are over the supporting base. The most economical way to carry a load is that observed in more primitive peoples, namely, carrying the load directly in line with the body, which means over the head.

Pushing and pulling

Both activities call for a broad base of support. Consideration must be given to the direction one wishes to move the object and the relationship of the body to the object. Find the proper place to put the hands in order to exert force on the object, and the proper angle to place the body in relation to the object, or the object in relation to the body.

To push a heavy object, the hands should be placed (body weight in line with arms) below what would be considered the center of gravity of the object (see page 51, center of gravity). If the object tends to tip, the position of the hands must be lowered.

An object may be pushed so as to turn it end-over-end or to half rotate it, turning first one side, then the other, and so moving it along. In the end-over-end movement, the hands should be placed above the center of gravity, thereby tipping the object on each move. (See Fig. 5-22.) On the rotary movement, the hands should be placed as far toward the edge of the object as possible (away from the line of gravity).

In pulling, the same principle is applied as in pushing, e.g., that of inclining the body in the direction one wishes to move the object. The body in this position exerts its force most economically by using the strong muscles. When pulling an object with a rope (e.g., a sled), it is advantageous to have a long rope so that the force exerted will move the sled forward (horizontally), rather than pulling it upward, as too short a rope will do.

RELAXATION

There are many causes for the neuromuscular or physical tensions which exist in our world. "Push-button" living, lack of opportunity for large muscles and physical exercise, and the quickened pace of present-day living are among the most readily identifiable. The student and the office worker both are forced to sit still for many consecutive hours. The fatigue resulting from many hours of mental work is not the good feeling of fatigue experienced after strenuous physical activity. Such mental fatigue often leads to restlessness and failure to sleep well. Individuals who experience tension or symptoms of it should be taught to relax tense muscles.

It is possible to relax a selected group of muscles, just as it is possible to contract them. As one learns the feeling of a good tennis swing, so the feeling of a relaxed arm and shoulder can also be learned. Both the contraction of a selected group of muscles for a sport or dance movement and the relaxation of muscles for the release of tension require practice. Tense students respond readily to instruction in relaxation, and find they can conserve energy by contracting only those muscles necessary for the completion of a specific task. Excessive tension not only interferes with movement by inhibiting free action and resisting natural physical forces, but also is responsible for the burning of more fuel. Thus we often find the tense person to be one who complains of chronic fatigue.

For practicing relaxation technique, it is best to lie on the back on a mat, arms at the side. A small pillow placed under the neck and under the knees may be used to relieve strain. In order to relax at will, the student must learn to identify the feelings of tension and of relaxation. As soon as this has been experienced, all lessons thereafter will begin with a period in which the individual remains quiet, giving attention to relaxing. Students having difficulty in this initial phase will benefit by holding an arm straight up, contracting all the muscles as completely as possible, then allowing the arm to collapse to the mat. This complete collapse is comparable to a complete relaxing, and one should learn to identify the feeling. The relaxed arm will tend to bounce slightly and roll somewhat when it reaches the mat. Through the teaching of the principles of relaxation, the student can readily learn to contract certain parts of the body in a definite order: the arms, legs, abdomen, spine (including the neck), and facial muscles. At first only forcible contraction and a vague sensation of relaxation will be felt. However, after a repeated practice one should become sensitive to slight increases in tension and will know how to reduce this tension in whatever part of the musculature it occurs. In each lesson, the technique of contracting and relaxing a group of muscles, and identifying the feeling associated with each, must be repeated two or three times. The time devoted to learning the relaxing phase should be approximately twice that spent on the contracting phase. At the close of each lesson, ample time should be allowed to attempt total relaxation of the entire body. The ultimate objective is to be able to relax any muscle tensions without first contracting.

Free swinging exercises serve to loosen tight muscles. Any type of swing action requires some relaxation of muscles to enable the body to move freely. Momentum will aid a swing if it is not resisted by excessive tension.

Some simple exercises which help the physically inactive individual to reduce tension are: (1) circling the arms from the shoulders, allow momentum to carry them around; (2) lying on the back, raise the legs so that the body weight is on the neck and shoulders, support the hips with the hands, circle the legs in a bicycle-like action; (3) feet astride, bend at the waist and allow the arms and shoulders to relax and swing easily from side to side in pendulum-like action.

To help prevent muscle tension from building up, one should use every opportunity to move around and so reduce rigid or static type of contraction; walk with an easy, free swing of the arms and legs; lift the shoulders and then drop them down and back into good posture position; allow the neck muscles to relax by tucking in the chin and carrying the head high; breathe slowly, deeply, and allow the breathing muscles to relax.

Many people suffer from tensions created by poor postural habits such as forward head, sagging abdominal muscles, and exaggerated lower back curve. Others have habitual responses to stress, such as clenching a fist, crossing the legs with excessive contraction of the leg muscles, or twisting a strand of hair. The first step toward correcting these nervous habits is to become aware of them. The second step is to apply the learned technique to produce relaxation in the muscles involved under conditions of stress. To break long-standing habits is not easy; students must be ready to practice often, and not to expect immediate results, particularly in very tense individuals.

Tension-producing thoughts of work or of troubles and anxieties may cause muscular contractions in many parts of the body. When attempting to relax, it is helpful to replace "worry thoughts" with passive (unemotional) attention to visualizing or imagining a pleasant scene. Imagine a beach with the waves rolling in and out, giving attention to the colors of the water, the foam, and the continuous motion of the surf. Should the original thoughts recur, the passive attention should again be resorted to. Whatever visual imagery is used, it is essential that it be non-emotive and completely impersonal.

Given five, 15, or 45 minutes in which to relax the body, one can utilize such time to the fullest advantage; total relaxation or release from tension provides a feeling of having rested, and better equips one to meet the sudden demands of present-day living.

YOGA

Yoga is another form of relaxation that can be used to gain relief from tension, and to develop body control and mental poise. It was developed in India as a Hindu philosophy of living from the writings and teaching of Patanji in about 300 B.C. It is considered by its followers as a science to gain adequate strength to execute the prescribed body positions that feature high levels of body flexibility, and mental concentration that may even develop some voluntary control over the autonomic nervous system.

Those who practice yoga see great therapeutic value in the stress of extending joint structures to the fullest and in the inverted body (head stand) held for long periods of time. It is designed to produce an equanimity of spirit that is beneficial to the whole nervous system. Many great musicians and artists practice yoga, believing that it fulfills their need for exercise (including breathing exercises) and introspection, raising the mind to its highest level in order to study its activities on lower levels of consciousness. It may also serve as an applied religion, requiring self-discipline, the understanding of man, and devotion to God.

Anyone interested in pursuing yoga should read the literature and seek training from reputable leaders.

TERMINOLOGY

Body alignment   The position of the weight-bearing parts of the body in relation to each other.

Center of gravity   A point around which the body balances in all directions.

Gravital (weight) line   The line of intersection in the body of two planes, one dividing the body antero-posterior, the other left and right.

Kyphosis   Increased curve in upper back.

Lordosis   Increased curve in lower back.

Scoliosis   Deviation of the spinal vertebra from the normally straight midline position.

SELECTED REFERENCES

Broer, Marion R., *Efficiency of Human Movement* (2nd ed.). Philadelphia: W. B. Saunders Co., 1966.

Clayton, Irene A., *A Study of the Evidence of Motor Age Based on Technique of Standing Broad Jump.* Unpublished thesis. University of Wisconsin, 1936.

Cooper, John M., and Ruth B. Glassow, *Kinesiology* (2nd ed.). St. Louis: The C. V. Mosby Co., 1968.

Jacobson, Edmund, *Progressive Relaxation.* Chicago: University of Chicago Press, 1944.

————, *You Must Relax.* New York: McGraw-Hill Book Company, Inc., 1942.

Kendall, Henry O., Florence P. Kendall, and Dorothy A. Boynton, *Posture and Pain.* Baltimore: The Williams and Wilkins Co., 1952.

Kennedy, Joseph A., *Relax and Live.* Englewood Cliffs, N.J.: Prentice-Hall, Inc., 1953.

Morton, Dudley J., and Dudley D. Fuller, *Human Locomotion and Body Form.* Baltimore: The Williams and Wilkins Co., 1952.

Movement Group Report, *Workshop Report: Purposeful Action.* Washington, D.C.: The National Association for Physical Education of College Women, 1956.

Rathbone, Josephine L., *Teach Yourself to Relax.* Englewood Cliffs, N.J.: Prentice-Hall, Inc., 1957.

Scott, M. Gladys, *Analysis of Human Motion* (2nd ed.). New York: Appleton-Century-Crofts, 1963.

Steinhaus, Arthur H., *Toward an Understanding of Health and Physical Education.* Dubuque, Iowa: William C. Brown Company, Publishers, 1963.

Wakefield, Frances, Dorothy Harkins, and John M. Cooper, *Track and Field Fundamentals for Girls and Women.* St. Louis: The C. V. Mosby Co., 1966.

Wells, Katherine F., *Kinesiology* (4th ed.). Philadelphia: W. B. Saunders Co., 1966.

Wessel, Janet A., *Movement Fundamentals.* Englewood Cliffs, N.J.: Prentice-Hall, Inc., 1961.

Angling

ORIGIN AND DEVELOPMENT

Fishing with line and hook was probably originated by the Egyptians. They used a rather crude line of woven animal hair and a sharpened bone for the hook. Other nations devised methods of catching fish and it is not definitely established just when and where fly-casting originated. The origin of the reverse barb and the metal hook, although of rather modern invention, is not known. Menke [1] claims that Aelian, an Italian (A.D. 170–230), is credited with being the first to write about fly-casting, but that William Radcliffe of England, who wrote *Fishing from the Earliest Times,* believed that Martial wrote about it between A.D. 10 and 20. Historians agree that the reel came into existence during the fifteenth century, but no one seems to know just when and where. The modern reel with free-running spool geared to four revolutions to one turn of the handle was in-

[1] Frank G. Menke, *The Encyclopedia of Sports* (New York: A. S. Barnes & Co., Inc., 1947), p. 17.

vented by George Snyder, a watch-maker of Paris, Kentucky, between 1800 and 1810.

Izaak Walton, the Englishman, who published his *Compleat Angler* in 1653, is considered the patron saint of anglers because, more than any other man, he changed fishing to angling. In other words, fishing became a sport for pleasure rather than a means of supplying food. Many angling clubs sprang up in England following this publication, but it was some time before such clubs were formed in this country. The first was the Schuylkill Fishing Company, founded in Philadelphia in 1732. This organization has existed more or less continuously since that time. The first fly-casting championship was held in Chicago during the World's Fair in 1893.

Angling has increased in popularity until today innumerable persons engage in the sport. There are over 25,000,000 fishing licenses issued in the United States each year, while at least another 10,-000,000 people fish without licenses, making it the most popular sport in the country. It is also estimated that they spend more than any other sport minded group on their sport—at least $3 billion annually.

THE NATURE OF ANGLING

As was indicated before, angling is fishing for sport. More than that, it is the employment of the skill of casting to catch fish. A true angler receives a great deal of pleasure out of the testing of his skill and the outdoor adventure even though he fails to catch fish. He is also one who is interested in conservation, and especially in observing the fishing laws. Nature makes this enjoyable outdoor sport possible, and, to keep the sport flourishing, every angler and fisherman should follow a few simple rules:

1. Know the state game laws and obey them.
2. Don't keep more fish than are needed and handle with care those that are thrown back.
3. Be careful with fire and do not destroy plant life.
4. Join a local Izaak Walton League or Sportsman Club and do your part in restocking streams and conserving fish life.

The basic skill in learning to become an angler is casting. Despite the fact that this is a relatively simple skill, very few become masters of it because they do not learn properly under skilled guidance. The general objectives of this sport might be:

1. To master the skill of casting.
2. To learn to select and care for proper equipment.
3. To study the habits of fish and how to catch them.
4. To become a part of the conservation movement.

There are two types of casting: fly and bait. These two types are quite similar but employ different tackle and somewhat different techniques. In *fly-casting*, a longer, more flexible rod is used, the line is controlled from the hand, and the light bait is propelled entirely by its own weight and that of the line. The purpose of fly-casting is to make it possible to use very small lines and to secure accuracy and not distance. *Bait-casting* requires a shorter, less flexible rod. Distance is gained by the weight of the bait or lure. In bait-casting the line is controlled at the reel, rather than by the line as in fly-casting.

We shall treat fly-casting first because it is the aristocrat among anglers and probably should be learned first.

FLY-CASTING

Equipment

The beginner should first enlist the assistance of an experienced fly fisherman in selecting his equipment, as proper equipment in the beginning is very important. He should purchase a minimum of good, but not necessarily expensive, fishing equipment. As he becomes more skillful in casting and experienced in selecting lures, he will want to secure better and more elaborate equipment. The equipment, of course, should be suitable for the type of fishing to be done.

The most important piece of equipment is the rod. For general purposes, one of eight and one-half feet, weighing between four and one-quarter and five ounces is recommended. The fiberglass rods are best suited for general use. A single action reel with a large diameter should be selected. The automatic reel is not recommended for beginners. Some experts recommend that the reel and line weight be one and a half times as much as the rod. The choice of the line depends on the action of the rod. A limber rod requires a line of small diameter and a stiff rod a heavier line. The manufacturer's recommendations of line size for the rod should be closely followed. For the rod recommended here, a line of size "D" level is suitable. The leader should not exceed the length of the rod, and usually six feet is sufficient.

There are two types of fly-rod artificial bait: surface and underwater. The surface type includes dry fly bass bugs and all floating bait. The underwater type includes wet flies such as nymphs, streamers, spinners, and small deep-running lures. The dry fly selected should vary in hook-size from #4 to #18. There are innumerable kinds of each type of

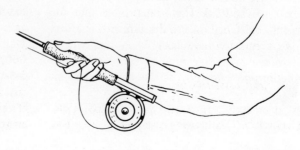

FIGURE 6-1. The most common grip for casting

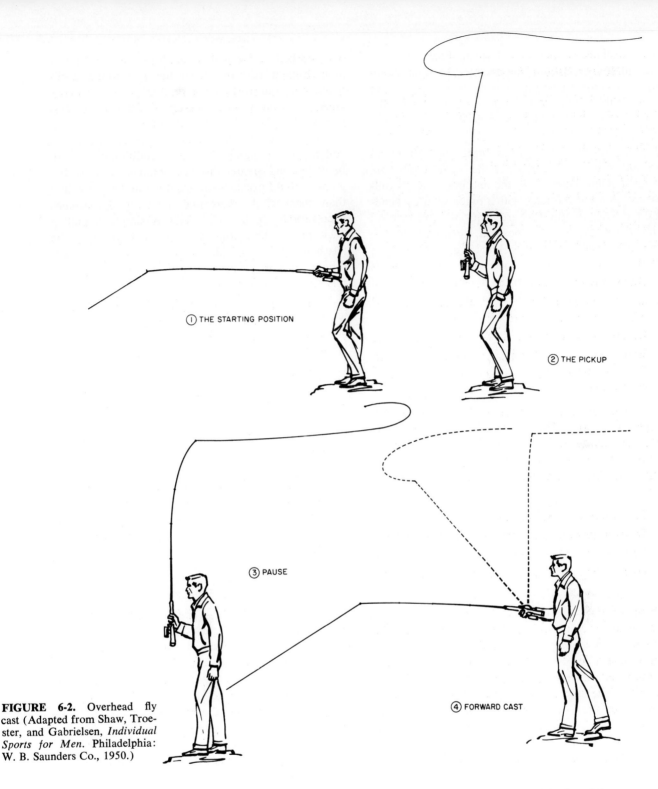

FIGURE 6-2. Overhead fly cast (Adapted from Shaw, Troester, and Gabrielsen, *Individual Sports for Men*. Philadelphia: W. B. Saunders Co., 1950.)

① THE STARTING POSITION

② THE PICKUP

③ PAUSE

④ FORWARD CAST

bait, but the beginner should purchase just a few of each for the kind of fishing he expects to do. As he progresses, he may learn to tie his own, or can purchase a more extensive variety.

Techniques and fundamentals

The overhead cast should be mastered first. The first step is to learn the proper grip. The rod is grasped at the center of the grip with the right hand, fingers around the shaft and the thumb placed on top "opposite the reel." (See Fig. 6-1.)

With the line and leader about six to ten feet longer than the rod and extended in front (in the water if possible), lift the rod to clear all of the line and part of the leader. (See Fig. 6-2.) Then, after the fly is on the surface, snap the rod sharply upright with enough force to propel the bait an equal distance to the rear. Instead, however, bring the rod straight up into the air over the right shoulder to a vertical position. The rod should not move back of the shoulder. It must be kept in mind that this is a wrist and forearm action with the elbow acting as a pivot. The elbow must be kept close to the side of the body. Then bring the rod to an abrupt stop when it reaches the vertical position. After a slight pause while the line moves to its fullest extension to the rear, with a quick snap by bending the wrist sharply forward, bring the rod forward and down again to a position horizontal to the ground or water. The fullest force is exerted at about midway down on this movement. This action is often likened to that of using a tack hammer, and precaution must be taken not to throw the rod with a long sweep of the arm, but to emphasize the definite snap with the wrist and forearm.

Beginners will have difficulty with the line and leader entering the water before the bait. This can be avoided by aiming the lure about a foot above the water or imagining that the level of the water is higher. It will help also to draw the rod backward a few inches an instant before the leader straightens out.

At the same time one must learn to handle the line with his left hand. Slack is taken and the line grasped between the thumb and the forefinger and stripped (drawn) from the reel to an arm's length. Repeat this action so that three or more coils are formed. The pick-up of the back cast is executed, and then at the end of the forward motion of the line, the line should be released from the coil in the left hand. Each time additional line can be coiled and greater distance obtained, but the beginner should practice for accuracy and form rather than distance. As more line is let out, it becomes necessary to "pull back." This is simply a pulling back of the line after reaching forward with the left hand and seizing the line at the first guide. Additional line may also be stripped from the reel at this time in preparation for a longer cast.

There are other types of casting that the novice will eventually want to learn, such as the side cast, the roll cast, and the false cast, but space prohibits an elaboration of them.

BAIT- AND SPIN-CASTING

Equipment

The beginner should select (with the aid of his instructor) a good rod that is five to six feet

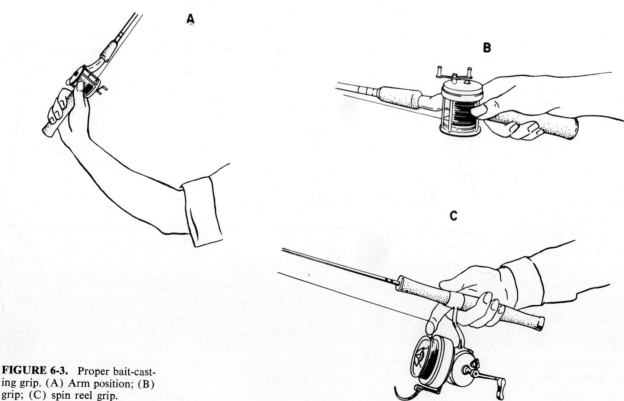

FIGURE 6-3. Proper bait-casting grip. (A) Arm position; (B) grip; (C) spin reel grip.

long and has good action. Despite the fact that a good rod is very strong and durable, it must be given special care. After use, it should be wiped off and replaced in its case. It should never be laid on the ground or in the bottom of the boat, where it can be stepped on or where the reel may be harmed by water. The ferrules must be oiled occasionally and if too tight should be returned to the factory for refitting.

The best reel for bait-casting is the spin-cast pushbutton type, but the old reliable quadruple multiplier is still popular. The spin-casting reels may be obtained in various gear ratios, with the three to one or four to one being most common. The beginner should select a reel of moderate price which contains approximately 100 yards of eight to twelve pound test monofilament line. It is important that the rod and reel balance. A heavy reel would "kill" the action of a light rod.

The reel must be given good care. It should be carefully cleaned and oiled before and after each use. Sand and dirt are especially harmful, so the reel must not be placed on the ground or allowed to gather dust when stored. After cleaning, a drop of oil or other lubricant should be placed under the spool bushing. (The conventional type of reel should be oiled at each end of the spool bushing, line carriage, and crank shaft.) Use only the type of lubricant recommended by the manufacturer.

Techniques and fundamentals of casting

In general, the action in bait-casting is the same as described for fly-casting, but there are several very different fundamentals. We shall describe these differences and not repeat any more of the fly-casting technique than necessary.

The grip for bait-casting is different in that the thumb must be placed on the button for the spin-cast or the spool flange for the conventional type, and the reel turned sidewise (see Fig. 6-3) so that the handle points straight up. The index finger should grip the finger trigger while the other fingers grasp the handle firmly but not rigidly.

As in all sports, the first essential for good casting is to remain relaxed. In fishing, a good caster learns to cast from any position and with either hand. In target casting, which is the only method of learning accuracy, the caster may stand directly facing the target or slightly sidewise, with the right side (if casting right handed) toward the target and the right foot slightly advanced. The arms should be held in a relaxed "natural" position with the el-

bow at or near the side. The target should be aligned by looking at it through the top of the tip.

The casting action has two parts: the backward and the forward motion. Each is equally important. When the rod and target are properly "lined up," the tip of the rod is brought in and up sharply to a vertical position and stopped suddenly the instant the backward motion of the tip stops. The forward motion is started straight forward and is twice as fast as the backward motion. This is important to bring out the action of the rod. (See Fig. 6-4.)

All the action is given the rod with the wrist, the elbow being held stationary. Using the arm destroys accuracy.

In order to control the line, it is necessary to *thumb the spool* when using a conventional reel. By varying the pressure of the thumb on the spool, one regulates the speed of the spool and prevents back-lashing of the line. The tip of the thumb may be placed entirely on the line or, better for beginners, it may be placed partially on the line and partially on the flange of the spool. (The spool should be full of line but not touching the posts.) The thumb should apply firm pressure as the rod is

FIGURE 6-4. Overhead cast (Adapted from Shaw, Troester, and Gabrielsen, *Individual Sports for Men.*)

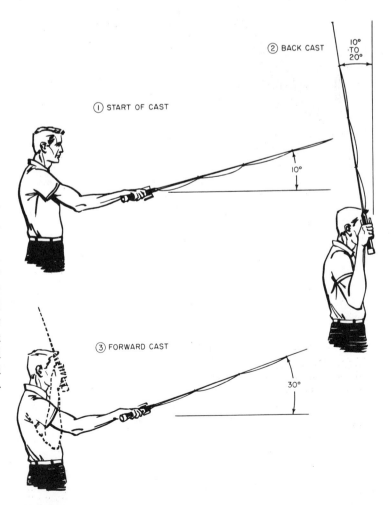

brought back for the cast and held until the rod completes its forward movement. The pressure is eased on the forward cast at about the ten o'clock position, allowing the line to run (but never fully released, touching the line or flange at all times), and then increased again just before the bait hits the target. When using a spin-cast reel, the line is controlled by pressure on the button. Only practice will teach one this technique.

As the rod reaches the vertical position, the grip of the three fingers is relaxed so that the rod breaks away from the palm. Beginning the downward movement they should be closed again so that impetus is added to the cast. In bringing the rod down, one must be careful to pass again through the "aiming zone" sighted at the beginning of the cast. The eyes should "pick-up" the plug soon after it is released, keeping the rod, line, and target in alignment.

The rod must be shifted to the left hand in order to retrieve the plug. The right hand then grasps the handle of the reel and begins to reel in the line.

After learning to cast from the standing position, it is wise to learn from a sitting position because it is often necessary to fish while sitting.

Retrieving

The method of retrieving depends, of course, on the type of bait being used. There is such a variety of lines and they become so specialized that the manufacturer supplies printed instructions on their proper manipulation so the angler may secure the best results from each type. These instructions should be studied carefully. The same method of using any line will not always be successful and the fisherman should experiment until he finds the method most suitable to his technique of handling it. This being the case, there is no "only" method of using any one lure or type of lures. However, the practices generally used on the three different types are as follows:

1. When using most types of underwater lures, the lure should be allowed to sink a little, then be jerked to the surface. The lure is then allowed to sink again while slack line is rolled onto the reel.

2. The top water type of lure imitates a mouse or other small animal swimming on the surface. The line should be wound slowly back onto the reel with slight pauses.

3. The underwater type are the spoons and spinners. The spinners should be wound back just fast enough to get the proper spinning action.

The spoon should be allowed to sink for at least 30 seconds, then brought back with a steady winding interspersed with jerks of the rod, allowing the lure to settle a few feet each time while slack is taken in.

4. The bottom-bumping type of lure includes the lead-headed jigs, weighted plastic worms, and other sinking types of bait. These type of lures has proven most effective when retrieved slowly with intermittent twitches of the rod. This gives the effect of natural movement.

SPINNING

Spinning is the newest form of bait-casting in America, but it has been used in Europe for many years. It was introduced here a few years ago by the importation of one of the most popular French spinning outfits. This reel has been widely copied and improved by American spinning-reel manufacturers.

The spinning reel

The spinning reels are divided into two general classes: (1) *Open type*—The spool upon which the line coils has no cover, leaving the spool and line fully exposed. This is the original type which was first introduced from Europe; (2) *Cone type*—A cone covers the spool and line to protect the line from dirt, to prevent its being touched by lures, twigs, weeds, and other foreign objects, and especially to prevent gusts of wind blowing it off the spool and causing "gnarling." The line passes through a hole in the center of the cup, directly in front of the axis of the spool shaft (See Figs. 6-5 and 6-6.)

FIGURE 6-5. Spinning reels. (*Top*) Open face on a straight seat. (*Bottom*) Cone face on a curved seat.

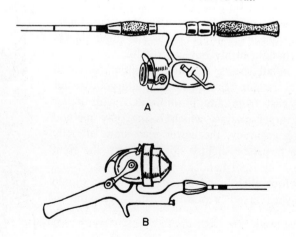

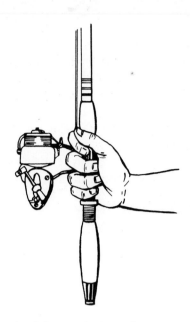

FIGURE 6-6. Grip on spinning rod

Although this cone does protect the line, most spinning authorities think this cover interferes with the free action of the line while leaving the spool, thus reducing the length of the cast. For this reason, the open type is generally preferred.

Most reels are equipped with left-hand action handles, but some of the later types have handles for right-hand use.

The action of the reel spool is the basic difference among the spinning, spin-casting, and standard bait-casting outfit. The spool of a spinning reel does not rotate to release the line on the cast or to re-spool it during the retrieve. On most reels, it advances and recedes as the line is being coiled on, in order to spool the line uniformly, but it never rotates. On the cast, the line slips off the exposed end of the spool. This action can best be visualized by thinking of a spool of thread. If one end of the spool of thread is held firmly in one hand and the thread end grasped by the other hand and stripped off straight over the opposite end of the spool, the action would be similar to that of the spinning line leaving the reel. The spool also remains stationary on the retrieve. A metal "finger" rotates around the spool, picking up the line and placing it back around the spool. For this reason, there are no backlashes such as frequently happen with the standard reel. This feature especially appeals to the inexperienced caster.

The spinning rod

Since light lures are to be cast, a light, flexible rod must be used. The length is also important. Most rods are seven feet long, a few are six feet six inches, and very few, very light rods are only six feet long. Fiber glass and nylon are the materials used.

The base or butt of the rod is straight, with a cork grip about ten inches long and two metal bands to secure the reel by sliding over either end of the rod clips.

The spinning line

Since the light lures and rod are used, it is necessary to use a light line. Most spinning lines are from four to eight pounds test strength of mono-filament nylon. Braided lines, especially those of heavier tests, are made by some companies.

When putting on a line, it is very important to follow carefully the instructions from the manufacturer in order to avoid twisting the line. Nothing is more troublesome than a twisted line, whether spin-, fly-, or bait-casting.

Making the cast

The cast with the spinning outfit is made in the same manner as with the bait-casting outfit. The only difference is in the control of the line during the cast. With the standard outfit, the control is exercised by varying the pressure of the thumb upon the line *on* the rotating spool. With the spinning outfit, it is done by pressure upon the line between the forefinger and the rod grip *after* the line has left the spool.

In starting the cast, the line (ahead of the reel) is held firmly against the rod grip with the forefinger of the hand with which the cast is made. While holding the line securely, the pick-up bail or finger is released and moved aside so that it will not interfere with the line during the cast. This is done by turning the handle very slightly in reverse, by pressing a release button, or as required for the particular make of reel.

As with the conventional rod and reel, the direct overhand cast is recommended until proficiency with the new outfit is acquired.

The pressure upon the line is released at the same time and in the same manner as the thumb pressure upon the spool would be released with a bait-casting outfit. During the flight of the lure, control is exercised by decreasing or increasing the finger pressure on the line against the cork grip.

For the experienced bait-caster, the "timing" of the spin cast requires some readjustment. The tendency is to release the pressure too quickly, thus permitting the lure to travel up instead of forward. However, with practice, proper control can be secured.

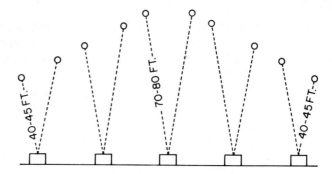

FIGURE 6-7. Ten targets, five stations

Most experienced casters feel that there is nothing they can do with a spinning outfit that they cannot do better with one or the other bait or fly outfits. However, many have discarded bait and fly outfits for a spinning outfit, once they have learned to use it.

There are several erroneous ideas about the spinning outfit. The most general concerns the comparative distances secured in spin- and bait-casting. The impression among the inexperienced is that almost anyone with a spinning outfit can make longer casts than can an experienced caster with a conventional casting outfit. While it is true that the average fisherman can consistently spin-cast 50 to 100 feet, tournament records show that with good casters much greater distances are secured with the conventional bait-casting than with the spinning outfit.

Another mistaken idea held by many not familiar with the principle of casting is that weightless lures such as flies, nymphs, and bugs, can be cast alone, just as are the one-quarter ounce and one-third ounce casting lures. The reason this is impossible should be perfectly obvious. Any object that can be cast must have enough weight to develop sufficient momentum to strip the line from the spool during the cast. These light flies can be cast, but with other lures or objects to supply the weight.

Spinning's popularity increased rapidly very soon after it was first introduced here, until it appeared that it might replace the older methods of casting. However, its fall in popularity was almost as rapid as its growth, and now it is only one of the three recognized forms of casting, bait-casting still being by far the most common method.

All who enjoy casting or fishing certainly should learn to use the spinning outfit. It definitely has a place in casting equipment and in fishing enjoyment.

SKISH

Skish is a dry-land game designed to improve one's skill in casting with regular bait and fly-casting tackle. It is an excellent "game way" to master the skills of accuracy and the control of distance.

Bait-casting rules call for the plug not to exceed five-eighths of an ounce, and the line no smaller than nine-pound test. Ten targets, rings not to exceed 30 inches, are randomly scattered at unknown distances (to the caster). The closest target is not less than 40 feet or more than 45 feet from the casting box (four feet × four feet), while the farthest one should be not more than 80 feet or less than 70 feet. Each target has its own casting box and the contestants move from box to box, taking two casts at each target. (See Fig. 6-7.)

SCORING. Six points are scored for perfect cast on first trial; four points for perfect cast on second trial.

The play must fall within the target to score. In the event of tied score, the one having the greatest number of points on initial casts is declared the winner.

Fly-casting rules call for regular fly-casting tackle, tied in approved dry fly style and the hook broken off back of the barb. Five targets are placed at unknown distances (to the casters) between 20 and 40 feet from the casting boxes.

FIRST ROUND. Caster must start with fly in hand and no slack in line, and is given two and one-half minutes at each target to make three casts.

SCORING. Five points are scored for perfect cast on first trial; three points for perfect cast on second trial; two points for perfect cast on third trial. Maximum score is 50 points. (On water, fly must rest on water until judge calls for score.)

SECOND ROUND. Time limit is one and one-half minutes (90 seconds) for each target. The caster rolls casts until a "perfect" has been scored on all five targets or until the official calls time. Time begins when fly drops on surface. Each perfect score counts five points, with a possible score of 25.

THIRD ROUND—WET FLY. Time limit, one to one and one-half minutes. Caster starts with fly in hand and no slack in line. To begin, he extends line to nearest target by false casting and time begins when the fly drops on the surface as a measured cast. Two casts are made, without false casts, at each of the five targets from left to right, stripping the necessary line to reach each target.

SCORING. Three points are scored for perfect cast on first trial; two points for perfect cast on second trial. Maximum possible score is 25 points. In case of tie, the caster having made the greatest number of initial perfects is declared winner.

SAFETY

1. Care and skill must be employed if the angler is to avoid being "hooked" by the fishhook in bait- and fly-casting. Even experts must be careful when casting on windy days. The overhand cast is safest to use in almost all situations. The fly-caster should not jerk the fly out of the water too quickly, and the bait-caster should not pick his lure out of the water so long as there is slack in his line. Both mistakes tend to endanger the caster. The rebound of a hook that has been forcefully extricated from a bush may also be dangerous. It is best to let a physician remove a hook that has been imbedded in the flesh, but if one is not available, the hook can often be pushed on through or pulled back if the barb or eye is cut off. If possible, the remaining end should be sterilized before being pushed through.

2. All the precautions of camping and water safety must be practiced to avoid accidents in these areas while fishing. Such hazards as the following must be recognized and proper precautions must be taken: use of gasoline or kerosene to start fires; poisonous snake areas; fishing from a boat if you are not a swimmer or are with non-swimmers; changing positions in water craft, especially a canoe; capsized craft; remaining on a lake when a storm comes up; handling dangerous fish, such as the sting ray or Portuguese man-of-war; encountering dangerous animals, such as a bear with a cub; and eating poisoned food or drinking unfit water.

3. Wading with boots in unknown waters or wearing them in a boat is hazardous and the angler must realize the danger involved. Very few persons are good enough swimmers to survive if wearing boots when a boat capsizes.

4. Lures should not be left in the bottom of a boat or on the shore because they may become imbedded in one's foot or leg.

5. To avoid injuring the thumb, the bait-casting reel may be coated with lacquer or covered with adhesive tape.

TERMINOLOGY

Back cast Drawing the rod back; the initial movement in the cast.

Back-lash A faulty casting technique that results in a tangling of the line.

Bait Artificial or natural lures that are used to attract fish.

Bait-casting The throwing and placing of a lure and line from the rod and reel.

Bucktail A fly used for bass fishing.

Cork arbor The part of the reel to which the line is attached.

Dry fly fishing Casting a surface fly so that it resembles an insect on the water.

Ferrules The metal connections between sections of the rod.

Flies Artificial bait resembling insects.

Fly-casting Throwing a line with an artificial lure by means of a fly rod.

Forward cast The last movement forward with the rod that throws the bait on the line to the desired spot.

Gaff A hook used to land fish.

Guides Small loops on the rod through which the line is run.

Hooking the fish Setting the hook after the fish takes the bait.

Leader The strong, transparent material that connects the line to the hook or lure.

Level-wind reel A reel which has a carriage that distributes the line evenly on the spool.

Lures Artificial or natural bait used to attract fish. A hook or hooks are attached to the lure.

Net A device to take the fish safely out of the water.

Reel The mechanism which winds or unwinds the line.

Reel set A part of the rod handle to which the reel is attached.

Rod tip The end of the rod.

Skish A competitive game of accuracy in casting.

Spin-casting A term used to describe "push-button" casting, using a casting rod and a closed-face spinning-type reel.

Spinner An artificial bait that spins when it is drawn through the water.

Spinning A type of casting in which the line leaves the spool much in the same manner as thread leaves the end of a spool.

Spoons Artificial bait shaped something like a spoon.

Still fishing Fishing with the baited hook held motionless.

Streamer An artificial fly resembling a May fly.

Strike When a fish grabs the bait.

Tackle Fishing gear; usually refers to the rod and reel only.

Thumbing   Controlling the speed of the cast with pressure on the reel with the thumb.

Weedless bait   Lures which have guards that prevent the hooks from catching on weeds.

SELECTED REFERENCES

American Association for Health, Physical Education and Recreation, *Casting—Outdoor Education Project*. Washington, D.C., 1201 Sixteenth Street, N.W., 20036, 1960.

American Casting Education Foundation, *Tournament Fly and Bait Casting Guide*. Nashville: The Foundation, 1965.

Bauer, E. A., *The Bass Fisherman's Bible*. New York: Doubleday and Company, Inc., 1961.

Brooks, Joe, *Complete Book of Fly Fishing*. New York: A. S. Barnes and Co., Inc., 1958.

Bueno, B., *American Fisherman's Guide*. Englewood Cliffs, N.J.: Prentice-Hall, Inc., 1960.

By-Laws, Rules and Regulations of Casting (current publication). National Association of Angling and Casting Clubs, University City, Missouri.

Evanoff, Vlad, *Natural Baits for Fishermen*. New York: A. S. Barnes and Co., Inc., 1959.

Janes, E. C., *Fresh-Water Fishing Complete*. New York: Holt, Rinehart and Winston, Inc., 1961.

Macdonald, Alexander, *On Becoming a Fly Fisherman*. New York: David McKay Co., Inc., 1959.

National Skish Guide. Washington, D.C.: National Skish Board, Bond Building (latest edition).

Owington, R., *The Sportsman's Guide to Fresh Water Fishing*. New York: Thomas Nelson & Sons, 1961.

Paust, G. H., *Fishing*. New York: Sterling Publishing Co., Inc., 1962.

Sell, F. E., *Practical Fresh Water Fishing*. New York: The Ronald Press Company, 1960.

Walton, Izaak, *The Compleat Angler*. New York: E.P. Dutton & Co., Inc., 1906.

———, *The Complete Angler*. New York: Doubleday and Company, Inc., 1961.

Archery

ORIGIN AND DEVELOPMENT

Although the time and place of the origin of archery are unknown, evidence of its existence has been found on practically every continent and in every habitation of man. Archery was first used for hunting, and was changed into a weapon of war by the Egyptians, who overthrew Persia, their conquerors, and successfully waged war on many other nations. The bow and arrow remained the principal weapon of war from many centuries before the Christian era until about A.D. 1600. The first Egyptian bow was from four and one-half to five feet long. The arrows ranged from 24 to 32 inches in length, and had tips made of bronze, flint, stone, or pointed wood. It was found that increased bow length meant increased range, so that length was increased up to six feet. Longer lengths were unwieldy and of little value because a six-foot bow would shoot as far as most archers could score hits.

In the fourteenth century, archery practice was compulsory in England, with the result that England had the best bowmen in Europe. England was also the first country in Europe to mount her archers, which increased the shooting range. Ghengis Khan, however, was the first war lord to use mounted archers. The successful use of English firearms in the invasion of England by the Spanish Armada in 1588 relegated the bow and arrow to a secondary place as a weapon of war. Its use decreased, and it was used for the last time in battle by the Chinese in 1860.

A small group of archers created the "Ancient Scorton Arrow" contest in England in 1673. Still being conducted, this is the oldest continuous archery tournament in existence. King Charles II of England fostered archery as a sport in 1676. Other nations also approved archery as a sport, and it flourished and expanded through the seventeenth, eighteenth, and nineteenth centuries.

Archery was introduced into the United States as a sport in the seventeenth century, but had little following until 1879, when a revival in interest led to the formation of the National Association of Archery, which was later changed to the National Archery Association. The first archery tournament was started in 1879 in Chicago, and, with the exception of the years 1917, 1918, 1942, 1943, 1944, and

1945, there has been an annual tournament ever since.

NATURE OF ARCHERY

Archery is primarily a sport of shooting arrows at a target. Each year, however, more and more archers are turning to the use of the bow and arrow for hunting, and many participate in clout and flight shooting. Archery is a healthful sport because it is usually practiced out of doors and is not too strenuous. This allows persons of both sexes and all ages to participate, and many find it a most enjoyable lifetime recreational sport. It also has some remedial posture value.

Archery tackle need not be expensive, and most of it can be handmade by the enthusiast. In fact, one of the real pleasures of the sport for many archers lies in the joy of making the bows and arrows.

RULES FOR COMPETITION

1. Any bow, except a crossbow, and any arrows may be used.
2. An archer may change tackle at any time.
3. One may shoot at the same target as used in practice.
4. Women may shoot in a men's event or in junior or senior events, but men may not shoot in a women's event.
5. Arrows must remain in the target until scored.
6. An arrow that cuts two areas scores the higher one.
7. Seven (red) is assigned an arrow that passes through a target, unless the field captain determines its true value.
8. Six arrows (an *end*) is the scoring unit. Usually the archer shoots three arrows consecutively.
9. An archer is allowed to retrieve an accidentally loosed arrow if he can reach it from his stance by the aid of the bow.
10. An arrow hitting the wrong target counts as a shot, but its value is forfeited.

OFFICIATING

The archery tournament is under the direction of a *field captain* for men and a *lady paramount* for women. This person acts as the referee and has full charge of conducting the competition and en-forcing the rules. He calls the target captains together five minutes prior to the match and checks their duties and assignments. After a second call, "ready to start," the shooting begins. When an archer finishes his end (six arrows) he steps back from the line, and when all have finished the field captain blows his whistle and they all advance to the targets to score and retrieve their arrows.

The shooters on each target elect a captain, a scorer (women, two), a drawer, an observer, and an arrow hound.

The *target captain* (usually the first in order of assignment) presides over the contestants at a given target and sees to it that they shoot in turn, draw arrows from the target, and announce their values; he calls the field captain to witness ends, and takes an archer's place in event of an unavoidable delay.

As the *drawer* pulls the arrows (the scorer's arrows are drawn first, beginning with those nearest the center) he calls their values and then draws his own, and then those of the observer and of the arrow hound.

The *scorer* records each arrow's score on the official score card as well as the total number of hits and scores for each end, group of ends, or range scores, and the total hits and scores of that round.

The *observer*'s duty is to see that no careless errors are made, and the *arrow hound* retrieves the misses. After the first round the archers are reassigned to targets according to their scores. For the third and remaining rounds those who shot on various targets rotate—those on one move to two, those on two to three, and those on three to one. The object is to match archers of similar abilities.

EQUIPMENT

Selecting archery tackle

BOWS. Probably the smoothest shooting long bow for target archery is made of a rare wood called yew. The laminated recurve bow with fiberglass backing is also very popular with experts because of its beauty, efficiency, and smooth shooting cast. Both, however, are too expensive ($30 to $100) for most schools to furnish. Most schools have found the fiberglass bows best suited for beginners. They lack this "smooth-in-hand" quality that the more experienced archer demands, but they have proven to be durable and have good shooting qualities. Regardless of the kind of bow selected, there are seven tests it should pass in order to give satisfactory service:

1. Bend the bow, place the lower nock on the ground with the string up, rest the upper nock on the index finger, close one eye and look up and down the bow. *The bow must be straight,* and if it is, the bowstring will bisect both limbs and the handle.

2. Thickness of a bow should taper from one and one-eighth inches at the handle to about five-eighths inch, not more than three inches from the handle on both limbs. These sharp changes in thickness at the handle are called dips.

3. A bow should have more bend in the upper limb than in the lower limb and the limbs should bend uniformly from handles to tips. The distance from the string to the middle of the upper limb should be one-quarter inch greater than the distance from the string to the middle of the lower limb. A bow that bends the same amount in both limbs will probably break in the lower limb.

4. Bows should be at least a third wider than they are thick.

5. A bow should have no tool marks, humps, or gouges. Tool marks break the wood fibres and make the bow more susceptible to breakage. The finish should be smooth and well polished. Bows with horn nocks should have the nocks well glued onto the limbs.

6. The bowstring should be made of dacron, laid in glue, be thicker at both ends than in the center and taper gradually, have the end of the upper loop spliced into the string, and have a glue-laid service about six inches long with the center of the service opposite the junction of handle and upper limb when the bow is strung.

7. Recommended bow weights:

	WOMEN	MEN
Target archery (beginners)	18–22	22–26
Target archery (experienced)	25–30	30–38
Field archery	25–32	35–42
Hunting and fishing	30–45	42–52

ARROWS. The best wood for arrows is Norwegian Pine. Another excellent wood, though less durable and not practical unless the majority of your shots hit the target, is the Port Orford Cedar. Birch arrows are the cheapest, but they warp easily. Aluminum and fiberglass arrows are quite successful and generally more durable than those with wood shafts. Qualities to look for in an arrow are:

1. Footing—a footed arrow is more durable and less susceptible to warping.

2. Straightness—slightly crooked arrows may be straightened.

3. Roundness—twirl the arrow shaft on the thumb nail. If it is not round, it will jump up and down.

4. Nocks—wedge horn nocks and aluminum nocks are the best. Aluminum is more expensive, but will not break and can be reshaped if spread or squeezed together.

5. Fletchings—balloon-shaped fletchings are the best and should be so placed that the base of the fletch-

FIGURE 7-1. (A) Target; (B) bow; (C) arrow. (From Donna Mae Miller and Katherine L. Ley, *Individual and Team Sports for Women.* Englewood Cliffs, N.J.: Prentice-Hall, Inc., 1955.)

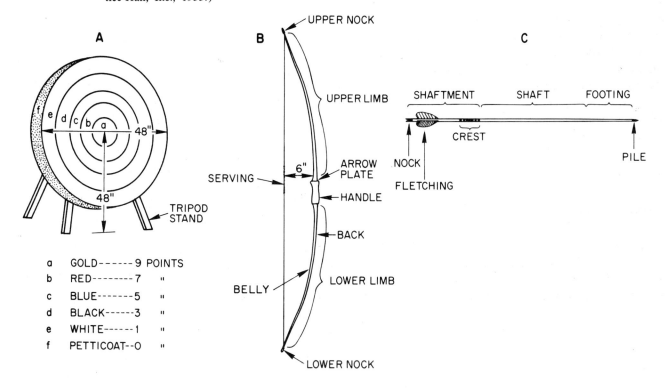

a	GOLD------9 POINTS
b	RED--------7 "
c	BLUE-------5 "
d	BLACK------3 "
e	WHITE------1 "
f	PETTICOAT--0 "

ings are parallel to the shaft and equidistant from each other. All fletchings on an arrow must curl in the same direction.

6. Finish—the better the polish, the better the durability. All sets should have some distinctive coloring just below the fletchings to serve as a means of identification. This is called the "crest."

7. Weight—arrows should not vary more than 5 per cent in weight within a set. It is best to state the arrow length, bow weight, and length, and let a reputable manufacturer send the proper weight arrows.

8. Pile (point)—the parallel pile is generally considered superior to the bullet shaped pile, and the piles should be fastened to the shaft by "knurling." Knurling is done by a machine that presses metal indentations into the shaft.

9. Length—the length of an arrow should be such that when you have drawn the arrow back to the proper position, the point of the arrow will be even with the back of the bow. It is important to use a bow long enough to handle your arrow length. To determine the proper length, a beginner should place the nock of the arrow on the center of his chest and extend his arms full length forward, palms facing, so that the point of the arrow extends past the fingertips.

TARGETS.   The best targets, and the most expensive, are hand made, coiled rye straw, sewn with tarred lobster marline (twine). The new styrofoam targets may replace the heavier and less durable straw ones.

TARGET STANDS.   Target stands should be made of soft wood, preferably white pine or cypress. The target can be tied to the stand or placed on dowels projecting from the two front legs. Target stands should be constructed so the front legs tilt back from 10 to 15 degrees. Lightweight metal-frame target stands with wheels are becoming quite popular.

Care and repair of tackle

BOWS.   Wooden bows dry out during the winter. Before using them at the beginning of the season, it is well to place them where it is particularly moist. It does not help to oil them. Improperly made nocks may cause the bowstring to break. They may be filed out smooth by a good carpenter or craftsman, or returned to the manufacturer for repair. Cracks and breaks can be repaired by waterproof glue and wrapped tightly until dry. Remove the wrapping, scrape off excess glue, wrap ends at breaks (or cracks with thread), and cover with Duco Household Cement or shellac.

ARROWS.   Arrows should be stored standing in an airtight, warm, dry, and mothproofed place. Fletchings may be replaced by using the previously mentioned cement and wrapping with light thread. The base of the fletching must be parallel to the arrow shaft. Arrows whose points or nocks have broken off should be sent to a manufacturer for repair. Broken arrows, when the break is long, can be mended the same as bows. Paint from the target

FIGURE 7-2.   (A) Stringing the bow; (B) nocking; (C) addressing the target. (From Miller and Ley, *Individual and Team Sports for Women.*)

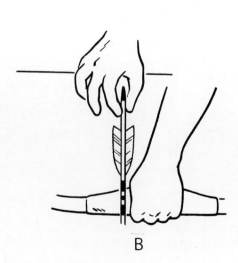

A   B   C

FIGURE 7-3. Method of stringing a recurve bow

face can be cleaned from the arrow shaft with gasoline or steel wool. Arrows should be waxed with floor wax; white shellac is good for refinishing arrows.

TARGETS. Targets should never be rolled but carried to help prevent their becoming loose. Once loosened, they may be tightened by starting at the center and pulling the string tight, working around and around.

BOWSTRINGS. Broken bowstrings cannot be repaired. The only replaceable part is the service, which may be sized with glue. It is well to check the arrow nocks for rough edges, for they cut the string.

TECHNIQUES AND FUNDAMENTALS

Stringing the bow

By this term we mean engaging the upper loop of the bowstring in the upper nock of the bow. (See Fig. 7-1 A.) The procedure is as follows:

1. Take the bow handle in your left hand with the back of the bow toward you.
2. Holding the left arm in front of the body and angling the bow's upper limb toward the right,

place the lower nock against the instep of the left foot, but not touching the ground.
3. Place the right hand on the upper limb just below the upper loop of the bowstring; then, keeping both arms straight, pull with the left and push with the *heel* of the right hand, and slide the string into the upper nock with the fingers.

TO STRING A RECURVE BOW. Step through the bow with the right leg, hook the lower limb over the ankle of the left foot, press the upper limb forward with the open right hand and slide the string into the nock with the left hand. (See Fig. 7-3.)

To unbend, merely bend the bow more by taking the position described above, flexing the bow, and picking the string out of the nock.

Addressing the target

By this term we mean taking the proper stance for shooting. It is done by facing the target and then turning to the right. A line drawn through one's heels and extended to the target should go through the gold. (See Fig. 7-4.)

Nocking the arrow

By nocking the arrow is meant placing the arrow on the bowstring in preparation for drawing. There are three methods of nocking an arrow, any of which may be used.

1. Hold the bow in shooting position, take an arrow by the nock and run it between the string and

FIGURE 7-4. Correct stance at full draw (From Dorothy Ainsworth, *et al., Individual Sports for Women,* 3rd ed. Philadelphia: W. B. Saunders Co., 1955.)

bow from right to left, and bring the nock back onto the bowstring service.

2. Hold the bow in shooting position, turn it over to a horizontal position with upper limb to the right, and, holding the arrow by the nock, merely lay it on top of the bow and place the nock onto the bowstring service.

3. Bend the bow arm, resting the bow on the hip with the string on the inside of the forearm. Grasp the arrow by the shaft and place the nock on the bowstring with the arrow under the bow and the cock-feather pointing down.

Regardless of the method used, there are four conditions that must be satisfied: (1) the arrow shaft must be on the left side of the bow, (2) the arrow shaft must be on the upper limb just above the handle, (3) the odd or cock-feathers must be to the left, and (4) the arrow must be perpendicular to the bowstring. If one is asked to explain how to nock an arrow on the examination, he should be sure to include these four points.

Drawing

This is the act of pulling the bowstring back into shooting position. To draw, curl the thumb and little finger into the palm of the drawing hand, place the tips of the first, second, and third fingers on the string with the arrow nock separating the first and second fingers, and pull the string back in one smooth, deliberate motion, keeping the drawing hand near the bow arm and shoulder all the way back to the shooting position. All three fingers pull with equal force. They must be kept parallel with the ground and perfectly straight from the first joint to the elbow. Do not have the string as far as the first joint of the fingers.

Loosing

Loosing is the act of releasing the bowstring with the drawing hand. It is performed by relaxing the fingers quickly and smoothly and without any other movement of the body.

Point of aim

The point of aim is the spot at which you look over the point of the arrow when aiming. This spot can be on the gold at only one distance with each shooting situation. By situation, we mean length of the arrow, weight of the bow, and physical characteristics of the individual archer. There are two factors that prevent aiming at the gold, and these are explained by Figs. 7-5 and 7-6. When aiming

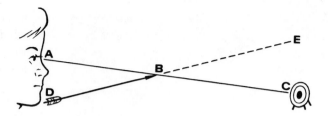

FIGURE 7-5.

at the gold, the flight of the arrow DBE must necessarily be above the target, because the nock is below the eye A, and the point of the arrow is on the line of sight ABC. (Fig. 7-5.)

If the arrow nock were at the level of the eyes and you aimed along the arrow at the gold ABC, the pull of gravity would cause the arrow to fall below the gold or even below the target D. (Fig. 7-6.)

When the rise in the arrow flight BE (Fig. 7-5), due to the difference between the level of the eye and the arrow nock, is equal to the fall in the flight of the arrow, EC, then and only then can you aim at the gold. This distance is generally between 40 and 60 yards. At short ranges, the rise in flight is greater than the drop, so it is necessary to aim under the target. At long ranges, the drop is greater than the rise, so it is necessary to aim above the target.

The scoring values are as follows:

Gold or "Bull's Eye" . . . . . . 9 points
Red Ring 7
Blue 5
Black 3
White 1
Outside of white ring 0

An arrow that goes *completely through the target* counts 7 points regardless of the part of the target through which it passed. An arrow that *hits the target* and bounces off counts 5 points regardless of the part of the target it hits. An arrow that *touches the line* between two rings counts as hitting the inside or higher value ring.

The hits are designated by the scoring value or color ring in conjunction with the position of the hits as would be recorded on the face of a clock. The six hits on Fig. 7-7 would be designated as:

1. Gold (or 9) at 6 o'clock.
2. Red (or 7) at 6:30 o'clock.
3. Blue (or 5) at 3 o'clock.
4. Black (or 3) at 10:30 o'clock.
5. White (or 1) at 7 o'clock.
6. Skirt (or 0) at 5:30 o'clock.

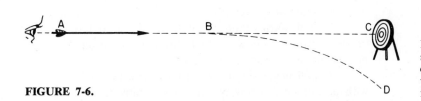

FIGURE 7-6.

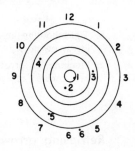

FIGURE 7-7. Scoring the position of the hits (Note: unless otherwise indicated, an archer will always shoot six arrows before retrieving and scoring.)

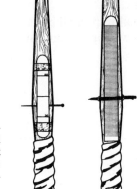

FIGURE 7-8. Homemade bowsights. (*Left*) Large pin placed behind a tongue depressor that is held by Scotch tape. (*Right*) A matchstick or toothpick supported by a rubber band.

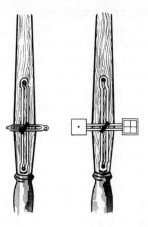

FIGURE 7-9. Manufactured bowsights. (*Left*) A peep-sight. (*Right*) A combination prismatic and common sight.

Shooting position

Following are the six fundamentals of target-shooting form necessary to a good archer.[1]

1. Bow arm slightly bent with the point of the elbow to the rear.
2. Wrist of bow arm bent so the bow bisects the "V" formed by the thumb and forefinger, and so the force of the bow comes through the wrist and not on the thumb.
3. Shoulder of bow arm low.
4. Index finger of drawing hand under jawbone.
5. String in center of nose and chin.
6. Left eye closed.

Bowsights

Bowsights are becoming more popular among the championship archers and are practical for the intermediate or advanced archer. There are numerous homemade and manufactured types. Two of the most common homemade sights are the adhesive tape or tongue depressor with a large-headed pin type, and the matchstick rubber band type. These and a manufactured sight are shown in Figs. 7-8

[1] Phillip Rounsevelle, *Archery Simplified* (New York: A. S. Barnes & Co., Inc., 1931), p. 10.

and 7-9. The advantage of the bowsight is that the point of aim is the target itself.

HELPFUL HINTS

Movements of certain parts of the body upon "loosing" results in faulty arrow flight. The most common errors are:

ERROR	RESULTING ARROW FLIGHT
a. Peeking (looking up to watch arrow)	High
b. Relaxing (letting your drawing hand move forward)	Right
c. Jerking (jerking drawing hand away from face)	Right
d. Hunching (hunching the left shoulder)	Left
e. Throwing the bow arm (moving bow arm toward target)	Left
f. Dropping the bow arm	Low

An arrow will fall off bow hand because of:

CAUSE	CORRECTION
a. No shelf on which to rest due to raised forefinger of bow hand.	a. Place forefinger of bow hand around bow with tip under the thumb.

CAUSE	CORRECTION
b. Tight shooting tab, squeezing arrow nock.	b. Increase size of arrow slot in shooting tab.
c. Pinching of arrow nock by fingers of drawing hand.	c. Separate fingers of drawing hand, being sure all fingers pull with equal force.

Retrieving arrows

FROM THE TARGET. Place the back of either hand against the target, with the arrow separating the first and second fingers. Holding the target face tight against the target with this hand, grasp the arrow by the shaft close to the target with the other hand and pull directly backward with a slight twisting motion. When the arrow is free of the target, place it between the thumb and forefinger of the hand on the target with the nock down.

FROM THE GROUND. (1) When fletchings are covered by the grass, grasp the point of the arrow and pull it forward until free. (2) When fletchings are free of the ground and grass, grasp the shaft near the ground and pull out backward. Care must be taken to pull out in the same path in which the arrow entered the ground in order not to bend it.

Safety hints

I shall always remember that bows and arrows are not toys, but weapons capable of inflicting serious injury and death.

I shall never point an arrow (in a bow) at another person, even in sport.

I shall never attempt to demonstrate my skill by permitting another to hold the object at which I shoot.

I shall never stand farther away from the target than others, so that I have to shoot over or past them, and I shall do all I can to prevent another archer from doing so.

I shall faithfully obey the starting and stopping signals when I shoot with others.

I shall never attempt to recover my own or another's arrows while someone is shooting, and I shall try to restrain others from so doing.

I shall call out, "Fast," before I loose on a field course, so that people about me may be warned.

I shall never leave my bow and arrows about unguarded where young or careless people can get their hands on them.

I shall never shoot unless I am certain that my target or its backstop will stop my arrows; and that there is no road in use or unpoliced area back of the target.

I shall never try to shoot far, except on a safe flight range; and I shall never shoot straight up into the air under any circumstances.

I shall warn others when I am about to test or demonstrate a bow; I shall draw with an unnocked arrow of safe length toward a solid wall.

I shall never shoot, or permit others to shoot, with a splintered arrow or one that I think unsafe, with a bow badly out of balance, or with a bowstring unserved.

I shall never brace another's bow without his permission, and I shall never draw it under any circumstances.

I shall respect all bows and arrows, and I shall give my own equipment careful, correct treatment at all times.

In short

I shall never take chances with a bow and arrow.

I shall seek to make known the safety rules of archery, and I shall work for archery safety every way I can.

I shall be a good sport, and I shall obey promptly if I am told to stop shooting for the infraction of any of these rules.

FIELD ARCHERY AND HUNTING

When hunting wild game, it becomes impossible to use a sight or point of aim because the animal very seldom stands still for the hunter to shoot. It is therefore necessary to revert to the natural or instinctive method of shooting—which was used throughout the ages by man to kill his game.

In the natural or instinctive method one must learn to judge distances quickly with the bow hand. The National Field Archers Handbook lists the following shooting details:

1. Feet well apart (aids balance and confidence).
2. Bow slightly inclined (brings right eye directly over arrow).
3. Head tilted (keeps string out of the way).
4. Bow held in a firm but not tight grip (avoid tension).
5. The bow resting against the thumb side of the palm (doesn't pound the wrist).
6. A straight bow arm (don't lock elbow and wrist or tense every muscle).

7. A comparatively high and solid anchor (runs from the jawbone to the cheekbone).
8. Both eyes open (measures distance of triangulation by natural method).
9. A full draw on all shots (various sized draws add complications).
10. A "hold" of a second, or so, on all shots to get set (all good shooters are deliberate).

The next step is to practice this instinctive method of shooting with field targets. (Hunting does not provide sufficient practice in shooting.) The archer must focus his eyes on the small black spot in the center of the target. He will see peripherally the bow hand, the bow, and part of the arrow. As one progresses he will slowly begin to disregard the arrow and to concentrate more and more on the spot on the target. It is then that he discovers that his bow hand is automatically taking care of the problem of elevation.

After mastering this technique the archer is ready to hunt. This calls for all the cunning of a hunter stalking his game. It is necessary for him to take his animal unaware, so he must move cautiously through the woods. He should move quietly and against the wind. Occasionally the conditions are suitable for the archer to remain stationary by concealing himself and shooting his game as it passes. He must not, however, move too much in order to assume a shooting stance or his game will be scared away.

SAFETY PRECAUTIONS

Field archery

1. Always call "timber" before starting to shoot, as warning to others who may not have cleared the shooting line or target area.
2. Always leave one member of your party standing in front of the target while you are looking for lost arrows as warning to others following on the course. If you are alone, leave your bow.
3. Never release an arrow when you cannot see where it will land; never "flight shoot" an arrow in the woods. Never shoot straight up.

Hunting

1. Hunt only during specified bow and arrow hunting periods and areas. (Most states provide those times and areas.)

2. Abide by the apparel and license regulations of your state.
3. Observe all hunting safety rules, such as not shooting at unidentified objects and not hunting with more than one other person.

TERMINOLOGY

American round For men and women; 30 arrows from 60 yards, 50 yards, and 40 yards, respectively.

Anchor point A definite point on one's face to which the index finger, bowstring, or arrow nock is brought in drawing for each shot.

Archery golf An adaptation of the game of golf to the sport of archery. Players shoot for the holes and score according to the number of shots required to hit the target—a four-inch ball.

Arm guard A leather or composition pad with or without reinforcing metal stays, worn on the bow forearm for protection.

Arrow plate A piece of hard material set into the bow, where the arrow crosses it, to protect the bow.

Arrow rest A small projection at the top of the bow handle.

Back The side of the bow away from the string.

Backed bow A bow whose back and belly are of different composition.

Belly The side of the bow nearest the string.

Bowyer A bow maker.

Brace To string the bow.

Broadhead A large flat hunting head with razor-sharp blades.

Butt A target built of bales of hay or straw.

Cast The distance a bow can shoot.

Clout shooting Shooting at a 48-foot target laid on the ground at 180 yards for men, and at 140 or 120 yards for women; usually 36 arrows.

Cock-feather The different colored feather which is set at right angles to the arrow head.

Columbia round For women; 24 arrows shot at 50-, 40-, and 30-yard ranges.

Composite A bow made up of more than one substance.

Creeping Letting the drawing hand move forward at the release.

Crest The identifying marks just below the fletchings on the arrow.

Double round A round shot twice in succession.

Drift The drift to either side of a mark caused by a cross wind.

End   Six arrows shot in succession.

Field captain   The one in charge of a tournament.

Finger shooting   A method of practicing the proper release of the string by using the partner's index finger as the string.

Fistmele   The distance between handle and string when the bow is strung. It is an old Saxon measurement. The distance from the base of the hand, when clenched, to the tip of the extended thumb.

Fletching jig   A device for securing feathers to an arrow.

Fletchings   The shaped and cut feathers secured to the arrow to keep it on its course.

Flight arrow   An arrow used for distance shooting. It is long and light and has very small feathers.

Flight shooting   Shooting an arrow the farthest possible distance.

Flirt   An arrow jumping out of its steady line of flight.

Follow   A tendency of some bows and bow woods to take for their permanent form their strung shape.

Handle   The grip at the mid-section of the bow.

Hen feathers   The two feathers that are *not* at right angles to the arrow neck.

High-braced   When the distance between handle and string of a strung bow is over seven inches. It is better to high-brace a bow than low-brace one.

Holding   Holding the arrow at full draw before release.

Instinctive shooting   Aiming and shooting instinctively, rather than using a bowsight, pre-gap, or point of aim method.

Keeper   A string used to secure the upper eye of the string onto the upper limb when unstrung.

Lady paramount   Lady in charge of a women's tournament.

Limbs   Upper and lower parts of the bow; divided by the handle.

Loose   To release the bowstring following the draw.

National round   For women; 48 arrows shot at 60 yards, 24 at 50 yards.

Nock   The groove in the end of the arrow in which the string is placed. The notch in arrows.

Nocking point   The point on the string at which the arrow is placed.

Overbowed   Using too strong a bow.

Overdrawn   Drawing the bow so that the pile of the arrow is inside the bow.

Overstrung   When the string is entirely too short for the bow.

Perfect end   Shooting of six perfect arrows into the gold.

Petticoat   That part of the target face beyond the white ring.

Pile   The pointed metal tip of the arrow.

Point blank   The type of range when no allowance is made for trajectory.

Point of aim   A mark used in sighting upon which the tip of the arrow is aimed.

Quiver   A receptacle for carrying or holding arrows.

Range finder   A device for determining varying points of aim.

Reflexed bow   Any bow whose limbs spring toward the back when it is unstrung.

Release   To let the arrow and string go; to shoot an arrow.

Round   The term used for shooting a definite number of arrows at definite distances. (See N.A.A. rules.)

Roving   A game in which the archery-players select random targets and shoot a predetermined number of arrows at them in turn. The targets are usually selected by the winner of the previous target.

Self   A bow made of only one wood, e.g., yew. A self arrow is unfooted.

Serving   The thread wrapped around the bowstring at the nocking point.

Shaft   The main part of the arrow.

Shaftment   The part of the arrow that holds the crest and the feathers.

Shooting glove   A glove so made that the two shooting fingers have protection across the tips.

Spine   The characteristic of an arrow's rigidity and flexibility.

Tab   A flat piece of leather used on the hand to protect the fingers of the archer.

Tackle   All archery equipment.

Target face   The painted front of a target, usually replaceable.

Timber   Same as "Fore" in golf; a warning to others in field archery.

Timber hitch   The knot used to secure the bowstring to the lower limb.

Toxophilite   A student of the history, as well as a master of the art, of archery.

Trajectory   The path of the arrow in flight.

Underbowed   Too weak a bow for the archer.

Vane   A feather of an arrow.

Wand shoot   Shooting at a narrow upright stick.

Weight   The total pull required to draw a bow the length of its arrow, measured in pounds; or the actual weight of an arrow in grams.

Wide   The flight of the arrow to either side of the target.

Windage   The influence of the wind upon an arrow in flight.

SELECTED REFERENCES

American Association for Health, Physical Education and Recreation, Division of Girls' and Women's Sports, *Archery and Riding Guide* (current edition). Washington, D.C.: The Association, published biennially.

The Athletic Institute, *How To Improve Your Archery*. Chicago: The Athletic Institute.

Burke, Edmond, *The History of Archery*. New York: William Morrow and Co., Inc., 1957.

Cavanaugh, James F., ed., *Bowhunting Manual* (2nd ed.). Redlands, Calif.: National Field Archery Association, 1962.

Edwards, C.B., and E.G. Heath, *In Pursuit of Archery*. London: Nicholas Kaye, Ltd., 1962.

Gillelan, G. Howard, *The Young Sportsman's Guide to Archery*. New York: Thomas Nelson and Sons, 1962.

Hochman, Louis, *The Complete Archery Book*. Greenwich, Conn.: Fawcett Publications, 1957.

Jaeger, Eloise, *Archery*. Athletic Institute Series. New York: Sterling Publishing Co., Inc., 1961.

Keaggy, Dave, Sr., *Power Archery*. Riderwood, Md.: Archery World Magazine, 1964.

National Field Archery Association, *Official Handbook of Field Archery* (current edition). Redlands, Calif.: The Association.

Niemeyer, Roy K., *Beginning Archery*. Wadsworth Sports Skills Series. Belmont, Calif.: Wadsworth Publishing Co., Inc., 1962.

Periodicals

The Archer's Magazine. 1200 Walnut Street, Philadelphia. 12 issues.

Archery—A Sportsman's Magazine Devoted to Hunting and Field. Official Publication of the National Field Archery Association, P.O. Box H, Palm Springs, Calif.

Archery World. Official Publication of the National Archery Association of the United States. Boyertown, Pa.: Archer's Magazine Company, 19512.

Badminton

ORIGIN AND DEVELOPMENT

Badminton was first known as "Poona" and was first seen in India. English army officers learned the game there and introduced it into England sometime between 1870 and 1880. Little enthusiasm was shown for the sport until the Duke of Beaufort really launched it at his home, "Badminton," at Gloucestershire.

The original Indian rules governed the activity until 1887, when the Bath Badminton Club laid down its basic regulations. These were supplemented and completed by the Badminton Association of England, established in 1895, to form the present rules.

Badminton was brought to Canada in the 1890's and to the United States shortly thereafter. Although it spread widely at first, its popularity soon waned, and the game had few followers until a second wave of popularity, starting in 1929, carried it to its status today.

As a result of its present popularity, the American Badminton Association, which now controls the sport and sanctions all badminton tournaments in the United States, was formed. It is affiliated with the International Badminton Association, which has its headquarters in England. There are approximately 300 badminton clubs in the United States, divided into 19 "Class A" associations. The official publication of the organization, *Bird Chatter,* is issued quarterly. The subscription rate is low and the magazine is available from the subscription manager, Grace Devlin, Dolfield Road, Owings Mills, Maryland.

NATURE OF THE GAME

Badminton is a more or less new addition to the family of sports in America. Despite the late date of its recognition as a valuable leisure-time activity, its popularity has recently grown by leaps and bounds due, primarily, to its adaptability. It is one game that can be played fast or slow, hard or easy, in or out of doors; by men, women, and children, young or old, fat or thin.

It is only fair, however, to point out some of its disadvantages. To be played out of doors, badminton requires that there be little or no wind (because of the light weight of the shuttlecock), a condition seldom to be found. The outdoor shuttlecock is too heavy to make for a satisfactory game. Another drawback is that the difference in score does not reflect the difference in playing ability between players. A slight superiority in playing ability will make for a very one-sided game.

When properly played, badminton requires a great deal of speed, endurance, and power. Team play of partners in a doubles game and deception demand the utmost in cooperation, concentration, and initiative in the use of strokes. It is an especially fine game for mixed doubles because the girl can play the net successfully while the boy covers the remainder of the court.

EQUIPMENT

Game equipment required for badminton includes only three items, unless the court is laid out temporarily with tapes. These items are the net and its supports, the rackets, and the shuttlecock or bird.

COURT. The playing court for doubles is the entire court (outsides lines 44 feet × 20 feet), while for singles it is the same length (44 feet) but only 17 feet wide. The service court for doubles is short and wide while the singles service court is longer (longer than the doubles service court) but narrower. (See Fig. 8-1.) This is difficult for a beginner to understand, but after more experience he will see the logic of the different service areas for singles and doubles.

NET. The net is woven from a light cord into a small mesh and supported on the upper side by a comparatively light rope, making it extremely vulnerable to improper care and rough usage. Two purposes for which the net is commonly used improperly are: (1) serving as a highjumping obstacle, and (2) serving as an object on which a player vents his ire by hitting it with his racket after making a poor play or missing a shot. The net should serve one and only one purpose—to stop birds that are not played sufficiently high to pass over it.

RACKET. Badminton rackets are light and fragile, and require the best of care. The best rackets are made of laminated wood, and some of them have a steel shaft. The more laminations the better the racket. Steel, aluminum, and plastic rackets are available, but have not proved as satisfactory as the wooden ones. The best rackets are strung with lambgut, which is usually too expensive for class use. Nylon is less expensive and quite satisfactory, especially the perfected nylon which has several strings enmeshed with the larger strings.

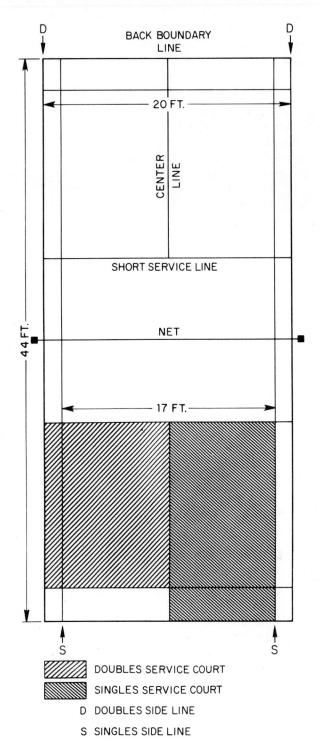

FIGURE 8-1. Badminton playing courts

When not in use, the rackets should be kept in a press to prevent damage to the head of the racket by warping. One should not hit the racket against the knee, calf of the leg, or other object. This loosens the strings and/or covers them with perspiration. Nor should one hit the net with the racket. Not only is it against the rules while playing, but it indicates a lack of control and emotional instability. Of course, one should never throw the racket.

SHUTTLECOCK. A shuttlecock weighs approximately one-sixth of an ounce and consists of a leather-covered cork base in which feathers are inserted at regular intervals and held in place with glue and string. A good shuttlecock is expensive—primarily because of the difficulty in obtaining good feathers, the best of which come from Czechoslovakia. The nylon and plastic birds have proved quite satisfactory and are recommended for class play. To get the most service from a shuttlecock, the following rules concerning its care should be learned and practiced:

1. Keep feathered birds in a humidor.
2. Always remove birds from containers base first and replace them the same way.
3. Take time to check and straighten out the feathers after every rally.
4. Always put the bird in play with an underhand stroke—otherwise the bird will be hit on the feathers.
5. Never kick or knock the bird along the floor or ground. Pick it up and throw or bat it where you want it to go.

RULES

1. Fifteen points constitute the usual game except for women's singles, in which 11 points are played. When the score is tied at 13-all, the side reaching 15 first chooses to finish the game at 15 or to set the game at 5 points. When tied at 14-all, he chooses to play 1 or 3 points. Similarly, in 11-point games, the score may be set at 3 when the score is 9-all and at 2 when 10-all.
2. The service must be delivered to the diagonal service court. A bird that lands on a line is considered good. In singles the bird must land in the long, narrow court and in doubles in the short, wide court. (See Fig. 8-1.) A let serve is one in which the bird touches the top of the net, but lands in the proper service court and is served over. It is a fault unless it lands in the service court.
3. Only one service (trial) per player is allowed per inning (not like tennis, where two trials are allowed), unless the bird is missed entirely. The service alternates courts, starting in the right-hand court for doubles at all times. In singles, the service starts in the right-hand court at the

beginning of the game, but thereafter service is made from the right-hand court when the score is even (for that side) and from the left-hand court when the score is odd (for that side). Only one hand is allowed the side beginning the serve in doubles the first inning, and two hands are allowed each inning thereafter. However, a member of the team can be in either court when the score is even (or odd), but each member must be in his proper court, i.e., the same sides they were in when they made their first point. An easy way to remember: When their score is even partners should be in the courts (sides) in which they started the game.

4. It is a fault (loss of service or hand for the serving-side and loss of point for receiving-side) when:
    A. Service is illegal, i.e., the bird is struck when above the waist or the head of the racket is higher than the hand when hit.
    B. Service or played shot lands outside the specified court (see Fig. 8-1), passes through or under the net, or hits a player or obstruction outside the court.
    C. If server or receiver steps out of his proper court before delivery of serve or feints in any way before the service. Only the person served to may return the bird.
    D. A player reaches over the net to hit a bird (he may follow a shot over).
    E. A player touches the net with his racket or any part of his body.
    F. A player hits the bird twice or momentarily holds or throws it with his racket.
    G. A player fails to return the bird to the opponent's proper court. (He cannot hit, catch, or be struck by a doubtful bird and call "out" as permitted in some sports.)
    H. The server steps forward as he serves.
    I. In a doubles-serve a player may not "unsight" the server.

OFFICIATING

Officials are used in tournament play only. Needed is an umpire stationed at the net and two linesmen on the opposite side corners. Each linesman calls "out" or "fault" (never "good") on his sideline, back line, and service lines if requested by the umpire. Linesmen may signal "out" with thumb up and "good" by palm down.

The umpire must check net height and shuttles, toss for service or side, announce players, keep score and announce it, supervise setting at deuce, announce "game point" or "game and match point," announce winner or winners and score, recording the same; call double hits, slung shots, let serves, service violations, and, during doubles contests, exercise great care in recording the number of "hands" in, and after each rally announce the score and the number of "hands" in.

TECHNIQUES AND FUNDAMENTALS

The grips

To acquire the proper grip for a forehand stroke, hold the racket by the shaft in the left hand with the face of the racket perpendicular to the floor, and shake hands with the handle with the right hand. Grasp the handle lightly with the little finger on the leather base and the forefinger slightly separated from the others. Care must be taken not to grasp the handle too far up from the end, or the wrist action will be prevented by the protruding end. The thumb should be on the left side of the handle with the "V" formed by the thumb and forefinger being on top of the handle, resting above the third finger. Basically, the grip should permit the palm of the hand to be parallel to the face of the racket. There is too great a variation in individuals to say exactly where each part of the hand should be. Many players like to touch the thumb and the third finger.

This same grip may be used for backhand shots, but most of the better players today use what is known as the "thumb-up" grip. To take this thumb-up grip, turn the top edge of the racket frame over slightly to the right and place the thumb along and parallel to the wide side of the handle. The power of the thumb is thus added to that of the

FIGURE 8-2. (*Directly below*) Forehand grip. (*Below*) Backhand grip.

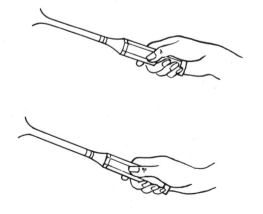

body, arm, and wrist on the wrist snap during the forward swing of the racket. This grip permits a longer reach, more power, and, in strokes where the bird must fly long distances, greater accuracy. Another advantage is that a quicker recovery can be made because not as much body movement is required as when the same grip is used for forehand and backhand strokes. Beginners have a tendency to grip the racket too tightly.

Wristwork

In every stroke there is a swing within a swing. Not only does the arm make the stroke, but this swing is accentuated by the movement of the wrist during the arm motion. At the beginning of any stroke, whether backhand or forehand, the wrist is "cocked" by pointing the racket head back away from the point of contemplated contact between bird and racket. By taking the hand back first as shown in Figure 8-5, added snap may be secured. The wrist remains cocked on the forward swing until just before the bird is hit. At the last moment the racket head snaps through, and at the time of contact between racket and shuttlecock, there should be a straight line from shoulder through elbow and wrist to the end of the racket. As the arm continues forward, the wrist continues to bend until the entire swing is finished.

In the thumb-up grip the wrist is cocked sideways, bringing the thumb back toward the elbow.

A good wrist action permits more power and control with much less effort. In fact, it is impossible to make a good length clear from the back court or to put that extra "zip" into the smashes without it.

Footwork

Although footwork is easily understood, it is the one item of technique most often poorly executed. The term *footwork* merely implies that all shots are played with the body at right angles to the net, i.e., on forehand shots, the left foot is nearer the net than the right foot; on backhand strokes, just the reverse is true. In most cases, the foot nearer the net will also be nearer the sideline you are facing than the other foot, and the nearer the back boundary line you are, the more advanced this foot will be. In this position the weight of the body will be on the rear foot when the racket is swung back and transferred smoothly to the forward foot when the racket is swung forward. Such a transfer of weight adds power to the stroke and makes it more easily controlled.

When moving toward the spot from which a

shot is to be made, start with short steps and end with long strides. Short steps make for a quick start and longer strides leave you in position to make your shot.

More advanced players use a skipping or sliding technique in which one foot or leg leads the way. In retreating to the back court one can back-peddle, turn and run, or skip with the right foot going to that side and the left foot leading when going to the left.

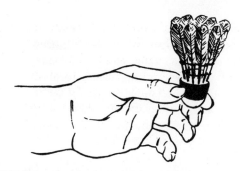

FIGURE 8-3. Holding the bird for delivery

Body control

Every player must develop the ability to get away from the bird so that, at the moment of contact, the arm and racket are extended to the greatest possible length, thus insuring complete freedom of movement. The most common error made in badminton, next to faulty footwork, is that of moving in too close to the bird and having to play it with a bent arm swing. It is best to go to meet the shuttlecock, playing it as soon as possible after it crosses the net.

Many shots are driven directly at the body. In this case, instead of going to the shuttlecock, it is necessary to get away from it. One way to deal with this type of shot is to reach forward and play it before it reaches the body. The only alternative is to wait, move sideways, and hit the shuttle very late.

Ready position

After every shot, move immediately to your base of operations (which in singles is approximately the center of the court and in doubles the center of your side), and take up a position of readiness for the return. Such a position means the racket is held with a forehand grip diagonally across the upper part of the body. It may rest lightly on the palm of the left hand if desired.

The better players often prefer holding the racket higher and not resting it in the other hand. The knees should be slightly bent, with the left foot in front of the right foot, the weight of the body on the balls of the feet. The elbows should be held at a comfortable distance away from the body, and the body may be slightly crouched.

Stroke production

Badminton strokes may be classified either according to the point of contact between bird and racket in relationship to the body, or according to the flight of the shuttlecock. According to bird flight, the strokes are the drive, lob or clear, drop (includ-

ing net shots), and smash. Any combination of overhand and underhand with forehand and backhand strokes constitutes the other classification. Because almost any shot is made with at least a minimum of upward or downward swing, the sidearm stroke is omitted, thereby simplifying the classification. Regardless of the stroke used, one must keep his eye on the base of the bird.

FOREHAND. The preparation or preliminary motion for all forehand strokes should be the same except for the direction in which the racket head is pointed on the backswing. By using the same motion for all bird flights, the opponent is unable to detect what shot you are going to make until the bird is actually hit. The same consideration is true for all backhand strokes.

On a forehand stroke, the body should face to the right with the left foot nearer the net, and possibly nearer the right sideline, than the right foot. The farther from the net the shot is to be made, the more the left foot should be advanced in front of the right toward the sideline, and the greater the turn of the body to the right. As the racket is swung back, the arm is bent, bringing the hand toward the right shoulder; the wrist is cocked, and the body weight placed on the right foot. From this position, the stroke is then made by throwing the hand at the point of contact between bird and racket with the wrist leading and the weight being transferred to the left foot. Follow through by having the arm and body move toward the spot at which the shuttlecock is directed. Always finish by facing the net in the ready position. The movement of the arm is identical to what would be used if a ball were to be thrown at the bird instead of hitting it with the racket. The wrist movement is also that used for throwing a ball, with the hand (and racket head) snapping forward only after the arm is fully extended. It makes no difference whether the stroke is to be made by throwing the arm up, down, or straight out to the side. The preliminary motion and the forward swing are made the same way except for the direction in which the hand moves.

BACKHAND. Allowing for reversed positions and body turn, essentially the same process can be followed for backhand shots. The main differences are: on the backswing the hand is brought toward the left rather than toward the right shoulder, and generally the foot nearer the net is more advanced toward the sideline, permitting even more body turning than on the forehand stroke.

A modified figure-eight system can be used to secure more wrist snap. When starting the backswing take the racket hand back first (with the racket head dragging) as shown in Figure 8-5. Then bring the racket forward with a snap of the wrist.

On both backhand and forehand strokes the back swing must be started in sufficient time to permit the rhythmical, unhurried, and unbroken forward swing.

While it is necessary to have proper footwork and bodywork to make a comfortable, accurate, and powerful forehand stroke with the least expenditure of energy, it is absolutely impossible to make any kind of backhand stroke without good body position, regardless of the amount of strength used in the attempt.

STROKES ACCORDING TO BIRD FLIGHTS.

1. *Lob or clear*: This stroke is a defensive shot used when in difficulty (off balance or out of position)

FIGURE 8-5. Starting the backhand. Added wrist snap may be secured by taking the racket hand back first so that the stroke forms a modified figure-eight.

FIGURE 8-4. Full movement of the overhead strokes. (A) Backswing. (B) Upswing with impact. (C) Follow-through for the smash: (1) impact of racket with shuttle for overhead clear, (2) impact for smash. (From Miller and Ley, *Individual and Team Sports for Women*.)

to slow up the game, to drive your opponent away from the net or forecourt, and (following the old football axiom of "when in doubt, punt") when in doubt as to what shot should be played.

The lob may be made either on the backhand or forehand stroke, from any part of the court, and from any height that is within reach. The technique used in making the shot is the same as described for any forehand or backhand stroke. To be successful, the lob must be made so the bird flies above the opponent's reach and falls within at least one foot of the rear boundary line. It takes a great deal of power to clear from one back line to the opposite back line, and, to get this power as effortlessly as possible, it is essential that footwork, bodywork, and wrist action be correct.

The greatest difficulty encountered in making this shot is that of judging where to stand

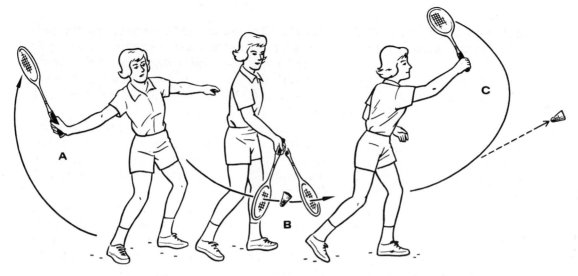

FIGURE 8-6. Underhand clear or high, long serve. (A) Backswing; (B) impact with wrist action involved; (C) follow-through. (From Miller and Ley, *Individual and Team Sports for Women.*)

with relation to the bird so the shot will not be too high and too short or too low and too long.

If possible, the lob should be made with an overhand stroke as the bird will then have less distance to travel, thus requiring less power. An overhand stroke is particularly desirable when the bird must be played from deep in your backcourt.

2. *Smash:* The smash is strictly an attacking shot and is made with all the power and speed one can put into it. Because of the required power, the feet may be placed slightly farther apart and the body may be twisted slightly more than for the other shots. Rise high on the toes to hit from the top. The shuttlecock must be stroked at the extreme limit of one's upward reach and slightly in front of the right shoulder, in order to hit down on the bird. At the moment of contact the racket face must be headed downward by "pulling the string" with the hand and wrist. Due to the power with which the shot is made, it is often necessary to take a step forward with the right foot as the follow-through is made, in order not to be off balance. A common fault is to point the elbow sidewise instead of forward just before hitting the smash.

The shuttle should just clear the net and land well up in the opponent's forecourt.

A smash should not be attempted unless there is time to get set and be well-balanced before the shot is made. Never smash when moving backward as the stroke will not have power and you will not be able to recover and play any shot returned to the forepart of your court. The ordinary player should not attempt to smash from the back fourth of the court. More advanced play-

ers use the half-smash as a defensive weapon. It should be hit sharply down across court.

The smash is one shot that cannot be executed on the backhand. Enough power cannot be generated to call even the severest backhand stroke a smash. The same basic principles can be used in attempting a smash on the backhand as are used on the forehand, but due to the slower speed with which the bird flies, it is important that the shuttle be even more accurately placed on the backhand.

3. *Drive:* The drive is a flat shot that is kept as low as possible and is second only to the smash as an attacking shot. It is used to run your opponent from side to side and should never be used when there is a chance of its being intercepted, as the speed of the stroke will be turned against you and the rally will probably be lost as a result.

The drive must be hit as near the net level as possible. It must never be hit upward unless it is driven above the opponent's reach and played to the back of the opponent's court (called a "driven clear").

4. *Drop shots:* A drop shot is any shot that drops immediately after crossing the net. If played from a position close to the net, it is called a "net shot."

The overhand drop should be made to look as much like a smash or lob as possible, and the underhand drop should be very similar to the underhand lob. It is extremely difficult to execute a drop shot similar to a drive or to hit it at the same level as the drive from the back court. The overhand is the easiest and most desirable stroke to use.

Even though played very lightly, the drop

shot requires as much wrist movement (though not power) as any other shot if accuracy is to be obtained.

Beginners should attempt only drop shots from the backhand until sufficient strength is developed to clear, half-smash, or drive the bird from that normally weak side.

5. *Net shots:* Net shots are controlled almost exclusively by wrist and forearm. Requiring no power, the net shots can be played while facing almost square to the net, and should be played as near the level of the top of the net as possible. However, the lower the bird is allowed to drop before being played, the more deceptive the return can be made, with the angled, cross-court shot being the easiest and safest to use when the bird is hit well below the top of the net.

After learning to play an accurate net game, a great amount of deception can be used by changing the flight of the shot through wrist action alone.

THE SERVE. The serve is an underhand stroke made on the forehand side of the body, but cannot be included in the classification of bird flights due to the variations in flight.

There are several types of serves considered from the standpoint of how the bird is actually put into play. The one requiring the most coordination, but by far the most practical when once it is mastered, is the "toss" serve. This is the proper type to learn and only as a last resort, due to inability of individuals to learn the toss serve, should the out-of-hand serve be used.

Inasmuch as the serve is a defensive shot hit to a waiting opponent, it is necessary for the server to use as much deception as possible to outwit his opponent. To this end, all types of serves should be made with identical action.

For a serve to be legal, the rules state that the shuttlecock must be hit below the server's waist and that, at the moment of contact, the racket head must be below the server's hand. In other words, the serve is definitely an underhand stroke.

Keeping these two points in mind, the best type of serve is executed as described below.

In singles, take a position near and on the proper side of the center line, as determined by the rules, and about four feet behind the short service line. (See Fig. 8-7.) In doubles, take a position closer to the front service line and more to the center of "your" side. Face slightly to the left with the right foot nearer the net than the left. Hold the bird by the base with the left hand and swing your racket back, cocking the wrist as the swing is made. Toss the bird wide across the body to the racket head, or merely drop the bird from shoulder height to the right front and swing the racket forward, hitting the bird to make the desired flight. Try to "rub" the bird over the net. The point at which the shuttle and racket make contact varies with the individual and the flight desired. If hit too far in front of the body, or too soon, the flight will probably be too high. If hit too far away from the net and near the legs, or too late, it will probably be too low.

The three possible service flights are: (1) a low, short serve, which should just clear the net and fall within an inch or two beyond the short service line of the receiver's court, (2) a long, high serve, which must be played so it travels above the receiver's reach and should fall within six inches of the rear boundary line in singles, or the rear service line in doubles, and (3) a drive serve that is generally made by a quick flick of the wrist and travels in a direct line to the desired spot. The latter serve may be directed straight at the receiver's chest, over the head of a receiver rushing forward for a contemplated short serve, or low and to the inside back corner of the receiver's court as formed by the center line and the rear service line in doubles, or the back boundary line in singles. This serve is especially effective from the right-hand court to the opponent's left-hand deep corner.

FIGURE 8-7. Serving and receiving positions in doubles. (A) Positions recommended in men's or women's doubles: (1) server; (2) server's partner; (3) receiver; (4) receiver's partner. (B) Positions recommended in mixed doubles using forward and back system: (1) server's position if a woman; (2) her partner's position (man); (3) server's position if a man; (4) his partner's position (woman); (5 or 6) woman's position when her partner is receiving. (Adapted from Shaw, Troester, and Gabrielsen, *Individual Sports for Men.*)

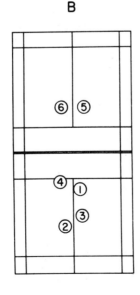

A   B

PLAYING STRATEGY

Although there is no set sequence of shots that one can use to win a rally, there are definite situations that call for a specific shot or demand that a specific shot not be used. Basically, shots made from below the net are *defensive* and those made from above the net are *offensive*. Also there are certain principles concerning the use of the body that make for a more enjoyable game.

Singles

1. Serve long the majority of the time unless opponent is playing back for just such a shot, then serve short to take advantage of his poor position. Serve short every so often to prevent opponent from consistently taking up a position near the back of the receiving court. A long serve puts the server and the receiver on an equal basis. It is difficult to drop accurately from the back court; it takes too much accuracy and power on the part of the waiting player to smash repeatedly back from the back court, and too much power to clear from the back court time after time for a receiver to have an advantage on a well-executed long serve.

2. To receive in your right-hand court, stand on the left side about mid-way back from the front service line so that most serves can be received by the forehand. Likewise, when receiving in your left court stand to the left, about mid-way back from the front service line, so that most serves can be received by the forehand.

3. Return a high serve with a drop or clear. Do not smash a high serve unless it is of insufficient length or unless your opponent has a very weak smash defense and you have accurate smashing ability. Even then, use sparingly. Drop shots to your opponent's forehand and clears to his backhand are usually the most difficult for him to handle. Variation is essential in returns to prevent successful anticipation of your shot by your opponent.

4. The safest reply to a short serve is a clear, although a net shot can be made if the bird is hit before it falls too low below the level of the net.

5. Do not return a net shot with another net shot unless you are sure of winning the rally, as the bird will probably be flicked quickly over your head to the back court without any possible chance to recover it.

6. After every shot, return to your base of opera-

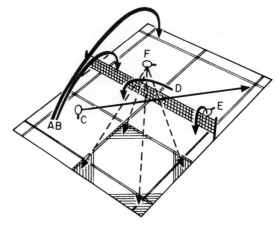

FIGURE 8-8. Line of flight and placement of basic strokes. (A) High clear; (B) drop shot; (C) smash; (D) cross-court net flight; (E) hairpin net shot. (F) Darkened areas indicate desired areas for placement of service.

tions located on the center line and from two to four feet behind the short service line. Do not make any shot that will not give you time to get back to this base, otherwise you will be out of position and unable to play the return shot properly, if at all.

7. Do not be moving at the time your opponent makes his shot or he will probably play the bird to the spot you vacated. On the other hand, if your opponent is moving to cover an open spot on his court when you make your shot, play the bird to the position he is leaving. The most difficult maneuver on the court is that which requires a quick change of direction in your movement, for a retracing of your steps demands the utmost agility and speed.

8. Other than shots played directly at your opponent, play the bird to a point within a foot of the restraining lines whether on the serve or during a rally.

9. When smashing, use the cross-court variety or smash at your opponent's right hip or shoulder.

10. Return a smash with a drop to the point on the court farthest from the point at which the smash was made.

11. Build your game on a basis of alternately dropping and clearing, then use smashes and drives as openings occur. Run your opponent from front to rear and from side to side on alternate shots unless the provisions of paragraph 7 will apply.

12. Do not drive cross-court unless the shot is a sure winner. The safest drives are those made straight down the sidelines passing your opponent.

13. Do not use net shots unless your opponent is

clearly out of position and will be unable to reach the shuttle for a reply.

14. Do not try to outguess your opponent by anticipating where he will play the bird and taking up a position for an easy return of his anticipated shot. By a glance at your position before he makes his shot he can change his stroke to take advantage of your poor position.

15. Take advantage of any weakness your opponent may have. Do not, however, play to it so much that the practice he gets on the shots increases his ability to such an extent that his weakness disappears. Before playing to a weakness, uncover it by first playing to the other side of your opponent's body or to the farthest part of the court from the point of weakness.

16. Do not try fancy shots unless they are the only ones possible under the circumstances, and do not try deception through wrist action until you have thoroughly mastered the basic strokes.

17. At the beginning of a game or match, play your shots near the center of the court and then spread gradually to the boundary lines.

18. Watch the bird closely. Most players have a tendency to take their eyes off the shuttle just before or at the time it is hit. This action will result in a miss, in a throw, or in a "bad" shot.

Doubles

Before considering the principles of doubles play, it is first necessary to understand the various formations used. This is important as it is the first decision that must be made by a doubles team in any game. In fact, the choice of formation and agreement on how the court is to be covered must be made even before the first service is made. Without this agreement, partners will be running into each other in some cases, and at other times the bird will hit the floor with neither partner having made an attempt to return it. There are any number of formations, only three of which will be discussed here—the side-by-side, the up and back, and a combination of the two.

1. Side-by-side

In the side-by-side formation, each partner is responsible for his half of the playing court. The base of operations for each player is mid-way between the center line and the side boundary line of his half court and approximately four feet behind the service line. The main disadvantage of this formation is that it is more difficult to cover 22 feet from net to rear boundary line than it is to cover 20 feet from side to side.

This fact is easily understood when it is realized that standing still, a player can reach out seven feet. By reaching seven feet to each side, the court can be covered laterally by moving only four feet to right or left from the center of the court. On the other hand, it is necessary to move three feet forward and 12 feet backward from the base of operations in covering the 22 feet from net to rear boundary. Only one reach of seven feet can be used due to the fact that you can't reach toward the rear to make a shot.

Another disadvantage of this formation is that it is almost impossible to determine who is going to hit those strokes played down the center line, despite the accepted rule that the player to the left should take these shots because they are on his forehand.

Still another drawback of this formation is that few players of average ability can move from the net to the rear court and still smash—often meaning a possible loss of attack.

2. Front and Back

In the front and back formation, one member of the team plays the front portion of the court, with a base of operations on the center line and just in back of the short service line, while his partner plays the rear portion of the court from a base on the center line and just in front of the doubles rear service line. The front player is then responsible for all drop shots and any other shots he can intercept and return with an equal or better shot than his partner, while the back player takes all shots that the net man cannot comfortably return while standing on the short service line. This system is ideal for mixed doubles because the lady is better suited to play near the net while the man can better cover the back court.

Although the front and back formation facilitates greater attacking power, it definitely has certain disadvantages. One of the most important is that it affords poor defense against smashes and drives down the sidelines. This formation also puts a premium on a very low, accurate short serve, as any bird over an inch above the net will be pushed back straight at the server, or quickly and completely put out of reach of both players.

3. Combination formation

The combination system, sometimes called the "in and out" system, combines the best of the other two systems, using the side-by-side position for defense, and the front and back formation for attack. The basic principles to be followed in the combination system are as follows:

a. When the receivers start in the front and back formation, the server's initial formation is determined by the server's ability to make a good short serve. If the server is an accomplished server, the team should start in the front and back formation, otherwise use the safer side-by-side formation.

b. On a long, high serve, the servers should play side-by-side and the receiver, going back for the serve, should play the back court, while the receiver's partner should move forward to play the front court as the receiver goes back.

c. On any high shot that gives the opponents the advantage and opportunity to smash, the team making the stroke should take up the defensive side-by-side formation. The player making the shot should cover the half of the court from which the shot was made.

d. The first opportunity should be taken to revert to the front and back formation, going clockwise or counterclockwise in the direction taken in playing the shot. Any shot returned, other than a lob, affords this opportunity. Which partner cover what part of the court on the return is determined by who played the return shot from what spot on the court. If the return stroke is made near the net and on the right side of the court, the partner playing the right half of the court would naturally make the shot. Since he had to move forward to make the shot, he would then play the front position while his partner would fade back and play the back court. If the right half-court guardian drifted back to play the return from the back court, he should then play the back position and his partner should move up and play the front court.

4. Tactics

Regardless of the system of teamwork selected, the following points of tactics and strategy will make for better play:

a. Always play for your partner. Make shots, the return of which will leave an opening for your partner to play his best shot and possibly finish the rally. Never play a shot that leaves your partner open to blistering smashes or scrambling about the court to play the return.

b. Always make an attacking shot unless any other return would leave you, your partner, or both out of position for the return. This implies that all shots should be hit down, thus preventing your opponents from doing the same. Your partner should move forward on all smashes (and drops from the backcourt) to protect against returned drop shots and cross-court drives.

c. Make most serves short and low, preferably to the off-hand corners. Use a high service only when your opponent is consistently rushing the serve, and then play the bird just over his reach, giving him little time to run back and get under it. When a lob serve is used, the best spot is to the receiver's backhand. The drive serve should be used sparingly and then to the corner formed by the center line and rear doubles service line.

d. Rush short serves by standing close to the service line with the left foot forward. As soon as the bird is served, step forward with the right foot, turn the racket so the face is parallel with the net, and push the right arm forward, hitting the bird while it is still above the level of the net. Hit it down. Neither power nor back swing is needed.

e. Usually smash a long serve, but occasionally play a drop shot for variation.

f. Do not play too close to the net, but rather take up a position around the short service line when playing net.

g. If the servers are playing a front and back formation, the best return of a low service is a half-court shot down the side boundary line. A drive clear to the backhand corner of the court is probably the best return against a team using the side-by-side system.

h. Avoid quick, flat shots and sharply angled shots unless opponents cannot intercept the bird and return it before you can recover.

i. Have the left-court player in the side-by-side system play the shots down the center of the court.

j. Make placements to the least obvious spots.

k. Keep your racket up in front of your body and weight on the balls of your feet.

SAFETY HINTS

Badminton is one of the safest of games. There are, however, a few suggestions for its safe conduct.

1. There should be sufficient clearance about the court. There should be at least four feet at the ends and sides of the court to a wall, bleachers, or another court—more is desirable.
2. Warming up properly is essential—the legs should especially receive a considerable amount of stretching and bouncing before beginning play.
3. In doubles, the players must be careful not to strike one another. The method of coverage must be thoroughly understood to avoid this; glasses should not be worn by those playing in doubles.
4. In mixed doubles, the girl at the net should protect her face against smashes with her racket.
5. Shuttlecocks not in use should not be left on the playing area.

PLAYING COURTESIES

Like tennis, badminton emphasizes sportsmanship and playing courtesies. Following are a few hints on how to conduct oneself in badminton:

1. If in doubt about the bird's landing, always call it in favor of the opponents.
2. Spin racket for the choosing of courts and service.
3. One never "rides" his opponent in badminton.
4. If there is any question of your fouling at the net, be sure to call it on yourself. Your opponent should be a good sport and disagree if there is some doubt in his mind.
5. If there is any question about your throwing of a bird, be quick to call it a throw.

TERMINOLOGY

Backhand   Any stroke made on the side of the body opposite the racket side.
Bird   The shuttlecock.
Clear   A high shot (or lob) which falls close to the back line.
Cross-court shot   A shot in which the bird crosses the net at a sharp diagonal, usually close to the net.

Drive   A hard driven stroke which just clears the net and does not rise high enough for an opponent to smash.
Driven clear   A drive which goes to the back court, but not high enough for an opponent to kill.
Driven serve   The flight of a serve similar to a drive. Used best in the right-hand court to a right-hand player.
Drop   A shot made from back court which barely clears the net, dropping sharply. A smash or clear shot is usually faked.
Fault   Any infraction of the rules whose penalty is the loss of the serve or the point.
Forehand   Any stroke made on the racket side of the body.
Hand-out   The loss of the serve.
Let   A bird which touches the top of the net but falls good.
Net flight   A shot in which the bird follows the net in a short flight.
Rally   A heated return of the bird several times, such as rallying for serve.
Receiver   The player to whom the bird is served.
Round the head stroke   A high stroke over the head to hit a bird on the offhand side.
Server   The player who puts the bird in play.
Setting the game   Choosing how many points to play when the score becomes tied.
Short serve   A serve that scarcely clears the net and lands barely inside the opponent's court.
Shuttlecock   The feathered (or plastic) object which is batted back and forth in badminton.
Smash   The most powerful overhead stroke that sends the bird downward over the net.
Smooth or rough   The two sides of a racket; end strings used when spinning the racket for the choosing of sides or serve.
Throw   A shot in which the bird is carried or thrown by the racket.
Toss serve   Throwing the bird up and across the body so that it comes down in a position to serve legally.

SELECTED REFERENCES

Ainsworth, Dorothy S., *et al., Individual Sports for Women.* Philadelphia: W. B. Saunders Co., 1963.

American Association for Health, Physical Education and Recreation, Division for Girls' and Women's Sports, *Tennis and Badminton Guide* (current edition). Washington, D.C., 1201 Sixteenth Street, N.W., 20036.

Davidson, Kenneth R., and L. R. Gustavson, *Winning Badminton.* New York: The Ronald Press Company, 1964.

Davis, Pat, *Badminton Complete.* New York: A. S. Barnes & Co., Inc., 1964.

Friedrich, John, and Ann Rutledge, *Beginning Badminton.* Belmont, Calif.: Wadsworth Publishing Co., Inc., 1962.

Miller, Donna Mae, and Katherine L. Ley, *Individual Team Sports for Women.* Englewood Cliffs, N.J.: Prentice-Hall, Inc., 1956.

Radford, Noel, *Badminton.* London: Sir Isaac Pitman & Sons Ltd., 1957.

Shaw, John H., Carl Troester, and Milton A. Gabriel- sen, *Individual Sports for Men.* Philadelphia: W. B. Saunders Co., 1964.

Sports Illustrated Editors, *Book of Badminton.* Philadelphia: J.B. Lippincott Co., 1964.

Vannier, Maryhelen, and Hally Beth Poindexter, *Individual and Team Sports for Girls and Women.* (2nd ed.) Philadelphia: W.B. Saunders Co., 1968.

Varner, Margaret, *Badminton.* Dubuque, Iowa: William C. Brown Company, Publishers, 1966.

Skills

Lockhart, Aileen, and Frances A. McPherson, "The Development of a Test of Badminton Playing Ability," *Research Quarterly,* XX (December 1949), 402.

Miller, Frances A., "A Badminton Wall Volley Test," *Research Quarterly,* AAHPER, 1951.

Scott, M. Gladys, and Esther French, *Evaluation in Physical Education.* Dubuque, Iowa: William C. Brown Company, Publishers, 1959, p. 74.

Basketball

Men's basketball

ORIGIN AND DEVELOPMENT

Basketball is the only major sport that originated in America. Dr. James A. Naismith introduced the game to a class at the YMCA College in Springfield, Massachusetts, on January 20, 1892. He wanted a winter sport that would appeal to his students as much as did football and baseball during their respective seasons. During the game's first season, it spread to all corners of the United States. Before the game was two years old, it was being played in several foreign countries. Its popularity and growth could be attributed to these factors: (1) a small or large floor could be used, depending upon the number of players in the game, (2) the equipment used was not complicated or expensive, (3) it was not a hazardous sport, and (4) it provided recreative exercise. The first rules of the game were printed in the school paper, *The Triangle,* and clearly show the game was a combination of the basic fundamentals of lacrosse and association football.

For the first game, Dr. Naismith had the school janitor attach a peach basket ten feet from the floor at each end of a large hall. He said to the 18 players as a soccer ball was tossed to them, "The winning team will be the one scoring the most goals." The baskets were about 15 inches in diameter across the opening and about 15 inches deep. The person designated to umpire the game had to remove the ball from the baskets by climbing a step ladder. As the game developed and became firmly established, A. G. Spalding & Bros. placed on the market a basket which, when a dangling string was pulled, released the ball. Early rules included the following:

1. The ball may be thrown in any direction with one or both hands.

2. A player cannot run with the ball. The player must throw it from the spot on which he catches it—allowance being made for the player who catches it on the run.

3. The ball must be held only in or between the hands.

4. No shouldering, holding, pushing, tripping, or striking in any way the person of an opponent shall be allowed; the first infringement of this rule by the player shall count as a foul; the second shall disqualify him until the next goal

has been made, or, if there were intent to injure the person, for the whole of the game—no substitute allowed.

5. If either side makes three consecutive fouls, it shall count as a goal for the opponents.

6. The time shall be two 15 minute halves, with five minutes rest between.

7. The side making the most goals in that time shall be declared the winner. In case of a draw, the game may, by agreement of the captains, be continued until another goal is made.

8. When the ball is out of bounds, it shall be thrown into the field of play by the person first touching it. In case of a dispute, the umpire shall throw it straight into the field. The thrower-in is allowed five seconds. If he holds it longer, it shall go to the opponent.

A referee and an umpire were the officials. The number of players composing a team depended largely upon the size of the floor space, but it could range from three to forty. Nine players on a team was the most popular—a goalkeeper, two guards, three center players, two wings, and a home man. When a team had 40 players, two balls, generally, were used in the game.

The first team was organized at the YMCA College in 1892, and it played its first game with the Twenty-sixth Separate Company of the United States Army. From that day, the military forces have been one of the chief proponents of the game.

The first men's institution of higher learning to play basketball was Geneva College, Beaver Falls, Pennsylvania, in 1892. In this same year Iowa University played the game, and is, along with the University of Minnesota, credited with bringing the sport to the midwest. Yale organized a team in 1894 and played the first intercollegiate schedule in 1896 with Trinity, Wesleyan, and the University of Pennsylvania. By 1905 the game was firmly entrenched in the athletic programs of the colleges. In the beginning of collegiate basketball there was no central agency in control, but in 1904 men's college teams came under the jurisdiction of the Intercollegiate Athletic Association, which was later named the National Collegiate Athletic Association (NCAA).

In the past two decades the game of basketball has been given an even greater impetus by the numerous tournaments that are held annually. Sectional tournaments and national tournaments are held both on the amateur and collegiate levels.

The NCAA University division tournament is organized into four regional tournaments. These include the Eastern, Mideastern, Midwestern, and Western regions.

In the Eastern regional tournament, the winners of the Mid-Atlantic, the Southern, and the Atlantic Coast conferences compete with four at-large selections.

The Mideast regional tournament is composed of the winners of the Mid-American Conference, the Ohio Valley Conference, and the Big Ten. These conference winners compete with two at-large representatives in order to determine their regional representative.

The Midwest regional tournament includes the champion of the Southwest Conference, the Big Eight Conference, and Missouri Valley Conference, along with three at-large selections, while the Western Regional tournament is composed of winners of the Western Athletic Conference, the Big Sky Conference, the West Coast Conference, and the A.A.W.U., along with two at-large selections.

At-large teams are selected by regional committees. In most cases these selections are made from schools which are not members of participating conferences, but have University division status and have established an outstanding season's record. The winners of the various regional tournaments then meet to determine the national champion.

The NCAA College Division is made up of eight regional tournaments. These include the Northeastern, Mideastern, Eastern, Midwestern, South Central, Southwestern, Great Lakes, and Pacific Coast regions. The regional winners meet to determine the college division champions.

The NAIA national tournament finds 32 district representatives competing in a single elimination tournament to denote the NAIA national champion.

The rapid growth of Junior colleges throughout the country has added to the interest of the National Junior College Athletic Association championship tournament. The NJCAA tournament is made up of 16 regional tournaments, with the regional champions meeting to determine the national Junior College champion.

Invitational tournaments, such as the National Invitation Tournament (NIT) in New York, make their selections, by tournament committee, from schools which have established excellent win-loss records. In addition, City and State tournaments are played on the high school level.

The national television networks televise some of these games into millions of homes, which has stimulated additional interest in the game. The increased popularity of the game has led to the development of better facilities, both from the players' standpoint and as regards spectator accommodation. The annual selection of all-star teams at all levels of competition throughout the country is now a standard practice and has led to a greater interest in the game of basketball. A new milestone was established in the history of basketball on January 20, 1968, when 52,693 fans attended a game at the Astrodome in Houston, Texas, between UCLA and the University of Houston.

NATURE OF THE GAME

The playing area on which basketball is played is called a court. The teams are composed of five players each. Two officials are needed to regulate the game, and they are assisted by two timers and two scorers. The ball is passed, thrown, bounced, batted, or rolled from one player to another. Each team has an offensive and a defensive basket. The purpose of the game is to score a larger total number of points than the opponent. The score is compiled by shooting the ball through the basket either from the field (court) or from the free throw line. Two points are scored when a basket is made from the field and one point when a basket is made as a foul shot from the free throw line.

In the game, the ball is put into play by a jump in the center circle of the court. From this point the team in possession of the ball is designated as the offensive team, and their opponents are the defensive team.

The game is divided into two 20-minute halves for college and university teams and into eight-minute quarters for high school teams, with a one-minute intermission between quarters. Teams composed of players younger than high school age should have six-minute quarters with intermissions equal to those of high school teams. For college and university teams there is a 15-minute intermission between halves, and for high school and younger teams there is a ten-minute intermission between the second and third quarters.

The popularity of this American game can be attributed to many factors. Some of these are the small number of players needed to compose a team, the limited space needed in which to play, and the low cost and maintenance of the playing equipment. The rules, despite their increasing number, are easily understood by the beginner. The constant speed of basketball has thrilled millions of participants and spectators around the world. The United States, dominating world basketball, won its 75th game in the 1968 Olympics against Yugoslavia.

Officials play an important part in the success of basketball, because the calling of fouls is largely a matter of judgment, and officials who are too strict or too lax will necessarily take away some of the spectator and player appeal.

Today, the rules of basketball are written by the National Basketball Committee of the United States and Canada, which is composed of representatives of the Canadian Intercollegiate Athletic Union, the Canadian Amateur Basketball Association, the National Collegiate Athletic Association, The National Federation of State High School Athletic Associations, the National Junior College Athletic Association, and the Young Men's Christian Association. Prior to 1915, several of these organizations had a separate set of rules for play. In that year, they formed a joint committee and standardized the rules.

Because of ease of organization, the low cost equipment available, and the learning situations that it presents, basketball is utilized in physical education programs on all levels of our educational system. The game presents the opportunity to teach skills, coordination, agility, speed, and body control. Participation in the game can contribute toward maintenance of total fitness of the individual, which is an important phase of physical education programs. In addition, concomitant learnings such as respect for others, sportsmanship, respect for rules, and proper competitive attitude are exemplified. These factors and the attractiveness of action have brought basketball into physical education classes.

Basketball has been an excellent recreational activity, and is so employed by the YMCA, CYO, Boys Club, community centers, and recreational departments. On the college level, basketball as a recreational activity in intramural programs is very successful.

In conclusion, we see that this American sport has very broad applications. A large age group can participate, it can be utilized for competitive as well as recreational purposes, and it has the necessary spectator appeal to make it a popular game for those who do not actually participate.

TECHNIQUES AND FUNDAMENTALS

Catching

This fundamental should be discussed in relation to the basic position of a basketball player. A player must have his weight evenly distributed between his feet (on ball of foot), the knees flexed, and head up. The hands should be held forward of the body with the elbows held in to maintain balance when moving in any direction to meet the ball. The ball should be caught with the fingertips and brought toward the body to prepare for the next play (a dribble, pass, or shot) at that spot. The thumbs are held inside on high passes and outside on low passes. As in most games that require catching a ball, the basketball player must relax and keep his eyes on the ball until it is caught.

Passing

THE TWO-HAND CHEST PASS. This is one pass that has been used for many years in basketball. It can be made anywhere on the floor by any of the players. The ball is held in both hands, the fingers spread on the sides of the ball slightly to the rear, with the thumbs pointed toward the inside. The ball is retained in a position about chest height directly in front of the body and about one foot from the body. The knees are slightly flexed and the body is slightly bent forward. The elbows are kept close to the body and the ball is released by extending the arms fully, snapping the wrists, and stepping in the direction of the pass. A good follow-through with the arms and body will assist in making a good pass.

THE TWO-HAND BOUNCE PASS. This pass is used as a short pass from out-of-bounds or into the pivot man. It is executed in the same manner as the two-hand chest pass except the ball is bounced into the hands of the receiver. A spin on the ball is not needed to get the proper bounce. The ball should strike the floor near the receiver's feet and bounce belt high.

THE ONE-HAND UNDERHAND PASS. This is a good short distance pass used to maneuver the ball into the pivot. If a defender is facing the passer, he steps to the right (if passing with the right hand) with the right foot, stepping outside the defender to avoid his interfering with the pass. The body weight is shifted to the right leg, with the left leg held nearly straight. The ball is carried in both hands on the backward swing until the right hand (slightly under and behind the ball) has control of the ball. The fingers of the right hand are spread and the right arm is extended forward and upward, driving the ball to the receiver. After the ball leaves the right hand, the palm of that hand should face upward and the fingers should point toward the receiver. This pass can be executed with the left hand from the left side of the body by stepping to the left with the left leg.

THE ONE-HAND BOUNCE PASS. This pass is also a short distance pass used anywhere on the court. For this pass, the ball is held with both hands about waist high in the center of the body. In ex-

ecuting the pass, the ball is released from the left hand, taken back with the right hand around the side of the body, and as the step is taken in the direction of the pass, the ball is thrown and bounced in the same manner that a side-arm throw in baseball is executed. The step is very important in this pass, because it can enable the passer to step to the side of his guard and then bounce the ball around him. In this instance the step would not be in the direction of the pass.

THE ONE-HAND JUMP PASS. This pass has been developed by the increasing popularity of the jump shot. The pass is executed by a right-handed player with the right hand while up in the air in the act of shooting. The ball is supported with the left hand (fingers spread) under the ball and the right hand with the fingers spread behind the ball. The ball is held slightly above the head, and the passer has a good view of the playing area. The pass is executed by the right hand and arm driving downward and forward toward the receiver. When the ball leaves the right hand, the passer is off the floor and the palm should be facing the floor with the fingers pointing toward the receiver. The left-handed player executes this pass in the same manner, using the left hand and arm to provide the force for the pass.

THE TWO-HAND OVERHEAD FLIP. In executing this pass, the ball is held overhead with both hands, thumbs under the ball and fingers spread on the sides of the ball. This should be done in the same manner as the two-hand overhead shot. The passer steps forward toward the intended receiver and transfers his body weight to the front foot. The arms, which are slightly bent, are brought forward sharply, with a snap of the wrists releasing the ball. The force of the pass comes from the step forward and the snap of the arms, wrists, thumbs, and fingers. This pass is best utilized by the tall player in basketball.

THE ONE-HAND OVERHEAD PASS (BASEBALL PASS). This pass can be used anywhere on the court and is used most frequently as a long pass initiating the fast break. When this pass is thrown with the right hand, the ball is brought in back of the right ear, close to the head, with the right hand (fingers and thumb spread well) in back of the ball. The left hand supports the ball when it is in position to be thrown. The weight of the body is then shifted to the rear right foot. As the pass is thrown, the left hand comes off the ball and the body weight shifts forward to the left foot, which points into the direction of the pass. The right arm is brought forward and downward sharply, driving the ball toward the receiver, the throw ending with the right foot in front of the left and the palm of the right hand facing the floor.

Shooting

THE TWO-HAND SET SHOT. This is one of the oldest shots in basketball and is considered the most effective one for shooting distances over 25 feet. The ball is held firmly in both hands with the fingers spread along the side and toward the rear of the ball. The thumbs are held along the side of the ball and the feet spread comfortably with the body weight slightly forward when in the set position. In executing this shot, the ball is brought to about eye level, and, after making a circular motion of the arms and wrists, the ball is released toward the basket by an upward extension of the arm in order to attain the proper arch. The follow-through is important, and after the ball is shot, the arms should be brought to a full extension above the head with the palms of the hands facing the basket and the thumbs also pointing toward the basket. The eyes are focused on the basket throughout the shoot.

THE ONE-HAND SET SHOT. For the right-handed shooter, this shot is executed by holding the ball in both hands, the left hand on the bottom of the ball, and the right hand on the back of the ball just in front of the face. The right foot is about one step in front of the left foot and the weight is slightly forward. In executing the shot, the knees are bent slightly, carrying the body downward, and the ball is pushed up with the left hand. The right hand moves down slightly so that it now rests more on the bottom of the ball. From this position the legs and right arm are extended in the direction of the basket. The follow-through with the right hand is high enough to insure the proper arch. (See Fig. 9-1.)

At the termination of the shot, the palm of the shooting hand should be facing the basket and the thumb of the shooting hand should be pointing toward the basket. The eyes should remain focused on the basket throughout the shot. Many players, collegiate and professional, use this shot—or some variation thereof—when shooting free throws.

THE ONE-HAND ON-THE-MOVE SHOT. This shot is made on a straight or diagonal drive in relation to the basket. At the last dribble the ball is firmly grasped by the fingers and thumbs of both hands and carried above the head. When shooting with the right hand the take-off is on the left foot, and at that moment the ball is being set in the shooting hand. The shot should be executed by extending the arm forward and upward. At the termination of the shot the weight should shift to

FIGURE 9-1. The one-hand set shot: Gary Gamble

the right foot, and the body should be slightly bent with the knees flexed. This shot is one of the many popular one-hand shots.

THE ONE-HAND JUMP SHOT (STATIONARY). This is one of the most popular shots in basketball today. The ball is held firmly in both hands and carried above the head before shooting. The shot is made while the shooter jumps into the air by pushing off with both legs. The ball is cradled in the left hand and the right hand is behind the ball. The fingers of the right hand, which are spread, and the wrist provide the force that drives the ball to the basket. At the termination of the shot the right arm should be fully extended. The eyes should be kept focused on the basket throughout the shot. The player should land in a balanced position. (See Fig. 9-2.)

THE TWO-HAND UNDERHAND FOUL SHOT. Stand with the toes just back of the foul line and with legs spread sufficiently to give good balance. Hold the ball in both hands with the fingers spread downward on the sides of the ball and the thumbs across the top of the ball. In executing the shot, the knees are bent slightly, as the elbows are bent. The ball is then brought forward and upward by extending the legs and carrying the ball toward the basket with a sweeping motion of the hands. The fingertips will be the last to touch the ball, giving a backward

FIGURE 9-2. The jump shot: Cazzie Russell (From David H. Strack, *Basketball.* Englewood Cliffs, N.J.: Prentice-Hall, Inc., 1968.)

FIGURE 9-3. Right-hand hook shot: Bill Buntin (From Strack, *Basketball.*)

spin. The follow-through should carry the hands high above the head.

THE HOOK SHOT. Stand with the ball in both hands with the fingers spread slightly forward and downward and the thumbs across the top of the ball. With your back to the basket, the shot is executed in the following manner: Take a step with the left foot to the side and slightly away from the basket, remove the left hand from the ball, and, as you take off on the left foot, bring the ball in a circular movement over the head with the right hand, toward the basket. The right arm follows through to its fullest extent, releasing the ball in a medium arch. (See Fig. 9-3.)

Rebounding

There are various ways of gaining possession of the ball, and an important one is by rebounding. Rebounding takes place in two areas: (1) at the defensive backboard, or (2) at the offensive backboard.

1. ***Defensive Backboard Play Hints.***

   (a) Get into good rebounding position not too far from the backboard or too far under the backboard.

   (b) Position yourself between the offensive rebounder and the basket to protect against the offensive tip-in.

   (c) Get up off the floor as far as possible, with both arms fully extended overhead.

   (d) On the downward move, after getting the ball, spread the legs and hold the ball high and away from your opponents.

   (e) Do not pass until an open path for the pass is evident, so as to minimize the chance of interception by your opponents. (See Fig. 9-4.)

2. ***Offensive Backboard Play.***

   This type of rebounding consists mainly of scoring by tipping the ball into the basket, which is primarily a tall man's play in basketball. Some points for emphasis in tipping are:

   (a) After a good position is assumed, the jump is made extending the arm that will be used to tip the ball.

   (b) The ball is tipped with the four fingers of the hand widespread.

   (c) The ball should be tipped at the height of the jump and played against the backboard into the basket as often as possible.

FIGURE 9-4. Rebounding: Bill Buntin (From Strack, *Basketball.*)

FIGURE 9-5. Offensive tip: Bill Buntin (From Strack, *Basketball.*)

A team that is outsized would find it difficult to utilize the tip; in that case, they may rely upon the defensive rebounding techniques under the offensive backboard in going after the rebound. (See Fig. 9-5.)

Dribbling

There are a few fundamentals that must be observed for all styles of dribbling. The most important factor to remember is to dribble low for the maximum protection. The wrist should be kept relaxed and the fingers nimble, because the ball is controlled by these parts. The fingers control the direction of the ball, and the wrist supplies the force. The ball should be pushed forward and downward as the player moves down court, and the body is in a crouched position with the weight forward. The eyes and head should be kept up at all times. The height of the bounce of the ball will vary with individuals and situations. A taller player will have a higher dribble than a shorter one, and when dribbling for speed the bounce of the ball will be higher and longer. A good rule to remember in relation to dribbling is never dribble the ball when a pass can be completed successfully.

OFFENSE

Offensive position

Principles to keep in mind are that you cannot travel without dribbling, nor do you want to lose possession of the ball by having your opponent steal it from you through your carelessness. Election of pivot foot is determined by the position of the feet when possession of the ball is attained. If feet are parallel to each other, you may elect the one to move and the one to remain as the pivot foot. If, upon attaining possession of the ball, one foot is in advance of the other, the rearmost foot must be the pivot foot and cannot be moved without first dribbling. A good technique for the beginner is to assume a spike has been driven through the pivot foot into the floor, which would afford him faking movements with the opposite foot and traversing movement with the pivot foot. This can be removed only through dribbling or passing. The ball is held close to the body, away from the opponent, with elbows out from the side. When faking left or right, the ball is held on the opposite hip of the faking step. Once you have lured your opponent off the direct line to the basket, step toward the basket with your faking left so that your body is between the opponent and your destination. The ball must be dribbled by the hand farthest from the defender when driving past the opponent. Other fakes such as the "rocker step" can be used to get your opponent off balance so that you might drive past him. (See Fig. 9-6.)

Offensive tactics in basketball will vary with the defensive tactics employed by the opposing team. Thus, the offensive patterns will vary in order that the most efficient attack may be developed against the particular defense. Generally speaking, there are two types of offense: (1) that which is employed against the zone defense, and (2) that which is employed against the man-to-man defense. Within each of these offensive patterns, there will be further variations in accordance with the peculiarities of each of the defense patterns mentioned. For example, the offensive team would not employ the identical attack against 2-1-2 zone defense that they would against a 1-3-1, a 2-3, or a 3-2 zone defense. Similarly, they would not employ the identical attack against a straight follow-your-man defense that they would against a switching man-to-man defense.

Offense employed against a zone defense

The offense used against the zone defense will be primarily one of moving the ball with short, quick, accurate passes to force the defensive players out of their assigned positions in order that a good shot

FIGURE 9-6. Low protective dribble using outside hand: Oliver Dardin (From Strack, *Basketball.*)

may be taken. The offensive players are placed in positions that will force the defense to alter their planned zone and thus weaken its strength. For example, against any 1-2 zone defense, offensive men would be placed about halfway down the sides, and three men would be located across the front of the court. Thus, in order to cover the three front offensive men, one of the two front defensive men would have to move out of his position. Similarly, the one center defensive man cannot cover the two offensive men placed down the sides, and one of the two back defensive men is forced to leave his assigned position near the basket. For each of the zone defenses, then, an offensive is employed that will force the defenders to move out of their respective positions, and thus weaken the zone.

Offense employed against a man-to-man defense

The offense used against the man-to-man defense will be a combination of passing and player movement. That is, against the man-to-man defense, players follow their passes to the basket, and try to get quick breaks from their individual guards in order to attain good position for shooting. Dribbling is more liberally utilized in this offense than it is in the offense against the zone. Set plays are practiced to be utilized in certain game situations, but during the game there is never a planned procedure for such plays. That is, these plays are spontaneous, and utilized when the defense permits the opportunity; they are never forced.

DEFENSE

Defensive position

Note fundamental defensive stances (Fig. 9-7) of the players: boxer's stance, weight evenly distributed on the balls of the feet, head up, knees flexed, seat low, approximately arm's distance away from opponent, same hand in air as lead foot, with opposite hand and forearm parallel to the floor. A player in this position must anticipate a quick move in any direction and be sure never to cross his feet in shifting position. A fundamental rule on defense is to guard your opponent in such a manner as to be able to see him, the ball, and the basket at all times. When guarding opponent, it is important the player learn to shift the hands and arms so that the same hand is in the air as the lead foot.

In moving laterally, slide first with the foot nearer the destination. The opposite foot then slides or closes halfway toward the first foot. Do not cross

FIGURE 9-7. Defensive guards meeting offensive at time line (From Strack, *Basketball*.)

the feet. In moving forward, slide the front foot forward—pushing off the ball of the rear foot—then slide the rear foot forward (halfway) toward the front foot. Keep the feet shoulder width or more apart throughout.

In moving backward, slide the back foot first, keeping the weight on the ball of the foot. The front foot then slides in a drag action halfway toward the rear foot. Keep the feet shoulder width or more apart throughout.

The zone defense

This style of defense calls for the placement of the defensive players in designated areas in and around the defensive basket in order to give a maximum protection against good shots. It is strictly an area defense in that each man is assigned a certain area on the court to cover, and guards only that offensive man who is located in his area. This type of defense is good on small courts, especially when the team is tall. It gives the maximum control of the defensive basket, since no matter when a shot is taken, there will be defensive men under the basket. The defensive men shift in relation to the position of the ball, and not in relation to the position of the offensive players. Some of the various patterns for the zone defense are the 1-3-1, the 1-2-2, the 3-2, the 2-1-2, and the 2-3. The pattern or patterns selected will necessarily take into consideration the size, speed, and ability of the players.

The man-to-man defense

The basic principle behind the man-to-man defense is the assignment of each player to guard one offensive man, and thus the area element that is prominent in the zone defense is eliminated. Instead of shifting in relation to the position of the ball, the players shift in relation to the positions of the men they have been assigned to guard. Variations from this style of man-to-man defense may incorporate such defensive maneuvers as switching, sliding, and double teaming. This style of defense is more individualistic than is the zone defense.

Pressing defenses

In recent years, pressing defenses have taken on great significance at all levels of basketball competition. The main objectives of pressing defenses are to harass opponents into ball-handling errors, to force opponents into changing their game strategy, and to attempt to prevent the offensive team from successfully crossing the division line in the required ten seconds.

The zone press

As in regular zone defenses, each player is responsible for an area of the court, with the emphasis being on harassing the player with the ball and forcing him into errant passes in his backcourt.

Zone presses commonly used are the 1-2-2, 3-1-1, and 1-3-1. Coaches usually encourage their players to constantly try to double team the man with the ball. This provides more opportunities for the pressing team to steal the ball.

When the offensive team crosses the division line, the zone press is usually abandoned and a more conventional defense employed. (See Figs. 9-8 and 9-9.)

FIGURE 9-8. The start of a zone press (From Strack, *Basketball.*)

FIGURE 9-9. Double teaming the man with the ball (From Strack, *Basketball.*)

The man-to-man press

The man-to-man press incorporates the basic principle of all man-to-man defenses: namely, each player is assigned to guard a specific man. However, due to the various methods used to defeat this type of press, rapid switching is utilized whenever necessary.

The man-to-man press is used when a team wishes to change the pace of a game, when an opposing team lacks speed or good ball handlers, and when a team is behind at the latter stages of a game. This particular type of press is usually maintained all over the court.

Attacking pressing defenses

When attacking a zone press, coaches usually position their players in vacant areas on the court. They encourage rapid, accurate passes which prevent the zone press from double teaming the man with the ball. Dribbling is encouraged when the situation warrants.

The man-to-man press is usually attacked in one of two ways. A man is placed in a post position in order that a direct pass may be made to him. The man making the pass, or another teammate, breaks free and receives a pass from the post man and advances the ball into forecourt.

Another technique is to isolate a good dribbler one-on-one, and allow him to dribble the ball into the forecourt.

When attacking either a zone or man-to-man press, it is recommended that the team take the ball out of bounds quickly, so as to prevent organization of the pressing defense.

PERSONAL EQUIPMENT

Purchase of equipment

1. Shoes are the most important item in the basketball player's equipment and should be selected with the greatest care, with the attention given to size, material, support for the ankles and arches, and durability.
2. Socks are to be selected with regard to size, material, and durability. They should be of heavy, soft wool to aid in absorbing shock and preventing blisters.
3. Supporters should be of good yarn material and rubber fibre, and should be able to withstand frequent laundering.

Care of equipment

1. Launder your socks, supporters, and T-shirts at least twice a week.
2. Shoes should be aired out frequently.
3. Do not put wet towels and other damp equipment in your locker overnight.
4. Never wear socks that have holes in them.
5. Have your shoes repaired as soon as they show signs of wear. Worn soles will lead to accidents due to the loss of gripping surface.

BASIC RULES [1]

Equipment and facilities

1. The playing area has both a minimum and a maximum size. The maximum is 94 feet in length and 50 feet in width, and the minimum is 74 feet by 42 feet.
2. The markings of the playing area are to be two inches wide and marked clearly.
3. The center circle for the game is to have a radius

[1] *Official Collegiate Basketball Guide* (New York: The National Collegiate Athletic Bureau, 1967).

of two feet measured from the inside edge of the circle, marked in the center of the court. A circle concentric with this center circle is to be drawn with a radius of six feet, measured from the outside edge of the circle on the court. The courts are divided into halves by extending the radius of the center circle until it intersects the side lines. If the court is less than 74 feet in length, two parallel lines 40 feet from the farther end divide the floor.

4. Free throw lanes are placed at each end of the court. Each lane is bounded by two lines 12 feet apart. The lane is further bounded by a circle having a radius of six feet with its center 19 feet from the end of the court. The free throw line is drawn parallel to and 15 feet from the surface of the backboard.
5. The backboards may be made of plate glass, wood, or any other material that is permanently flat and rigid. They may be rectangular or fan-shaped. The front face of the board will be perpendicular to the floor and parallel to the end line, four feet from it.
6. Baskets are made of metal rings 18 inches in inside diameter with a white cord net suspended beneath the ring. They are securely attached to the backboard with the upper edge ten feet from the floor and parallel to it. The nearest point of the inside edge of the ring is six inches from the plane of the face of the backboard. The ring and the attaching flange and braces are bright orange in color.
7. The ball shall be round and leather covered, unless the teams agree to use a composition cover. It should have a circumference of not more than 30 inches and not less than 29½ for adults and not less than 29 inches for players below senior high school age. The weight of the ball is not less than 20 ounces and not more than 22 ounces. It shall be inflated to an air pressure such that when dropped to a solid wood floor from a height of six feet—measured to the bottom of the ball—it will rebound to a height—measured to the top of the ball—of not more than 54 inches when it strikes on its most resilient spot nor less than 49 inches when it strikes on its least resilient spot. The channels between the panels of the ball shall not exceed one-fourth inch. If the home team does not provide a ball which meets the specifications, the referee may select one provided by the visiting team.
8. The imaginary line parallel to the division line is now clearly marked (Rule 4, sec. 18) and designates the mid-court area. Where the of-

fense is responsible for action in the mid-court area, a warning time of ten seconds will be given to the offensive team when defensive players are in the mid-court area, unless the defensive team is providing continuous action.

9. Any time a player has control of the ball in the mid-court area for five seconds and is closely guarded during the five seconds, a held ball shall be called.

10. It will be a violation for the offense or the defense to touch the ball or basket when the ball is in or on the basket, and to touch the ball when any part of the ball is on the cylinder above the basket. "Dunking the ball" is not permitted.

Officials

1. The officials for the game shall be a referee and umpire, or, by mutual agreement, two umpires and a referee, and two timers and scorers.

2. A single timer and a single scorer may be used if they are trained men acceptable to the referee.

3. The referee inspects and approves all equipment, including court, baskets, ball, backboards, timer(s)' and scorer(s)' signals. He designates the official timepiece and its operator. He does not permit any player to wear equipment which in his judgment is dangerous to other players or is unnatural and designed to increase height or gain a similar advantage. He is responsible for notifying each captain three minutes before each half is to begin.

4. The referee tosses the ball at center to start the game. He decides whether a goal shall count if the officials disagree. He has power to forfeit a game when conditions warrant. He decides matters upon which timers and scorers disagree. At the end of each half, he checks and approves the score. His approval at the end of the game terminates the jurisdiction of the officials.

Teams and players

1. Each team consists of five players, one of whom is captain. A team must begin with five players, but if it has no substitutes to replace disqualified players it must continue with less than five.

2. The captain is the representative of his team and may address an official on matters of interpretation or information in a courteous manner. Any player may address an official to request a time-out or permission to leave the court.

3. A substitute who desires to enter the game reports to the scorer(s), giving his name and number. The substitute remains outside the boundary until an official beckons him, whereupon he enters immediately.

Scoring and timing

1. A goal is made when the ball enters the basket from above and remains in or passes through it.

2. A goal from the field counts two points for the team into whose basket the ball is thrown.

3. A goal from a free throw is credited to the thrower and counts one point for his team. The try for goal is made within ten seconds after the ball has been placed at the disposal of the free-thrower at the free-throw line. This applies to each free throw. The free throw awarded because of a technical foul may be attempted by any player, including an entering substitute of the offended team.

4. For the length of games, see Nature of the Game.

5. Time-outs are restricted to a total of five. One additional time-out may be granted each team for each extra period of the game. A technical foul will be charged for any additional time-outs granted.

6. If the score is tied at the end of the second half, play continues without change of baskets for one or more extra periods, with a one-minute intermission before each extra period. In games played in halves, each extra period is five minutes. In games played in quarters, each extra period is three minutes. As many such extra periods are played as are necessary to break the tie. Extra periods are an extension of the second half.

7. Time-out occurs and the game watch is stopped each time an official blows his whistle (fouls, violations, jump balls, any unusual delay in getting a dead ball alive, conference with scorer or timer, and the like). Any player may request a time-out, such request being granted only when the ball is dead or in control of a player of his team and when no change of status of the ball is about to occur.

Play

1. Putting the ball into play at the start of the game and at the start of each succeeding quarter or half or extra period is by a jump ball in the center circle between two opponents. After each goal, the ball is put into play by the team that did not score from the out-of-bounds area at the end of the court at which the basket has been scored.

2. A player is out of bounds when he touches the floor on or outside of a boundary.

3. The ball is out of bounds when it touches a player who is out of bounds or any other person, the floor, or any object on or outside a boundary, or the supports or back of the backboard. When the rectangular backboard is used, the ball is out of bounds if it passes over the backboard.

4. The ball is caused to go out of bounds by the last player to touch it before it goes out, provided it is out of bounds because of touching something other than a player. If the ball is out of bounds because of touching a player who is on or outside the boundary, such player causes it to go out.

5. A player can not remain for more than three seconds in that part of his free throw lane between the end line and the farther edge of the free throw lane while the ball is in control of his team. Allowance shall be made for a player who, having been in the restricted area for less than three seconds, dribbles in to try for a goal.

6. The team that has continuous control of the ball in its back court (that part of the court between the opponents' end line and the entire division line) must advance the ball into the front court prior to the expiration of ten consecutive seconds.

7. Fouls are classified as (a) technical—involving delay of game, using unsportsmanlike tactics, illegal entry, excessive time-out(s), failing to raise hand at arm's length above one's head after being charged with a foul, and the like; or (b) personal—involving pushing, charging, tripping, holding, or using rough tactics.

   The penalty for technical fouls is one free throw, and the offended team's captain shall designate the thrower. If the foul is flagrant, a second free throw shall be awarded.

   For personal fouls offender is charged with one foul and, if it is his fifth personal foul, or if it is flagrant, he is disqualified. (1) Offended player (or his substitute, if such player is disqualified or injured) is awarded one free throw, unless it is a double foul or a common foul committed by a player while he or a teammate is in control. (*Note:* If a personal foul is committed by any player of the offensive team while his team is in possession of the ball [front or back court], a foul is charged to the offending player and the ball is awarded to the offended team at the nearest out-of-bounds spot, no free throw being awarded.) (2) Unless it is a multiple foul, a second free throw is awarded if the foul: (a) is flagrant or intentional, including one by a player who does not make reasonable effort to avoid contact and who tries to reach the ball from an unfavorable position; (b) is committed against a field goal thrower whose try is not successful; or (c) is a common foul [except as noted in (1) above] which occurs after the offending team has been charged during the half with six personal fouls in a game played in halves or with four personal fouls in a game played in quarters, and provided the first free throw for the common foul is successful. (Extra periods are an extension of the second half.)

8. Violations include causing the ball to go out of bounds, double dribbling, running with the ball, kicking the ball (positive act), striking the ball with the fist, excessively swinging arms or elbows even though there is no contact with opponents, interfering with basket, goal tending, illegal throw-in, putting the ball into play improperly, and failure to observe free throw regulations, the three second rule, and the ten second rule.

   Penalties vary considerably for violations and include loss of point(s), loss of ball, or the awarding of point(s) to the offended team.

Strategy

The strategy employed by an individual basketball player will necessarily vary in accordance with his special abilities. That is, some fast players will take advantage of their speed, whereas good fakers will utilize this capacity. Thus, the player will play the type of game best suited to his abilities.

Regardless of these individual characteristics, there are certain principles of individual strategy that will generally pertain to all situations. (1) When guarding a right-handed player, make him utilize his left hand as often as possible by guarding him more closely on his right side. (2) Press high scoring players very closely. Many times it is possible to pressure these players into an off-night by this type of guarding. (3) Stay away from speedy opponents. Guard them loosely if they are not good at long shots, and if they are, keep them faked off balance as much as possible without going in too close. (4) Keep tall men from gaining possession of the ball when playing under the basket, and when they move out, guard them on the side from which the pass may come. This will necessitate constant, rapid shifting. (5) If you are tall, and the man guarding you is short, play near the basket or in the pivot. (6) When guarding an opponent who seems uncertain, be aggressive and force him to maintain his uncertainty. This is usually good policy when guarding substitutes who are entering the game for the first time, or when guarding inexperienced players. (7) Poor ball handlers are usually distressed by a close guarding opponent, so watch for fumbled balls, telegraphed passes, and other miscues that will permit you to steal the ball. (8) Study your opponent early in the game and attempt to analyze his strengths and weaknesses so you will be able to play your best game.

Team strategy will also vary with the particular team in accordance with the style of play and the coach's methods. However, there are certain principles that may apply despite this variation. (1) When playing against a tall team, keep them off balance. Don't let them get into scoring position. (2) Use a fast break against a tall, slow team unless they get into position before you can get the fast break going. (3) Against a tight man-to-man defense, utilize screens, quick cuts, and criss-cross breaks. Do not attempt long passes, and dribble only when absolutely necessary. (4) If your opponents are getting tired, utilize a fast break, but not if your team is tired as well. (5) When playing a team that gets back fast, utilize set plays and omit the fast break. (6) When playing against a zone defense, set up plays on the weak side of the court by overloading one side. Bring the ball down the court quickly before the zone defense has time to get set. (7) When your opponents are guarding loosely, take long shots to force them to come out. (8) When you are ahead near the close of the game, play control ball and slow up your offense. Don't lose a close game because of your own mistakes. (9) If a team is using a fast break against you successfully, bottle up their rebound players, and drop two men back as fast as you can. (10) Never try to force a fast break.

SAFETY HINTS

1. Be sure your shoes fit properly and are laced to the top to prevent ankle injuries.
2. Be careful when playing on courts with unprotected backboard supports, or walls that are close to the end lines.
3. Before the game be sure to note all obstructions that are proximal to the playing court, such as players' benches, timer's table, cheer leader megaphones, and so forth.
4. Warm up properly before each game or practice session.
5. Be conscientious about training rules. Your best protection is top condition.
6. Wear two pair of socks to prevent blisters until your feet become toughened.
7. Treat blisters, floor burns, bruises, and abrasions immediately.

8. Report all injuries to your coach. Don't play when you feel sick or are in pain due to an injury.
9. Get the advice of your coach or trainer when using tape.
10. Watch for wet, slippery floors in the shower and locker rooms.

HELPFUL HINTS

Passing and Dribbling

1. Use bounce passes and underhand flips against tall opponents, and baseball, hook, and two-hand overhead passes against smaller opponents.
2. Fake with your head, eyes, and body when dribbling.
3. Practice receiving and passing in one motion.
4. Do not "give away" your passes.
5. Always fake before you pass.
6. Never pass across the court underneath your defensive basket.
7. Always lead a running teammate.
8. Go to meet passes thrown to you.
9. Step in the direction of your passes.
10. Learn to handle the ball well.
11. Know the role of dribbling in your team's offense.
12. If you are right-handed, learn to dribble with the left hand, and vice versa.
13. For speed, use a belt-high bounce; for control and deception, use a knee-level bounce.
14. Learn to dribble backward as well as forward.
15. In using the low-guarded dribble:
    (a) Keep the ball at the side of the body and legs—not in front of the body.
    (b) Allow the ball to bounce no higher than the knees.
    (c) Control the ball with the finger tips.
    (d) Keep the body over the ball.
16. In using the high-driving dribble:
    (a) Drive for speed when in the clear.
    (b) Allow the ball to bounce almost chest high.
    (c) Keep the ball in front of the body.

Shooting

1. Practice the shots that you take most in a game.
2. Relax and try to maintain body control.
3. Shoot when you are "hot," pass when you are "cold."

4. Do not attempt "prayer" shots.
5. Practice short shots, then gradually move away from the basket.
6. Always follow your shots.
7. Concentrate on the basket.
8. Study the backboards in pre-game drills.
9. Be a good team player—don't be selfish.
10. Maintain your poise.
11. Know the floor position from which you shoot the best.
12. Analyze each shot before you shoot—distance, arc, and power needed.

TERMINOLOGY

Air dribble   That part of a dribble during which the dribbler throws or taps the ball in the air and then touches it before it touches the floor.

Backcourt men (guards)   Players who set up a team's offensive pattern. Usually the smallest men on the team. They generally operate between the center court line and the foul line and are usually fast and excellent dribblers.

Basket   The 18-inch ring with a suspended cord-net through which players attempt to throw the ball.

Blocking   Personal contact by a player that impedes the progress of an opponent who does not have the ball.

Boxing out   A term used to designate a defensive player's position under the backboard which prevents an offensive player from achieving a good rebounding position.

Charging   Personal contact against the body of an opponent by a player with the ball.

Corner men (forwards)   Players who are basically responsible for the rebounding phase of a team's operation. On offense, they are usually located at the sides of the court between the foul line and the base line.

Double foul   When two opponents commit personal fouls against each other at approximately the same time.

Dribble   Ball movement caused by a player in control who throws or taps the ball in the air or onto the floor and then touches it. The dribble ends when the dribbler touches the ball with both hands simultaneously, permits it to come to rest while he is in contact with it, or loses control.

Drive   The quality of powerful and concerted effort.

Fast break   A rush to score after gaining the ball in the opponents' half of the court.

Follow-in   To move toward the basket for the purpose of securing a rebound if one results.

Foul   Any infraction of the rules for which the penalty is one or more free throws.

Free throw   The privilege given a player to score one point by an unhindered throw for goal from within the free-throw circle and behind the throw line.

Freeze   The attempt by the leading team in a game to maintain possession of the ball and run out the clock. It is usually employed during the latter stages of the game.

Give and go   A maneuver in which the offensive player makes a short pass to a teammate, and then goes in toward the basket for a return pass.

Held ball   Occurs when two opponents have one or both hands firmly on the ball, and neither can gain possession without undue roughness.

Holding   Personal contact with an opponent that interferes with his freedom of movement.

Hook shot   A shot made by extending the arm overhead and shooting the ball across the body behind the head.

Inside man (center)   Often the tallest man on the team. He is usually located on offense between the foul line and the basket (outside of the three second lane). He often plays with his back to the basket until a shot is taken. He, along with the corner men, has rebounding responsibility.

Jump ball   A method of putting the ball into play by tossing it up between two opponents in one of the three circles.

Multiple foul   A situation in which two or more teammates commit personal fouls against the same opponent at approximately the same time.

Pass   Movement of the ball caused by a player in control throwing, batting, or rolling the ball to another player.

Personal foul   A player foul which involves contact with an opponent while the ball is alive or after the ball is in possession of a player for a throw in.

Pitchout   A term used to designate a direct pass from a rebounder to a teammate, with the main objective being the start of a fast break.

Pivot   Takes place when a player who is holding the ball steps once or more than once in any direction with the same foot, the other foot, called the pivot foot, being kept at its point of contact with the floor.

Post   A pivot position.

Pressing defense   A defense designed to break up the offensive through constant guarding and forcing the offensive team to move the ball.

Rebound   A term usually applied when the ball bounces off the backboard or basket.

Restraining circles   Three circles of six-foot radius, one located in the center of the court and one located at each of the free-throw circles.

Screen   An attempt to protect a teammate's play by shutting off an opponent's approach without personal contact.

Set shot   A shot taken at the basket from a "set" or stationary position usually 20 feet or more from the basket.

Switching   A reversal of defensive positions.

Team's front court   That part of the court between the team's end line and the nearer edge or the division line, which includes its basket and the inbounds part of its backboard.

Technical foul   A foul by a non-contact player, a player foul which does not involve contact with an opponent, or a player foul which involves unsportsmanlike contact with an opponent while the ball is dead—except as indicated in the last clause of personal foul definition.

Throw in   A method of putting the ball in play from out of bounds.

Trailer   A player who follows behind a dribbling teammate.

Traveling   When a player in possession of the ball within bounds progresses illegally in any direction.

Weave   To run from side to side, passing the ball to a teammate.

SELECTED REFERENCES

Anderson, Forrest, and Stan Albeck, *Coaching Better Basketball*. New York: The Ronald Press Company, 1964.

Baisi, Neal, *Coaching the Zone and Man-to-Man Pressing Defenses*. Englewood Cliffs, N.J.: Prentice-Hall, Inc., 1961.

Bunn, J., *Basketball Techniques and Team Play*. Englewood Cliffs, N.J.: Prentice-Hall, Inc., 1964.

Cousy, Bob, Edward Linn, and Robert Riger, *The Last Loud Roar*. Englewood Cliffs, N.J.: Prentice-Hall, Inc., 1964.

Dobbs & Pinholster, *Basketball's Stunting Defenses*. Englewood Cliffs, N.J.: Prentice-Hall, Inc., 1964.

Harrell, B., *Championship-Tested Offensive and Defensive Basketball Strategy*. Englewood Cliffs, N.J.: Prentice-Hall, Inc., 1967.

McGuire, Frank, *Offensive Basketball*. Englewood Cliffs, N.J.: Prentice-Hall, Inc., 1958.

McLane, H., *Championship Basketball*. Englewood Cliffs, N.J.: Prentice-Hall, Inc., 1965.

Meyer, Ray, *Basketball as Coached by Ray Meyer*. Englewood Cliffs, N.J.: Prentice-Hall, Inc., 1967.

Newell, Pete, and John Bennington, *Basketball Methods*. New York: The Ronald Press Company, 1962.

Newsom, Heber, *Basketball for the High School Coach and the Physical Education Teacher*. Dubuque, Iowa: William C. Brown Company, Publishers, 1966.

Rubin, R., *Attacking Basketball's Pressure Defenses*. Englewood Cliffs, N.J.: Prentice-Hall, Inc., 1966.

Santos, Harry, *How to Attack and Defeat Zone Defenses in Basketball*. West Nyack, N.Y.: The Parker Publishing Co., 1967.

Strack, David, *Basketball*. Englewood Cliffs, N.J.: Prentice-Hall, Inc., 1968.

Van Ryswyk, R., *Ball Control Offense and Disciplined Defense in Basketball*. Englewood Cliffs, N.J.: Prentice-Hall, Inc., 1967.

———, *Complete System for Winning Basketball*. Englewood Cliffs, N.J.: Prentice-Hall, Inc., 1967.

Ward, C., *Basketball's Match-Up Defense*. Englewood Cliffs, N.J.: Prentice-Hall, Inc., 1964.

Wilkes, Glen, *Basketball Coach's Complete Handbook*. Englewood Cliffs, N.J.: Prentice-Hall, Inc., 1962.

Wooden, John R., *Practical Modern Basketball*. New York: The Ronald Press Company, 1966.

Women's basketball

ORIGIN AND DEVELOPMENT

Basketball was introduced in 1892 by Dr. James Naismith at the YMCA College in Springfield, Massachusetts. Soon thereafter a game adapted to women was played at Smith College. The game has grown steadily in popularity with girls and women in high schools, colleges, and recreational and industrial organizations. During this period the game has undergone many changes in recommended floor size, numbers of players, divisions of the court, and rules governing the play.

NATURE OF THE GAME

Girls' and women's basketball is played by two teams in an area divided into two courts. (See Fig. 9-10.) Each team has six players: two stationary guards who play in the back court, two stationary forwards who play in the front court, and two rovers who play in the full court, positioning themselves in relation to the ball. When the rovers are in their front court they become forwards, and when in their back court, guards. Any player acting as a rover may designate, whenever she wishes, any other player on her team to rove for her, thus minimizing the possibility of overfatigue.

If team X is in possession of the ball and in

FIGURE 9-10. Diagram of basketball court showing names of players and positions at the start of a game

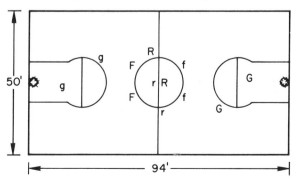

its front court, four of its players will be in the front court and two in the back court. Their opponent, team Y, will have four players in its back court and two in its front court.

The object of the game is to pass the ball among the players, advancing it toward a player in the front court who is in a good position to shoot for the basket. A goal is made, and thus a score, when the ball is dropped through the basket from the front court, scoring two points, or from the free-throw line on a foul shot, scoring one point. The game is played in quarter periods of eight minutes each, with a ten-minute intermission between halves, and a two-minute intermission between the first and second quarters and the third and fourth quarters.

TECHNIQUES AND FUNDAMENTALS

Receiving

When catching the ball, the player must absorb the force on the oncoming ball. This will be accomplished by "giving" with the ball as it is caught. Finger control is important. The hands should be cupped with the fingers pointed upward when the ball is caught above waist height, and with fingers pointing downward when the ball is caught below waist height. The hands, arms, and body should be relaxed.

Moving toward the oncoming ball and getting the body in line with the ball will lessen the possibility of interception by the opponent and aid in making a good catch.

In order to avoid the common basketball violation called *traveling* (walking with the ball), players should learn to receive the ball in a skip-step. This will permit a legal two-step stop, enabling the player gradually to slow down her forward momentum. The skip-step can be learned by skipping toward the ball as it is passed. The forward leg is lifted high in a bent position, the rear leg slightly bent with the foot just off the floor. As contact is made with the ball the rear foot comes down to the floor, with the knee and ankle joints flexing to absorb

FIGURES 9-11, 9-12. Two-hand overhead pass. (*Left*) Starting position. (*Right*) Follow-through.

the shock. The second step is made to complete the check of forward momentum. Fouls as well as violations can be avoided if the head and shoulders are kept in good alignment when receiving a pass, thus preventing falling forward as the two-step stop is executed.

Passing

Accurate, controlled passing is essential to a good basketball game. Players should learn to execute several passes well, both to the right and the left. The ball should be held with the fingers and snapped with the wrist when thrown. Transfer of weight and follow-through provide the force and direction of the ball. In general, accurate, short passes aimed about chest level are superior to long, looped ones.

Passes should be thrown so that the receiver can easily catch the ball. This is accomplished by anticipating the speed and direction in which the receiver is moving, passing the ball so that it and the receiver will reach the space at the same time. In order to accurately time a pass for the use of a "cut," the catch and throw are executed as one continuous motion.

CHEST PASS. The ball is held on the sides and slightly to the back with fingers spread, thumbs pointing to the inside, wrists flexed. The ball is in front of the body about chest level; elbows are close to the body. The body should lean forward slightly and the knees should be easy. As the ball is released, the arms extend, the wrists snap, and the body moves forward with a step. The follow-through should be a full extension of the body in the direction of the pass. This pass is used in many situations during a game.

ONE-HAND SHOULDER PASS. The ball is held with the fingers of one hand slightly behind the shoulder at shoulder height. It may be balanced in place with the other hand just prior to passing. The wrist is cocked, weight slightly back on the same foot as throwing hand. As the ball is thrown the arm extends forward, the wrist snaps, and the body weight shifts forward. The follow-through is in the direction of the desired pass and the body weight continues to move through on the same foot as the throwing hand. This pass is used when distances are desired.

TWO-HAND OVERHEAD PASS. The ball is held high over head and in front of the body with the fingers gripping the ball on the sides and slightly to the back. The wrists are cocked. The body weight is slightly forward. The ball is released with an extension of the arms and snap of the wrists. The follow-through is in the direction of the desired path of the ball. This pass is used often from a rebound position. It is also effective when passing to a player who is in the key. It should be snappy and accurate. (See Figs. 9-11, 9-12.)

TWO-HAND UNDERHAND PASS. The ball is held with two hands at either right or left hip and close to the body. The ball is released with an extension of the arms and a strong wrist snap. When passing to the right, the left foot should be forward; when passing to the left, the right foot should be forward. This is an effective "hand off" pass when players are close to one another. It is also useful to a pivot player in the key.

BOUNCE PASS. The ball is held with the fingers of one or both hands (frequently about waist height). The ball is released with an extension of the arms and wrists and is directed toward the floor. The ball should bounce about three feet in front of the receiver. To avoid weakness in the pass, the wrist snap should be emphasized. This pass must be used with discretion, although it can sometimes be an effective way to pass the ball. The speed of the pass must be determined by the particular situation.

HOOK PASS. The ball is held in one hand (the other hand can be used to guide the ball to position) and taken to one side of the body. The outstretched arm is then raised to a vertical position with the upper arm almost resting alongside of the head. From this position the ball is released, with the wrist snap, over the head. The opposite shoulder should point in the direction of the desired path of the ball. This pass can be very effective when the passer is closely guarded. It is a difficult pass to execute but an asset to the more advanced player.

Shooting

Scoring baskets is generally the result of long practice. Very few individuals have a "natural" ability to shoot accurately. To become a proficient shooter it is necessary to have confidence, perseverance, and relaxation. Good body balance and strong wrists and fingers are essential. In all shooting, the ball should be held with the fingers in a position which would permit a pass to be held with the fingers in a position which would permit a pass to be made if the shot is not attempted. The knees should be easy, with the body slightly crouched. The elbows should be flexed and close to the body prior to the shot. One-hand shots should be practiced with both the right and left hand. The rim of the basket serves as a consistent point of aim, although some shots are dependent upon banking the ball against the backboard. Keeping one's eye focused on the basket, and the follow-through of the arms and body, are essential to good shooting. It is important that both set and moving shots be practiced.

LAY UP SHOT. The lay up is an angle shot taken close to the basket. When shooting from the right, the take-off is from the left foot with the right knee lifting up to gain additional height. The ball is held in both hands with the right hand on the back of the ball, toward the top, and the left hand under the ball. The right arm is extended, still holding the ball, while the body is being thrust upward. At the top of the upward thrust, the ball is released by the finger tips with a gentle push that will "lay" the ball against the backboard about 10 to 12 inches over the basket. This shot should be practiced also from the left side with the left hand.

CHEST SHOT. The chest shot is used most frequently for a long set shot. The shot is executed like a chest pass but with more elevation. The aim should be above the rim and the follow-through in the direction of the basket. (See Figs. 9-13, 9-14.)

ONE-HAND PUSH SHOT. This shot can be

FIGURES 9-13, 9-14. Chest shot. (*Left*) Starting position. (*Right*) Follow-through.

FIGURES 9-15 and 9-16. One-hand push shot. (*Top*) Starting position. (*Bottom*) Follow-through.

used either as a set or a moving shot. The ball is held (for a shot from the right) with the fingers of the right hand on the back of the ball at chest level and the fingers of the left hand on the bottom of the ball. The right arm is extended upward and outward toward the basket, releasing the ball with a flexion of the wrist as full extension of the arm is reached. The aim is over the rim and the follow-through toward the basket. If the shot is stationary, the right foot is ahead of the body, knees flexed, and body inclined forward. If this is a moving shot, the take-off is from the left foot. The shot should also be practiced moving in from the left side and using the left hand. (See Figs. 9-15, 9-16.)

TWO-HAND OVERHEAD SHOT. This shot requires a good deal of wrist strength. It is a good shot to develop because the ball is caught high and shot high with little time wasted between catching and shooting. The fingers are placed to the side and under the ball. The follow-through is out and toward the basket.

JUMP SHOT. This is a difficult shot to guard and requires a great deal of practice. It can be a moving or a stationary shot. The ball is held on the sides at chest level. As the player jumps straight up off the floor, the ball is brought up overhead, elbows slightly flexed and wrists well cocked. Just before reaching the peak of the jump, the right hand moves behind and under the ball and the left hand moves slightly to the front and side of the ball. When the player has reached the peak of the jump, the ball is released by extending the right elbow and snapping the wrist. Powerful wrist and finger action are necessary. The aim should be over the rim of the basket and the follow-through toward the basket. Care should be taken to bring the body straight down from the jump to avoid moving forward, which could result in fouling the defending player.

Common shooting errors

Some common errors are caused by: (1) carrying the elbows too far from the body, extending the arms too forcefully or abruptly, failing to achieve finger and wrist snap, (2) throwing the ball at the backboard too hard, which causes too much rebound, (3) tossing the ball with insufficient arch in those shots requiring arch, and (4) neglecting to concentrate on aiming for the basket.

The fake

The fake is a move made with the ball, head, eyes, shoulders, or feet, with no intention of actually following through with the movement in that direc-

FIGURE 9-17. Evasive tactics. (A) The bounce; (B) rear pivot in several directions, from either a side stride or forward stride position; (C) feint and front pivot around opponent. (From Miller and Ley, *Individual and Team Sports for Women.*)

tion. It is done to put the guard off balance. To fake effectively, the knees must be bent, the body weight must be carried low, and the player must be able to move quickly. Fakes should be practiced to the right and to the left of the opponent. The faker should be certain that the opponent is committed to the fake direction before moving in the opposite direction, otherwise the opponent will remain a hindrance.

The dribble

The player causes the ball to be bounced, using one or both hands on the first bounce but only one hand (either) on the other bounce until she regains possession of the ball. If the player uses two hands on the ball after the first bounce, she may not continue to dribble. For good body control on the dribble, a player should keep her head and shoulders in line, bending the knees to keep low with the ball. Impetus is given to the ball with a pumping-like action of the arm and fingers. A player should keep her head and eyes up. For a good control of the ball, the dribble should be kept low. However, for gaining distance at greater speed when unguarded, the dribble can come nearer waist height. A player who can dribble well with either hand will be an asset to her team. The dribble should not be used to excess.

The pivot

The pivot is a means of protecting the ball and evading an opponent. The toes of one foot (called the pivot foot) remain in contact with the floor on the spot where they were at the time the player received the ball. The other foot may step in any direction causing the body to turn away from an opponent or toward a teammate. (See Fig. 9-17.)

TEAM DEFENSIVE PLAY

Guarding

The man-to-man and zone systems of defense are effective only if each player guards her opponent well. A good guarding stance is one where the knees are bent, the body weight is centered over both feet, one foot slightly ahead of the other, and the body slightly inclined forward. One arm is held out to the side and the other arm forward. Quick sliding steps should be used when moving to the side, forward, or backward, to remain on the goal side of the opponent. When guarding the opponent with the ball, the guard should keep her feet on the floor, knees bent until after the opponent has released the ball. Only then should the guard jump to block the shot or pass. Good guarding requires the ability to anticipate and to analyze the moves of the opposite team.

The zone defense

In the zone defense the fundamental principle involved is that the guards are given a prescribed area to cover, regardless of the forward play. Within this system of guarding there are several variations, the most common being the 2-2 zone with two guards playing one on the right and one on the left sides near the basket, and the other two guards playing also on the right and left sides of the basket but at approximately the free-throw line. The roving players will most often be the two near the free-throw line. Other possibilities of defense are a 1-3 zone, or a 1-2-1 zone. In all three types of zone defense there must be definite shifts of the guards in relation to the position of the ball. It will be noticed that the pattern of the four guards during defense is usually diamond shaped. The 1-3 and 1-2-1 types ultimately shift into a 2-2 zone.

Zone defense enables the guards to concentrate on that portion of the court from which forwards shoot with a high degree of accuracy. Thus it is hoped that the forwards will be forced to take long shots and, at the same time, the guards will be in good position to get the rebounds from these long and usually inaccurate shots by blocking out the offense. Zone defense also serves to conserve energy. Finally, zone defense is a team effort with definite shifts and moves, enabling one guard to take the place of another who has temporarily been avoided.

In the zone defense it is essential that the players thoroughly understand the exact system being played so that there is no confusion on the part of the guards. The forwards are making every effort to draw a guard out of her zone, or to pass faster than a guard can shift.

The man-to-man defense

Man-to-man defense depends upon having guards, each of whom is quick and able to anticipate correctly the moves of her forward. Since the forward need avoid only one guard to be free to shoot, each guard must be aggressive, confident, and quick to move to remain between her man and the basket. Man-to-man defense requires the guard to play the entire half-court area and to stay close to her opponent at all times. The distance between the guard and player for whom she is responsible will depend upon their relation to the goal and whether or not the opponent has dribbled. The guard can move in closer after an opponent has used the dribble. Playing an opponent too closely will often result in being outmaneuvered. The man-to-man defense can be very effective if the team has enough stamina. It is especially useful against a team which stalls the ball. This type of defense requires much practice as a team unit so that the guards know when it is necessary to switch opponents, should a teammate be outmaneuvered.

TEAM OFFENSIVE PLAY

Offensive play should be the result of good team play and ball control on the part of each member of the team. The offensive play will be varied as the defensive tactics being used against it are recognized. Moving the ball efficiently down the court into scoring position, with accurate, well-timed cuts and passes, is essential for good offensive play. The player must anticipate the forthcoming moves of the ball and teammates so that she avoids wasting time trying to decide what to do with the ball after she receives it. The offense should be quick to analyze the system of guarding being used and should be ready to strengthen its attack with its own diversity of play. As players become more experienced, they will include the "screen" and "pick-off" plays, techniques which will need to be practiced many times along with other techniques. These techniques will require the team to move its players, causing the zone defense to move out of its prescribed area, thereby weakening the defense. To break a man-to-man defense the forwards must employ a series of quick short passes, bounces, and the dribble. By breaking fast from the guards and cutting in toward the basket, the players and the ball are worked into a good shooting position.

BASIC RULES

Equipment and facilities

1. The playing area will vary in size from a maximum of 94 feet in length by 50 feet in width to a minimum of 74 feet by 42 feet. It will be divided into two courts by a two-inch line drawn from side to side parallel with the end lines.

2. All markings are two inches wide, except a narrow broken line drawn three feet inside the boundary lines.

   (a) A center circle is drawn in the center of the court with a two-foot radius and a concentric circle is drawn with a six-foot radius.

   (b) Free-throw lanes will be placed at each end of the court, 12 feet in width, extending from the end line toward the free-throw line and ending in a circle with radius of six feet. The circle will continue through the lane with a broken line.

   (c) A two-inch line will be drawn parallel to the end line, 15 feet out from the backboard, and extending across the circle. The midpoint of this line determines the center of the six-foot circle enclosing the free-throw lanes.

3. Backboards made of flat, rigid material, preferably wood or glass, from which the baskets are suspended, will be placed at the end of each area.

4. Baskets are metal rings, painted orange, to which are attached nets of cord or sometimes leather.

5. The ball is round, usually leather covered, with a circumference of about 30 inches. It is inflated to the manufacturer's specifications usually found on the ball.

Officials

Officials shall be an umpire and a referee assisted by two scorers and two timers.

Play

Preliminary to the start of the game the officials and team captains will decide which basket each team will have for the first half. Sides are changed at the beginning of the third quarter of play. Play is started each quarter by a jump ball taken by two opponents standing in the center restraining circle. After a basket has been made from the field the ball is put in play by a guard of the opposing team from any place behind the end line. When a foul is called, the girl fouled must attempt her own free throw. If the foul occurs in a team's back court, the player moves to her team's front court and so becomes the fourth forward, who is called the *roving player*.

When a foul is called, guards and forwards line up at the free-throw lanes in alternate positions. The offensive team has the choice of either right or left lane line position nearest the basket. A defensive player, then, is on the opposite lane line near the basket. A minimum of two players must line up along each line. There must be the same number of players from each team on each lane line. A third player of each team may be on the lane line, but a fourth (defense) player must be either three feet behind the lane line or outside and beyond the free-throw line. Players shall not line up along the free-throw lanes for free throws following double fouls.

If a goal is scored on the final free throw of any one penalty, the ball is put in play by the opposite team out of bounds at the end line. On a free throw that is missed, the ball is in play if it touched the ring. If it did not touch the ring, the ball is awarded to an opposing player out of bounds at the side line opposite the free-throw line.

A *jump* ball resulting from a tie ball, double foul, double violation, or other reasons covered by the official rules, is taken by two opponents who will stand in the restraining circle designated. The ball will be tossed between them by the referee or the umpire. A *tie ball* results when two players of opposing teams simultaneously place one or both hands on the ball or when a player places one or both hands on a ball already held by an opponent. It is legal to tap or take a ball already held by an opponent. Only one bounce or a dribble are permitted as ways to advance the ball on the floor. Other than this, the ball is advanced from one player to another by various types of passes, until a forward is in position to shoot a basket. Infringements of the rules are classified as either fouls or violations. A game ending in a tie shall be played off in extra periods. Overtime periods shall be of three minutes duration. Overtime shall continue until one team is ahead by at least one point at the end of the period. Intermission between such periods shall be two minutes.

Fouls

Fouls are classified as (1) those involving personal contact resulting in roughness, e.g., overguarding a player by holding, charging a player, blocking and tagging, and (2) those without personal contact, e.g., illegal substitution, delaying the games, and unsportsmanlike tactics.

The *penalty* for a foul is one free throw awarded the player fouled against *unless* that player was in the act of shooting for a basket, in which case the goal, if made, counts and one free throw is awarded. If the field goal is missed, the player receives two free throws. During the last two minutes of the fourth quarter and in all overtime periods, individual fouls are penalized with two free throws by the opposite team—unless the fouled player scores the field goal, in which case only one additional shot is awarded.

Violations

Violations are technicalities such as line violations, traveling with the ball, field goal and free-throw violations, goal tending, and so forth.

The *penalty* is that the team not committing the violation is awarded the ball, and it is put in play outside the side line by a player on that team, except in the case of an end line violation, in which case the ball is played from outside the end line of the court.

Official Rules for Basketball for Girls and Women are compiled by the National Division for Girls' and Women's Sports and are reviewed constantly and revised as deemed best.

SUMMARY

Basketball, to be played well, demands that you determine both your own and your opponents' strengths and weaknesses. The objective of the game is scoring, so it becomes essential to have a smooth working forward shooting combination, capable of analyzing and understanding the guard pattern used against them. They, accordingly, will vary their plays and shots and change the tempo so as to play a truly offensive game. They will be alert to the guard play from out of bounds, whether guards or forwards are more successful in gaining possession of the ball from rebounds, whether the forward plays from the center toss and out of bounds are working or being intercepted, or whether a specific area is so guarded as to prevent the forwards from getting through.

The guards must likewise analyze the opposing forwards in terms of plays used from the center jump, from out of bounds, and on the court. They must be quick to adjust to any guarding weakness such as an area not covered well or an opposing player who scores consistently. They must be ready, if necessary, to change their tactics and style. They must quickly adjust to an offensive game when one of their players has the ball so that it can be passed down the court to the forward area.

The team must have a knowledge of the rules of the game, must always be ready to accept the decision of the officials, and must maintain a good spirit with enthusiasm yet calmness under tense situations or when one's team is lagging far behind in the score. The team captain, by calling "time-out" at crucial points, can do much to help control the game by way of making suggestions both to individual players and to the team. Much of the attitude of the coach is reflected in the team on the floor. A coach, therefore, recognizing her team's assets and liabilities, will always strive to remain objective in criticism and personal in her understanding of individual weakness, knowing the players will strive to do their best.

PERSONAL EQUIPMENT

1. Tennis shoes or regulation basketball shoes must be worn at all times to insure safety.
2. Guards for those wearing glasses should be required. Such guards are now available in light weight but durable plastic material.
3. Recommended costumes include shirts and shorts, one-piece gym suits, or gym tunics. If shirts and shorts are worn, care should be taken that they are properly tailored and that size and style are in good taste.

SAFETY HINTS

1. Wear the proper kind and fit of shoes.
2. Wear clean socks to avoid blisters.

3. Wear guards for glasses.
4. Report injuries promptly and have them treated promptly.
5. Warm up before the start of the game.
6. Have a jacket or sweater convenient to wear between halves or whenever you are not playing.

HELPFUL HINTS

Passing

1. Always be ready to practice ball handling and passing.
2. Pass so that a person can receive the ball—usually about chest high.
3. Pass to a player coming toward you.
4. Move to meet a pass coming to you.
5. Do not pass across the court under your opponents' basket.
6. Learn to vary your passes.
7. Learn to "fake" a pass.

Shooting

1. Practice shooting constantly.
2. Practice short and then long shots.
3. Try to relax.
4. Practice free throws until they are "mechanical." To establish a "feel" for this shot, attempt it with your eyes closed.
5. Follow-up your field shots.
6. Study the backboard to be aware of the amount of rebound it gives.
7. Shoot when you are in a position to do so, but don't be selfish and forget to pass to others who might be in a better position.
8. Use an equal amount of force in both hands on all two-hand shots.
9. Extend the arms fully as the shot is being released.
10. Practice shots on the move and in game-like situations.

TERMINOLOGY

Air dribble   A throw or tap of the ball by a player who then obtains possession of it before another player has touched it or it has touched the floor.

Back court   That half of the court which contains the opponent's basket.

Basket The 18-inch ring with a suspended cord-net through which players attempt to throw the ball.

Blocking Personal contact by a player that prevents progress of an opponent with or without the ball.

Bounce When a player gives impetus to the ball once and it bounces on the floor one or more times before she regains possession of it. An *illegal bounce* means that a player regains possession of the ball after a bounce, then bounces it again.

Charging Personal contact against the body of an opponent by a player with the ball.

Double foul When two opponents commit fouls against each other at approximately the same time.

Dribble When a player bounces the ball at least twice, giving impetus to it for the first bounce with one or both hands but only with *one* hand for the following bounces.

Foul An infringement of the rules resulting in one or more free throws for the team or teams fouled against. Types of fouls include:

> *Individual*—blocking, charging, pushing, tagging, holding, tripping, encircling an opponent without the ball, trapping an opponent without the ball at boundary line, in general any personal contact; also threatening the eyes of a player, illegal substitution, and delaying the game.
>
> *Team*—too many time-outs, players and position not officially entered on score book, coaching from side lines during playing time.
>
> *Disqualifying*—for any player who has five fouls charged against her.

Free throw A throw for goal by a player, unguarded, made from behind the free-throw line, scoring one point if made.

Front court That half of the court which contains the team's own basket.

Goal A basket made by a player in that half of the court, the ball having entered the basket from above. *Own goal* is the basket for which a team is shooting.

Jump ball The method of putting the ball in play by tossing it between two opponents who are in one of the restraining circles.

Rebound A term usually applied when the ball bounces or bounds from the backboard or basket.

Restraining circles Three circles of six-foot radius, one located in the center of the court and one located at each of the free-throw circles.

Roving player A player who crosses the division line to become her team's third or fourth player.

Screen An attempt to protect a teammate's play by shutting off an opponent's approach without personal contact.

Set shot A shot taken at the basket from a "set" or stationary position, usually 20 feet or more from the basket.

Starting play Jump ball in center circle.

Tagging Contact with opponent by using hand, elbow, or body constantly or repeatedly.

Three-second lane violation A forward without the ball may not remain inside the free-throw lane for more than three seconds while her team has possession of the ball in her half of the court.

Throw in A method of putting the ball in play from out of bounds.

Time-outs Taken when the ball is dead or when a coach or a team in possession of the ball requests it. Time-outs are taken for all fouls and jump balls, substitutes, injuries, or official's decision. A *team* may call time-out not more than five times during a game for no more than one minute each time. One additional time out is permitted in each additional overtime period.

Traveling When a player in possession of the ball within bounds progresses illegally in any direction.

Violation An infringement of rules resulting in the ball being put into play from out of bounds. Violations can occur on the center throw and on a jump ball. Common violations include handling the ball, traveling with the ball, holding the ball for more than five seconds on the court when closely guarded, or ten seconds on the free-throw line, or five seconds out of bounds; line violations, and the three-second violation.

SELECTED REFERENCES

Barnes, Mildred J., *Girls' Basketball*. New York: Sterling Publishing Co., Inc., 1965.

Bell, Mary, *Women's Basketball*. Dubuque, Iowa: William C. Brown Company, Publishers, 1964.

Division of Girls' and Women's Sports, *Basketball Guide*. Washington, D.C.: American Association for Health, Physical Education and Recreation (current edition). (Selected articles, rules, visual aid listings, drills, questions and answers contained in current and past guides.)

Meyer, Margaret, and Marguerite Schwarz, *Team Sports for Girls and Women* (4th ed.). Philadelphia: W. B. Saunders Co., 1965.

Miller, Donna Mae, and Katherine L. Ley, *Individual and Team Sports for Women*. Englewood Cliffs, N.J.: Prentice-Hall, Inc., 1955.

Neal, Patsy, *Basketball Techniques for Women*. New York: The Ronald Press Company, 1966.

Pinholster, Garland F., *Illustrated Basketball Coaching Techniques*. Englewood Cliffs, N.J.: Prentice-Hall, Inc., 1960.

Vannier, Maryhelen, and Hally Beth Poindexter, *Individual and Team Sports for Girls and Women* (2nd ed.). Philadelphia: W. B. Saunders Co., 1968.

Bowling

ORIGIN AND DEVELOPMENT

Existing records indicate that a form of bowling may be traced back as far as 7000 years. Archeological studies of ancient Egyptians provide us with evidence of implements for playing a game similar in some respects to our modern game of bowling. Variations of the modern game were developed in Europe around 1000 to 1500 years ago, with alleys consisting of outdoor areas on open greens. The original bowls were spherical stones, probably not equipped with holes for the fingers as we find in modern equipment, but held in the open hand. The ninepin game was developed in Germany. Martin Luther was an enthusiastic bowler and is credited with having standardized the number of pins at nine. The game was brought to America by the early settlers who utilized the sport as a recreational activity in the colonies.

The ninepin game became increasingly popular with the colonists and in 1840 the Knickerbocker Alleys were built in New York City. The game lost favor with governmental authorities when gamblers began wagering on the outcome of matches, and in 1841 the game was outlawed in Connecticut. In order to circumvent the law and continue the game of bowling a tenth pin was added, thus changing the name to tenpins. Tenpins soon became popular over the country but there was a wide variation in size of pins, length of alleys, rules of play, and general regulations governing the game. The American Bowling Congress (ABC) was organized in 1895 and was given the task of establishing a standardized set of rules governing play, equipment, and tournament competition. The Woman's International Bowling Congress was organized in 1916 and was followed soon afterwards by the American Junior Bowling Congress. Bowling is now one of the fastest growing indoor sports in America; it is estimated that over 30,000,000 persons engage in the sport with varying degrees of regularity.

In addition to tenpin bowling there are two other forms of bowling played in various sections of the country and promoted by National Organizations. Duckpin bowling is governed by the National Duckpin Bowling Congress, and lawn bowling is under the direction of the American Lawn Bowling Association. In duckpin bowling the pins and balls are

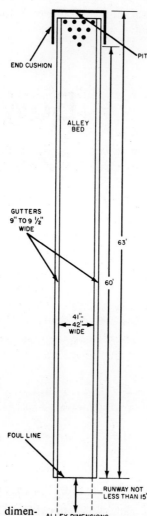

FIGURE 10-1. Lane dimensions

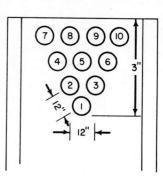

FIGURE 10-2. Position and number of pins

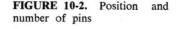

FIGURE 10-3. Dimensions and shape of bowling pin

smaller than in regulation tenpin bowling, and, as the name implies, lawn bowling is played on an outdoor surface.

NATURE OF THE GAME

The modern game of tenpins is played on indoor wooden lanes, 60 feet in length from foul line to number one pin, and 41 or 42 inches in width. (See Fig. 10-1.) The tenpins are located in diamond formation on pin spots 12 inches apart, center to center. (See Fig. 10-2.) A regulation tenpin is 15 inches high with a diameter at the base of two and one-fourth inches, and is constructed of clear, hard maple. (See Fig. 10-3.) A bowling ball is actually constructed of a mixture of natural and synthetic rubber, cotton, sulphur, and carbon black, which acts as a softener to accelerate the mixing process. Balls may not exceed 27 inches in circumference, with weights ranging from a minimum of ten pounds

to a maximum of 16 pounds. Balls are bored with two or three holes in which the player places his fingers to hold the ball in preparation for delivery on the lane. The game is played by rolling the balls down a wooden lane in an effort to knock down the pins stationed at the end of the lane opposite the bowler.

Bowling is an excellent recreational activity for all ages and both sexes. Because of the relatively small expenditure of energy required to participate in the game, it may be played for years after more strenuous activities have been abandoned.

BASIC RULES

Two lanes immediately adjoining each other are used in all games of league or tournament play, and the bowling of ten complete frames on these lanes constitutes an official game. Members of contesting teams successively and in regular order bowl one frame on one lane, and for the next frame alternate and use the other lane, so alternating each frame until the game is completed. Each player bowls two balls in each frame unless a strike is made on the first ball, in which case the second ball is not rolled, except in the tenth frame if a strike or spare is made the player immediately rolls on the same lane the additional balls or ball to which the strike or spare entitles him.

In case of a tie game, each team bowls one complete frame on the same lane in which the tenth frame was bowled, bowling and scoring said extra frame in exactly the same manner as the tenth frame. If, at the completion of the first extra frame, a tie still exists, teams must change lanes for additional frames that may be required to determine the winner.

It is a foul if a bowler permits any part of his foot, hand, or arm, while in contact with the lanes or runways, to rest upon or extend beyond the foul line at any time after the ball leaves the bowler's hands and passes beyond the foul line. No count is made on a foul ball, and any pins knocked down are immediately respotted. A foul ball counts as a ball bowled by the player. If a player commits a foul which is apparent to both captains or one or more members of each of the opposing teams competing in a league or tournament on the same pair of lanes where the foul is committed, and the foul is not seen by the foul judge or umpire, or recorded by an automatic foul detecting device, a foul shall nevertheless be declared and so recorded.

Pinfall—legal

Every ball delivered by the player shall count, unless declared a dead ball. Pins must then be respotted after the cause for declaring such dead ball has been removed.

1. Pins knocked down by another pin or pins rebounding in play from the side partition or rear cushion are counted as pins down.
2. If, when rolling at a full setup or in order to make a spare, it is discovered immediately after the ball has been delivered that one or more pins are improperly set, although not missing, the ball and resulting pin fall shall be counted. It is each player's responsibility to detect any misplacement of pins and have the setup corrected before he bowls.
3. Pins knocked down by a fair ball, and which remain lying on the lane or in the gutters, or which lean so as to touch kickbacks or side partitions, are termed dead wood and counted as

pins down, and must be removed before the next ball is bowled.

Pinfall—illegal

When any of the following incidents occur the ball counts as a ball rolled, but pins knocked down shall not count.

1. When pins are knocked down or displaced by a ball which leaves the lanes before reaching the pins.
2. When a ball rebounds from the rear cushion.
3. When pins come in contact with the body, arms, or legs of a pin setter and rebound.
4. A standing pin which falls upon removing dead wood or which is knocked down by a pin setter or mechanical pin setting equipment shall not count and must be replaced on the pin spot where it originally stood before delivery of the ball.
5. Pins which are bowled off the lane, rebound, and remain standing on the lane must be counted as pins standing.
6. If in delivering the ball a foul is committed, any pins knocked down by such delivery shall not be counted.

Bowling on wrong lane

When only one player or the lead-off men on both teams bowl on the wrong lane and the error is discovered before another player has bowled, a dead ball shall be declared and the player, or players, required to bowl on the correct lane. When more than one player on the same team has rolled on the wrong lane, the game shall be completed without adjustment and the next game shall be started on the correctly scheduled lane.

Scoring

All players should learn how to score because it adds considerably to the enjoyment of the game if the player can keep an accurate record of the score as it progresses throughout a game. As indicated earlier, a complete game consists of ten frames. If a player does not get a strike or spare in any frame, scoring is just a matter of adding the number of pins knocked down in each frame, and carrying the cumulative total in each succeeding frame. If all pins are knocked down with the first ball, it is called a strike and a cross (X) is marked in the small square in the upper right-hand corner of the frame on the score sheet. If all pins are knocked down with two balls, it is a spare and is indicated by a diagonal mark (/). A strike means that the bowler is credited with ten pins in the frame in which he obtained the strike, plus the number of pins knocked down on two successive balls. Hence no numerical score is marked down when a strike is made, but is delayed until the player has again taken his turn and bowled two more balls. A spare means that a player is entitled to ten pins in the frame in which he obtained the spare, plus the number of pins knocked down on his next ball.

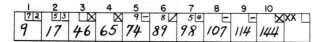

FIGURE 10-4. Score sheet showing method of indicating score

In order to illustrate scoring we shall score a hypothetical game. (See Fig. 10-4.) A bowler starts a game by getting seven pins on his first ball and two of the remaining three pins on his second ball in frame one, giving him a score of nine, which is marked down immediately on the score sheet in frame one. In frame two, the bowler knocks down five pins on his first ball. This number is marked down immediately in the left-hand box of the small boxes located in the upper right-hand corner of the frame area. If he happens to be using a score pad with only one small box, he writes the results of the first ball to the left of the small box. On his second ball in frame two, the bowler gets three of the remaining five pins. This number is written in the right-hand box and the total of the two, eight pins, is the bowler's score for frame two. This number is added to his total for frame one, nine pins, which gives a cumulative total of 17 pins to be marked down in frame two. In frame three, he rolls a strike, so no score is recorded, only a strike mark (X) in the small box in the upper right-hand corner. In frame four, he rolls another strike and still no score is recorded in frame three because he has not yet rolled two additional balls after the strike in frame three. In frame five, he hits nine pins on his first ball, so this number is immediately recorded in the upper box. Now the score may be computed for frame three, because he has rolled two balls after his strike in that frame. We obtain the score for frame three by totaling the score of two strikes and nine pins, or 29 pins, which is added to his total of 17 pins in frame two, making a total score of 46 pins for frame three.

On his second ball in frame five, he misses the single pin, for an error, so his score may be totaled

for frames four and five. The score in frame four is obtained by adding 19 pins (ten for the strike and nine for the two additional balls in frame five) to the score of 46 in frame three, for a total of 65 in frame four. Since he did not strike or spare in frame five, his score is increased by nine, the number of pins obtained in this frame, making a total of 74 pins through frame five. On his first ball in frame six, he obtains eight pins, so this number is marked down in the upper box. On the second ball he gets the remaining two pins for a spare, so a mark (/) indicating this is marked down in the upper box. This means that his score in frame six is ten, plus the number of pins that he obtains on his first ball in frame seven. On his first ball in frame seven, he obtains five pins, which gives him a total of 15 pins to be added to his previous total of 74 in frame five, or a total of 89 in frame six. On his second ball in frame seven he obtains four of the remaining five pins for a total of nine pins, giving him a total of 98 pins through frame seven. In frame eight he obtains nine pins on two balls, which added to 98 gives a total of 107 pins through frame eight. In frame nine, seven pins are knocked down on two balls, giving a score of 114 through frame nine. In frame ten our bowler gets a strike, which entitles him to roll two additional balls. He obtains strikes on both additional balls, giving him a score of 30 pins for frame ten, or a total of 144 for the complete game. A careful study of these directions and the accompanying score sheet should enable anyone to learn the fundamentals of scoring in a short time.

Automatic scoring machines have been developed which record the score immediately after a person bowls, but the machines are rather expensive and it will probably be some time before they are in general use. Knowing how to score adds to the interest and enjoyment of the game, so all students should acquire this knowledge and skill.

TECHNIQUES AND FUNDAMENTALS

If one is to become proficient at bowling, he must give proper attention to such fundamentals as selection of correct equipment, employment of proper stance, and adoption of a standard number of steps in the approach which will enable him to move toward the foul line with a smooth, rhythmical movement.

Equipment

It is important to select a ball equipped with holes that fit the fingers. Balls are bored with two

FIGURE 10-5. Position of fingers in three-hole ball

FIGURE 10-6. Bowling shoes

or three holes. One should try both and determine which feels more comfortable and which can be controlled with the least effort. If a bowler's fingers are weak, he may feel the need of three fingers in order to properly control the ball, although many expert bowlers who have strong fingers use the two-hole ball because they feel it can be handled with greater accuracy. The holes should be large enough for the fingers to slip in and out easily. The thumb hole should be comfortably loose, the finger holes comfortably snug. To determine the correct fit of a bowling ball, place thumb completely in thumb hole, fingers relaxed and spread over finger holes. The crease of the second joint of the fingers should extend a quarter of an inch beyond the inside edge of the finger holes. The holes should not be too large, as extra pressure will have to be exerted to hold the ball in the act of delivery. As one progresses in bowling, he may wish to own his own ball, in which event he should purchase one with holes bored to fit his particular needs. Women generally use balls lighter in weight than those used by men. Most modern lanes have an adequate supply of both types of balls for use by bowlers. (See Fig. 10-5.)

Another important item in the bowler's list of equipment is proper footwear. Most commercial lanes will not permit bowlers on the lanes unless dressed in regulation bowling shoes. The right-handed bowler should use a shoe with a leather sole on the left foot (to facilitate sliding at the release) and a rubber sole on the right shoe. The left-handed bowler reverses this order. While bowling establishments have shoes to rent, it is more economical for a person to own his own shoes if he bowls regularly. Shoes are available in a variety of colors and styles and range in price from $5 to $15. (See Fig. 10-6.)

Stance

There is no definite or prescribed stance assumed by all bowlers in preparation for the start of their delivery movement. Whether one stands erect or crouched, the feet should be slightly spread and the ball held in a comfortable position in front of the body. The ball should be held with both hands, somewhere between the waist and chin, the left hand giving major support to the weight of the ball until the right arm is lowered as a part of the approach and delivery. On the backswing, the ball should not be raised higher than a plane parallel with the shoulders.

Approach

Bowlers vary in the number of steps taken in the approach. The number of steps ranges from three to five, with more bowlers using four steps than any other number. One should experiment with the delivery and decide upon a definite number of steps—it is not advisable to be continually changing delivery form. Using a four-step approach, the right-handed bowler will take his first step with the right foot, following with the left, then right, and completing the delivery with the left foot forward. If three or five steps are used in the approach, the first step will be taken with the left foot. In proper execution of the approach, the bowler should move from his starting position toward the foul line in a smooth rhythmical motion that will allow him to keep control of his body and the ball both while in motion and at the completion of the last step when the ball is released on the lane.

Starting from a comfortable standing position, either erect or crouched, with ball held in both hands in front of the body, step first with the right foot

FIGURE 10-7. Beginning stance and steps used in 4-step approach

(in four-step delivery) and at the same time prepare to push the ball forward in front of the body. (See Fig. 10-7.) As the second step is taken the ball is continued on the downward and backward swing, reaching the peak of the backswing as the right foot is planted on the floor in completion of the third step. While taking the fourth and last step, the bowler starts the ball forward and releases it as he completes the fourth step. The first and second steps should be short, natural steps, with momentum and step-length increasing on the last two steps. The last step is the longest, and forward momentum should be checked by a slide on the left foot at completion of the approach. The toe of the left foot should be pointed toward the target and the right leg and foot should be behind the body.

Release of ball

The ball should be released out in front of the body and laid, not dropped, on the lane. The bowling ball, when properly delivered, has a double motion. When first released it slides and revolves, sliding in the direction toward the pins and revolving toward the left gutter in the case of a right-handed bowler throwing a hook ball. After sliding a certain distance, friction decreases the slide action and the revolving effect takes over, causing the ball to hook, back up, or roll straight forward, depending upon the direction of the rotation movement. A hook ball breaks toward the left and a backup ball toward the right for a right-handed bowler.

The straight ball

Beginning bowlers should concentrate on perfecting the straight ball before attempting to roll a hook or curve. In rolling a straight ball, the thumb should be held in the twelve o'clock position with the fingers underneath the ball. This position should be maintained throughout the delivery, with no rotation of the arm during release of the ball. (See Figs. 10-8 and 10-9.) The ball should be started from the right side of the lane and directed so that it will strike in the 1-3 pocket. (See Fig. 10-10.)

The hook ball

Most good bowlers use a hook ball; beginning bowlers will want to learn this delivery as soon as

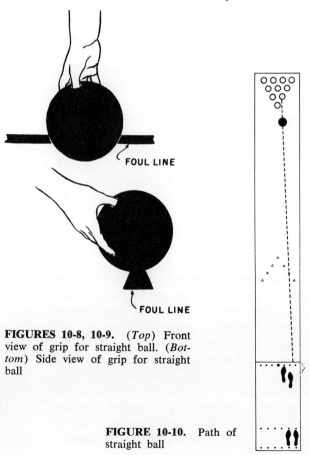

FIGURES 10-8, 10-9. (*Top*) Front view of grip for straight ball. (*Bottom*) Side view of grip for straight ball

FIGURE 10-10. Path of straight ball

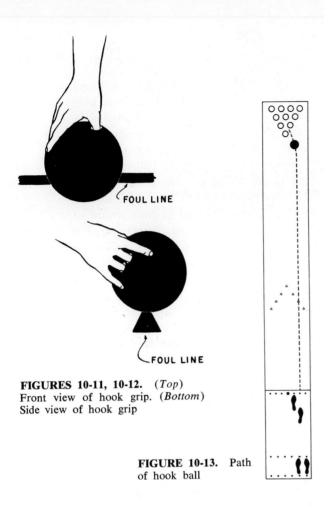

FIGURES 10-11, 10-12. (*Top*) Front view of hook grip. (*Bottom*) Side view of hook grip

FIGURE 10-13. Path of hook ball

combine arm rotation and forceful lift of the fingers in order to obtain maximum hook on the ball. This is perhaps the most difficult of hook ball deliveries to master and should be used only by bowlers who bowl regularly. (See Fig. 10-13.)

The curve ball

The curve ball is difficult to control and is not recommended for beginning bowlers. In this type of delivery the ball travels more slowly and the ball follows a wide curve in approaching the pins. (See Fig. 10-14.)

The backup or reverse hook delivery

In a backup delivery the ball travels first straight forward or to the left, and then breaks to the right for a right-handed bowler. (See Fig. 10-16.) This type of delivery is not recommended because it is difficult to control, gives fewer strikes than the hook ball because of reduced pin-mixing action, produces more splits than other deliveries, and often results in difficult pin leaves. A backup ball results when the forearm is rotated clockwise, or the thumb comes out of the ball late, imparting a lift to the ball, instead of the lift coming from the fingers. (See Fig. 10-15.)

possible. To obtain maximum pin action, the ball should strike the pins at an angle, but the angle of the straight ball is limited by the width of the alley. The straight ball revolves forward, but the hook ball revolves at an angle, thus giving it greater pin splash or action by imparting a revolving action to the pins themselves. To obtain a hook on the ball, the bowler should release the ball with the V formed by the thumb and first finger pointing toward the target. The thumb is released first and as the ball leaves the fingers a rotation effect is imparted to the ball. (See Figs. 10-11 and 10-12.) This delivery is sometimes called the "handshake" delivery because the position of the hand is similar to that used in an ordinary handshake. After release of the ball the hand should be carried upward and forward toward the pins in the follow-through. Some bowlers obtain an increased hook on the ball by rotating the arm in the counter-clockwise direction as the ball is released. Other bowlers increase the hook by forcefully lifting the fingers upward as the ball is released. In this delivery the fingers leave the ball last and impart a vigorous lift to the ball, which gives it a strong counter-clockwise spin. Many professional bowlers

FIGURE 10-14. Path of curve ball

FIGURE 10-15. Release of backup ball

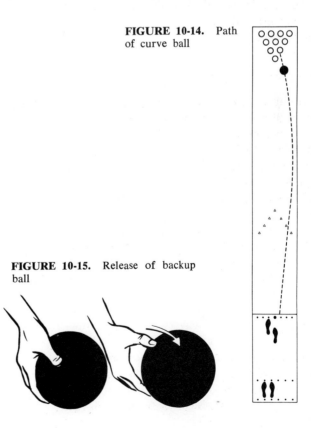

FIGURE 10-16. Path of backup ball

FIGURE 10-17. Lifting ball from ball rack

PLAYING STRATEGY

Being an individual sport, bowling has no complicated playing strategies similar to those found in many team sports. One should plan his game so as to knock down the greatest number of pins possible. This is accomplished by individual control and accuracy, rather than cooperation with teammates in execution of plays.

Playing strategy should include first a mastery of a definite approach and delivery style. The good bowler will settle upon a definite pattern as early as possible, making every effort to throw each ball with the same motion. Most bowlers are classified as "spot" or "pin" bowlers. The spot bowler selects a spot on the alley a few feet from the foul line over which he attempts to roll his first ball in each frame. The pin bowler looks at the pins while approaching and making his delivery. Whether throwing a hook or a straight ball, the bowler should follow his selected style on all balls and concentrate on developing accuracy with a smooth and rhythmical delivery. To make a decent score the bowler must pick up spares consistently. Accuracy is essential for good spare bowling.

SAFETY

Bowling is about as safe an activity as is found in our list of recreational activities. Accidents have been caused by bowlers releasing the ball on the backswing and permitting it to strike spectators or fellow-bowlers in the rear of the lane. Obviously this may be prevented by having the ball well under control at all times. Slippery or rough surfaces on the approach may cause the bowler to fall, so it is wise to test the approaches and become aware of any irregularities before beginning competition. Pin setters have been injured when bowlers rolled the ball into the pits before the pins were spotted. See that workers are ready before rolling and this danger element can be eliminated. Bowlers have been known to have their fingers crushed by improper removal of the ball from the retaining rack. In order to eliminate possibility of injury, the bowler should always pick up the ball with the palms of the hands parallel to the sides of the bowling rack. (See Fig. 10-17.)

HELPFUL HINTS

1. Select a ball that fits your hand.
2. Practice your approach at home; some object such as an old flat iron may be carried to simulate the bowling ball.
3. Dress properly for bowling. Wear loose-fitting clothing and, if bowling on a strange lane for the first time, find out requirements regarding use of bowling shoes. Managers in most lanes require that regulation bowling shoes be worn.
4. Having taken your stance, concentrate on your delivery and ignore any remarks that may come your way from the spectators.
5. Control your temper. Public exhibition of anger disturbs fellow bowlers and detracts from your efficiency.
6. Bowl, do not throw the ball.

PLAYING COURTESIES

1. Do not talk to or otherwise disturb a bowler who is on the approach and ready to bowl.
2. Do not walk in front of a bowler to secure your ball from the rack when the bowler is ready to bowl. Use one ball only—wait for its return.
3. When bowlers on adjacent lanes are both ready to bowl, the one on the right should always be permitted to bowl first.

4. Do not use a ball that is the personal property of some individual unless given permission to do so by the owner.

5. Be at your post ready to bowl when your turn comes.

6. After delivering the ball and noting the result, turn and walk back immediately to the rear of runway, being careful to stay in your approach lane.

7. Do not argue with the foul line judge over decisions even though you think an unjust call has been made against you.

8. Be punctual when scheduled to bowl. Nothing upsets a team more than having to wait for a late member.

TERMINOLOGY

Anchor   The person who shoots last on a team. An anchor is the symbol of hope.

Baby split   The 1-7 or 3-10 railroads.

Backup   A reverse hook. A backup rotates toward the right for a right-handed bowler.

Bed posts   The 7-10 railroad.

Blow   An error; missing a spare that is not a split.

Box   The same as a frame.

Brooklyn   A cross-over ball, one that strikes in the 1-2 pocket.

Bucket   The 2-4-5-8 or 3-5-6-9 leaves.

Cherry   Chopping off the front pin on a spare.

Cross-over   Same as a Brooklyn.

Double   Two strikes in succession.

Double pinochle   The 7-6 and 4-10 split.

Dutch 200 or Dutchman   A score of 200 made by alternating strikes and spares for entire game.

Error   Same as a "blow." Failure to make a spare that is not a split.

Foul   To touch or go beyond the foul line in delivering the ball.

Frame   The box in which scores are registered. There are ten frames to each game.

Gutter ball   A ball that drops into either gutter.

Handicap   A bonus score or score adjustment awarded to individual or team based on averages.

Head pin   The number one pin.

High hit   Hitting the head pin full in the face or head-on.

Hook   A ball that breaks to the left for a right-handed bowler.

Jersey side   Same as a Brooklyn.

Kegler   Synonym for bowler, derived from the German "kegel."

Lane   A bowling alley.

Light hit   Hitting the head pin lightly to the right or left side.

Line   A complete game as recorded on the score sheet.

Mark   Obtaining a strike or spare.

Open frame   A frame in which no mark is made; at least one pin remains standing after rolling both balls in a frame.

Pocket   Space between the head pin and pins on either side.

Railroad   Terms used by some for a split. There are several kinds.

Sleeper   A hidden pin.

Spare   All pins knocked down on two balls.

Split   A leave after first ball has been thrown in which number one pin is down and an intervening pin is down between pins that remain standing. Indicated by 0 on score sheet.

Spot   A place on the alley at which a bowler aims.

Strike   All pins knocked down on the first ball.

Striking out   Obtaining three strikes in the last frame.

Tap   When a pin is left standing on an apparently perfect hit.

Turkey   Three strikes in a row.

SELECTED REFERENCES

ABC *Bowling Guide.* Milwaukee, Wis.: American Bowling Congress, 1572 East Capitol Drive (current edition).

Andsley, J., *Bowling for Women.* New York: Sterling Publishing Co., Inc., 1964.

Archibald, John J., *Bowling for Boys and Girls.* Chicago: Follett Publishing Company, 1963.

Canter, *et al., The Complete Guide to Better Bowling.* New York: Maco Magazine Corporation, 1959.

Casady, Donald, and Maria Liba, *Beginning Bowling.* Belmont, Calif.: Wadsworth Publishing Co., Inc., 1962.

Clause, F., *How to Win at Bowling.* New York: Fleet Publishing Co., 1962.

Day, Ned, *How to Bowl Better*. New York: Arco Publishing Co., Inc., 1960.

Dawson, Taylor, *The Secret of Bowling Strikes*. New York: A. S. Barnes & Co., Inc., 1960.

Division for Girls' and Women's Sports, *Official Bowling, Fencing and Golf Guide*. Washington, D.C.: American Association for Health, Physical Education and Recreation (current edition).

Forslund, E. M., *Bowling for Women*. New York: The Ronald Press Company, 1964.

Fraley, Oscar, *The Complete Handbook of Bowling*. Englewood Cliffs, N.J.: Prentice-Hall, Inc., 1958.

McMahon, Junie, and Murray Goodman, *Modern Bowling Techniques*. New York: The Ronald Press Company, 1958.

Vannier, Maryhelen, and Hally Beth Poindexter, *Individual and Team Sports for Girls and Women* (2nd ed.). Philadelphia: W. B. Saunders Co., 1968.

Weinberg, J., *Duck Pin Bowling*. New York: A. S. Barnes & Co., Inc., 1954.

Dance

ORIGIN AND DEVELOPMENT

That dance in some form has existed since primitive times is an accepted fact. Whether the dance is an expression of war and combat; the portrayal of religious rites; a more stilted form involving complex techniques and artificialities; the informal expression of man's work and play experiences; the attempt to interpret by means of movement the life of earlier peoples as depicted through sculpture, painting, and poetry; the attempt to seek novel steps with little artistic, cultural, or aesthetic value; or the desire of the individual to express through movement his own reactions to the world in which he lives—we have continued to recognize the need of man to give expression through bodily movement. Thus in studying the various ages of culture that preceded our present forms of rhythmic expression, we note the activities of primitive man; the aesthetic age of the early Greek civilization followed by its decline with the conquest of the barbaric Romans; the medieval period and the influence of asceticism; the order of the Renais-

sance with the recognition of individual rights, and our recent, so-called contemporary period.

In the United States, many of the forces that have had an impact on the development of the dance have been those with a direct bearing on the history of our country. The Indians with their tribal and ceremonial dances, the conservative Puritans, the people of many countries bringing their folk lore with them, the southern Negroes, the western cowboys, are but a few of the groups from which we draw our dance heritage. We cannot fail to recognize, in addition to the historical-geographical factors affecting the dance of today, such ever-present and tremendous powers as those exerted by the rapid progress of science, the economical and political status, and the pace of the present-day world.

As types of dance typical of the United States we have the Indian, Tap and Clog, Folk, Square and Country, Social, and Modern dance. Of these, the most commonly found in the college physical education program at present are Folk, Square, and Modern dance. Probably because of its generally accepted recreational value, square dancing has become a very popular activity. Various centers in the

United States have done much to promote this wholesome and thoroughly enjoyable type of dance. Among such centers, mention should be made of Michigan (particularly Dearborn), Colorado, the New England States (with concentration especially about the Boston area), the southern mountain groups, and California.

Modern dance, because of its great scope of possibilities in creative, artistic, and aesthetic forms, has a strong appeal to the college student. From an educational point of view, it affords an opportunity to every student to understand and appreciate body movement, and to learn how it in turn may be used as a means to a creative experience. Although not everyone has the potential ability of achieving the high level of the dance artist, every student should experience the techniques and fundamentals that will enable him to progress to his own potentialities.

FUNDAMENTALS OF LOCOMOTOR MOVEMENT COMMON TO ALL DANCES

In order to dance, one must move. Although such movement may at times be confined only to the body, more commonly it requires a special consideration requiring the use of various forms of locomotion in which the body weight is transferred by the feet, or foot. All forms of locomotion can be reduced to five fundamental steps: walk, run, leap, jump, and hop. Any other type of locomotor activity is a combination of these basic steps. Closely related to the five fundamental steps are the skip, slide, and gallop, and often reference is made to the eight fundamental means of locomotion.

WALK. The weight is transferred from one foot to the other, alternately, one foot always being in contact with the ground. The usual foot action is a transfer of weight from the heel to the ball of one foot, during which time the other leg is pushing off, then swinging through to assume its position in the sequence of action.

RUN. The speed of the walk is increased and there is a brief period when neither foot is in contact with the ground.

LEAP. By means of a strong push-off from *one* foot, the body is lifted off the ground momentarily; the body weight then returns on the *opposite* foot. The leap differs from the run in that more energy is needed, and there is a longer period between transfer of weight due to a longer period of suspension in the air. The leap may be either for height or distance.

JUMP. The body springs into the air by one of the following means:

1. A single-foot take-off, landing on both feet.
2. A two-foot take-off, landing on one foot.
3. A two-foot take-off, landing on two feet.

A jump may be made for either height or distance.

HOP. By means of a strong push-off from one foot, the body is lifted off the ground momentarily; the weight then returns to the *same* foot.

These five steps are all done to an even beat, sometimes designated as *long*. Thus all these forms could be done to a beat graphically represented as ——— ——— ——— ——— ———. Should the pattern become uneven (long-short), one of the three related remaining forms of locomotion would fit into the beat: skip, slide, gallop. The graphic presentation would be ——— – ——— – ——— – ——— – or in reverse order.

SKIP. A combination of a step and a hop, done to an uneven beat in which the step is given the long time value and the hop the short value: ——— – ——— – ——— –.

st hop st hop st hop

Note: Were each part given equal time value, a step-hop would result instead of a skip.

——— ——— ——— ——— ——— ———

step hop step hop step hop

In performing the skip, there is a feeling of elevation resulting from the natural tendency to swing the free leg forward and upward.

SLIDE. The weight is transferred from one foot to the other by means of a step on one foot followed by a quick drawing up of the other foot with an immediate transfer of weight to it.

GALLOP. A leap step combination in which the foot executing the step is brought up to but not beyond the foot that has completed the leap. The leap is done with slight height, and distance is not a factor.

SQUARE AND FOLK DANCE

Before describing the terms common to the square dance, mention must be made of the related quadrilles that may or may not have been the stem from which emerged square dancing as we know it today. Although square dancing has existed for many years among our western cowboys and southern mountain folk, quadrille dancing is believed to be derived from European dances, and was danced by early Americans. The quadrille is executed precisely

FIGURE 11-1. Circle eight hands round

and in a stately manner. It is done in sets of four couples forming a square, opposite couples numbered one, two, and three, four. Most figures are performed by opposite couples or in a circle of four.

The square dance, however, is energetic, lively, and bouncy, with many changing figures involving combinations of couples or single man or single woman, or the entire group. In square dancing, the starting formation is always that of four couples facing the center of a square, one couple on each side of the square. At all times in every couple formation, the lady must be placed to the right of the gentleman. The head couple (couple number one) is commonly designated as the one with its back to the music, which is usually located at the head of the hall. The couple to the right is couple number two, and so on around the square. If, for any reason, this arrangement is not followed, the leader of the dances will indicate the head couple.

Music for square dancing usually consists of the frequently heard and well-known melodies such as *Comin' Round the Mountain, Little Brown Jug, Turkey in the Straw, Arkansas Traveller,* and other similar and rather simple tunes. Frequently the accompaniment is played by a fiddler, and at times piano, banjo, or guitar is added to the accompaniment. For class work, the piano is very satisfactory. Excellent inexpensive recordings of square dance music and calls have become available recently, and that type of accompaniment is very satisfactory.

Calling for square dancing requires a great amount of practice, understanding, voice control, and ability to handle a large group. Old-time callers, or those with considerable experience and ability,

have a jargon or patter of their own that adds to the spirit of the true square dance. The student, however, can find many references from which he can obtain calls. Anyone attempting calling must have a loud, distinct, and clear voice, a sense of timing, so the calls will immediately precede the figure and produce continuity in the dance, and a thorough knowledge of the dance figures.

Folk dance originated with peasants of the country, who gathered together to express various feelings through dance. Thus we have expression of work (*Shoemaker's Dance*), feeling for environment (*Mountain March*), or the pure joy found in so many folk dances. The early dancers, the folk people, took pleasure in these meetings and emphasized freedom rather than exactitude of step or formation. As these dances were passed along from one generation to another, they tended to lose either the step pattern or the formation. This accounts for the differences in descriptions of the same dance as reported by various authors. The most outstanding effort to preserve the true folk dance of many countries was made by Elizabeth Burchenal. Since then others have visited the countries and described the dances as they have come to be performed.

Terms and figures common to square and folk dance

ALLEMANDE LEFT. Gentleman gives his left hand to the lady on his left (his corner lady). With left hands joined, they walk around one another and then both return to place. This is sometimes followed by an allemande right in which the gentleman executes the same figure but with his right hand lady (his partner). More frequently the allemande left is followed by a grand right and left.

BALANCE. There are three ways this step is performed, the difference due partly to locale, and also due to the use to which the step is put. (1) Done as a step swing, partners (or whatever the call may be) will face each other and execute a step right followed immediately by a hop right, at which time the left leg is swung across the body, then continue with a step-hop left and a right swing. (2) Another type of balance is done with partners facing, each stepping backward four steps followed by a curtsey, and then stepping forward four steps. Sometimes it is done with two steps back, curtsey, and two steps forward. When "balance home" is called for, this type of balance step is preferred to the step-swing type. (3) The third kind of balance is actually a sashay (or *chassé*) step—a slide step to the right or left—as called.

CIRCLE EIGHT HANDS ROUND. Four couples join hands, and with a walking step circle to the left and frequently follow with a circle to the right. "Circle four hands" (two couples) or "six hands" (three couples) is often called. Different parts of the country will offer variations to the way the walk is done. In some sections it becomes a shuffle of the feet, in others it is done as a semi-sideways walk with an occasional two-step inserted into the sequence.

CORNER. In square formation, all couples facing center, your corner is the person to the man's left and the woman's right.

DO-SI-DO (*dos-a-dos, docey-do*) PARTNERS (corners, opposites). Face the person with whom the step is to be performed, advance toward him, pass right shoulder. Without turning around, pass back to back, cross over right and then, walking backward, return to place. Each person always remains facing in his starting direction.

DOWN. Toward the foot of the formation, if long-wise. Sometimes means through the center, as "down the center and cast off two."

DOWN THE CENTER AND AROUND THE OUTSIDE. The couple, number one for example, walks forward and between man and woman standing opposite and, depending upon the call, will either separate (see *Separate*) or, still in couple formation, go to the man's left around the outside of the set and back to position.

ELBOW SWING. Couples link elbows and make a complete turn, not advancing. Frequently done as a "grand right and left with an elbow swing," in which case the formation of a grand right and

left is used, but when couples meet they hook elbows and make a complete swing before advancing to the next person. In this call, elbow swings will alternate right and left on around the set.

TO FALL BACK. Retract from lead forward.

FACE FORWARD. Refers to the line of direction, the position at the start of the dance.

FIGURE EIGHT (as in Lady 'Round the Lady). With couple number one facing couple number two, each lady walks forward as if to go between the facing couple, around the approaching lady, moving to the left and back to back, then back to place. As the women start back, the men will perform the same figure with one another. As soon as the man starts moving back to place, the lady will start forward toward the opposite man, pass back to back, and back to place. The men, on this same part, will advance slightly to take part in the figure "gent 'round the lady and lady 'round the gent."

FOOT. The opposite of *Head*, thus the foot of the hall or the foot couple, facing head couple. Couple number three is the foot couple.

FORWARD AND BACK. To lead forward and back, done singly, in partners, threes, fours, sixes, and so on. In English folk dancing it can be "forward and back a double," meaning three steps and close forward, and three steps and close backward.

FORWARD AND PASS THROUGH. Couples, threes, or fours, etc., lead forward and each person crosses over to the opposite side. When done in couples, each lady passes as if to give right hand to opposite man.

GRAND RIGHT AND LEFT. Partners face one another in a circle or square formation that will always remain the line of direction. The man then moves counterclockwise and the lady clockwise around the circle unless a change of direction is called. Partners give right hands to one another, pass right shoulders, and walk in the direction each is facing. As another person is approached, the left hand is extended and the right hands dropped. This continues on around the circle—right hands, left hands, and so on—until each person has returned to his original starting position. This will mean that partners pass once when half way around the circle. Sometimes the call is "Grand right and left half way round and promenade home," in which case the grand right and left continues only until partners meet half way around. From there the lady turns about in the direction her partner was moving and promenades with him until they reach their original position.

HEAD. Can refer to the top of the hall (where orchestra is located), or to the head couple (with its back to the head of the hall), or to couple number one.

HONOR (*salute, address*) **YOUR PARTNER** (*corner, opposite*). The gentleman bows and the lady curtsies to the person named in the call.

INSIDE (*in*), OUTSIDE (*out*). When couples are in double-line formation, partners facing one another, *inside* (in) means the couples toward the center of the hall or the center of the formation, as for Fireman's Dance. *Outside* (out) means the couples toward the outside of the hall. *In* and *out* can refer also, then, to the direction in which the step is to be performed.

LADIES' CHAIN. This is done with two couples. The ladies advance across the set, touching right hands as they pass in the center and extending left hands to the opposite gentleman, who turns the lady around in front of him, as in the figure right and left through. The lady repeats the figure, returning to her own partner, who turns her around, and both couples are face to face, having completed the ladies' chain.

GRAND LADIES' CHAIN. All ladies meet in the center, join right hands high and circle half way around the square, in clockwise direction. They give their left hands to the opposite gentleman, who turns the lady in front of him around. The figure is repeated, thus finishing in the original position from which the figure was begun.

TO LEAD. Advance forward, usually with a walk or slight springing step (English)—done in single, partner, or other formation.

ONES, TWOS, etc. Refers to single, partners, threes, etc. *Threes* can be partners plus one, two women and one man, or two men and one woman.

PARTNER. The person with whom you dance. In a side-by-side position, the woman is always on the right. Sometimes partners are changed and you will have a new partner, or you will temporarily dance with another and return to your partner.

PROMENADE. Walk with partners wherever the call indicates—usually around the square. Partners join hands in the promenade, right hand in right hand, left in left, so that the gentleman's right arm is over the lady's left. This is sometimes referred to as the "skating position" in other dances.

HALF PROMENADE is done only half way around the square.

RIGHT-HAND STAR, LEFT-HAND STAR, STAR PROMENADE, RIGHT-HAND MILL. The call will indicate whether the figure is to be performed by all men, all women, opposite couples, and so on. On the right-hand star, indicated persons advance for-

ward, all raise right arms toward center, and, touching hands, walk around the circle. Star promenade means that all will participate with right or left hands, depending upon the call.

RIGHT AND LEFT THROUGH. Two couples facing advance toward each other and, as they pass, the gentleman touches right hands about shoulder height with the opposite lady. As soon as opposites have passed, the gentleman takes his partner's left hand in his left hand and places his right arm about her waist. As he turns his partner around in front of him, both couples will be face to face. The figure is repeated so couples return to their original position to complete the figure right and left through. "Half right and left" is sometimes called, in which case the figure is completed when couples have exchanged places.

SEPARATE. Partners go in different directions, usually man to the left and woman to the right. Common to square dance when couple goes down the center and separates, or when the couple separates and each goes 'round the outside of the set.

SWING YOUR PARTNER. This is a modified social dance position in partners. The gentleman's left arm is extended to the side, his right arm around the lady's waist. The lady puts her right hand in the the gentleman's left, her left hand on the gentleman's shoulder. Stand to the side so that right hips and right feet are in line with one another and almost touching. Using the right foot somewhat as a pivot, push with the left foot so that partners circle about in place, in a clockwise direction. More advanced dancers tend to vary the arm position by giving left hands to each other and each placing right hands on partner's right shoulder. As the swing is performed, partners lean away from one another which results in a vigorous turn.

UP. Toward the head of the formation or head of the hall.

Steps common to square and folk dance

BUZZ STEP (as originally used in Folk Dance) or PIVOT (as commonly used in Square Dance). When done in circle formation, moving to the left, hands joined, step left to side, and with accent step right in front of left. Continue moving left, toes pointed to center of circle, accent on right foot. For Square Dance, see *Swing Your Partner*.

HEEL AND TOE POLKA. This step starts with a hop on the left foot, while at the same time the right leg is extended with heel on the floor, toe up. With another small hop left, the right foot is brought back with toe touching the floor near the left foot.

A polka step follows, starting hop left. The entire step is repeated starting hop right, touching left heel, and so on.

MAZURKA. This is a high brush step right to the side, an immediate close and transfer of weight left, and a hop left. At the time of the hop the right leg is swung out, then the right knee is bent so that the foot comes close to the left knee. The foot is then lowered to the left ankle in readiness for the next muzurka step. This is a strong, vigorous step, done continuously to the same side unless a variation is introduced.

POLKA. Depending on which part of this step one selects as a starting point, it becomes either a hop-step-close-step or a step-close-step-hop. To suggest one of the most satisfactory methods of learning it, let us use the second analysis. Students who have experienced difficulty in executing the step in sequence have picked it up readily by using a forward slide as a basis. A slide four times with the left foot leading, then a change to four slides with the right foot leading, will establish a pattern that can then be reduced to two slides with one foot followed by two slides with the other foot. When this pattern is fixed, the tempo can be increased, and a hop substituted for the second close in the two-slide sequence. Thus we have slide-close-slide-hop, slide-close-slide-hop and the polka step results.

SASHAY (or Chassé). A slide step to right or left, for man or woman or four couples, as call directs.

SCHOTTISCHE. This step is most frequently done by taking three small runs followed by a hop. It is an easy, smooth pattern.

TWO-STEP. A pattern consisting of step, close, step, executed by the transfer of weight from foot to foot similar to the waltz; thus step left, close right, step left.

WALTZ. A pattern consisting of step, step, close, in which it must be remembered that the weight is transferred from one foot to the other; thus step left, step right, close left. The pattern is then repeated, starting with a step right.

Formations common to square and folk dance

SINGLE CIRCLE. Partners side by side, woman *always* on the right of her gentleman partner, all facing center of circle or counterclockwise.

DOUBLE CIRCLE. (1) Partners facing, man with back to center of circle, woman facing center of circle; (2) Partners side by side, each couple facing line of direction, usually counterclockwise to start; (3) Alternate couples facing each other. Thus every other couple faces clockwise.

LINES. (1) Two couples facing two couples (Portland Fancy); (2) Four couples, one in back of the other, all facing head of hall—preferred number for many English Country Dances; (3) Six couples all facing head of hall—preferred number for Virginia Reel.

Representative square and folk dances frequently taught

American:

Long dances: Virginia Reel, Pop Goes the Weasel, Portland Fancy

Quadrille: Lancer's Dance, Uncle Steve's Quadrille

Round dances: Rye Waltz

Circle dances: Old Dan Tucker, Chester Schottische, Cowboy Schottische, Glow Worm, Black Hawk Waltz

Square: Texas Star, Sally Goodin', Lady 'Round the Lady, The Basket

Danish:

Crested Hen, The Hatter, Little Man in a Fix, Totur

Czechoslovakian:

Kanafaska

English:

Sweet Kate, Gathering Peascods, Bean Setting, Black Nag

Finnish:

Pretty Sister-in-Law

German:

At the Inn, Bummel Schottische, Broom Dance

Greek:

Gerakina, Syrtos

Hungarian:

Czebogar, Cifra, Tingi-Lingi Boom

Irish:

Irish Lilt, Rinca Fadha

Israeli:

Hora, Hanoded, Mayim, Kol-Dodi

Italian:

Sicilian Tarantella

Lithuanian:

Turning Dance

Macedonian:

Kolo

Mexican:

La Raspa, Corrido

Norwegian:

Mountain March

Russian:

Koroboushka, Troika, Hopak, Vo Sadu

Scottish:

Gay Gordons, Road to the Isles, Highland Fling

Swedish:

Bleking, Schottische

Swiss:

Weggis, Meitschi Putz Di

Ukrainian:

Hopak

Yugoslavian:

Jovano-Jovanke, Kolo, Krici-Krici

BALLROOM DANCE

Dance positions

CLOSED. Partners facing, standing toe to toe, looking over opposite's right shoulder, man facing line of direction. Man's left hand holds lady's right hand about shoulder height, arms are relaxed and slightly bent at elbows. Man's right hand, fingers closed, placed on partner's back below her left shoulder blade or slightly above her waist. Lady's left hand placed on man's right shoulder, forearm relaxed on man's right upper arm.

SEMI-OPEN. From closed position partners turn slightly away from one another looking in line of direction—man's right and lady's left sides are near each other.

OPEN. From semi-open position, turn so that both are facing in line of direction.

REVERSE OPEN. Partners turn so that both are facing in reverse line of direction—man's left and lady's right sides are near each other. Man's left arm and lady's left arm may be down near side.

Line of direction

In general, couples move about the floor in a counterclockwise circle known as the line of direction (LOD). One may, however, move forward, backward, or sideward within this pattern. On the other hand, there are many new dances such as the frug in which the couples dance in much the same spot.

Style and manners

Every type of dance is performed with a style. The particular dance form, its tempo, and rhythm determine the style with which a particular dance is executed.

The man asks a girl to dance in a simple and direct way. "May I have the next dance?" or "Will you dance with me?" are the two customary approaches. The girl expects to be escorted to and from the floor. A gentleman always thanks the girl for the dance.

At a private party, unless there is a contrary rule, a man may cut in on any couple. At a public dance cutting in is not condoned.

Every dancer should avoid being a show-off, a chatterbox, an iceberg, a crooner, a wrong-way Charlie, or a great lover on the dance floor.

How to lead and follow

The man must indicate his steps and leads sufficiently in advance so that the woman can follow with confidence. He does this primarily with his upper torso, shoulders, and right arm and hand. The right hand becomes the steering rudder.

The woman's principal method of following is to remain relaxed so that her partner may guide her easily.

Fwd—Forward
Bck—Backward
R—Right
L—Left
S—Slow
Q—Quick
Close—Bring one foot to another and
take weight on it.

Man's part is described. Lady's is opposite.
All steps indicated as slow use two beats of
the music, and all steps indicated as quick use one
beat of the music.

Foxtrot 4/4 time

MAGIC STEP.   Basic Rhythmic Pattern S S Q Q
For Man (Lady's part opposite)

1. Closed Position

Fwd Left—S
Fwd Right—S
Side Left—Q
Close right to left—Q

Lead Cue
Lift right arm, lean forward.

2. Semi-open Position

Side Left—S
Cross Right over Left—S
Side Left—Q (return to closed position)
Close right to left—Q

Lead Cue
Pressure with heel of right hand.
Pressure with finger tips of right hand.

3. Turn—Under

(Man's part same as semi-open position varia-
tion)
For Lady:
Side right; start to turn under right arm—S
Complete turn under right arm on to left
foot—S
Side right—Q (return to closed position)
Close left to right—Q
Lady's right and man's left hands are released
during turn.
BOX.   Basic Rhythmic Pattern S Q Q
For Man (Lady's part opposite)
Fwd L—S
Side R—Q

Close L to R—Q
Back R—S
Side L—Q
Close R to L—Q

Waltz 3/4 time

Basic Rhythmic Pattern Q Q Q
For Man (Lady's part opposite)

1. Box

Same as Foxtrot except each step is Q

2. Crossover

Do one-half Box
Cross R over L; semi-open position
Side L; return to closed position
Close R

Lead Cue
Pressure with heel of R hand.
Pressure with finger tips.

Tango 4/4 or 2/4 time

Basic Rhythmic Pattern S S Q Q S
For Man (Lady's part opposite)

1. Basic

Fwd L—S
Fwd R—S
Fwd L—Q
Side R—Q
Draw L to R, weight remaining on R—S

2. Semi-open position

Side L—S
Cross R over L—S
Fwd L—Q
Side R—Q
Draw L to R—S

Lead Cue
Pressure with heel of R hand.
Pressure with finger tips of R hand.

Rhumba 4/4 time

Basic Rhythmic Pattern Q Q S
For Man (Lady's part opposite)

1. Box (closed position)

Side L—Q
Close R—Q
Fwd L—S
Side R—Q
Close L—Q
Back R—S

2. Cuban Walk

Walking forward or backward in the quick quick slow rhythm.

Cha cha cha 4/4 time

Basic Rhythmic Pattern S S Q Q S
For Man (Lady's part opposite)

1. Basic Step (closed position)

dancing to each other with hands held
Forward L—S
Back R—S
Back L—Q
Back R—Q
Back L—S
Back R—S
Fwd L—S
Fwd R—Q
Fwd L—Q
Fwd R—S

2. Cross Step

Cross L—S (reverse open position) Man's L and Lady's R hand joined
In Place R—S
Side L—Q
Close R—Q
Side L—S
Cross R—S (open position) Man's R and Lady's L hand joined
In Place L—S
Side R—Q
Close L—Q
Side R—S

Jitterbug 4/4 time

Basic Rhythmic Pattern S S Q Q

1. Basic Step (closed position)

Place L, then take weight on L—S
Place R, then take weight on R—S
Back L—Q (semi-open position)
Fwd R—Q (return to closed position)

2. Man's part same as for basic step

Lady:
Start to turn to R under R arm on R foot—S
Complete turn under R arm on L foot—S
Back R—facing partner—Q
Fwd L—Q
Start to turn to L under R arm on R foot—S
Complete turn under R arm on L foot—S
Back R—facing partner—Q
Fwd L—Q

MODERN DANCE

Modern or contemporary dance began in the early twentieth century in this country and was another manifestation of the many changes that were occurring in politics, the society, and the art of the day. The "natural" life had great appeal, as did the growing place of women in a society outside the home. Ballet had become ineffectual for the dance expression of young Americans. Isadora Duncan became a primary leader in the protest against weakened dance forms by removing her shoes, donning flowing draperies, becoming an expatriate, and dancing to the loftiest music of Gluck and Beethoven. But it was difficult for Americans to accept her. In Germany, Mary Wigman and Rudolph von Laban were also experimenting in movement forms as media for communication of non-verbal feeling and action. Soon, again in the United States, Martha Graham began experimenting to find the fundamental, original impulse of movement in the body. Gradually she evolved a whole technique of dance movement based on the idea that such movement begins in the center of the body and follows sequentially out to the limbs. Whereas in classical ballet peripheral or limb movements were of prime importance, purity of line preceded motivation, and the central axis of the body was held firmly under control, in the Graham technique motivation was of utmost importance. The central axis was rotated, contracted, or released for expressive and aesthetic purposes, and the floor used as a medium itself for falls, rolls, and heavier, earthy movements. At this same time, Doris Humphrey and Charles Weidman were likewise working on new techniques, and the male contribution to dance was recognized. For the woman also, movement began from the center of the torso and was a result of the play of gravitational forces on the body and the body's reaction to them. Falls, suspensions, and recoveries were the core of her early vocabulary. All of these and other "early moderns" were basically trying to communicate a twentieth century point of view by means of expressive movement that was not derived from arbitrary classical standards, such as ballet. Humanity and our psychological and social heritage were the concern. Most of the major choreographers today are the direct or indirect successors of the above innovators. Scores of experiments and valuable methods have evolved since then, some of which will be mentioned under "Elements of Choreography." Recently, however, there has been a swing back to searching for the purely kinesthetic, abstract (from human emotion), non-dramatic meanings and forms in dance. While the source material for movement may be more "non-human," the techniques used are not balletic, but modern in style.

In the early 1920's, through the efforts and convictions of Margaret H'Doubler, University of Wisconsin, dance found its place in educational institutions along with other art forms. Many colleges and universities now offer undergraduate majors in dance, and some offer advanced degrees.

PRINCIPLES OF MOVEMENT

Movement determined by the body structure

Students of dance must train their instruments, their bodies, to be as fully receptive as possible to the demands that beautiful, skilled movement require. Flexibility, coordination, strength, control, and balance are among the basic tools one should acquire in technical classes. These abilities also enable the dancer to perform special skills such as complex turns, spirals, and falls. A student of the dance may also wish to pursue ballet training, an invaluable discipline for specific development of footwork, precision, and elevation. The beginner should be helped to align her body parts correctly so as to enable her to move as freely and clearly as possible. Each bony portion of the body should be lined up directly over or under another. The head is held level and tall above relaxed (not collapsed) shoulders, under which is a very high (not forward) chest, narrow waist, and pulled up abdomen. The hips are lined directly under the chest, not pushed forward or back. The legs are pulled up straight and high from the feet. Ankles should be straight, not inverted. The body weight is held up from the center of each relaxed foot. The posterior and anterior torso should be high and strong enough to allow the extremities to remain relaxed and free to move. Nothing should be "gripping." Poor posture or alignment not only means limited technical facility, but can ultimately lead to injuries and distortions, or their increase should they already exist.

The beginner should also be encouraged to use her body as openly and fully as possible. This enables her to appreciate movement easily and to feel she is really dancing. Later, as her instrument becomes more lucid and finely "tuned," she is trained to isolate or control specifically all body parts for more subtle, easy, economical expression. Should a dancer wish to display effort, strain, or awkwardness because of the emotional content of the dance (despair, frustration) she is free to do so. Movement may be consciously distorted, for example, by an angular elbow, flexed or extended ankle, or a torso twisted from its normal center. The modern dancer has many ways to portray the emotional and psychological content of her performance, and searches for ways to move to our modern, dissonant, and rhythmically complex music and sounds. She must develop an acute kinesthetic sensitivity so that the sensation of movement, not the visual appearance, becomes her guidepost. Depth, quality, and dynamics of the sensation are conveyed by the dancer to the observer, both of whom thereby have an enriching experience.

Beside such training, the dancer should clearly comprehend the limited number of ways a human being can move:

1. AXIAL MOVEMENTS. Occur in space but do not transport the body from place to place
   (a) Flexion—bending
   (b) Extension—raising or stretching
   (c) Rotation—twisting
   (d) Adduction—moving a body segment toward the central axis of the body
   (e) Abduction—moving a body segment away from the central axis of the body
   (f) Circumduction—circling the entire torso or any body part; a combination of the above
2. LOCOMOTOR MOVEMENTS. Moving from one place to another in space
   (a) Walk-step
   (b) Run
   (c) Leap
   (d) Hop
   (e) Jump
   (f) Combinations of these: skip-step and hop; gallop-step and leap; slide-step and leap moving sideways

Movement determined by the environment and the demands of dance

There are a number of elements of movement that can be analyzed. We move within a specific rhythmic structure, with a variety of muscular forces all having relationship to physical forces such as gravity, acceleration, and momentum. We move in space making designs and through space by means of locomotor patterns.

1. **RHYTHM.** Organizes the movement into repeatable units of time. It is composed essentially of both force and time factors. Dynamics is a frequently preferred term for describing the relationship between force and time.

Rhythmic factors include:

(a) Tempo—variation from fast to slow.

(b) Underlying beat—the steady pulse inherent in a particular movement phrase. Three ways to arrive at a basic beat are through:
   1. Metric or movement counts determined by the accompaniment of movement.
   2. Breath rhythm determined by the intervals of inhalation-exhalation and carried like a pulse through the body.
   3. Emotional rhythm determined by the inner forces of the dancer as she moves and motivates the expressive content of the work.

(c) Phrase—sequence of long and short beats with a feeling of unity; an idea suggested but not complete in itself, though having its own beginning and dynamic line followed by a pause before a new phrase begins.

(d) Accent—emphasis given in movement, sound, force, space, tempo in the beat. Silence, or arrested movement, can be as much an accent as a loud sound or abrupt movement.

(e) Syncopation—an unexpected accent in the general pattern. This engenders surprise and excitement as heard in jazz or felt in clapping two beats while walking three in the same given time. ——— —— —— walk
————— ——— clap
————————— time length

2. **FORCE.** Conveys the quality, texture, or kinesthetic and emotional energy underlying a dance. Energy or force is that factor which enables one to feel these qualitative differences. Muscles and joints are capable of moving with varying degrees and combinations of forces; each is as different as the texture of velvet is from silk or tweed. These forces may be expressed as:

(a) Sustained—an evenly timed, controlled flow of energy. The muscles resist gravity in varying degrees from very very strong to light and airy. There is an equalization of muscle tension, as in movements requiring careful balance or slow motion.

(b) Swing—an alternate swaying, suspended, to and fro use of energy. There is a passive acceleration as the dancer gives in to gravity and a more active retardation as she completes the arc of the swing. The swing has a characteristic beat of three for each phase.

(c) Ballistic—a piston-like thrusting use of energy. The dancer attacks out against gravity and recovers with an equal action before momentum is overcome. There is a gradual dying down of the movement between the two attacks. Such movements usually have an underlying beat of two and need far more energy than does the relaxed swing. A series of vigorous leaps or fast, stiff-kneed high marching steps require ballistic force.

(d) Percussive—a sharp, explosive use of energy. The muscles fixate against gravity as the movement comes to an abrupt halt, rather than "following through." The halt usually occurs in one beat, though the preceding and following movements may be in any other quality and time. Percussive moments are the strongest peaks of a movement. Much of the excitement felt in watching primitive and jazz dance is due to a continual use of percussive energy.

(e) Vibratory—a continuous back and forth use of energy. Short, percussive movements done very rapidly produce this effect but are difficult to prolong because of the high tension and control required to keep them even.

(f) Collapsing—a letting go of muscular energy. The dancer's body or a part of it gives in to the force of gravity. To recover from the fall requires any other use of energy called for to convey the idea in mind. A true collapse occurs in one time interval, a long or short beat.

3. **SPACE.** Limits and defines the movement through the factors of:

(a) Direction
   1. Line of motion—forward, backward, sideward, diagonal, turning, circular.
   2. Focus—use of eyes or a body part, such as a leg, to emphasize a point of attention.

(b) Range
   1. Distance covered—by locomotion.
   2. Degree and number of *joint actions*—in axial movement, from narrow to broad. For example, a greeting by a slight nod or a deep, sweeping bow.

(c) Levels—low through high.

(d) "Body facing"—front, side, diagonal, back,

up, down—all in relation to the location of the *front* of the given work space.

ELEMENTS OF CHOREOGRAPHY

As in music, painting, and the other arts, dance must have both a subject and structure, or content and form. The subject may be something as concrete as a story or character study (representative, denotative) or as abstract as an emotional or mood idea (manifestative, connotative). Movement itself is often used as an initial stimulus to begin a dance; the gestures, principles of movement, and kinesthetic experience of the dancer will suggest further material. For example, she may move forward three beats with her arms raised, then discover a natural swaying of the arms could be used to good advantage by making them move in small arcs. This may suggest a leg gesture of a similar sort the next time she wants to advance forward; this could be done in five beats, then, and with stronger tension and different focus. Eventually, a whole phrase or dance assumes shape.

Modern dancers have been experimenting with many abstract ideas as subject matter. Among these, a student may find interest in explorations of physical principles, such as the movement and structure of the atom, and the effects of centrifugal force on the body. Atonal and 12-tone music, as well as sounds from nature, cities, and electronic machines, are other fields of interest. Objects, such as elastic ropes or large discs, innovations in costume design and material, such as stretchable tent-shapes, and stage sets, such as slanting boards and mesh-wired enclosures, all open many possibilities for original and meaningful dances. There is virtually little in life that could not be the source of creative work. A student may find that nature ideas, the wind, seas, birds, fire, and seasons, suggest qualities and themes that can become a full-length work. Themes based on work, play, and routine—sowing and harvesting, a basketball game, the daily life of a college girl—are all fruitful sources for beginning choreographers.

After the subject has been chosen, the dancer must begin to find the movements she wants to use as a theme or basic material from which many of her later combinations will come. Improvisation is one of the most valuable tools for discovering movement. The student simply moves spontaneously, with or without music, then employs dramatic actions or dances freely with other people. Gradually she must mold her movements into a concrete, rhythmic, spatial form. New ideas will arise from work on the dance itself. One should take care to be specific about what one is trying to say. Work habits, including the ability to make decisions, change something, and remain with the exact problem at hand, are necessary qualities to develop. It may be best to ask someone to observe parts of a dance to determine whether what one is feeling or attempting to say is really conveyed in the movement!

Another way to begin a dance is within an already set form, among which are poetry, plays, and short stories. Musical forms lend themselves well to dance: ABA, rondo, ABC, theme and variations. Different instruments in a quartet may be copied in movement—the oboe, drum, violin, and flute, for example. Pre-classic dance forms, now in music, the pavanne, gigue, or gavotte, can bring excellent results.

Whether or not a dancer works within a set framework, she must still deal with the over-all design. Some aesthetic principles here listed apply to a finished dance and are equally a part of any art work:

1. *Balance* Alternations of length, energy, symmetrical and asymmetrical designs, and so on.
2. *Repetition* For familiarity of the themes; for making one "whole" of a piece, for emphasis.
3. *Contrast* In force, time, space, for interest, heightened drama.
4. *Unity* Again, to make a dance a satisfying whole structure.
5. *Sequence* Phrases and sections should follow each other coherently.
6. *Transition* The way in which movements and phrases change from one to another. Transitional movements must not be important within themselves, but should be smooth and part of the dance proper.
7. *Variety* For interest, by manipulating any principle or dramatic idea.
8. *Climax* A definite, fully realized, classical approach to composition.

In today's dance theater, the more searching and avant-garde choreographers go far afield from many of these principles. However, it is more fruitful and clear when a novice is given disciplines to follow.

To compose a dance, the beginning student may find it best to use one or only a few dancers and stay within the limits of an idea small in scope and length. She should wisely select an idea about which she has some knowledge or experience. Choreographing for a large number can become as complex as writing for a symphony orchestra. Simplicity and honesty in staying with one idea, no matter how limited it may seem at first, are necessities in learning the discipline demanded by dance, like any art. Too many philosophical ideas incorporated into a dance tend to weaken the real value of the piece. The value lies in the movements, not in words. The medium of the dance is movement; its province is one in which moods, feelings, and meaningful activities in space and time can put into visual forms what words cannot express. Every human being who can move can find personal and shared values in the dance.

CONCLUSION

To attempt to put satisfactorily into a few words how one creates a dance, the technique involved, the procedures necessary, and all other elements of which dance is composed, is not only impossible, but undesirable. The fact that dance is an art form suggesting ideas and conveying emotional feelings on the part of the dancer to the observer, precludes any attempt to set in words the exact method of creating dance. Although emotions may be the same, reactions vary from one individual to another, and from one time to another. The foregoing material is presented in the hope of offering the beginning student of the dance some basic understanding of the elements of modern dance, and a hint of where such necessary components can take one if he has an interest in that direction.

SELECTED REFERENCES

Andrews, Emily, *et al., Physical Education for Girls and Women*. Englewood Cliffs, N.J.: Prentice-Hall, Inc., 1963.

Astaire, Fred, *The Fred Astaire Dance Book*. New York: Cornerstone Library, 1962.

Cohen, Selma Jeanne, *The Modern Dance*. Middletown, Conn.: Wesleyan University Press, 1966.

de Mille, Agnes, *To a Young Dancer*. Boston: Little, Brown & Company, 1960–62.

Ellis, Havelock, *The Dance of Life*. New York: Modern Library, Inc., 1923.

Hall, J. Tillman, *Dance: A Complete Guide to Social, Folk, and Square Dancing*. Belmont, Calif.: Wadsworth Publishing Co., Inc., 1963.

Harris, J., A. Pittman, and M. Swenson, *Dance a While*. Minneapolis: Burgess Publishing Co., 1955.

Horst, Louis, and Carroll Russell, *Modern Dance Forms*. San Francisco: Impulse Publications, 1961.

Catalogues and records for folk, square, and social dance

Educational Activities, Inc., P. O. Box 392, Freeport, N.J. 11520. (Formerly Square Dance Assoc.—Honor Your Partner)

Educational Recordings of America, Inc., P. O. Box 6062, Bridgeport, Conn. 06606. (Physical fitness; square, social, and folk dances)

Elektra Records, 51 W. 51st Street, New York, N.Y. 10019. (Hora and others, with booklet of directions)

Kismet Record Co., 227 E. 14th Street, New York, N.Y. 10003. (Square, folk dances; records of various companies)

R.C.A. Victor Albums, obtainable at local music/record stores. (Folk dances of many countries)

Fencing

12

ORIGIN AND DEVELOPMENT

Fencing has not always been a sport. Originally it was one of the required skills of war and personal combat. Its mastery was an essential element of self-preservation through the ages of conflict.

The crude force that so often typified the heavier sword-play of the days of heavy armor disappeared before the quicker and more efficient action permitted by lighter weapons. The rapier, the forerunner of modern fencing weapons, had its first extensive use in the sixteenth century. This lighter and more graceful weapon launched the development of new techniques of combat out of which grew the modern school of the sword, with its great speed and precision. The highest peak of this development was attained in western and southern Europe.

Originally a tool of deadly personal combat, it was natural that the purpose of the weapon have considerable effect on the spirit and techniques with which it was employed. If the modern use of the sword has largely lost its more serious purpose, the sense and spirit of that original purpose is retained in the application of old techniques to modern sporting competition. Perhaps it is the recognition of this element of personal combat that attracts the growing interest that modern fencing is receiving in this country.

NATURE OF FENCING

The purpose of the sport is to touch the opponent with the sword in such a manner that a valid point is scored. Before there can be any consideration of the various techniques and skills, there should be some knowledge of the sword, the target, and other limitations under which the sport must function.

Among the famous schools of fencing are the French, Italian, Spanish, and Hungarian. The French school emphasizes dexterity and relies on deception and quickness of movement. The French foil has a slightly curved handle. The Italian school stresses strength in preference to lightness of movement. The

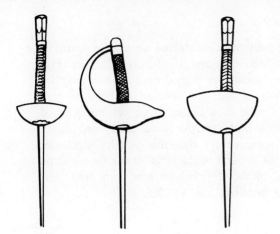

FIGURE 12-1. Types of weapons: (A) French foil; (B) saber; (C) épée.

Italian foil has a short handle and a cross bar which adds to the strength of the grip. The Spanish school combines elements of both French and Italian techniques.

In the modern sport of fencing, there are three diversified weapons: the foil (fleuret), the saber (sabre), and the dueling sword (épée). (See Fig. 12-1.)

The foil

The foil (see Figs. 12-2, 12-3) is a light weapon of no more than 17.637 ounces. Its blade is about 35 inches in length, and is rectangular. The blade tapers from a relatively thick and inflexible section at the guard, to a slim, flexible section toward the end. The tip is flattened into a small, button-like end. The guard is usually circular and concave, seldom more than four inches in diameter. The handle is either wood or cord-wrapped, and ends in a balance weight known as the pommel.

The French foil usually has a pommel of larger size than that of the Italian foil. This tends to balance the weight of the blade and make it seem lighter. The Italian foil has a cross bar at the guard, for the purpose of strengthening the grip of the fingers on the sword. This strength is often increased by strapping the pommel to the wrist.

It is the contention of advocates of the French school that greater accuracy is the result of the lighter grip and balance of the French foil. Devotees of the Italian school claim equal accuracy while having the added strength provided by the strap and cross bar.

As this chapter is not intended as an exhaustive treatment of fencing, no reference is made to

FIGURE 12-2. Types of foils

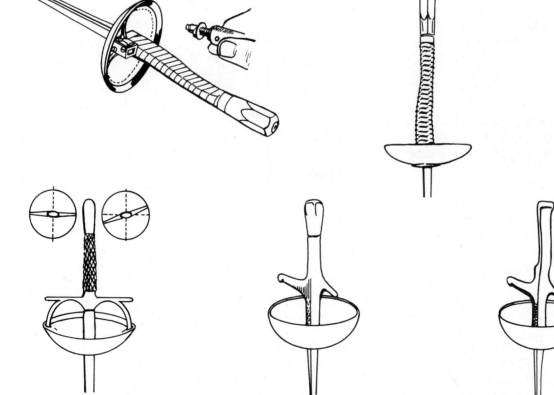

the other weapons of modern fencing, the épée or dueling sword and the saber. The foil only is considered in this short chapter since it is generally considered that initial training with the foil enhances one's eventual success with the other weapons.

Scoring

Points are scored in foil-fencing by direct thrusts arriving point first against the valid target. A grazing thrust, a slap, or a direct thrust against an invalid part of the target will not score a point. The first fencer to score five touches wins in men's competition, while four is sufficient in women's competition.

The target

The foil target excludes head, arms, and legs, extending from the top of the collar to the groin lines in front and in the back to a horizontal line passing across the top of the hip bones. (See Fig. 12-4.)

Just recently, the foil target for men and women has become the same.

Playing area

Competition is conducted on a strip approximately 40 feet long and six feet wide. (See Fig. 12-5.) The fencers are placed opposite one another at the center of the strip and are obliged to stay within its limits. If a fencer steps off the side of the strip with both feet, he is penalized one meter from that spot, except that this penalty shall not place him off the end of the strip. If the fencer steps off the end of the strip behind him with both feet, he shall be penalized one touch.

RULES

Perhaps the most important section of the rules is that having to do with the regulation of sequence. Because of the rapid exchange of sword play that occurs in competitive fencing, it has been necessary to establish certain regulations by which orderly sequence can be enforced.

Basically, each offensive action should be executed with an extension of the sword and sword

FIGURE 12-3. Parts of the French foil

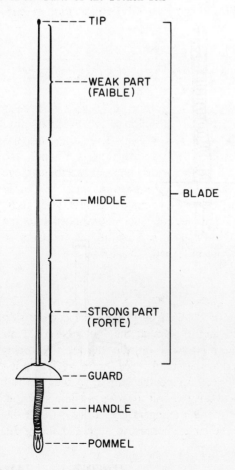

FIGURE 12-4. The foil target

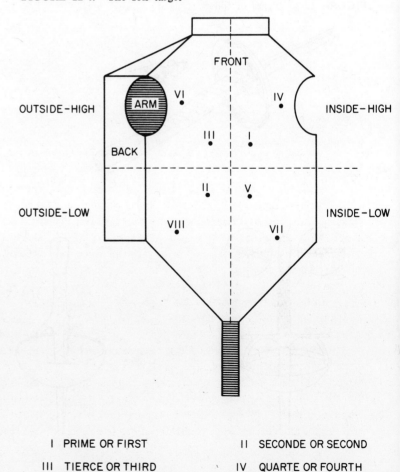

I	PRIME OR FIRST	II	SECONDE OR SECOND
III	TIERCE OR THIRD	IV	QUARTE OR FOURTH
V	QUINTE OR FIFTH	VI	SIXTE OR SIXTH
VII	SEPTIME OR SEVENTH	VIII	OCTAVE OR EIGHTH

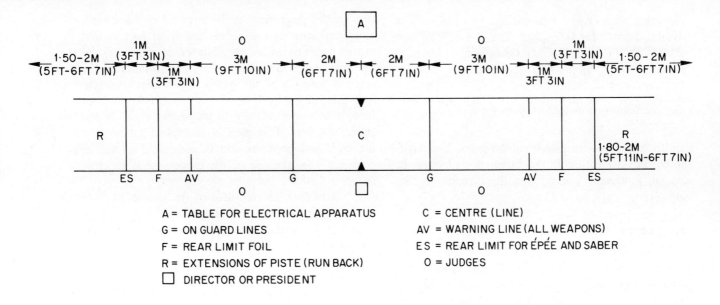

A = TABLE FOR ELECTRICAL APPARATUS   C = CENTRE (LINE)
G = ON GUARD LINES   AV = WARNING LINE (ALL WEAPONS)
F = REAR LIMIT FOIL   ES = REAR LIMIT FOR ÉPÉE AND SABER
R = EXTENSIONS OF PISTE (RUN BACK)   O = JUDGES
☐ DIRECTOR OR PRESIDENT

FOR ELECTRIC FOIL AND ÉPÉE THE METALLIC PISTE MUST COVER THE WHOLE OF THE LENGTH AND BREADTH OF THE PISTE INCLUDING ITS EXTENSIONS (RUN BACK)

NOTE: MEASUREMENTS GIVEN TO NEAREST INCH, THE DISTANCE FROM ES TO AV IS 6FT. 7IN

FIGURE 12-5. The regulation piste for all three weapons (From Amateur Fencing League of America, *Fencing Rules and Manual*, p. 17.)

arm toward the opponent's target. Such an extension, executed ahead of any such action by the defense, takes the right of way, and must be parried before any counter action may be taken.

Any loss of time or withdrawal of the point or arm results in a losing of the right of way, in the event that the defender responds by an immediate and timely extension of his sword and arm. This extension is known as a stop thrust, and takes the right over a continued attack, which scores simultaneously. An improper extension against a properly executed attack has no rights in the event the attack scores.

Assuming an attack is parried successfully, the defender takes the right to execute a counter action. The immediate extension of the arm in a riposte has the right of way over a renewal of the attack. It must be parried. If, however, the riposte is delayed, the renewal of the attack takes the right of way.

Following the successful parry of a riposte, the original attacker then retakes the right of way for counter ripostes.

It must be apparent that this discussion of the important rules regulating sequence of play is at best general. The technicalities of the rules require careful study for the serious fencer contemplating competitive fencing. If the fencer observes the basic techniques of fencing, and applies them to the rules

of right of way, it is safe to say that he minimizes the difficulties that might otherwise be experienced in competitive fencing as far as officiating is concerned.

TECHNIQUES AND FUNDAMENTALS

Because it is an ancient skill, fencing has been so developed that its techniques and practices have been reduced to a near-science. Even the basic differences between the two great schools, French and Italian, would not be readily apparent to the average spectator observing opposing fencers of those schools. The technique of the use of feet, legs, body, arms, and hands has all been coordinated into the service of the weapon, serving its requirements of distance, precision, speed, and force.

The grip

The grip is taken by placing the convex side of the curve in the palm at the heel of the thumb with the thumb placed on the top of the broad surface close to the guard. (See Fig. 12-6.) The index finger wraps around the handle so that the foil is resting between the first and second joints of this finger. The remaining fingers are curled so that the tips rest on the concave, narrow surface, holding the

FIGURE 12-6. Side view of the grip (From Shaw, Troester, and Gabrielsen, *Individual Sports for Men.*)

handle firmly, but not tensely, in the palm. The wrist should be straight with the pommel flat upon it forming a straight line through the forearm to the blade.

The guard

The position or stance with which fencers oppose one another is known as the guard. This is the position from which all offensive and defensive movements originate. In the guard position, the feet are at right angles, heels in line, the forward foot pointed along the axis of the strip. The distance between the feet is approximately twice the length of the fencer's own foot. A wider stance tends to decrease mobility, while a smaller interval between the feet tends to reduce the firmness of the stance. The legs are bent at the knees at an angle of approximately 45 degrees. The front knee is over the instep or ball of the front foot. The rear knee is slightly forward of the rear foot so that the leg, along its outside, is in approximately the same plane. The body is erect and effaced so as to reduce the target presented to the opponent. The body is relaxed, the normal posture unaffected by the positions of the arms and legs. The sword arm should be extended about two-thirds toward the opponent, the sword hand being at a level approximately even with the lower edge of the breast. The rear arm is raised so that the upper arm is horizontal with the floor, the forearm being perpendicular with the floor and forming a right angle with the upper arm at the elbow. The hand is relaxed and the head is turned toward the opponent. (See Fig. 12-7.)

The advance and retreat

The basic foot movement from the position of the guard is that of the advance and retreat. This is a quick, short step, either forward or backward, along the strip. To advance, the front foot is first moved forward about the distance of one foot and the rear foot is brought up the same distance to the original position of the guard. To retreat, the rear foot first moves back about one foot and the front foot follows immediately to its proper place in the guard position. This step is controlled entirely by the legs, and body motion is minimized as far as possible. The purpose of the movement is to close or open distance between the fencers.

A further development of the simple advance is the jump advance, or balestra. In this instance both feet leave the floor at the same time and arrive at the same time.

The lunge

The lunge is the final foot movement in the attack. As such, it is one of the most important single movements in fencing. Considerable practice is required to develop its advantages to the utmost.

The lunge is a long and forceful reach with the legs, and takes the sword to the opponent. It is always preceded by an extension of the sword and sword arm, in a thrust, toward the opponent.

The execution of the lunge combines several simultaneous movements. The front foot is raised from the floor and the whole body is impelled forward. This forward lunge of the body comes primarily from the explosive and forceful straightening and extension of the rear leg. The rear arm is flung down and back so it ends parallel with the rear leg. The body is balanced slightly forward, the forward lean aiding in overcoming the initial inertia. The foot arrives in a position at right angles to the rear foot, which has remained flat on the floor. There is no settling or sagging into position. The forward speed and lunge is at this moment complete. The thigh and lower leg should form a right angle at the knee, in the full lunge, with the front knee over the heel of the foot. (See Fig. 12-8.)

In recovering from the lunge, there is a simultaneous thrust back with the front leg, a pulling of the rear leg against the rear foot, and a pulling back of the rear arm, all aiding in returning to the

FIGURE 12-7. The guard

FIGURE 12-8. The lunge

148

guard position. The guard position may also be resumed by closing to the fore in those instances where the defending opponent retreats out of range on each attack.

The fleche

The fleche, or running attack, is simply a crossing of the legs in a running movement toward the opponent. It has the value of surprise, variation, and differing of timing and speed. It has the disadvantage of disturbing the accuracy of the sword and the fencing balance of the one employing it. The fleche is illegal in scholastic, college, and women's fencing.

Use of the sword

Although the sword is employed on both offense and defense, it is necessary first to discuss its employment in defense, because this must be understood before the defense can be penetrated by a successfully conceived attack.

ON DEFENSE. The sword protects the target from attacks, both high and low as well as on either side of the body. Dividing the target in half at breast level, we determine the high and low lines of defense.

In the high line, the point of the sword is held slightly above eye level and the hand is slightly below the level of the breast. In the low line, the hand remains at the same level, while the point of the sword is at the level of the knee. Against offensive movements in these areas, these positions of the sword assure sufficient leverage with which to deflect the attacking blade to one side or the other. (See Fig. 12-9.)

Attacks deflected past the chest are known as passing by on the inside line. This is opposite the inside of the arm. Attacks deflected past the back pass on the outside, being past the outside of the sword arm. In the inside line, the defensive sword places the hand at the edge of the chest, bringing the blade to the edge of the body by placing the point at a corresponding position. On the outside line, the hand is brought across the body to the edge of the body at the back, and the point is brought across to a corresponding position. The position of the blade on either side (in deflecting the threatening or attacking blade) is known as "closing the line" on that side. Going on guard with the line closed on one side or the other leaves fewer lines in which feints can be made by an opponent. (See Fig. 12-9.)

The movement of the sword across the body

FIGURE 12-9.
On defense

to one of the guard positions, thereby deflecting the attacking blade, is known as a parry. This simple movement across the body is known as the simple parry. It may be a simple pushing movement in opposition to the attacking blade, or it may be executed with the forceful snap of authority known as a beat-parry. The terminal position of the parry is also the position of the guard, for all intents and purposes.

Thus, there are four positions: inside-high; inside-low; outside-high; and outside-low. In each of these positions the hand may be in either pronation or supination. This gives eight parries or guards, in their terminal position. These are known as: *prime,* inside-low or high, hand in pronation; *second,* outside-low, hand in pronation; *tierce,* outside-high, hand in pronation; *quarte,* inside-high, hand in supination; *quinte,* inside-high or low, hand in pronation; *sixte,* outside-high, hand in supination; *septieme,* inside-low, hand in supination; and *octave,* outside-low, hand in supination. (See Fig. 12-4.) As a matter of practice, some of the low line parries are used almost exclusively as high line parries, and vice versa. Each high line parry may be executed by dropping to the low line, as may each low line parry be executed by raising to the high line.

The simple parries, back and across the body, may be supplemented by what is known as the counter parry. This is executed with the hand remaining in the same position, the point being moved around the attacking blade in an elliptical or circular movement, contacting the blade and carrying it off the target in the line opposite from the one in which the attack is being made. The parry is clockwise or counterclockwise, depending on the direction in which the blade is to be deflected.

Further versatility is provided for the defense by dropping the point from high line defensive positions, across the line of attack and the attacking blade, into a low line parry. The reverse can be done from low line to high line. This is known as breaking the line.

A further parry is known as the envelopment. It is a parry that moves from inside to outside line or outside to inside, accompanied by a sweeping encircling movement. It is calculated to cover every line of attack. As an occasional movement it is very serviceable, but it is extremely susceptible to evasion by a skillful fencer because of its wide nature.

A series of succeeding parries, simple and counter, serves to lend variety to the defense. Varying combinations increase the difficulty of analyzing the defense. Although all these parries are available, for practical use they are usually confined to quarte (fourth), sixte (sixth), and second. Basic instruction and practice should be confined to these parries.

ON ATTACK.   The attack is executed by the sword, either in movements that avoid the defending sword's parries or that seek to beat aside the blade or control it, in either case seeking to reach the target prior to a successful parry.

Initial practice and instruction should be limited to the deceptive or avoiding movements. Such an attacking movement is known as a deceive.

Against simple parries in the high line, the deceptive movement is executed by merely dropping the point of the sword under the defending sword as it moves across in a parry, raising the point after the defending sword has passed over. This is known as a disengage. Against low line parries the point is raised so the defender's hand passes under the point. Where two disengages are required in succession, the attack is known as a one-two. Where three are required, the attack is known as a one-two-three.

To deceive the counter parry, the point of the attacking sword does, in a sense, follow the circular parry, returning to the original line of attack. This movement is known as the double.

Another deceptive movement, more difficult to execute and seldom employed by a fencer until he has mastered the more basic movements, is the cutover or coupe. This may be described as a disengage over the adversary's blade. Executed from the guard position, the point is raised so that the blade passes over the other sword to threaten on the other side by lowering the point and extending the arm. Perhaps the most effective use of this movement is after an initial feint has drawn a parry from the defender. Keeping the arm extended with hand at shoulder level and turning the thumb uppermost, raise the point by wrist movement so that the blade clears the parrying blade, after which the point is dropped to the target. This evades either a simple or counter parry.

The attacks that seek to knock the defending blade aside, or control it, are known as attacks on the blade. One is a beat, executed much as a parry would be executed. This tends to knock the blade aside so the attacking blade can continue to the target. Also, the defending blade may be pressed aside, the attacking blade continuing to the target. Further, the attacking blade may merely glide along the defending blade and to the target. These are known as the beat, the press, and the glide attacks. They may be intended to arrive directly against the target or they may be executed to draw a parry that may be deceived on the other side.

Another attack on the sword is known as the bind. It seeks to control the defending blade, carrying it diagonally either from high to low line, or from low to high line, levering its way in to the target as it changes the line of the defending blade.

Additional movements of the sword

After the attack or the parry, the play does not cease. There may be successive movements that keep the fencing a continuing exchange of sword play.

THE RIPOSTE.   Following the successful execution of a parry, the defender acquires the right to take the initiative. Immediately following the parry, he should extend his sword arm and sword toward the target of the opponent. This should be an explosive movement that seeks to reach the opponent before he can recover from the lunge or execute his own parry against this return movement. This return is known as the riposte.

REMISE.   Sometimes following the attack, the defender delays his riposte. Without recovering from the lunge, the attacker may merely move his sword and sword arm so that his point is replaced in the target area of the defender. This is known as a remise. If a remise is attempted while the defender executes an immediate riposte and both fencers are touched at the same time, the riposte counts and the remise is annulled. In such an instance, the remise must be scored a full measure of fencing time ahead to count.

REDOUBLED ATTACK.   Following the attack, the attacker may recover from his lunge and immediately lunge again in attack. This taking of the attack again, without any intervening movement by the defense, is known as a redoublement of the attack.

COUNTER RIPOSTE.   Following the attack and a riposte, the original attacker may parry the defender's riposte, and following that make his own riposte against the defender. This is a counter riposte.

PLAYING STRATEGY

The fencers are usually placed on guard either in or out of distance. When in distance, they are at the interval where the lunge of one will reach the other. Out of distance is when an advance is necessary to come within lunging distance. Distance varies with each fencer, so that two fencers may have a different distance. Each seeks to have the other take his own distance.

When in distance, the fencers may fence in or out of engagement. In engagement means that each fencer closes either the inside or outside line, and crosses his blade with that of the opponent. When out of distance, the fencers fence out of engagement. When out of engagement, the fencers usually assume an outside guard with their swords.

Fencers often seek to vary distance by moving in and out, attacking with simple lunges as well as preceding a lunge with advances. These disturb the opposing fencer's ability to estimate the distance from which he can expect an attack to be launched.

Initial feints, by the rapid and smooth extension of the blade with the point threatening the target, often draw a parry that can be deceived. A movement against the blade often causes the defender to parry, thus opening his defense and target for attack. Occasionally a stamping of the front foot aids the feint with the sword, although this is more often dramatic than effective.

SAFETY

The mask should be of good quality and in repair. It should be carefully inspected at regular intervals to ensure its continued good condition. It should always be worn when opposing another fencer, even when merely demonstrating certain movements.

The canvas jacket should also always be worn while fencing. It is protection against possible broken blades and also serves as padding against the hard touches that are sometimes scored. Women fencers should use breast protectors in their jackets, which are manufactured so as to be adaptable for this purpose. Many instructors insist on men wearing a similar protector.

The tip of the foil should either be covered by a protective rubber tip or be taped carefully with adhesive tape. For beginners, it is suggested that the tip be taped to a distance of about eight inches. The blade should be inspected at regular intervals for possible flaws.

The gauntlet should be used for the protection of the hand. This also ensures a better grip of the weapon.

If permitted, the fleche attack should be used with care. The attack usually brings the fencers to-gether rapidly in such a way that there is danger of breaking the blades.

PLAYING COURTESIES

It is not an anachronism that the salute with sword is still required in competition. It is a gesture of courtesy toward the opponent, and additional salutes should be given the officials.

Remember not to hold the point against the other fencer's vest too long, especially after you hear the word "Halt."

It is considered unsportsmanlike to make facial expressions of surprise, anger, or mockery either at the jury or the other fencer.

It is always appreciated if you call a touch against yourself when you are hit.

OFFICIATING

The officials are five in number. There are four judges and one director. Two judges stand behind each fencer, watching for touches against the other fencer. The director stands to one side of the strip and between the fencers. His duty is to start and stop the action. The judges have one vote apiece and the director has a vote of one and one-half.

In judging with electrical apparatus, the president does the whole job by moving up and down the piste in order to follow each movement. At the same time he is able to see the light signals of the apparatus. He always checks on the spring in the point of the foil. The fencers do not change sides.

HELPFUL HINTS

As in any sport where technique is of primary importance, attention to detail is particularly necessary for the beginning fencer. Because of the different muscular coordination and reflexes that fencing requires, the beginner should pay particular attention to mastery of the fundamental requirements of the sport. Although initial development may be retarded by attention to details, the final reward in better performance is well worth the extra initial effort and difficulty. The best fencing is based on techniques and form developed by the hardest kind of experience over many, many years.

It must be remembered that the sword is used quite differently than the instruments employed in other sports. This use is thrusting rather than swinging. Further, instead of being a running or walking sport in the ordinary sense, fencing requires a type of precise and controlled footwork peculiar to that sport.

A careful practice of the guard position, with a continuing execution of the advance and retreat, will accustom the body and legs to the movements and physical demands of this stance. Practice of the lunge will serve further to condition the legs and body to meet the requirements of the sport. Practice with the sword, with particular attention to the smooth but rapid extension and retraction of the sword arm, will accustom the hand to the balance and control of the sword. Practice of these positions and movements before one's own reflection in a mirror will facilitate the gaining of proper execution.

Following a mastery of position and footwork, the next type of practice is that of drill against another fencer. This should usually be in the form of predetermined movements, the fencers alternating in attack and defense positions. This type of practice provides the first real sense of distance, control, and timing. It will also serve to demonstrate to the fencer errors in execution that require further correction. Of course, if an instructor is available to conduct these drills personally, then the benefit to be derived from them is increased.

The final type of practice is fencing for touches. Here the fencer learns the competitive application of the techniques already practiced, and the development of the competitive sense essential to good fencing. This type of practice should be with as many varied styles of fencers as possible.

However expert a fencer may become, he should always practice basic movements and engage in technique drills. The question of physical conditioning, as in other sports, depends on the individual and the seriousness of his intentions.

TERMINOLOGY

Advance   Move forward to get within attacking distance.

A.F.L.A.   Amateur Fencers League of America (founded April 22, 1891).

Attack   Attempt to hit an opponent by moving the body and/or weapon forward.

Attack of second intention   An attack that is intended to be parried so that the attacker may score on a counterattack.

Attacks on the blade   A beat, pressure, or glide attack to deviate the defensive point.

Balestra, or jump advance   A forward body movement with a quick jump before the lunge.

Benefit of doubt   If the two side judges disagree and the director has no opinion, no score is awarded.

Blade   *Strong:* near the guard or parrying surface; *middle:* the center section of the blade; *weak:* near the tip, least force exerted.

Bout   A contest between two fencers.

Competition   A contest with one type of weapon, organized on an individual or team basis.

Deceive   Elude or escape control of the blade.

F.I.E.   (Federation Internationale d'Escrime) The International Fencing Federation.

I.C.F.A.   Intercollegiate Fencing Association.

Invitation   Inviting an attack by purposely exposing target or by closing the distance.

I.W.F.A.   Intercollegiate Women's Fencing Association.

Jury   The officials, usually four judges and a director.

Mask   A wire mesh protector for the face.

Match   A contest between two teams in any one weapon, consisting of a series of bouts.

Meet   Competition between two or more teams in which two or more weapons are fenced.

N.F.C.A.A.   National Fencing Coaches Association of America.

Pass (or miss, flat, slap, etc.)   A touch which would not inflict a puncture or wound.

Phrase   No cessation of action for a period during a bout.

Pool   A group of fencers or teams competing in round-robin tournament.

Retreat   The opposite of advance; to step back and to open distance.

Right of way   (See fencing rules.) Established by fencer who just extends his arm with point in line.

Riposte or return   After a successful defense; an offensive action that may be a simple or compound return.

Touch   A hit on the target which would inflict a puncture or wound if the weapon were pointed.

Tournament   A series of competitions in one or more weapons and organized as individual and/or team bouts.

SELECTED REFERENCES

de Beaumont, C. L., *Fencing: Ancient Art and Modern Sport*. New York: A.S. Barnes & Co., Inc., 1960.

Breckinridge, S.D., *Sword Play*. New York: A.S. Barnes and Co., Inc., 1941.

Castello, Hugo, and J.M. Castello, *Fencing*. New York: The Ronald Press Company, 1962.

Castello, J.M., *Theory and Practice of Fencing*. New York: Charles Scribner's Sons, 1961.

Crosnier, R., *Fencing With the Electric Foil*. New York: A.S. Barnes & Co., Inc., 1961.

Fencing Rules. New York: Amateur Fencers' League of America (current edition).

Garret, Maxwell R., *Fencing*. New York: Sterling Publishing Co., Inc., 1961.

————, *Fencing: Instructor's Guide*. Chicago: The Athletic Institute, 1960.

Official Bowling, Fencing and Golf Guide. Washington, D.C.: Division for Girls' and Women's Sports, American Association for Health, Physical Education and Recreation (current edition).

Palffy-Alpar, Julius, *Sword and Masque*. Philadelphia: F. A. Davis Company, 1968.

Sports Illustrated Book of Fencing. Philadelphia: J.B. Lippincott Co., 1961.

Vince, J., *Fencing* (2nd ed.). New York: The Ronald Press Company, 1962.

Field Hockey

13

ORIGIN AND DEVELOPMENT

Field hockey is thought to be one of the oldest games played. Figures with hockey sticks appear in early Greek art and Egyptian hieroglyphics. In England, where the game has existed for a long time, it is a popular man's sport, with the woman's game holding a secondary position to it. In the United States, field hockey has been played principally by women. It was introduced in 1901 by Miss Constance Applebee, an English lady, at a Harvard summer session. The game was accepted with great favor and Miss Applebee was asked to teach it at several eastern women's colleges—Bryn Mawr, Mount Holyoke, Smith, Vassar, and Wellesley.

The United States Field Hockey Association, an entirely amateur organization, was founded in 1922 to spread, further, and advance the best interests of field hockey for women and girls. This objective is promoted through the teaching of the game, offering opportunity for competition, and the training of officials. Clubs have been formed in many areas throughout the country and sectional and na-

tional tournaments take place annually, the U.S. team being selected at the latter.

The International Federation of Women's Hockey Associations was formed in 1927 and it meets for conferences and tournament play every three years. The United States has sent teams to all such tournaments since 1933. It served as the hostess nation in 1936 and also in 1963, when six continents were represented among the 26 nations taking part.

There is also the Field Hockey Association of America (for men), organized primarily for the purpose of entering teams in the Olympics.

NATURE OF THE GAME

The game is played by two teams of 11 players each, designated as five forwards, three halfbacks, two backs, and a goalkeeper. (See Fig. 13-13.) Each player carries a hockey stick. With the exception of the goalkeeper, who is permitted certain kicking privileges and the roll-in play from out of bounds, the only way players may move the ball is by use of the stick.

Goals count one point and can be scored only if an attacker's stick touches the ball inside the striking circle. The official game is played in two periods of 35 minutes each. There is no time-out allowed, except for injury or replacement of a broken stick. The game is started by the center forwards taking a bully on the center line. After each goal, the center bully is repeated.

The field is about the size of a football field, approximately 100 yards long and 60 yards wide, with a goal at each end. Goal posts are four yards apart and seven feet high, joined by a cross bar. The posts and cross bars are square and painted white. The goal is usually enclosed with a net or screen, supported by two additional posts approximately six feet behind the goal.

EQUIPMENT

The official ball is hard and slightly larger than a baseball. It is made of cork and string, covered with leather, and painted white. The Chingford ball is also approved for games. Practice balls used for stickwork should be painted yellow or red to designate them from official balls. Official balls should be used for all shooting practice and in games because practice balls tend to rise dangerously.

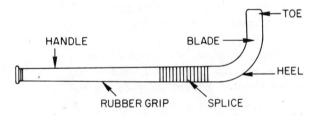

FIGURE 13-1. A hockey stick and its parts

A good stick has a handle made of cane with rubber or cork inserts, and a blade made of wood. The left side of the blade is flat and is used for hitting the ball. The other side of the blade is rounded and may not be used for hitting the ball at any time. (See Fig. 13-1.)

CHOOSING A STICK. Two types of sticks are in common use, one with a long blade made of ash and the other with a shorter blade made of mulberry. The grain of the wood in the blade should follow around the curve to the toe to prevent splintering. The stick should be light enough to facilitate techniques and ease of control, the usual weight being 18 or 19 ounces. The proper length of a stick is determined by the distance of the player's hands from the ground, and has nothing to do with her height or the length of her legs. The most common lengths for a stick are 36 or 37 inches, but 35- and 38-inch lengths are not unusual. To determine the length required, grasp the stick as for a drive, stand erect, and swing it in front of the body. A long-toed stick should just clear the ground; the short-toed may be slightly shorter and should feel a bit heavier in the toe.

CARE OF THE STICK. The blade of the stick should be treated at the beginning and end of each season, using linseed oil on mulberry wood and a hard waterproof wax on ash. It should be kept clean and again treated after use on wet fields and occasionally during the season. When splinters appear, they should be rubbed down with fine sandpaper and covered with a small strip of adhesive or electrician's tape. Too much tape is not recommended inasmuch as it will change the balance of the stick. The stick should be stored in a cool, dry, preferably unheated place. Never put a stick near a radiator or heat outlet.

Players may not wear shoes with metal cleats. Leather or rubber cleats are permitted and there are several types of good rubber-cleated hockey shoes available. Shoes with cleats are recommended to prevent slipping and dangerous play. The goalkeeper's shoes should be well padded along the sides, have a hard toe, and should be large enough to allow several pairs of heavy socks to be worn. Rubber sponges often are used to protect sensitive places on the ankle or instep. There is a type of "kicker" for the use of the goalkeepers. It is well padded and covers the whole foot. These are particularly good for practice in that they are worn over the player's own shoes and thus eliminate the problem of shoe sizes.

Light shin guards are wise protection and will not interfere with a player's ability to run. They will protect the ankle bones as well as the shins. Goalkeeper's pads should cover the leg from the thigh down. If the pads do not extend over the instep, kickers should be worn.

TECHNIQUES AND FUNDAMENTALS

Too much stress cannot be laid on the importance of doing all practices while moving. The proper relationship between ball and feet is most important and can only be gained by always practicing strokes while one is running or walking. The essence of stickwork is footwork. Make the feet assume the proper relationship to the ball, not the ball to the feet. Keep the eye on the ball at all times.

Holding the stick

With the heel of the stick resting on the ground in front of the left foot, allow the top of the handle to fall into the fingers of the left hand. Grip the stick easily. Lift the stick to a horizontal position in front of the body with the toe of the stick pointing up. Place the right hand immediately below the left in the same relative position. The V formed by the thumb and index finger of each hand will be in line with the toe of the stick. Allow the stick to drop to a perpendicular position so the heel of the stick is in front of and very slightly to the right of the right foot with the flat face pointing directly ahead. The left forearm should be in a straight line with the stick. The grip with both hands should be easy and relaxed, not tense. This is the fundamental position for all stroke production. The left hand will never change its position. For some strokes the right hand will be farther down the handle.

Dribble

This is a series of short strokes used to carry the ball down the field. As running speed is increased, the ball is hit harder but should be close enough at all times to be under complete control. The position for the dribble is the fundamental position except that the right hand is about four inches lower on the stick. The arms are relaxed, the left arm away from the body, the left shoulder leading slightly. The stick is almost perpendicular and moves straight forward and backward, with most of the impetus coming from a wrist motion. The player should be in a proper position for running, with the ball in front of the right foot but slightly to the right to prevent kicking the ball. The hands are separated only for better stick control and should be as near to the top of the handle as possible so as to maintain a good running position. Bending over, crouching, or running sideways should be avoided at all times.

FIGURE 13-2. The follow-through on the drive

Drive

The drive is a hard stroke used for passing and shooting. The hands are always close together for this stroke. The stick swings in a perpendicular plane with a pendulum-like motion in the direction the ball is to travel. The stick may not be lifted above the shoulder on either the back swing or the follow-through. Body weight, shoulders, arms, and wrists, all combine to give the stroke its force. However, one must be careful not to bend the wrists at either end of the stroke because this will cause the stick to rise illegally. To be assured of an accurate stroke, allow the body weight to follow through with the stick pointed in the direction of the pass. (See Fig. 13-2.)

DRIVE STRAIGHT AHEAD. The ball should be ahead of and slightly to the right of the path the right foot is to take. The stroke can be executed with either foot forward, and should be practiced that way so it can be executed at any instant.

DRIVE TO THE LEFT. The ball should be in front of the body and so placed that at the moment of impact of stick and ball, the weight will be behind the stroke and the stick will be in a position perpendicular to the ground.

DRIVE TO THE RIGHT. The ball is to the right of the body. The farther to the right the ball is to be passed, the more its position will be behind that of the fundamental position. The right foot should be forward as the stroke is made. The body pivots from the hips so the right shoulder drops back and the left shoulder is brought around in the direction of the pass.

HARD DRIVE FOR GOAL. This is the same as a straight drive, but the emphasis should be on pointing the left shoulder toward the path the ball is to take. The ball should be in front of the forward foot at the moment of contact so the weight of the body is behind the stroke. Follow-through by reaching toward the path the ball has taken. Avoid pulling back on the stroke, which will occur when the ball is behind the forward foot at the moment of impact of ball and stick.

Push-pass

This stroke is used for short, accurate passing or shooting when there is not time or necessity for a drive. The body crouches more for the push-pass and flick than for other strokes. Either foot may be forward when the stroke is executed, but it is found easier to practice first with the left foot forward. The right hand is well down the stick, about six to eight inches lower than in the fundamental position. There is no back swing. The stroke is started with the stick facing the direction of the pass and in contact with the ball, as shown in Figure 13-3b. The top of the stick is slightly ahead of the blade. Both arms move forward, sweeping the stick along the ground. When the arms come to the limit of reach, the stick is used as a lever, the left hand pulling back and the right hand pushing forward. The stroke ends with the stick and weight following the direction of the pass, the stick not completely parallel to the ground and the left forearm and handle of the stick maintaining a straight line. (See Fig. 13-3c.) The ball travels along the ground. When executed smoothly, the push-pass can have great force and accuracy and is invaluable for short passes at close quarters, especially in the circle. It is an easy stroke to receive.

Flick

This is also a wrist stroke without back swing. The ball usually rises slightly. It is used for shooting when deep in the circle and for passes to a marked player. The hand and foot position are the same as that for the push-pass. In this stroke the stick starts in contact with the ball on its right side and is brought around the ball, the top of the handle swinging in a greater arc than the blade. The stroke is finished in the same way as a push-pass. The flick is especially valuable for shooting at close range inasmuch as the direction the ball is to take is concealed. Also it is off the ground, making it more difficult to stop. Neither the flick nor the push-pass should be practiced with a stationary ball because it will be extremely difficult to adjust a moving ball. (See Figs. 13-3 a, b, c.)

Job

This is a weak stroke, useful only to spoil another player's shot. It should not be used except in extreme necessity. It is used when the player finds himself on the left side of his opponent with no opportunity for a circular tackle. The stick is held in the left hand with the blade traveling close to the ground and facing up. Without touching or impeding an opponent, the stick is thrust forward with a reach so the ball is temporarily pushed away from the opponent. This spoiling stroke must be followed up immediately with another play controlling the ball.

Fielding and passing

The ball must be fielded or controlled when it comes to a player and before it is passed or played. *Point, possess, place, pass* are often used for keys to fielding and passing. *Point* the stick at the ball as it approaches, keeping the eyes constantly on the ball. As the ball comes within reach, the stick is lowered so that it grazes the ground. The blade meets the ball squarely. The hands are slightly apart as for the dribble and have an easy grip. *Possess* the ball. (See Fig. 13-4.) On impact, the blade gives slightly, so the top of the handle will be ahead of the blade. The grip must not shift on the handle. The left wrist will be over the top of the handle in such a position as to have the left arm a continuation of the stick and not in a bent wrist position. *Place* the ball before playing it. Place it into a space slightly ahead and to the right of the body so that the weight will be behind the passing stroke. With the ball now under control, the player is ready to execute whatever stroke he chooses. *Pass* the ball. All strokes should be done with the feet in running position. No balls should be hit on the fly. Fielding and passing should always be practiced while moving, not while standing still.

Stop

To stop a ball dead still, the technique is the same as for fielding except that there is more give to the stick, which will cause the ball to stop on the stick and not rebound. (See Fig. 13-4.)

FIGURE 13-3. (A) First stage in the execution of a flick. (B) Second stage in execution of a flick; also, beginning of a push-pass. (C) Follow-through for a flick or push-pass.

FIGURE 13-4. Fielding or stopping the ball

Carrying the stick

A player when running and not near the ball, carries the stick in a horizontal position in front of the body, with arms bent in a comfortable position for running. The left hand remains in its place and the right hand slides down the handle a comfortable distance. Be sure the hands are brought together when the stick is lowered to play the ball. The stick should be carried across the body in the position described only when there is no possibility of a pass reaching the player.

Tackle

This is a play used in an attempt to take the ball from an opponent who is in control of it. A player should be able to tackle from right, left, or front. Since a successful tackle is dependent on timing, practice should always be with two players, both moving. The instant to tackle is when the opponent's stick is away from the ball.

STRAIGHT-FORWARD TACKLE. This is used to tackle an opponent who is approaching from directly in front with the ball in her possession. Do not stand still to tackle. Meet the opponent stick to stick. This necessitates having the body slightly to the left, and so doing will avoid collisions. Points to remember:

1. Keep the eye on the opponent's stick and the ball, anticipating any move the opponent may make to deceive.
2. Time the tackle so it is unexpected. Slow or increase the pace to achieve this deception.
3. Have the weight of the body behind the tackle so as to control the ball and cause the opponent to overrun.
4. Keep the body weight controlled so as to be alert and ready to move quickly in any direction.

LEFT-HAND LUNGE. This stroke is used to rob an opponent of the ball when both the opponent with the ball and the player are running in the same direction, the opponent on the player's left. The stroke has great reach. It is used by players in all positions. The stroke starts with two hands on the stick and ends with one hand on it. Approach the opponent with the stick in the carrying position. Do not get too close to the opponent to be tackled. When on a line with her, draw the stick off to the right of the body. As the opponent taps the ball, the stroke is started. Forcefully swing the stick to the left with both hands. When the right arm can no longer reach, continue to direct the stroke with the left hand so that the ball meets the stick in its path and is trapped.

The weight is on the left leg, which is in a lunge position. The left arm is straight and firm, as shown in Fig. 13-5. The run is now checked and the right foot brought forward. At the same time there is a pivot. The right hand is replaced on the stick, which gives the player the ball in the fundamental position. The opponent will overrun. Points to be remembered:

1. Keep the stick low throughout the stroke.
2. Time the lunge.
3. Allow plenty of room—do not get too close to the player with the ball.
4. Finish the stroke by pivoting and taking possession of the ball.
5. Keep the blade closed and so trap the ball.

This stroke may also be used as a pass, in which case the lunge is used intentionally to direct the ball off to another player. It can be very effective in shooting when the ball might appear to be out of reach. The left-hand lunge should not be used recklessly or without objective.

CIRCULAR TACKLE. This play is used when the opponent with the ball is on the player's right—and both are moving in the same direction. Before executing this stroke, the player must get at least a stride or two ahead of the opponent with the ball. She then crosses in front of the opponent in a circular course, taking possession of the ball as she goes, using a series of short taps, and continues until she is going in the direction of her attacking goal. The player travels in a semicircular course, with the ball traveling in a smaller arc than that of the player. The entire play must be executed without touching the opponent or causing her to break her stride. The player's position will be similar to that for the drive to the right in that her trunk rotates so her left shoulder comes forward, the right shoulder drops, and the ball is played to the right of and slightly behind the right foot. (See Fig. 13-6.) It is fre-

FIGURE 13-5. Left-hand lunge

FIGURE 13-6. Finish of circular tackle

quently used by the left half who wants to stay between her opponent and the goal. In other situations the tackler should try to approach on the stick side of her opponent.

Points to be remembered:

1. Player must be well ahead of the opponent with the ball.
2. The tackle must be timed so that the player takes possession when her opponent's stick is not in contact with the ball.
3. The ball must travel in a small circle while the player runs in a larger one. The left arm and shoulder will lead and the right shoulder will drop back, as shown in Fig. 13-6.
4. The ball must be kept behind the right foot in order to avoid obstruction.

Dodge

The dodge is used when a player who is in possession of the ball wishes to evade an opponent who is approaching from in front. The effectiveness of the dodge is derived from deceiving the opponent. Therefore the player should learn a variety of dodges.

RIGHT DODGE. Sometimes called "dodge to non-stick side." The player in possession of the ball sends the ball ahead and close to the non-stick side of the approaching opponent. The player herself passes on the stick side of the opponent and meets the ball again behind her. In other words the ball goes right and the player goes left. The stroke has only the force of a dribble and the ball goes just enough off line to the right to miss the opponent's left toe. This is not a pass and should have neither the force nor change of direction of a pass. (See Fig. 13-7.) Remember to execute this dodge before the opponent can reach the ball but be close enough to her so that she has no opportunity to move to her left and thus block the ball.

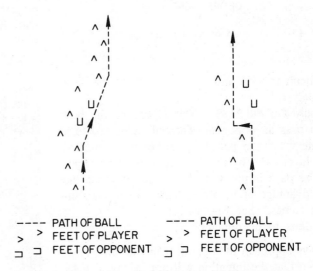

---- PATH OF BALL   ---- PATH OF BALL
>   > FEET OF PLAYER   >   > FEET OF PLAYER
⊐   ⊐ FEET OF OPPONENT   ⊐   ⊐ FEET OF OPPONENT

FIGURES 13-7, 13-8. (*Left*) Diagram of a right dodge. (*Right*) Diagram of a left dodge.

LEFT DODGE. In this play, both ball and player go to the left of the approaching opponent. Shortly before the ball is within reach of the opponent, the player steps left, pulls the ball left a short distance (not more than six inches), then continues straight ahead. For success, the timing must be accurate and the ball must be played squarely left, not diagonally. The ball must remain on the player's right throughout the dodge. (See Fig. 13-8.)

SCOOP. As the name implies, the ball is scooped or lifted on the toe of the stick over the tackling opponent's stick. The hands remain in the dribble position. The player turns the stick so the flat side of the blade is up, then, by flicking the toe of the stick under the ball, lifts it an inch or two over her opponent's stick. The ball should be kept close enough to the dodger's stick for her to control it throughout the play. She herself passes on the opponent's stick side. When this stroke is well done

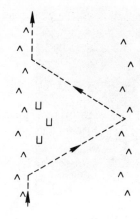

---- PATH OF BALL
>   > FEET OF PLAYER AND TEAMMATE
⊐   ⊐ FEET OF OPPONENT

FIGURE 13-9. Diagram of a triangular pass

it is difficult to stop and in no way slows the pace of the player.

TRIANGULAR PASS. This is one of the best plays to pass an opponent. The ball is passed to a teammate who is in parallel position, then returned to the player, who by this time is behind the opponent. The pace is not slowed and the play has the added advantage of involving team rather than individual tactics. (See Fig. 13-9.)

Points to be remembered when dodging:

1. Always approach the opponent in the same position so that the intention will not be revealed by movement of hands or changes in body-ball relationship.
2. The player herself must pass on the opponent's stick side, regardless of which side the ball is to go. This will avoid collisions.
3. Increase pace to change timing. Do not slow down to do a dodge.
4. Execute the dodge just before the opponent is within reach of the ball. Remember that both players are moving, thus this point will be considerably farther away than might be expected.

Bully

This is the play used to:

1. Start the game at the beginning, after half time, and after a goal has been scored.
2. Re-start the game after the ball has passed over the side line off the sticks of two opponents.
3. Re-start the game after simultaneous fouls by two opponents.

4. Re-start the game after a penalty bully.

FORMATION. The players of both teams must be on their defending side of an imaginary line drawn across the field through the point where the ball is placed. One player from each team takes the bully. They stand with feet astride the line, facing the side lines squarely, so the ball will be between them. They may not move their feet until the bully is completed.

EXECUTION. The hands are well apart on the stick to give strength to the stroke to be used. Some teachers advocate rotating the right hand slightly to the right, thus enabling the player to execute any play following completion of the bully without making the intention obvious. To bully the ball, each player strikes the ground on her own side of the ball with the heel of the stick, then strikes the opponent's stick over the top of the ball, as shown in Fig. 13-10.

FIGURE 13-10. The bully

This is done three times. With the third meeting of sticks, the bully is technically completed and all players are free to move into attacking areas.

PLAY FOLLOWING A BULLY. Every player should know at least three plays to be used following a bully and be able to execute them interchangeably.

1. *Reverse stick:* After hitting sticks for the third time, the stick is turned over, without a shift of the hands, so the toe is down and the ball is tapped back with a firm wrist motion. It can be tapped back and immediately passed by the same player to a teammate on the right, or it can be tapped back harder to the defense who is backing up the bully. This last play opens up the game and is difficult for the opponents to stop.
2. *A pass right:* After the completion of the bully, one of the players will play the ball between the

opponent's stick and right foot, thus passing to a teammate on her right if the play is well executed.

3. *A pass left*: The ball is drawn slightly toward the player, enough to be out of reach of the opponent.

FIGURE 13-11. A pass left after the bully

At the same time, the player will step back with the left foot and, without obstructing her opponent, pass forward to the left inner or left wing. (See Fig. 13-11.)

Penalty bully

This is given for a foul by the defense:

1. That prevented a goal from being scored.
2. That was a willful breach of the rules.
3. That was part of deliberate or repeated fouling.

The penalty bully is taken five yards out from the center of the goal line by the player who fouled and any player chosen by the attacking team. All other players, including the goalkeeper, if she is not the defense member participating, are beyond the 25-yard line and must remain there, not taking part in the game until the penalty bully is over. The penalty bully will result in one of the following situations:

1. A goal is awarded to the attacking team and the game re-started at the 50-yard line when:
   (a) The ball goes between the goalposts off the stick of either player.
   (b) The defender fouls.
2. There is no score, the penalty bully is completed, and the game is re-started with a bully in the center 25 yards from the goal line when:
   (a) The ball goes outside the circle into the field of play.

(b) The attacker hits the ball over the goal line but not between the goalposts.
(c) The attacker fouls.

3. The penalty bully is repeated when:
   (a) The defender hits the ball over the goal line but not between the goalposts.
   (b) The ball, off the sticks of both players, goes over the goal line but not between the goalposts.
   (c) There is a double foul or improper bully.
   (d) Any other player interferes.

Corner

This formation is awarded as an advantage to the attacking team and has two variations:

1. *Long corner*: Sometimes called only a *corner,* awarded when the ball is unintentionally sent over the goal line, not between the posts, off the stick of a defender. The ball is placed five yards from the corner on either the goal line or side line, preferably on the goal line, on that side of the goal where the ball went out.
2. *Short corner*: Sometimes called a *penalty corner,* awarded when:
   (a) The ball goes over the goal line off a defender's stick with no attempt being made to keep it in the field of play.
   (b) The ball goes over the goal line off the person of the defense.
   (c) The defense fouls in the circle.

The ball is placed on the goal line not less than ten yards from the nearer goal post on either side of the goal according to the choice of the attacking team.

FORMATION. A member of the attacking team, usually the wing, takes the corner hit. The other forwards arrange themselves around the circle, their sticks and feet outside the line. The halfbacks are in position to back up the forwards. The defending team has six players, usually the defense, with their sticks and feet behind the goal line. Each player should be opposite the stick of the person she is marking. No player may be nearer than five yards to the player taking the hit. These players may move as soon as the ball is hit. The other members of the defending team, usually the forwards, may not be nearer than the 25-yard line and may not cross that line until the ball has either been touched by a player other than the hitter, or has come out of the circle.

THE PLAY. The wing hits the ball to one of the other forwards, who stops the ball and should immediately try to score. There may be no shot for goal until the ball has been stopped on the ground, not necessarily motionless, or has touched the stick or person of a defender. This stop does not have to be made by the first attacker who touched the ball. The success of a corner lies in a hard hit from the wing that stays on the ground (does not bounce), a good stop, and a quick shot for goal.

Free hit

WHEN AWARDED. A free hit is awarded to the opposite team when a foul is committed anywhere on the field, except by a defending player inside the circle.

A free hit, frequently called a "defense hit," is awarded to the defending team when:

1. An attacking player hits the ball over the end line:
   (a) Not between the goal posts.
   (b) Between the goal posts but from outside the circle.
2. The ball goes over the end line off the sticks of two opponents.
3. The ball is unintentionally hit over the goal line by a defense player from beyond the 25-yard line.

FORMATION. For a free hit outside the circle, the ball is placed on the spot where the breach occurred and is played by the defense player of the team fouled against in whose area it lies. For a free hit inside the circle, the ball may be placed anywhere within the circle area, usually at the edge, and is played preferably by the back. For a free hit following out-of-bounds over the goal line, the "defense hit" regulation applies. For any free hit, all other players must be five yards away. The ball must be motionless.

THE PLAY. The player taking the free hit strikes or pushes the ball along the ground (any stroke causing the ball to rise is illegal), but after taking the hit may not play the ball again until it has been touched by another player. Free hits should be taken quickly so as to take full advantage of the penalty before the opposing team gets placed.

Defense hit

This is the method of putting the ball in play when, under certain circumstances, it has gone over the goal line. A free hit is taken by a player of the defending team, the ball being placed 15 yards in from the goal line (16 yards for men), exactly opposite the spot where it went out and always outside the circle. This rule, adopted in 1967 and replacing the 25-yard bully, is termed "Behind" in International Rules.

Roll-in

When the ball goes over the side line a roll-in is awarded to the team opposite that of the player who last touched the ball.

FORMATION. The player taking the roll-in, usually the halfback, must have her feet and stick outside the side line. She takes the ball in one hand and her stick in the other. The left half should roll the ball in with her right hand and the right half with her left hand, as shown in Fig. 13-12. All other players are in the field of play outside the alley (the area between the side line and the five-yard line).

FIGURE 13-12. Right halfback taking a roll-in

THE PLAY. The player taking the roll-in bends over but does not kneel, and rolls the ball onto the field of play. It must touch the ground within one yard of the spot where it left the field and it may not be thrown or bounced. This player may not play the ball again until it has been touched by another player. The other players may enter the alley as soon as the ball crosses the outside line. Many effective plays can be developed from this formation if the roll-in is taken quickly.

GOALKEEPING

Goalkeeping requires different skills from other positions. The goalkeeper should not only have good stickwork, but more than that, she must have alertness of mind, agility of movement, and a courageous spirit. Her feet and legs are well protected (see equipment). She has the privilege of using her feet for stopping and directing the ball and may stop the ball with her flat hand, although she may not bat it.

POSITION. The goalkeeper stands in front of

the goal line, never on it. Imagine a semicircle that meets the goal line at the posts and extends out about a yard. The goalkeeper stands on the part of this semicircle nearest the oncoming player. Thus, should the attack be coming from her left, the goalkeeper is on the left edge of this circle, covering the angle of a possible shot. She stands with her legs together, knees bent, weight slightly forward, ready to move quickly. She follows the ball closely, and constantly changes position as the angle of a possible shot changes, being sure that she knows where the goal cage is in relation to her position. She holds her stick in her right hand part way down the handle.

TECHNIQUE. The beginning goalkeeper should meet the ball with legs together and "give" on impact, so that the ball drops almost dead. It is then cleared with the inside of the foot hard and accurately, either toward the sideline or to a back or side halfback who is ready to receive it and relay it up the field. With more experience she may learn to reach out to catch and re-direct the ball with the side of one foot, especially a well-directed shot that is impossible to reach with two feet. The stick is used only for emergency clears.

Getting the ball out of reach of the oncoming forwards is as important as stopping the initial shot. Balls not aimed between the posts should be allowed to go over the goal line untouched. When a forward is coming down alone or loses control of the ball, the goalkeeper will learn to come out fast to meet her. Experience will best teach the goalkeeper when this should be attempted.

She should never allow a defense player to block her vision. It is the job of the defense to prevent a shot and of the goalkeeper to stop it. The goalkeeper must avoid fouls such as obstruction or keeping her foot against the ball. She must not fall down.

The goalkeeper should follow the game intently all the time. There are long periods when she has little to do, but she must be on her toes when the action comes. She can help her team by analyzing the play of both teams.

OFFICIALS

There are two official scorekeepers, two official timers, and two official umpires for a hockey game. The umpires each take one-half the field. To indicate how a penalty is to be taken, the umpire will raise one arm in the direction in which the ball should be played and will stand just outside the sideline opposite the spot where the ball shall be placed. The umpire will say "Corner," or "Penalty corner," or "Defense hit" when those are to be the plays.

FIGURE 13-13. Position of players for center bully

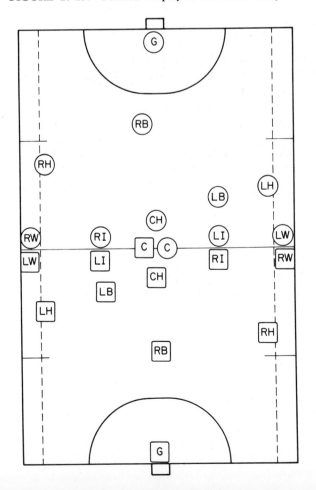

FIGURE 13-14. Position of players immediately following center bully

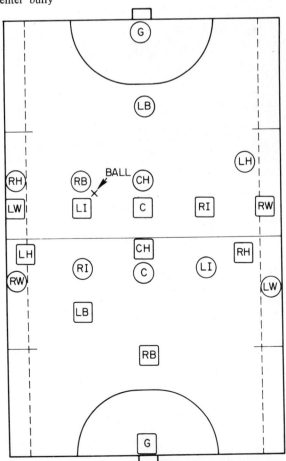

PLAYING STRATEGY

At the start of the game, the players are in the positions indicated in Fig. 13-13. This same relative formation is used for a bully in any part of the field. As soon as the bully is completed the forwards move in an attacking direction and the formation becomes similar to that seen in Fig. 13-14. This figure indicates the opponent for each player, and shows the spaces between the players and also between the lines of attack players and their defense. These spaces must be maintained to make openings through which passes may be sent and to prevent the game from becoming a muddle. Passes should be given by either a forward or defense player when a person on her team is in a good position to receive the ball. The ball should not necessarily be held until the player is tackled.

The area played by each forward is best described in Fig. 13-15. It may be seen that these areas run parallel between the 25-yard lines, but narrow toward the goal at the attacking end. In the attacking end, this division gives the inners and center forward most of the shooting and follow-up work. The wings have occasional opportunity to shoot from the edge of the circle but their responsibility on attack is more one of feeding and setting

FIGURE 13-15. Areas for forwards

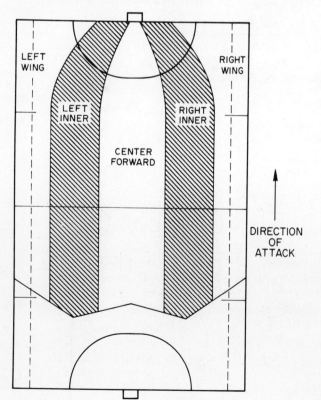

up shots than of scoring. In the defending end, the formation becomes a shallow "W" from which position the center is prepared to distribute the play; the wings are ready to carry the ball speedily down the field, the inners are deeper in the defending area waiting to relay a short pass from the defense to the wings.

Forwards on attack

When one forward has the ball, the other four forwards should be on line with and about a yard behind her. This enables each one to see the ball and also makes better spaces into which a pass may be placed. The ball should be passed from one forward to another as opportunity permits, so the defense cannot get set. A shifting attack is hardest to stop. As soon as the circle is reached, there should be a hard shot for goal quickly followed up. The attackers should make their greatest effort when they have brought the ball to this part of the field. When a shot is taken, it should be rushed fast by the center and inners with their sticks in readiness for a follow-up shot. The center goes toward the center of the goal and each inner converges so that her stick covers the area near the goalpost, thus covering the space for a possible clear by the goalkeeper. The left inner, in this play, will be farther out than the right inner. The main duty of the wings is to pass the ball in for a scoring shot by the inners or center. In the defending half of the field, the wings should be used as much as possible. This takes the play away from a possible set-up for a goal shot by the opponent, and also gives the ball to the fastest member of the team. Forwards must have initiative, speed, and determination, and be relentless in the striking circle.

Forwards on defense

When the team is defending, each forward has two main responsibilities:

1. To tackle back instantly on the opponent who takes the ball from her and to feel responsible for the opponent who marks her.
2. To position herself in such a way that a teammate with the ball can find an opening through which to pass so the forward can receive the ball while moving in the direction of their attack. (See Fig. 13-16.)

Defense

In very elementary tactics each defense is instructed to play the same area as the forward she

FIGURE 13-16. (*Left*) Position of forward receiving pass from behind on the left. (*Right*) Position of forward receiving pass from behind on the right.

FIGURE 13-17. Areas for defense

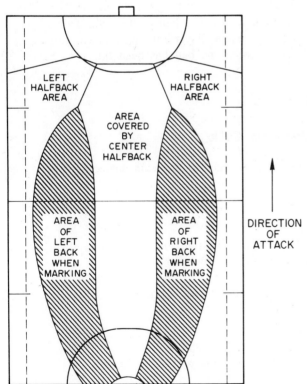

marks and to be responsible for only that person. After the first rudiments are mastered, the defense (halfbacks and backs) are given more specific areas and duties. (See Fig. 13-17.)

HALFBACKS. The halfback has two duties of equal importance:

1. When her team is attacking, she must back up her forwards. This means she must place herself between her own forward line and her opponent so as to press the attack and not allow the ball to reach the opposing forwards. When an opportunity occurs, she must be ready to take a quick hard shot for goal but not be drawn out of position.

2. When her team is defending, the halfback must mark her opponent in such a way that:
   (a) When her opponent has the ball, she is close enough to tackle her, preferably with a straight-forward tackle or a left-hand lunge.
   (b) When another member of the opposing team has the ball, she is positioned so that a pass cannot reach the forward for whom she is responsible.

The halfbacks must shift readily from attacking to defending tactics as possession of the ball changes from one team to the other.

BACKS. The backs do not come so far up the field as the halfbacks, but they have the great responsibility of stopping any attacker who breaks away. This involves two important features of defense play:

1. *Marking:* When marking, a defense player is:
   (a) Close to her opponent.
   (b) Slightly on the ball side.
   (c) Nearer the goal than the attacker.
   (d) Holding her stick down in a position to play the ball.

2. *Covering:* When covering, a player is:
   (a) Well behind the play.
   (b) In the center of the field, from side to side.
   (c) In a position of anticipation with stick down, and alert mind analyzing the play.

The back on the side of play marks her opponent, the other back covers. In Fig. 13-14, the defending right back, RB, is marking; the left back, LB, is covering. Should the play shift to the opposite side of the field, the right back will come back to cover and then the left back will mark. From the covering position, the back is ready to tackle an opposing, ball-possessing forward who has outwitted the defender marking her. Should the left inner in the diagram succeed in passing the right back, the play should be:

1. The right back turns quickly and tries to catch up and tackle again, probably with a left-hand lunge.
2. If this is impossible, the left back moves to the right and does a straight-forward tackle while the left half assumes the covering position.
3. It should be noted that the right half and the center half, the defense players nearest the play, do not enter into this interchange. They continue to mark their own opponents, thereby preventing an easy pass from occurring.

Should the wing break away from the halfback, it is unwise for the back to tackle. The wing can do no harm in the position she plays in the alley, but it is essential that the defense mark all other forwards to prevent their receiving a pass. The wing is not dangerous until she gets to the circle. At that time:

1. The halfback may have caught up to her.
2. The back can tackle her if the wing comes into the inner position.
3. The goalkeeper can handle the long shot.

A sound defense has:

1. All opposing forwards marked except the ones farthest from the ball.
2. One player in a covering position.

When the play reaches the circle, all defense players must mark closely with no covering player. Thus they can prevent a shot and avoid interfering with their goalkeeper.

FOULS AND OUT-OF-BOUNDS PLAY

Fouls

A. *When Playing the Ball, a Player Shall Not*

1. Raise any part of the stick above the shoulder at either the beginning or end of a stroke.
2. Hit the ball dangerously; i.e., into a player at close range, a hard ball that rises, or a ball hit on the fly.
3. Undercut—a drive type of stroke with the blade of the stick laid back.
4. Use the rounded side of the stick.
5. Stop the ball with any part of the body except the hand. When using the hand the ball must fall perpendicularly and not rebound in any direction. The foot may not be used to stop the ball. *Exception:* Pro-

vided she is within the striking circle, the goalkeeper is permitted to kick the ball or allow the ball to rebound from her hand (she may not bat it). She shall not be penalized if the ball is deflected off her body, providing she is within the striking circle.
6. Hit the ball between her own feet.
7. Back up her stick with her foot.
8. Take part in the game without having her stick in her hand.

B. *With Regard to an Opponent, a Player Shall Not*

1. Push, charge, shove, trip, strike at, or in any way personally handle her opponent.
2. Strike, hook, hold, lift, or in any way interfere with an opponent's stick.
3. Place her body between her opponent and the ball.
4. Allow her feet, shoulder, or any part of her body to interfere with an opponent playing the ball.
5. Run in front of an opponent so as to break her stride.

C. *Offside*

When the ball is last touched by one of her own team, a player may not be ahead of that teammate unless there are at least three defenders between her and the goal she is attacking, or she is in her own half of the field. This does not prevent a player running forward to meet a pass after the ball has been hit.

Penalties for fouls

A. *Outside the Circle*

A free hit is awarded to the team not committing the foul.

B. *Inside the Circle*

1. By the attack—a free hit anywhere in the striking circle, usually on the edge of the circle, taken by a member of the defense, preferably one of the backs.
2. By the defense—
   (a) A short, or penalty, corner is awarded to the attacking team.
   (b) A penalty bully.

Out-of-bounds play

A. Over the Sideline

1. A roll-in by a member of the team opposite that of the player who last touched the ball before it crossed the sideline.
2. A bully taken on the five-yard line opposite the spot where the ball left the field when it went out of bounds off the sticks of two opponents.

B. Over the End Line, Not between the Goal Posts

1. Off the attack—a defense hit.
2. Off the defense—
   (a) A long corner when the ball is unintentionally hit over the goal line.
   (b) A short or penalty corner when no attempt was made to keep the ball in the field of play.
3. Off the sticks of two opponents—a defense hit.

C. Over the End Line between the Goal Posts

1. A legal goal, when the ball was touched by the stick of an attack inside the striking circle. Play resumed by a center bully on the center line. The goal counts even if the ball was last touched by the stick or person of the defense.
2. When the ball was not touched by a stick of the attack inside the circle and:
   (a) was touched by a stick of the defense—a long corner.
   (b) was not touched by a stick of the defense inside the circle—a defense hit.

HELPFUL HINTS

1. Sticks may not be raised above the shoulder. It is better to keep them below the knee.
2. Use only the flat side of the stick.
3. Field the ball before hitting it. Never hit on the fly.
4. Each player should move only in her own territory.
5. Run straight up and down the field.
6. When receiving a pass from behind, the player should be looking back over her shoulder, and be in a running position with her feet going in the direction of her attacking goal.
7. The player should go to meet a pass coming toward her and leave a ball going away from her.
8. A player should move away from a teammate with the ball to make a space into which the ball may be passed.
9. In order to avoid obstruction, the player herself must turn in a clockwise direction around the ball, and never pull the ball around her.
10. Do not touch an opponent with the stick or the body.
11. Do not run in front of another player whether she has the ball or not.
12. A forward should not get ahead of another forward who has the ball until the offside rule is thoroughly mastered.
13. Keep a space between the line of forwards and the line of defense through which passes may be sent.
14. Pass when a teammate is free to receive the ball rather than wait to draw an opponent.

MEN'S FIELD HOCKEY

The basic differences between men's and women's game are:

1. The striking circle for men is 16 yards in, and the alleys are seven yards wide.
2. The penalty bully for women is replaced in men's game by a penalty flick which is played eight yards from the center of the goal.

TERMINOLOGY

Advancing   Foul committed when the ball rebounds from a player's person.

Alley   Area of the field between the side line and the five-yard or alley line.

Backing up   Describes play of defense who stands directly behind a bully.

Bully   Play used to start or re-start the game. Opposing players alternately strike the ground and each other's sticks three times before touching the ball.

Circle   Same as striking circle.

Circular tackle   Play used to attempt to take the ball from an opponent on the player's right.

The situation should be avoided when possible.

Corner A play following certain infringements of the rules; the formation used in such a play. See long corner and short corner.

Covering Defensive anticipatory position much nearer the defending goal than the play. Usually refers to a fullback. As opposed to marking.

Defense hit Method of putting the ball in play when, under certain circumstances, it has gone over the goal line.

Dodge Play used to evade an opponent while maintaining control of the ball.

Dribble Series of short strokes used to take the ball down the field while maintaining constant control of it.

Drive Hard stroke with a back swing. May be done to right, left, or straight ahead.

Fielding Controlling an approaching ball before it is passed or played.

Flick A wrist stroke having no back swing. Ball rises slightly. Stick is brought around the ball during execution. Good for close shooting or passing to a marked player. Illegal for a free hit.

Foul Infringement of rules. Penalty may be a free hit, short corner, or penalty bully.

Free hit A play following some infringements of rules. Taken by a player on the team fouled against.

Fundamental position Term used in this book to define the position of player, stick, and ball that is basic to most strokes.

Goal The part of the end line between the goal posts; a score made when the ball crosses that goal line, having been touched by an attack inside the circle. Each goal counts one point.

Holding the whistle Term used when the umpire allows play to continue after a foul when, in her opinion, this is more advantageous to the team fouled against than stopping play and awarding a penalty.

Left-hand lunge See *Lunge*.

Long corner The play awarded to the attack after the ball goes over the end line unintentionally,

off the stick of a defense; the ball is placed five yards from the corner.

Lunge Stroke used in attempting to take the ball from an opponent on the player's left. It is a useful tackle that has great reach. May be used for a pass or follow-up shot when a long reach is necessary.

Marking Defensive position when the player stays close to her opponent.

Obstruction A foul made by placing the body or any part of it between the opponent and the ball so as to interfere with the opponent's effort to play or reach the ball.

Off-side The foul committed by a player receiving the ball while in an illegal position.

Own goal The goal one's own team defends.

Own half The half of the field one's team defends.

Penalty bully Penalty following a serious breach of rules by the defense in the circle. Not common.

Penalty corner See *Short corner*.

Push-pass A quick wrist stroke having no back swing. The ball does not rise. When the stroke is executed the stick faces the direction of the pass in contact with the ball. Accurate and easy to receive.

Reverse sticks Turning the stick over to play a ball on the left, or to tackle a player on the right. A weak play often resulting in a foul by obstruction, therefore better attempted by experienced players.

Roll-in Method of putting the ball in play after it has gone over the sideline.

Scoop Stroke without back swing in which the ball is lifted slightly with the toe of the stick. Good as a dodge. Illegal for a free hit.

Short corner The play awarded to the attack for a foul by the defense inside the circle or when the defense intentionally hits the ball over the end line. The ball is placed ten yards from the goal post. Also called penalty corner.

Stick side The player's right side. So-called because the stick meets the ball on that side of the body.

Sticks Raising the stick above the shoulder at either the beginning or end of a stroke. It is a foul.

Striking circle The goal-shooting area; the curved line that encloses it.

SELECTED REFERENCES

Delano, Anne Lee, *Field Hockey*. Dubuque, Iowa: William C. Brown Company, Inc., 1967.

Division for Girls' and Women's Sports, *Field Hockey —Lacrosse Guide*. Washington, D.C.: American Association for Health, Physical Education and Recreation.

Lees, Josephine T., and Betty Shellenberger, *Field Hockey for Players, Coaches, and Umpires*. New York: The Ronald Press Company, 1957.

Ley, Katherine, and Donna M. Miller, *Individual and Team Sports for Women*. Englewood Cliffs, N. J.: Prentice-Hall, Inc., 1955.

Meyer, Margaret, and Marguerite Schwarz, *Team Sports for Girls and Women* (4th ed.). Philadelphia: W. B. Saunders Co., 1965.

Pollard, Marjorie, *Hockey for All*. New York: Thomas Nelson & Sons, 1957.

Vannier, Maryhelen, and Hally Beth Poindexter, *Individual and Team Sports for Girls and Women* (2nd ed.). Philadelphia: W. B. Saunders Co., 1968.

Golf

14

ORIGIN AND DEVELOPMENT

The game of golf as it is played today had its origin in Scotland in the early fourteenth century. However, the origination of the game has been ascribed to many peoples and many lands. Probably a game of striking a ball or pellet with a knobbed stick is as old as the spirit of play.

In 1754, the first rules to govern the sport were established by a committee at the St. Andrew's Golf Club in Scotland. These were 13 in number and some remain in the rules of today's game. St. Andrew's has come to be the world shrine of golfdom. It is considered one of the most outstanding courses in the world today and was built in 1552.

The game came to the United States in about 1885. However, there is evidence that it was played in Canada as early as 1873. The first golf club in this country, St. Andrew's of Yonkers, New York, was established in 1888. John G. Reid is called the "Father of American Golf," for he first introduced it to his friends at Yonkers at this time. Play took place in a cow pasture and the course consisted of six holes

of from 150 to 250 yards in length. Since the players had no lease from the owner for use of the land, it wasn't long until they were forced to move to another site. The first permanent course with a club house was established at the Shinnecock Hills Golf Course in Westchester County, New York.

The United States Golf Association was established in December, 1894. Two annual championships were set up. One was open and one for amateurs. These carry over today as the United States Open and the United States Amateur Golf Tournaments. Anyone was eligible for the Open, including those who taught the game and professionals, but the Amateur was restricted to members of any club associated with the United States Golf Association. This rule remained in effect, despite the growth of public course and public links players, until the last decade.

Since that day in 1888, the game has shown tremendous growth. A recent survey reveals that there are in excess of 13,400 nine and 18 hole courses in 50 countries throughout the world—from one in Israel to over 9000 in the United States. Australia has approximately 1200; England 1100; and Scotland 450. In addition to the courses, there are innumerable driving ranges—some of these having two and three levels—par 3 courses, and miniature courses.

It is estimated that there are in excess of 15 million golfers in the 50 countries. The United States leads with approximately nine million, followed by Japan with two million, and England with one and one-half million. New Zealand has the highest per capita golf population.

The growth of golf courses has not kept pace with the tremendous increase in the number of persons who desire to play. As a result, starting times must be obtained and more time allotted for playing nine or eighteen holes.

OFFICIALS

In stroke play—a Rules Committee.

In match play—a Referee accompanies each group of players in the final rounds.

NATURE OF THE GAME

One of the greatest advantages to the game lies in the age range of those able to participate. Youths of 12 may become quite proficient, and the game can be played at a much earlier age. On many courses, men in their 70's may be found participating. Moreover, increasing age does not seem to cause a great loss of skill, as is the case in many sports. Many older golfers pride themselves by *shooting their age*. The game offers a chance for fellowship in the open air, and is good exercise without calling for undue exertion, since it can be played at a leisurely pace. The concentration necessary to play the game properly serves as a cathartic for the mental strain of present-day life. An 18-hole round of play may consume most of an afternoon, or fewer holes may be played in the summer at the end of a full workday. Nine holes can often be completed in an hour and a half.

Golf may be played by strokes or by holes. In stroke play, the winner is the player using the least number of strokes over the entire distance of the game. In match play, or play by holes, the winner is the golfer who wins the greater number of holes despite the final total in strokes. Stroke play is considered the more exacting, since each shot is of equal value, whereas in match play a loss of two or more strokes on one hole may be recouped by a one-stroke victory on a later hole.

Handicapping is a means of equalizing competition among golfers of differing abilities. The player with the lower average score is required to give strokes to the higher average golfer. In stroke play the higher average player subtracts these strokes from his total to get a *net* score. This is compared with the other player's *gross* or total score to determine the winner. In most handicap play the strokes are usually computed in relation to the difference between par and the average score of the player. Thus, many can compete in a tournament on a handicap basis. In match play the strokes are subtracted from the higher average player's score on holes designated as the most difficult. That is, a handicap of five would allow the player to subtract one stroke from his score on the five most difficult holes.

Sometimes a Nassau system of scoring is used. This would be two players matched against each other, or as a team matched against another pair.

SCORE CARD

HOLE	1	2	3	4	5	6	7	8	9	OUT	10	11	12	13	14	15	16	17	18	IN	Total
Championship BLUE	440	545	250	350	175	385	420	385	480	3430	520	440	525	420	205	350	385	185	405	3435	6865
Men's WHITE	365	515	245	325	160	380	415	350	455	3210	450	420	510	405	150	325	380	180	395	3215	6425
PAR	4	5	3	4	3	4	4	4	5	36	5	4	5	4	3	4	4	3	4	36	72
Men's Handicap	5	3	13	15	17	7	1	11	9		12	2	6	4	18	14	10	16	8		
Won + Lost - Halved 0																					
Women's YELLOW	360	490	245	320	160	365	410	350	440	3140	440	405	510	405	150	320	370	175	395	3170	6315
PAR	4	5	4	4	3	4	5	4	5	38	5	5	5	5	3	4	4	3	4	38	76
Women's Handicap	5	1	17	9	15	7	11	13	3		4	10	2	16	18	12	8	14	6		

DATE _____ PLAYER _____ ATTEST _____

Each match is worth three points, one point being awarded the winner of the first nine holes, one point for the second nine, and one point for the winner of the eighteen holes. As many individual matches as necessary can be played in this manner, thus allowing for team competition—one school or club versus another.

There are many recreational types of play. These are used in friendly games and by clubs staging special tournaments. The "Hole-in-One" contest is one of the most popular. Each participant is given a certain number of shots on a short hole in an attempt to score a hole in one or come as near it as possible. The winners are those who come nearest. In the Scotch Foursome, a team of two plays one ball and each player alternates hitting. In "Bingle-Bangle-Bongle," the group competes for points on the basis of a point for the first player to reach the green, for the first to go into the hole, and for the nearest player to the hole after all players are on the green. A Flag Tournament is a means of conducting a one-day, one-round tournament where the average of those competing is known. Each player is given his average number of strokes for the round, and when he has used them up he plants his flag. Prizes may be awarded for the one whose flag is planted farthest along the course, or for those whose flags are planted in specific holes or in unusual spots. These should be known, however, only to the planners of the tournament. Another unusual type of game is the "Blind Bogey" tournament. Certain holes are selected as the only ones to be counted in the total. Prizes may be given for low totals, for low particular holes, and for high on certain other holes.

The "Dogfight" is a method of foursome competition. Here the foursome may be played for low ball for the group or points may be set up to be awarded for particular types of scoring. For example, four points may be given for each eagle, three points for each birdie, two for each par, and one for each bogey. This system is excellent, since each member of a group may make a contribution to his team even though his is not the lowest score.

The "Specialist" tournament is one in which each member of a group of players plays only the particular type of shot in which he specializes. A variation of this for recreational use is where each member of a group is given only one club, but the players must alternate shots. Thus, the player with the driver may be putting or the player with the putter may be called on to get out of a trap. The golf may not be the best, but the players enjoy it.

Putting, approaching, and driving contests may also be part of recreational competition.

THE COURSE

The course is the whole area within which play is permitted. It is the duty of authorities in charge of the course to define its boundaries accurately. Most courses consist of eighteen holes. However, there are many nine-hole courses. Golf scores are based on eighteen holes of play, with the par usually varying between 70 and 72. Each hole consists of a tee, tee markers, fairway, rough, boundaries, a green, cup, and a flag. Most courses include hazards in the nature of traps, bunkers, water, and trees found in strategic areas so as to penalize poorly played shots.

DIRECTIONS FOR COMPUTING PAR ON A GOLF COURSE

For Men

Par 3 Up to 250 yards, inclusive
Par 4 241 to 470 yards, inclusive
Par 5 471 yards and over

For Women

Par 3 Up to 210 yards, inclusive
Par 4 211 to 400 yards, inclusive
Par 5 401 to 575 yards, inclusive
Par 6 576 yards and over

EQUIPMENT

In choosing equipment, it is wise to consult a golf professional. He can give invaluable advice. The beginner may not wish to invest in a complete set of expensive clubs. Many of the less expensive clubs will suffice in the beginning. A minimum set should contain one wood, four irons, and a putter. The recommended choices would be a Number 3 wood, the 3, 5, 7, and 9 irons, and a putter. The Number 1 wood, which completes the basic set, can be added when it is warranted by the player's progress. While it is possible to obtain a full set by gradually adding the missing clubs, such as the Numbers 4 and 2 woods and the 8, 6, 4, and 2 irons, as well as the sand wedge, a better plan is to play with the basic set until a fairly high level of skill is reached. At this time, the professional should be called upon to fit the player with a better and completely matched set of 14 clubs of his choice. The most popular 14 clubs are the driver; numbers 3 and 4 woods; numbers 2 through 9 irons; a pitching wedge; a sand wedge; and a putter. It is usual practice for the professional to allow a trade-in on the beginner's set of clubs.

Golf clubs are precision instruments. If you were to apply a piece of tape to the heel of a wood

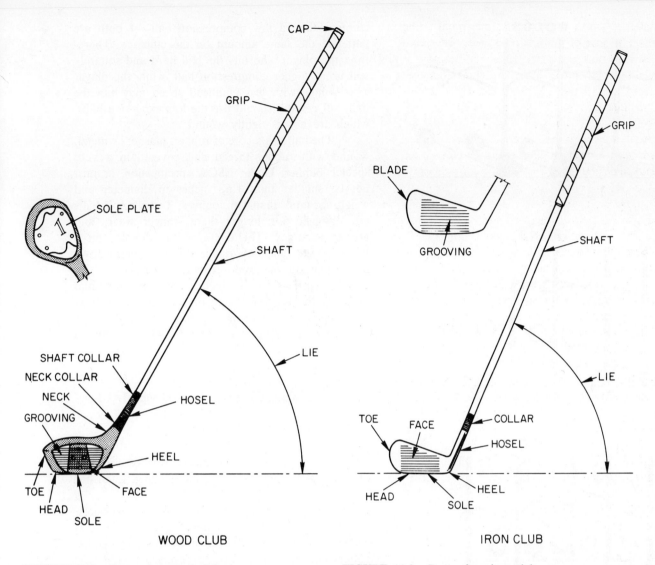

CAP

GRIP

SOLE PLATE

SHAFT

SHAFT COLLAR

NECK COLLAR

NECK

GROOVING

LIE

HOSEL

HEEL

TOE

FACE

HEAD

SOLE

WOOD CLUB

BLADE

GROOVING

GRIP

SHAFT

LIE

TOE

FACE

COLLAR

HOSEL

HEAD

HEEL

SOLE

IRON CLUB

FIGURE 14-1. Parts of a wood club

FIGURE 14-2. Parts of an iron club

club, it could change the club swingweight. This would affect a skilled golfer's shotmaking ability considerably.

Swingweight, determined by a swingweight scale, is the relationship among the weights of a club's component parts—grip, shaft, and head. Such scales may be found in most pro shops.

The length of the clubs is most important. Most men find that a 43-inch driver is the best; most women prefer a 42-inch. A longer club might give you more distance, as it would widen your swing arc and increase the clubhead speed. A man who uses a 43-inch driver would most probably use a 38½-inch 2 iron. A woman using a 42-inch driver would most probably use a 37½- to 38-inch 2 iron.

Shaft flexibility plays an important role in golf, as it determines the golfer's "feel" of the clubhead. The various types of clubshafts are: the extra-stiff, used only by very long hitters; stiff or firm, used by

the average hitter; medium-stiff, suitable for most men; medium flex, used by lighter-hitting men and long-hitting women.

The design of the clubhead is important in the selection of clubs. Players who drive less than 175 yards are advised to use wood clubs with relatively shallow faces and with a loft of 10 degrees in order to gain additional height. Those who drive between 175 and 225 yards should have a deeper-faced club with a loft of 9 degrees, and the players who drive over 225 yards usually use the deepest-faced club with a loft of 8 degrees. The difference in face-depth of the irons is not too important, as most irons have practically the same face-depth.

Grips for men and women players vary from the thin, for short-fingered players, to the standard size, for big-handed and/or long-fingered players. A good guide is, "If it feels right, it is for you."

Tees are made of wood, plastic, or even light

WOODS

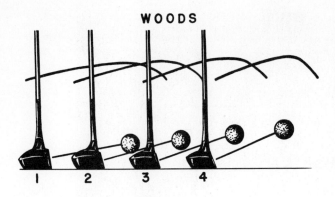

IRONS

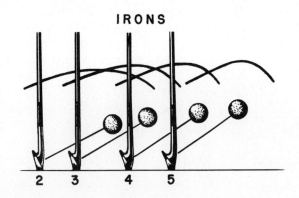

IRONS

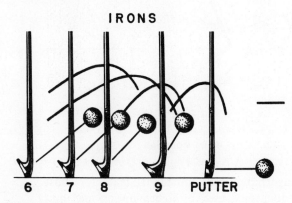

FIGURE 14-3. Club lofts. The loft of any one club will vary a few degrees. The above are manufacturers' recommendations.

metals. Wooden tees are considered best and are usually least expensive. There is very little difference among the types of tees that would give anyone a particular advantage.

Golf balls come in a variety of types and in a wide price range. In the case of a beginner, it is not always necessary to buy the most expensive balls. Less expensive balls will serve the purpose equally well.

The distance a ball travels is largely determined by the amount it is compressed by the clubhead at impact. A ball which is tightly wound and has a high compression rebounds farther from the clubface than a low compression ball—if both are flattened the same amount on the clubface. Therefore, the player who hits the ball hard and squarely will use a higher compression ball, while the player who swings with less clubhead speed and hits the ball "off center" should use the less expensive balls, which are not as tightly wound.

The ball has a core of rubber, plastic, or metal, wound with rubber thread and covered in a very special manner. Under USGA specification, it must not be smaller than 1.68 inches in diameter and weigh not more than 1.62 ounces. Today's golf balls are designed for longer flight, longer wear, and greater accuracy. The depth of the dimples on a ball is of extreme importance. Manufacturers have, through years of experimentation, learned that a dimple depth of 0.0135 inches produces maximum distance, the highest degree of accuracy, and maximum usage. A decrease of 0.002 inches in the dimples would reduce a drive of 240 yards by 20 to 30 yards.

TECHNIQUES AND FUNDAMENTALS

The grip

There are two acceptable grips of the golf club: the overlapping and the interlocking. Each has its proponents. The overlapping grip, however, is more widely accepted by teachers and professionals. For this reason, the overlapping grip will be discussed here. Descriptions are given for right-handed golfers and must, naturally, be reversed to suit left-handed players.

The left hand should be placed on the club first. This should be done by keeping the fingers as close together as possible and the thumb close to the hand at the first joint, as in Figure 14-4a. The hand is held so that the wrist is directly above the shaft. The V formed by the thumb and the forefinger points over the right shoulder, as in Figure 14-4b. The right hand is easier to place. Again, keep the fingers close together and the thumb close to the hand at the first joint. When placing the right hand on the shaft, the palm faces the target, as in Figures 14-4c and 14-4d.

The right-hand grip is mostly in the fingers, and the little finger of the right hand overlaps the forefinger of the left, resting between the forefinger and the middle finger. The shaft is gripped by the other three fingers of the right hand, and the thumb is placed at the left of the center of the shaft. The V formed by the right thumb and forefinger should point to the necktie. It is generally possible, in the

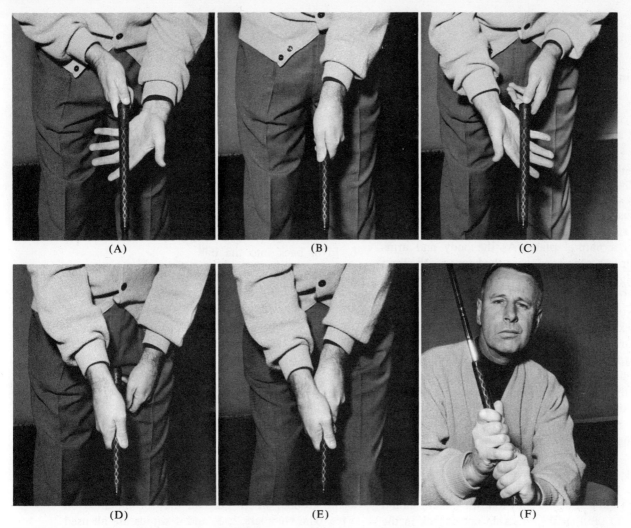

FIGURE 14-4. The overlapping grip. (A) Position of the club in the left hand—open. (B) The left hand closed. (C) Position of the club in the right hand—open. (D) The right hand closed. (E) Positions of both hands on the club. (The complete overlapping grip.) (F) Rear view of the overlapping grip.

overlapping grip, for the golfer to see three knuckles on the left hand and one or two on the right. Figures 14-4e and 14-4f show the compactness of the grip.

The stance

There are three types of stance that may be taken when addressing the ball preparatory to hitting it. The open stance is taken with the left foot pulled farther away from the intended line of flight than the right foot. The closed stance has the right foot pulled farther away from the intended line of flight than the left foot. The square stance, with both feet lined up equidistant from the line of flight, is probably the best for almost all shots, especially for the beginner. It is considered better to instruct the beginner with the fundamentals of the swing from one stance and explain to him the various adaptations. As he gains

mastery of the game, he may adapt these modifications to fit his own situations.

In assuming the proper stance, the player should be careful to keep the weight of the body equally distributed on both feet, resting between the ball and the heel. The knees are slightly flexed as they are just prior to sitting. The body is bent at the waist only to the extent necessary for the club to rest flat on the ground.

The feet should be about as far apart as the width of the shoulders. Too wide a stance tends to restrict free movement, and too narrow a stance makes for difficult balance. However, the amount of separation between the feet will be determined largely by the individual. The distance one stands from the ball is controlled by the extension of the left arm. Care should be taken not to stand too far away, thus shifting the weight to the toes. On the other hand, crowding the ball causes the arms to break badly at the elbows.

The swing

In swinging a golf club, the attempt is to swing it back and through a large circle. True, an elliptical circle, but this is of slight importance in the primary stage. The important point is that the club head leaves the ball and returns to the same point each time it is swung. The player should consider his body as the center of this circle and his arms as the radius. It is necessary for him to pivot his body around a vertical axis and allow his arms to follow firmly in a natural plane. As the body and arms start their backswing and when the hands reach about waist height, the wrists begin to cock. They continue cocking to the top of the swing. At the top, the left hand is parallel to the line of flight. Here, the left arm is extended comfortably away from the body, and the right arm is bent, with the elbow pointing downward. The length of the backswing varies with individuals and the clubs used. The woods generally require the longest backswing. The swing shortens as the clubs for shorter distance and more accuracy are brought into play. In the use of any club, the backswing should be leisurely, avoiding any tendency to hurry.

In the downswing, the initial movement is from the waist down. The weight returns to the left foot, with the rest of the body following. Care should be taken to see that the wrists do not uncock in the early stages of the downswing. The speed is accelerated through the reverse pivot of the body and arms.

The release point of the wrists should be as late in the downswing as possible. Momentum will cause the release of the wrists close to the point of impact in a natural way. The club continues on to complete a follow-through position, with the arms extended and the body maintaining a vertical line of balance.

In order to maintain the vertical line of balance, both back and through, the eye should be kept on the ball during the backswing and downswing. Only after the ball is struck should the head be allowed to turn and follow the flight of the ball.

The thought required to swing the club should be kept as simple as possible. Cluttering the movement with excess thought is detrimental, rather than helpful. In practicing, care should be taken to follow a simple sequence of motion each time the player addresses and swings at a ball. Habit will be formed along correct lines if this advice is followed. Haphazard practice is almost as bad as no practice at all, and it should be avoided.

A simple sequence of motion for address and swing follows:

1. Center the club face behind the ball and adjust the shaft square to the intended line of flight.
2. Grip the club.
3. Place the feet. They should be parallel to the line of flight, with the ball just inside the left heel. Arms should be extended only enough to clear the body and to allow balance to be maintained.
4. In the backswing, the arms and body should move as nearly in one piece as possible.
5. At the top of the backswing the wrists should be cocked.
6. Pivot back into the ball.
7. Release the wrists and continue on into the follow-through position.

Figures 14-5 through 14-10 show the basic positions for the swings necessary to play various shots. They will serve as a guide to a simplified procedure.

TYPES OF SHOTS

The wood shots

The woods are used for the longest shots in golf. The driver is primarily used for shots from the teeing ground, where the ball may be mounted on a tee. The Numbers 2, 3, and 4 woods are all used for extra distance when hitting from the fairway. Each is graded for a slightly shorter distance than the lower numbered club. The higher the number of the club, the greater the height of the shot.

For the drive, the ball should be approximately in line with the instep of the left foot. With the Numbers 2, 3, and 4 woods, the ball can be played slightly on the inside of the left heel.

In playing shots from the fairway where the ball is resting on depressed ground, it is often best to choose an iron. In selecting a wood for a fairway shot, the lie should always be carefully considered. If there is doubt of success, an iron should be chosen. A poorly played wood shot is never as effective as a well-played shot with one of the irons. In the rough, the lie must be exceptionally good to warrant the use of one of the woods.

The long irons

The Numbers 2, 3, and 4 irons are considered the long irons. They are used on the fairway when maximum distance is desired, but the lie is such that the use of a wood is not deemed advisable. The irons, being shorter, allow the plane of swing to be more upright. Consequently, the player is closer to the ball. Irons give greater accuracy and offer more control of the shot. They also impart backspin to the ball, allowing better placement of the shot.

In choosing the proper club, always select one that does not require straining for distance. Underclubbing may cause the player to press and sacrifice accuracy for distance. A Number 3 iron swung with a three-quarter swing is more easily controlled than a Number 5 iron swung as hard as possible. There is no premium for an exceptionally long shot with a particular iron when another, longer iron might be used and more accuracy obtained. The irons are graded to be used at various distances, and there is a proper club for each distance. This may vary with individuals, but each player must determine what club is proper for him. There is no disgrace in using a Number 2 iron when a stronger player used a Number 5 iron for the same distance. The question is who went the closest to the hole with the club he used.

With the longer irons, the stance involves a somewhat shorter stride and the ball is played between the left heel and the center of the body. The golfer stands closer to the ball, since the shaft of the club is shorter than the wood. In hitting all iron

FIGURE 14-5. Sequence of the full swing for woods. (A) Addressing the ball. *Note:* club is perpendicular to the line of flight, the feet are about shoulder width apart, and the ball is opposite the left heel for the driver. (B) Pivot around vertical line of balance. (C) Continue back, allowing wrist to cock. (D) Return back into the ball; wrists have not yet released. (E) Swing continues through the ball; wrists have been released; arms follow flight. (F) Full follow-through position; vertical line balance is maintained; grip is still kept firm on club.

(A)   (B)   (C)

(D)   (E)   (F)

(a)   (b)   (c)

(d)   (e)   (f)

FIGURE 14-6. Sequence showing full swing for long irons. Ball is played a little more on the inside of the left heel. *Note:* club does not go back as far as with wooden clubs. Shorter shaft and shot being played slightly firmer causes this.

shots, the club meets the ball just prior to the bottom of the downswing, taking a little turf after the ball is struck. (See Fig. 14-6.)

The medium irons

This name applies to the Number 5, 6, and 7 irons. They are the middle-distance clubs, so far as the irons are concerned. They offer greater accuracy and also allow the player to achieve some distance. These can often save strokes on the score. Many holes can be negotiated with a good tee shot and a well-placed one with an iron—leaving only an average length putt. These clubs can substitute for an approach shot if played well onto the green. They can also compensate for a slightly missed tee shot in many cases. Out of the rough, they give enough loft to the ball to get out of trouble and still give fair distance. These clubs are often used for chip shots close around the green, where entry is not obstructed by traps or hazards. All in all, they are very useful clubs for a multiplicity of purposes. (See Fig. 14-7.)

The short irons

These are the Number 8 and 9 irons and the sand wedge. They have a high pitch to the face of the club and are used for short shots around the green and in getting out of the rough, hazards, and traps. These clubs are designed so that they impart a great deal of backspin to the ball and therefore little roll at the end of the shot. The ball is hit on the downstroke and some turf is taken. Here, accuracy is the main concern and thus the backswing is shortened. The pivot and body action is reduced and more

of the swing is produced in the action of the arms and hands. More advanced golfers play these shots with a slightly open stance. (See Fig. 14-8.)

In making a shot from a sand trap, address the ball with a slightly open stance—toes pointed slightly toward the target, ball played opposite the left foot, clubface open, and weight on the left foot at address and during the swing. (See Fig. 14-9.) There should be little body and leg movement during the swing. Make certain that the clubhead accelerates into and through the sand. Practice with the sand wedge is very important, as the type of

FIGURE 14-7. Sequence showing full swing for medium irons. *Note:* As shafts of clubs get shorter, player is closer to ball, but body and arm position remain the same.

(a) (b) (c)

(d) (e) (f)

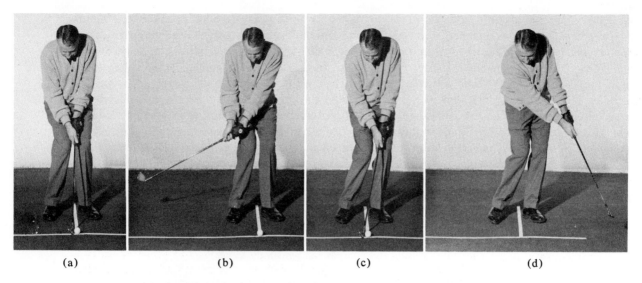

(a)   (b)   (c)   (d)

FIGURE 14-8. Proper position and swing sequence for playing part shots (short approach shots). *Note:* Ball is played between the feet. Because of the shorter shaft, player is closer to the ball. The body remains in fundamentally the same erect position and the arms are still extended. The backswing is shorter. Notice that the hands are past the ball before the wrists are released, and that the follow-through is shorter and firm on the line of target.

(a)   (b)   (c)

FIGURE 14-9. The sand shot. *Note:* stance is slightly open; the ball is opposite the left foot; the clubface is open; and weight is on the left foot at address and during the swing.

sand in the bunker will determine the amount of force required, the position of the clubhead, and where the clubhead enters the sand. If the sand is of the coastal type, the clubhead should enter it at approximately three-quarters of an inch behind the ball; if "dirt" sand, at approximately one inch; and if very loose sand, at approximately two inches.

The putt

This is probably the most important phase of the game, and too often one of the most neglected. Half the strokes allowed for par on most courses are allotted to play on the greens. The greens are therefore the places on which the average golfer can achieve par figures and also where strokes lost in other phases of the game can be regained. Concentration and confidence are two of the primary requirements for good putting, and can be gained best through practice of fundamental techniques. Forms of putting differ widely. However, basic fundamentals are much the same. The stance can vary more than in other shots. It should be one that is comfortable and in no way cramps the shot. Stand well up to the ball so that the eyes are directly over it. The feet should be fairly close together and with a slightly open stance. The weight of the body should be comfortably placed on both feet. There is a slight variation in the grip used for the putt. To permit the hands to swing the club in a loose pendulum movement, turn the hands so that both wrists face each other. The left arm should be kept rather close to the body and the right forearm should be kept rather close to the right thigh in order to permit the club head to be brought back in a straight line and to swing through on a direct line to the hole. The right elbow should be resting lightly on the right hip. The ball should be played from a position midway between the feet or toward the left foot. Many golfers play the ball from a position off the inside of the left foot. The backswing should be low and along the line of flight and the stroke should be followed through in the same manner. The stroke should be sharp and crisp and one that is fairly short.

By approaching the ball from the rear, the golfer can "read" the green. Since few greens are absolutely flat, the golfer must determine which way the ball will curve and to what extent. More important, however, is the distance the ball must travel. The player should study each green to determine its speed by considering the way the grass grows, how it is cut, and how hard the turf is. If the distance of the putt is accurately judged, the golfer will seldom leave himself a difficult second putt. On the other hand, if the distance is badly misjudged, even though the direction is accurate, there may be a long, bothersome putt waiting. (See Fig. 14-10.)

SAFETY HINTS

1. Never hit a shot until you are sure those in front of you are out of your range. If you hit another player you may be liable for damages.
2. Never swing a club, especially on the tees, unless you are sure no one is standing close to you.
3. If the warning "Fore" is given, it is often dangerous to turn to see where the ball is coming from. It is best to cover the head for protection and turn away from the direction of the warning.
4. In the event of a thunderstorm, it is not wise to remain outdoors. Shelter should be sought in a closed building protected against lightning. Large or small unprotected buildings are alternatives in the order given. If remaining outdoors is unavoidable, keep away from open spaces and hilltops. Also, stay away from isolated trees, wire fences, and small shelters in exposed locations. Protec-

FIGURE 14-10. Putting. (A) Ball is played from the left heel, feet fairly close together, palms facing each other, blade square to direction line. (B) Clubhead follows direction back, little or no movement above the elbows. (C) Club follows through toward the hole with the blade square to direction line.

(A) (B) (C)

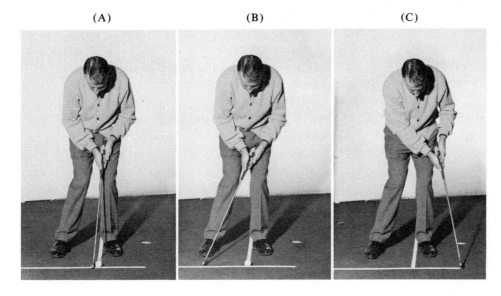

tion may be sought in caves, depressions or deep valleys and canyons, the foot of a cliff, or in a dense stand of trees. Umbrellas held overhead in exposed places are dangerous.

5. Never practice in an area where others are playing. Most golf courses have special practice areas.

6. Never hit practice shots while playing a round. It not only wastes time, but is dangerous.

7. Only one person should hit at a time. The person farthest from the hole should play first.

8. Knowing the rules of golf and golfing etiquette and practicing them will increase one's safety on a golf course.

HELPFUL HINTS

1. For downhill shots, use a lofted club, a wide stance, and play the ball back so as not to hit the hill on the downswing.

2. For uphill shots, use a straight face club, feet well apart for balance, and play the ball opposite the left foot. Let the club follow the contour of the hill.

3. For sidehill shots (standing below the ball), use a shorter grip, aim to the right and open the stance, and play the ball back to make certain you hit the ball first and not the turf.

4. For sidehill shots (standing above the ball), use a longer grip, close the stance, and flex the knees to get down to the ball—don't lean.

5. If you slice, try closing your stance, closing the left hand, and placing the right hand farther over the shaft. If you hook, do the reverse.

6. Remember there is a maximum body pivot and backswing on woods for distance. As the clubs become shorter and the distances decrease, the body pivot and backswing also decrease.

7. Study each shot carefully, but don't delay other players.

8. Learn to control your shots before trying for distance.

9. Learn the distances you hit each of your clubs. Play your own game—not your opponent's.

10. Always select the club that will not require straining for distance.

11. Learn to judge distances.

12. Study the roll of the green by approaching your ball from the rear.

13. Concentrate on each shot and take your time.

14. Relax before hitting every shot. Taking a fairly deep breath and then exhaling just before starting the swing is a good method of relaxing.

15. Study the speed and direction of the wind, condition of the course, and the terrain to be covered on each shot.

16. After you have played, attempt to analyze your game and work on those phases that need improvement.

17. Remember that good golfers not only play, but practice as well.

18. Learn the rules of golf and golfing etiquette.

19. Hit drives to the center of the fairway except in unusual circumstances.

20. Play to the safe side of the greens if there is no contour; play to the downhill side if they slope.

PLAYING COURTESIES

1. Do not talk, move around, stand too close or directly in line of a shot when another player is preparing to shoot.

2. Never play a shot until the group ahead is completely out of range.

3. As soon as a hole has been completed, the players should leave the green. Do not total the scores and record them on the green.

4. While looking for a lost ball, do not unduly delay the play of others. Allow a group playing behind you to go through by signaling them to do so and do not resume play until they are out of range.

5. Replace all turf and press it down after each shot in which you displace turf.

6. Allow the person farthest from the hole to shoot first.

7. Fill holes made in bunkers and smooth sand after playing from a trap.

8. Only the person with the honor should tee his ball on the teeing ground. Only one ball should be teed at a time.

9. When lifting a ball on the green, mark it with a coin.

10. Never lay a bag of clubs down on the green.

11. Do not throw the flag stick off to the side. Always lay it down gently, away from all play, and replace it when the hole has been completed.

12. Do not damage the hole with the flag stick or by standing too close to the hole.

13. Repair ball bruises on the green.

RULES

The United States Golf Association, 40 East 38th Street, New York, New York 10016, is the official ruling body for golf in this country. It publishes a rule book each year and offers it for sale at minimal cost. It is strongly recommended that serious students obtain a copy. Here is a list of the basic rules a golfer should observe:

1. Players must play by the rules. Players shall not agree to exclude the operation of any rule or local rule or to waive any penalty incurred. Failure to abide by this means disqualification.

2. Legal clubs and golf balls must be used. The specifications for both are listed in the rule book.

3. A player may have a maximum of 14 clubs.

4. The tee markers will be found on each tee. A player must tee his ball between these markers or anywhere in a rectangle two club-lengths behind them. If he tees up ahead of the markers, his opponent in match play may recall his shot and force him to re-play properly with no penalty. In stroke play the player must shoot again, counting his first stroke and adding one stroke penalty.

5. Every time a player intentionally strikes at the ball he must count a stroke, even though he "fans" it. But on the tee, if he accidentally knocks the ball off the wooden-peg tee, he may replace it without penalty. If a player accidentally touches the ball after it is put in play from the tee, and the ball moves out of position, the penalty is one stroke.

6. A ball is lost when not found within five minutes or when another ball is played under the rules.

7. The honor of the first tee shall be decided by lot. After the first hole, the honor is changed when a hole is won by one other than the man with the honor. Subsequently, the honor goes to the individual or team winning the last hole played.

8. The ball must be fairly struck at and not pushed, scraped, or spooned with the head of the club.

9. The ball must be played where it lies. It may not be touched, except as provided in the rules.

10. Any flag stick, implement, vehicle, or loose impediment may be removed. A ball lying near an immovable obstacle, such as a shelter, bridge, drain, hydrant, exposed waterpipe, or a ball lying in a hole made by a greenskeeper may be lifted and dropped as provided in the rules. The ball should not be moved more than two club-lengths and must not get moved nearer the hole.

11. In dropping the ball, the player should stand facing the hole and drop it over his shoulder. If the ball falls into a hazard or back into the place it formally rested, it may be dropped again without penalty. If it is impossible to drop the ball without causing it to roll nearer the hole or more than two club-lengths from the spot, it should be placed.

12. The lie of the ball or the player's stance may not be improved. However, anything which hinders a golfer from fairly taking his stance may be removed or held back by the golfer himself in order to address the ball.

13. A player may request the lifting of any ball he considers might interfere with his play. A ball so lifted is replaced in its original position after the player has played his shot.

14. (a) If a ball is lost or out of bounds, the player shall play his next stroke as nearly as possible at the spot from which the original ball was played, adding a penalty stroke to his score for the hole, or he may play a provisional ball. (b) In both match and stroke play, if a player deems his ball to be unplayable, he shall: play a ball as provided in (a) above; drop a ball under penalty of one stroke, keeping the point where the ball was unplayable between him and the hole; or play a provisional ball. A provisional ball is one that is played until the player reaches the place where the original ball is likely to be. He shall then elect to play either the original ball—in which case there is no penalty—or the provisional ball under the penalty provided for in this particular case. (c) If a ball lies in or is lost in a recognized water hazard, the player may drop a ball behind the hazard, keeping the spot at which the ball crossed the margin of the hazard between himself and the hole. There is no limitation as to how far behind the hazard the ball may be dropped. He may also go back to the spot from where the original ball was played. Penalty: one stroke. (d) If the ball is in a lateral water hazard, he may choose either alternative in (c) under the same penalty, or he may drop a ball within two club-lengths of the margin of either side of the lateral water hazard. Penalty: one stroke.

15. If a ball lies out of bounds, the player shall play his next stroke as nearly as possible to the spot from which the ball that is out of bounds was played, adding a penalty stroke. If it was hit out

of bounds from the tee, he may re-tee it. The penalty remains the same.

16. Casual water is any temporary accumulation of water not constituting a water hazard. A player is allowed to drop his ball out of casual water, but not nearer the hole. When the ball to be dropped from the casual water is in a hazard, in the rough, or on the putting green, the ball must be dropped in same.

17. If the ball moves after a loose impediment has been removed within one club-length, there is a one-stroke penalty.

18. Touching the line of the putt is not permitted, except in removing loose impediments, repairing ball marks, cleaning ball, and immediately in front of the ball while addressing it before putting. The player's caddie, partner, or partner's caddie may point out a line for putting, but they cannot touch the ground or place any marks while guiding the putter.

19. In match and stroke play, a player may require any ball lying on the putting surface to be lifted if he considers that the ball might interfere with his play. The lifted ball is replaced in its original position after the player has played his shot. When a ball on the putting green is to be lifted, its position should be marked. A recommended method of marking the ball is to place a small coin or similar object immediately behind the ball. If this interferes with another player, the coin should be moved one or more putter head-lengths to one side.

20. If a player's ball strikes an opponent's ball in match or stroke play, the opponent may replace his ball on the original spot, and no penalty is incurred. The player must play his ball as it lies after hitting the opponent's ball. If a player strikes an opponent's ball while both balls are on the putting green or within 20 yards of the hole, stroke play rules dictate that the player add two strokes to his score for the hole, and the opponent immediately replace his ball. In match play, no penalty is incurred, but the displaced ball must be replaced.

21. Effective January 1, 1968, the croquet or straddle style of putting became illegal. Penalty: Loss of hole in match play; two strokes in stroke play. Maximum penalty per round: four strokes in stroke play and loss of two holes in match play.

22. Club shafts must be straight from the top of the club to a point not more than five inches above the sole, and the putter shaft must diverge from the vertical by at least 10 degrees.

LOCAL RULES

In constructing the rules which uniformly govern all golf play in the United States, the United States Golf Association recognizes that certain local conditions such as climate, variable physical conditions, and characteristics of golf courses may necessitate modifications of the rules. These modifications are termed Local Rules and are designed to protect the golf course and make the game more enjoyable. A player is responsible for acquainting himself with the Local Rules before playing. Sources of information concerning Local Rules include the golf professional, the score card, golf course bulletin board, and players familiar with the golf course.

The United States Golf Association limits the extent to which Local Rules may modify the U.S.G.A. rules, and the player should refer to the United States Golf Association Rules of Golf Appendix to familiarize himself with the limitations.

TERMINOLOGY

Ace   A hole in one.
Address   The position taken by a player in preparing to start a stroke.
Apron   The area immediately surrounding the green.
Banana ball   A slice.
Barber   A player who talks too much.
Best ball tournament   Competition in which the better score of a partnership on each hole is used as the team score.
Birdie   The score of one under par on a hole.
Bladesman   An excellent putter.
Bogey   A score of one over par on a hole (United States). In countries playing the British rules, the score an average golfer should make on a hole—on easier holes, par and bogey might be the same score.
Can   To hole a putt.
Casual water   Temporary accumulation of water which is not recognized as a hazard on the course.
Course rating   The comparative difficulty of a specific course. Usually computed by a committee of a local association in order to have uniform handicapping for all courses within a district.
Divot   Sod cut with the clubhead when executing or attempting to execute a shot.
Dog-leg   A hole which has a sharp bend in the fairway.
Driver   Number one wood.

Eagle A score for a hole played in two strokes under par.

Fairway The course between the teeing ground and the putting green, exclusive of hazards.

Flag Banner on top of the flag stick identifying the cup.

Fore A warning cry to anyone of a stroke about to be played or one that has been played.

Go to school Learning the roll of a green by watching a previous putt over the same area.

Hole The hole is four and one-quarter inches in diameter and at least four inches deep.

Home The green.

Honor The side which is entitled to play first from the teeing ground is said to have the honor.

Hook A ball in flight that curves from right to left for a right-handed golfer.

Lie The position of the ball on the playing ground. Also refers to the angle of the clubhead.

Loose impediments The term loose impediments denotes natural objects not fixed or growing and not adhering to the ball, and includes stones not solidly embedded, leaves, twigs, branches, and the like, dung, worms, and insects, and casts or heaps made by them.

Match play Competition in which the winner is decided by the number of holes won.

Mulligan or Shapiro Permitting a second hit of a badly played ball—usually on a tee shot. (Not permitted under the rules but by mutual agreement in friendly matches.)

Par The standard score for a hole.

Pigeon An easy mark (opponent).

Pull-shot To hit a ball straight, but to the left of the target for a right-handed golfer.

Push-shot To hit a ball straight, but to the right of the target for a right-handed golfer.

Red Grange or Sunset Strip A round of 77 for 18 holes.

Rough The unmowed terrain on either side of the fairway.

Scotch Foursome A competitive round in which two partners play the same ball, taking alternate shots.

Slice A ball in flight that curves from left to right for a right-handed person.

Stony A ball that comes to rest very close to the pin.

Stroke play (medal play) Competition in which the winner is decided by the total number of strokes taken from a specific number of rounds, not by individual holes won, as in match play.

Stymie A situation on the putting green when an opponent's ball lies in the line of a player's putt to the hole, providing the ball is not within six inches of the other, and the nearer ball is not within six inches of the cup.

Summer rules Playing the ball as it lies from tee through green.

Trap A hazard, technically known as a bunker.

Waggle Body or club action prior to starting the swing.

Wedge A heavy iron club that is used to loft the ball high into the air. It is also used for special situations, such as getting out of heavy grass or sand.

Winter rules The privilege of improving the lie of the ball on the fairway of the hole being played.

SELECTED REFERENCES

Boros, Julius, *How to Play Par Golf*. Englewood Cliffs, N.J.: Prentice-Hall, Inc., 1953.

———, *Swing Easy, Hit Hard*. New York: Harper & Row, Publishers, 1965.

Casper, Bill, Jr., *Chipping and Putting*. New York: The Ronald Press Company, 1961.

Dey, Joseph C., Jr., *Golf Rules In Pictures*. New York: Publication of the United States Golf Association; Grosset & Dunlap, Inc., 1962.

Finsterwald, Dow, *Fundamentals of Golf*. New York: The Ronald Press Company, 1961.

Golf Magazine editors, *Winning Pointers from the Pros*. New York: Harper & Row, Publishers, 1965.

———, *Your Long Game*. New York: Harper & Row, Publishers, 1964.

Grimsley, W., *Golf: Its History, People, Events*. Englewood Cliffs, N.J.: Prentice-Hall, Inc., 1966.

Jones, Robert Tyre, *Golf Is My Game*. Garden City, N.Y.: Doubleday & Company, Inc., 1960.

King, Leslie, *The Master Key To Success At Golf*. New York: Harper & Row, Publishers, 1962.

Nance, Virginia L., and E.D. Davis, *Golf*. Dubuque, Iowa: William C. Brown Company, Publishers, 1966.

Nicklaus, Jack, *My 55 Ways to Lower Your Golf Score*. New York: Simon and Schuster, Inc., 1964.

Palmer, Arnold, *Arnold Palmer's Golf Book "Hit It Hard."* New York: The Ronald Press Company, 1961.

Price, Charles, *Pro Pointers and Stroke Savers.* New York: Harper & Row, Publishers, 1960.

Robinson, Lawrence, and James Graham, eds., *Golfer's Digest.* Chicago: Follett Publishing Company, 1966.

Smith, Horton, and Dawson Taylor, *The Secret of Holing Putts!* New York: A.S. Barnes & Co., Inc., 1962.

Snead, Samuel, *How To Play Golf, and Professional Tips on Improving Your Scores.* Garden City, N.Y.: Garden City Books, 1962.

Sports Illustrated, *Golf Lessons from the Pros.* Englewood Cliffs, N.J.: Prentice-Hall, Inc., 1961.

Suggs, Louise, *Golf for Women.* Garden City, N.Y.: A Rutledge Book, published by Doubleday & Co., Inc., 1960.

Wright, Mickey, *Play Golf the Wright Way.* Garden City, N.Y.: Doubleday & Company, Inc., 1962.

Magazines

Golf Digest. 88 Scribner Ave., Norwalk, Conn. Published monthly; $6.00 subscription.

USGA Golf Journal. 40 E. 38th St., New York. Published 8 times yearly; $3.00 subscription.

Gymnastics, Tumbling, and Trampolining

15

Men's gymnastics

ORIGIN AND DEVELOPMENT

Gymnastics may have originated in ancient Greece, for records of Spartan civilization indicate that its men and women placed great emphasis on gymnastic activities. The peculiar type of gymnastics practiced by the Greeks was centered around the idea of working with apparatus, rather than on it.

Modern gymnastics began in Germany. Johann Basedow (1723–1790) was the first teacher of organized gymnastics, which were included as a part of regular school work. His idea that gymnastics have a significant contribution to make toward the general education of the child was further promoted by Johann Guts Muths (1759–1839), who wrote the first book on gymnastics, *Gymnastics for Youth*. Muths is commonly referred to as the "Great Grandfather of Gymnastics."

Frederick Jahn (1778–1852) presented a plan in Germany to promote national strength and unity through *Turnverein* organizations. His plan was partially the result of the Napoleonic victories over the Germans. He also invented such equipment as the horizontal bar, side horse, and parallel bars. His contributions have brought him the title of "Father of Gymnastics."

American development of gymnastics received its principal impetus from the activities of European immigrants who settled in this country. The strongest agency promoting this development in the United States was the Turnverein organization. In 1865, the American Turners established the Normal College of the American Gymnastic Union in order to train future gymnastic teachers.

After World War I, the trend in physical education was toward the recreational type of activity and away from the gymnastic type. But World War II reemphasized the need for a more strenuous conditioning program for American youth. Where such a program was established, gymnastics played a very important part. As a result, it has become a part of post-war physical education programs throughout the country. More and more colleges and high schools are initiating complete programs of activities that include gymnastics and tumbling.

Gymnastics as a sport dates only as far back

as the 1850's. It was in Switzerland that the first gymnastic competition, more or less as we know it today, was started. Clias was the founder of that movement.

The Larousse *Encyclopédie des Sports* states that gymnastics is the youngest of all sports in its present form. The statement seems to be true, since the last changes in competitive gymnastics were made in 1932. That year rope climbing and Indian clubs were abandoned. Women's gymnastics is much younger, as will be seen later in the chapter.

People usually confuse the sport of gymnastics with the term gymnastics as used in the past, denoting almost all kinds of physical activities. It was in 1936 at the Olympic Games in Berlin that the leaders of this sport saw that if gymnastics was to progress and be recognized as a sport, it was imperative to give it a personality of its own. They limited its program to activities not found in any other sport. Since 1936 gymnastics has become a sport in itself, an individual sport that comprises the following activities: for men, high bar, parallel bars, floor exercise, side horse, trampoline, long horse, rings, and all-around. Special events for women include tumbling and rebound tumbling (trampolining). The all-around event for women consists of floor exercise, uneven parallel bars, balance beam, and side horse vault.

Events for men in Olympic competition include individual all-around, free standing exercises, side horse, parallel bars, rings, long horse vault, and the horizontal bar. Japan won the team championship in 1960, 1964, and in 1968.

NATURE OF THE ACTIVITY

Gymnastics is an individual sport, and one that lends itself to recreational use. In its most elementary form it is seen in the swings, slides, rings, teeter-totters, and jungle gyms that are so prevalent in community recreational areas. In its more advanced form, gymnastics necessitates such equipment as flying rings, side horses, parallel bars, mats, high bars, and trampolines. Such equipment will be found in the gymnasiums of YMCA's, colleges and universities, athletic clubs, and many secondary schools.

The area necessitated for participation in gymnastics varies with its use. That is, in most situations the ordinary gymnasium is sufficient as the playing area, or such area may be larger or smaller as the demand warrants. The important thing is that the area must be sufficient to permit participation with maximum safety conditions prevailing, and this latter

is probably the only restriction insofar as the area of participation is concerned.

The sport lends itself to recreational use because it does not require any definite group to permit participation. That is, the interested individual may at any time utilize the facilities available to him without having to wait for a team to form. Also, there is unlimited freedom of selection, which permits the individual to select various stunts to satisfy his particular needs and attain the objectives he may set up for himself.

Gymnastics is also adaptable to an outdoor program, which permits its use during the summer months as well as the winter months when the gymnasium is usually the focal point of physical activity. Mats for tumbling, parallel bars, horses, vaulting fences, spring boards, balance beams, and ropes may be constructed to permit the inculcation of gymnastics in the summer recreational program.

BASIC RULES [1]

1. List of events in order of competition for championship meets is as follows: Floor Exercise, Side Horse, Long Horse, Parallel Bars, Rings, Horizontal Bar, and All-Around. The All-Around event is not contested for points in a dual meet. Trampoline may be included as an exhibition event.

2. All-Around—the All-Around event consists of a gymnast competing in Floor Exercise, Side Horse, Horizontal Bar, Parallel Bars, Still Rings, and Long Horse.

3. In dual meets, each team shall be allowed to enter four men in each event providing two men work the All-Around event. However, should the designated All-Around men fail to compete in any of the six Olympic events the team limit will be three entries for that event. Any gymnast competing in the six All-Around events will be considered an All-Around competitor even though he is not a designated All-Around contestant.

4. A gymnastic team will be limited to a maximum of twelve men in both dual and championship meets.

5. In championships and other qualifying meets the contestants who elect to compete in the All-Around event will be required to complete the current international compulsory exercises in the

[1] Official NCAA Rules, National Collegiate Athletic Bureau, New York, 1969.

188

six Olympic events in addition to the optional exercises as a part of their All-Around total.

6. The team score will be determined by adding the best three competitors' scores of each team on every event. This system of team scoring will be used in both dual and championship meets.

7. For all events the judges shall award scores on the basis of 10.0 for a perfect routine. The 10.0 points are awarded as follows: for difficulty—3.4, for combination—1.6, and for execution—5.0 points.

8. Four judges shall be used per event in dual and championship meets with the exception of the final championships, where a fifth superior judge will be used only to determine whether the middle scores are within range (i.e., the difference between the two middle scores must not exceed: a. 0.2 if the average is 9.5 or more; b. 0.3 if the average is between 8.5 and 9.45; c. 0.5 if the average is between 7.0 and 8.45; d. 1.0 in all other cases). The scorers shall note on score sheets the marks of each judge, and then eliminate the highest and lowest marks, using the average of the two intermediate marks for the evaluation of the performance, i.e., if the marks of the judges on one routine are 9.0, 8.9, 8.7, and 8.6, the highest mark (9.0) and the lowest mark (8.6) are discarded and the two intermediate marks of 8.9 and 8.7 are averaged, making the valuation of the routine 8.8. In the event that there are two or more identical high scores, only one will be discarded. The same applies for the low marks.

9. The routines on every piece of apparatus must be composed of eleven or more stunts. If the performer falls from any apparatus or touches the springs of the trampoline, the contestant has 30 seconds to remount and continue the exercise from the point of interruption, with the automatic deduction of 1.0 points.

10. Floor Exercises—the NCAA rules do not specify a time limit for Floor Exercise. However, the F.I.G. (Olympic rules) specify a maximum time limit of 70 seconds and a 50 second minimum time limit. The routine must start and finish in the prescribed area of 39′ 4½″ by 39′ 4½″. The area shall be covered with protective material which is at least one inch thick. Stepping outside the free exercise area will constitute a deduction of 0.1 to 0.3 points for each violation depending upon the number of body parts outside the area.

11. Trampoline—it is required that spotters be posted at the end and the sides of the trampoline. All exercises should begin and terminate on the trampoline. There will be no audible counting. It is also required that a minimum area of five feet surrounding the trampoline be covered with mats.

12. Uniform—complete uniforms must be worn by all competitors. Minimum uniform shall be socks, pants, and shirt.

13. In dual meets each competitor shall perform only one optional routine or exercise in each event in which he is entered. The only exception is the long horse event where vaults are required. The competitor is judged according to his score on two different vaults. The second of his two vaults must be of a different family from the first of the two vaults.

14. Coaching or talking to a contestant during his performance is prohibited. Infringement of the rule may result in a maximum penalty of 0.3 of a point.

15. In order to prevent accidents, a guard, or spotter, is permitted to stand near the apparatus. Touching or helping a gymnast, however, may draw a penalty up to 1.0 point.

OFFICIALS

In addition to the necessary number of judges, other officials may include a referee, clerks, scorers, timers, an announcer, and a physician.

TECHNIQUES AND FUNDAMENTALS

Side Horse

This piece of apparatus consists of a leather-covered body measuring 63 inches (1.60 m.) in length and 13 and $^{13}\!/_{16}$ inches (plus or minus three-eighths inch) in width, and is usually mounted on four iron legs. On the top of the horse there are two pommels (curved wooden handles) four and three-quarter inches (12 cm.) (plus or minus one-sixteenth inch) high, adjustable within a range of 15 and ¾ to 17 and ¾ inches. The height of the horse is also adjustable (when used for vaulting purposes especially) within a range of 35 to 57 inches. The regulation height for competitive purposes is 48 inches (plus or minus three-sixteenths inch) from the floor to the top of the pommels.

FIGURE 15-1. Front support position

1. Elementary Positions

(a) *Jump to a front support position:* Grasp the pommels firmly with both hands, jump to a front support position. The body may be touching the horse slightly, and the weight of the body is supported by the hands. Keep the back arched. (See Fig. 15-1.)

(b) *Front stand:* This position is attained by running, taking off on either foot or both feet, and landing on the horse with either foot or both feet and assuming a standing position.

(c) *Jump with a half turn (left or right):* Stand facing the horse, and with the right hand grasp the opposite pommel firmly, with the back of the hand upward. Jump, rotating the body away from the horse, and grasp the free pommel with the left hand. The body may be slightly touching the horse, the hands supporting the weight of the body.

2. Stunts

(a) *From rest position:* Assume the front rest position; swing the left leg laterally and upward over the horse; release the pommel grasped in the left hand to permit the left leg to come to a position between the two pommels on the opposite side, and quickly re-grasp this pommel. The body weight is supported by the hands. (This stunt may also be performed with the right leg.)

(b) *From back rest position:* Swing the right leg laterally and upward over the horse; release the pommel from the right hand to permit the leg to come to a position between the two pommels on the opposite side, and quickly re-grasp this pommel. The body weight is supported by the hands. (Stunt may also be performed with the left leg.)

(c) *From front rest position:* Swing the right leg to the left laterally and upward between the horse and the body, release the pommel from the left hand to permit the leg to pass up and over the horse, and quickly re-grasp this pommel. The leg comes to a position between the two pommels on the opposite side of the horse. The weight is supported by the hands. (Stunt may be performed with the left leg also.)

(d) *Squat vault:* Stand facing the horse, grasp the pommels firmly; jump upward and forward; tuck the legs under the body and allow the body to pass over apparatus. Push with the hands and extend the legs as you dismount. This stunt may be done with a running start.

(e) *Straddle vault:* Stand facing the horse; grasp the pommels firmly; jump upward and forward, and as the body begins to pass over the horse, spread the legs as far as possible and push with the hands. Land with the feet together.

(f) *Front vault:* Stand facing the horse, jump upward and forward so the weight of the body rests on the hands, and swing the body to the right or left over the horse with the body facing downward. The body is arched, and in landing, the body has made a quarter turn (right or left) from the starting point, with the hand (right or left) still grasping the pommel. (See Fig. 15-2.)

(g) *Flank vault:* Stand facing the horse, jump upward and forward so the weight of the body rests over the hands. Swing the body over the horse, with the side facing downward. Release the pommel on the side over which the body passes. Release both hands on landing, with the back to the horse. (See Fig. 15-3.)

FIGURE 15-2. Front vault

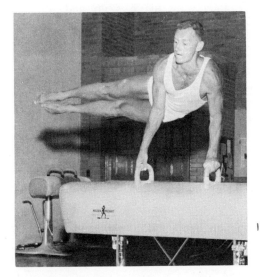

FIGURE 15-3. Flank vault

Long Horse and Board

The long horse body is the same size and shape as the side horse, but if the side horse is used in competition, pommel-securing holes must be covered or filled in. The height from the floor to the top of the horse is 53 and ⅛ inches (minus three-eighths inch). The body must be marked with three-eighths inch wide lines as follows: measuring in from each end, the first lines are placed at 15 and ¾ inches and the second lines are placed at 23 and ⅝ inches. A minimum distance of 65.6 feet must be provided for the run-up. The board must be covered with a non-slip material and provisions

made for fixing the springboard at two inch intervals from the horse. The board is 23 and ⅝ inches (plus or minus one-eighth inch) wide and 47 and ¼ inches (plus or minus three-sixteenths inch) long.

Long Horse

THE TAKE-OFF FROM THE BEAT BOARD. The performer should begin his preliminary run from a distance of 60 to 75 feet from the beat board. Start the run with a few trotting steps and increase the speed as the horse is approached. The eyes should be kept not only on the beat board but also on the horse and the immediate surroundings. Just prior to reaching the beat board, take a hurdle step (a step similar to the one used in diving, only much slower and longer). In executing this step, the take-off is negotiated from one foot. The other foot is then raised and both feet should land close together and simultaneously on the beat board for the final take-off prior to the flight over the horse. It is important to land on the balls of the feet (not flatfooted) on the section of the beat board which will release the greatest amount of spring. The purpose of the board is not only to gain height but also to obtain distance. For this reason, the beat board should not be too close to the horse—at least three or more feet depending upon the height of the vaulter and the type of vault being executed. The body-lean necessary on hitting the beat board depends upon the vault being performed. In general, the performer "sits" into the board with the trunk leaning slightly forward.

THE LANDING. The performer should land solidly in one spot with the feet together. The knees should be slightly flexed to absorb the shock. The arms should be extended sideways and upward (palms facing out) for balance. The arms are brought down as the performer straightens to a stand.

The following vaults may first be mastered over the buck (a small vaulting horse) or over the side of the long horse prior to advancing to the lengthwise position of the horse.

JUMP TO STAND ON CROUP AND STRADDLE FROM NECK. Following the take-off, vault to a stand on the croup (nearer end of the horse), pushing with the hands on the croup. Reach for the neck (farther end of horse) with the hands and jump forward, kicking the legs nearly to a handstand position. The legs are then straddled over the horse as the hands push down on the neck. This thrust raises the chest and enables the vaulter to clear the horse.

STRADDLE FROM THE NECK. After hitting the beat board, lift the hips upward, kick the legs backward, and reach for the neck of the horse. By the time the hands have touched the neck, the body of the vaulter should be in a three-quarter handstand position with the feet still together. As the performer pushes down on the horse, his legs are separated and driven downward and his chest is raised. Complete the vault with a stand on the mats—feet together.

SQUAT FROM THE NECK. The take-off (a 30 degree angle or near handstand over the horse) and landing of this vault are the same as in the straddle vault. However, in the squat vault, the knees bend and the feet remain together as they drive down between the hands. It should be emphasized that the chest is raised following a vigorous push from the hands.

STOOP FROM THE NECK. This stunt is similar to the squat vault in all respects except that the knees are perfectly straight as they drive down while a deep pike (a position in which the body is bent at the hips and the legs are kept straight) is negotiated.

JUMP TO STAND ON CROUP AND SQUAT FROM NECK. Following the take-off, vault to a stand on the croup. From this position, reach for the neck. Jump forward, kicking the legs upward nearly to a handstand; bend deeply at the knees; and drive the legs downward between the hands as the hands push on the neck. Land with a slight bend in the knees and come to a standing position.

Still rings

The rings are made of wood, are hung 98 and 7/16 inches off the floor, have an interior diameter of seven and three-thirtyseconds inches, and are one and one-eighth inches thick. They are attached to adjustable cables and straps hanging from the ceiling. Provisions should be made to prevent twisting of the cords by use of swivels.

1. Elementary Position

Front hang: Stand directly beneath the apparatus, reach upward and grasp the rings with a forward upward motion of the hands. This is the initial starting position for all stunts.

2. Stunts

(a) Chins: From the front hang position, pull up until the chin is level with the bottom of the rings, keeping the rings close to the chest. This should be repeated several times.

(b) Inverted hang: From the front hang position, swing the legs into the kip position and then extend them straight up to bring the body into a vertical position with the floor. Keep the body arched, the head back, and the arms fully extended.

(c) Bird's nest: From a front hang position, place the insteps in the rings and push backward with the feet so the body faces the floor. Keep the head up and the body arched. (See Fig. 15-4.)

(d) Bird's nest with one arm and one foot: From the front rest position, place one foot in one of the rings; release the ring from the hand in which the foot has been inserted.

(e) Skin the cat: From the front hang position, chin slightly and swing the legs up and through the arms; allow the legs to pass through and drop down as far as possible. Pull the legs back through the arms. Repeat as many times as possible without releasing hold on the rings.

(f) Monkey hang: Skin the cat, let go with one hand, and do a full turn; then re-grasp the free ring.

Flying rings

The flying rings and the still rings are the same apparatus. The distinction between the two comes

FIGURE 15-4. Bird's nest

from the manner in which the stunts are performed. That is, to perform flying ring stunts the rings must be in motion, thus the term "flying." Although flying rings are no longer a competitive event in Olympic and NCAA meets, it is still widely used in gymnastic circles to provide training and conditioning exercises for the gymnasts. It is a thrilling event, and it is relatively easy to arrive at some level of performance without many years of practice.

1. *Elementary Positions*

   (a) *Front hang:* This position is attained by standing beneath the apparatus and reaching upward, grasping the rings by a forward, upward motion of the hands. This is the initial starting position. The swing is generally obtained by a push from a fellow gymnast.

   (b) *Kip position:* Pull up on the rings and swing the legs forward and upward so that the feet are above the head between the two rings and the body is in pike position.

2. *Stunts*

   (a) *Dismount backward:* While swinging backward, pull up on the rings, bring the body vertical to the floor, and then release the rings to drop straight to the floor on both feet.

   (b) *Bird's nest:* Roll into the kip position on the end of the front swing; place the insteps in the rings and push backward with the feet so the body faces the floor. Keep the head up and the body arched. (See Fig. 15-4.)

   (c) *Inverted hang:* On the front swing pull the legs up into position between and parallel to the straps, so the body is in a position vertical to the floor. Look at the toes and keep arms fully extended.

   (d) *Kip position on back, stretch on front swing:* On backward swing, pull up into kip position, extend the legs upward and outward on front swing and swing from the shoulders.

Parallel bars

This apparatus consists of two wooden, adjustable hand rails not less than 137 and $1^3/_{16}$ inches

(plus or minus three-eighths inch) in length and connected to two steel uprights. The uprights are part of a large steel base. The bars are adjustable in height from three feet nine inches to five feet eight inches and in width from 15 inches to 21 inches. The competitive regulations, however, are 66 and $^{15}/_{16}$ inches (plus or minus three-sixteenths inch) high and an optional width between 18 and $^7/_8$ to 20 and $^1/_2$ inches.

1. *Elementary Positions*

   (a) *Jump to cross rest position:* Stand at the end of and between the two hand rails, place the hands on the inner top side of the bars and spring upward and forward. Keep the arms extended, so the weight of the body is supported by the hands.

   (b) *Jump to cross upper arm hang:* After a short run, take off from both feet, keeping the body in a slight forward lean position. Jump high enough to carry the shoulders above the bars. The hands swing upward and forward and come to rest on the top of the bars. At first the weight is supported by the hands, and when the forward motion ceases, it is supported by the upper arms.

2. *Stunts*

   (a) *Swing from shoulders:* From a cross rest position, swing from the shoulders backward and forward. When swinging backward, lean slightly forward; when swinging

FIGURE 15-5. Swing from shoulders

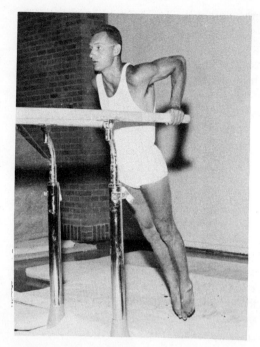

FIGURE 15-6. Dips

forward, lean slightly backward. Keep the body arched and the head up. (See Fig. 15-5.)

(b) *Dips:* From a cross rest position, drop to a bent arm position and push back to the cross rest position. (See Fig. 15-6.)

(c) *Walk length of the bars:* From a cross rest position, walk the length of the bars, keeping the elbows locked, the body arched, and the toes pointed. Take only small "steps."

(d) *Forward roll from straddle seat position:* From cross rest position, swing to straddle seat position. Place the hands on the bars in front of the thighs and start to roll forward. Spread the elbows, complete the forward roll, and return to the straddle seat position. Place the hands under the buttocks and arms along the bars to help the body complete the roll to straddle seat position. (See Fig. 15-7.)

(e) *Inverted hang and walk forward:* Stand in between the bars. Grasp the bars from the outside and swing to an inverted hang position. Walk the length of the bars with small "steps."

(f) *Single leg cut-off:* From a cross rest position at the end of the bars, swing the leg (right or left) up over the bar. Push off with the hands backwards, carrying the leg over and outside, landing on both feet.

(g) *Double leg cut-off:* From a cross rest position at the end of the bars, swing the legs up over the bars, push off with the hands backwards, carrying the legs over and outside the bars, landing on both feet.

Horizontal Bar (High)

The specifications of this piece of apparatus for competition are: (1) the cross bar must be 1.102 inches (plus or minus 0.0039 inch) in diameter; have a minimum tensile strength of 199,127 psi (pounds per square inch); and be 94 and ½ inches (plus or minus one-sixteenth inch) in width. The top of the bar must be 98 and $\frac{7}{16}$ inches from the floor (with provisions made to increase this height to 100 and ⅜ inches). With the bar set at 98 and $\frac{7}{16}$ inches, a test weight of 485 pounds, placed in the middle of the bar, must produce a dip of three and fifteen-sixteenths inches (plus or minus three-eighths inch). (2) The guying cables must be a minimum of one-quarter inch in diameter and have a minimum tensile strength of 1,323 pounds. (3) The floor plates must be spaced at 216 and $\frac{9}{16}$ inches (plus or minus three-quarters inch) across the width of the unit and must be spaced at 157 and ½ inches (plus or minus nine-sixteenths inch) down the length of the unit.

1. Chins: Grip the bar with a forward grip at shoul-

FIGURE 15-7. Forward roll from straddle seat

der width. Keep legs extended throughout performance with the head forward. Pull up with your arms until chin reaches the bar level. Extend the arms and repeat the procedure. Practice with a backward grip.

2. *Swing and dismount:* Take a chinning position. Pull up with your arms until chin reaches the bar level. Kick up, out, and down, immediately extending the arms on the forward swing. As body reaches under the bar on the back swing, start pulling toward the bar and dismount at the peak of the back swing. Land with a straight body, slightly bending the knees.

3. *Backward single knee circle:* Take a forward grip on the bar (knuckles toward the body). Pull up until thighs are resting at bar level, body erect. Step over bar with left leg, hooking at the knee. From this stationary position extend the right leg back, keep left knee hooked to the bar, then throw the head and shoulders back on the down swing. As body reaches under the bar bring the right thigh close to bar, bending the arms at the top of the swing. Repeat the procedure for consecutive spins. Practice with assistance.

4. *Backward hip circle:* Assume forward grip on bar. Pull up to a front rest position, thighs touching bar. Throw the legs slightly upward and off the bar. As legs come down and forward to start the circling of the bar, throw the head and shoulders backward. The lower stomach region sticks to the bar at all times, making a complete circle. Finish with a front rest position and repeat the stunt.

5. *Kip:* Start the swing as you do for the *dismount* exercise. Once the beginning swing is initiated, keep the arms straight. Start arching the back on the forward swing to slow down the speed of swing. At the peak of the front swing quickly bend at the hips and bring your feet up toward the bar. Snap legs up, out, and down, pulling down on the bar with straight arms. The last snap is the kip. Finish at a front rest position and repeat the exercise.

6. *Kip up:* From a hanging position on a horizontal bar, propel the body forward, with the trunk flexed and the legs raised overhead to a support. The kip up can be completed at the end of the forward swing, or from a still position with a short forward swing.

7. *Skin the cat:* From the front hang position, chin slightly and swing the legs up and through the arms; allow the legs to pass through and drop down as far as possible. Pull the legs back through the arms. Repeat as many times as possible without releasing hold on the bar. (See Fig. 15-8.)

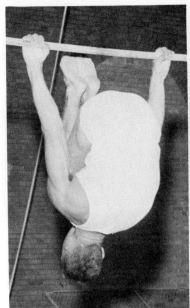

FIGURE 15-8. Skin the cat

Horizontal Bar (Low)

1. *Fence vault (flank vault):* Take off and kick hard over the bar with one foot. Shift weight on the supporting arm, pushing down on the bar and throwing free arm upward. Get legs parallel to bar and land with the knees bent.

2. *Straddle vault:* Grasp bar with both hands shoulder width. Keep head up, slightly bending the knees. Spring legs upward, at the same time lift hard with hands. Straddle legs over the bar and release the hands as the body goes forward and over. Keep head up and finish with bent knees.

3. *Squat vault:* Start this stunt in the same manner as in the straddle vault. Spring feet upward and at the same time lift hard with hands. Pull knees toward the chest and between the hands. Push off and over the bar, releasing the hand grip. Keep head up and finish with bent knees.

TUMBLING

Equipment

MAT. A padded mat is all that is required. It is generally two inches thick, and may be of several dimensions: five feet x ten feet, 5 feet x 60 feet, and so on.

Stunts

1. *Forward roll:* From a squat position at the end of the mat, place the hands slightly forward,

FIGURE 15-9. Front handspring

with the fingers pointed inward and the knees between the arms. To start the forward roll, tuck in the head so the chin is on the chest. Roll forward on the neck and shoulders. Keep the feet spread and close to the body, grab the shins when coming out of the roll, and balance on both feet.

2. *Shoulder roll:* From a standing position at the end of the mat, rotate the body slightly by turning the head and dipping the shoulder to the side. Use the arm to break the fall and roll on the "dipped" shoulder to a standing position.

3. *Backward roll:* Take a position with the back to the mat and the feet together. Place the hands on the mat with the arms extended. Push off backwards with the hands into a sitting position with the buttocks close to the heels and the hands contacting the mat on the sides to break the fall. Quickly move the hands up over the shoulders with the palms facing upward and continue to roll backward. When coming up on the shoulders and neck, the hands come in contact with the mat. Push off with the hands; spread the legs, and come up on both feet.

4. *Dive and forward roll:* From a short run, dive toward the mat, land on the hands to break the fall. Bend arms to permit rolling forward on the neck and the shoulders. Continue as in the forward roll.

5. *Hand balance in squat position:* From a squat position, move slightly forward by pushing with the toes until the weight is supported by the hands. The legs are outside the arms and the knees are resting on the upper arm above the elbow with the feet off the mat. This may be prac-

ticed by beginning with the head on mat and then, after knees are resting on the arms, lifting the head.

6. *Forearm balance:* Place the forearms on the mat with the palms down and the elbows slightly behind the shoulders. Move the feet up as close to the elbows as possible, keeping the head up. Bring the legs upward, with the feet directly over the head, the body well-arched, and the weight of the body supported by the forearms. The toes should be pointed. (This stunt should be practiced with assistance until proficiency has been attained. It may also be practiced with the head on the hands and the head gradually raised.)

7. *Head stand:* Place the hands on the mat with the fingers pointed forward; put the head on the mat to form a triangle with the hands. Swing the legs up so the feet are directly over the head. Keep the body well-arched with the weight supported slightly more on the hands than on the head. To come out of this position, bend at the hips and lower the legs to the mat.

8. *Hand balance:* Place the hands forward on the mat with the shoulders ahead of the hands. Keep the head up and look ahead slightly. Swing the legs up so that the feet are over the head, keeping the body arched and the toes pointed. The weight of the body is supported by the hands. (Practice with assistance.)

9. *Cartwheel:* Stand with the feet spread apart and the hands over the head; lean to the left (or right) and throw the left hand down to a spot about two feet from the left foot, the right hand following. The hands should be about 18 inches apart. Bring the right leg up and over the body,

the left leg following. The body is straight. Land on the right foot first, then the left foot; the distance between the feet when landing is about 24 inches.

10. *Neckspring:* Start from a lying-down position. Roll back and have the weight on neck and shoulders, then suddenly kick the legs upward and forward at approximately a 45-degree angle. A sharp hip-snap is brought into play with the kick. Simultaneously push off with the hands and head, landing with the feet *under* the body and with the knees slightly bent.

11. *Headspring:* Place the head and the hands on the mat with the body in a pike position and feet on the mat. Push off with the feet, swing the legs over the body, and, when passing the vertical position, shoot the legs forward and push off with the hands. Land on both feet with legs bent.

12. *Front handspring:* Begin with a short run, skipping on the last step and placing your hands directly in front of the take-off foot. Keep the hips loose at this point. The back leg comes up as the hands reach the floor. Keeping the arms slightly bent, give a hard push-off with the hands using a quick hip-snap to bring the legs under the body. Finish with a good leg-snap, maintaining an arch position and landing with the feet under the body. (See Fig. 15-9.)

13. *Chest roll:* From a hand-balance position, slowly let the body fall forward in a rolling motion to the chest.

14. *Forward somersault (from flip):* Start with a short run, skipping on the left foot on the last step;

bring the right foot forward, and at the same time throw both arms upward, then forward, then downward, and place the chin on the chest. Continue the circular motion with the hands by grasping and pulling at the shins into a tuck position. During the somersault (flip), the chest should be close to the knees and the heels close to the buttocks. After completing the somersault, a full 360 degrees, shoot out of the tuck position and land on the mat in an upright position with the knees slightly flexed. (See Fig. 15-10.)

15. *Back handspring (flip-flap):* Start from a standing position with the feet shoulder-width apart and the arms held straight out in front of the body. Swing the arms down and at the same time bend the knees and sit back as though you were going to sit in a chair. As the body falls off balance swing the arms overhead and force the head backwards. Straighten the legs and push off with the toes, forcing the hips upward, and make a big arc with the hands. As the hands land on the mat, the body is in a handstand position. From this position, snap the legs down from the waist and land in a standing position with the knees slightly flexed. (See Fig. 15-11.)

16. *Fish flop:* Otherwise known as the egg roll; roll the body backward to a momentary head balance, then force the shoulders forward, rolling down in a rhythmic motion to the chest and stomach and finish in a stand.

17. *Backward (snap up):* From a standing position, move into a backward roll—to a momentary hand balance—to a snap down—to a stand.

FIGURE 15-10. Front somersault

FIGURE 15-11. Back handspring

TRAMPOLINING

Although the trampoline is a newcomer to physical education, it has been used by circus performers since the 1920's. Circus acts used the nets as a rebound device to end their performances. Performers seized upon this idea and built a rebounding net on which they would do acrobatic stunts. In the late 1930's, an American, George Nissen, standardized this apparatus and made it available to the public, thereby changing the concept of the trampoline as being suitable only for the professional acrobat or tumbler.

In recent years, trampoline tumbling has proved to be a dynamic, stimulating sport which is safe and adaptable for all age groups; requires little space or equipment; and produces outstanding physical benefits. It provides both student and instructor with ample opportunities for the exercise of creative initiative. It is important to note that trampolining is not limited to the men's program.

For competitive purposes, the bed must be constructed of white nylon webbing—one inch in width—and stitched with nylon thread, using a lock stitch. The bed must be marked with a color that contrasts with white in the following manner: (1) the center web—full length of bed, (2) the center web—full width of bed, (3) the fourth web in from either side—full length of bed, and (4) the eighth web in from either end—full width of bed.

Protective frame pads must be provided to cover the top of the perimeter frame. These pads must be securely attached. Spotters are required at the end and sides.

1. Elementary Position

Feet bounce: Stand in the middle of the trampoline bed with the feet approximately 12 to 15 inches apart. The arms are lifted up to the sides with the body weight on the balls of the feet. The arms are then rotated and swung sharply downward with the elbows flexed and the hips and knees bent. As the arms reach the bottom of their swing, the hips and knees are forcefully extended, and the heels brought down against the bed. As the arms again swing up, the toes are pushed down, the body is tensed, and the recoil of the bed thrusts the body into the air. The arms continue to swing upward, slowing in a "floating" movement as the body reaches the peak of the bounce. As the body descends, the arms are brought into position to repeat the strong, downward beat on landing.

2. Stunts (Beginning)

(a) *Seat drop:* From the bounce, land in a sitting position so that the backs of the legs and the seat contact the canvas simultaneously. The body is inclined slightly forward on landing, and the hands are about six inches behind the body, with the fingers pointed forward. Bounce to the feet after the stunt.

(b) *Back drop:* From the bounce, land on the back with the legs extended vertically from the canvas. The hands are retained on the fronts of the legs, or in a semi-extended position above the chest. Keep the chin on the chest during the entire stunt.

(c) *Front drop:* From the bounce, land in a prone position with the elbows extended laterally and the palms downward. One should land simultaneously on the legs, the abdomen, the forearms, and the hands.

(d) *Knee drop:* Take off with hips slightly flexed. As body descends toward bed, knees are bent and toes extended back. Rotate arms back and down, bending elbows to insure small radius of swing. Land on knees and lower legs, with most of weight on knees, keeping hips slightly flexed and firm. After making contact, drive down on bed and extend hips. Swing arms up on take-off, extending body on the rise. Land on feet with body erect. (See Fig. 15-12.)

(e) *Hands and knees drop:* Hips thrown back slightly at take-off. Hips rise during ascent, with arms forward and downward and head and shoulders in same direction. Body descends with head and shoulders forward and downward, and hips and knees flexed and raised. The back is horizontal on contact, arms down and knees bent forward under hips. Flex and extend arms, driving down on bed. Simultaneously, in rapid movement, legs beat down, then up. During rise, head

FIGURE 15-13. One-half twist to front drop

and shoulders go up, hips and knees extend, landing erect on feet.

(f) *Hands drop:* In trampoline tumbling, hands usually assist in low-bounce exercises. Take off from knees for low bounce with body forward. Sharply lift and flex hips as head and shoulders go forward and downward into very low bounce. Land on hands and flex knees. Body rebounds with arms and knees extended from bed. Land upright with head and shoulders up.

(g) *One-half twist to back drop:* From the bounce, start as for a front drop. As the top of the bounce is reached, turn the body in a one-half turn by throwing the arm across the chest and turning the head in the same direction. Land in the back drop position.

(h) *One-half twist to front drop:* From the bounce, proceed as if doing a back drop. When at the top of the bounce, turn the body by throwing the arm across the body and turning the head in the same direction. Land in the front drop position. (See Fig. 15-13.)

(i) *Back drop to front drop:* From the bounce,

FIGURE 15-12. Knee drop

do a back drop; kick forward with the legs. In coming off the canvas, draw the legs up to a semi-tuck position. Land in the front-drop position.

3. *Stunts (Advanced)*

(a) *Swivel hips:* This exercise consists of a seat-drop take-off, half twist, and a seat-drop landing. The half twist may be executed either right or left. Hands push off at take-off, starting twist as body rises. Throw arms up slightly to left, drop legs, turn head in direction of twist. Arms swing high to right near peak of bounce. Reacting to arm swing, shoulders and hips turn to left, completing twist. Flex hips, raise legs, bring arms into landing position.

(b) *Half-turntable (Bluch):* Take off in front-drop position. Push thighs against the bed with hands pushing down and to the left, causing body to spin right. As body clears the bed flex the knees and hips. The arms are semi-flexed with head and shoulders low, keeping the back parallel to the bed. As body drops near completion of half spin, extend knees and hips, raise legs and head momentarily. Land in front-drop position.

(c) *Forward somersault progression:*

(1) Hands and knees take-off, forward turnover to seat-drop.

(2) Knees take-off, forward turnover to seat-drop; hips are flexed, thrust back for take-off. Feet push off as body rises, head and shoulders go forward. Flex hips and knees, tip body forward, and grasp legs above ankles. For rapid rotation make tucking action forceful. As tuck is broken at three-fourths completion, legs straighten, bringing body into semi-pike position. Place arms down and back to support body on seat-drop landing.

(3) Bent dive, feet take-off to three-quarter somersault landing in the back-drop position: make take-off with hips flexed to rear of vertical line passing through head and feet. Carry legs high, hips upward, bringing head down in semi-tuck position. Face down until about three feet above the bed. Quickly duck head under with hips down for a flat, back-drop landing. Variations: full tuck, pike, or layout position.

(4) Feet take-off, forward turnover to seat drop.

(5) Front somersault. Feet take-off, forward somersault to feet. At take-off, thrust hips back, swing arms forward and down to start forward rotation. Throw head forward, flex knees and hips, grasp legs near ankles, pulling body against thighs with heels against buttocks. Kick out at three-fourths completion. Raise head, extend arms up, straighten body to slow rotation, extend legs down with body in erect position. Separate feet just before landing. Have spotters or use the

FIGURE 15-14. Front somersault progression. *Note:* performer executing from a knee-drop position.

FIGURE 15-15. Back somersault progression

"mechanic" (safety belt). (See Fig. 15-14.)

(d) Backward somersault progression:

(1) Back-drop take-off, backover to hands and knees. Hold legs high at take-off, swing over and back as body rises. On peak of height, throw head back quickly, flex hips and knees, arms pulling legs against chest for fast tuck. Hold tuck momentarily. As body reaches horizontal, swing head and shoulders up, extend arms and land on hands and knees.

(2) Back-drop take-off, backover to feet.

(3) Feet take-off, backover to hands and knees. At take-off, thrust hips forward to start backward body rotation. During ascent, throw head and shoulders back and legs up and back. Flex hips and knees into a semi-tuck position. As body rotates and head reaches position looking down, eyes should spot a landing point. Body comes to horizontal level momentarily. Swing head up, adjusting body for landing. Hold body rigid; land on hands and knees.

(4) Feet take-off, backward somersault to feet. Use "mechanic" or "guards" on each side of trampoline. (See Fig. 15-15.)

(e) Forward one-and-a-quarter somersault: This exercise combines the forward somersault and the front drop. The tuck is held until the somersault is slightly overturned, then a come-out is made to a semi-tucked position, the body assumes a horizontal position, and is extended for a front-drop landing.

(f) Back somersault, feet to seat: The take-off and tuck used in this exercise are similar to those employed in executing the backward somersault from feet to feet. However, more rapid rotation or a higher bounce must be attained to make the seat-drop landing possible. Hips are thrust forward at take-off, and legs pulled over toward chest in a fast, tight tuck. Tuck is held until somersault is three-fourths completed. Arms and legs are extended to retard rotation. As head and shoulders rise toward erect position, hips are flexed and legs are swung down under the body. Rotation is completed as legs swing up and are extended at right angles to upper part of the body. Arms are brought down and back and body is held rigid for seat-drop landing.

(g) Trampoline back (Loose layout back somersault: Rotation is slower than when a tuck is used, consequently a moderately high bounce is desirable. During take-off, hips are rocked forward and shoulders are

thrust back. Hip action imparts a forward "gaining" movement to the body as it rises, counteracting travel to the rear. During ascent, hips rise up and forward, and head and shoulders drop as body revolves in loose layout position. Head is thrown well back; as body assumes a head-down position, eyes locate landing spot on the bed. The body remains in layout position, back arched, until rotation is almost complete. Then head is raised, hips are flexed, and legs are swung under the center of weight into landing position.

FLOOR EXERCISE

The floor exercise area is 12 meters x 12 meters. The surface of the area must be covered with protective material which is at least one inch thick. Touching the floor outside the area by a performer during competition will constitute a deduction of 0.1 to 0.3 points for each violation.

The floor exercise event is highly creative, consisting of compulsory and optional exercises, and provides opportunities for the execution of stunts requiring strength, flexibility, balance, agility, and rhythm. Among the many stunts performed are handsprings (forward and backward), forward and backward somersaults (with or without twists), double leg circles, and splits.

HELPFUL HINTS

Equipment

1. The most effective uniform for a gymnast is one that allows complete freedom of the arms and legs.
2. The gymnast's equipment should include a T-shirt, trunks, a supporter, socks, and gym shoes. It is advisable to substitute light gymnastic slippers for the heavier gym shoes when possible.
3. If the lighter gymnastic slippers are not available, it is better to work in stockinged feet. This makes the gymnast feel lighter, and protects the equipment.
4. For varsity or exhibition purposes, teams or groups of performers should be dressed alike in regular gymnastic pants and shirts. Wool gabardine and wool rayon are the best materials for this purpose.

5. Hand guards may be constructed from one-inch lamp wicks or half-inch skate straps for the protection of the performer.
6. A safety belt is a *must* in the equipment for gymnastic work. The type that permits twisting tricks is best for tumbling or trampoline stunts.

PLAYING COURTESIES

1. Do not monopolize any piece of apparatus. Remember that someone else may be waiting to use it.
2. Never distract a performer while he is in the process of performing a stunt. This may lead to a serious accident.
3. Be concerned with the safety of others. Do not wait to be asked to "spot" for a performer—volunteer.
4. Always leave the apparatus in the same condition you found it. This is a courtesy to be shown those in charge of equipment.
5. Always be appreciative of the progress and ability of those with whom you participate.
6. Be receptive to the suggestions of others.
7. Observe the rules and regulations of the playing area on which you are participating.
8. Do not walk on mats with your street shoes.
9. Never alter the position of apparatus until you have the permission of the person in charge.

SPOTTING

One of the major considerations in administrating a program in gymnastics, or in any other active sport, is the problem of safety. Being cognizant of the inherent danger in attempting new or difficult stunts, gymnastic instructors employ a skill known as "spotting" or "guarding." Spotting, as it is more frequently designated in gymnastic nomenclature, is any technique utilized by the teacher and/or students to stand by alertly or to actually assist in insuring the safety of the performer as he executes a routine or specific stunt. Whenever a gymnast is performing on the horizontal bar or the trampoline, there should be at least one "spotter" present regardless of whether the athlete is a neophyte or an Olympic level gymnast. In one type of spotting, the guarder is only standing by to assist should the performer get into difficulty. Spotting of this nature should also be utilized on any apparatus when the gymnast is attempting a routine or dismount that he is not absolutely certain of completing. There is no penalty for spotting in gymnastic competition unless actual contact has taken place.

When actually assisting a performer, there are basically two methods of spotting employed: (1) hand spotting and (2) belt spotting. When using a hand spotting technique, it is obvious that the spotter must get close to the gymnast, generally from the side, and yet not interfere with execution of the movement. The duty of the spotter is to break the fall of the gymnast or to prevent him from hitting the uprights of the apparatus, cables, or other obstacles. The guard may also increase the velocity of rotation in order to prevent the performer from landing on his head or other vulnerable area.

Belt spotting may best be negotiated by using an overhead rig which consists of a long section of rope attached from the ceiling by a double pulley and a single pulley spaced about 20 feet apart. The ends of the rope are attached to metal hooks in the right and left side of the safety belt that the performer is wearing. The coach or teacher standing under the double pulley can then pull on the loop of the rope and lift the gymnast when help is required.

A traveling suspension system is also available for spotting tumbling sequences. A less expensive belt spotting technique can be employed by simply using a safety belt and two short lines which are controlled by two guards. For twisting movements, a special twisting belt can be purchased from gymnastic equipment companies. A regular belt system may also be used for twisting by wrapping the ropes around the performer in the opposite direction of the anticipated twist. However, this is not an effective method, particularly for spotting multiple twisting action.

GENERAL SPOTTING RULES

1. Use a safety belt when initially attempting advanced stunts.
2. The spotter should know exactly what trick or routine the gymnast will attempt to execute.
3. The gymnast also should be aware of how he will be spotted so that he will not be "psyched out" during a stunt by the spotting technique utilized.
4. The spotter must be alert at all times.
5. The instructor should know exactly when the performer will go for a trick (e.g., after the second giant swing, on the third bounce, and so on).
6. A minimal number of bounces or swings should be used before attempting a stunt.
7. Do not stop once a stunt is begun.
8. Keep the slack out of the ropes when using a spotting device, especially on the trampoline. Too much tension in the early phases of a trick, however, will tend to pull the gymnast off balance.
9. Do not spot anyone on a new stunt unless he has mastered the necessary prerequisites. If in doubt, consult an expert.
10. Good belt spotting is an art. The gymnastic teacher should develop his ability to spot in a progression from mechanically simple tricks to more difficult ones.
11. Do not give unnecessary assistance to a performer. Over-spotting can also be dangerous.
12. Be careful not to interfere with the movement being attempted.
13. Make certain that the ropes of the mechanicism are in the proper position before the stunt is practiced so that the gymnast does not become entangled in the lines (e.g., the ropes should be under the arms and over the shoulders when attempting a back toss on the Parallel Bars).
14. The spotting lines should be wrapped around the apparatus in the opposite direction of the movement being learned. The number of times the rope is wrapped around should be carefully determined.
15. Particularly in high school, the use of an overhead spotting device should, for the most part, be restricted to the instructor.
16. The spotter should recognize fatigue and make a performer rest at appropriate intervals. Many gymnasts are so enthusiastic about learning a new trick that they ignore signs of exhaustion.

SPOTTING FLOOR EXERCISE

1. The spotter is generally at the side of the performer (e.g., when spotting a back hand-spring, stand at the side, lift with the right hand on the small of his back, and flip the tumbler over by pushing on his thigh with the left hand).
2. In spotting tumbling moves, pressure may be exerted on the upper back to keep the performer from landing on his head (e.g., dive roll and front somersault).

3. Use a traveling mechanic for learning complicated tumbling sequences.

SPOTTING SIDE HORSE

1. Spotting on the side horse is difficult because of the continuous circular movement of the performer's feet.
2. Mounts or dismounts can be spotted by standing in back of the gymnast and lifting his hips by placing one hand on each of his hips (e.g., spotting loops).
3. A special side horse mechanic has been developed recently and is now on the market.

SPOTTING TRAMPOLINE

1. There should be at least one spotter on each side and on each end of the trampoline whenever possible.
2. A guard should not reach in for a performer because the man may then fly over the spotter's head.
3. To prevent serious injury, push the trampolinist back onto the trampoline bed, if possible.
4. If the gymnast is flying off high and far from the side of the trampoline, attempt to break his fall and insure that he lands on his feet.

SPOTTING HORIZONTAL BAR

1. Stand on the side and to the left of the performer on overhand stunts. Stand to the right of the performer on reverse grip stunts.
2. Spot under the horizontal bar for in-bar work. Make certain that the movement is being achieved toward or on the same side of the bar as the spotter.
3. Watch the hands! When they release the bar, move quickly in the direction of the maneuver.

SPOTTING PARALLEL BARS

1. Spot from under the bars rather than putting the hands between the parallel bars and the performer.
2. Some stunts can be spotted more easily from low benches or by adjusting the bars to a lower height.

3. The parallel bars may be moved off to the side of the overhead mechanic for easier spotting of dismounts.

SPOTTING RINGS

1. Watch the performer's hands, as in horizontal bar spotting.
2. For a dismount, spot with one hand under the chest and the other on the upper back of the gymnast.
3. Use an overhead device for spotting difficult dismounts.

SPOTTING LONG HORSE

1. Generally, the guard should stand to the side of the long horse at the croup and move with the performer as he goes over the horse. In the landing phase of the vault, have one hand under the chest and the other on the upper back of the athlete.
2. A traveling mechanic can be used for more difficult vaults.

OFFICIALS

Refer to number eight of Basic Rules. In dual meets, fewer than four judges may be used in an emergency, in which event their scores shall be averaged. Officials used in a dual meet must have been agreed upon by the participating coaches.

It is recommended that in addition to the judges and scorers there be a meet director (when five or more schools are competing), an announcer, and a physician.

SAFETY HINTS

1. Inspect all apparatus before using it.
2. Do not use defective apparatus.
3. Help keep mats as clean as possible by:
   (a) Carrying mats rather than dragging them.
   (b) Not walking on mats with street shoes.
   (c) Always placing mats with the "tied" side down.
4. Report any defective equipment.
5. Place mats around and under all apparatus being used.
6. Do not overlap or leave gaps between mats.

7. In placing mats in a line, it is advisable to tie them together.

8. Do not "horseplay" in the apparatus area.

9. Be sure, when you practice a stunt, that it is within your capabilities.

10. Remember that once you have committed yourself to the execution of a stunt you must follow it to completion in the best interests of your safety.

11. The performer should have a complete idea of what he is about to attempt.

12. Use carbonate of magnesium on the hands to lessen hand friction and possible torn palms from the apparatus.

13. Keep apparatus sanded with solidified "mag" or "chalk."

14. No distractions should be present in activity area.

15. Participate only when safety pads are provided for the metal frame of the trampoline.

16. All beginners should learn to "kill" their spring by flexing the knees immediately upon landing on the canvas to prevent an uncontrolled bounce off the trampoline.

17. Do not jump from the canvas to the floor (trampoline).

TERMINOLOGY

Approach   The manner in which the performer walks toward his apparatus before starting his routine.

Arabesque   A one-foot balance with one leg raised backward with arms placed in various positions.

Balance   To maintain equilibrium.

Break   To halt or lessen the rebound while bouncing on a trampoline.

Bridge   Done by lying on the mat using the head and legs as support, raising the body from the floor.

Check   A halt or slowing of the body revolutions when performing on a trampoline.

Croup   The straight end of a long horse.

Dip   A maneuver performed on the end of the parallel bars by lowering and raising the body by arm strength alone.

Dolly   A small low platform on rollers used for moving bulky or heavy objects.

Fan   A stunt on the parallel bars; starts with a swinging pirouette but finishes with a half turn away from the bar.

Flex   To bend.

Gainer   A back flip, in which the performer lands ahead of the take-off spot.

Jackknife   A position with the legs straight, the hips flexed.

Kip   A movement utilizing forceful extension of the hips from a hand position to a support position.

Lunger   A strong leather or webbing belt to circle the body of a gymnast with ropes attached to its sides by swivels.

Pommels   The curved iron handles of a side horse.

Shinny   To climb.

Somersault (Flip)   A movement in which the body makes a 360 degree arc without touching apparatus or mat during the turn-over.

Spotter   Guard assisting the performer in order to prevent injury.

Tassels   The bottom side of a mat.

Tinsica   A front handspring with a cartwheel action, one hand being ahead of the other.

Vault   A leap, jump, or swing in which the hands assist the performer to clear an obstacle.

Whip   A vigorous powerful drive with a part of the body, usually the legs, to get sufficient force to execute a stunt.

Women's gymnastics

Women's gymnastics is actually the only sport typically feminine. The events comprising this sport are not found in any other sport. It is only in gymnastics that women do not copy men. For this simple reason it is the only feminine sport.

As is the case with men's gymnastics, competitive gymnastics for women is relatively young. The sport in its form today has existed only since 1952. Women's gymnastics, as conceived since that time, requires and develops qualities strictly feminine: grace, rhythm, beauty of movement and body, and elegance.

Women in the United States who desire to participate in competitive gymnastics may do so under the jurisdiction of the National AAU Gymnastics Committee assisted by the Women's Technical Committee of that organization.

Recently, a Commission on Intercollegiate Athletics for Women (formed by the Division for Girls' and Women's Sports of the American Association for Health, Physical Education, and Recreation) was established. This Commission will hold its first gymnastics championships for college and university women in March or April of 1969.

International competition is under the jurisdiction of the International Gymnastics Federation (FIG). Events for women in Olympic competition include individual all-around, free standing exercise, balance beam, uneven parallel bars, and long horse (vaulting). The U.S.S.R. won the team championship during the competitions of 1952 through 1968.

BASIC RULES [2]

1. The minimum age limit shall be 15 years for championship competition.
2. The competitors shall perform in rotation in the order selected by the committee. No competitor shall be required to perform first in more than one event.
3. Proper gym attire (leotards) shall be worn at all times. The leotards must be modest and

[2] 1969 Official Gymnastics Guide of the Amateur Athletic Union.

made of non-transparent cloth. Gymnasts may work either in sandals or barefoot.

4. Approved events for district and national championships shall be as follows: Individual Events —Floor Exercise, Uneven Parallel Bars, Balance Beam, and Side Horse Vault; Special Events—Tumbling and Rebound Tumbling (Trampolining) as of 1961; All-Around Event —consisting of Floor Exercise, Uneven Parallel Bars, Balance Beam, and Side Horse Vault.
5. In the Balance Beam event, the performance must not be carried out at a too slow or monotonous rhythm, but must be full of life and make use of the entire body. The exercise, lasting one minute 20 seconds to one minute 45 seconds, should include steps, running, jumping, turns, some held positions, and minimal sitting and lying positions.
6. With the exception of Floor Exercise, any gymnast may repeat without loss of points a compulsory exercise which she thinks she has missed or performed badly.
7. In Side Horse Vaulting, a gymnast is entitled to two vaults both for the compulsory and optional exercises. The better performance will count. In the Balance Beam competition, if a gymnast falls from the apparatus, she can repeat the exercise from the moment of the fall to the end with a penalty of one point per fall.
8. Judging and marking: The compulsory exercises will be awarded from zero to ten points, in tenths of a point. Optional exercises will be marked from zero to ten points. On the Side Horse, compulsory vaults will be marked from zero to ten points and in tenths of a point, as are the optional vaults. In Rebound Tumbling, a minimum of six spotters is required. Each gymnast will perform a compulsory and an optional routine consisting of ten to twelve movements. The method of judging and scoring (except where otherwise specifically noted) will be governed by applicable rules and regulations currently prevailing for the men's gymnastic competition.
9. On the apparatus and in floor exercises, each

competitor performs two exercises, one of which is compulsory.

10. The performance of the compulsory exercise is judged solely on its execution.

11. The optional exercises are evaluated from zero to ten points by tenths of a point. The ten points are allocated as follows: Three points for difficulty, two points for composition and technical value, five points for execution and general impression. Optional exercises should contain five higher elements of difficulty, of which one must be of supreme difficulty. For the general beauty of movement and in order to avoid regrettable excess, it is highly recommended not to exceed the set standard (that is, five higher degree of difficulty moves).

12. In judging and scoring, five women judges are used plus a superior judge (although if necessary four judges may be used). The highest mark and the lowest mark are eliminated and the average of the three middle marks is posted. The rules require that the spread between the highest and the lowest of the three middle marks cannot exceed 0.3 of a point when the average score is 9.0 or above; 0.5 of a point when the average score is 8.0 to 8.95; and 1.0 when the average score is below 8.0. Should this occur, the judges will consult and the superior judge will be responsible for making the necessary adjustment.

13. The compulsory and the optional Floor Exercises must be executed to the accompaniment of music utilizing a single instrument. The exercises should be performed in time with the music.

14. The Tumbling event consists of an optional routine of not more than two minutes duration with four trips across the five feet by 60 feet mat. Short rests are allowed between passes. Only tumbling moves are to be performed. Dance moves, for instance, are not considered appropriate.

TECHNIQUES AND FUNDAMENTALS

Women's floor exercises

This event for women is quite similar to the men's event. The performer does the exercises on the floor or on a thin mat for a maximum time of one and one-half minutes. The performer must confine herself to an area of 12 meters x 12 meters. The women's activity differs basically from the men's in the type of exercise performed. The women use more ballet type movements as contrasted with the power movements usually found in the men's routine. A typical sequence for the women would be tumbling, ballet movements, balancing and agility exercises, and finishing with additional tumbling stunts. The event is one of the most flexible in competition for women. In competitive meets in this event, the voluntary exercise, like the required one, must be accompanied by music utilizing a single instrument.

TOE STAND.   From a standing position with arms at sides of body, rise on the toes and extend the arm outward to shoulder height with the palms down. Return to standing position. (See Fig. 15-16.)

STAG LEAP.   Leap into the air and before landing move one foot up and under the other leg in such a way that the foot almost touches the knee. Lift and balance are provided by the hands during the leap by raising them at the sides. (See Fig. 15-17.)

STRADDLE STANCE.   From a standing position, slide the feet outward into a one-half split. Bend slightly forward, keeping the head erect. The arms may be extended at shoulder height. (See Fig. 15-18.)

SPLITS.   The same as in the straddle stance except the feet are extended farther, permitting the performer to come to a "sitting position."

STRADDLE LEAN.   Do a split and finish by leaning forward until the chest makes contact with the floor. The hands should grasp the ankles.

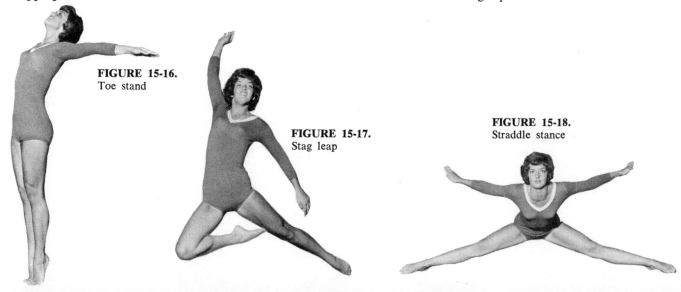

FIGURE 15-16.
Toe stand

FIGURE 15-17.
Stag leap

FIGURE 15-18.
Straddle stance

FIGURE 15-19.
Needle scale

FIGURE 15-20. Balance seat
(V seat)

FIGURE 15-21.
Side seat

SPIRAL. This usually involves a full turn. Take little steps to turn in place while in a trunk-bending position with knees flexed. The arms and body move to one side in a twisting motion to a toe stand and stretched body.

NEEDLE SCALE. The person leans forward into a front scale and then continues moving downward until the forehead touches the shin of the supporting leg. The other leg is extended directly overhead. Diligent practice is needed to accomplish this trick because of the extreme flexibility involved. (See Fig. 15-19.)

BACK WALKOVER. Bend backward from a standing position until the hands touch the floor. When this happens, kick smoothly with one leg up and over. The other leg will follow so that the standing position will be achieved. During the learning stage of this stunt a spotter should be used.

BALANCE SEAT (V SEAT). While sitting on the floor with the legs together, elevate the legs so that they form a V with the trunk. The performer may either keep the hands on the floor behind the body or may raise them outward as shown in the picture. (See Fig. 15-20.)

VALDEZ. While sitting on the floor, one hand is in back of the hip as the other is held straight out from the body. One leg is straight and the other is flexed with the foot close to the body as shown in the picture. From this starting position, the arm held straight is thrust backward and overhead while the straight leg is lifted upward. The other arm and leg are used for support. A fast backbend

motion allows the performer to finish in a handstand position or a standing position by continuing the motion.

Women's even and uneven parallel bars

The dimensions of the parallel bars are very similar to those used by the men. In the uneven bars, the height of the high bar is seven feet six inches (to the top of the bar) and the height of the low bar is 59 inches. Between the inside of the two bars the distance varies from 17 inches to 19 inches. As in other events, a beat board may be used for mounting.

Whereas the even parallel bars have been a standard event for women for many years, the uneven bars, as a competitive event, was first introduced in the 1952 Olympic Games held in Helsinki. The event has since been accepted in Olympic, international, and national competition.

Even bars

SIDE SEAT. The performer, from the straight arm support position, swings forward, passes both legs up and over one of the bars, finishing in a side seat position, the hands being behind the body on the bars. The performer may then do a series of side seats by swinging the legs upward into the side seat from the straight arm position and then back again. (See Fig. 15-21.)

UPPER ARM BALANCE (SHOULDER STAND).

The performer begins from a straddle seat position, the hands in front of the body on the bars. Then leaning forward and placing the upper arms on the bar, the performer slowly lifts the hips and legs up and into the shoulder balance position. Keeping the head up, the performer moves slowly into a shoulder balance, the back arched, legs straight, and toes pointed. (See Fig. 15-22.)

SINGLE LEG CUT-OFF FORWARD DISMOUNT. The performer facing away from the bars in a straight arm support position swings back and forth a few times. On reaching the back end of one of the swings, the performer lifts one leg over the bar. Then the grip on one hand is released, and the leg passes between it and the bar. The performer continues to move forward and lands on the mat in a dismount fashion.

SINGLE LEG FLANK DISMOUNT. The performer begins with the body in a resting position sideways across the bars—one leg over the forward bar and the other leaning on the rear bar. The performer then swings the back leg up and around the bars, pushes off the front bar, and drops to the mat.

REAR VAULT DISMOUNT. Swinging back and forth a few times in a straight arm support position, the performer on forward position swings both legs up and over the bar. The movement is continued to the side, passing over the left bar if the dismount is to the left side, and the performer finishes facing the same direction, the left hand free and the right hand holding the bar for support. (See Fig. 15-23.)

STRAIGHT ARM SUPPORT. The performer jumps into a straight arm position on either the middle or the ends of the bars. The arms are kept straight, the head up, the back arched, and the toes pointed. This position is used in many of the stunts for the parallel bars. (See Fig. 15-24.)

Uneven bars

BACK PULLOVER MOUNT. This mount is started by facing the low bar and clasping it with an overgrip. Both legs are swung over the bar almost simultaneously by pulling in towards the bar with the arms. Continue pulling until both legs are over the bar and so that the body eventually finishes in a straight arm support position.

SHOOT OVER LOW BAR FROM HANG ON HIGH BAR. Start from in back of the high bar facing the low bar. Approach and take off, clasping the high bar and swinging both legs over the low bar. Finish with the back of the thighs resting on the low bar and the hands holding the high bar. The body should now be in a hanging lying position.

REAR VAULT WITH QUARTER TURN DISMOUNT. The body should be between the bars, leaning forward with the hands holding the high bar and low bar. Swing the legs up and over the low bar. Pushing off the high bar, turn the body to an L seat position over the low bar. Continue the motion by placing both hands on the low bar and dismounting to the feet.

SWAN SUPPORT. This is done on the high bar from a straight arm support position. Execute a swan arch position and hold the arms straight out at the sides.

FIGURE 15-22. Upper arm balance (shoulder stand)

FIGURE 15-23. Rear vault dismount

FIGURE 15-24. Straight arm support

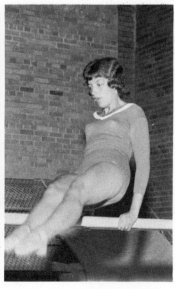

THIGH REST. Take a front rest position on the high bar. Drop slowly downward and grasp the low bar with the hands, keeping the arms straight. Slowly lift the legs and arch the back. The body is now resting on the hands and thighs.

CROSS SEAT MOUNT. Stand between the bars (near the middle) with the left shoulder toward the high bar. Jump up and grasp the high bar with the left hand and the low bar with the right hand, and swing the legs up and over the low bar to a cross seat position.

KICK OFF LOW BAR TO HIGH BAR SUPPORT. From a hanging position, hands holding the top bar, place one foot on the low, and hold the other leg stretched close to the top bar. Whip that leg down and simultaneously push with the leg on the low bar, keeping your body as you ascend as close as possible to the top bar so that the body ends in a straight arm support position on the top bar.

Women's balance beam

This activity is performed on a beam approximately four inches wide and 16 feet long which rests on tripods about four feet high. The event also utilizes the beat board. In competition, the performer is allowed one and one-half to two minutes during which she may execute her routine—a routine consisting of a mount, a series of movements on the beam, and a dismount. In this particular event running movements, jumps, rolls, turns, and side steps must predominate over held positions and balance positions. The performer should during each routine exhibit confidence, poise, grace, flexibility, and rhythm.

STRAIGHT ARM SUPPORT MOUNT. From a standing position place the hands on the beam at shoulder width. Jump up to a straight arm position with the thighs resting on the beam. The head should be up and the body arched, with the toes pointing outward. Two or three running steps may also be

used to mount the beam in this manner. If this is done, use a double foot take-off.

SQUAT MOUNT. From a straight arm support pull both legs up between the arms so that the feet may be placed on the beam between the hands. (See Fig. 15-25.)

STRADDLE MOUNT. From a straight arm support spread the legs and place the feet on the beam outside of the hands to a straddle support position. When starting this stunt, have a spotter on the opposite side of the beam. (See Fig. 15-26.)

FRONT SCALE. Perform this stunt on the beam by standing on one leg with the other leg raised so that it is parallel to the beam. The arms are spread outward and are used for balance.

ONE LEG SQUAT. From a standing position on the beam, lower into a squat position on one leg. A full squat position is attained when the other leg lifted is parallel to the beam.

KNEE SCALE. In the starting position, one knee should be behind the other on the beam. Place both hands on the beam in front of you by leaning forward. As you begin to lean forward, lift the back leg into the air and hold the position. (See Fig. 15-27.)

Women's vaulting

The horse for women's vaulting is five feet three inches long and 13¾ inches wide. The pommels have been removed and the vaulting is done over the side of the horse. During competition, the height of the horse is $43\frac{5}{16}$ inches; each vault has a difficulty rating; and each competitor performs two vaults. A springy-type beat (take-off) board may be used to gain height. The hands, upon landing on the horse, usually rest on the middle part (saddle) of the apparatus. Men's and women's vaults bear similar names—flank, squat, straddle, thief, stoop, handspring, and the like.

STRADDLE STAND FORWARD JUMP OFF. In

FIGURE 15-25. Squat mount

FIGURE 15-26. Straddle mount

FIGURE 15-27. Knee scale

this exercise, the performer jumps to a straddle stand on the outside of the arms. The performer then straightens up and jumps forward to the mat.

THIEF OR WINDOW VAULT. The performer takes off from one foot, then lifts the other leg upward in the direction of the take-off foot and goes over the horse in a sitting position. As the body goes on over the horse, the hands drop to the horse and push strongly. A neat shoot forward is accomplished by having the feet elevated as the hands touch the horse.

HANDSPRING. The performer springs from the beat board upward to a handstand position on the saddle of the horse, the arms straight. The performer from this position continues on over with a handspring or arch-over motion to the mat.

FLANK VAULT. The performer goes over the horse with the side of the body nearest the horse. The body is kept straight while leaning on the supporting arm and in going over the top of the horse. (See Fig. 15-28.)

SQUAT VAULT. The performer in this exercise takes off from the beat board; puts the hands on the horse; and brings the knees up and between the arms; then pushes hard with the arms; goes over the horse in a squat position; and lands on the mat.

FRONT VAULT. This is similar to the flank vault, with the exception that the front of the body is nearest the horse while passing over it. The body forms a graceful arch when the legs and feet are lifted into the air. The performer lands on the mat, resting the inside hand on the horse for support.

REAR VAULT. The performer goes over the horse in a sitting position with the seat nearest the horse. While taking off, lift the legs to the side and pass them over in a pike position. Continue on over; then change the hands and land on the mat facing the direction of the turn, using the inside hand on the horse for support. (See Fig. 15-29.)

HELPFUL HINTS

1. Practice many of the stunts before a mirror—especially those in free exercises and balance beam.
2. Use spotters for the more difficult stunts.
3. Practice the stunts in free exercises first on a mat.
4. Concentrate on rhythm, balance, and coordination.
5. Develop specific routines.

FIGURE 15-28. Flank vault

FIGURE 15-29. Rear vault

6. In your routines, emphasize individuality and originality and make an effort to mold the movements into a harmonious pattern.

7. Strength and endurance are essential for excellence of performance.

8. Confidence is extremely important for successful execution of many of the stunts. To build it requires that you practice and practice the stunts.

9. In vaulting stunts, set the height of the horse at a low level when first learning the vaults. Raise it gradually as you gain in skill and confidence.

10. Spend considerable time in practicing take-offs from the beat board.

11. In learning balance beam stunts, first practice on a straight line on the gymnasium floor. Use tape or water-solvent paint to represent the four-inch beam.

12. Change from the painted line to a beam just a few inches high after you have gained in skill and in confidence.

13. Learn all stunts in a progressive order.

14. Learn stunts on the even parallel bars before proceeding to the uneven bars.

15. Several of the stunts on the uneven bars may first be practiced on a low horizontal bar.

SPOTTING

Spotting balance beam

1. New stunts should, whenever possible, be spotted on the tumbling mats, floor, or the low balance beam before progressing to the standard beam height. (Chalk lines the size of the beam may be drawn on the floor and mats.)

2. While spotting ballet moves on the balance beam, the guard may walk alongside the beam with one arm raised so that the gymnast may steady herself on the hand of the spotter without falling or dismounting from the balance beam.

Spotting uneven parallel bars

1. Spotting sometimes can be facilitated by removing one of the bars or by using an adjustable horizontal bar.

2. Generally, it is advisable to spot from the side standing between the uneven parallel bars. However, various stunts necessitate a move to the front or rear of the bars. (Dismounts are usually completed in front of the lower bar. Therefore, these maneuvers are better spotted to the front and side of the low bar.)

3. The spotter should watch the hands of the gymnast to make certain that she has re-grasped the bars properly.

Spotting side horse vaulting

1. The horse may be lowered to facilitate spotting.

2. It is advisable to have two spotters on side horse vaulting—one in front of the horse and one in the rear.

3. The front spotter can best help the performer by lifting her hips. (When spotting a front handspring vault, the spotter should face the gymnast.)

SELECTED REFERENCES

Babbitt, Diane, and Werner Haas, *Gymnastic Apparatus Exercises for Girls*. New York: The Ronald Press Company, 1964.

Cooper, Phyllis S., *Feminine Gymnastics*. Minneapolis: Burgess Publishing Co., 1967.

Hughes, Eric, *Gymnastics for Men*. New York: The Ronald Press Company, 1966.

Kenney, Charles J., *Fundamental Tumbling Skills Illustrated—With Floor Exercise*. New York: The Ronald Press Company, 1966.

————, *Trampolining Illustrated*. New York: The Ronald Press Company, 1961.

Loken, N., and R. Willoughby, *Complete Book of Gymnastics*. Englewood Cliffs, N.J.: Prentice-Hall, Inc., 1967.

Norman, Randi, *Gymnastics for Girls and Women*. Dubuque, Iowa: William C. Brown Company, Publishers, 1965.

Ruff, Wesley K., *Gymnastics: Beginner to Competitor*. Dubuque, Iowa: William C. Brown Company, Publishers, 1959.

Ryser, Otto E., *A Teacher's Manual For Tumbling and Apparatus Stunts*. Dubuque, Iowa: William C. Brown Company, Publishers, 1961.

Handball

16

ORIGIN AND DEVELOPMENT

The game of handball was originated by the Irish around the tenth century and since that time has been a popular sport in Ireland and England. Championship tournaments were held in the 1800's, John Cavanagh of York being the outstanding player during this early period. William Baggs of Tipperary followed Cavanagh and is credited with developing the technique of imparting "English" to the ball so that it would hop and curve on rebounds.

During the 1800's, several Irish handball players migrated to the United States and were surprised to find there were no courts in this country. Phil Casey, one of these Irish players, began developing an interest in the game around Brooklyn and in 1887, after winning the handball championship of the United States, arranged a 21-game series with John Lawlor, champion of Ireland. A side bet of $1,000 was placed on the match. The first ten games were to be played in Cork and the remaining 11 in the United States. Lawlor won six of the first ten games, but Casey won seven straight when

the series was resumed in the United States, thereby becoming the world champion. Casey retained his championship until the turn of the century, when he retired from championship play. He is known as the father of handball in America.

One of the greatest players of modern times was Joe Platak, who won the singles championship of the United States nine times between 1935 and 1945. He is recognized by many authorities as the greatest handball player in history.

Today, handball is widely played throughout the world.

PADDLEBALL

Paddleball is a version of handball in which a paddle is used instead of the hand to strike the ball, and the same basic rules apply to both versions of the game. Paddleball was originated by Earl Riskey at the University of Michigan in 1930, and since the game was played in a regulation handball court, Riskey utilized handball rules, with some minor adaptations, for the game of paddleball. The National Paddleball Association was organized in

213

1952 with Riskey as the first president. The first national paddleball tournament was held in 1961, with 11 entries in singles and a like number in doubles. The game has grown in popularity throughout the country, and, although played primarily by men, it has grown in favor as a corecreational activity in many colleges and universities.

PADDLE.   The official paddle is made of wood or plastic and is 15 inches in length, approximately eight inches wide, and weighs about 16 ounces. Attached to the end of the handle is a leather thong, which must be worn around the wrist during play. (An "official" paddle is manufactured by the National Paddleball Association, Sports Building, Ann Arbor, Michigan.)

BALL.   The official paddleball is the Pennsy Official National Paddleball made by General Tire–Pennsylvania Athletics Products, Akron, Ohio. When dropped from a height of six feet, the ball should rebound approximately four feet.

NATURE OF THE GAME

The game of handball is played by batting a small rubber ball with either hand against a wall. The game may be played on one-wall courts or on enclosed courts with four walls. One-wall courts are frequently constructed out-of-doors, but the walls of a gymnasium may be utilized for the game by including boundary lines on the walls and floor.

The unified rules require that players use gloves when playing the game of handball. Any close-fitting glove is helpful as a protective device, but players will find regulation handball gloves to be most desirable. Gloves are available with padded and unpadded palms. (See Fig. 16-1.)

FIGURE 16-1.   Handball glove

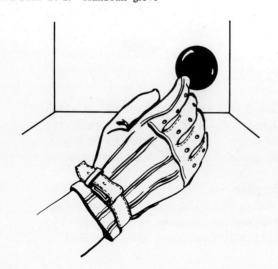

Handball is a desirable game for recreation because the players may play at any speed they desire and it is not necessary to get a large group of persons together in order to have a game. Older persons will find the doubles game less fatiguing than the singles game because two players share the responsibility of covering the court area. Handball courts are standard equipment in most YMCA buildings, athletic clubs, and recreation centers. A person can get a good workout in a short time and have fun while doing it. Instructors are generally agreed that while they often fail to find many enthusiastic supporters of the game in a class of beginners, there is universal enthusiasm for the game after the students have learned the fundamentals and have had a taste of competition.

BASIC RULES

Another strong point in favor of handball is the simplicity of the rules governing the game. Any person can become familiar with the basic rules in one or two class sessions. In 1958 the AAU, the USHA, and the YMCA agreed upon a unified set of handball rules that would be applicable throughout the country, and in 1959 these rules were officially accepted by the Jewish Welfare Board. Included below is a summary of these rules.

THE GAME.   The game may be played by two, three (cut-throat), or four players. A game shall be won by the side first scoring 21 points and only the side serving may score points. Only one hand, at any one time, may be used in striking the ball. It is illegal to use the foot, or any part of the body, except one hand, to play the ball. Violation of this rule results in a point or handout as the case may be. In attempting to play the ball, it cannot be struck more than once.

In the act of serving, the server drops the ball on the floor (between the short and service lines) and on the first rebound it is struck in such a manner that it will first hit the front wall and on the rebound land upon the floor back of the short line, either before or after striking one of the side walls. After the ball is legally served, one of the players of the receiving team returns the ball by striking it either on the fly or on the first bounce so that it will strike the front wall before striking the floor either directly or after having struck one or both of the side walls, back wall, ceiling, or any combination of these surfaces. The receiving side then returns the ball to the front wall, and play continues until one side is unable to return the ball legally, which will then constitute either a point or a handout.

EQUIPMENT. The standard four wall handball court is 40 feet × 20 feet × 20 feet, and an outdoor single wall court is 34 feet × 20 feet × 16 feet. The court shall be divided into a front court and a back court of equal dimensions by a line called the *short line,* running parallel to the front wall. Five feet in front of the short line shall be another parallel line called the *service line.* Eighteen inches from and parallel with each side wall a line shall be drawn to form a box, termed the *service box,* where the partner of the server, in doubles, must stand while the ball is being served.

The ball shall be made of black rubber, one and seven-eighths inches in diameter, and weigh 2.3 ounces. The ball should rebound 42 to 48 ounces from a 70-inch drop in a temperature of 68 degrees.

Any glove consisting of soft material or leather, light in color, may be used. Fingers of gloves shall not be webbed or connected. No foreign substance, tape, or rubber bands shall be used on fingers or palms of gloves. Gloves must be worn at all times.

PLAYING REGULATIONS. The choice for the right to serve shall be decided by the toss of a coin, and the player or side winning the toss starts the first and third games. The server may stand any place in the service zone. When the server or serving side loses the service, he or they shall become the receiver; the receiver the server; and so alternately in all subsequent services of the game. The serve must be made within the service area; stepping on the line, but not beyond, is permitted. In serving, the ball must be bounced on the floor and struck on its first rebound from the floor. If the server attempts to hit the ball on this rebound, and fails, he is out. The server may not bounce the ball more than three times in the service zone in making a service. Violation of this rule retires the server. A server shall not serve until his opponent has had a fair opportunity to get placed. The server's partner, in doubles, must stand within the service box with his back to the side wall, both feet on the floor, until the ball passes the short line on its return from the front wall.

If a player's partner is hit by a served fly ball while standing in the service box it counts as a "dead ball" without penalty, but does not eliminate any short or long fault preceding this service. If he is hit by a served ball on the bounce, it is a short ball. If the served ball should pass behind the partner and strike the floor back of the short line, it is a dead ball.

In doubles the side starting each game is allowed one handout only. After that both partners are permitted to serve. Players in doubles must follow the same order of service throughout the game. It is not necessary for players to alternate serves to their opponents.

If a ball be swung at and missed it may be played again, providing it is hit before bouncing twice on the floor. If a player swings at and completely misses the ball in play and in his, or his partner's, attempt to again play the ball there is an unintentional interference by an opponent, it shall be a hinder. If the completely missed ball should on the fly or first bounce strike an opponent it is a penalty against the opponent—a point or handout as the case may be.

RECEIVING SERVICE. The receiver or receivers must stand at least five feet back of the short line while the ball is being served. The receiver may play the ball on the first bounce or volley it, provided he does not cross the short line. The receiver may not play an illegally served ball.

ILLEGAL SERVICE. Any two of the following serves in succession retires the server.

1. When the served ball hits the front wall and fails to strike the floor back of the short line on the fly.
2. When a served ball hits the front wall and two side walls before striking the floor.
3. When a served ball hits the front wall, side wall, and back wall before striking the floor.
4. When a served ball hits the front wall, then the ceiling or back wall before striking the floor.
5. When stepping beyond the short line or service line in the act of serving.

HINDERS. A returned ball that strikes an opponent before striking the floor is dead even if it continues to the front wall, and must be played over. It is a hinder if a player unintentionally interferes with an opponent in such a way as to prevent him from having a fair chance to play the ball. In doubles, both players on a side are entitled to a fair and unobstructed chance at the ball and either one is entitled to a decision on a hinder even though it naturally would be his partner's ball and notwithstanding the fact that his partner may be attempting to play the ball, or that he may already have missed it. It is no excuse that the ball was "killed" or that the opponent "could not get it." A player is entitled to a fair chance to play the ball. A player cannot be interfered with by his partner.

OUTS. Outs shall be declared under the following conditions.

1. On an avoidable hinder—when an opponent deliberately moves to obstruct an opponent.
2. A partner serving both hands in doubles.

FIGURES 16-2 through 16-4. Low drive serve

3. A legally served ball touching the server on the fly.
4. A legally served ball which strikes the server's partner when the latter is outside the server's box.
5. A legally returned ball striking the partner of the one returning the ball.
6. Failure of the server to properly return a ball in play.
7. A served ball hitting the ceiling, floor, or side walls before striking a front wall.
8. A served ball which hits the front and side wall, or front wall and floor, or front wall and ceiling at the same time (crotch ball).

TECHNIQUES AND FUNDAMENTALS

The good handball player observes certain fundamentals common to all sports. These include position on the floor, balance, accuracy in placing the ball, and the use of correct arm movements in playing the various shots. The beginning player will usually have difficulty in playing an experienced player, because the latter will always be in position to hit the ball, while the beginner will frequently find himself out of position. The player who learns to station himself in a position of maximum coverage of the floor as soon as he strikes the ball will find it easier to return difficult shots from an opponent.

Proper use of footwork is essential if a player is to become proficient in handball. When striking the ball with the right hand, the left foot should be forward. The legs should be slightly bent at the knees and the body kept in a crouched position in order that quick movements may be made instantly in any direction. The player should keep his eyes on the ball as it comes off the front wall until it strikes his hand and then watch the front wall for the return of the ball from the opponent. On balls that the player strikes with such force that they go over his head, he should watch the ball until it passes him and then watch the front wall. Players should not turn around to watch the flight of a ball they have hit to the back court area. Watch the front wall—if the ball is not returned, it is a point for the player. If the ball does not return to the front wall the player has won a point or a side-out, but if he turns around to watch his opponent play the ball in the back court area he may find himself out of position for a play on the return—or in a position to get hit in the face with an unexpected return.

Serving

There are several types of serves in common use by good handball players. We shall list four types and the player can develop others as he perfects his game.

LOW DRIVE SERVE. In this serve the ball is hit close to the floor so that it returns just past the short line. (See Figs. 16-2, 16-3, 16-4.) The ball

FIGURE 16-5. Lob serves high along side wall

FIGURE 16-8. Putting a "hop" on the ball

should not go more than two and one-half feet high and should be hit so that it drops dead in the back corner or hits the wall and floor just back of the short line.

THE HIGH SIDE WALL LOB SERVE. In this serve the player stands about an arm's length from the side wall and strikes the ball so that it hits high on the front wall and stays close to the side wall on its return. The ball should not be hit hard but should be kept close to the side wall. (See Fig. 16-5.)

THE SHARP ANGLE SERVE. The player stands on one side of the court and hits the ball at an

FIGURES 16-6, 16-7. (*Left*) Sharp angle serve or placement to back corner. (*Right*) Serve to side wall and back corner.

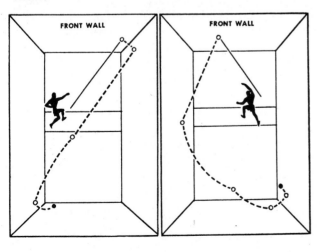

angle so that it strikes the front wall, then the side wall opposite the server, in such a position that it lands back of the short line behind the server. This serve may be started from either side and is quite effective for those who take time to master it. (See Fig. 16-6.)

THE TWO-WALL SERVICE TO BACK CORNER. The server stands close to the right wall and serves to the front wall about five or six feet high and four to six feet from the side wall. The ball, on its return from the front wall, strikes the left side wall just back of the short line, drops to the floor and bounces into the back right corner, hitting the back wall, and then the right side wall. This serve is sometimes called the "run around" and may be started from either side of the court. (See Fig. 16-7.)

Players who become adept at putting "English" or a "hop" on the ball can use this technique quite effectively in the serve. (See Fig. 16-8.)

Arm strokes

There are three basic arm strokes in handball: the underhand, the overarm, and the sidearm.

THE UNDERHAND STROKE. The beginning player should concentrate on the underarm stroke because it is one of the most widely used strokes in the game and is most effective in obtaining "kill" shots in which the ball is driven to the front wall so close to the floor that the opponent is unable to play it before it bounces twice. There are variations of the underarm stroke that include an arm motion similar to that used in throwing a rock so that it skips on a lake, a "wrist snap" much like the motion used in cranking a car, and a motion that simulates the action of a softball pitcher.

THE OVERARM STROKE. This stroke usually involves one of two different motions. In one, the arm is bent like the baseball catcher's throw to second base. The stroke begins with the hand behind the ear and is completed with a cupped hand as the player steps forward. The other overarm stroke involves an extended arm in which the arm is straight and the swing starts farther back than in the bent arm stroke.

THE SIDEARM STROKE. This is used with the feet facing the side wall and the body usually in an erect position. The wrist is kept flexible and the shot is often used to stop balls that would otherwise go for "pass" shots.

Kill shots

These are shots that hit the front wall so close to the floor that they bounce twice before the opponent has an opportunity to play the ball. (See Fig. 16-9.) There are several types of kill shots of which the following are the most common.

REGULAR STRAIGHT KILL. In this shot the ball is driven straight against the front wall close to the floor. The underarm stroke will be found effective for this kill, and if the player can wait until the ball is near the floor before striking it, he will find it easier to drive it on a straight line toward the front wall.

RIGHT OUTSIDE CORNER KILL. In this play the ball strikes the right wall and then the front wall close to the floor.

RIGHT INSIDE CORNER KILL. The ball strikes the front wall first, then the right side wall so close to the floor that the opponent cannot get under the ball. These two kills may also be used on the left side of the court, but the outside corner kill is rather difficult for the right-handed player.

FLY KILL. In this play the ball is hit on the fly as it comes off the front wall with such force that it passes the opponent before he has an opportunity to play the ball.

Variations of these skills may be mastered by the player as he develops skill in directing the ball to areas impossible for his opponent to cover.

PLAYING STRATEGY

Handball is a game in which a premium is placed on analyzing the opponent's strong and weak points. Some players are unable to use their left hands with any great effectiveness. When facing such an opponent, a player should direct a majority of his shots so the opponent is placed at a disadvantage. Players should vary their strategy by employing fast balls alternated with lobs in sufficient frequency to get the opponent off balance. The change of pace is particularly effective on the serve and many good players use it to advantage. In playing doubles, partners should agree on the area each is to cover and assign the areas so each player may take advantage of any particular strong points he may have.

Players should work for a desirable position on the court. It is usually good strategy to maintain a position in the well—near the middle of the court and close enough to enable one to play low balls and corner shots. By skillful placing of shots, a player can keep an opponent in such a position that he will be at a disadvantage in returning cross-court angle shots. Think ahead and make the first play a forerunner to a second or third play that will result in an error by the opponent, or afford the opportunity to place a passing or kill shot. If an opponent persists in playing close to the front wall, he can be driven out of position by high lob shots that go over his head but do not strike the back wall with sufficient force to rebound any distance. In the final analysis, a careful scrutiny of your opponent and his style of play is the first step in planning a campaign that will be most effective. Pick out his weak points and take advantage of them.

FIGURE 16-9. Outside corner kills

FIGURE 16-10.

FIGURE 16-11.

SAFETY

1. Dress properly for the game. Always wear rubber soled shoes to insure firm footing.
2. Do not damage the hands in the beginning before they become toughened sufficiently to withstand the pounding of the ball.
3. Always warm up thoroughly before beginning competition.
4. Do not play a dead ball because your opponent may turn and get struck in the face.
5. Do not deliberately hit an opponent with the ball in the hope that he will call a hinder on the play. You may both get hurt and ill feeling will develop.
6. After you play the ball to the back court, do not watch the ball; you may get hit in the face by a returning ball.

HELPFUL HINTS

1. Practice "kills" alone. Play the ball around an imaginary opponent and work on the various arm strokes.
2. If your hands swell from playing, soak them in hot water before entering the court and swelling will be minimized.
3. Gloves are worn by a majority of handball players. Your enjoyment of the game will be increased if you wear a pair of gloves that fit your hands well. Always hang gloves up to dry after using them.
4. Do not rush the ball. Wait for it and you will not only save energy but play a better game.
5. Control is more desirable than speed.
6. Serve each ball so that it is difficult for the opponent to return it. Try to get several ace serves in each game.
7. A ball hit close to the floor has less bounce and is more difficult to return. The underarm stroke is best for this shot; practice regularly on this play.
8. Watch good players and pattern your play after after those who have mastered the game.

PLAYING COURTESY

The opponent is entitled to a fair and unobstructed opportunity to play the ball.

If there is any doubt about a play, it is advisable to play the point over.

TERMINOLOGY

Ace   A service which completely eludes the receiver.

Ball   Made of black rubber, inflated, about one and seven-eighths inches in diameter, and weighing about two and three-tenths ounces.

Box (service)   Denotes where the server's partner

must stand in doubles when serve is being made. It is an area within the service zone, bounded by the sidewall and a parallel line 18 inches away.

Ceiling crotch shot A shot that hits the ceiling about a foot in front of the front wall.

Crotch The juncture of any two playing surfaces, as between the floor and any wall.

"Cut-throat" A three-man game in which the server plays against the other two players, with each player keeping individual scores. Not played in official competition.

Run-around-shot Ball that strikes one side wall, the rear wall, and other side wall.

Screening Method of blocking an opponent from making a shot. Legal if the screener remains in the position from where he made his shot and does not move into opponent's way.

Server Person, or persons in doubles, in the "hand-in" position and eligible to serve.

Service court The area in which the ball must land when returning from the front wall on the serve.

Service line The line behind which the server must stand when serving the ball.

Service zone Where the server must stand when serving the ball. The area between the service line and the short line, usually five feet wide, and extending across the court.

Sharp angle service Serve delivered underhand from left side of the court, which strikes the front wall close to the floor near right wall, bounds off front wall to right wall and back toward the server.

Short line A line on the floor parallel to front wall and equidistant from front and back wall. Serve must carry over this line on its return from the front wall.

Sidearm A stroke made with sidearm motion. Used to distinguish from usual stroke which is the underhand.

SELECTED REFERENCES

Fait, Hollis, John Shaw, and Katherine Ley, *A Manual of Physical Education Activities* (3rd ed.). Philadelphia: W. B. Saunders Co., 1967.

Kozar, Andrew J., Rodney Grambeau, and Earl Riskey, *Beginning Paddleball*. Belmont, Calif.: Wadsworth Publishing Company, 1967.

O'Connell, C. J., *Handball Illustrated*. New York: The Ronald Press Company, 1964.

Official Handball Rules. New York: The Amateur Athletic Union (current edition).

Robertson, R., and H. Olson, *Beginning Handball*. Belmont, Calif.: Wadsworth Publishing Co., Inc., 1962.

White, Jess R., *Sports Rules Encyclopedia*. Palo Alto, Calif.: National Press, 1961.

Yessis, Michael, *Handball*. Dubuque, Iowa: William C. Brown Company, Publishers, 1966.

Horsemanship

ORIGIN AND DEVELOPMENT

Horseback riding in sport, in battle, and in hunting appears in records from the dawn of history. Horses were raced in Egypt as early as 1500 B.C., and riding races were included in the thirty-third Olympiad in 648 B.C. Early mention of horses ridden in war is found in the Bible in Genesis, Exodus, and Job, and there is recorded on clay tablets an account of Ashurbanipal riding his horse hunting in 667 B.C.

All early riding was done bareback and apparently with some sort of jointed bit in the bridle. The Romans appear to have been the first to use saddles about 400 B.C., although the Syrians had used a blanket on the horse's back about four centuries earlier. Stirrups were not added until a much later date. One of the first accounts of them occurs in the writings of St. Jerome about A.D. 400.

Before 360 B.C., Xenophon wrote the earliest extant treatise on horsemanship, and it is still a sound guide. He may also have been the originator of the curb bit.

The Middle Ages was a time of knights in armor and of great companies of armored horsemen on their lumbering, broad-backed horses clashing in battle.

In England, hunting has been popular for over three centuries. The style was for the rider to sit well back on his trim and agile hunter with his stirrups long and weight thrown back. In great contrast, the style on the continent for most of this period placed emphasis on dressage and extreme collection of the horse. At the beginning of the twentieth century, Federico Caprilli, an Italian, introduced a form radically different from either of the older methods. It stressed greater freedom for the horse than the style on the continent and a much more forward position of the rider than was popular in England. Although there was considerable hesitancy in adopting the new form, cavalries of various nations as well as racing jockeys proved that there was merit in it.

The style of riding in the United States was first patterned very largely after the English style; however, the present trend for hacking, hunting, or racing is definitely toward the forward seat.

Today, interest in riding for recreation is spreading and is a part of the physical education offering in many schools, colleges, and camps. Hacking or hunting are the types of riding for which most students will wish to prepare. Therefore, teaching usually emphasizes the forward seat because, for these types of riding, this is the most satisfactory for the performance of both horse and rider.

THE HORSE

Riding, unlike most other sports, introduces an element entirely separate from the performer. This element, the horse, holds equal importance in the successful mastery and enjoyment of the sport. Both horse and rider must be trained to know and understand each other. Figure 17-1 will give the student the nomenclature for the parts of the horse and a knowledge of his conformation.

Understanding the horse

Before he takes his first lesson, the novice rider will do well to learn something of what to expect from his horse—his instincts, disposition, temperament, training, and so forth.

The horse is timid and easily frightened. A sharp noise, a sudden movement, or an unusual object will make him shy or bolt. The horse is always in fear of being trapped, confined, or restrained, which accounts for his timidity to go certain places or enter a strange building, van, or similar structure. If tied too short, he will jerk back and scare himself, break his halter, and run away. The same thing will occur if the rope is too long, because when he puts his head down he may get his foot over it and the rope will be tight when his head is raised.

The horse is responsive to sympathetic handling. In anticipation of something that may frighten

FIGURE 17-1. Points of the horse

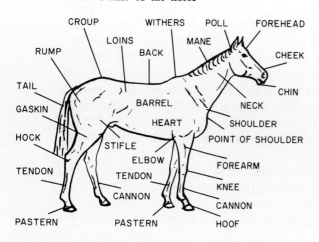

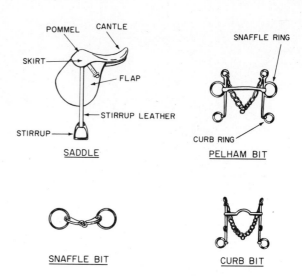

FIGURE 17-2.

him, a pat on the neck and a soft word spoken in a confident tone will reassure him that there is nothing to fear, though his curiosity may cause him to take a good look.

Some of the horse's senses are highly developed. He has acute hearing, and his ears are constantly moving to focus on sounds. His eyes are set so that he can see behind as well as in front. Because his body is sensitive, a light application of the aids is usually sufficient, and strong handling may make him rebellious. He has a good memory and will remember such things as what hurt him, where he was frightened, or what roads lead home.

The training of the horse is the repeated association of the application of the aids and rewards. The *aids* (which sometimes might feel unpleasant for the horse) include the rider's legs, hands, weight, voice, spurs, and whip, which are applied in definite sequences to elicit definite responses. The reward is the stopping of the application. The rider must remember that every experience, every ride has its influence on the memory pattern of the horse. Do not spoil the horse, be firm, do not frighten him, and be sure to give the signals so that he can understand them.

Handling the horse

Horses vary a great deal in regard to such things as training, temperament, abilities, and nervous response. For a beginner, it is well to have an experienced horse that is quiet and has reasonably good habits.

If the rider is not familiar with horses, he should first become acquainted with his mount. Among the first things to learn are:

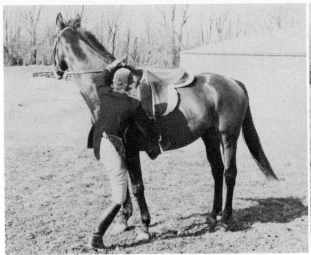

FIGURE 17-3. Mounting. (*Left*) Starting position. (*Right*) Leaving the ground.

1. Approach him on his near (left) side. This is what he will expect because a horse is led, saddled, fed, or mounted from this side.
2. Approach confidently but not suddenly.
3. If approaching from behind, speak to him as you come and put your hand on his rump.
4. Stand close to him, not reaching for him.
5. Lead him around a little to get used to him. Lead him from the near side, holding the rope or reins rather close to his head with the right hand and further down with the left hand. Walk beside him, but do not try to pull him. (Do *not* wind the rope around the hand.)
6. Carry a bit of reward and give it to him when you finish or for a job well done. Horses like carrots and apples, and most of them like sugar lumps. Let him have it on the flat palm of the hand with the fingers together so that he will not accidentally nip them.

TECHNIQUES AND FUNDAMENTALS

Before mounting

Before mounting, the girth should be checked to see that it is properly adjusted. It should be tight enough to hold the saddle firmly in place but not too tight. If the fingers will slip under without forcing, it needs tightening. Many horses will swell up when being saddled, making a final check of the girth necessary. If it should be necessary to tighten the girth while mounted, put the reins in the right hand, move the left leg in front of the saddle and tighten with the left hand.

Mounting

Mounting (see Fig. 17-3) should be one continuous motion done smoothly and without sharp or sudden movements.

1. Approach the horse on the near side and stand close to his shoulder facing the rump.
2. Gather the reins in the left hand just short enough to feel the horse's mouth but not short enough to pull him. With a little experience, the reins will be taken properly in the left hand before mounting.
3. Put the left hand, now holding the reins, just in front of the horse's withers. Grasp his neck or a lock of mane.
4. Take the stirrup in the right hand and put the left foot in so that it comes against the heel of the boot, keeping the toe down as much as possible to prevent the foot from slipping out. Bend the knee so that the weight is directly over the stirrup.
5. Grasp the cantle of the saddle with the right hand. (If the horse is tall and the rider short, he may not be able to reach the cantle and will have to take hold of the flap.)
6. Spring off the right foot and rise into the saddle. As the weight comes on the left foot, release the right hand from the cantle and place it on the pommel. Swing the right leg smoothly over the horse's croup and settle into the saddle easily and quietly.
7. The right foot is placed immediately in the stirrup.
8. Adjust both stirrups under the balls of the feet.
9. Take the reins in the customary manner—usually in two hands.

FIGURE 17-4. Dismounting

To be avoided:

1. Digging the horse in the ribs with the left toe.
2. Dragging on the saddle rather than springing from the ground.
3. Falling heavily on the saddle instead of settling quietly into it.
4. Holding the reins either too loose or too tight, so as not to control the horse properly.

At first, it is well to have someone hold the head of the horse as the rider mounts and dismounts. Later he may do it unaided.

Adjusting stirrup length

The stirrup length is measured by hanging the legs free of the stirrups as the rider sits squarely in the saddle. The bottom of the stirrup should be at the ankle bone for most riding purposes. A longer stirrup may be used for park riding and shorter for jumping. Be sure that both stirrups are the same length.

If the stirrups must be adjusted after mounting, take one foot at a time out of the stirrup and make adjustment with the hand on that side while the reins are held in the opposite hand.

It is well to learn to measure the stirrup length before mounting, as it is much easier to make adjustments from the ground. Hold the stirrup under the armpit and extend the arm up the leather to where the buckle is seated close to the saddle. The fingers should rest on the tongue of the buckle. With a little experience the rider will be able to adjust his stirrups to the proper length before he mounts.

Dismounting

There are several ways of dismounting. Two will be mentioned here. Dismounting, like mounting, should be one continuous, smooth motion. (See Fig. 17-4.)

1. (a) Take the reins in the left hand and place them in front of the horse's withers. Place the right hand on the pommel.
   (b) Take the right foot out of the stirrup.
   (c) Transfer the weight to the left foot, swing the right leg back across the horse's croup and move the right hand back to the cantle.
   (d) Put the weight on both hands and free the left foot from the stirrup.
   (e) Slide gently to the ground.
2. (a) Take the reins in the left hand and place the hand on the horse's withers.
   (b) Put the right hand on the pommel.
   (c) Take both feet out of the stirrups.
   (d) With the weight on the hands, vault quietly and smoothly to the ground.

Things to remember:

1. Be sure that the horse stands still. Have him standing quietly before beginning to dismount.
2. Do not kick the horse as the right leg swings across the croup.
3. Never let go the reins. After the rider is on the ground he may grasp the reins near the bit to hold or lead the horse.

Holding the reins

One method of holding the reins will be described here. Holding the reins in two hands is the manner most usually seen and is considered best for the beginner. There may be times when one hand is used, especially when standing still or when the rider wishes to carry something. It is customary to use the left hand, if using only one, but the right hand must be kept forward so that the shoulders will remain square. Whatever way is used, the following principles are imperative:

1. Reins on both sides must have equal tension. This is to keep the horse straight and going in the desired direction.
2. Snaffle rein should be tighter than the curb. The snaffle is less severe and should be used for guidance.
3. When shortening or lengthening the reins, be sure the above tensions are maintained continuously and at all times. This is particularly important at the faster gaits and in emergency.

Considerable practice is necessary before the handling of the reins becomes natural and instinctive. Practice on a bridle that is on a dummy or on a hook is helpful. This dexterity must become an unconscious, smooth, and intuitive reaction, just as the movement of the foot from accelerator to brake is instinctive when there is reason to slow down an automobile. The mind must be free for other things.

TWO HANDS. The reins on the left side are to be held in the left hand with the snaffle rein on the outside and slightly tighter than the curb. Put the little finger between the two reins from the top, run the bight of the reins between the thumb and first finger, and grasp just firmly enough to keep the reins from slipping. Grasp the reins on the right side in the right hand in a similar manner.

To shorten the reins, relax the fingers of one hand and pull the reins through the fingers by taking hold of the bight with the thumb and forefinger of the opposite hand. Shorten one side at a time, making sure that both sides are kept at even tension at all times.

To lengthen the reins, either allow them to slip through the fingers, or use the opposite hand as in shortening them. Be sure that the proper tension on the snaffle is maintained.

If the bridle has only one pair of reins, they should have the same position in the hands as the snaffle reins when the bridle has both snaffle and curb.

The aids

The *aids* are the means that the rider uses to control and guide his horse. They are the language by which the horse is told what to do and the means by which he is coerced into doing it. There are natural aids (rider's legs, hands, weight, and voice) and artificial aids (such as crop, spurs, and martingale). Only a few of them which need concern the beginner will be discussed here.

LEGS. The legs control the hind quarters of the horse where forward movement is initiated. When the rider wishes to change to a faster gait or go faster in the gait he is in, he applies the leg aids.

The action is to squeeze with the calf of the leg, or tap—usually just behind the girth—with the foot or heel, without unbalancing the rider or getting the leg out of position.

HANDS. The hands control the forequarters of the horse and are used to slow him down, stop him, or make him turn or back.

The action is the application of pressure on the reins evenly with both hands for slowing or stopping, and greater pull on the side of the turn with

corresponding release on the opposite side when a change of direction is desired. The tension should be applied smoothly without jerking the horse's mouth. The pull should *not* be steady and hard but should have a give-and-take quality to keep the horse's mouth sensitive. A steady, hard pull will irritate the horse and make him pull back against the rider.

VOICE. The voice can be used to great advantage. A soft word will do wonders in settling the nerves of a horse that has become excited or fidgety. But he will also respond to a nervous voice or a sharp command. The rider must remember to be quiet around his horse, unless he wants to rouse him.

CROP. The crop or whip is used most often in conjunction with the legs when the horse is slow to respond. The purpose is to startle the horse by the sting and noise it makes, rather than to hurt him. It is only used for punishment under special circumstances such as chronic refusal in jumping. Like other aids, it should be used sharply and precisely, remembering that the timing is most important.

The crop is ordinarily carried in the palm of the right hand, along with the reins, with the handle up and the length paralleling the horse's shoulder.

It may be used by turning the hand so that the crop strikes the horse's shoulder. More often the crop will be used by a quick, sharp stroke on the horse's side behind the saddle. To do this, the reins are put in one hand and the crop used in the free hand.

A type of whip sometimes carried is a feathered bat. It is flexible and covered with braided leather. About two-thirds of the way down it continues with leather fringes. The novice often will carry a plain, straight, flexible whip.

It is very unwise for a beginner to carry a crop. He is sure to use it accidentally when he least wants to, which will cause trouble. However, when he becomes more proficient, he may want to carry one, since a horse often performs better when the rider has a crop.

SPURS. Spurs are not for the novice and will not be discussed here.

Essentials for the proper use of the aids:
1. Apply them clearly and concisely so that the horse may understand what is demanded of him.
2. Stop their application as soon as the horse responds.
3. Control the horse at all times, and do not tolerate disobedience or laziness.

The rider must have quiet, relaxed arms and steady legs. Sudden or constant motion or tension of the limbs excites and confuses a horse. He does not know what the rider wants, he gets jabbed with bit or legs, which makes him nervous, and soon both horse and rider are in trouble.

When a person is beginning his riding experience, he should ride a horse that will respond reasonably well to simple hand and leg aids and will maintain a gait on a loose rein. The rider's chief concentration must be on learning security in the saddle—position and balance. He should ride with the reins loose so as to be sure not to snatch them for balance and thus abuse and confuse his mount. When he has developed a good seat he may go on to the finer points of horsemanship and equitation.

The seat

There are many different styles and schools of riding that have been developed for various purposes, from various theories, and at various times. After learning the fundamentals, the rider may develop a method to suit his needs and desires based on his experience, his horse, and the style of riding that he wishes to pursue.

The instructions which follow will be based on two considerations; namely, security in the saddle and ease of performance of the horse. Security is acquired by practice and experience. It is a matter of balance and equilibrium based on the rider's position and firm contact with the saddle. His center of gravity should be as near as possible to the center of gravity of the horse so as to keep interference with the horse's natural gaits and movements to a minimum.

Standstill

POSITION. (See Fig. 17-5.)

1. *Foot*
   (a) Stirrup on the ball of the foot with the foot to the inner edge of the stirrup.
   (b) Heel down.

FIGURE 17-5. Position at standstill

(c) Weight on inside border of the foot.
(d) Toe turned out slightly—about 15°.

2. *Lower leg*
   (a) Pulled back slightly so that the stirrup leather is perpendicular to the ground. If a plumb line were dropped from the knee, it would also touch the toe.
   (b) Ankle flexible. This acts as a shock absorber and makes it possible for the foot to remain in the stirrup when the horse is in motion. (Do *not* try to grip with the lower part of the calf of the leg. This will throw the whole leg out of position.)

3. *Knee*
   (a) Tucked in against the saddle.
   (b) Joint relaxed. There will be considerable flexion, especially at the trot.

4. *Upper leg*
   (a) Close to the saddle.

5. *Seat*

   Sit down in the saddle so that:
   (a) Crotch is near the pommel.
   (b) Nearly the width of the hand remains between the seat and the cantle of the saddle.

6. *Upper body*
   (a) Body should be erect, but not stiff.
   (b) Shoulders held squarely.
   (c) Back kept straight.

7. *Head*
   (a) Held high.
   (b) Eyes up. Look between the horse's ears.

8. *Arms*
   (a) Upper arms hang naturally from the shoulders and slightly forward, close to the body, neither artificially tucked in nor sticking out.
   (b) Lower arms, hands, and reins should form a straight line from the rider's elbows to the horse's mouth.

9. *Hands*
   (a) Just above the horse's withers.
   (b) Apart—about six to eight inches.
   (c) Turned so that the thumbs are slightly inward and the knuckles at about a 45 degree angle, turned neither upward nor outward.

10. *Grip*
    (a) The upper calf, knee, and lower thigh in

FIGURE 17-6. Be alert when leaving the barn, for horses tend to be more spirited outside.

contact with the saddle give the rider firm balance.

(b) Conscious grip is unnecessary for security and leads to tension rather than the desired relaxation. Muscular tension is increased at increased speeds and when the horse misbehaves.

CONTROL. When standing still, the reins should be without tension, the hands down, and the legs steady. If the horse starts to move about, the hands and legs may be used to steady him, but the reins should be relaxed as soon as he starts to respond. A quiet word and a pat on the shoulder often have a soothing effect on a fretful horse. (See Fig. 17-6.)

The walk

The walk is a four-beat gait, each foot striking the ground separately in an even cadence. (See Fig. 17-7.)

POSITION. The rider's position is essentially the same as at a standstill. In maintaining this position, the:

1. Upper body is slightly forward and the eyes up and looking ahead.

2. Arms are relaxed at the joints so that there is no jerk on the horse's mouth as his head moves forward and back.

3. Waist, hip, and knee joints must be particularly supple to absorb the motion of the horse and allow the rider to remain firmly in the saddle.

FIGURE 17-7. The walk

FIGURE 17-8. The trot

4. Thighs, insides of the knees, and upper calves maintain contact with the saddle for balance.
5. Lower leg from the knee down should remain stationary with the heels down.

CONTROL. To make the horse walk from a standstill, shorten the reins a little if necessary, and apply both legs simultaneously. A squeeze or a light tap should be sufficient. Repeat the signals if he goes too slowly, and pull back with the hands if he starts to break into a trot.

The trot

At the trot (see Fig. 17-8), the horse moves forward with the near fore foot and the off hind foot simultaneously, followed by the off fore foot and the near hind foot. These are termed "diagonals." The horse's back rises with each forward step, and this movement raises the rider in the saddle. The rider will usually post to the trot.

POSTING. The rider rises on one diagonal, lowers himself back into the saddle with next diagonal, and goes up again with the following one. It may be helpful for him to sit to the trot as a preliminary, until he gets the feel of the rhythm. When posting, he should:

1. Lean forward slightly from the hips.
2. Allow the action of the horse's hind quarters to help raise him from the saddle.
3. Only rise out of the saddle as far as necessary for smoothness.
4. Meet the saddle again rhythmically and gently, without a bump.

5. Take the weight in the stirrups, keep the lower legs steady, let the ankles act as shock absorbers. The knee and hip joints must extend and flex freely.
6. Never pull on the reins for balance. This jerks the horse's mouth. When learning, the rider may drop his hands on the horse's withers or take hold of the mane or neck strap for an instant for balance, but he should immediately resume proper position.

CONTROL. To trot, give a tap or kick with both legs and simultaneously lean slightly forward. The reins will need to be shortened a little. It is important that the rider not squeeze with his legs or jerk the reins to keep his balance as that will make the horse break the trotting rhythm.

Like learning to ride a bicycle or to skate, trotting must be practiced until the feel of the motion is obtained. The rider should trot only a short distance at first so as not to lose his balance. He should feel at home in this gait before going on to the canter. He does not want to be unseated by the fast trot, or by the horse breaking from one gait to another.

The canter

The canter (see Fig. 17-9) is a three-beat gait with a sort of rocking horse motion when the horse is going smoothly. The horse's feet strike the ground in the following order: one hind foot, diagonal feet, remaining front foot, and a period of suspension when no feet are touching. The beginner will probably go into the canter from the trot.

POSITION. The rider should:

1. Sit almost as for the walk.
2. Keep the upper part of the body slightly forward and straight.
3. Maintain constant contact with the saddle.
4. Relax, particularly at hip and knee joints.
5. Roll with the motion, with the body breaking at the hips, not at the waist.
6. Be sure the lower legs remain steady, with heels down and ankles flexed and supple.
7. Allow shoulder and elbow joints to move freely and smoothly to absorb the motion of the horse's neck and head withut changing the tension on the reins or jerking them.
8. Maintain balance by proper inclination and flexibility of the body rather than by too strong a grip, which leads to tension.

CONTROL. To make the horse canter, both hand and leg aids should be used. Shorten the reins

FIGURE 17-9. The canter

and, at the same time, lean forward and use both legs. If the rider is in a trot, he should stop posting in preparation for the new gait. Just as the horse is about to canter, the rider may give a light kick with the outside leg (the left leg if circling to the right) and relax the tension on the reins. The use of the hands in conjunction with the legs signifies a change of gait rather than an increase of speed in the same gait.

Practice is necessary to get the feel of the gait. If the joints are rigid or muscles tense, the rider will be thrown out of the saddle by the action of the horse's hind quarters. Never let the balance get behind the motion.

The gallop

The essential elements of riding should have become instinctive reflexes rather than thought-motivated actions before increasing speed to the gallop. This gait will be discussed later, under Coordination of the Aids.

Stopping

To stop the horse from any gait, apply tension on the reins. The weight may be thrown back slightly for greater power when necessary. Use a give-and-take motion and relax the tension completely when the horse has stopped.

Backing

To back up, use the hands and legs to bring the horse to attention. Then apply stronger pressure on the reins, keeping the hands low. When the horse

steps back, relax the pressure, then apply it again for the next step. Only three or four steps should be required at one time. Pressure on the horse's mouth should never be so great that he will open it.

CONTROL

Control is much more than merely changing gaits and speeds. It involves the physical and emotional condition of the horse, his training, and the mechanics of his movements, as well as the rider's kinesthetic ability and his feeling for his horse. Control is to be gained through experience, and is much better practiced in a ring than by going off along a bridle path. Both horse and rider should feel good but relaxed, and the rider must continually out-think and out-guess his horse.

When the rider has become sufficiently secure and balanced in the saddle so that his arms and legs are free to move independently of his body motion and independently of each other, then he is ready for a more complete understanding of the use and application of the aids. Also, he may be privileged to ride horses that are better trained, have more comfortable gaits, are less phlegmatic, and perhaps less patient with the awkwardness of the inexperienced rider. The arms, hands, and legs must be quiet and passive except when applying the aids.

Hands

CONTACT. When there is no longer a likelihood of the rider snatching the reins for balance, he must acquire a closer understanding with his horse through the reins. This is called "feel" or "contact" with the horse's mouth. The reins are shortened so that, with the arms in proper position, a slight but even tension on the reins is maintained without changing the horse's carriage or interfering with his gait. This should *not* be a pull. It is maintained by keeping the horse up on the bit and by using the leg aids rather than pulling back with the hands.

The rider will have discovered that in the walk and canter there is considerable movement of the horse's neck and head. This is necessary, in these gaits, for balance. (At the trot, there is considerably less action of the neck because of the more balanced movement of the legs in diagonal pairs.) Therefore, to maintain an even and constant feel of the horse's mouth, the action of his neck and head must be followed by the rider's arms. The joints must be supple and the arms relaxed so that much of the action may be absorbed by the shoulder and elbow joints.

This feel of the horse is the mark of a fine horseman and essential to a good performance. The horse will move with more energy and spirit, be more agile, and act more alert.

GIVE AND TAKE.   The rider controls the pace by a give-and-take motion with the hands. This is accomplished by alternately strengthening and releasing the pull on the reins. With experience, this can be achieved efficiently and inconspicuously, sometimes by the mere flexion of the fingers, but normally by using the wrists or even the shoulders and back if the horse is heavy on the bit.

Some horses will take a stronger hold of the bit than others. Do not give a steady pull, but control him by a give-and-take motion. Others will tend to unobtrusively increase the pace and should be controlled in the same manner.

This same give and take is used to slow or stop the horse, but of course is applied more strongly than when just steadying the pace. In case of emergency, it may be very strong. But do not make the habit of fast starts and sliding stops. They may look good in the movies, but are very bad riding form.

All hand aids should be applied with the least amount of force that will produce the desired result. Never take a strong hold or pull with the reins. That means "heavy hands" which will make a horse pull or will spoil the mouth of a well-schooled horse. "Bad hands" are to be avoided at all costs. A steady pull on the reins gradually numbs the horse's mouth while producing less and less result.

Legs

As the rider becomes more relaxed and co-ordinated to the rhythm of the various gaits and aware of what movements he may expect from his horse, he must refine his use of the leg aids. A sensitive horse will respond to a squeeze of the lower legs or a light tap just behind the girth. Use both legs simultaneously for increase of forward speed. The use of one leg moves the horse's body to the side as for a turn, or straightens him out when he is crooked or sideways. For a turn to the right, apply pressure with the left leg behind the girth. When the horse is traveling sideways with his hind quarters out to the right, apply pressure with the right leg until he reacts as desired.

COORDINATION OF THE AIDS

So far we have discussed the aids separately. However, in practice, the hands and legs are most often used simultaneously. The coordination of the aids is the essence of good control and a good performance. As the novice gains experience, he must learn to combine the aids smoothly so as to get exactly what he wants from his horse. He must cease to be a passenger and become a rider.

General principles

The following general principles will be helpful:

1. *Contact:* Make sure there is contact before any change of pace or gait.
2. *To turn:* Pull straight back on the reins on the side of the turn. Release a similar amount of tension on the reins on the opposite side and touch the horse's neck with them. Shift the weight in the saddle to the turning side and apply pressure slightly behind the girth with the leg on the side opposite the turn. The horse will be bent around the inside leg at the girth—the sharper the turn, the more he is bent.
3. *To increase speed in the same gait:* Without moving the hands, squeeze or tap with both legs as necessary, except at the walk, when alternate legs are used.
4. *To change to a faster gait:* Establish contact, shortening the reins when necessary; relax the tension; and apply the leg aids while simultaneously moving the weight forward.

Walking

Relax the reins and urge the horse forward with the legs. Establish contact and stop leg action as soon as the desired speed is reached. Use alternate legs to increase the speed of the walk by applying the left leg when the horse's weight is on the near hind leg in anticipation of the movement of the off hind leg and vice versa. A horse usually walks at about four miles an hour.

Trotting

Relax the reins and bring the weight somewhat forward while applying both legs. Start to post and re-establish a feel of the horse's mouth as soon as he starts in the new gait. The hands should remain quiet with no up-and-down or forward-and-backward movement. The arm joints should be limber so the hands may remain quietly and steadily in the same position relative to the horse's withers.

To increase speed, use the legs on the downward beat of the post and keep them steady and relaxed on the upward motion.

After he has become proficient, the rider should learn to change diagonals. This means if he is rising with the near fore foot, he allows himself to bump once and then rises with the off fore foot. This is not difficult, and it will both rest the horse and allow him to travel in a square forward movement.

The usual trotting speed is about nine miles an hour.

Cantering on the proper lead

For a canter while circling to the right, the right foot should lead and vice versa. This avoids stumbling caused by the horse getting his feet crossed, is more comfortable, and makes a smoother performance. To know which lead a horse is on, listen for or watch his front feet. He will carry the lead foot higher and further forward, and it will come down after what seems almost like a half-beat with the other front foot.

The canter is a three-beat gait. On the right lead the sequence will be (1) left hind foot, (2) left fore foot and right hind foot together, and (3) right fore foot (lead foot). Then follows a period of suspension. The usual cantering speed is about twelve miles an hour.

To make the horse canter on the right lead, the rider should:

1. Have the horse well collected before starting the canter, that is, have good contact through the reins, and have the horse alert, with his feet well under him traveling with short steps.
2. As the left fore foot strikes the ground, increase the tension on the right reins so as to pull the horse's head slightly to that side (not enough to

turn). At the same time the left leg squeezes behind the girth and right leg at girth.
3. Bring his weight definitely forward by bending at the hip joint as the left hind foot strikes. (First beat of the canter.) The rider's back should remain straight.
4. As the lead foot (right fore foot in this case) strikes the ground, allow the arms to follow the movements of the horse's head and neck. Even tension is restored on the reins, and the rider's legs return to a normal position.
5. Remain firmly in the saddle, and allow the body to sway with the rhythm of the canter.

For a canter on the left lead, the opposite aids are used.

If the horse does not canter or goes into the wrong lead, come back to the slower gait, take time to get both rider and horse settled and collected, then try again. It is very poor form to race the horse into a canter from a fast trot. Some horses prefer one lead and are difficult to put into the other. The rider should practice first one lead and then the other. He will find it easier to get into the proper lead while circling, and it is recommended that it be practiced in the ring at first.

The gallop

The gallop should not be attempted until the rider is completely at home on his horse, has no fear, and has mastered the other gaits, the handling of the reins, and the use of the aids. As pace increases, everything happens faster, and it is very easy for the horse to become exhilarated and get out of control if the rider is inexperienced.

At the gallop, a four-beat gait, the feet strike the ground separately. For instance, right lead: (1) left hind foot, (2) right hind, (3) left front, and (4) right front. The speed is usually about fifteen miles an hour, but will increase at a fast gallop or run.

POSITION. The rider's position is well forward with his balance over the horse's front legs. The buttocks just clear the saddle and are pushed backward. The head is up so that the rider can look ahead and not down. The hip, knee, and ankle joints should be supple and act like springs to absorb the motion. The lower leg remains in the usual position. The hands should be low along the horse's neck with the line straight from bit to elbow. Because the rider is much further forward, the reins will be shorter than for other gaits. They should be short enough to give the rider good control but not so short as to give the horse the idea of racing.

CONTROL. To increase the speed to the gallop, the rider shortens the reins and brings his weight forward while applying the leg aids. There will probably be more tension on the reins, but there must continue to be a following motion to allow for the movement of the horse's head and neck.

HINTS ON HORSEMANSHIP

Going up and down hill

Ride straight up and straight down steep inclines with rider's weight well forward over the forelegs. Going up a hill, the hind quarters must be free to drive horse and rider up. In going down a steep slope, the forelegs will act as props and the hind legs can merely slide because of their anatomy, so they should not bear the weight of the rider nor be allowed to swing to the side.

Water

A horse may be hesitant about crossing streams, but once in, he usually does not mind. (See Fig. 17-10). If he shows signs of dislike, approach quietly at a walk and let him have a good look. Then turn around and approach again, driving him forward with legs and keeping him straight with the reins. A soothing word may steady him. He may plunge in and out, or he may step gingerly. The rider must be ready. Many horses will roll in water and putting the head down and starting to paw will be the first signs. Pull the head up, kick, and make him continue to move. The horse may be allowed to have a *short* drink if the ride is to be continued immediately. Cold water in large quantities when a horse is hot and not moved briskly may cause serious colic.

Eating

The horse must not be allowed to nibble while he is being ridden. Pull reins and kick when he tries to graze or snatch at the leaves on a tree. This is a bad habit which serves only to pull the rider out of the saddle and to dirty the bridle. It should not be allowed.

Pulling

If the horse is inclined to pull and not respond to the bit, use a give-and-take action to control him. It is well to work such a horse in the ring and not allow him to travel at the faster speeds. However, the rider must be sure that he is not taking too tight

FIGURE 17-10. When crossing swift water, ride upstream at a 45-degree angle.

a hold, perhaps in fear of being run away with, and thus making the horse pull more.

Running away

When a horse gets out of control, the principal thing is for the rider to keep from getting excited or tense so that he can no longer sit his horse. Use a strong give-and-take pull, using the back. If that does not work, pull back hard on the reins, set one hand against the horse's neck just in front of the withers, and then pull on the other side with the reins across the horse's neck so as to make him actually pull against himself. This is a severe pull and must be relaxed as soon as the horse submits. The rider may also seesaw the reins by alternately pulling harder on one side than the other.

If there is plenty of space, such as in a field, make the horse travel in a smaller and smaller circle until he is brought under control. If there are no dangerous obstacles or hard roads to worry about, the rider can bring the horse under control when he begins to tire.

Stumbling

Most stumbling will be avoided if the rider is alert and the horse collected. The rider should not allow his weight to fall forward if the horse does stumble. He should permit the horse freedom to recover and thereafter keep the horse alert.

Shying

It is the unusual or unexpected, such as a dog or a strange noise, that makes a horse shy. If you have a nervous horse, try to anticipate such situations. Introduce him to the strange object, and do not allow the unexpected to startle him. Stop and let him have a good look, pat him and get his confidence, then take him past. When he does shy, quick reflexes and balance will help the rider to stay in good position.

Kicking

If your horse is inclined to kick, keep him out of the middle of a crowd and tie a red ribbon on his tail to warn other riders. Give the reins a pull and move him away if he seems to be getting ready to kick. If this is impossible, quickly turn his head toward the horse or object he is laying for.

Avoid being kicked by keeping at least a length behind other horses, and never ride up on another horse's tail. Most horses will not kick unless surprised or jostled.

Bucking

On a crisp or windy day when a horse feels good, he may try to buck a little. Remember, he has to get his head down to buck. Keep his head up, or get it up even if a sharp jerk of the reins is necessary, make him move forward, and the effort will be short-lived. Balance and a firm seat will keep the rider on.

Rearing

Few horses rear. If the horse does rear, the rider must throw his weight well forward and drive the horse forward with the legs or crop. He will then come down. Do *not* pull on the reins because, if he goes high, this is liable to pull him over and the rider will be on the bottom.

What to wear

Riding clothes should be worn not only because they look better and are correct, but because they are designed for ease and comfort. The costume should include:

1. Breeches that fit tightly below the knee and button on the inside of the knee. They should be tan or another conservative color, not gaudy shades such as red or green.
2. Boots that fit snugly in the legs and come up high.
3. Shirt and tie, or sport shirt.
4. Riding coat and hat or cap are optional.
5. Gloves will save the hands.

Jodhpurs with a snug leg fit and that reach the ankles when sitting, and Jodhpur boots or shoes, may be subsituted for breeches and boots.

Do not wear blue jeans or slacks. They are not proper. Also, they will chafe the knees and legs, because they wrinkle and have rough seams.

Be sure to dress warmly in cool weather. Hands and feet can get achingly cold.

Manners

1. If another rider has dismounted, wait until he has remounted before moving away.
2. Pass other riders slowly with your horse under control.
3. Do not cluck to your horse to make him go when riding in company.
4. Warn the riders behind you of tree branches, wire, holes, and so forth.
5. Do not gallop past or away from other riders.
6. Have the owner's permission before riding over private property.
7. Do not let the horse eat along the way.
8. Bring your horse in cool.

SAFETY HINTS

1. Ride a horse you can manage.
2. Check the tack before starting, particularly the girth.
3. Walk the first ten minutes and the last ten minutes of a ride.
4. Be alert and anticipate situations so as to be ready to meet them.
5. Always have the horse under control.
6. Walk along the side of hard-top roads. When crossing, go at right angles to the crown to prevent the horse from slipping.

7. Walk over wooden bridges, and watch for bad boards.
8. Stay a length away from other horses, and stay out of a crowd if your horse kicks.
9. Walk down steep inclines or over rocks.
10. Frozen ground is treacherous.
11. If your horse loses a shoe, do not continue the ride. Walk him home over soft ground.
12. If you fall off, let go of the reins and try to roll free of the horse.
13. Do not chase a runaway horse. It will frighten him and make him run more.
14. Do not water a horse when he is hot. It may give him spastic colic, or founder.

OBJECTIVES

Seat

1. Rider positioned at all gaits so that his center of gravity is adjusted to approximate that of the horse.
2. Firm and erect seat in the middle of the saddle with the inside of thighs, knees, and upper calves against the saddle.
3. Lower legs always steady, heels down.
4. Hands quiet, arms close to the body with elbows slightly forward.
5. Position maintained by coordination and equilibrium, not excessive or periodic gripping.
6. Post to the trot smoothly and with a minimum of motion.
7. Canter rhythmically while staying firmly in the saddle.

Control

1. Ability to make the horse walk, trot, and canter by correct application and coordination of the aids.
2. Ability to make changes of gait, both faster and slower, at a given time or spot.
3. Ability to keep the horse at a steady, even pace in any gait, with his body straight.
4. Make turns at a walk, trot, and canter.
5. Slow or stop the horse at will with smooth give-and-take movements.

Performance

1. Make transitions from one gait to another quietly and without having the horse fuss.

2. Put the horse in the proper lead at the canter.
3. Properly follow with the hands, the horse's head and neck movements.
4. Keep the body supple and resilient so that horse and rider move together as a well-coordinated unit.
5. Avoid stiffness, tension, and fear which will produce awkwardness and poor balance.
6. Interfere as little as possible with the horse's natural movements.
7. Always be in control. If discipline is necessary, the horse should not remain upset but return to quiet, smooth performance.
8. Be able to ride different horses.
9. Have good manners in the ring or on the road or bridle path that will not interfere with another rider's performance or pleasure.

TERMINOLOGY

Aids   The means used to guide and control the horse. They include hands, legs, weight, and so forth.

Bight   The loop of the reins behind the rider's hands —runs between the thumb and first finger and falls along the horse's shoulder.

Bit   The metal part of the bridle that goes in the horse's mouth and to which the reins are attached.

Bridle   Horse's headgear, used when riding.

Canter   A three-beat gait to which the rider usually sits. (For sequence, see text.) Usual speed is about 12 miles an hour.

Cantle   Rear of the saddle.

Collected   A horse is said to be collected when he is alert, with stride shortened, feet under him, and the reins taut.

Contact   The rider is said to establish contact when the reins are not slack, yet exert no real pull.

Crop   A riding or hunting whip.

Croup   The part of the horse's back behind the saddle.

Curb   A type of bit, more severe than a snaffle; the rein attached to the lower ring on the shank of a bit.

Diagonal   Term used to describe one step of the trot.

Double bridle   One having both curb and snaffle bits.

Feel   Light contact with the horse's mouth through taut reins. Same as "contact."

Gallop   A horse's fastest gait—usually about 15 miles an hour, but may be much faster. Term not to be used interchangeably with "canter."

Girth   Wide band of leather or webbing used to hold the saddle in place. It passes under the horse's belly and is buckled to the saddle at both ends.

Good hands   Ability of the rider to control his horse with ease through light feel and use of the reins.

Hack   To ride for pleasure. A horse used for pleasure riding.

Halter   Headgear on the horse, used when he is being led or tied.

Heavy hands   A rider is said to have heavy or bad hands when he pulls a horse hard and rides him roughly, giving him a hard (insensitive) mouth.

Lead   The forward foot of a canter. When the right foot is forward, the horse is said to be on the right lead.

Martingale   Harness used to prevent or discourage the horse from carrying his head too high. There are two kinds: (1) *Standing martingale*—one end of the strap is attached to the girth, the other to the nose band; (2) *Running martingale*—same as standing martingale except that it divides at the chest and terminates in two rings through which the reins pass.

Near side   Left side of a horse, from which he is fed, led, saddled, mounted, and so forth.

Off side   Right side of a horse.

Pelham   A type of bit with snaffle and curb reins.

Pommel   Front of a saddle.

Post   Action of the rider at the trot when he rises from and returns to the saddle.

Reins   Leather straps from the bit which the rider uses to guide and control the horse.

Rump   Hind end of a horse.

School   To teach a horse something; to practice such a lesson.

Seat   The position of the rider in the saddle; a type or method of riding.

Shying   When a horse jumps sideways as when frightened.

Snaffle   A type of bit which is jointed in the center and has large rings for the reins; the rein from such a bit or from the center ring of a bar-type bit. Less severe than a curb bit.

Stirrup   Part of the saddle which supports the rider's foot.

Tack   General term for equipment used on the horse in riding.

Trot   A two-beat gait in which the horse's feet move in diagonal pairs. Usual speed is about nine miles an hour.

Walk   A four-beat gait in which each foot strikes the ground separately in even cadence. Speed is about four miles an hour.

Withers   The highest point on the horse's back, where the neck meets the shoulder blade. This is the point from which a horse is measured.

SELECTED REFERENCES

American Horse Shows Association Rule Book. New York: The Association (40 East 54th Street), published annually.

British Horse Society and Riding Club, *Manual of Horsemanship* (5th ed.). London: British Horse Society, 1961.

Churchill, Peter, *Progressive Steps in Riding*. New York: Arco Publishing Co., Inc., 1965.

Division of Girls' and Women's Sports, *Riding Guide*. Washington, D.C.: American Association for Health, Physical Education and Recreation (current edition).

————, *Technique Charts*. Washington, D.C.: American Association for Health, Physical Education and Recreation, 1960.

Froissard, Jean, *Equitation: Learning and Teaching*. New York: A. S. Barnes & Co., Inc., 1967.

Griffen, Jeff, *Book of Horses and Horsemanship*. Englewood Cliffs, N.J.: Prentice-Hall, Inc., 1963.

Kearley, B. L., *You and Your Horse*. New York: A. S. Barnes & Co., Inc., 1965.

Kirschner, Michael, *Forward Freely*. New York: A. S. Barnes & Co., Inc., 1967.

Lewis, Benjamin, *Riding*. New York: Grosset & Dunlap, Inc., 1958.

Licart, Jean C., *Start Riding Right*. Princeton, N.J.: D. Van Nostrand Co., Inc., 1966.

Littauer, Vladimir S., *Common Sense Horsemanship* (2nd ed.). Princeton, N.J.: D. Van Nostrand Co., Inc., 1963.

Romaszkan, Gregor de, *Fundamentals of Riding*. Translated by M. A. Stoneridge. Garden City, N.Y.: Doubleday & Company, Inc., 1964.

Self, Margaret Cabell, *Horseback Riding Simplified* (2nd ed.). New York: The Ronald Press Company, 1963.

Seunig, Waldemar, *Horsemanship.* Translated by Leonard Wins. Garden City, N.Y.: Doubleday & Company, Inc., 1960.

Sports Illustrated, *Sports Illustrated Book of Horseback Riding.* Philadelphia: J. B. Lippincott Co., 1960.

Steinkraus, William, *Riding and Jumping.* Garden City, N.Y.: Doubleday & Company, Inc., 1968.

Summerhays, R. S., *Elements of Riding.* Brattleboro, Vt.: The Stephen Greene Press, 1963.

Wright, Gordon, *Learning to Ride, Hunt, and Show* (new and revised edition). Garden City, N.Y.: Doubleday & Company, Inc., 1966.

Judo

ORIGIN AND DEVELOPMENT

Early development in Japan

Judo, one of the fastest growing sports in the world today, is an ethical refinement of jujitsu—an Oriental martial art that began to take a systematized form in Japan during the latter half of the sixteenth century.

Following the establishment of the first jujitsu school in 1532, hundreds of other schools were soon organized and jujitsu flourished under Japanese feudalism for the next three centuries. However, because of its abuse by those skilled in its violent and dangerous techniques, jujitsu began to diminish in popularity as knowledge of this art became more widespread among the common people. This disesteem, along with the abolition of feudalism, left jujitsu a dying art in the latter half of the eighteenth century.

It was under these social conditions that a new sport called "judo" was born—a sport that included inculcation of certain basic philosophic principles as a part of its training. The change from jujitsu to judo was, in fact, the elevation of the sport's purpose from mere fighting to physical, mental, and ethical training.

In 1878, Jigore Kano, a frail student at Tokyo Imperial University, took up the art of jujitsu in order to overcome the bullying of his larger companions. Although this enthusiastic student soon recognized jujitsu's potential for developing both the mind and body, he realized that its dangerous and crude techniques were not suitable for physical education. Selecting the good points from the various training schools of the period, Kano founded the Kodokan School of Judo in 1882 in Tokyo. This "mother school" of modern judo was based not only on physical culture, but on moral and intellectual training as well.

From its humble beginning—nine registered students practicing on 12 mats in the hall of a tiny Buddist temple—the Kodokan has developed into the largest and best known judo school in the world. Today, with its complex of dormitories, training rooms, and offices, the Kodokan is generally accepted throughout the world as the foremost authority on all techniques and rules.

Professor Kano, a recognized educator by the

time he established the Kodokan, made many notable contributions to athletics and education during the ensuing years; e.g., he was the founder and first president of the Japan Athletic Association, the first Oriental to be honored as a member of the International Olympic Committee, and holder of many governmental posts and principalships in the field of education. Dr. Jigoro Kano—educator, fighter, philosopher, gentleman, and "father" of modern judo—was an active participant in judo until his death in 1938 at the age of 78.

Judo development in the United States

Judo was formally introduced in the United States in 1902 when Dr. Kano, recognizing the great judo potential of this country, sent his ablest associate, Professor Yoshiaki Yamashita, to promote the sport on the east coast. Yamashita's most famous student was President Theodore Roosevelt, an avid judo enthusiast who practiced three times a week over a three-year period in a specially converted judo training area of the White House.

Despite the early efforts of Professor Yamashita and other visiting Japanese masters to advance the cause of judo throughout the United States, it was on the west coast that judo gained its real foothold. Following the establishment of the first American judo club in Seattle in 1903, the sport began to grow and flourish as clubs sprang up in those west coast communities populated by the increasing flow of Japanese immigrants. Although most of its participants were nisei (second-generation Americans of Japanese descent), American judo continued to grow and develop at a slow but steady rate—a pattern that was abruptly altered on December 7, 1941.

Although World War II and its attendant "anti-anything Japanese" feeling dropped American judo to the nadir of its popularity, three significant postwar developments paved the way for the future widespread growth of judo throughout the United States.

The first of these developments was the release and return of Japanese Americans from relocation camps at home and military service with the United States Army in Europe. Many of these returnees migrated to large urban areas throughout the Midwest and East Coast and became instrumental in developing high-quality judo clubs in these areas. Unfortunately, however, membership in these clubs was still largely confined to Americans of Japanese descent. Judo, in the minds of most Americans, remained synonymous with the brutal unarmed-combat techniques used on the battlefields by the Japanese army.

A second key postwar development, the military occupation of Japan, played a far more significant role in helping to shatter this "Causasian barrier" by providing thousands of American servicemen with the opportunity to observe and study judo in the land of its birth. Many G.I.s rose to the occasion and studied under some of the greatest judo teachers in the world. On their return to the United States, these men started clubs of their own or otherwise promoted the sport in "home towns" all over the country.

The third significant milestone in the postwar development of judo was the establishment, in 1950, of an official combat aircrew training program in judo within the Strategic Air Command (SAC) of the United States Air Force. By sending a yearly class of up to 50 judo instructor trainees to the Kodokan in Tokyo, the Air Force manned "Combative Measures" (judo) teaching positions at its bases throughout the country. These qualified physical conditioning and judo specialists, not content at confining their teaching to SAC's combat crews, were extremely active in promoting judo during their off-duty hours. Consequently, evening judo classes for both military and civilian personnel sprang up on military bases and in YMCA's and colleges throughout surrounding communities. Yearly refresher clinics that were held in the United States for these instructors and official Air Force support of a competitive judo recreation program further insured the continuous and rapid growth of these newly organized programs. Within ten years (1961) the Air Force Judo Team was able to win the National AAU overall team championship.

The ultimate impact of these three developments can best be demonstrated by listing a few of the more recent milestones that serve to indicate the establishment of judo as an amateur sport in the United States and throughout the world.

1952 The Amateur Athletic Union (AAU) appointed Henry A. Stone to head a subcommittee on judo; the United States Amateur Judo Association was organized; and the International Judo Federation (IJF) was formed. The AAU was recognized as the governing body for United States judo and the official United States member of the IJF.

1953 San Jose State College hosted the First National AAU Judo Championships.

1955 The SAC Judo Society was formed; the Amateur Judo Association changed its name to the Judo Black Belt Federation (JBBF).

1956   The United States Judo Team participated in the First World Judo Championships (held in Tokyo, Japan).

1958   An American Judo Team participated in both the Pan American Judo Championships and in the Second World Judo Championships (held in Tokyo).

1961   Dutch champion, Anton Geesink, defeated all opponents to become the first non-Japanese World Champion of Judo (at world championships in Paris); the United States Armed Forces Judo Association (AFJA) was formed from the old SAC Judo Society. This 10,000-member organization today plays an important leadership role in the United States Judo Program.

1962   The newly formed National Collegiate Judo Association (NCJA) sponsored the first Annual National Collegiate Judo Championships, which were hosted by the United States Air Force Academy. The first step in the development of an organized judo program for women was also taken during this year with the formation of a JBBF-AAU Women's Committee and the inclusion of rules for women in the *Official AAU Judo Handbook*.

1963   Two youth judo programs were created by the National AAU Judo Committee, i.e., the AAU Age-Group Judo System and the AAU Junior Olympic Judo Program.

1964   The JBBF inaugurated an AAU-sanctioned National Junior Judo Tournament; the newly formed JBBF High School Judo Committee sponsored their first Annual National High School Judo Tournament; and judo made its debut in the eighteenth Olympic Games at Tokyo, Japan.

1965   The United States Olympic Team enhanced its international prestige by finishing 4th, in terms of total wins and losses, in a field of 27 countries. The United States medalist, James Bregman, won a third-place bronze medal.

1965   A United States team competed in the Fourth World Judo Championships and James Bregman earned a third-place finish in the middleweight category of this event.

1967   The United States hosted the Fifth World Judo Championships in Salt Lake City, Utah.

Judo in the United States today, therefore, consists of a wide variety of programs in existence at local, regional, and national levels to serve American judo enthusiasts of all ages and both sexes throughout the fifty states. The failure of many American judo instructors to register either their clubs or their students with the AAU precludes the compilation of accurate descriptive figures pertaining to these programs, but reliable surveys indicate that approximately 250,000 judo students are currently practicing in 1500 clubs—800 of which are local YMCA and independent AAU clubs, 200 are college clubs, and 500 are Armed Forces judo clubs.

NATURE AND BASIC RULES OF JUDO CONTESTS [1]

Although judo or the "gentle way" (*ju* means "gentle" and *do* means "way" or "principle") comprises many of the dynamic and effective throwing, strangling, and joint locking techniques of jujitsu, the development of guiding principles and strict rules that regulate the use of these techniques distinguishes judo the sport from jujitsu the art. It is this emphasis on the "manner" or "way" that techniques are applied that makes judo both popular and safe as a physical education activity and international sport.

The two principles upon which Dr. Kano based the whole fabric of this art and science are:

1. *Seiryoku zenyo* or "maximum efficiency with minimum effort."

2. *Juta Kyoei* or "mutual welfare and benefit."

The principle of "maximum efficiency" is followed when one skillfully defeats a stronger opponent by yielding to his attack while maintaining his own balance, thus throwing him off balance to a point where he is weaker and vulnerable to one's counterattack. In his second principle, Dr. Kano advocated the maximum-efficient use of one's mental and physical energy for the mutual benefit and welfare of all mankind.

Description of the judo contest

The best way to acquaint the reader with this personal contact sport is to provide a brief description of a judo contest, which in AAU sanctioned matches is conducted in the following weight divisions: lightweight (139 lbs. or under); light middleweight (154 lbs. or under); middleweight (176 lbs. or under); light heavyweight (205 lbs. or under); heavyweight (over 205 lbs.); and open (any weight).

[1] "Contest Rules of the Judo Black Belt Federation of the United States," *Official AAU Judo Handbook* (New York: Amateur Athletic Union of United States, 1964), pp. 21–52; *International Judo Federation Rules*, published by the Armed Forces Judo Association, Barksdale AFB, La., 1967.

The two contestants come onto the mat and stand facing each other at a distance of about 12 feet. Each wears a judogi, the special three-piece soft cotton judo uniform that is designed for the participant's comfort and safety. The loose jacket, worn over buttonless and pocketless lightweight pants, is held in place by a colored belt (refer to discussion of judo ranking system) looped twice around the body and tied in front with a square knot.

At the referee's signal, the contestants bow to each other (a traditional judo custom analogous to the handshake used in boxing and wrestling or the salute in fencing), grasp each other's jackets, and begin the match. Each tries to defeat the other by (1) scoring one full point or two one-half point scores, which immediately terminates the match, or (2) displaying superior skill resulting in an official's decision at the termination of the regulation match period, which varies in length from three minutes for young beginners to 15 minutes in world championship matches.

One full point may be earned by:

1. Throwing an opponent with good form so that he strikes the mat on his back with appreciable force.
2. Holding (not pinning) an opponent under full control on the mat for 30 consecutive seconds. Many collegiate wrestling techniques are variations of judo "holds."
3. Applying a reverse lock to the elbow or a choke against the windpipe or against the carotid arteries on either side of the neck that (a) forces a participant to signal his surrender by tapping his opponent or the mat, or (b) causes the referee to stop the match to prevent injury to a stubborn competitor who refuses to submit to a well-applied technique. Contest rules, however, generally prohibit the use of reverse elbow locks against other than advanced contestants (black belt ranks).

One-half point (almost a full point) is awarded if:

1. One contestant throws his opponent with skill and in good form which does not merit a full point but which does deserve major credit. It is said that an "almost" ippon (point) is 90 to 95 per cent of a full point.
2. One contestant, who has already received a one-half point for a previous technique, holds his opponent under control for 25 seconds.
3. A contestant is given a second warning for a rules violation.

The complex and exciting nature of this sport is indicated by the fact that a highly skilled judo student may have as many as 200 different techniques in his judo repertoire—each capable of producing a match-terminating score in a split second.

During the course of this action, competitors are prohibited from performing such acts as:

1. Applying a leg scissors to the opponent's trunk, neck, or head.
2. Applying joint locks to other than the elbow joint.
3. Applying any technique which might injure the neck or spinal vertebrae of the opponent.
4. Intentionally falling backwards on an opponent who is holding him from the rear.
5. Forcing the release of his opponent's hand or hands from his costume by striking, kicking, or wrenching with his knee, foot, hands, forearm, or any other part of the leg or arm.
6. Intentionally preventing action by avoiding contact or holds with his opponent.
7. Leaving the contest area for any reason, except as a result of a technique or action of the opponent.
8. Adopting an excessively defensive posture in order to stall or avoid defeat.
9. Gripping the ends of the opponent's sleeves or bottom of his trousers by inserting his finger or fingers into them.
10. Intentionally disarranging judo costumes or untieing and retieing the belt without the referee's permission.
11. Pulling an opponent down to the mat in order to start groundwork.
12. Holding the opponent's jacket or costume in or against his (the opponent's) mouth or any part of the face, or putting his foot, hand, or forearm directly on any part of the opponent's face.
13. Winding the end of the belt or jacket around any part of the opponent's body.
14. Attempting any technique outside the contest area (a recommended mat area of 30 feet × 30 feet).
15. Making unnecessary calls, remarks, or gestures derogatory to the opponent.
16. Disregarding the referee's instructions.
17. Taking any other action which may injure or endanger the opponent or otherwise violate the spirit of judo.

Any contestant failing to abide by these and other contest rules of the International Judo Feder-

BELT COLOR SYSTEM

RANK	UNITED STATES	EUROPEAN	STUDY TIME
Rokkyu (6 kyu)	White	White	1st day
Gokyu (5 kyu)	White	Yellow	4–8 mo.
Yonkyu (4 kyu)	White	Orange	8–12 mo.
Sankyu (3 kyu)	Brown	Green	1–1½ yrs.
Nikyu (2 kyu)	Brown	Blue	1½–2½ yrs.
Ikkyu (1 kyu)	Brown	Brown	2–4 yrs.
Shodan (1 dan)	Black	Black	3–5 yrs.
Nidan (2 dan)	Black	(U.S. and Euro-	4–8 yrs.
Sandan (3 dan)	Black	pean systems are	6–11 yrs.
Yodan (4 dan)	Black	alike for Ikkyu	Over 9 yrs.
Godan (5 dan)	Black	and higher)	Over 11 yrs.
Rokudan (6 dan) *	Black or Red and White sections		
Shichidan (7 dan)	Black or Red and White sections		
Hachidan (8 dan)	Black or Red and White sections		
Kudan (9 dan)	Black or Red (about 25 awarded)		
Judan (10 dan)	Black or Red (only six have been awarded— recipients now deceased)		
Juichidan (11 dan)	Black or Red (none awarded to date)		
Junidan (12 dan)	Black or Wide White (none awarded)		
Shihan (Doctor)	Black or Wide White (awarded only to Dr. Kano)		

* Promotions to Rokudan and higher are based largely upon teaching ability, research, and other contributions to judo. Consequently, it is difficult to estimate the study time required to attain these ranks.

ation is liable for disqualification or other disciplinary action by the officials in accordance with the rules.

JUDO RANKING SYSTEM

A unique feature of judo is its system of ranks (identified by the colored belts) which are awarded by instructors through an examination based upon promotion standards that are suggested by the JBBF and adopted and approved by the AAU. Included in these rank requirements are a general knowledge of judo, possession of sound moral character, the ability to demonstrate various techniques (throwing, grappling, choking, armlocks, countertechniques, escapes, and combination techniques), and contest proficiency as measured by wins in promotional or other certified contests.

These ranks constitute a valuable incentive system and are listed above in ascending order along with appropriate belt colors and approximate training time required to attain them (based on at least three practice sessions per week).

TECHNIQUES AND FUNDAMENTALS

Judo, because of its free and flexible nature, is probably one of the most enjoyable and unrestricting sports among the personal contact activi-

ties. The beginning judo student, however, will be amply rewarded by accelerated progress if he thinks through the ideas presented in the next few sections and concentrates on putting them into practice on the mat.

Posture

Good players, as can be noted in the photographs that follow, adopt a stance somewhat like that of a tennis player getting ready to receive a fast service; i.e., the body is quite erect, but not stiff, and the knees are slightly bent. From this posture, both attack and defense maneuvers are easier to execute.

Your greatest obstacles to maintaining this good judo posture will probably be your fear of falling and your overdefensiveness—both of which can be gradually overcome by (a) learning to fall correctly under the guidance of your instructor, and (b) practicing many drills with your partner throwing you without any resistance on your part. Removal of these obstacles will enable you to develop a fast-moving and highly effective attacking style.

Gripping

The manner in which you hold or grip your opponent is almost the unknown science of judo. Even though it is given little treatment in textbooks on the sport, the art of gripping is one of the most important aspects of judo technique. In fact, grips

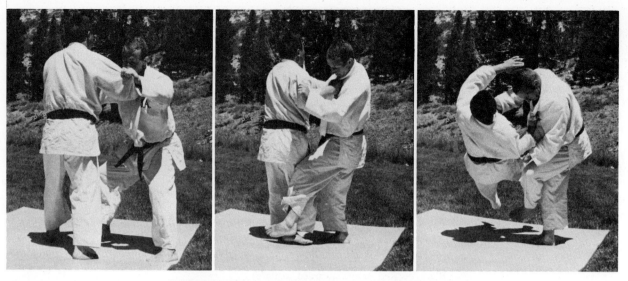

FIGURES 18-1 through 18-3. Minor outside reaping (*kosotogari*) is executed here by United States champions Bill Paul (the thrower) and Leroy Abe. Left photo shows the important pulling action of the thrower to get his opponent stepping forward with the left foot. He then quickly pulls down and back with his left hand while simultaneously sweeping his opponent's legs away to complete the throw. (Photographs in this chapter courtesy of the Armed Forces Judo Association.)

FIGURES 18-4 through 18-6. Foot Stop (*Sasae-tsuri-komiashi*), an important "break-up" throw, can be used with a major outside reaping on the other side if it fails. Left photo shows the thrower snapping his opponent forward and blocking his foot to turn him over. Thrower maintains his balance throughout by twisting his body.

and grip breaking is considered by the National Coaching Staff of the Armed Forces Judo Association as one of the "Eight Elements of Judo Contesting."

The traditional grip in judo is to take the sleeve of your opponent in one hand and the lapel in the other. That is, you grip your opponent's right sleeve with your left hand and his left lapel with your right hand if you intend to throw him to his right side. This traditional grip would, of course, be reversed for a throw to the left side.

In actual practice, however, top-caliber judo players hold any way they want to. For example, you can see Zeelenberg throwing left with a right grip (Figs. 18-4 through 18-6), and Carter throwing to the left with a left hand grip deep behind

FIGURES 18-7 through 18-9. Inner thigh throw (*uchimata*) is demonstrated here with a high collar grip with the left hand. This is the most common contest throw of judo and is a favorite of many players. It can be used in combination with both inside reaping throws to the rear. Photos show clearly the three parts of a judo throw: off-balance, entry, and execution.

his opponent's neck (Figs. 18-7 through 18-9). These and other top competitors have successfully integrated such varied grips into their fighting or matching style.

In general, in order to throw you, your opponent must get a firm grip on your judo jacket with his lifting hand. He must, therefore, keep his wrist straight and his elbow under his hand in order to generate greater lifting power. You, on the other hand, should try to take any grip which prevents your opponent from getting this efficient hold and which enables you to apply these "laws of leverage" in your own grip. Any such grip is satisfactory— whether it involves holding both lapels, both sleeves, or a lapel and a sleeve. In other words, you should take hold of your opponent in a manner that enables you to throw him, but that prohibits him from throwing you—which is really what the game of judo is all about.

Movement

In standing judo, the most important element to learn—even more important than grips and grip breaking—is how to move. During practice your opponent will always be trying to break your balance so that he can throw you. You, of course, will be trying to do the same to him. Essentially, breaking balance consists of getting the top part of the opponent's body moving faster than his feet—thus tipping him over. Before he can regain his balance, you try to place your body under or against his, depending upon the throw involved, so that he can-

not regain his balance. You then turn him over so that he lands flat on his back.

Therefore, the secret is, obviously, to move your feet with smooth short steps so that you can not have your balance broken. Although this is more difficult than it sounds, you can start trying to perfect this skill on the first day you start judo. This method of sliding the feet over the mat, with one following the other, is called "tsugi ashi" in judo language—literally, "following foot."

In your practice drills always try to move smoothly—in the suggested manner—so your balance is never broken. You will thus maintain the correct judo posture as you move around. However, any method of moving which permits you to keep your balance and break your opponent's is good.

Methods of falling

In judo the art of falling without injury has been developed to a science. If you have seen judo demonstrated, you may have gotten the impression that the person being thrown was in great danger of being injured. This is not true, however, since the judo student receives extensive instruction in falling when he begins his judo training. Recent scientific studies indicate that judo is as safe as any other generally accepted body contact activity.

The three parts of a judo throw

As you know from reading the preceding sections on how a judo contest is conducted, you can

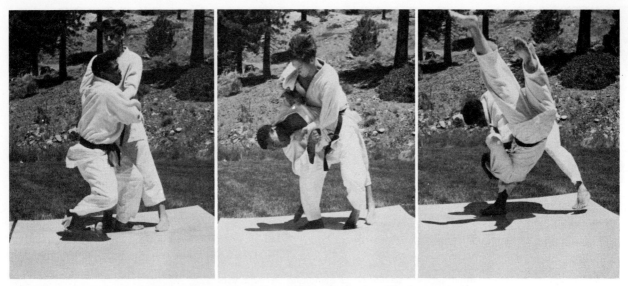

FIGURES 18-10 through 18-12. Lifting hip throw (*tsuri-komi-goshi*) by United States Interservice Champion Robey Reed shows the off-balance (*left*), entry (*center*), and execution (*right*) of this very powerful hip technique. Figures 18-1 through 18-9 demonstrate foot techniques. This page shows throws that are called waist or hip techniques because the hip is the primary agent in executing them.

FIGURES 18-13 through 18-15. Sweeping loin throw (*Harai-goshi*), executed as in a contest with a spinning entry. This type of dynamic action is characteristic of judo and takes many hours of practice to develop. The left and center photos demonstrate superior gripping and a strong upward pull that keeps the opponent's balance broken during the entire spinning entry.

beat your opponent in four different ways (or combinations thereof); i.e., throwing, holding, choking, and arm locking. Since throwing is considered to be the most complex of these "methods of winning," a great deal of research has gone into devising the best methods of executing judo throws.

The general theory of judo throwing divides the actual throw into three parts: (1) off-balancing your opponent; (2) the entry or placing of your body into a position that both prevents your opponent from regaining his balance and enables you to throw him on his back; and (3) the actual execution of the throw by twisting your body around and down in order to deliver your opponent to the mat. The exact manner in which the last phase (the body twist and turn) of the throw is executed depends,

FIGURES 18-16 through 18-18. Body drop (*tai-otoshi*), a hand technique, as demonstrated by United States and Pan American Gold Medalist Allan Coage. Very difficult to stop or counter, this throw is the favorite of many experts. In the center photo, notice the upward driving action of the thrower's left hand that breaks the grip and resistance of his opponent and turns him over in the execution.

FIGURES 18-19 through 18-21. Spinning left shoulder throw (*seoi-nage*) as executed by three-time National Junior and Senior High School Champion Tony Gonzales. This movement can be executed when the opponent is moving to either side, forward, or backward. Like the inner thigh throw, it can be integrated with both inner reaping rear throws if the opponent resists to the rear.

of course, upon the particular throw in use. These three steps are illustrated and commented upon in the sequence of photos in this chapter.

The eight elements of judo contesting

After years of study, in both this country and Japan, the National Coaching Staff of the Armed Forces Judo Association has systematized judo training so that it will develop in the student the eight factors of technique that produce an effective contest style. These eight elements of judo are given below, not necessarily in order of importance.

1. *Your favorite throwing technique.* This should be a major forward throwing technique; i.e., one

FIGURES 18-22 through 18-24. This valley drop counter (*tani-otoshi*) for a forward throw shows the counter man catching the attacker in the middle of the throw and driving him over backward toward his weak point to score a full "ippon" or point. Sequence demonstrates that the defense shown in the left photo leads naturally to the countering action illustrated in the remainder of the sequence.

FIGURES 18-25 through 18-27. Minor outside dash of the second leg (*nidan-kosoto-gari*) is a counter for the most common rear throw, major outside reap (*osoto-gari*). Left photo shows the attacker (on right) entering attempting to sweep both of his opponent's legs out from under him. The opponent drives up with his right arm to stop the attack and reaps both of the attacker's legs instead.

of the wrist or hand techniques illustrated in this chapter. It is the center of your technique, and all other elements are integrated around it.

2. *Opposite side throw.* When your favorite technique becomes really sharp, your opponents will take special defensive grips and body positions to prevent your using it. If your favorite is to the right, you must develop an efficient method

of throwing to the opposite side to overcome these strong defensive measures. Obviously, if your favorite throw is to the left side, the opposite side throw will be to the right, and vice versa.

3. *The rear throws.* As you develop the ability to throw your opponents toward the front and on both sides, they will begin to dig in and lean back

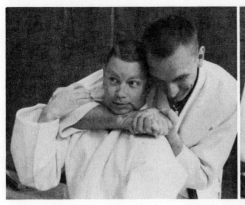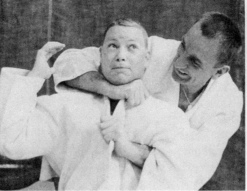

FIGURES 18-28 through 18-30. Two judo chokes are shown in the left (*hadaka-jime*) and center (*okuri-eri-jime*) photos, while the scarf hold (*kesa-gatame*) is illustrated in the right photo. The attacker in the left is using his wrist and forearm to force his opponent to submit to the "naked strangle"; the center photo illustrates the use of the sliding lapel choke.

to stop you. You must, therefore, have the ability to throw to the rear. The four most effective rear throws are the inner and outer major and minor reaping actions. The minor outside reaping throw, "kosoto-gari" (Figs. 18-1 through 18-3), is the first throw illustrated in this chapter. All competent judo players can execute these four rear throws well, though they may specialize in only one or two of them.

4. *Grips and grip breaking.* This element is very important in both offensive and defensive judo techniques and was discussed in the section on fundamentals.

5. *Defenses and counters.* Defenses to the throws and mat holds of judo follow along as an extension of learning to grip properly for defense. In addition to resisting with the hands and arms, you must learn to move and twist the body so that your opponent cannot break your balance. Counters are a further natural extension of defenses. Usually, if you stop your opponent's at-

tack, you will have broken his balance and be in a position to apply a counter throw before he can recover. Two counter throws (Figs. 18-22 through 18-24; Figs. 18-25 through 18-27) are illustrated in this chapter.

6. *Combinations.* Combinations or fakes are specialized methods of getting your opponent to make a sudden defensive move against your pretended attack—and then to throw him the other way by taking advantage of his defensive move. For example, you might repeatedly pull him forward and then throw him to the rear as he leans back to resist your forward pull.

7. *Break-up throws.* We use this term to characterize the minor foot techniques (i.e., Figs. 18-1 through 18-3) which you can use to break up the opponent's balanced defensive posture. Because a skillful player's balance is very difficult to upset, you cannot sufficiently prepare him for a throw by just moving and pulling him about. Thus, you must either fake him with a combi-

FIGURES 18-31, 18-32. Two judo holds, the smothering hold (*kuzure-kami-shiho-gatame*) on the left and the side hold (*joko-shiho-gatame*) on the right, are illustrated below. The side hold is very similar to the half nelson and crotch hold of wrestling and is extremely effective.

nation or attack him with a technique which, though it may fail, will break his defense enough for you to try another, more effective attack.

8. *Take-downs and mat work.* Several throwing techniques are especially suited to taking your opponent to the mat for grappling, should you fail to score a full point on the throw. Other methods that form an important phase of judo training can also be used to take an opponent to the mat; i.e., arm locks and counters. On the mat itself, both chokes and arm locks are included in the general category of mat work. There are nine major mat holds, each of which has many variations, that can be used to hold the opponent under control (not pinned) for 30 consecutive seconds and thus win a full point. As previously mentioned, any opponent who can no longer resist either a choke or arm lock signifies his defeat by tapping his opponent (or himself or the mat) two or more times in rapid succession.

Integration of technique

Although there are many separate techniques in each of the eight elements of judo contesting listed above, the skillful player, although he can execute most throws, does not specialize in them all. He does, however, try to perfect one or two techniques in each of the eight categories. The secret is that these techniques must fit together into a unified whole. For example, an expert in the right shoulder throw might also develop the right minor

inside reaping throw as a rear throw, and the right inside reaping with a winding action to the mat as a take-down technique. If your opposite-side throwing technique is easy to apply when you miss your favorite throw, then the two throws fit together or are integrated. It takes a lot of practice to develop a mature style in judo, but the end result is a player who (1) has an answer for everything, (2) can stop any attack, and (3) can crack any defense. This degree of perfection can only be achieved by integrating the elements of one's own technique—with a special emphasis given to becoming proficient in all of the "Eight Elements of Judo Contesting."

HYGIENE AND SAFETY

Since cleanliness and personal hygiene are important in judo, each student should (1) assist in keeping the mat clean by wearing clogs or thongs to and from the mat area, (2) keep toe- and fingernails trimmed short to prevent their being torn or cutting the judo partner, and (3) keep his judo uniform clean—it is white to show dirt and encourage frequent washing.

The primary cause of judo injuries is a lack of alertness. Think always of the safety of your opponent and of preventing injuries to yourself. After you become really interested in judo you will find that an injury which keeps you off the mat is very discouraging. Therefore, the best way to prevent the loss of practice enjoyment is to be constantly alert for those situations conducive to injury.

FIGURES 18-33 through 18-35. The standing arm or "armpit" lock (*wake gatame*) is generally considered to be part of the "grips and grip breaking" element of judo contesting. This technique is particularly effective against the stiff-armed opponent who is very difficult to attack because his arms hold the attacker away from his (opponent's) body.

FIGURES 18-36 through 18-38. The cross-arm lock (*juji gatame*) is the most common reverse elbow lock used in the grappling phase of judo. There are many variations of arm locks which can be used in virtually every situation where an opponent permits one of his arms to straighten out and leave his body. The lock shown below can often be used when a throw is only partially successful.

Horseplay with judo techniques off the mat is strictly forbidden. In fact, most instructors will dismiss from their classes those students who abuse this privilege. Talk about judo off the mat—but practice it only on the mat under supervision.

JUDO TERMINOLOGY [2]

Because Japanese is the international language of judo, the student must have some understanding of the basic terminology used in judo training sessions and contests. Since command of the vocabulary list constitutes a minimum requirement, the more advanced student is referred to the cited reference for a complete glossary of important Japanese terms.

Ashi waza   Foot techniques.
Awase waza   Victory by adding two waza ari.
Dan   Degree or step in judo. There are 13 grades of dan.
Dojo   Judo exercise or training hall.
Hajime   "Begin!" This command is given by referee.
Hantei   Call for a decision by judges.
Hiki wake   Indicates a "draw" decision by match officials.
Ippon   One or "full" point when given by referee.
Jikan   Time out.
Jime   (also *shime*) choke.
Judoka   Judo practitioner.

Kata   Form, shoulder form practice, or one of the nine prearranged form routines used in the Kodokan.
Kiai   A yell used to summon supreme energy.
Kime   Decision.
Koshi waza   Hip techniques.
Kuzushi   Off-balance.
Kyu   Ungraded judo student below a judansha grade yet holding a class grade in judo.
Maitte   "I surrender."
Matte   "Stop!" Given by referee.
Nage waza   Throwing techniques.
Ne waza   Grappling techniques in general; i.e., holds, chokes, and joint locks.
Osae komi   "Hold down!" Given by referee.
Osaekomi toketa   "Hold down broken!" Given by referee.
Osae komi waza   Holding techniques.
Randori   Free practice.
Rei   Bow or salutation.
Shiai   Contest.
Sono mama   "Don't move!" Given by referee.
Tori   Throwing partner in the performance of techniques.
Tsukuri   Preparation for a throw by moving into position.
Uchikomi   Repetitive practice attacks without throwing.
Uke   Receiver of throws in performing techniques.
Ukemi   The art of falling.
Waza   Technique.
Waza ari   One-half point (said to be 95 per cent of a full point).
Waza ari awasete ippon   Full point by addition of two waza ari or one-half point techniques.
Yoshi   "Go" or "all right!" Given by referee.

[2] "Glossary of Japanese Terms," *Official AAU Judo Handbook* (New York: Amateur Athletic Union of United States, 1963), pp. 230–36.

SELECTED REFERENCES

Many publications on the art of judo have appeared during the past few years, but unfortunately most of them are of little value to the serious student of judo. The following books and periodicals are recommended for their technical content and clarity.[3]

American Judoman. A monthly publication of the Armed Forces Judo Association, Drawer D, Barksdale AFB, La. 71110.

Illustrated Kodokan Judo. Prepared by the Kodokan. Tokyo: Kodansha, 1955.

Kobayashi, Kiyoshi, and Harold E. Sharp, *The Sport of Judo.* Rutland, Vt.: Charles E. Tuttle Company, 1956.

Kudo, Kazuzo, *Dynamic Judo.* 2 vol. Translated by Richard L. Gage. New York: Japan Publications Trading Company, 1967.

Matsushita, Saburo, and Warwick Stepto, *Contest Judo.* London: W. Foulsham and Company, Ltd., 1961.

Mifune, Kyuzu, *Canon of Judo.* Translated by K. Sugai. Tokyo: Seibundo-Shinkosha Publishing Company, 1956.

Official AAU-JBBF Judo Handbook. New York: Amateur Athletic Union of United States, 1963 and 1964 editions.

Otaki, Tadao, and Donn F. Draeger, *Judo for Young Men.* Tokyo: Kodansha International, Ltd., 1965.

Smith, Robert W., ed., *A Complete Guide to Judo.* Rutland, Vt.: Charles E. Tuttle Co., 1964.

Takagaki, Shinzo, and Harold E. Sharp, *The Techniques of Judo.* Rutland, Vt.: Charles E. Tuttle Co., 1956.

[3] A complete and detailed book list on judo may be obtained free of charge from the AFJA, Drawer D, Barksdale AFB, La. 71110.

Shuffleboard

ORIGIN AND DEVELOPMENT

The exact founding date of the game of shuffleboard is not known, but it has been established that a similar game was played in England during the fifteenth century under the reign of King Henry IV. The game has been played under several names, including "shove groat," "slide groat," "shovelboard," and "shovel-penny," with "shovelboard" being the most common prior to adoption of the present name. The English brought the game on shipboard where it proved to be a very popular activity. Targets were painted on the deck floors and cues were used somewhat in the same manner that the present game of shuffleboard is played in the United States.

It is thought that the game was introduced into the United States around the middle of the nineteenth century. Some reports state the game was banned in the New England area during this period because of its connection with gamblers. The game was resumed in the late 1890's, but the participants consisted mainly of children. The game was introduced to Daytona, Florida, in 1913 and met with immediate approval. Many courts were installed,

but because of an absence of standardized rules, courts were of varying lengths and widths, causing considerable difficulty when players moved from one location to another. In order to effect certain standards in courts and playing rules, the Florida State Shuffleboard Association was formed in 1928. In 1931 the National Shuffleboard Association was formed and began immediately to hold national tournaments, a winter event being conducted at St. Petersburg, Florida, and a summer meet at Traverse, Michigan.

It is estimated that there are over 3,500 shuffleboard courts in the United States at the present time, with more than three million participants using these courts. The sport is now a well-established recreational activity in our culture and will probably continue to grow as new facilities become available and additional persons are introduced to the game.

NATURE OF THE GAME

The game of shuffleboard may be played by two people (called "singles") or by four (called "doubles"). The game is played by propelling round,

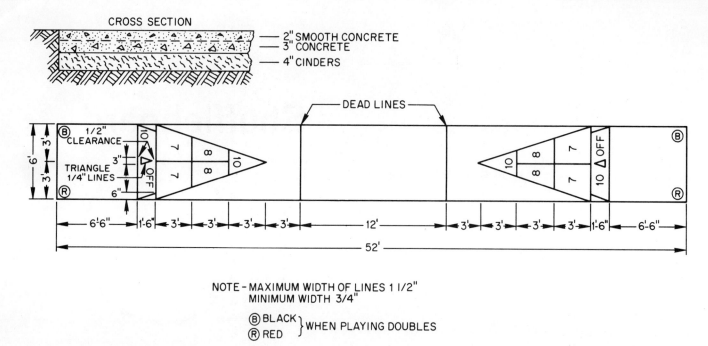

CROSS SECTION
— 2" SMOOTH CONCRETE
— 3" CONCRETE
— 4" CINDERS

NOTE-MAXIMUM WIDTH OF LINES 1 1/2"
MINIMUM WIDTH 3/4"

ⒷBLACK }
ⓇRED } WHEN PLAYING DOUBLES

FIGURE 19-1. Shuffleboard court

wood discs by a cue over a hard, smooth surface on which the outlines of a court have been drawn. The court is 52 feet long and six feet wide, and is equipped with a target and scoring diagram at each end. (See Fig. 19-1.) One end of the court shall be designated as the Head of Court and one as the Foot of Court. The wood discs shall be six inches in diameter, weigh not less than 11½ ounces nor more than 15 ounces, with thickness ranging from three-quarters of an inch to one inch. The cue shall not be longer than six feet three inches, and shall have no metal parts touching the playing surface.

Equipment shall consist of one cue for each player and two sets of discs, one set painted red and one black. Choice of discs is made by playing one disc to the farthest deadline, with player of the disc closest to it receiving his choice of colors. In starting a game, the owner of red disc shoots first, followed by black, then by red, alternating thus until all discs are shot. In singles play, after all discs are shot from Head of Court, the players walk to Foot of Court and, after tallying the score, continue play toward Head of Court with owner of black discs shooting first.

In doubles, with two players at each end of the court, a game is started with the owners of red discs shooting all discs first from the Head of Court, followed by owners of black discs. Owners of red discs again shoot first from the Foot of Court, followed by black. On the second round, owners of black discs shoot first at each end of the court, followed by owners of red discs. Playing of all discs

from one end of the court and back constitutes a round, so in doubles play the lead in starting to shoot changes after each round, while in singles play the lead changes after each half round.

Shuffleboard requires a minimum expenditure of energy and has become a popular activity for people of all age levels. While the rules of the game are easy to learn and the game can be played with a minimum of practice, considerable skill is required to propel the discs so as to clear the deck of opponent's discs and leave his own in scoring territory.

TECHNIQUES AND FUNDAMENTALS

Skills involved in playing shuffleboard are few, hence a reasonable degree of proficiency can be attained with a minimum of practice. To compete against topflight players, one must master the minimum fundamentals required to direct the disc to the right spot with the right amount of speed.

In making a shot, the player should place his cue against the disc before starting the forward thrust and maintain contact with the cue through the forward stroke. The cue should not be jabbed at the disc, but placed in contact before starting the stroke. (See Figs. 19-2 through 19-4.)

Since the surfaces of different courts often vary, it is advisable to play some practice shots before engaging in competition on a strange court.

FIGURES 19-2 through 19-4. (*Left*) Cue against disc, ready to push. (*Center*) Forward movement underway. (*Right*) Forward thrust completed, disc on its way.

BASIC RULES [1]

SCORING. The scoring area contains one 10-point area, two 8-point areas, two 7-point areas, and one 10-off area. To count, a disc must lie entirely within one of the scoring areas with no part of the disc touching any side line, except that the separation line in the 10-off area is not considered. A game may end at 50, 75, or 100 points. Play continues until all discs have been shot, even if game point has been reached during the early part of a half round. In doubles, if a tie score results at game point or over, two additional rounds shall be played. If the score is still tied, play continues as outlined. In singles, one additional round shall be played to determine the winner in a tie game.

PENALTIES. From five to ten points shall be deducted from the score of players for certain infractions of playing rules. Five points shall be deducted for the following infractions:

1. All discs not in respective half of 10-off area when ready to shoot.
2. Discs not played from respective half of 10-off area (red played from right side, black from left).
3. Players stepping on or over baseline in making their shot.
4. Players not remaining seated when play is toward their end of the court.
5. Interfering in any way with opponent while he is making a play.

[1] *Official N.S.G.W.S. Recreational Games and Volleyball Guide.* Washington, D.C.: The American Association for Health, Physical Education and Recreation, latest edition.

6. Players touching live discs at any time.

Ten points shall be deducted for the following infractions:

1. Player making hesitation or hook shot.
2. Player making remarks to disconcert opponent.
3. Making any remarks which may be construed as coaching a partner while making a play.
4. Player shooting before opponent's disc has come to rest.

PLAYING RULES. A disc returning or remaining on the court after having struck any object other than a live disc, shall be called a *dead disc* and shall be removed from the court before play is resumed. If a dead disc strikes a live disc, that half round shall be replayed. A disc that stops in the area between farthest deadline and starting point shall be considered dead and removed from the court. Any disc that stops just beyond the farthest baseline shall be moved a distance at least eight inches from baseline. Any disc stopping more than halfway over sidelines, or which rests or leans on the edge, shall be removed from the court.

PLAYING STRATEGY

Shuffleboard is an individual sport and involves little or nothing in the way of team strategy found in many other sports. The player must concentrate on developing skill in propelling the discs in such a manner as to knock opponent's discs off the scoring area and leave his own discs in a scoring position. Players must learn to gauge the ricochet angle of discs when hit by another moving disc, and the importance of blocking areas when attempting to protect a disc that has stopped in a favorable area.

SAFETY

Shuffleboard constitutes one of the safest games in our present list of recreational activities. Since no bodily contact is involved, or equipment used which in any way endangers partners or opponents, the game can be played with the assurance that accidents will be a rarity. Occasionally, playing surfaces may be slippery, but if proper precautions are taken in the selection of footwear and in drying any moist playing area, this danger can be eliminated.

HELPFUL HINTS

1. When playing on strange courts, take time to become acquainted with the surface of the playing court. Not all courts have the same type of playing surface.
2. Be sure that discs are perfectly round and equipped with a smooth surface.
3. Spend considerable time in practicing difficult shots, e.g., stopping the disc in the 10-point area, or dislodging opponent's disc while leaving your own in scoring territory.

PLAYING COURTESIES

1. Do not heckle or in any way try to disconcert opponents during play.
2. Encourage partner, but make no remarks that might be construed as coaching while he is making a play.
3. Commend both partner and opponents after making a good play.
4. Give opponent choice of cues if cues are in such a condition that a choice would be desirable.

TERMINOLOGY

Court Area 52 feet in length and six feet in width, with playing surface of terrazzo or concrete, preferably concrete.

Cue A stick, not longer than six feet three inches, used to propel discs toward the target.

Dead disc One that returns to or remains on the court after having struck an object other than another live disc. Disc is also dead that stops between farthest deadline and starting line. If a dead disc moves or displaces a live disc, that half round shall be played over.

Discs Round wooden discs, six inches in diameter and from three-quarters of an inch to one inch in thickness. Four are colored red and four black.

Foot of Court That end of the court opposite the head.

Game A game is based on 50, 75, or 100 points and match play shall be on the basis of the best two out of three games.

Head of Court That end of the court from which play starts to begin a match.

Hesitation shot This is illegal—forward motion of the disc must be continuous.

Round The playing of all discs from one end of court and back constitutes a round.

Scoring One 10-point area, two 8-point areas, two 7-point areas, and one 10-off area.

SELECTED REFERENCES

Fait, Hollis, John Shaw, and Katherine Ley, *A Manual of Physical Education Activities* (3rd ed.). Philadelphia: W. B. Saunders Co., 1967.

Haslam, Charles S., *How-to Book of Shuffleboard*. St. Petersburg, Fla.: Great Outdoors Association, 1955.

Official N.S.G.W.S. Recreational Games and Volleyball Guide. Washington, D.C.: The American Association for Health, Physical Education and Recreation (current edition).

Official Rules, National Shuffleboard Association. Kissimee, Fla.: National Shuffleboard Association, Inc., 1965.

White, Jess R., *Sports Rules Encyclopedia*. Palo Alto, Calif.: National Press, 1961.

Skiing

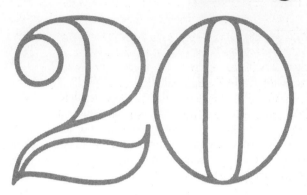

ORIGIN AND DEVELOPMENT

There is considerable doubt and speculation about the origin of skiing. Since it is a form of locomotion as well as recreation, its beginning probably came early in the development of life in the northland. The earliest example of prehistoric skis is the Swedish Hoting ski, discovered in a peat bog, that dates back to at least 2000 B.C.

Other early skis have been discovered in the northern countries and most of them have been curved, made of pine, ash, or birch, and covered with leather. Often one ski, shorter than the other, was worn on the left foot as a guide.

The early explorers from the Scandinavian peninsula probably brought skis to America. The early settlers used them for transportation and mail carrying.

With the advent of the telemark-turn in about 1880, skiing began as a sport. Some highlights in the evolution of the sport of skiing include: development of the snowplow and the stem turn by Zdarsky, the father of the Alpine technique, in 1896. The National Ski Association of America was formed

(1904) by Carl Tellefson and competitive skiing was officially recognized. Hannes Schneider developed the stem christiania (1909). Hoschek and Wolfgang introduced the stem swing which emphasized rotation, up-weighting and uphill swing (1935). After stunning the world with wins in the F.I.S. downhill and slalom races, the Allais parallel technique was adopted (1937). The National Ski Patrol was formed in 1938. Kruckenhauser and the Austrian system of employing counterrotation, comma position, and wedeln, caused a flurry in the ski world (1950–55). The Professional Ski Instructors of America was formed (1961) and *The Official American Ski Technique* was first published in 1964.

In the spring of 1968 the Eighth Interski, International Congress for Ski Instruction, met in Aspen, Colorado. Interski, which is international in the broadest sense of the word, has become so important that every national ski school presented something special or something new in skiing. Because of the dynamic nature of this sport, one can expect that ski technique and ski instruction will constantly undergo change, revision, and development.

There are many approaches to teaching ski technique. There are the American, Austrian, Canadian, French, Italian, Swiss, Natur-Teknik, GLM (Graduated Length Method), etc. No one system is best, but from the standpoint of the students learning to ski in this country, it would be wise to pursue a program that is widely accepted throughout this country and that provides consistency in approach. The Official American Ski Technique best fills the bill at this time.

THE NATURE OF SKIING

Skiing is a sport of propelling oneself over snow upon two skis, each about two feet to eight feet long and approximately three inches wide. It is a sport for all ages and social classes, and for both sexes. It gives one a feeling of being one's own master, yet at the same time there exists a wealth of camaraderie. Skiing is an exhilarating and vigorous fun sport.

There are many types of skiing: downhill, slalom, cross-country, jumping, touring, specialty, and trick. Downhill is the most popular and the only form of skiing treated in this limited text.

EQUIPMENT

Unless a person has a lot of time to spend in researching how and what to buy in the line of ski equipment, he should shop at a store specializing in ski equipment in order to obtain equipment that will meet his individualized needs. Price is usually a good barometer in determining quality of equipment.

Skis

There are special skis for each of the types of skiing mentioned above, but the beginner will be concerned only with the selection of downhill skis. To learn about skis, you may seek advice of other skiers, read each company's sales brochure, read the back issues and current issues of periodicals containing articles about skis, and try as many different skis as possible. Learn all you can about what the skis are designed to do.

Today's skier is vitally concerned about whether the skis are made of wood, fiberglass, epoxy, or metal. Each type has certain advantages as well as disadvantages. It is very difficult to say which material is the best with complete objectivity. Wood skis are cheaper but less durable. The fiberglass and epoxy skis perform extremely well but there is some question as to their durability, repair-

ability, and camber retention. Metal skis are very durable and ski excellently; they are easily repaired, thus providing years of service.

The purchase of skis can be an exciting event and can be quite an investment. Therefore it is important that you get the ski best suited for you. Generally, to determine the proper ski length for yourself you must answer these questions. How well do you ski? What is your physical condition? How old are you? How much can you spend? If you are an expert, young, and in good physical condition, a ski 12 to 15 inches over your head is correct. As these attributes decrease so should the length decrease to about your height.

After you have determined the length and make or model ski you want, there are other common features that you should check. Check the flex pattern, camber, cut, torque, groove, bottom or surface uniformity, and that the skis are matched in every way. Remember, a competent dealer or instructor can aid you by checking your selection.

Bindings, boots, and poles

There is no question that release bindings are a must for skiing. There is a great variety to choose from, with a substantial range in price. They are generally easier to get into and, if adjusted properly, offer the skier a safer experience. A word of caution: it is better to buy toe and heel releases of the same make than to mix models.

Boots are perhaps the most important item of a skier's equipment. All of the force applied to controlling the skiis passes through the boots. They must provide the skier with adequate support and comfort. Be sure to try on boots while wearing your normal ski socks (two pairs) and ski pants. Walk around the shop in them for a few minutes and check them for comfort. Be sure they are neither too long nor too short, wide nor narrow, and that the heel stays snug in the heel pocket when you flex forward. Today the skier has a choice of single and double laced or buckle boots, as well as leather and plastic boots. The life expectancy depends upon the quality of the boot purchased and on the power, speed, and frequency with which one skis.

Ski poles should be light, durable, and well balanced, with a comfortable hand grip. (See Fig. 20-1.) With the tip on the floor, arm at the side, the handle should pass comfortably under the armpit.

Accessories

Some accessories are necessities and others are frills, but they all make your skiing more enjoyable. Here is a short list that may prove helpful: ski wax for different conditions, file or edge sharpener, repair kits for filling in gouges, boot press, tool to adjust bindings, retention straps, goggles, sunglasses, lip balm for protection against sun, cold, and wind, and clothes that are specifically designed to provide protection and to be functional.

Care of equipment

Wooden skis without plastic bottoms should be sandpapered and treated with a liquid base lacquer. Those skis with plastic bottoms including wood, epoxy, and metal can be repaired with special kits which are available at most ski shops. All skis, including metal skis, should be waxed. The first wax job should be done with hot wax which fills the pores of the base and offers much greater protection to the running surface. As a rule of thumb, the drier the snow the harder the wax, the wetter the snow the softer the wax applied to the ski. Never wax the groove of the ski. Check edges for nicks and burrs and file them off, always leaving the edges sharp. Before putting away your skis for the year, be sure to oil the edges to protect them from rusting.

Ski boots are expensive and worthy of the best of care. Leather boots should be polished with a wax base once or twice a week. Be sure to keep them in a boot tree whenever they are not on your feet. Remember to take good care of your equipment and it will serve you well.

TECHNIQUES AND FUNDAMENTALS

It is extremely important to learn skiing under proper tutelage because it can be a hazardous sport

FIGURE 20-1. How to grasp the ski pole

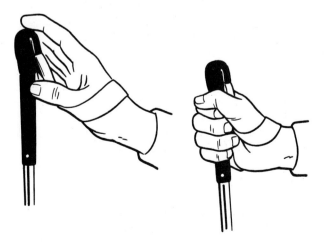

when not properly learned. The recommended order of progression is to learn: (1) to put skis and poles on and to take them off, (2) to ski on the level, (3) the correct running positions, and (4) the fundamentals of changing direction and how and when to employ the various turns and positions.

The skis are put on by simply stepping into them and fastening the straps. The buckles and binding clamps are always on the outside. If it is necessary to put them on while on a slope, put the lower ski on first. The poles are properly gripped by inserting the hand into the strap from below and grasping the pole over the top. (See Fig. 20-1.)

Walking

In walking, the skis are kept parallel and close together and the legs are moved as in normal walking, except that the feet must glide forward. The poles are used alternately—the right going forward with the left leg and the left with the right leg. The elbows should be kept in and the pole not planted beyond the foot.

The easiest way to turn around on skis is to lift the tip of the right ski and move it to the right, leaving the tail in place. Then lift the tip of the left ski to the right, bringing it parallel to the right ski. Continue this process until the desired direction is reached. This turn may be accomplished in either direction. Also, you can try it by moving the tails rather than the tips. Be sure to take small steps. You may use your poles for support and balance.

Skating is another useful form of forward motion that is faster than walking. This is accomplished by pushing off with one leg with the ski turned out slightly, while gliding on the other ski. Then lift the back ski up sufficiently to clear the surface, place it in the gliding position, and push off again with the other leg. The weight should be carried well forward with the weight-bearing knee bent and the heel flat on the ski.

The kick turn

After locomotion and balance have been learned, the kick turn should be attempted. This turn is used to face about. In turning to the right, place the left pole close to the tip of the left ski and the right pole back of the left ski, then lift the right ski clear and swing it completely around parallel to the left ski, but pointed in the opposite direction. Then, after transferring the weight to the right ski and balancing on the right pole, swing the left ski and left pole around until it points in the same direction as the right ski.

Uphill climbing

Hill climbing is the drudgery of skiing that can be lightened by mastering the proper techniques. There are three different methods of climbing: the sidestep, the diagonal sidestep and the herringbone. They should be practiced on level terrain before trying even a gentle slope.

The diagonal sidestep is used on gentle slopes. It is merely walking with short strides uphill at an angle. Each ski is carried to the side and slightly uphill as each forward step is taken.

The sidestep is used on steep slopes and is the same as the diagonal sidestep, except that no forward motion is made. The weight is always carried upon the lower ski while the upper is being lifted to the new position. The steps should be firmly taken.

The herringbone is used for short, straight ascents and is accomplished by turning the tips out and lifting the tail of each ski over the top of the tail of the other. The poles are held behind each ski and the skis are edged slightly on the inner side. The weight is carried on the back ends of the skis.

Falling down and getting up

When a fall seems inevitable, the skier should assume a low crouch, controlling his fall to the uphill side by sitting to the side of his skis. To rise, the skis should be moved downhill to the body, parallel to each other and horizontal to the slope. Both ski poles are placed together. Then with the skis tucked under the body and one hand on the top and one hand on the bottom of the poles, push to stand.

Downhill

Downhill skiing is the goal of most skiers. As with any sport there are some fundamental principles. Probably the most important principle of proper downhill position is balance. To maintain a natural balance position a skier must ski with total motion, that is, a unity of action by the entire body. This action implies that the joints are flexible and that a properly controlled and relaxed skier is able to absorb blows. Balance is essentially maintained with the ankles, knees, and torso slightly bent and with the body perpendicular to the skis; the weight is evenly distributed on the balls of the feet. Since balance is a dynamic rather than a static position, it follows that when actions such as counterrotation take place, compensating body action occurs. Other principles involve unweighting by either an upmo-

tion or a downmotion, turning of body by rotation or counterrotation, weight transfer, and angulation or comma. Counterrotation and upmotion for unweighting are the methods used by the American Ski Technique.

Straight run

Straight run is first practiced on a gentle slope with an adequate runoff. The skis are flat, slightly apart and parallel to each other. There is no lead with either ski; the tips are always aligned. The ankles, knees, and torso are slightly flexed, with the body at right angles to the skis at all times.

FIGURE 20-2. Straight running (Figures 20-2 through 20-7 adapted from *The Official American Ski Technique*, by permission of The Professional Ski Instructors of America, Inc. © 1966 Professional Ski Instructors of America, Inc.)

Ski poles are pointed down and back. They are held with elbows flexed near the body, hands hip-high, forward and slightly off the body. Always look ahead. Practice various body positions and movement of the skis. (See Fig. 20-2.)

Traverse

The traverse position is used when crossing a slope. The skis are together with the uphill ski, leg, hip, and shoulder advanced. The uphill leg is bent more than the downhill leg, thus allowing the downhill ski to carry most of the body weight. Body angulation is added to insure proper edge control

FIGURE 20-3. Traverse

FIGURE 20-4. Straight snowplow

keeping the center of gravity over the inside edge of the downhill ski. The traverse should be run in a relaxed and natural position. The poles should be held parallel and pointed back uphill in line with the shoulders. It is the most important position in skiing. Be sure to practice the traverse in both directions. (See Fig. 20-3.)

Braking

The beginner should turn his attention to braking only after he becomes proficient in straight running and the traverse. There are two techniques of braking—sideslip and snowplow.

SIDESLIPPING. This is the most important controlled braking and serves as a basis for the christies. To initiate the sideslip, start from a traverse position, up-unweight the skis. This will cause the center of mass to move downhill, thus flattening the edges. Weight distribution in sideslipping is the same as in the traverse. The body always faces the direction of the sideslip, thus insuring proper balance. By shifting weight forward and backward a slow, controlled sideslip can be made. The sideslip can be checked and the traverse position resumed by resetting the edges through angulation.

SNOWPLOW. This is used to slow down or stop at times when a more natural turning stop cannot be used. To snowplow from a straight running position, the skis are unweighted with an up-motion and tails displaced at equal angles approximately a ski pole width apart, keeping the tips together. The knees are bent toward the tips of the skis. The skis are at right, lateral angles to the lower legs with the weight equally distributed and slightly for-

ward. The control of the braking force in the snowplow is essentially the skier's weight, not simply muscle power. The poles should be kept well back. To return to a straight running position, again the skis are unweighted by an up-motion and the tails are allowed to slide back together. (See Fig. 20-4.)

The single stem is used to achieve slight braking. The outside ski is stemmed while the inside ski bearing the weight is kept straight. The single stem is often used in a systematic drill for stem turns and stem christie. It relates to an unweighted uphill ski.

Turns

Turns are simply changes in direction that require the following conditions: motion, muscular energy, and resistance.

SNOWPLOW TURN. This is started from a straight snowplow. From this position more weight is transferred to one ski, which becomes the outside ski in the turn. Weight transfer is accomplished by a slight bending of the knee and angling the upper body over the weighted ski as the outside shoulder comes slightly back. The tips are kept together and the skis remain at equal angles. To turn right the left ski is weighted; to turn left the right ski is weighted. (See Fig. 20-5.)

STEM TURN. This is a slow, deliberate, controlled turn initiated from a traverse position. The uphill ski is stemmed rather than the downhill. This keeps the skier's weight on the downhill ski, making it easier to control the direction of the traverse. After the uphill ski is stemmed, the weight is gradually shifted to the stemmed ski by angling the upper

FIGURE 20-5. Snowplow turn

FIGURE 20-6. Stem turn

FIGURE 20-7. Parallel christie

body over it while the outside shoulder moves slightly back. The stem is continued across the fall line until the downhill ski points in the direction you want to go. The edging of the downhill ski is increased in preparation for a new traverse. The uphill ski is then gradually allowed to run alongside the downhill ski and a new traverse position is assumed, thus completing the turn. (See Fig. 20-6.)

UPHILL CHRISTIE. This is important because it develops confidence on steep slopes and is the last half of a christie turn. The uphill christie is initiated from a traverse position by unweighting with an up-forward motion and slight counterrotation. This is followed immediately by a sinking motion, angulation, and slight countermovement which combine to displace the tails downhill. The turn is completed when the skier rises to resume normal traverse position.

STEM CHRISTIE. This is perhaps the most difficult turn to master. The turn is started from a traverse position. The uphill ski is stemmed, accompanied with a sinking motion, and keeping the downhill ski edged and weighted. With an up-forward motion the weight is transferred to the stemmed ski. The inside ski is advanced slightly and brought immediately alongside the outside ski prior to crossing the fall line. The remainder of the turn continues as an uphill christie.

PARALLEL CHRISTIE. This has been the precursor of many variations of parallel skiing, e.g., parallel christie with check, wedeln, short swing, serpent, mambo. It is considered an advanced form of skiing. The parallel christie is initiated from a traverse position with a sinking motion accompanied by a pole plant. With an up-forward motion and counterrotation, weight is transferred to the outside ski and edge set is changed. Pressure is then exerted on the edges by a down motion, angulated position with knees and hips pressing forward, and slight counter motion. Rising to a new traverse completes the turn. Note: don't let the tails of the skis swing too much past the fall line. (See Fig. 20-7.)

SKI SAFETY:* HOW YOU AND YOUR FRIENDS CAN ENJOY SAFE SKIING

1. Be physically fit. Get a good night's sleep.
2. Eat a good breakfast. Stop for lunch. When skiing, as when driving, don't drink alcoholic beverages.

* Courtesy of The Professional Ski Instructors of America, *The Official American Ski Technique*, 1966, p. 70.

3. Drive safely to and from the ski area.

4. Dress for the weather; wear non-breakable sunglasses or goggles; use sunburn cream even on cloudy days; check for frostbite on cold days.

5. Use proper equipment; check it often.

6. Use properly adjusted release bindings with a ski retaining device.

7. Follow posted instructions at ski lifts and on slopes.

8. Learn the meaning of the uniform trail signs: green square—easiest; yellow triangle—more difficult; blue circular—most difficult. Consult a ski area map for slope difficulty.

9. Be aware of danger spots. Look for the red diamond-shaped sign. It means EXTRA CAUTION.

10. Obey trail closure signs. A fluorescent orange octagonal sign means AVALANCHE CLOSURE.

11. Ski within your ability. Improve by taking lessons from a CERTIFIED SKI INSTRUCTOR. Ski in control; don't be a schuss boomer.

12. Loose clothing and long hair are hazards on rope tows and ski lifts.

13. When riding any lift, carry ski poles by the shafts with the points back. Don't have straps around your wrists. Take straps off wrists when skiing in trees or bushes. The jerk caused when the ski pole basket becomes caught may dislocate a shoulder.

14. Keep ski tips up with riding chair lifts.

15. Avoid deep snow until you've learned how to ski in ski school.

16. When ski touring away from the ski area, check out and check back in with the Ski Patrol or other responsible individuals. It may be worth your life.

17. Ski with companions when skiing remote runs or areas. Four or more is recommended. If an accident occurs, one stays with the victim, two go for help.

18. When an accident occurs, cross a pair of skis upright in the snow ABOVE the victim. Be sure to report the EXACT location of the accident to the Ski Patrol or lift operator. At least one person should stay with the injured person until the Ski Patrol arrives.

19. Stop skiing when you are tired or when visibility is poor. Allow sufficient time to complete your last run before the Ski Patrol "sweeps" the slopes.

20. Ski defensively; be aware of other skiers; be ready at all times to react to the unpredictable movements of beginners.

BE COURTEOUS—BE SAFE—SKI IN CONTROL—HAVE FUN!

TERMINOLOGY

Angulation (comma)   In the traverse, the knees are slightly bent and pressed into the hill. The upper body leans away from the slope over the downhill ski. The downhill shoulder is back in line with the hips, thus describing a comma.

Camber (bottom)   The built-in arch of the ski as seen from the side view; designed to distribute the weight over the entire length of the ski.

Camber (cut)   The built-in arch on each side of the ski designed to enable a ski to carve a turn when the edge is set.

Countermotion   The change from one traverse to the other and the body motion is always contrary to ski motion.

Counterrotation   A quick turning motion of the upper body while the skis are unweighted resulting in an equal counteraction in the lower body.

Edge set (edging)   Steel edges biting the snow by angulating.

Fall line   The shortest distance down a hill.

Flex   Bending properties of the ski.

Forebody   The section of the ski in front of the binding.

Garland   An exercise which alternately links a traverse and sideslip.

Groove   The indentation on the base of the ski and running nearly the entire length of the ski to improve tracking stability.

Heelthrust   The vigorous displacement of the tails of the skis sideways with the turning point near the front of the skis.

Hip   The widest part of the tail section.

Inside edge   The left edge of the right ski and the right edge of the left ski.

Inside ski   The ski describing the inside arc of a turn.

Linked turns   A series of turns made one right after the other in opposite directions.

Mogul   Mounds of snow created by skiers turning in the same spot where the terrain is steep and snow is deep.

Outside edge   The left edge of the left ski and the right edge of the right ski.

Outside ski   The ski describing the outside arc of a turn.

Reverse shoulder   In a traverse, the downhill shoulder is back and the uphill shoulder is advanced in line with the hips.

Rising motion   A slow rise resulting in a change of edge position.

Rotation   Turning the body in the direction of the turn.

Ruade   Vigorously lifting the tails off the snow and turning with the tips acting as pivots. Usually used on moguls.

Schuss   Skiing straight down the fall line without turns or checks.

Short swing   Linked parallel christies without traversing, using definite edge set and pole plant. Used to control speed down steep slopes.

Shoulder   Widest part of the forebody of the ski.

Sinking motion   A slow down motion in preparation for up-motion or rising motion.

Sitzmark   A hole left in the snow by a skier who has fallen.

Tail   The rearmost part of the ski.

Tip   The frontmost part of the ski.

Torsion   The amount a ski twists. The stronger the torsional properties of a ski, the better the edge setting and holding characteristics.

Total motion   All exercises in skiing should be performed with a unity of movement by the entire body in a controlled, relaxed, and balanced state.

Track   A warning to a skier in front of you that you are about to have difficulty in avoiding hitting him.

Up-motion   Used to unweight the skis in preparation for some exercise.

Waist   The narrowest part of the ski near its center.

Wedeln   A series of consecutive parallel turns without traversing or appreciable edge setting.

SELECTED REFERENCES

Bradley, Miller, and Merrill, *Expert Skiing*. New York: Holt, Rinehart & Winston, Inc., 1960.

Genasci, Jean, and James Genasci, *Skiing*. Springfield, Mass.: Springfield College, 1967.

Hutter, Clemens M., *Wedeln*. Garden City, N.Y.: Hanover House, 1960.

O'Rear, John, and Frank O'Rear, *Skiing Illustrated*. New York: A.S. Barnes & Co., Inc., 1956.

The Professional Ski Instructors of America, *The Official American Ski Technique*. Salt Lake City, Utah: Quality Press, 1967.

Ski Life Magazine editors, *Ski Pointers by Experts*. New York: Harper & Brothers, 1961.

Ski Magazine publishers, *The New Way to Ski*. New York: Universal Publishing & Distributing Corporation, 1964.

Skin and Scuba Diving

ORIGIN AND DEVELOPMENT

The earliest reference to diving as a utilitarian activity occurs in the *Iliad* where Patroclus compares the fall of Hector's charioteer to the action of a diver diving for oysters. This suggests that the art of diving was known 1000 years before the Christian era. It is not definitely known when man first began to use aids to enable him to remain under water longer than would be possible with normal breath-holding capacity. Aristotle mentions the fact that divers used instruments of respiration which enabled them to draw air from above the surface of the water and thus remain submerged for longer periods of time. In 1819 Augustus Siebe was successful in developing an "open" dress suit that was connected with a tube extended to the surface of the water through which air was pumped to the diver wearing the suit. In 1830 Siebe developed a "closed" dress diving suit which enabled the diver to operate under water with much greater freedom. The basic principles underlying Siebe's inventions have governed the development of diving equipment since his time. It is well known that Polynesian natives and inhabitants of other tropical areas have been diving for pearls and fish for many centuries, but it was not until after World War II that skin diving, as a sport, was practiced to any great extent by inhabitants of the United States.

During World War II, the Armed Forces, particularly the Navy, gave considerable attention to the development and refinement of underwater diving equipment. The "frogmen," as they were called by the public, became particularly skilled in diving and performed remarkable exploits in wartime pursuits, including the placing of demolition charges on beaches prior to invasions, attaching "limpet mines" to the hulls of enemy ships, detonating enemy mines, and so forth. Considerable publicity was given this activity by the press and radio during the war, and many individuals became intrigued by the possibility of utilizing this activity as a sport during peacetime. The motion picture industry helped fan the imagination of the public by releasing several interesting movies based on underwater exploits. The thrills and adventure associated with exploring underwater areas, viewing denizens of the deep at close range, or spearing fish was so appealing that the number of

FIGURE 21-1.
Swim fins

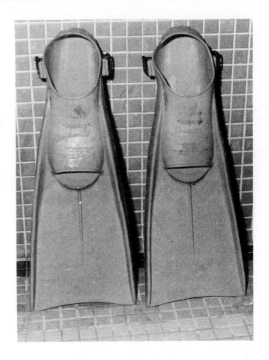

adherents to the activity grew by leaps and bounds. Spear fishing has become so popular in some areas that local legislative bodies have been forced to place limitations upon the kind of equipment used and the number of fish that may be taken by this method. It seems reasonable to assume that interest in skin diving will continue to increase. For that reason, this chapter has been presented to help the swimmer understand the basic principles of the sport and to avoid the mistakes made by beginners in this activity. At the present time there are diving clubs located all over the country. Since many of these clubs provide good training courses for beginning skin divers and maintain rigid rules for members, it is recommended that the individual contemplating skin diving join such a club if one is available.

NATURE OF THE SPORT

Underwater diving and swimming is called by two different names depending upon the type of equipment used. In ordinary skin diving, the swimmer is usually equipped with swim fins on the feet (Fig. 21-1), a face mask and a snorkel (Fig. 21-2), and any optional equipment the swimmer may elect to carry such as camera, spear, gun, knife, or compass. With this equipment, the swimmer is limited by his individual breath-holding capacity in the length of time he may stay under water. Beginners will be limited to a few seconds under the water in early trials, but experienced divers can learn to remain under for about two minutes. The face mask

enables the diver to see under water, and his range of vision depends upon the clarity of the water and amount of natural light present. The swim fins, which enable the swimmer to attain considerable speed in traveling through the water, allow him to submerge to greater depths than would be possible without their use.

In scuba diving, the swimmer carries, in addition to the swim fins and face mask, an aqualung

FIGURE 21-2. Face mask (side view) with snorkle

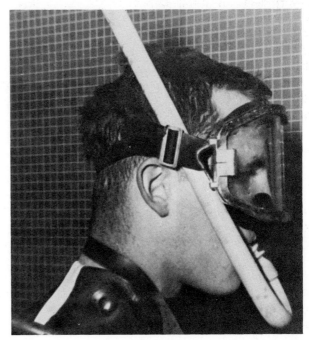

FIGURE 21-3. Aqualung strapped on diver

(trade name for a form of scuba), which is strapped to his back. (See Fig. 21-3.) The aqualung is an open circuit device which enables the user to breathe compressed air from the tank and exhale the expired air into the water. The length of time a swimmer may stay under water using this device is limited to the volume of air in the cylinders and the amount of oxygen his body requires. Obviously, this equipment increases appreciably the distance a swimmer may travel under water, but its use also involves some safety hazards which will be discussed later. In addition to the open-circuit aqualung, there is an oxygen rebreathing unit which was developed during the war to prevent the swimmer from being detected (there are no bubbles to give away the swimmer's location). With this unit the swimmer breathes oxygen under pressure from a container and then exhales back into another container for purification of the oxygen before reuse by the swimmer. This equipment may not be used beyond a depth of 30 feet because of the danger of oxygen poisoning and its resultant symptoms. Obviously, the swimmer should limit himself to the use of the open-circuit type of scuba because of the safety

features and the increased range of movement it provides.

TECHNIQUES AND FUNDAMENTALS

It should be obvious that an individual must master the techniques and fundamentals involved in swimming the various strokes before attempting to use any skin diving or scuba equipment. In addition to the ability to perform the various strokes in an effective manner, the individual should develop his endurance to a degree that will enable him to swim for considerable distances without tiring. For example, the Los Angeles County Department of Parks and Recreation recommends that any swimmer contemplating skin diving should meet the following minimum performance standards: swim 200 yards without swim aids; swim 10 yards under water without swim aids; swim 50 yards with ten pounds of weight without swim aids (the weight should be iron or lead in a belt around the waist); tread water for five minutes; tread water with hands out of water for 30 seconds.[1] Individuals who plan to use scuba equipment should have even greater swimming ability and have a thorough knowledge of the special hazards involved. No one should dive who suffers from sinusitis, ear trouble, or a respiratory infection. People who have pulmonary or cardiovascular disorders should consult their physician before attempting to dive.

If there is any question about the performance of the various strokes, the swimmer should refer to the chapter on swimming included in this handbook. After the swimming strokes have been mastered, the swimmer should start using the swim fins on the feet. The use of this equipment enables him to attain greater speed in swimming. The techniques involved in securing the maximum forward thrust provided by the fins should be mastered. The swimmer should use the fins in surface swimming for development of endurance and skill before attempting to use them for diving, either with or without underwater breathing equipment.

Swimming with fins

The beginner should select fins that fit and feel comfortable. Fins provide greater propulsive power to the swimmer, increase endurance, and enhance relaxation. Swimmers should select large fins although women will probably be more comfortable

[1] *Underwater Recreation Manual.* Los Angeles: Department of Parks and Recreation, latest edition.

with fins smaller than the large "pro" size. The best kick is a form of the flutter kick, in which the legs are moved up and down in a rhythmical fashion, legs bent slightly at the knees, ankles relaxed, with fins pointed backward and passing each other at a reasonable distance as the legs move up and down. The leg movement should originate at the hips, so the thigh muscles are an important source of power in swimming with fins. If the swimmer feels any indication of muscular cramps developing, he should stop action immediately and relax until the pain has ceased. The hands and arms are used primarily to change direction under water and are not ordinarily needed to help propel the body through the water, as in surface swimming. Sufficient force to drive the body through the water is available from the leg kick, so that hands may be used to handle accessory equipment or allowed to hang loosely at the sides.

HINTS FOR THE BEGINNER

1. After mastering the techniques suggested above, take advantage of supervised instruction in the use of the face mask.
2. Limit yourself to clear, shallow water when first using the face mask.
3. Mask fogging may be minimized by rubbing saliva over the inside surface of the glass lens and then rinsing. If water gets under mask it may be cleared by exhaling through edge of mask under surface of water.
4. To become acquainted with the use of scuba, use it first in shallow water by simply breathing in and out while resting on the bottom. As skill and confidence develop, take slow, easy swims around a shallow area, breathing as you proceed. Use of any scuba equipment should be done under competent supervision to prevent disabling or fatal accidents.
5. Practice removing the mouthpiece, reinserting it, and then clearing the air hose by blowing air through it. At first, small amounts of water may be swallowed, but as proficiency develops, the swimmer should be able to remove and replace both the face mask and mouthpiece without difficulty while under water.
6. Practice use of the equipment on short, controlled swims. Gradually increase the distance until you are able to submerge and expend a tank of air without surfacing.
7. Study the following pages for information on dangers involved in skin and scuba diving.

EQUIPMENT

Swim fins

With the expenditure of a moderate amount of money, the swimmer may purchase the essential equipment necessary for skin diving. Swim fins are manufactured by several companies and have varying degrees of flexibility. The beginner will likely prefer the more flexible fin over the rigid type. Fins may be had with either open or closed toes, the former usually being more comfortable. Fins with their flippers set at a downward angle to the foot give greater driving power with less strain on the foot. Fins should cover the heel of the foot completely to facilitate walking. An anti-skid surface on the bottom of the fin makes it easier to walk on slippery surfaces. Fins should be tried on before purchase to see that they provide a snug and comfortable fit.

Face masks

Face masks may be purchased with face plates equipped with plain glass, laminated safety glass, or plastic. Plain glass masks are not recommended because glass splinters when breaking. Plastic faceplates scratch easily and have a tendency to fog more readily than glass, but although they will break, they are not as dangerous as plain glass. When buying a face mask, a person should select one with a faceplate made of tempered safety glass. The part of the mask that touches the face should have a soft feathered or tapered edge to insure a watertight fit. Straps to hold the mask to the face should be attached toward the front of the mask in order to facilitate the use of a snorkel tube and to insure a tight seal. Before buying a mask, it should be tested for fit, comfort, and ability to provide a tight seal without leaks. In using a face mask, the swimmer should know that he will have a distorted view of things seen under water; objects will appear larger and nearer at hand. In time, however, the swimmer learns to allow for these differences and can judge size and distance with reasonable accuracy.

Snorkels

The snorkel consists of a tube which projects above the water at one end and terminates in a mouthpiece at the other end. (See Fig. 21-2.) The swimmer uses the snorkel while lying face down on the surface of the water, enabling him to breathe without having to lift his face out of the water. This equipment has definite advantages in surface swimming because surface air may be breathed without lifting the face from the water or using air from the scuba, if the swimmer is carrying this equipment.

The simplest snorkel consists of a J-shaped tube and a mouthpiece designed so that the tube will curve up around the diver's face to the surface of the water. The tube should be flexible so that it will bend when striking an object and not be torn from the swimmer's mouth, possibly displacing the mask. If the swimmer elects to submerge with snorkel in use, he deliberately maintains enough air pressure to keep the water from entering his mouth, although the snorkel tube will fill with water. Upon surfacing, he "spouts" like a whale, blowing the water out of the tube before taking a breath. Some snorkels have an intake check valve to keep water from flowing into the tube when it is drawn under the surface, but these devices do not work satisfactorily under all conditions and are not recommended.

FIGURE 21-5. Mask and breathing apparatus

Aqualung

The most common type of scuba is the aqualung, which was invented by Captain Jacques Yves Cousteau, of the French Navy, and Emile Gagnan, a French engineer, in 1942. Trained persons commonly reach a depth of 130 feet with the aqualung, and in 1948, Fredrick Dumas, a famous French

FIGURE 21-4. Divers equipped for underwater swimming (Courtesy of the National Recreation Association. Photo by Jasper Nutter.)

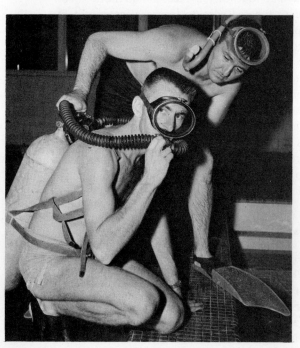

diver, reached a record of 306 feet. These achievements are limited to the well-trained diver, however, and anyone just beginning this sport should limit his dives to a few feet until he masters all the necessary skills and techniques associated with the use of the aqualung.

The main components of an aqualung are the cylinders which contain compressed air to around 2250 pounds per square inch, the shoulder straps for securing the lung to the swimmer's back, the regulator which automatically adjusts the pressure of the air inhaled to the pressure of the water surrounding the diver, and the air tube which is connected to the swimmer's mouth. The diver inhales air from the cylinders and expels it into the water as he swims under the surface. As mentioned earlier, their is also a closed-circuit unit in which the expired air is used again, but this system is not recommended for amateur swimmers.

Spear guns

Divers in search of water game may wish to use one of the many spear guns on the market, but before deciding upon a particular gun, they should check with local authorities to see what limitations are imposed upon spear fishing. Probably the safest type of spear gun is the so-called Hawaiian sling, powered with either a spring or rubber bands. This gun operates on the same principle as a sling shot. Other guns, powered by springs or bands which must be pre-cocked, are subject to accidental discharge if inadvertently dropped or struck. Guns powered with

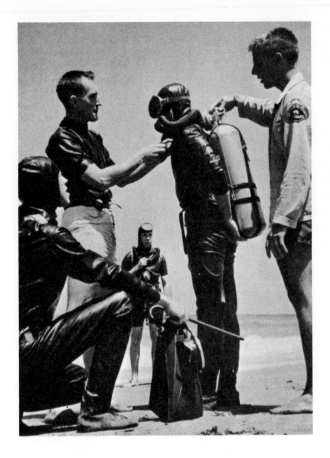

FIGURE 21-6. *Protective swimming suits* (Courtesy of *Recreation Magazine,* National Recreation Association.)

carbon dioxide gas from a cylinder are more powerful, but constitute a definite hazard because the cylinder is subject to accidental discharge if dropped or exposed too long to heat from the sun.

Other equipment

Other items which the diver may wish to have are a knife, encased in a sheath and attached to a lanyard, for use in cutting kelp, nets, and lines in which the diver may become entangled. If weighted belts are worn to facilitate the descent in scuba diving, the belts should be of the quick-release type for instant jettisoning. Cotton or canvas gloves are helpful when swimming around coral or sharp rock, and a T-shirt will help protect the skin from excessive sunburn. If diving in cold areas, a rubber suit may be desirable for protection. (See Fig. 21-6.)

CARE OF EQUIPMENT

Most skin diving equipment is durable and will give years of service if properly maintained. Salt and

chlorinated water tend to have a corrosive effect upon metal, so all equipment should be thoroughly cleaned with fresh water after each use. A light coat of oil may be applied to the knife, but oil should never be placed on rubber tubes or acqualung because of possible contamination of air. After thorough cleansing with fresh water, the equipment should be hung up to dry. After storage, the equipment should be checked thoroughly to see that all parts are in perfect working order.

SOME BASIC PRINCIPLES THE DIVER SHOULD KNOW

Since the diver will be using air under circumstances somewhat different from those which exist on land, he should understand not only something of the basic properties of air, but something about the laws of physics that govern certain conditions.

FIGURE 21-7. Ready for diving

Composition of air

The main constituents of the air we breathe are approximately as follows:

CONSTITUENT	PER CENT OF VOLUME
Nitrogen	79.00
Oxygen	20.94
Carbon Dioxide	.03
Miscellaneous	.03

The elements exert a force of 14.7 pounds per square inch at sea level, the nitrogen exerting 11.6 and the oxygen 3.07 pounds per square inch. This force is referred to as atmospheric pressure and increases as the diver descends under the surface of the water. The increase in pressure is at the rate of 0.445 pounds per square inch for each foot of depth in sea water. A depth of 33 feet is known as "one atmosphere below sea level," and the pressure at this point is 29.4 pounds per square inch; in other words, the 33 feet of water have added 14.7 pounds of pressure per square inch to the 14.7 pounds present at sea level. The reader should understand the operation of two laws of physics which have special implications here. According to *Dalton's law*—the law of partial pressures—the total pressure exerted by a mixture of gases is equal to the sum of the pressures exerted by each gas acting alone in the total volume. For example, at a depth of 132 feet, the absolute pressure is 73.3 pounds per square inch. The percentage of the gases remains the same, however. The pressure of the gases has increased to 57.9 pounds per square inch for nitrogen and 15.4 pounds per square inch for oxygen, which means that the partial pressure of oxygen at 132 feet approximates the breathing of pure oxygen at sea level. This fact is important for the diver because the breathing of oxygen under pressure has toxic effects.

According to *Boyle's law,* if the temperature is constant, the volume of gas varies inversely as the absolute pressure, while the density varies directly as the pressure. That is, if the pressure of the gas is doubled, the density is also doubled, but the volume is decreased to one-half of the original volume. In going from atmospheric conditions to a depth of 33 feet, the pressure becomes twice that at the surface, but the volume of gas is only one-half what it was originally (neglecting temperature differences). Therefore, in addition to furnishing air at increased pressures, it is necessary to furnish twice as much air to obtain the same volume at this depth.

SOME DIVING AILMENTS OR DISEASES

The diver is susceptible to certain ailments if he does not observe the proper safety precautions when under the water, or when his equipment is not functioning properly. Some of these ailments are described below.

Caisson disease ("the bends")

This is probably the best known of the ailments suffered by divers. It is caused when a diver breathes compressed air, under greater than normal pressure, for extended periods of time. This results in an excess accumulation of nitrogen in the bloodstream, which tends to expand as the diver ascends to the surface. The nitrogen bubbles in the bloodstream gravitate first to the leg and arm joints, where they cause severe pain (hence the name "bends"), then to the heart and finally to the brain, which may result in paralysis or death. The bends can be avoided by diving only once a day and limiting the depth to less than 33 feet. Nitrogen is cumulative in the body system and requires 24 hours to be assimilated by the blood.

Air embolism

This is one of the most serious of the ailments afflicting divers. It is caused when swimmers who are breathing compressed air attempt to surface while holding their breath. As the pressure exerted by the water decreases during ascent, the volume increases (Boyle's law), forcing lung tissues outward (like the sides of a balloon when expanded) until the lung tissues are torn, permitting air to enter the internal cavities of the chest. Air embolism can be avoided if the diver never holds his breath while surfacing, but continues to breathe normally.

Carbon monoxide poisoning

Carbon monoxide poisoning is caused when the diver breathes an excess of this gas from his air supply. To avoid CO poisoning, the diver must be sure that his supply of air is always pure.

Carbon dioxide poisoning

CO_2 poisoning results when the diver exerts himself to excess, or when CO_2 is allowed to collect in the air supply. An excess of CO_2 in the bloodstream can lead to unconsciousness. When the diver feels the onset of this ailment, he should surface immediately because continued exertion in diving will only aggravate the situation.

Oxygen poisoning

Although oxygen is necessary to sustain life, an excess in the bloodstream over and above the body's normal needs can produce harmful results. At sea level an individual can breathe 100 per cent oxygen for long periods of time with safety, but under the additional pressure of two atmospheres (33 feet in depth) the oxygen tends to concentrate in the bloodstream causing painful symptoms and possibly death if the situation is not remedied. Because of the danger in breathing 100 per cent oxygen, the diver should never attempt to fill his supply tank with this concentration.

Nitrogen narcosis

This ailment is induced when the diver descends to a depth at which the nitrogen in the air supply tends to produce a narcotic effect. The physiological aspects of this ailment are not thoroughly understood. Individuals vary in their susceptibility to this ailment, but not even experienced divers should descend to a depth below 130 feet.

SAFETY HINTS

Skin and scuba diving probably have more dangerous aspects associated with the activity than any other sport the individual is likely to encounter. For this reason, it is especially important that the reader study and observe these suggested safety procedures.

1. Never dive alone. Always use the "buddy" system, and be sure that your buddy is a strong, sensible swimmer.
2. Master the use of your diving equipment in shallow water and never attempt diving feats that may require skill and stamina beyond your ability.
3. Never dive into water head first when wearing a face mask because of the danger of breaking the face plate.
4. Never wear ear plugs when diving (especially with scuba), because their use can lead to rupture of an eardrum. If you are unable to equalize the pressure on your ears, stop diving for the day, and if ear pains persist, see your doctor.
5. Never attempt scuba diving until you have mastered the use of the face mask and swim fins and have developed your endurance through long periods of swimming.
6. When scuba diving, "buddies" should assume responsibility for checking on each other's equipment. Before and after submerging, check for air leaks, position of aqualung, proper fastening of harness, and so forth.
7. Always breathe normally when under water. If breathing becomes labored for any reason, signal your "buddy" and commence surfacing.
8. Never ascend more rapidly than 25 feet per minute. A good rule is never to pass your smallest bubbles on ascent.
9. During descent, if difficulty is experienced when attempting to equalize pressure, stop, ascend a few feet, and attempt to relieve the pressure by bobbing, or blocking the nostrils and blowing. Never try to force equalization by going deeper.
10. Do not dive deeper than 75 feet unless proper emergency facilities are available at the diving site—for example, recompression chambers, medical assistance, and so forth.
11. Never use homemade diving equipment. Failure of this type of equipment has been responsible for many diving accidents.
12. If any unusual difficulty is encountered when diving, stop and think before rushing into some action that may be detrimental. For example, jettisoning an aqualung should be the last resort, because it contains your air supply.

TERMINOLOGY

Absolute pressure The addition of 14.7 pounds to the indicated gauge pressure. True pressure.

Air embolism Ailment caused when diver attempts to surface while holding his breath.

Anoxia An insufficient supply of oxygen.

Aqualung A trade name frequently used interchangeably with "scuba." Tank containing compressed air carried by divers.

Atmospheric pressure Air pressure at sea level is 14.7 pounds per square inch. It increases at the rate of 0.444 pounds per square inch for each foot of depth in sea water.

Boyle's law At a fixed temperature, the volume of a given quantity of gas varies inversely with its absolute pressure.

Buddy line A line connecting two divers to maintain contact, relative position, and communication.

Buoyancy The upward force exerted by a fluid on an immersed or floating body.

Caisson disease Commonly called the "bends." An excess accumulation of nitrogen in the bloodstream, which tends to expand as the diver ascends.

Complemental air The volume of air which can still be inhaled at the completion of a normal tidal inspiration.

Compressor A mechanical device which provides a high-pressure air supply in filling scuba tanks.

Cylinder Used in diving to denote tanks holding compressed air.

Dalton's law The total pressure exerted by a mixture of gases is equal to the sum of the pressures exerted by each gas acting alone in the total volume.

Decompression A release from pressure or compression.

Dry suit A waterproof rubber exposure suit used by divers.

Embolism The presence of air bubbles in the circulatory system.

Hyperoxia Excess oxygen in body tissues.

Hyperventilation Respiratory activity in excess of that required to meet the body's normal requirements.

Face mask A mask placed over the face equipped with faceplates for enhancement of underwater vision.

Fins Rubber fins or flippers worn on the feet to increase speed in swimming.

Mae West A standard life jacket used by persons who may need safety devices in or on the water.

Nitrogen narcosis Diving ailment resulting when diver goes too deep and nitrogen in air supply begins to have a narcotic effect.

One atmosphere Pressure at sea level. Pressure at this point is 14.7 pounds per square inch.

Recompression Treatment of decompression sickness or air embolism by utilizing a recompression chamber.

Regulator A device for automatic maintenance and adjustment of air flow.

Scuba Self-Contained Underwater Breathing Apparatus.

Skin diving Diving without the use of scuba equipment.

Snorkel A J-shaped tube which projects above water at one end and terminates in a mouthpiece at the other end.

Spear gun Guns used in killing underwater life; may be powered by springs, rubber bands, or gas.

Tanks Term used to describe air cylinders.

Tidal volume The volume of air entering and leaving the lungs at each normal inspiration and expiration.

Toxic Poisonous in nature.

SELECTED REFERENCES

Barada, B., *Let's Go Diving.* Santa Anna, Calif.: United States Divers Company, 1962.

Carrier, Rick, and Barbara Carrier, *Dive: The Complete Book on Skin Diving.* New York: Funk & Wagnalls, 1957.

"Poet of the Depths," *Time,* LXXV, No. 13 (March 28, 1960).

Rahn, H., ed., *Physiology of Breath Hold Diving and the Ama of Japan.* Washington, D.C.: National Academy of Sciences—National Research Council, Publication 1341, 1964.

Tillman, Albert A., *Skin and Scuba Diving in Underwater Education.* Dubuque, Iowa: William C. Brown Company, Publishers, 1962.

Underwater Recreation Manual. Los Angeles: Department of Parks and Recreation (current edition).

Soccer

22

ORIGIN AND DEVELOPMENT

Games played with a ball have their origins in antiquity, and soccer appears to be one of these games. While it is popularly thought to have originated in England, there is considerable evidence to show that a form of soccer was played by the early Romans, who learned it from the Greeks. There seems to be little doubt of the fact that the early Romans played a game in which a round ball was kicked, and that this game or activity was the forerunner of other games such as cricket, croquet, and hockey. A form of soccer was played in Chester, England, as early as the tenth century and inhabitants of Derby, England, claim that soccer football was played there on Shrove Tuesday to celebrate a victory over a troop of Roman warriors.

With the standardization of rules, the sport assumed a place of international significance, being played in over 70 different countries under uniform rules. In Europe, Asia, Africa, Australia, and South America, the game is more popular than tennis, football, or baseball and often draws crowds of 150,000 spectators to important matches.

Soccer was introduced into the United States around 1870, but has not attained the prominent position here that it holds in many other countries. The game has had its greatest success in this country where there is a high proportion of foreign-born people who came from countries where soccer was a popular sport.

The first regulation game in America was played between Princeton and Rutgers in 1869. In 1923 the Intercollegiate Soccer Football Association of America was formed, comprising 12 eastern colleges and universities. The greatest performance record for colleges in soccer competition belongs to Pennsylvania State College for going eight seasons in a row, 1930–40 inclusive, without a defeat. In this period they played 65 games, winning 60, with 5 games resulting in ties. In 1919, after the rules had been modified to eliminate the rougher elements, soccer was introduced for the first time in a women's college at Bryn Mawr. It was not until 1927, however, that the National Section on Girls' and Women's Sports published the first soccer rules for women.

Currently, over 200 NCAA member senior colleges promote soccer as an intercollegiate sport and play on regular schedules. The 1966 National Collegiate Championship was won by the University

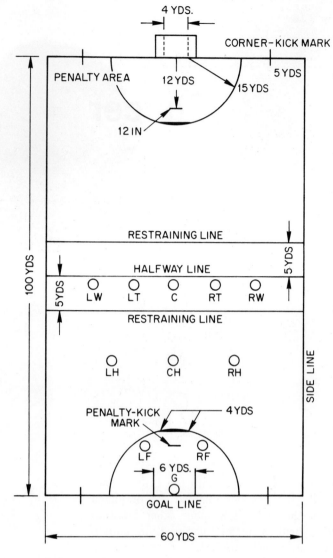

FIGURE 22-1. Diagram of women's soccer field, showing names of players in position.

of San Francisco and the 1967 title was shared by St. Louis University and Michigan State when inclement weather and wet grounds caused cancellation of the final game.

A vigorous effort is currently under way to promote professional soccer in the United States. Two professional leagues, the United States Soccer Association and the National Professional Soccer League, operated during the 1967 season, but the two leagues merged into one group for 1968 and decided to call themselves the North American Soccer League. Following the close of the 1967 season, the Tornado Soccer Club of Dallas, Texas, engaged in a worldwide tour in which the team traveled over 40,000 miles, playing some 47 contests against teams from 20 different countries. The trip was made in order to publicize American soccer around the world

and to help condition the Dallas team for play in the 1968 season. The paucity of topflight professional soccer players in the United States is indicated by the fact that player personnel for the 12 teams in the United States Soccer League for the 1967 season were recruited from countries outside the United States. Supporters of soccer are hopeful that as interest in the sport increases in this country, there will be a corresponding increase in the development of local talent for use on all teams, both amateur and professional.

NATURE OF THE GAME

The regulation team for both men and women consists of eleven players, and the game is put in play by a place kick from the center of the field. All players must be in their half of the field at the kick-off. The offensive object of the game is to get the ball across the opponent's goal line, with the entire ball traveling between the uprights and beneath the crossbar of the goal. The ball must be kicked or headed across the goal; no goal will be allowed if the ball has been thrown, carried, or propelled across the line by hand or arm. The ball may be played by any part of the body except the hands or arms, goalkeeper excluded, and is usually moved around the field by kicking or heading.

Since the ball must be played with parts of the body other than the hands, the skill of controlling the ball with the feet is more highly developed in this game than in any other. The rules for women are more strict than for men in prohibiting body contact, so the women's game is not as rough as the men's version. Differences between the two versions are noted below.

BASIC RULES FOR MEN [1]

Soccer is played on a rectangular field with a length of not more than 120 yards or less than 110 yards, and a width of not more than 75 yards or less than 65 yards. It is recommended, in the interest of uniformity, that soccer fields be 120 yards in length and 75 yards in width. The length of women's fields ranges from 80 yards to 100 yards and the width from 40 yards to 60 yards. The field is marked with distinctive lines, called touchlines in men's rules and sidelines in women's rules. (See Figs. 22-1 and 22-2.) A flag is placed at each corner of the field

[1] Official N.C.A.A. Soccer Laws, in *Official N.C.A.A. Soccer Guide.*

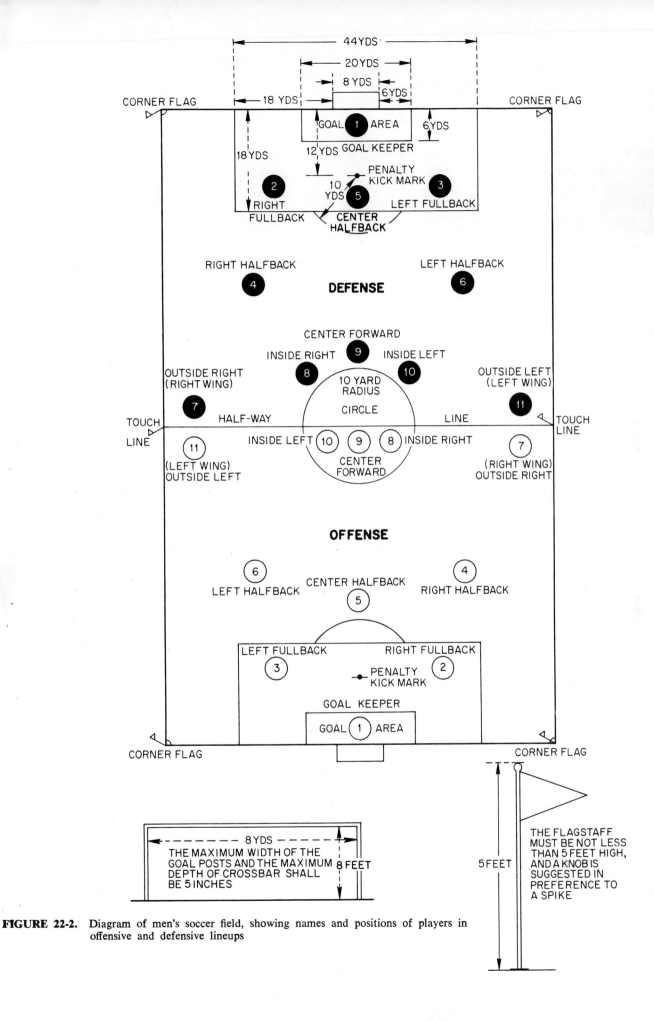

FIGURE 22-2. Diagram of men's soccer field, showing names and positions of players in offensive and defensive lineups

and a line drawn across the field equidistant from each goal line, dividing the field into equal halves. Penalty areas are designated at each end of the field and a penalty kick mark is indicated at each goal.

Soccer football is played with 11 men on each side and consists of four equal periods, each 22 minutes long, unless other time periods are mutually agreed upon by competing teams. In case of a tie at the end of a regulation game, two extra periods of five minutes each are to be played, the score then standing as official. A referee and two linesmen officiate. The referee has control of the game, enforcing all penalties and settling all disputed points.

The start of play

At the beginning of the game, choice of ends and the kick-off shall be decided by the toss of a coin. Upon signal from the referee a player of the kicking team shall place-kick the ball from a stationary position on the ground in the center of the field. The ball shall be kicked toward the opponent's half of the field, and every player on the kick-off shall be in his own half of the field and every player of the receiving team shall remain at least ten yards from the ball until it is kicked. The ball must travel the length of its own circumference, and if this distance (27 inches) is not attained, the ball must be kicked again. A goal may not be scored direct from a kick-off. After the ball has been properly put in play at the kick-off it can be kicked in any direction by the second and other players. It is a dead ball if, while in play, the ball touches the referee or linesman. Play shall resume by a drop ball at the point where the infringement occurred, unless it occurs in the penalty area, in which case the ball is put in play at the nearest point outside the penalty area.

Scoring

A goal is scored when the whole of the ball has passed over the goal line, between the goalposts and under the crossbar, provided it has not been thrown, carried or propelled by hand or arm, or carried by a player of the attacking side. (See Fig. 22-3.) If the defending team other than the goalie deliberately stops or deflects the ball with hand or arm to stop a goal, it should be scored a goal if it crosses the goal line between the uprights. Goals may also be scored on "direct free kicks," penalty kicks, and corner kicks. A goal counts one point for the team scoring the goal. After a goal is scored, a kick-off shall be made by the team scored against at the center of the field. Teams shall change ends after each regular and extra period.

Off-side

A player is off-side if he is nearer his opponent's goal line than the ball at the moment the ball is played unless:

1. He is in his own half of the field of play.
2. Two of his opponents are nearer to their own goal line than he.
3. The ball last touched an opponent or was last played by him.
4. He receives the ball when it is dropped by the referee or direct from a goal-kick or a corner-kick.

The position of the ball with respect to the player is the controlling factor in off-side. A player is not off-side under the following conditions:

1. If he is behind the ball when it is played.
2. If ahead of the ball, with two opponents between him and the opposing goal.
3. When he receives the ball from an opponent.

A player once off-side can be put on-side in one of three ways:

1. If an opponent next plays the ball.
2. If he is behind the ball when it is next played by one of his own side.
3. If he has two opponents between him and their goal line when the ball is played by one of his own side farther from the opponents' goal than he is.

A player should remember that he cannot be off-side in the following instances:

1. When an opponent last plays the ball.
2. On a corner kick.
3. On a goal kick.
4. On a drop ball.

The penalty for violation of the off-side rule shall be an indirect free kick taken by a player of the opposing team at the point where the infringement occurred. Off-side shall not be penalized unless, in the opinion of the referee, the off-side player is interfering with the play or with an opponent, or is seeking to gain an advantage by being in an off-side position.

Fouls and misconduct

The following offenses are penalized by a "direct" free kick at the point of the foul. The ball may be kicked in any direction and a goal may be scored on this kick.

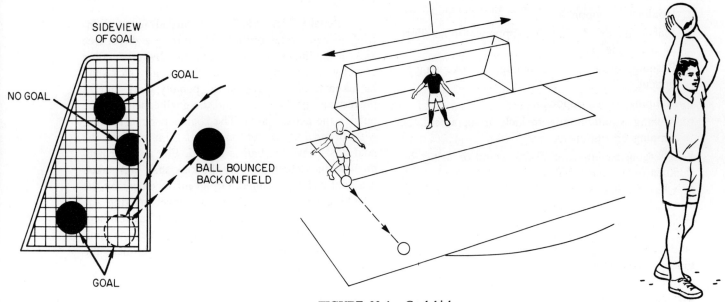

FIGURE 22-3. Scoring a goal

SIDEVIEW
OF GOAL

GOAL

NO GOAL

BALL BOUNCED
BACK ON FIELD

GOAL

FIGURE 22-4. Goal kick

FIGURE 22-5.
Throw-in

BALL OVER GOAL LINE
THIS SIDE OF FIELD

KICK
FROM THIS CORNER

FIGURE 22-6.
Corner kick

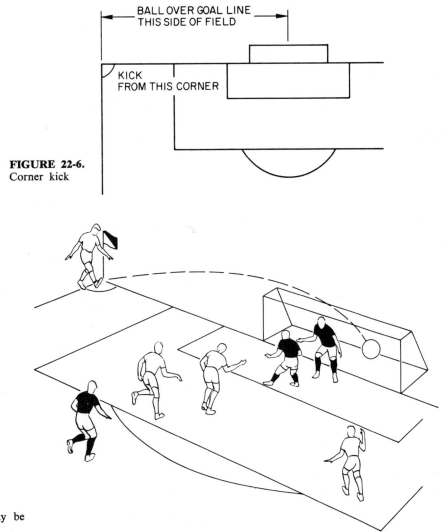

FIGURE 22-7. Goal may be
scored on a corner kick

1. Handling the ball with hands or arms.
2. Holding an opponent.
3. Placing hands or arms on an opponent in an effort to reach the ball.
4. Pushing, striking or attempting to strike an opponent.
5. Jumping at an opponent.
6. Kicking or attempting to kick an opponent, or tripping an opponent.
7. Charging an opponent from behind or using the knee on an opponent.
8. Charging goalie in the penalty area unless he is obstructing an opponent.

The following offenses are penalized by an "indirect" free kick. A goal may not be scored on this kick unless the ball is touched or played by a player other than the kicker before going through the goal.

1. A player playing the ball a second time before it has been played by another player on the kick-off, kick-in, corner kick or goal kick if the ball has passed outside the penalty area.
2. Ball not kicked forward on penalty kick.
3. Goalkeeper carrying ball more than four steps within penalty area.
4. Substitution made when ball is not dead, or for failure of substitute to report to the referee.
5. Persistent coaching from the sidelines after warning.
6. Ungentlemanly conduct.
7. Off-side.
8. Interfering with goalie or impeding him in any manner until he clears the ball.

Execution of free kicks

Free kicks shall be classified under two heads: "direct" (from which a goal can be scored against the offending side), and "indirect" (from which a goal cannot be scored unless the ball has been played or touched by a player other than the kicker before passing through the goal).

When making a free kick all members of the opposing team must be ten yards away, unless standing on the goal line between the uprights, until the ball is kicked. The ball must be stationary when kicked and must travel the length of its own circumference. If the kicker, after attempting a free kick, shall play the ball before it has been touched by another player, an indirect free kick shall be awarded the other team.

Penalty kicks

Penalty kicks shall be awarded for any infringement of rules ordinarily requiring a direct free kick, if the infringement is committed by a defending player within the penalty area. The penalty kick shall be taken from any spot on the penalty mark and all players except the kicker and the goalkeeper must be outside the penalty area. The goalkeeper must stand, without moving his feet, on the goal line between the goal posts until the ball is kicked. For any infringement by the defending team the kick shall be retaken if a goal has not resulted. On an infringement by the attacking team, other than the player making the kick, the kick shall be retaken if a goal has resulted. An infringement by the player making the kick shall result in an indirect free kick at the spot where the violation occurred for the opposing team.

Goal kick

When the offensive team forces the ball across the goal line, and not between the goal uprights, the ball shall be put in play by the defensive team from a point within that half of the goal area nearest to where it crossed the goal line. (See Fig. 22-4.) Opposing players must remain outside the penalty area while the kick is being made, and if the ball is not kicked beyond the penalty area, the kick shall be retaken. The kicker cannot hold the ball for the kick—it must be kicked from the ground.

The throw-in

When the ball passes completely over a touchline, either on the ground or in the air, it shall be thrown in from the point where it crossed the line by a player of the team opposite to that of the player who last touched it. The player making the throw-in must face the field of play and part of each foot must be on the touchline or on the ground outside the touchline. The thrower shall use both hands and shall deliver the ball from over his head. See Figure 22-5.

Corner kick

When the ball is caused to cross the goal line but not between the goal uprights by a member of the defending team, it shall be put into play by the offensive team by a corner kick within the quarter-circle at the nearest corner flag-post. (See Figs. 22-6 and 22-7.) A goal may be scored on this kick, and the same restrictions apply to opposing players on the kick as in other kicks in scoring area.

Privileges of goalkeeper

The goalkeeper enjoys certain privileges not granted to other players while in the penalty area. He may use his hands and arms to stop a ball from scoring, take four steps with the ball in his possession, place-kick or punt the ball, and he is free from interference by opponents while in possession of the ball. He loses these privileges when outside the penalty area.

BASIC RULES FOR WOMEN [2]

Teams

An official team shall be composed of 11 players. The five players in the forward line are called left wing, left inner, center, right inner, and right wing. The other players are the halfbacks —right, center, and left; the full backs—right and left; and one goalkeeper. Substitutes may enter the game when time is taken out, and a player who has been taken out of the game for any reason other than disqualification may reenter the game once.

Playing rules

A goalkeeper within her own penalty area may:

1. Pick up the ball.
2. Bounce the ball once.
3. Punt the ball.
4. Drop-kick the ball.
5. Throw the ball.
6. Combine a bounce with a punt, drop kick, or a throw.
7. Take two steps with the ball in the hands preceding a punt, drop kick, or throw. This privilege is denied if the punt, drop kick, or throw is combined with a bounce.

Privileges of other players:

1. A player may dribble, shoulder, or head the ball.
2. A player in possession of the ball may place herself between her opponent and the ball.
3. A player may stop the ball by trapping it under her foot, between her feet, or between the front of her legs and the ground.

FIGURE 22-8. Blocking a ball at chest height

4. A player may kick the ball while it is trapped by an opponent, provided she does not commit a foul.
5. Any player may stop the ball by blocking it with any part of the body except the hands or arms. Note: In blocking a ball at chest height, a player should fold her arms across her chest as a means of protection. The arms must be held in contact with the body. (See Fig. 22-8.)

Fouls

A foul is an infringement of the rules of the game for which a free kick or a penalty kick is awarded the opponents. Fouls include charging, playing the ball with the hands or arms, holding, off-side, kicking, pushing, tripping, and carrying (when goalkeeper takes more than two steps while holding the ball).

Penalties

1. Inside the penalty area:
   a. For any breach by the attacking team, a free

[2] *Official N.S.G.W.S. Soccer-Speedball Guide.* Washington, D.C.: American Association for Health, Physical Education and Recreation, latest edition.

kick shall be awarded by the defending team at the spot where the breach occurred.

b. For any breach by the defending team, a penalty kick shall be awarded the attacking team from the penalty kick mark.

c. For any breach committed simultaneously by both teams, a roll-in shall be awarded at the spot where the double foul occurred.

2. Outside the penalty area:

a. For any breach by either team, the penalty shall be a free kick awarded at the spot where the foul occurred.

Note: A goal may be scored directly from a free kick awarded for tripping, kicking, striking, jumping at, holding, pushing, charging an opponent, and handling the ball. A goal may not be scored directly on a free kick inflicted on the goalkeeper for "carrying" the ball.

Off-side

A player is in an off-side position if she is nearer her opponent's goal line than the ball at the moment it is played by one of her own team, unless: (1) she is in her own half of the field, or (2) there are three of her opponents nearer their own goal line than she is. A player shall not be penalized for being off-side unless she is playing the ball, interfering with another player, or gaining some advantage from standing in an off-side position.

Once off-side, a player can be put on-side only in the following ways: (1) if she is behind the ball when it is next played by one of her own team, or (2) if there are three opponents between her and their goal line when the ball is played by one of her own team farther from her opponent's goal than herself. A free kick is awarded as a penalty for off-side, but a goal cannot be scored directly on this kick.

Scoring

A field goal counts two points and a penalty kick one point.

TECHNIQUE AND FUNDAMENTALS

The basic fundamentals of play in soccer are dribbling, heading, trapping, shooting, passing, blocking, position play, and field generalship. Because the game of soccer is primarily a kicking game, it is essential that players master the technique of controlling the ball with the feet. In observing good soccer players, one will see that they control the ball with their feet and keep it reasonably close to their bodies when advancing it down the field. The ball should be kept close to the ground and not kicked into the air where it is impossible for the player to keep possession and control. Players should master the technique of kicking the ball with the instep, keeping the body over the ball. One practice technique involves dribbling the ball around various objects on the field. If a player can first learn to control the ball while dribbling it in and around stationary objects, it will be easier to maneuver around moving players in actual competition. Players are usually more adept with one foot than the other, but good performers must learn to control the ball with either foot. (See Fig. 22-9.)

TRAPPING. Beginning players should learn to trap or stop high bounding balls by stopping them with the feet or body. Such balls may be stopped by bringing the sole of the shoe down over the ball the instant it strikes the ground. (See Fig. 22-10.) If the player gets in front of the ball, he may stop it with his body, rather than his hands or arms, if it should be missed by the foot. Figure 22-11 shows the knee trap.

SHOOTING. This technique involves kicking the ball toward the goal in an effort to score. This skill may be practiced by kicking the ball toward a wall on which a mark has been placed to serve as a target. The ball should be kept low and players should practice this skill from a standing position by placing the left foot alongside the ball and kicking with the right, or vice versa. As control is gained, the player should attempt to shoot from a moving position.

FIGURE 22-9. Start of foot dribble

FIGURE 22-10. Trapping ball with foot

FIGURE 22-11. Trapping ball with knee

FIGURE 22-12. Passing the ball

FIGURE 22-13. Heading the ball

FIGURE 22-14. Dark-shirted man blocking white to obtain ball. Permissible in men's rules only

PASSING. Soccer is a team game and players must master the art of passing the ball to a teammate who may be in a position to score or advance the ball into scoring position. This skill may be practiced by two or more players while dribbling the ball down the field. The ball may be passed back and forth, using both the inside and outside of the foot to direct the ball, depending on the direction of the pass and the location of the ball when the pass is made. (See Fig. 22-12.)

HEADING THE BALL. This skill may be practiced by two or more players standing a few yards apart. The ball may be kept in the air and directed from player to player, using the head as the propeling agent. Heading the ball with the forehead should be mastered first and later the technique of striking the ball with the side of the head may be developed.

Heading the ball in competition is often a great time-saver and can frequently be used to direct a high ball through the goal when the defense is massed in front of the scoring area. (See Fig. 22-13.)

TACKLING. This term does not have the same meaning in soccer that it does in American football. Tackling in soccer (men's version) refers to techniques of gaining possession of the ball by playing the man or by playing the ball. Playing the man involves contact with the player possessing the ball in which the defensive player charges the man with the ball by hitting him with his shoulder below the opponent's shoulder. This contact is designed to force the opponent from the ball. Playing the ball involves taking the ball away from the opponent by intercepting it with the feet. (See Fig. 22-14.)

Under women's rules, no body contact is

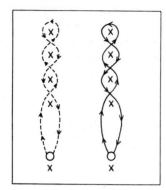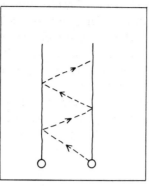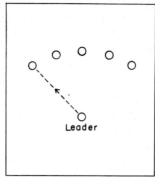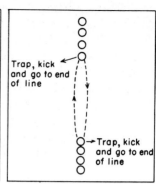

FIGURES 22-15 through 22-18. (*Left*) Player starting at X, dribbling ball around object, and returning to starting point. (*Left center*) Two-man pass drill. (*Right center*) Trapping drill. Players trap ball passed to them by leader. (*Right*) Trap and kick drill.

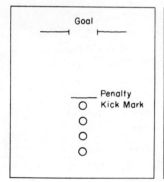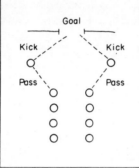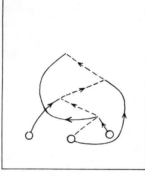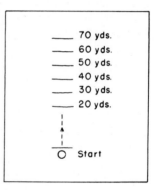

FIGURES 22-19 through 22-22. (*Left*) Penalty kick drill; each player tries five kicks. (*Left center*) Pass and kick drill. (*Right center*) Three-man weave. Player passes ball to man in front and then goes behind him. (*Right*) Kick for distance.

permitted in tackling. Tackling is executed by approaching an opponent from the front and gaining possession of the ball by intercepting it with an appropriate foot tackle as the ball leaves the opponent's foot. The tackles are described as straight, hook, or split, depending on the method employed to intercept the ball.

Soccer is a rugged game requiring a high degree of stamina. Because of the speed with which the game is played and the complexity of situations that arise in competition, there are few rules governing skills and techniques that operate in all situations. The player must be able to adapt his style of play to meet the situation as it arises. (For elementary soccer drills, see Figs. 22-15 through 22-22.)

PLAYING STRATEGY

Teamwork, coupled with individual skill, is the key to a winning combination in soccer. Because of the large area to be covered on a soccer field, it is essential that position play be mastered. Teams that allow all their players to congregate in one section of the field will find themselves at a great disadvantage in combating teams which practice position play. Playing the ball as soon as it can be reached, short passing, quick throw-ins, feinting an opponent, blocking, and leading a teammate when passing the ball to him are common-sense strategies employed by all winning teams. Throw-in plays, kick-off plays, corner kicks, and goal kicks should

282

all be worked out before game time and tried out in practice sessions. Finding the weaknesses in the opponent's play, looking for the man who tires or is slow, and directing the attack toward these vulnerable points is good soccer strategy.

PLAY OF THE GOALKEEPER. The goalkeeper represents the last line of defense, and if the ball gets by him all is lost. Since the goalkeeper may use his hands on the ball, he should always catch fly balls and stop bounding balls with his hands when he has time to use this method. When the play is close to the goal and the offense is pressing hard in an effort to score, it may be necessary for the goalkeeper to kick the ball out of dangerous territory. In such cases the ball should be kicked out toward the wings and not directly up the field, since this minimizes the opponents' chances of returning the ball. The goalkeeper may stand for long periods with little or no activity, but when the play calls for action on his part he must make decisions quickly and accurately. He must decide whether to rush out and play the ball or wait near the goal line and try to intercept the ball on an attempted scoring play. It is a good policy always to be in a position to go and meet the ball rather than be forced to run back for it.

PLAY OF THE HALFBACK. The halfback is the backbone of the soccer team. He will have to do more running than any other player and must, therefore, be in excellent physical condition. The halfback must be able to dribble, tackle, and pass accurately. He must know when to back up on defense, when to make a play for interception of the ball, and where to play in relation to his wing men.

PLAY OF THE FULLBACK. One of the most important skills for the fullback to master is that of accurate kicking. He represents the last line of defense in front of the goalkeeper, so must make every effort to intercept the ball before it passes his position. The fullback must study the style of play employed by the offensive wings and be ready to meet any situation that arises. He should remember that defense is his primary responsibility, and after intercepting the ball his next assignment is to get it to his teammates, who are responsible for advancing it down the field.

PLAY OF THE FORWARD LINE. The players in the forward line consist of center, inside left, inside right, outside left, and outside right. The forward line constitutes the offensive element of the team, and it is the duty of these players to advance the ball into scoring territory. Two styles of play are usually employed by soccer teams in advancing the ball down the field; one involves the fast, long passing game and the other a short passing game. Ama-

teur players frequently use the long passing game while professionals prefer the short passing style. An effective offense makes judicious use of both systems. The short passing game permits more effective control of the ball and its successful execution requires players who are expert in dribbling, passing, and shooting.

Soccer is a game for everyone. You don't have to be tall to play it, as in basketball; neither do you have to weigh 200 pounds or more, as in football. Men soccer players usually weigh from 145 to 175 pounds and range in height from 5 feet 6 inches to 6 feet 1 inch. The one thing that is essential, however, is physical fitness. It has been estimated that a soccer player runs between eight to ten miles during a regulation game. The players on a soccer team are called by the name which best describes the position from which they are called upon to perform during the game. Various formations are used at the start of a game and two traditional ones are indicated below. England won the World Cup in 1966 using the starting formation indicated in Figure 22-23. In this formation you have a goalkeeper, four fullbacks (defenders), three midfield linkmen (halfbacks), and three strikers (forwards). In Figure 22-24 the team has a goalkeeper, four defenders (fullbacks), two midfield linkmen (halfbacks), and four strikers (forwards). During play each team is constantly shifting from offense to defense as control of the ball shifts from one team to another.

FIGURE 22-23.   FIGURE 22-24.

The game requires a minimum of equipment and is truly an international sport, being played in more countries than any other team activity.

SAFETY

Soccer can be played to a safer degree by adhering to some of the following rules.

1. Know the game. Learn all rules pertaining to play and equipment.

2. Do not jump at an opponent.

OFFICIAL SOCCER SIGNALS

1. GOAL
2. OFF SIDE
3. TRIPPING
4. STRIKING
5. JUMPING
6. HANDLING BALL
7. HOLDING
8. PUSHING
9. CHARGING VIOLENTLY. CHARGING—BEHIND.
10. GOALKEEPER CARRYING BALL
11. DANGEROUS PLAY
12. BALL DEAD
13. TIME OUT
14. CORNER KICK Point to corner flag on side kick is to be taken.
15. INDIRECT KICK Forward underarm swing point direction of kick (1 arm).
16. DIRECT KICK Forward underarm swing both arms point direction of kick.
17. OBSTRUCTION Hit the chest with palms.
18. PLAY ON

FIGURE 22-25.

3. Do not head low bounding balls with the opposition close by.
4. Do not charge the goalkeeper or try to kick ball while he is holding it.
5. Always keep one foot on ground when kicking.
6. Learn to fall relaxed and roll with your falls.

HELPFUL HINTS

1. Practice ball control by dribbling the ball around the field before and after class periods.
2. Keep your eyes on the ball.
3. Learn to play your position properly.
4. Do not spend all your energy during the first few minutes of the game. Pace yourself.
5. Warm up thoroughly before all games.

6. Learn to use your physical attributes in beating an opponent to the ball.

PLAYING COURTESIES

1. Control your temper. Do not make derogatory remarks to your opponents during a ball game.
2. After a foul, move the required distance from the ball quickly and do not stop to argue with the referee or an opponent.
3. If an opposing player retrieves an out-of-bounds ball for you, wait until he is back on the field of play before you put the ball in play.
4. When the referee blows the whistle for the start of play, line up quickly and be ready for play.
5. Congratulate opponent after all games, whether won or lost.

TERMINOLOGY

Blocking   Girls' rules. Intercepting progress of the ball with some part of the body. It is legal to block with arms and hands if they are in total contact with the body.

Charging   Attempting to unbalance an opponent who possesses the ball or is attempting to gain possession of it.

Corner kick   A kick made by the attacking team from a corner arc. Awarded when the ball is last touched by a defensive player and crosses the goal line without resulting in a score.

Defense kick   Girls' rules. When ball is caused to cross the goal line, outside the goal posts, by a player of the attacking team, it shall be kicked in by any player of the defending team at a point anywhere on the quarter circles marking the penalty area.

Direct free kick   A kick awarded for committing personal fouls and major rule infractions. A goal may be scored from this kick.

Dribbling   A technique of advancing the ball down the field using the feet.

Drop ball   Ball put into play by the referee by dropping it between two opponents. The ball is in play as soon as it touches the ground and a goal may be scored directly following the drop.

Drop kick   A ball dropped to the ground and kicked as it rebounds. Limited to goalkeeper in girls' rules.

Goal   A one-point score for boys (two for girls) resulting when the ball passes entirely over the goal line, between the uprights and under the cross bar.

Goalkeeper   A player assigned to guard the goal. Unlike other players, the goalie may carry the ball while in the penalty area (four steps for boys, two for girls), may also throw it or kick it.

Goal kick   A kick-in made by a member of the defending team from the goal box. Goal kicks are awarded when the ball crosses the goal line without a score having been made and last touched by an offensive player.

Heading   A technique of directing the ball with the head. An important skill employed by competent soccer players.

Indirect free kick   A free kick from which a goal cannot be scored until the ball has been touched by another player. Awarded for minor violations of the rules.

Instep kick   Kick performed by making contact with the ball at the instep of the foot.

Kick-in   Girls' rules. Ball leaving field of play on side lines shall be put into play by a kick-in by a player opposite to the team that caused the ball to go out of bounds.

Kick-off   An indirect free kick used to put the ball in play from the center circle at the beginning of each quarter and after each score.

Live ball   One that has been kicked by a free kick or throw-in, or has touched the ground after a drop, or after a kick-in or roll-in under girls' rules.

Off-side   Refers to the position of a player on the field in relation to his opponents when the ball is put in play.

Penalty kick   A direct free kick made from the penalty mark. Awarded to offensive team for fouls committed by defensive team within its own penalty area.

Personal foul   One which results in a direct free kick (including a penalty kick).

Roll-in   Girls' rules. Method of putting the ball in play by umpire who rolls the ball between two opponents standing five yards apart. Used to start play after a double foul; after two players simultaneously cause ball to go out-of-bounds; and to start play after a temporary suspension.

Save   A good defensive play made by the goalkeeper in which he prevents the scoring of a goal.

Tackling   The process of kicking or attempting to kick the ball away from an opponent. Sliding tackles, in which one or both feet slide in an attempt to tackle the ball, are illegal. Opponents may not be held in tackling.

Touchlines   The side boundary lines on a soccer field. Called sidelines in girls' rules.

Throw-in   A two handed, overhead throw whereby the ball is put into play after crossing the touchlines. Girls use kick-in to put ball in play.

SELECTED REFERENCES

DiClemente, Frank F., *Soccer Illustrated*. New York: A. S. Barnes & Co., Inc., 1955.

Menke, Frank G., *The Encyclopedia of Sports*. New York: A. S. Barnes & Co., Inc., 1963.

Nelson, Richard L., *Soccer For Men*. Dubuque, Iowa: William C. Brown Company, Publishers, 1967.

Official N.C.A.A. Soccer Guide. Phoenix, Ariz.: College Athletics Publishing Service of the National Collegiate Athletic Association (347 East Thomas Road), published annually.

Official N.S.G.W.S. Soccer-Speedball Guide. Washington, D.C.: American Association for Health, Physical Education and Recreation (current edition).

Schmid, Irvin, John L. McKeon, and Melvin Schmid, *Skills and Strategies of Successful Soccer*. Englewood Cliffs, N.J.: Prentice-Hall, Inc., 1968.

Soccer News. New Rochelle, N.Y.: Soccer Publications, Inc., Box 153, published monthly.

Vannier, Maryhelen, and Hally Beth Poindexter, *Individual and Team Sports for Girls and Women* (2nd ed.). Philadelphia: W. B. Saunders Co., 1968.

White, Jess R., *Sports Rules Encyclopedia*. Palo Alto, Calif.: National Press, 1961.

Softball

23

ORIGIN AND DEVELOPMENT

Softball has had the most rapid and remarkable growth of all sports in the United States. Indoor baseball was first played in the United States about 50 years ago, but the game was not played out of doors to any extent until the late 1920's, when the Canadians began to use it on small playground areas. The game developed rapidly in Canada and returned to the United States, where it received impetus from the National Recreation Association. This organization supported the game because of its similarity to baseball and its wide appeal to all ages. The game has been called playground ball, kitten ball, recreation baseball, ladies' baseball, and soft baseball; but, in 1933, the name "softball" was generally adopted and a national tournament was held at the World's Fair in Chicago. Leo H. Fischer and M. J. Pauley were largely responsible for forming the Amateur Softball Association, an organization that made a great contribution to the game by effecting standardization of the rules and conducting national tournaments which attracted teams from all parts of the country.

It is estimated that over 5,000,000 active players engage in the game of softball and spend some $20,000,000 annually for equipment. Because of its wide appeal to all ages of both sexes, the game is increasing in popularity each year and is well on its way to becoming one of the most popular recreational activities in our sports program.

A softball field is small enough to be accommodated on most playgrounds. The bases are not as far apart as in regulation baseball, and the outfield boundary is much shorter. Because of the larger ball (12 inches in circumference) and smaller bat, it is not possible to drive the ball as far as a hard baseball, hence diamonds may be located on areas that would be far too small for baseball. The large ball is less likely to cause finger injuries than the baseball, so the game, while retaining many of the desirable qualities of regulation baseball, is particularly valuable for use on playgrounds and recreational areas. Equipment generally is less expensive than that required for baseball, making softball more acceptable for use in informal groups often found in parks, playgrounds, churches, and other community groups. Although softball lends itself to such informal use, it can be and is played on a level requiring a high degree of individual skill and team strategy; where teams develop these qualities, the game has often provided an attraction for fans that rivals that of baseball.

BASIC RULES

The rules of softball are patterned after those of baseball, making softball as nearly like the parent game as possible. The rules are compiled by an International Joint Rules Committee on Softball composed of representatives from the National Recreation Association, the Amateur Softball Association, the American Association for Health, Physical Education and Recreation, the YMCA, the Division of Girls' and Women's Sports of the AAHPER, the National Industrial Recreation Association, and several members at large. Included below is a brief summary of the rules, but players should study a copy of the Official Rules in order to become familiar with all regulations governing the game.

Equipment

The official bat shall be round and made of one piece of hard wood not more than 34 inches long and not more than two and one-quarter inches in diameter at its largest part.

The official ball shall be a regular smooth-seam concealed stitch or flat surfaced ball, not less than eleven and seven-eighths nor more than twelve and one-eighth inches in circumference and shall weigh not less than six ounces nor more than six

FIGURE 23-1. Pitcher on rubber

and three-fourths ounces. The home plate shall be made of rubber or other suitable material and shall be a five-sided figure 17 inches wide across the side facing the pitcher. The pitcher's plate shall be made of wood or rubber, two feet long and six inches wide, with the front line of the plate 46 feet from home plate for men and 38 feet for women. The bases, other than home plate, shall be made of canvas, or other suitable material, and shall be 15 inches square.

Gloves may be worn by any player, but mitts may be used only by the catcher and the first baseman. Shoes may have uppers of either canvas, leather, or similar materials, and may be equipped with smooth soles or soft or hard rubber cleats. Metal sole and heel plates may be used if they do not extend more than three-fourths of an inch from sole or heel of the shoe. Masks must be worn by catchers behind the plate and women catchers must wear both masks and body protectors.

Players and substitutes

A team shall consist of nine players (ten in "slow pitch") and a team must have a full lineup to start and continue a game. A substitute may take the place of a player whose name is in his team's batting order. A player removed from the game shall not participate in the game again except as coacher.

The game

A regulation game shall consist of seven innings, or of six and one-half innings if the team second at bat has scored more runs than its opponent. A game called by the umpire shall be regulation if five or more innings have been played. The score of a forfeited game shall be 7-0 in favor of the team not at fault.

Pitching regulations

The pitcher shall take a position with both feet firmly on the ground and in contact with the pitcher's plate. Before pitching the pitcher must come to a full and complete stop facing the batter with both shoulders in line with first and third base and with the ball held in both hands in front of the body. (See Fig. 23-1.) The pitcher may not take the pitching position without having the ball in his possession. The pitcher may use any wind-up in his delivery provided he does not stop his forward motion or reverse the direction of the arm swing. The release of the ball and the follow-through of the hand and wrist

FIGURES 23-2 through 23-4. Pitcher's delivery. *Note:* arm alongside of body in center figure.

must be forward past the straight line of the body; and, when the arm passes the body in the forward swing, the hand shall be below the hip and the wrist not farther from the body than the elbow. (See Figs. 23-2, 23-3, and 23-4.)

Batting

The batter must stand within the confines of the batter's box and may be called out for stepping on or over the lines. Players must bat in regular order as indicated in the starting lineup. Batting out of order is an appeal play and if the error is discovered while the incorrect batter is at the plate, the correct batter must take his place and assume the ball and strike count held by the incorrect batter. If the error is discovered after the incorrect batter has completed his turn at bat and before there has been a pitch to another batter, the player who should have batted is out, and the next batter is the player whose name follows that of the player declared out. Any runs scored are canceled and base runners must return to bases held when the incorrect batter came to the plate. If the error is not discovered until after a pitch is made to the next batter, no one is declared out.

A foul tip is a foul ball which goes directly from the bat, not higher than the batter's head, to the catcher's hands. The ball is in play and base runners may advance with liability to be put out.

The batter shall be declared out when he hits an infield fly with runners on first and second, or on first, second, and third with less than two outs.

Base running

Base runners must touch the bases in regular order and if forced to return while the ball is in play, the bases must be touched in reverse order. If two players find themselves on one base at the same time the player first on the base is legally entitled to it and the other player must return or be put out. A base runner is out for running more than three feet from a direct line between bases in regular or reverse order to avoid being tagged with the ball in the hand of a fielder, or for passing a preceding base runner before that runner has been put out. The base runner is also out if he leaves his base before the ball leaves the pitcher's hand.

Dead ball

The ball is dead and not in play under the following circumstances: on an illegally batted ball; when batter steps from one box to another as pitcher is ready to pitch; on an illegal pitch; when a pitched ball touches any part of the batter's person; when a foul ball is not caught; when a base runner is called out for leaving a base too soon; when a block ball is declared; and when a wild pitch or passed ball goes over, under, or through the backstop.

Scoring

A base hit results when a batted ball permits a hitter to reach first base safely when no fielding error is involved. A base hit shall not be recorded when a base runner is forced out by a batted ball, or would have been forced out, except for a fielding error.

Sacrifices are scored when with less than two out the batter advances one or more base runners with a bunt and is retired at first base, or when runners are advanced after a fair fly ball is caught.

Assists are scored to each player who handles the ball in any play or series of plays which results in a put-out, but only one assist is credited to a player in any one put-out.

Errors are recorded for the player who commits a misplay that prolongs the turn at bat of the batter or the life of the base runner.

Put-outs are credited to players who catch a batted fly ball, catch a thrown ball that retires a base runner, or touch a base runner with the ball while the runner is off the bag.

Winning and losing pitcher

A pitcher shall be credited with a win if he starts and pitches at least five innings and his team is not only in the lead when he is replaced but remains in the lead the remainder of the game. When a game is ended after five innings of play and the starting pitcher has pitched at least three innings and his team scores more runs than the other team when the game is terminated, he shall be declared the winner.

"SLOW PITCH SOFTBALL"

In the "slow pitch" version of softball certain deviations from the above rules are observed. In brief, these differences are:

1. No stealing of bases is permitted.
2. The base runner cannot leave his base until the pitched ball has crossed home plate.
3. Bunting is not allowed.
4. In delivering the ball the pitcher must throw it with moderate speed, below the hip, and with a perceptible arch (from the time it leaves the pitcher's hand) of at least two feet and not more than ten feet above the ground, before the ball reaches home plate.
5. A team shall be composed of ten instead of nine players.

TECHNIQUES AND FUNDAMENTALS

Softball, while adaptable for general recreational use, is a game that demands a good performance of certain fundamental skills and techniques if one hopes to play on a first-class team. One will find that enjoyment from participation in the game intensifies as skill increases. A careful study of the suggestions outlined here should help give a clearer picture of correct techniques necessary for performance of the fundamental skills. Observance of these suggestions while on the playing field under the guidance of an instructor should enable one to improve the quality of his play.

THROWING. This is a natural activity ordinarily engaged in by most boys and girls, but not all persons throw correctly. A player certainly will not be an asset to his team if he throws poorly. Throws should be made quickly, accurately, and to the correct base. Players should be able to throw using an overhand, sidearm, or underhand motion, but more time should be spent on perfecting the

FIGURE 23-5.
Overarm throw

FIGURE 23-6.
Follow-through

FIGURES 23-7 through 23-9. (*Left*) Fielder's stance while waiting for the ball. (*Center*) Fielding the ball. (*Right*) Catching the ball above the waist.

overhand throw than any other because with it one can attain the greatest accuracy. (See Figs. 23-5 and 23-6.) Practice throwing for accuracy when warming up and always concentrate on hitting the target whether throwing for fun or in competition. Use a natural rhythmical movement and step toward the target with the left foot when making a right-handed throw.

FIELDING THE BALL. Catching the ball is another fundamental that players must master if they expect to be on a team when sides are chosen. When catching ground balls, the fingers should always be pointed down. The ground ball should be watched closely and played so that it is caught just after the peak of the bounce, or just as it comes off the ground on the start of a hop. The body should face the ball in such a position that the ball is caught in the front of the center of the body. (See Fig. 23-7.) "Centering of the ball" enables one to handle balls that may take bad bounces to the right or left, and the body may be used to block the ball if it should be missed with the hands. Ordinarily, ground balls should be fielded with the feet apart, the knees slightly bent, and the body crouched, but on hard hit balls it may be advisable to close the feet or drop on one knee to block the ball. While ground balls and fly balls below the waist should be caught with the fingers pointed down, it is advisable to point the fingers up when catching fly balls above the waist. (See Fig. 23-9.)

BATTING. The key to offensive baseball lies in effective use of the bat, coupled with base running. To become effective in hitting the ball, there are certain fundamentals that should be observed. Occasionally good hitters will deviate from some of these suggestions, but one will find it helpful to follow these rules for hitting. (See Figs. 23-10 through 23-12.)

1. Assume a comfortable stance at the plate with feet apart and arms away from the body to allow complete freedom in swinging the bat.

2. Swing the bat parallel to the ground and follow through with the swing.

3. Refrain from taking a long stride; if a step is taken, make it a short one and step directly toward the pitcher. A long stride may cause one to swing under the ball.

4. Keep the bat poised in the air ready to swing if the ball is in the strike area. Don't rest the bat on the shoulder while waiting for the pitch.

5. Keep rear foot steady. Don't dance around in the batter's box.

6. Keep looking at the ball from the minute the pitcher starts his wind up until it reaches the plate.

7. Don't swing too hard.

8. Swing only at good pitches—balls that cross the strike area.

9. Select a bat that feels comfortable and use a grip that insures complete control of the bat at all times.

10. Be on the way to first base as soon as the ball is hit. John McGraw used to say that "pennants are won and lost by that last step to first base."

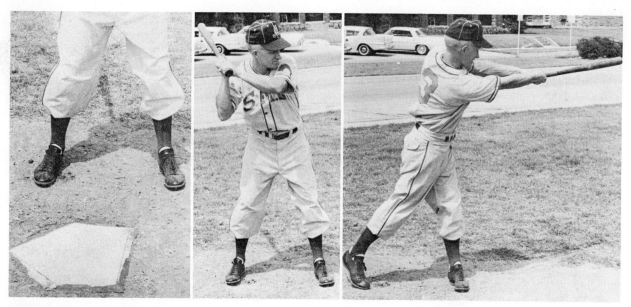

FIGURES 23-10 through 23-12. (*Left*) Stance at the plate. (*Center*) Bat poised, ready to swing. (*Right*) Follow-through, body under control, both feet on ground.

FIGURE 23-13. Sacrifice bunt position; feet pointing toward the pitcher, bat parallel to ground

BUNTING. This is an effective offensive weapon in softball. Although the fielders are closer to the batter in softball than in baseball, it takes just as much time to field and throw a softball as a baseball. Therefore, the batter in softball should have a slight advantage over the baseball player in using the bunt as a means of reaching first base safely.

The easiest bunting position is one in which the player faces the pitcher with the bat extended over the plate parallel to the ground, in such a po-sition that the ball may be directed toward first or third. The bat should not be swung at the ball but should remain stationary over the plate where it makes contact with the ball. (See Fig. 23-13.)

BASE RUNNING. Because of the short dis-tance between bases, certain restrictions are placed on the runner in softball that are not applicable in baseball. The runner must hold his base until the ball leaves the pitcher's hand before starting for the next base. Preparatory to advancing to the next base (whether on a steal or a batted ball), the runner should stand with one foot on the base in a sprinter's start, ready to leave the instant the pitcher releases the ball. When advancing from first to second, watch the third-base coach for directions. The coach is usually in a better position to see the entire field of play and tell the runner whether to stop at second or continue on to third base. Concentrate on hitting the base with one foot when running for extra bases, and stay close to the base line. Running in a wide circle outside the base lines takes too much time.

Runners should learn to slide correctly in order to keep from overrunning a base, and to prevent injury. The hook slide, performed by sliding on the thighs and hips while touching the bag with the left foot when sliding to the right side of the bag, is an effective technique and provides a small target for the fielder. In performing this slide, be careful to keep the right leg bent or extended in the air to prevent spikes from catching in the ground and injuring ankles and knees. Start the slide early enough to slide into the bag and not strike it with full force. The left leg should slide on the ground

FIGURES 23-14 through 23-16. (*Left*) Hook slide. (*Center*) Bent leg slide.

in approaching the bag in such a fashion that the front of the toe hooks the bag. (See Fig. 23-14.) The bent leg slide is used by players who wish to get to their feet quickly in order to advance to another base on an overthrow or misplay. In this slide the player slides on his bent, underneath leg with the upper leg making contact with base. The forward momentum of the slide is utilized to raise the body to an upright position after making contact with the base. (See Fig. 23-15.) Never attempt to slide in competition until the sliding technique is perfected by practice in a soft place, such as a sliding pit.

PITCHING. This is the only skill in softball that differs radically from regulation baseball. Certain restrictions are imposed upon the softball pitcher, because of the short distance between the pitcher's rubber and home plate. The pitcher in softball must use an underarm motion in delivering the ball to the batter.

FOOTWORK OF FIRST BASEMAN. The first baseman must learn to perform the proper footwork when receiving thrown balls at first base from the other infielders. After the ball has been hit to an infielder, the first baseman should rush to his bag and take a position on the inside of the base with his heels just touching the inside corner of the bag. (See Fig. 23-17.) After the infielder throws the ball, the first baseman performs his shift according to the direction of the thrown ball. If the ball comes toward the outfield side of the bag, the first baseman steps toward second or outfield side of the base with his right foot and touches the bag with his left foot. (See Fig. 23-18.) If the throw is toward the home plate side of first base, he reverses the process, stepping into the diamond toward home plate with his left foot and touching the base with his right foot. (See Fig. 23-19.)

SECOND BASE PLAY. The second baseman may take throws from other infielders at second

FIGURES 23-17 through 23-19. (*Left*) First baseman ready to receive throw. (*Center*) Taking throw to his right. (*Right*) Taking throw to his left.

FIGURE 23-20. Ready to receive the pitch

FIGURE 23-21. Ready to throw to a base

base, using footwork similar to that described for the first baseman, when a third-out force is made at second and no further throw is required. On an attempted double play when the second baseman is taking a throw from the third base side of the diamond, he must touch the bag, pivot, and throw to first base. If the second baseman has sufficient time, he may take a position on the third base side of second, similar to that employed by the first baseman, step with his right foot toward the throw, tag the base with his left, and then step with his left foot into the infield and toward first to complete the throw to first base. If the second baseman arrives late at the bag, he may have to hit the bag with his right foot as he catches the ball, then step into the infield and toward first with his left foot as he pivots and completes the throw to first base. In any event, he must maneuver so as to avoid contact with the runner coming down from first base.

The shortstop usually has a longer distance to run when taking throws at second on an attempted double play, therefore he should learn to catch the ball on the run, tag the bag, and throw to first. One method is to strike the bag with the right foot, hop with this foot toward the outfield side of the bag so as to avoid the runner, and then step toward first with the left foot in completing the throw to first. Both the second baseman and shortstop should practice on their footwork until they are able to make the put-out at second and continue the ball toward first base without being upset by the base runner.

CATCHING. The catcher is frequently called the "defensive center of the infield" because he not only handles all pitched balls, but is the only infielder who can see all infield proceedings all of the time. The catcher should wear a mask and an appropriate catcher's mitt. (See Figs. 23-20, 23-21.) He should direct the infield play by calling "infield flies," tell the pitcher and other infielders where to throw the ball on bunts, and keep all players informed of the number of outs. With runners on base he must exercise every effort to stop all wild pitches and help steady the defense by directing the pitcher's throwing pace during a streak of wildness, or during display of offensive power by the batters.

PLAYING STRATEGY

Softball permits most of the team strategies used in baseball. The winning team is one that not only masters individual fundamentals but functions as a unit in the execution of team plays. The team should understand and be able to execute the following offensive plays:

1. *Sacrifice bunt.* This play is usually executed with runners on first, or first and second, with none out. The batter bunts the ball toward first or third in an effort to advance the runners one base, in order to get them in scoring position and prevent the possibility of a double play set-up on the next hitter. In softball, however, the bunt may be used as an offensive weapon at any time, regardless of the number of outs, when there is a fast man at the plate.

2. *Hit and run.* In this play, the runners start for the next base on the pitch and the batter tries

to hit the ball between first and second behind the runner, in order to make it more difficult to retire the advancing base runners. A runner on first can often go to third on a single made to right field.

3. *Squeeze play.* With a runner on third in the late stages of a close game with less than two out, it may be advisable to attempt to score the runner on a bunt. In this play, the runner starts for home on the pitch and the batter bunts the ball on the ground. If the ball is bunted properly, this play will prove successful in most instances. The squeeze play may be used in any stage of the game with a runner on third and a weak hitter at the plate.

4. *Double steal.* This play is usually executed with runners on first and second, or first and third. In the latter case, the play may be used to score a run if the catcher throws the ball through to second base in an effort to retire the runner coming from first.

5. *Delayed steal.* In this play, the runner does not start for the next base until the catcher has caught the ball and has started his motion to return the ball to the pitcher. Seeing the runner break for the next base, the catcher must repeat his throwing action in making his throw to a base. A variation of this play calls for the runner to break just as the ball leaves the catcher's hand in his throw to the pitcher, requiring the pitcher to turn and relay the ball to the proper base. These plays succeed best against mechanical batterymen who do not watch the runners closely.

SIGNALS. In order to use the above plays effectively, teams should have a set of offensive signals so that the players concerned may know what play is to be executed. Signals are usually given by one of the baseline coaches, usually the third base coach. On some plays, e.g., the hit and run, the batter may give the signal.

DEFENSIVE STRATEGY. In order to combat offensive team plays, the defense must have a specific plan ready to meet any situation that may arise. In combating the sacrifice bunt with a runner on first, the first and third basemen, along with the pitcher, should play in close, ready to field the ball if it is bunted in their direction. The second baseman should cover first and the shortstop, second. With runners on first and second, the third baseman should cover his base for a possible force-out at that base, unless the ball is bunted so far to the pitcher's right that he can't field the ball, in which case the third baseman must come in and field the ball. Good defensive play requires a high degree of cooperation among all defensive players who keep one another informed by calling out plays, backing up bases for overthrows, and not throwing the ball unless absolutely necessary.

SAFETY

The following safety procedures should be observed in order to minimize the possibility of injuries:

1. Grip the bat tightly so it will not slip from your hands when swinging at the ball. Other players should always keep in mind the possibility that the batter may lose control of the bat, and they should station themselves where they will not be hit.
2. Catchers should always wear a mask. The game may be called "softball," but the ball is hard enough to break your nose.
3. Perfect a sliding technique before trying to slide in competition. This precaution will help eliminate skin abrasions and broken bones.
4. Use a glove; it will enable you to catch the ball more effectively and minimize broken fingers.
5. Wear proper equipment.
6. Warm up thoroughly before beginning competition—and don't throw too much in early season until your arm is in condition.

HELPFUL HINTS

1. Learn the rules and follow the instruction of your coach or teacher.
2. If you are having particular difficulty with certain skills, take extra time to master these fundamentals.
3. Learn to slide in a sawdust or sand pit before trying to slide in competition on a hard diamond.

PLAYING COURTESIES

1. While a certain amount of "razzing" is apparently an integral part of baseball and softball, it is certainly not sportsmanlike conduct to direct words of personal abuse toward any opponent.
2. Tell the base runner that it is not necessary to slide if you can see there is no possible play at the base you are protecting.
3. Accept without complaint decisions of the umpires that involve judgment. If a rule violation

is concerned, let your team captain discuss the matter with the umpires.

4. Never deliberately spike an opponent. No game is important enough to tolerate tactics designed to injure the participants.

TERMINOLOGY

Assist Credit an assist to each player who throws or deflects (with hand or glove) a thrown or batted ball in which a put-out results, or would have resulted except for a subsequent error by a teammate.

Battery Pitcher and catcher. Hence they are each other's *battery-mates*.

Batting average Number of hits divided by times at bat.

Bean ball A ball pitched at or near the batter's head in order to frighten him away from the plate.

Clean-up Usually the fourth position in the batting order and occupied by the team's heaviest hitter.

Double-play Two consecutive put-outs occurring between the time the ball leaves the pitcher's hand and its return to him, except when an error intervenes between the two put-outs.

Double steal Two base runners stealing a base at the same time.

Earned run Runs scored as a result of base hits, sacrifice hits, stolen bases, put-outs, bases on balls, hit batter, wild pitches, and balks before fielding chances have been offered to retire the side.

Error Charged against a player when a misplay prolongs the life of a base runner or batter, or permits a runner to advance a base, when perfect play would have resulted in batter or runner being retired.

Fielder's choice When defensive player elects to retire a base runner rather than the batter on a batted ball.

Fielding average Put-outs, assists, and errors divided into put-outs and assists.

Fungo bat Light-weight bat used in hitting balls to fielders in practice.

Hit Ball hit in such a way that batter or preceding base runners may not be retired by good defensive play.

Hot corner Third base.

Infield fly With runners on first and second, or on first, second, and third with less than two down, a fly ball hit that can be handled by the infielders. Batter is out.

Initial sack First base.

"In the hole" Having an unfavorable count when batting or pitching. If the count is two strikes and no balls, the batter is "in the hole." Also used to describe the player who is two turns away from batting.

Keystone sack Second base.

On deck Player in line to follow hitter at the plate; just ahead of the player "in the hole."

Passed ball Charged against catcher when he fails to hold a pitch he should have controlled and base runner is permitted to advance. An error, and not a passed ball, is charged if catcher drops third strike and permits batter to reach first base.

Portsider Left-handed pitcher; also called south-paw.

Put-out Credited to the fielder who last handles the ball on a play that retires a base runner. Automatic put-outs are credited to defensive players on certain violations by base runners and batters.

Running squeeze Runner on third starts for home with the pitch, hoping batter will bunt the ball safely on the ground.

Sacrifice bunt Batter bunts ball to advance base runner and is himself thrown out, or would have been if played properly.

Sacrifice fly Credited to batter who hits a fly to the outfield permitting runner to advance a base after the catch.

Safety squeeze Runner on third starts for home after batter bunts the ball.

Stolen base Base runner advancing without aid of a base hit, put-out, force-out, fielder's choice, passed ball, wild pitch, or balk. On attempted double or triple steal, no one is credited with a stolen base if one player is thrown out.

Switch hitter Batter who bats both right- and left-handed.

Texas leaguer Fly ball hit over heads of infielders that falls safely between infield and outfield.

Three and one A count of three balls and one strike on the batter.

Three for four Three hits out of four times at bat.

Wild pitch Ball, legally delivered by pitcher, so wide of the plate that catcher cannot handle it.

SELECTED REFERENCES

Coombs, Jack, *Baseball* (revised by Danny Litwhiler) (4th ed.). Englewood Cliffs, N.J.: Prentice-Hall, Inc., 1967.

Fait, Hollis, John Shaw, and Katherine Ley, *A Manual of Physical Education Activities* (3rd ed.). Philadelphia: W. B. Saunders Co., 1967.

Kneer, Marion E., and Charles L. McCord, *Softball.* Dubuque, Iowa: William C. Brown Company, Publishers, 1966.

Litwhiler, Danny, *Baseball Coach's Guide to Drills and Skills.* Englewood Cliffs, N.J.: Prentice-Hall, Inc., 1963.

Meyer, M. H., and M. M. Schwarz, *Team Sports for Girls and Women* (4th ed.). Philadelphia: W. B. Saunders Co., 1965.

Official Guide and Rule Book. Newark, N.J.: Amateur Softball Association and International Joint Rules Committee for Softball, published annually.

Official Softball—Track and Field Guide. Washington, D.C.: N.S.G.W.S. Guide, American Association for Health, Physical Education and Recreation (current edition).

Reichler, Joe, *Ronald Encyclopedia of Baseball.* New York: The Ronald Press Company, 1962.

Vannier, Maryhelen, and Hally Beth Poindexter, *Individual and Team Sports for Girls and Women* (2nd ed.). Philadelphia: W. B. Saunders Co., 1968.

White, Jess R., *Sports Rules Encyclopedia.* Palo Alto, Calif.: National Press, 1961.

Speedball

24

ORIGIN AND DEVELOPMENT

The game of speedball was developed by E. D. Mitchell at the University of Michigan in the early 1920's because of the need for a vigorous team game that could be played outdoors in the fall and that combined many of the elements found in other rather well-known sports. Many of the boys and girls who had gone to high school in the Middle West had been introduced to basketball in public schools and did not like soccer very well because of the restrictions regarding the use of the hands on the ball. Touch football, while a popular game, has certain limitations in that many players on the team did not get to handle the ball regularly. Speedball eliminated many of these objections by providing a game that permitted all the players to participate in all aspects of the game. The game has developed rapidly and is now a widely played sport in physical education and intramural programs throughout the country.

NATURE OF THE GAME

The game of speedball is played on an outdoor area comparable in size to the touch football or soccer field. The ball used is slightly larger than a soccer ball. Many schools use a soccer ball instead of the regulation speedball. The ball is put in play by a kick-off at the center of the field and may be advanced down the field by dribbling with the feet as in soccer, or by passing from player to player as in basketball, or by punting.

Eleven players constitute a regulation team, but the game may be played with a smaller number. When a smaller number of players is used, the tempo of the game is increased for individual players. No special equipment is needed for the game other than a field and a ball so the game is readily adapted for use on playgrounds and other recreational areas.

BASIC RULES

The official game consists of four quarters, with a ten-minute rest interval between halves, and a two-minute rest interval between quarters in each half. Time-out may be taken three times during a game; an additional time-out constitutes a technical foul for boys, or a team foul in girls' rules. Officials are a referee and two linesmen.

Women should refer to the *Official N.S.G.W.S. Soccer-Speedball Guide* (latest edition) and men to

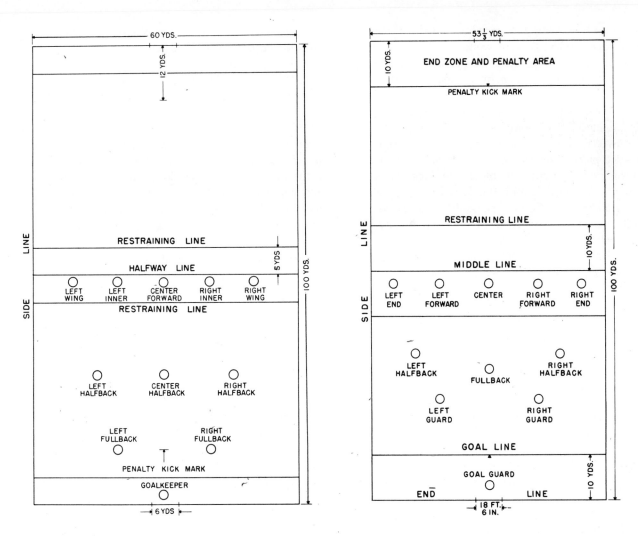

FIGURE 24-1, 24-2. (*Left*) Diagram of women's speedball field, showing names of players in position. (*Right*) Diagram of men's speedball field, showing names of players in position.

the *Official Speedball Guide* for a complete text of the rules. In general the rules are similar, but different terms are used in women's rules to describe certain fouls, e.g., personal fouls in men's rules are called individual type fouls in the women's version, while technical fouls are called team type fouls. There is also considerable variation in the enforcement of fouls. Individual skills and styles of team play are similar for both men and women.

Fields vary in size from 80 to 100 yards in length. (See Figs. 24-1 and 24-2.) In front of each goal post and extending across the field is a penalty area, and fouls committed in this area by the defense are penalized more severely than fouls committed outside the area.

The ball is put in play by a free kick at the center of the field and all members of the kicking team must be behind the ball when it is kicked. The ball must travel forward the length of its circumfer-

ence before it may be recovered by the offense. Defensive players must remain behind the restraining line, ten yards distant, until the ball is kicked. When a team causes a ball to go out of bounds on the sidelines, the opponents may put the ball into play by a pass. If the ball goes over the end lines without a score resulting, the opponents may put the ball in play by a pass or a kick. In the event of a "tie ball" where two players are contesting for possession of the ball, the ball is put in play by the official with a jump ball between the contesting players, as in basketball.

SCORING

Scoring may be accomplished by five methods in boys' rules; four methods in girls' rules.

FIELD GOAL. Ground ball kicked under the

cross bar and between the uprights. Counts three points in men's rules, two for women.

DROP KICK. Over the cross bar from outside the penalty area; counts one point for men, three for women.

TOUCHDOWN. Ball passed from field of play to a teammate back of goal line; counts two points.

PENALTY KICK. An attempt to score a goal by offended player from the penalty kick mark. Goalkeeper only may attempt to block the kick; boys must stand on end line until ball is kicked, girls must stand behind end line. Counts one point, if successful.

END GOAL. Applicable in boys' rules only. Ground ball that receives its impetus (kicked or legally bodied) from any player, offensive or defensive, in the end zone and passes over the end line but not between the goal posts. Counts one point.

PLAYING PRIVILEGES

AERIAL OR FLY BALL. The ball may be caught, or otherwise played with the hands, whenever it is clearly a "fly ball"; i.e., one that has been raised into the air directly from a kick by one or both feet. A ball thus raised into the air remains a fly ball until it again hits the ground. A fly ball that has been caught may be held, passed, punted, drop-kicked, or played as an overhead dribble, at option. A loose fly ball (not in the possession of a player) may not be kicked or "kneed" (permissible in women's rules), but otherwise may be played in any manner by the hands or body.

GROUND BALL. A ground ball is one that is stationary, rolling, or bouncing. Even though it may be in the air, as in the case when it is bouncing, the ball is ruled a ground ball until it is in the air from a direct kick. While a ground ball, it cannot be played with the hands or any part of the arms, but must be kicked, "headed," or bounced off the body.

DRIBBLING THE BALL. A player may dribble the ball with his feet at will. He may bat or tap a fly ball, or drop a caught fly ball to the ground and play it as a drop kick or kicking dribble.

A player may use one overhead dribble in advancing the ball without the aid of his teammates; that is, he may throw the ball in any direction and run and catch it before it strikes the ground. He may not score a touchdown by this method.

A player kicking the ball into the air is eligible to catch it before it hits the ground. In order to be eligible for such a catch, the player must give some impetus to the ball. If he stands still and merely permits the ball to hit his feet and bound upward, it is not considered a kicked ball. The foot or feet must actually leave the ground as the ball is lifted upward and the ball must have left the foot before being touched with the hands.

GOALTENDER. There is no distinction between the goaltender and the other players as regards privileges and restrictions in playing the ball.

TRAVELING. A player who is standing still when catching the ball from a kick or pass may take one step in any direction from the point at which he caught the ball, but must get rid of the ball before a second step is completed. If running, he is allowed two steps, and if at full speed the referee shall decide whether he stopped as soon as possible. Violations of this rule are known as "carrying the ball." A player cannot take a step over the goal line to score. He must be completely over the line when the ball is caught in order to score.

DEFENSIVE PLAY. A player may legally guard an opponent who has the ball. He must play to secure the ball, and in no way hold an opponent.

TIE BALL. In case a ball is held by two opposing players simultaneously, or where the officials are in doubt about which side last played the ball out-of-bounds, the official declares a "tie ball."

No score may result from a tip-off that is caught in the end zone, although the ball is still in play.

A tie ball at the center of the field is used to commence play after a double foul or at the beginning of an overtime period. (Jump ball at spot of foul for double foul in women's rules.)

PLAYING RESTRICTIONS (MEN'S RULES)

1. *Personal Fouls*

   (a) Kicking, tripping, charging, pushing, holding, or blocking an opponent.

   (b) Unnecessary roughness of any description.

2. *Technical Fouls*

   (a) Making an illegal substitution.

   (b) Taking more than three time-outs in a game.

   (c) Unsportsmanlike conduct.

   (d) Either team having more than 11 men on the field at one time.

   (e) Unnecessarily delaying the game. This includes persistent interference on out-of-bounds plays and unreasonable delay in taking positions on free kicks, penalty kicks, etc.

3. Violations

(a) Carrying the ball (also popularly known as "steps" or "traveling").

(b) Touching a ground ball with the hands or arms.

(c) Making two successive overhead dribbles.

(d) Violating the kick-off rules.

(e) Violating the penalty kick restrictions.

(f) Violating out-of-bounds rules by offensive player when returning the ball to field of play.

(g) Violating the tie ball rule.

(h) Kicking or kneeing a fly ball unless player had first caught it. (If opposing player is kicked or kneed in such an attempt, a personal foul is charged against the offender.)

PENALTIES AND THEIR ENFORCEMENT

1. Personal Fouls

(a) In case a personal foul is committed by a player outside his own penalty area, the opponents are awarded one penalty kick to penalize the personal contact. The offended player attempts the kick. If missed, the ball is dead and a touchback is declared.

(b) In case a personal foul is committed by a player within his own penalty area or end zone, the opponents are awarded two penalty kicks, one without a follow-up, to penalize the personal contact; the second, with a follow-up, to afford a chance to recover the score that the foul may have prevented. The offended player must attempt the kicks.

    (1) The ball is dead after the first attempt in all cases.

    (2) The ball is in play after the second attempt if it is missed.

2. Technical Fouls

(a) In case a technical foul is committed by a player outside his own penalty area, the opponents are awarded one penalty kick. Any member of the offended team may attempt the kick. The ball is dead on this play and no follow-up is allowed. If missed, a touchback is awarded.

(b) In case a technical foul is committed by a player inside his own penalty area, the opponents are awarded one penalty kick. Any member of the offended team may attempt the kick. As soon as the ball is kicked, it is considered in play and a follow-up is permitted.

3. Violations

(a) In case a violation is committed by a player outside his own penalty area, the opponents are awarded the ball out of bounds.

(b) In case a violation is committed by a player inside his own penalty area, the opponents are awarded a penalty kick, with the opportunity of a follow-up if missed. Such a violation is considered as possibly depriving the attacking team of a chance to score and therefore is penalized by a penalty kick with a follow-up.

PLAYING RESTRICTIONS (WOMEN'S RULES) [2]

Rule 13, Section 1 of the *Official Soccer-Speedball Guide* states that individual-type fouls shall include:

(a) Kicking, tripping, charging, pushing, obstructing, holding, blocking an opponent, or boxing up.

(b) Unnecessary roughness.

(c) Unnecessarily delaying the game.

(d) Traveling with the ball.

(e) Touching a ground ball with the hands or arms.

(f) Juggling the ball more than once.

(g) Holding the ball more than three seconds on the field.

(h) Drop-kicking for a goal or attempting a forward pass for a touchdown while within the penalty area.

Section 2 states that team-type fouls shall include:

(a) Taking more than three time-outs in a game.

(b) Having more than 11 players from the same team on the field at the same time.

(c) Failure to report to the scorer or umpire before going into the game.

[2] From the *Official N.S.G.W.S. Soccer-Speedball Guide*, latest edition, published by the American Association for Health, Physical Education and Recreation.

PENALTIES FOR FOULS (WOMEN'S RULES)

SECTION 1 of the *Official Guide* states that individual-type fouls are made by:

(a) A player outside her own penalty area: A free kick where the foul occurred.

(b) A player within her own penalty area, or behind own goal line: One penalty kick.

(c) An attacking player behind opponent's goal line: A free kick on the goal line opposite the place where the foul occurred.

SECTION 2.   Team-type fouls shall award the opponent one penalty kick each.

SECTION 3.   A player may be disqualified and removed from the game if she plays roughly or dangerously, or after being warned that she is displaying poor sportsmanship. A free kick or a penalty kick, as the case may be, is awarded the opponents.

SECTION 4.   Double foul made anywhere on the field including the penalty area: A toss-up where the fouls occurred between two offenders.

Double foul behind the goal line: A toss-up between the two offenders on the five-yard line opposite the place where the fouls occurred.

TECHNIQUES AND FUNDAMENTALS

FOOT DRIBBLE.   This is an effective method of moving the ball down the field, especially in crowded quarters where an individual pick-up or kick to a teammate is not advisable. One should keep the ball under control at all times, which means the ball must not be kicked with force but controlled by the feet, and kept close to the player. Players should use the inside of the foot to propel and guide the ball.

FIGURES 24-3 through 24-6. Lifting the ball in two-foot pickup

FIGURES 24-7 through 24-9. (*Left*) Start of one-foot pickup. (*Center*) Ball in midair. (*Right*) Completion of one-foot pickup.

FIGURES 24-10 through 24-14. The foot-toss pickup from start to finish

PASSING. This aspect of the game differs from soccer and permits a passing attack as in basketball. All types of basketball passes may be used in speedball with the baseball pass used extensively because of the wide playing area involved. Players should drill on the various types of passes from both the stationary and running positions.

PLACE KICKING. A place kick is used in attempting to score after a foul has been committed by an opponent. The player should practice for accuracy on this play in order that he may kick the ball past the goaltender, the only player who is permitted to block the try for the goal.

DROP KICKING. The round speedball is easier to drop kick for accuracy than the football because it is not necessary to strike the ground with the ball at any particular point; being round, the speedball always rebounds the same. Bend forward when dropping the ball so the ball drops only a short distance before striking the ground.

PUNTING. It is often advantageous for a player to punt the ball down the field in order to get it into scoring territory as quickly as possible. The techniques involved in punting a speedball are similar to those in punting a football. The ball should be kicked with the upper part of the instep and again, since the ball is round, it need not always be released with a certain side facing the foot, as in football. Players should practice punting and catching the ball by arranging teammates at either end of the field and kick the ball back and forth.

DEFENSIVE PLAY. Players should become adept in covering a player on defense because a man-to-man defense will be necessary when opponents are approaching scoring territory. This is especially true if the opponents use a passing type of game on offense. Players find that speedball requires good physical condition because of the large amount of running involved. You cannot cover a man if you can't keep up with him.

INDIVIDUAL PICK-UPS. Players will frequently find themselves with a ground ball in their possession and the occasion calling for a pass play. A player may be near the opponent's goal line, near the sideline where a field goal attempt is not practical, with a teammate standing in the end zone to whom the ball could be passed for a touchdown. One will find many other occasions during actual play when it would be desirable to be able to get a ground ball into the air so that it may be used in a passing attack. If no teammate to whom the ball may be kicked is available, it is desirable that one be able to kick it up and catch it himself. There are four methods that may be used to get a ground ball into your hands legally.

1. *Kick-up with both feet:* In this play, straddle the ball with both feet, grasping the ball with the insides of the feet. With the ball firmly held by the feet, jump into the air, lifting the ball upward and slightly forward with the feet when jumping and catch the ball in the hands after it leaves the feet and before it strikes the ground again. This is one of the easiest pick-ups to use and should be mastered by every player. (See Figs. 24-3 through 24-6.)

2. *One-foot pick-up:* Place the left foot alongside the ball and the other foot just behind the ball. Bend the body over the ball and form a pocket with the hands in front of the ball with thumbs together, palms facing the ball, and fingers extended. Kick the ball easily with the right foot

and catch it in the hands. The ball must be caught after it has left the foot and before it strikes the ground for the pick-up to be legal. Principal errors in this play consist of kicking the ball too hard and not forming a proper basket with the hands. Obviously the position of the feet may be reversed. (See Figs. 24-7 through 24-9.)

3. *Foot toss pick-up:* Place one foot on top of the ball with the leg extended slightly forward. To make the pick-up, pull the foot toward the body using enough pressure on the ball to cause it to roll toward the body. Slide the foot to the ground and allow the ball to roll up on the toe, from which position give it a toss into the air by kicking the foot upward. This is a more difficult pick-up than the other two, but some players become quite adept at it and prefer it to the other methods. (See Figs. 24-10 through 24-14.)

4. *Rolling or bounding ball:* Players should become adept at kicking rolling and bounding balls into the air so they may catch them in their hands and thus start a passing play. Players may practice this skill by having a teammate bounce a ball toward them in such a position that they can practice kicking the ball into the air for a catch.

PLAYING STRATEGY

SIZE OF TEAM. A regulation speedball team consists of 11 players with positions as indicated below. Five players constitute the first line, three the second, two the third, and one the fourth.

FOR MEN

4	2	1	3	5
Left end	Left forward	Center	Right forward	Right end

7	6	8
Left half-back	Fullback	Right half-back

9	10
Left guard	Right guard

11
Goal guard

DEFENSIVE PLAY. A man-to-man defense is effective, particularly when the opponents are using a passing game in their offensive maneuvers. If a kicking game is being employed by the opponents, defensive players need to cover the ball, being careful to keep the goal well defended when the opponents have the ball in scoring territory. The following defensive assignments are widely used, although variations may be devised to meet situations as they arise.

MAN-TO-MAN DEFENSIVE ASSIGNMENTS

Number	1	covers	number	6	on	opposing	team
"	2	"	"	8	"	"	"
"	3	"	"	7	"	"	"
"	4	"	"	10	"	"	"
"	5	"	"	9	"	"	"
"	11	"	"	11	"	"	"

This arrangement assigns defensive players to cover offensive opponents on their side of the field and leaves the goalkeeper free to protect the goal and cover an opponent who might momentarily elude his man in scoring territory.

OFFENSIVE MANEUVERS

KICKING GAME. If you have mastered the skill of dribbling the ball with the feet, as in soccer, an attack that features this aspect of the game will be found most effective. (See Figs. 24-14, 24-15.) You should keep the location of teammates in mind in order that the ball may be kicked to a teammate in the open when you are in close quarters and in danger of losing the ball. Whether playing a passing or a kicking game, all players should remain near their assigned positions on the playing field and not congregate the full team around the ball. Confusion and roughhouse play is usually the result when all players follow the ball all over the field.

PASSING GAME. This style of play is effective when you have mastered the skills of passing and catching the ball. Various offensive plays may be set up in which the ball is moved rapidly from one player to the other until an opportunity to score presents itself. Players should maintain their relative positions on the playing field and keep moving in

FIGURE 24-15. Kicking ball to teammate

FIGURE 24-16. Kicking ball with inside of foot

FIGURES 24-17, 24-18. Speedball in action

order to stay away from defensive players. The overhead dribble is an effective offensive weapon when using the passing game, and all players should learn to use it. Teams should learn not to depend on the passing game alone, but should combine it with the kicking game for an effective offense that is easily adapted to any situation that may arise.

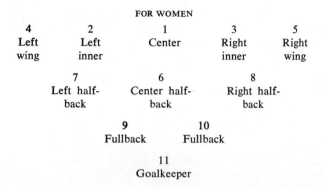

FOR WOMEN

4 Left wing	2 Left inner	1 Center	3 Right inner	5 Right wing

7 Left half- back	6 Center half- back	8 Right half- back

9 Fullback	10 Fullback

11
Goalkeeper

OFFENSIVE TEAM PLAYS. A few offensive plays have been shown above for illustrative purposes. Players can easily devise their own plays by varying these. The principal thing to keep in mind in offensive play is position of players on the field. The front line should head the attack down field, while the backs and guards should stay in position to cover on defense if the ball should be lost or intercepted by the opponents. The ends should be the first players across the goal line to receive forward passes from the forwards and center while the halfbacks remain between the front line players and their own goal. The right end should seldom cross to the opposite side of the field but should play in his territory. This serves two purposes—his teammates always know where he is located, and it keeps the defense spread. If all players follow the ball, team play is impossible and the game degenerates into a kicking scramble devoid of any teamwork.

FIGURES 24-19 through 24-22. (*Upper left*) Kick-off play. 1 kicks ball to 3; 3 passes to 2; 2 passes to 1. 1 passes to 4, who can drop kick, pass to 5 for a touchdown, or pass to 6 for a try for field goal. (*Upper right*) Free kick play near goal. 1 lifts ball to 3 with foot, 3 passes ball back to 1, who may drop kick or pass to 4 or 5, or reverse and pass to 6. (*Lower left*) Out of bounds at opponents' goal. 4 and 2 rush toward 3. 6 moves toward center of field to receive pass from 3. 6 passes to 1, who may drop kick or pass to 4, 2, or 5. (*Lower right*) Out of bounds on side line. 1 rushes past 5 to draw defense. 3 follows 1 and receives pass from 5. 3 passes to 1 who may kick or pass to 2 or 5.

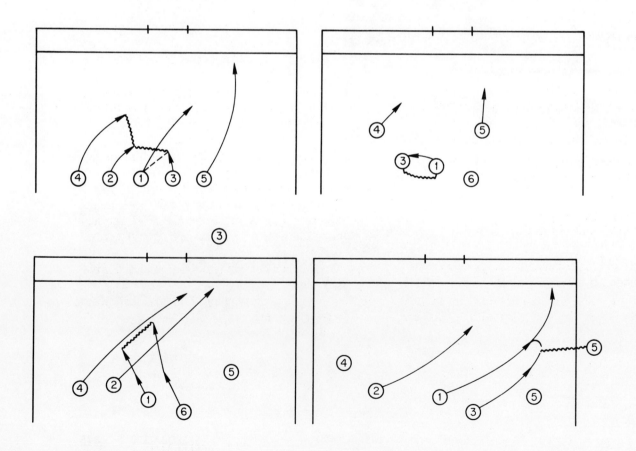

KEY TO DIAGRAMS
○ PLAYER   ----KICK   ——PATH OF PLAYER   ⌇⌇⌇⌇PASS

SAFETY

1. Refrain from wearing shoes with cleats or spikes that may injure other players.
2. Goal posts should be padded to a height of six feet to minimize possibility of injury in collision of players with posts.
3. The playing area should be smooth and free from holes, rocks, glass, and any other items that might cause ankle sprains or other injuries.
4. No obstructions should be placed near the end-lines or sidelines because players frequently run off the playing area and may be injured by contact with these objects.
5. Rough play should not be tolerated, because players attain considerable momentum in this game and injuries often occur if strict observance of the rules is not maintained.

HELPFUL HINTS

The following may be used in practice and in competition to develop your skill in playing the game. Arrange with your teammates to practice on these skills before class and during recreational periods.

1. Dribbling the ball for control.
2. Dribbling the ball for speed with and without obstacles.
3. Drop kicking for accuracy and distance.
4. Place kicking for accuracy and distance.
5. Catching forward passes and punts, stationary and running.
6. Punting the ball for accuracy and distance.
7. Throwing the ball for distance and accuracy.
8. Overhead dribble for distance.

PLAYING COURTESIES

1. Refrain from indiscriminate kicking when the ball is surrounded by several players.
2. Observe the rules and refrain from rough play just because you can get away with it. Because speedball is a fast-moving game, it is difficult for officials to observe all players.
3. Give assistance to the player who may not be as skilled as you are.

TERMINOLOGY

Attackers Members of team in possession of the ball.

Dead ball Ball is dead following a score, after a foul, during time-out and on a tie ball.

Defenders Members of team attempting to gain possession of the ball.

Drop kick A caught ball that is dropped to the ground and kicked just as it leaves the ground.

End goal Ball caused to cross the end line, not between the goal posts; counts one point for men, no score for women.

Field goal Ground ball kicked between the uprights and under the cross bar. Counts three points for men, two for women.

Fly or aerial ball Ball sent into the air by a kick of one or both feet.

Foot dribble Method of advancing the ball by a series of kicks with the feet.

Foul An infringement of the rules which is penalized by a free kick or a penalty kick.

Goaltender Player on team assigned to defend the goal.

Ground ball Ball that is rolling, bouncing, or stationary on the ground.

Handling the ball Touching a ground ball with the hands or arms.

Juggle Means of advancing the ball by throwing or tapping it into the air and catching it before it strikes the ground.

Own goal The goal a team is defending.

Passing Means of advancing the ball in the air by one- or two-handed pass.

Penalty kick Opportunity afforded to score a point by place-kicking ball from penalty kick mark between uprights and under the cross bar for boys. Girls must drop kick ball over the cross bar.

Pick-ups Methods of picking up a ground ball with the feet.

Trapping Method of stopping a moving ball with one or both feet.

SELECTED REFERENCES

Fait, Hollis; John Shaw, and Katherine Ley, *A Manual of Physical Education Activities* (3rd ed.). Philadelphia: W. B. Saunders Co., 1967.

Meyer, M. H., and M. M. Schwarz, *Team Sports for Girls and Women* (4th ed.). Philadelphia: W. B. Saunders Co., 1965.

Official N.S.G.W.S. Soccer and Speedball Guide. Washington, D.C.: American Association for Health, Physical Education and Recreation (current edition).

Speedball For Men. Washington, D.C.: American Association for Health, Physical Education and Recreation, 1967.

Vannier, Maryhelen, and Hally Beth Poindexter, *Physical Activities for College Women* (2nd ed.). Philadelphia: W. B. Saunders Co., 1968.

White, Jess R., *Sports Rules Encyclopedia.* Palo Alto, Calif.: National Press, 1961.

Squash Racquets

25

ORIGIN AND DEVELOPMENT

Like many of our games, squash racquets originated in England in the early seventeenth century. It was originally played out of doors, often on dead-end streets where three walls were available to bat the small hard rubber ball around. The racquet resembled a bat more than the present day shape. The fashionable boys' schools, Rugby, Harrow, Eton, and others, played racquets (or harder) as early as 1825. A softer ball was developed following the discovery of the rubber vulcanizing process in 1846 and from its sound of hitting came the name "squash." The development of the present racquet probably is an adaptation of the tennis racquet, but the date and place of its origin are unknown.

Squash came to the United States from Canada about 1885, with one of the first courts being built in Philadelphia in 1893. The first tournament was held in that city in 1907, and it has long been a stronghold of squash enthusiasts. From the beginning, squash was considered a rich man's game because of its very origin, the expense of building a

court, and the fact that it appealed to wealthy businessmen. Eastern universities were the first American schools to adopt the game. Harvard built a squash building with 28 courts in 1930, and since then practically all large universities have built courts, often adapting handball courts to squash play.

NATURE OF THE GAME

Squash is a form of handball played with a racquet by hitting a small rubber ball. The object of the game is to make the ball bounce off the front wall of the four-wall court, so that the opponent cannot return it from the air or before the second bounce. It may hit the side walls or back wall before reaching the front wall, but must hit the front wall above the telltale. Either the server or receiver can win a point, but the winner becomes the next server.

Squash can be played singles or doubles, by either sex of any age, but is usually considered a very vigorous game. For this reason, it is a good reducing exercise, and many athletes play squash during their off-season to stay in shape. Professional people and artists who do not want to injure their hands playing handball often take up squash. The play is extremely fast and calls for instantaneous decisions, good coordination, and quick response. It is also a good developer of endurance because of the hard play.

EQUIPMENT

A squash player should wear white gym clothes and tennis shoes. Other than dress, the only equipment needed in squash is a good racquet and ball. The ball is of black rubber, one and three-quarter inches in diameter, and becomes more lively as it warms up. The racquets are much like tennis racquets except that the handle is longer and the head smaller and more round. The best are made of laminated wood, strung with gut, and the handle is covered with good leather. Nylon strings are almost as satisfactory as gut, cost less, and usually last longer. It is advisable to buy a good racket because inexpensive ones are easily broken and are not guaranteed.

BASIC RULES

COURT.   The court is of four walls 18½ feet wide, 32 feet long and 16 feet high, with a metal telltale 17 inches high on the front wall. Any shot hitting this telltale is a fault.

SERVICE.   Serving or receiving is decided by the spin of the racquet (smooth or rough) and the server may choose to serve from either box and alternate thereafter until service is lost. If the server serves from the wrong box and the receiver plays it, the service shall count. If, however, the receiver does not attempt a return he may demand that it be served from the proper court.

The server must stand with at least one foot completely in the box until the ball has left the racquet. The ball must be served to the front wall above the service line (6 feet 6 inches) and below the 16-foot line before it touches any part of the court. On its rebound it must first strike the floor within (not touching) the lines of the opposite service court, either before or after touching any other wall or walls. Otherwise the service is a fault. If a player fails in his second attempt to make a legal serve he loses a point.

RETURNING THE SERVE.   The opponent must return the ball before it has bounced twice on the floor. He may hit it before it touches the floor (on the volley) or after one bounce. His return must reach the front wall on the fly above the telltale, and it may touch any wall or walls within the court before

or after reaching the front wall. If the receiver fails to return the serve he loses a point.

If, on the first bounce from the floor, the ball hits on or above the 6 feet 6 inches line on the back wall, the point shall be played over.

If at any time the ball hits outside the playing surface of the court, which includes the ceiling and lights, except as provided under the rules for service, it is a point against the player who hit the ball.

HINDER.   Each player must get out of his opponent's way immediately after he has struck the ball. A hinder is called whenever he fails to give his opponent a fair view of the ball as well as restricting him from getting to or striking the ball. The point is replayed when a hinder is called. This rule also applies if the player refrains from striking at the ball because of reasonable danger of injuring his opponent.

LET.   A let is the stopping of play and playing the point over. A player struck by the ball which, if unimpeded, would have been returned directly to the front wall, loses that point. But if the ball was *not* traveling directly toward the front wall, a let is called and the point is replayed. No let shall be called unless the striker could have made a good return.

SCORING.   A point is awarded a player when his opponent:

1. is unable to return the ball to the front wall before it bounces twice on the floor.
2. hinders his play.
3. hits the telltale.
4. hits the ball so that it strikes above the out-of-bounds lines or hits the ceiling or lights.

Fifteen points is game. At 13-all the one who reached it first may elect to finish the game at 15, to set it to five points (making the game 18 points) or to set it at three points (making the game 16 points). At 14-all (provided the score had not been tied at 13-all) the receiver must elect before the next serve to finish the game at 15 or to set it at three, making a 17 point game.

Match—Tournament play calls for the winning of three out of five games, but the usual friendly match is the best two out of three.

TECHNIQUES AND FUNDAMENTALS

The grip

To assume the correct grip hold the racquet by the throat with the left hand with the face of the racquet perpendicular to the floor at waist height and out in front of the body. Grasp the leather handle

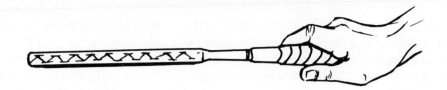

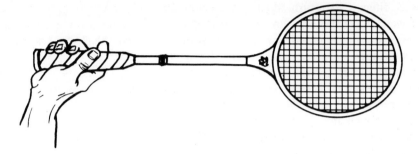

FIGURE 25-1. Continental grip. Used for both forehand and backhand shots.

with the right-hand fingers slightly spread as though shaking hands. The thumb is wrapped around and the index finger is extended. Be sure to hold the racquet as near the butt as possible to permit flexibility. The pressure should be felt not on the palm but on the inner part of the thumb, the inside of the forefinger (index), and the heel of the hand. This is called the continental grip. (See Fig. 25-1.) This grip should be used for both forehand and backhand strokes.

Hitting the forehand

To play the most common stroke in squash, the forehand, the player should face the right-hand wall, with the left foot slightly advanced, assume a semi-crouched position, and bring the racquet back, keeping his forearm parallel to the floor. He cocks his right wrist so that the racquet is straight up and down, with the racquet head about even with the right ear. There is a momentary pause; the weight is transferred to the right leg while the right forearm moves back until it is nearly parallel to the side wall. Led by the cocked wrist, the racquet then starts forward as the hips and shoulder pivot to the left and the weight shifts forward to the left leg, moves forward, parallel to the floor, to the intended contact point. The wrist whips the racquet to meet the ball, controlled mainly by the index finger and the thumb. The follow-through should be a smooth continuation of the stroke and the wrist should continue to rotate so that the face of the racquet will turn over from the vertical to the horizontal. The player should immediately assume his ready position.

The squash stroke differs from the tennis stroke in that the elbow rather than the shoulder becomes the focal point.

Uncoiling the backhand

To play the backhand, the player faces the left wall in the same position described above. The backswing is a motion of the forearm pivoting and a cocking of the wrist to the left and upward as the player holds the shaft at about a 45 degree angle to the floor with the racquet head about eye level. He pivots with his hip and shoulders to the left until the left shoulder is lower and the racquet is further back. After a slight pause he uncoils forcefully with his hips and shoulders.

The cocked wrist is whipped through until the ball is struck at a point about six inches in front of the right foot. In this stroke the pressure comes primarily from the thumb. When the player follows through he should immediately assume the ready position.

The ready position

The play is so fast in squash that the player must be alert and assume the ready position quickly. After playing his own shot he should take the center of the court with his heels just in front of the service line, facing the front wall. He should assume a semi-crouched position, head up, with the feet apart shoulder width and the weight resting on the balls of the feet. The racquet should be held up across the body with the right wrist cocked and the left hand placed lightly on the throat of the racquet. If his opponent is about to make a return from behind, the player should not face him but should keep his back to him, and turn the head and upper trunk sufficiently to see his opponent peripherally. The racquet head should be raised somewhat by the left hand for protection.

Serves

The underhand *lob serve* is most popular because it is difficult to return when it falls close to the side wall, it can be hit with little effort, and it permits time for the server to move to a position of advantage without hindering his opponent. The serve is made from either service box in practically the same way as described for the forehand stroke. The player faces the right wall, when in the right court, drops the ball with the left hand about one or two feet in front of the left toe and the racquet makes contact when the ball is about knee high. The lob service is a gentle stroke made with very little backswing and a lifting stroke.

The ball should hit the front wall about four to six feet to the right of the left wall and below the ceiling and rebound coming close to or hitting the left wall just back of the service line about eight or ten feet high. It should bounce on the floor about four or five feet from the back wall. (See Fig. 25-2.) This makes a very difficult shot to return if the serve is hit gently so that it hugs the wall and does not rebound from the rear wall well into the court.

When serving from the left court the above fundamentals apply except that the ball is hit high to the front wall of the opposite court. Also, the racquet should not cross the body but should follow the path of the ball.

The *side serve* is a smash with the ball thrown and struck at shoulder or head height with a forearm stroke. The placement may be the same as the lob serve or it may be played just about the front wall service line near the middle of the court so that it will hit the rear wall before touching the floor or side wall. It should then follow the side wall closely. (See Fig. 25-3.)

This serve should be used only occasionally from the left-hand court. A variation should be used in which the ball hits the front wall within a few inches of the left wall, rebounds to the left side wall across the court, bounces up the back wall (in the right court) and thence to the right wall, coming out in the middle of the right court. (See Fig. 25-4.)

The *overhead smash serve* approximates the tennis serve. The ball should hit the front center wall

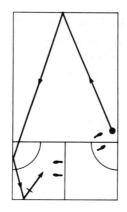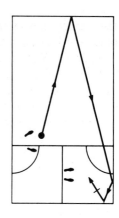

FIGURE 25-2. Serving and receiving positions for lob serves. (*Left*) From right-hand court. (*Right*) From left-hand court. (This and all the following diagrams are adapted from Louis E. Means, *Physical Education Activities, Sports, and Games.* Dubuque, Iowa: William C. Brown Company, Publishers, 1952.)

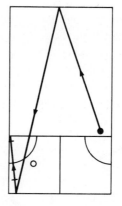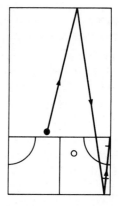

FIGURE 25-3. Side service placement from right and left courts

FIGURE 25-4. Side service variation placement

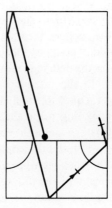

as close to the service line as possible. If hit hard enough it should travel to the rear wall, hitting about a foot above the floor. When it strikes the rear wall this low it will rebound low and make the return difficult, but if it strikes the floor first the rebound from the rear wall makes an easy return. This serve is useful against an opponent perplexed by its speed or against a tired opponent. A good player receiving this serve will usually volley it (play it before it bounces).

Return of service

The receiver should stand two or three feet back of the service line in the middle of the service court facing the wall away from the server. He should look at the front wall but be prepared for a smash serve. As soon as the ball is served he must adjust himself to the course of the ball. If the ball is going to be close to the back wall, he should move back, but if it is hard hit he may move forward to get into better position. It may also be necessary to move closer or away from the side wall.

He should return a smash by a volley off the wall, if possible. If it continues and hits the back wall, the receiver must come around (turn with it), hitting the ball as it rebounds off the back wall.

To return a good lob serve, choose one of three ways: (1) move forward and volley the ball, (2) move back and take it off the side wall just after the rebound, or (3) move back against the rear wall near the middle of the court, place the racquet against the wall, and lift the ball with wrist action. This return should be placed high on the front wall close to the side so that it rebounds down the alley.

To return a poorly hit lob serve that hits the side and back walls and bounds into the midcourt, back up toward the opponent, forcing him to the wall while the shot is being made.

Basic shots

As in all racquet games, the purpose of each shot is to either place the ball so that the opponent cannot return it or to "set him up" so that he will be unable to return the next shot. Two of the most basic shots in squash are the *alley shot* and the *crosscourt shot*.

The *alley shot* is made with the usual forehand stroke in the right court (and the backhand in the left court) when the ball is low and close enough to the right wall. It is hit hard and low to the front wall just above the telltale and as close as possible to the right side wall without touching it upon the rebound. (See Fig. 25-5.) This shot is best played when close

to the front wall. Exactly the same shot can be played in the left-hand court with a backhand stroke.

The *crosscourt shot* is played from the same position as the alley shot, but the stroke starts earlier so that the ball hits the front wall at a point near the center, which will cause it to rebound to the opposite side from which it was hit. It is also hit hard and low so that the opponent cannot tell which return to expect. On the rebound it should strike the floor and then bounce to the side wall at a point as far back as the opponent is standing. (See Fig. 25-6.) It must be hit hard enough to pass the opponent and force him out of position. The backhand shot is played in the same manner from the left-hand court. (See Fig. 25-7.)

Advanced shots

The drop shots and corner shots are advanced tactics that should be learned after mastery of the basic shots. The *drop shot* is used occasionally from well up in the front court as a change of pace from the alley and crosscourt shots. The wind-up for this shot is the same as for the others, but the stroke is slowed down before meeting the ball so that it is struck just hard enough to carry to the front wall. There it should be hit just above the telltale into the corner so that in rebounding it will come as close to the side wall as possible without rebounding from it. (See Fig. 25-8.)

Corner shots should be stroked lightly as with the drop, but shot should cross the court (from the right-hand court to the left corner, and vice versa), hitting the front wall low and near the left side wall. Played correctly, it will hit the side wall very close to the floor with practically no bounce. If it hits the crack it is called a "nick" and is impossible to return. (See Figs. 25-9 through 25-11.) A reverse corner shot that strikes the side wall first and then the front can be even more effective.

Hints for shots

1. Face the side wall for practically all shots.
2. Begin all shots the same.
3. Meet the ball above the knee.
4. Always grip the racquet the same way.
5. Make all shots with a flexible wrist.
6. Meet all alley shots in the middle of the swing on the inside of the front foot.
7. Make all crosscourt shots in advance of the front foot.
8. Meet all angle or corner shots late, behind the front foot.

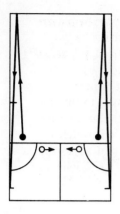

FIGURE 25-5. Alley shots placement, right and left courts on same diagram

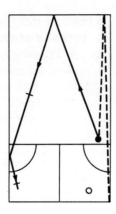

FIGURE 25-6. Forehand cross-court shot placement (alternate alley shot)

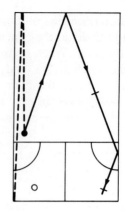

FIGURE 25-7. Backhand cross-court shot placement (alternate alley shot)

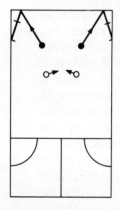

FIGURE 25-8. Drop shots, both shots diagramed (on same court) with opponent on opposite court

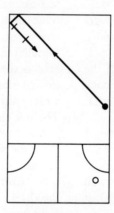

FIGURE 25-9. Corner shots with forehand and backhand shots

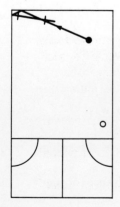

FIGURE 25-10. Corner shot from close to front wall

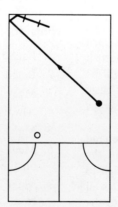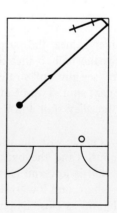

FIGURE 25-11. Reverse corner shots, right court, left court

9. Drop shots are played in the middle of the swing, just off the heel of the inside of the front foot.
10. Try to play the ball six inches to a foot above the telltale.
11. Follow through on all shots.

PLAYING STRATEGY

The type of tactics and strategy used in any game depends upon the strength and weakness of one's opponent. The ball should always be played so as to avoid giving the opponent a setup. This is best accomplished in squash by keeping the ball low, deep, and near the side wall. One's shots should be varied to keep the opponent guessing and out of position. Side alley shots mixed with crosscourt shots will keep most opponents busy, and if these are interspersed with well-planned drop or corner shots, victory should result.

Beginners must resist the urge to "kill" every shot and to make a point on every play. They must try to make every shot with a definite purpose: to keep the opponent out of position and to set him up for the kill. Remember the hardest hit shots in squash are often the easiest to return.

You should try to box your opponent so that he cannot start after the ball until after you have completed your stroke.

Try not to let your game get into a set pattern so that your opponent will know what to expect.

Vary the strokes between hard ones and soft easy shots. Delay the shot, direction, and force, so that your opponent cannot anticipate the play. Volley when possible.

Keep pressing to the forecourt ahead of your opponent. Remember, if you are winning, don't change your style of play, but if you are losing, alter your game.

SAFETY HINTS

The principal danger in squash racquets is being struck by the ball or racquet. This can usually be avoided if you:

1. Keep the eyes on the ball at all times.
2. Know where your opponent is and how he is swinging.
3. Call a hinder when your swing might hit your opponent.
4. Do not play doubles in a single court.

5. Do not turn your face backward when your opponent is about to strike from behind.
6. Keep racquet low. Do not use tennis strokes which are dangerous to your opponent.

PLAYING COURTESIES

1. Yield the right of way to your opponent.
2. The hinder is called by the hindered player and is not questioned by his opponent.

TERMINOLOGY

Ace   A point scored on one's service.
All   Score tied, i.e., 6–all, not 6 to 6.
Alley   Space (about two feet) along side walls.
Alley shot   A shot that travels in the alley.
Angle shot   A shot that hits side wall before the front wall.
Arc   The service box.
Back-wall line   A line 6 feet 6 inches from floor on back wall parallel to floor.
Balk   Interference with opponent's effort to hit the ball.
Boast   A shot hit from a corner to the nearest side wall at a sharp angle, then traveling to the front wall near the corner diagonally opposite from where it started.
Bow-shot   A shot hit into a side wall from the rear court traveling to the opposite side wall near the front wall and into the front wall at a sharp angle.
Box   Service box.
Corner shot   A shot that hits the side wall low and close to the front wall, then hits front wall close to telltale.
Crack   The angle formed by the wall and floor. When a ball is hit into the crack it is called a "nick" shot.
Double fault   The serving of two consecutive faults which results in the loss of a point and service.
Drive   A ball hit hard after it has bounced.
Drop shot   A soft shot that dies after hitting the front wall.
Fault   A serve that does not land in proper bounds. Point is lost after a double fault.
Flick   Used to return balls too close to rear wall for a full stroke.
Foot fault   Failure to keep at least one foot in service box.
Ground stroke   Hitting ball after it has bounced from the floor.

Half volley Hitting ball immediately after it has touched the floor. Also called a block shot.

Hinder Interference with opponent's effort to reach or hit the ball. It results in a "let" and the shot is played over. It results in a loss of point, however, if the ball has been hit and would have reached the front wall before striking any other wall.

Kill A hard placement that often results in a point being scored.

Let A hinder or interference. The point is played over and no loss of point is involved.

Lob An underhand service that strikes the front wall high and returns to the back wall or corner.

Love No score.

Nick See *Crack*.

Out A ball that is out-of-bounds or not playable and results in the loss of a point. Not a service fault.

Out of court A ball that strikes above the playing area.

Poach Playing balls that your partner (in doubles) should take.

Rally To warm up with practice shots or a good exchange of shots with your opponent.

Seeding Placing the best players in a draw tournament so that they do not meet in the early rounds.

Service Putting the ball in play.

Service box That area (arc) from which the ball is served.

Service court That half of the rear part of the court in which the service box is located.

Telltale A metal strip 17 inches high across the bottom of the front court. When a ball strikes it a point is lost.

Volley To strike the ball before it bounces off the floor.

SELECTED REFERENCES

Debany, Walter, *Squash Racquets*. New York: A. S. Barnes & Co., Inc., 1950.

Fait, Hollis, John Shaw, and Katherine Ley, *A Manual of Physical Education Activities* (3rd ed.). Philadelphia: W. B. Saunders Co., 1967.

Khan, Hashim, *The Khan Game*. Detroit: Wayne University Press, 1968.

Means, Louis E., and Harold K. Jack, *Physical Education Activities, Sports and Games*. Dubuque, Iowa: William C. Brown Company, Publishers, 1965.

Sports Illustrated, *Book of Squash*. Philadelphia: J. B. Lippincott Co., 1963.

United States Squash Racquets Association, *Official Year Book*. 470 Latch's Lane, Merion, Pa.

Swimming and Diving

ORIGIN AND DEVELOPMENT

It is difficult to determine when swimming was first used as a means of locomotion through water. Wall carvings of swimmers have been found dating back to 9000 B.C. The first written account of the teaching of swimming was found in the records from the Middle Kingdom in Egypt (2160–1780 B.C.). One of the earliest references to swimming in this country is an account of Benjamin Franklin teaching swimming to children on a visit to England.

Competition has always been the means of accelerating the development of all sports, and swimming is no exception to this rule. The 1880's furnish us with the first such records and from that date forward the development of water skills was very marked. Much of this development was due to further competitive swimming and much was done through the interest that competitive swimming has created.

Some swimmers from the United States who have won national and international acclaim for their

prowess in water skills during the past half-century are Charles Daniels, Johnny Weismuller, Adolph Kiefer, Alan Ford, Helene Madison, Ann Curtis, Charlie Hickox, Chris van Saltza, Debbie Meyer, Don Scholander. The United States led the world in competitive swimming for many years; Japan then led, then Australia; the United States regained the lead by winning 58 medals in the 1968 Olympics. Swimming records are broken faster than they are recognized because of any or all of the following factors: age group swimming, better training methods, recognition that strength is necessary for speed swimming, and the development of body-building programs that contribute to the conditioning of swimmers. In addition, there are more pools and more competition than ever before and any swimmer who has the desire to master the fundamentals and develop maximum endurance has a chance to succeed in topflight competition.

The American Red Cross has done much to advance safety in swimming and to popularize swimming as a recreational activity. Far too many people still lose their lives by drowning. One of the most effective means of reducing this mortality rate is through the mastery of basic water skills by all potential swimmers and the observance of safety precautions when in and around the water.

NATURE OF THE SPORT

Swimming is a seasonal sport as far as outdoor swimming is concerned, but with the ever-increasing number of indoor pools, it is fast becoming a year-round activity. Indoor pools are standard equipment in athletic clubs, YMCA's, YWCA's, and schools and colleges. Outdoor facilities include pools, lakes, seashores, rivers, and small streams dammed for this purpose, but only safe and unpolluted areas should be used. The popularity of swimming is not restricted to any locality because of climatic conditions, except the far north and the far south. Until recently, swimming in the United States had advanced most rapidly in the Midwest and eastern sections, probably because of the denser populations, with more money available for construction of facilities. It is rapidly spreading to other sections of the country, however, and is now a popular recreational activity.

Swimming finds expression in a multitude of activities, including recreational, competitive, synchronized water games, diving, life saving, water polo, water skiing, skin and scuba diving, and water safety. All of these activities have as their background certain fundamental water skills. Swimming is not restricted to any age group, and once these basic skills are mastered, the individual has many potential outlets for expression, plus a means of saving lives. Swimming is generally recognized as an excellent activity for all-around body development. It is frequently used in therapy that involves the re-education of muscles that have been immobilized or weakened through illness or injury.

TECHNIQUES AND FUNDAMENTALS

All forms of swimming have as their background certain fundamental water skills. The mastery of these skills is essential if the individual is to become at home in the water and succeed in mastering the various styles of swimming as exemplified in the combination of leg and arm strokes used by expert swimmers. These basic skills are:

1. Adjustment to the water.
2. Breathing or bobbing.
3. Buoyancy—floating or remaining afloat with a minimum of effort.

4. Propulsion through the water involving coordination of arms and legs in stroking, combined with breathing.
5. Safety.

After mastering these basic skills, the individual may work toward a development of skill in executing the various strokes and dives. These advanced skills are:

1. Backstroke, elementary and racing.
2. Sidestroke.
3. Breaststroke.
4. Butterfly (dolphin).
5. Crawl.
6. Treading water and sculling.
7. Surface diving.
8. Underwater swimming.
9. Diving.

Most of the above movements are not single skills but are coordinated movements that involve several single skills, i.e., the breaststroke consists of kicking, stroking, and breathing, all combined to form a unified and complete method of propulsion through the water.

Adjustment to water and breathing

Beginning swimmers must overcome fear of the water by gradual adjustment to the feel of the water and its effect. Some beginners will have no difficulty with this problem, while others require considerable time to feel at home in the water. The "sink or swim" approach to this problem may have been used successfully in some cases, but is not recommended as an acceptable method of becoming accustomed to the water. This problem should be approached in a way that will decrease or eliminate existing fears instead of exaggerating them. Beginners should first go in shallow water where they can feel the security of their feet on the bottom.

One of the early phases of water adjustment is that of getting the face accustomed to the feel of water. This skill may be practiced in the bath tub, the washbasin or in shallow water. A feeling of confidence and relaxation in the water cannot be attained until the individual is able to submerge his face in water without fear. As soon as the face can be submerged in the water with confidence, the beginning swimmer should learn the rhythmical or rotary breathing technique that is used in swimming the crawl stroke. Breath control in the water is different from normal breathing in that the time for performing the act is usually limited and there is always the possibility of inhaling water into the lungs.

RHYTHMIC OR ROTARY BREATHING. Breathing for water skills is done by exhaling under water through the nose and mouth and inhaling above water through the mouth. It is impossible to inhale enough air through the nose and, in addition, water may be inhaled, as small drops of water cling to the hairs in the nasal passage when inhaling through the nose. Air must be exhaled under water because there is not sufficient time to both inhale and exhale while the face is out of the water. Holding the breath creates extra tension in the muscles of the chest, causing fatigue to set in earlier, so regular breathing should be observed whenever possible. The inhalation must be done quickly and almost with a gasp. The rate of exhalation and inhalation will necessarily be coordinated with the speed of the swimming stroke being executed.

Helping hints for breathing

1. Do not force the air out too fast.
2. Inhale only when air is needed.
3. Keep forcing air out until the mouth is in a position to inhale.
4. Do not attempt to inhale until the mouth is above water.
5. Open the eyes for relaxation.
6. Keep body under water while performing this drill.

Floating

In true floating, a person is able to remain in or on the water for an indefinite period without any movement of the body. The body build is the determining factor in floating, which means that there is a wide range of floating abilities among individuals. If the body weight of the individual is such that it displaces less weight than an equal volume of water, the person will be able to float. Floating is rarely executed by a novice without some instruction. It should be learned, or practiced, before stroke instruction begins, as tension and a tendency to fight the water will be lessened if the individual is able to float. It has been found that a position on the back, chest well up, head back slightly, arms extended diagonally upward and outward with palms up, and legs bent slightly under the body will give the best results. (See Fig. 26-1.) Air must be inhaled quickly, held as long as is comfortable, and exhaled quickly. Many people will not be able to float even though these directions are observed, because their body weight is greater than the weight of the water they displace. Such individuals will have to move the hands in a sculling (backward and forward motion,

FIGURE 26-1. Floating

rotating at the wrists) motion or use a slight leg kick in order to remain afloat. Some forward progress usually results from this type of float and more energy will be expended than in the true float.

Frequently older and heavier persons will have difficulty regaining their upright position following this floating drill. This can best be done by quickly dropping the hips and bringing the head and shoulders forward. The exercise is almost like rocking in a chair.

The prone, or dead man's float, is executed by pushing off in a prone position with the face in the water and the arms extended, legs together. It is a useful drill when instruction in the dog paddle (human stroke) is first begun.

The jellyfish float is used to test buoyancy. It is executed by taking a deep breath, placing the face in the water and grasping the legs below the knees. If the individual is buoyant, the body will rise until the back breaks the surface of the water. The non-buoyant person will sink.

Helping hints for floating

1. Work in pairs with partners, assisting each other.
2. Practice first in shallow water.
3. Take a deep breath and lie back slowly and easily in the water.
4. Exhale and inhale quickly.
5. Attempt to relax as much as possible and still retain the same position.
6. Open the eyes, as this aids in relaxation.

The dog paddle (human stroke)

The dog paddle, sometimes called the human stroke, is the stroke usually taught beginners, particularly children, because it comes nearer to approaching the natural motion that most beginners would use if placed in the water and told to swim without previous instruction. In executing this stroke, the arms move in an alternate rotary motion with the legs using a modified flutter kick action. Since the head is kept out of the water, there is no problem of coordinating breathing with arm action and beginners can usually build up confidence more rapidly than if they started with the crawl stroke. Arm action should be kept under the surface in order to minimize splashing of water in the face of the swimmer. The dog paddle represents a relatively easy progression step from the face-down prone glide and the more complicated strokes are learned more readily after the swimmer has learned to move about in the water by using this elementary stroke.

Elementary backstroke

Many adults find this stroke the easiest to learn because it utilizes to the maximum the best floating position for the body and the added skill of coordinated breathing is not a problem as in the crawl. If the learner is able to master floating on the back, it is a relatively simple step to propel himself through the water by use of the elementary backstroke.

DESCRIPTION. (See Fig. 26-2.) The proper starting position is with the body in a dorsal position, legs straight and together, arms at the sides, head resting flat on the water and hips as high as possible. *Count 1* begins from this position with the arm recovery. The hands are drawn up, touching the sides, with the elbows dropping downward, keeping the arms in close. When the hands reach the armpit *count 2* starts. The wrists rotate and the palms are turned outward with the fingers pointing outward and upward. The leg recovery starts on this count also. The feet are drawn toward the body as the knees are bent and angled outward. *Count 3* finds the arms extending diagonally outward and at

the same time both feet are hooked and extended outward. *Count 4* is the propulsive phase of the stroke as the arms are swept to the sides and the legs are extended and squeezed together. *Count 5* is the glide phase and it must be observed if the stroke is utilized to its fullest. None of the movements should be too strenuous but there should be the feeling that both the feet and the hands have a hold on the water (the kick is often called the inverted frog kick). This stroke is occasionally taught in a three-phase coordination including stroke-kick-glide.

Helpful hints for elementary backstroke

1. Keep the hips as high as possible by arching the back.
2. Hands and arms must be kept close to the body on the recovery.
3. Always rotate the wrists before extending the arms in order to eliminate splash.
4. Turn the knees outward in order to keep the legs as high on the water as possible.
5. Elbows should be kept straight throughout the arm pull.
6. The glide should be unhurried.

Sidestroke

The sidestroke is not difficult to learn and it does have great value in every phase of swimming except competitive swimming. It is probably the most universally well-executed stroke of all. It is widely used in life saving.

FIGURE 26-2. Elementary backstroke

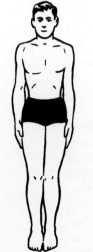
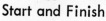
Start and Finish

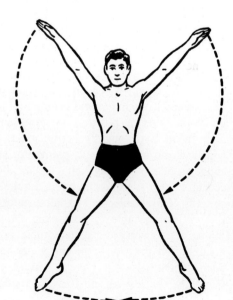

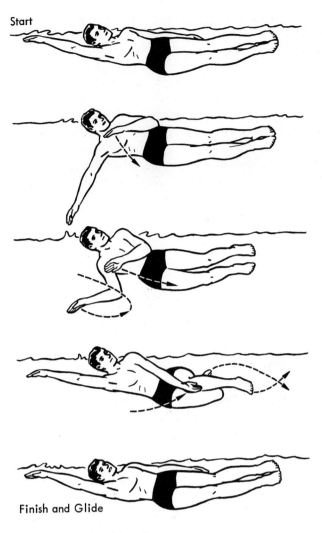

Start

Finish and Glide

FIGURE 26-3. Sidestroke

DESCRIPTION. (See Fig. 26-3.) The starting position for this stroke is on either side. More people swim on the right side than on the left. The starting position should find the lower arm extended in line with the body, the top arm resting on the body and legs straight and together. The head position should allow the face to be clear of the water. *Count 1* finds the lower arm pulling back with a bent arm pull in a diagonal, downward, and backward direction until it reaches a point under the shoulder. *Count 2* brings all of the limbs into action—lower arm, top arm, and both legs. The legs are drawn up with the heels in line with the backbone and knees held together. The side arm slides forward under the water until it reaches the lower armpit. The lower arm is tucked so the elbow is under the body and the hand is pointed forward and in line with the shoulder. *Count 3* continues the use of both arms and legs. The lower arm is extended to a position in line with the body and just under the surface; the top arm pulls back

parallel to the side of the body with the top leg stepping forward and the lower leg stepping backward, followed immediately by an extension and squeeze of both legs. *Count 4* is the glide phase following this propulsive action of the top arm and the legs. The position of the body on the glide is the same as the starting position of the stroke, and it should be maintained as long as the body continues to move forward and does not sink.

The sidestroke should be learned on both sides because this skill is helpful in life saving and in distance swimming where the body may become very strained in the same position.

Also the kick need not be the regular scissors described but it may be the reverse scissors, in which case the top leg reaches backward and the lower leg reaches forward. This kick variation is used in water safety work a great deal.

Helpful hints for sidestroke

1. Keep the body squarely on the side at all times.
2. Maintain the glide as long as possible.
3. Pull diagonally backward and not downward with the lower arm.
4. Keep the top arm close to the body on the recovery and do not overreach.
5. Keep the legs parallel to the surface on the recovery and kick.
6. Do not kick the legs apart forcibly on the leg recovery.

Breaststroke

The breaststroke is the most universal of all strokes and its usefulness is unexcelled. It is energy saving, graceful, and not too difficult to learn, although the timing does present some problems to children with their limited power of concentration. The high breaststroke is easier to learn, since coordinated breathing is eliminated. In this stroke, the head is held above the water and the legs are lower than in the conventional stroke.

DESCRIPTION. (See Fig. 26-4.) The starting position for this stroke is with the body in a prone position, arms extended, legs together and head up (lowered in the conventional). On *Count 1* the arm pull is executed. The hands are bent slightly at the wrists for the initial part of the press and the pull is a press back and somewhat down on the surface. It is a shallow pull and the arms should not be pressed to a point beyond the shoulder line, which would make it a 180 degree arc. *Count 2* involves both legs and arms. The legs are drawn up with the

Start

Finish and Glide

Glide

Sweep

Breathe

(Alternate style)

Kick

Glide

FIGURE 26-4. Breaststroke

knees dropped slightly and turned outward. The feet are together at first but spread slightly with the feet hooked in preparation for the propulsive action. At the same time, the arms are bent at the elbows and they are pulled in to the body to a position with the palms down and together in preparation for the extension of the arms. *Count 3* finds the legs going into the propulsive phase, which consists of extending and squeezing them. As this is done, the arms are extended forward to a position just under the surface where they are held. All through these

first three counts there is no hesitation or abrupt change, but a smooth, easy, flowing movement. *Count 4* is the glide phase of the stroke and this should be held as long as there is forward movement. The breaststroke kick is also called the frog kick.

In the high breaststroke there is no breathing problem. If the conventional stroke is tried the face will be in the water part of the time. The exhalation is done while the arms are extended, and as the arms are pulled back, the head is raised sufficiently to allow for inhalation through the mouth. It is immediately lowered when the arms are extended and it should remain there during the glide.

Competitive breaststroke

The breaststroke used in competition by many of the top swimmers differs in many respects from the conventional stroke just described. The kick recovery is narrowed, the breathing is executed following a stronger and faster pull, giving a faster cadence to the entire stroke. The faster turnover helps eliminate drag in the recovery stages of arm and leg movements, but presents timing problems for the swimmer, for basically the stroke is such that it is better adapted to a slower pace and looks graceful and tireless when so executed. In competition the swimmer is allowed but one kick and one pull under water both on the start and on the turns. The remainder of the time the head must be above the water.

Helpful hints for breaststroke

1. Arms should not be pulled beyond the line of the shoulders.
2. Arm pull should not be parallel to the surface but slightly down and back.
3. The back should not be arched and the hips should be slightly raised.
4. Start leg recovery by lifting feet and relaxing the knees, thereby streamlining the recovery.
5. The leg recovery should be easy and relaxed.
6. The leg kick and arm pull should not come together under any consideration.
7. The feet must be hooked before the kick, which means drawing the toes toward the knees.
8. Remember that the pull is not to be done hard but with a steady, firm press on the water.

Crawl

The crawl stroke is the fastest swimming stroke. This stroke has three distinct characteristics: a flutter kick with a regular beat, alternating arm recovery above the surface, and rotary breathing with the exhalation executed under water. The crawl stroke is the fastest of all strokes both in a prone and a dorsal position and so it has come into prominence mainly through competitive swimming. From a learner's standpoint, the first stage of this stroke is the dog paddle (human stroke). This is followed by an overarm stroke with the face out of the water and finally it becomes the crawl stroke in its last stage.
DESCRIPTION. (See Fig. 26-5.) The position

of the body should be as flat as possible, which means the hips should be high and the shoulders fairly level. The leg kick is an undulating, rhythmical, up and down beat with the power originating at the hips. The most common beat used is the six beat. This means there are six kicks (three by each leg) for each complete arm cycle. The ankles are kept loose with the feet toed in and the knees relaxed. The action of the legs is a great deal like the action of a fish tail, except the movement is up and down and not sideward.

FIGURE 26-5. Crawl

The arms are recovered alternately above the surface. The recovery starts as though the elbow were to be carried forward in a straight line and placed in the water. However, as the hand nears the shoulder the forearm swings forward and the hand enters the water directly in front of the shoulder with the elbow slightly raised, which means the arm is not fully extended. There should be immediate pressure on the water by the hand until it reaches a spot six or eight inches under the water. At this point the stroke becomes a pull until it reaches a spot under the shoulder. With no hesitation the elbow is flexed more and the forearm moves into a position that is more parallel to the surface than perpendicular to it. This last phase of the stroke is a push until the hand releases its hold on the water for the recovery. During the propulsive phase of this arm, the opposite arm is recovering above the surface. The second hand should always engage the water in the pressure stage before the first hand releases its hold in the push phase. The face should always be turned to the same side for inhalation. As the arm on the breathing side completes the pull, the head is turned back quickly and the breath is inhaled through the mouth. The face is turned back into the water as this same arm is carried forward on the recovery and exhalation starts immediately. The water should be at eye level when the face is in the water.

In the back crawl, the body position is on the back, so it is often called the inverted crawl. The action of the legs is similar to the crawl except that it is inverted. The arms are recovered alternately above the surface with a straight arm sweeping motion and they are placed in the water as far back as can be done without causing the body to roll or twist too much. The arm pull is parallel to the surface and not under the body as is done in the crawl stroke. The breathing is much simpler than in the regular crawl. The leg kick beat is similar to the crawl kick.

Helpful hints for crawl

1. Relax the legs, bend the knees slightly, keep the ankles and feet loose.
2. Keep the hips high.
3. Turn the head to the side and do not drop the shoulder as this is done.
4. Keep the elbow higher than the hand on the entry.
5. Break at the elbow more as the hand passes under the shoulder.
6. Carry the elbow forward on the initial phase of the recovery.

7. Strive for rhythm between the arms and legs.
8. Make certain that both hands do not lose hold on the water at the same time.

The dolphin stroke

The dolphin stroke, generally called the butterfly, is the latest member of the competitive stroke family and already it is the second fastest, bettered only by the crawl. (See Fig. 26-6.) This stroke is the creation of David Armbruster, retired swim coach at the University of Iowa, who created the stroke in 1935 but did not receive official sanction or gain recognition for the stroke until about 1956. It is a strenuous stroke and until it is mastered it is most exhausting in every respect. The arm recovery and pull is much like the old butterfly stroke (frog kick), and the kick is performed with the feet working simultaneously in a movement much like the flutter kick. The pressure of the feet on the downward beat forces the hips up and the swimmer looks a great deal like a seal bobbing up and down as he moves forward. When performed correctly it is a smooth and graceful stroke with the swimmer creating the impression of moving forward powerfully, yet easily.

MOVEMENT OF THE ARMS. The arms are recovered simultaneously over the water in a low arc with the elbows straight. As they are lifted from the water near the thighs the palms should be rotated outward which enables the swimmer to carry them low and still not catch water. When the arms reach a position forming a "Y" with the shoulders, the elbows are relaxed slightly, allowing the hands to enter the water in about the same position as in the crawl stroke. The elbows are slightly raised and bent. The hands should be placed or slid into the water and the first movement of the hands can be in one of two directions. Regardless of which direction is used, this action is the crux of the timing in the stroke, for without it the two-beat kick is most difficult to attain. When sprinting fast, most swimmers slide the hands forward much as is done in the crawl stroke, while others prefer the method of sliding them to the side. Following the slide there is a slight press downward on the water with the arms and then the pull is started towards the chest with the forearms catching the water and the elbows remaining somewhat stationary until the hands reach a point directly under the shoulders. At this point the swimmer turns his forearms inward so that they are parallel to the surface and quite close to the body. From this point backward the swimmer pushes and in order to gain the most from this action the wrist should bend so that the hands main-

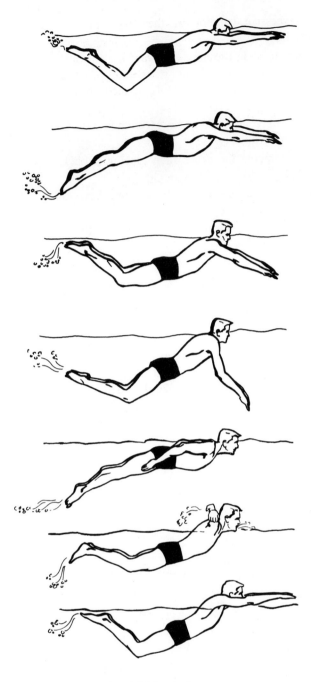

FIGURE 26-6. The dolphin stroke

point it should be noted that one of the greatest faults that a beginner experiences is bending the knees too much at this point. This tends to force the hips deeper, which is not desirable. The downward movement of the legs is started with emphasis on pressing the feet downward and continuing to press them to a point beyond straightening the knees. This final press causes the hips to rise and also propels the body forward. Both the upward and the downward action will afford propulsion. This two-phase movement of each kick should not be hurried and the swimmer should make every effort to get rhythm into these movements.

BODY POSITION AND BREATHING. The swimmer's body position should be much like the position when swimming the crawl. The hips should move slightly more although every effort should be made to maintain as level a position as possible. Breathing is done by raising the head just as the hands are pushing through the final phase of the propulsive act of the stroke. Breathing must be done quickly and the face must be placed back in the water as soon as possible. The butterfly swimmer should have special breathing patterns for races of different distances, e.g., in the 50 yard race it will not be necessary to breathe often, just as the 50 yard freestyler takes but few breaths (some take none). For a race of 100 yards, the swimmer may breathe three times in the first 25 yards and then breathe every other stroke or even every third stroke, if he is in good condition, for the remainder of the race. Ordinarily, the less breathing the better the body position, but swimming too far without breathing may cause a complete breakdown later in the race because of lack of oxygen. For races of 200 yards most flyers try breathing with every other stroke, and late in the race may need to breathe with every stroke. Many flyers attempt to breathe by turning their face to the side instead of lifting it forward, as this enables them to maintain a more level position in the water. However, this practice is not recommended, for when the swimmer tires it is almost impossible to breathe in this manner without dipping one shoulder which may cause disqualification.

COMPLETE STROKE IN ACTION. On assuming a starting position with the face in the water, arms extended and legs slightly bent, the hands should slide forward or outward slightly; the press on the water with the arms is then followed immediately by bending the arms at the elbows and pulling towards the chest. When the hands reach the push phase, the feet are lifted and pressed downward for the first kick, which lifts the body and aids propulsion. As the push phase is nearly com-

tain a position at right angles to the line of progress as long as possible. A final thrust is made with the hands as they both move outward from under the hips for the lift from the water followed by the recovery over the surface.

KICKING ACTION. The kick is executed with both legs and feet working simultaneously. Both the upward and the downward movements of the legs are initiated at the hips. On the upward movement the legs are lifted with a final whip of the lower legs, which will cause the knees to bend some. At this pleted, the face is raised for a quick breath and placed back into the water as soon as possible in order to maintain a flat position on the water. The armstroke will be completed and the arms will be coming out of the water as the face goes back into the water, and the arm recovery is started over the water. The second kick is initiated while the arms are in the air and as the arms slide into the water the downward press of the legs is made, giving the body a forward push over the water. Ultimately these two kicks should be evenly spaced and executed with about the same amount of force. Beginners will tend to have an uneven tempo with the kicks coming close together followed by a "dead spot," but this can be corrected by practice.

LEARNING THE STROKE.   This stroke is generally conceded to be the toughest of all strokes to learn, and mastering it takes much practice and perseverance. The *first step* in learning the stroke is to learn to kick properly, which can be started by hanging on the edge of the pool and practicing the leg movements just as the flutter kick was started. The swimmer must feel the movement starting at the hips and there must be a feeling of pressure against the water, on both the downward and upward movements of the feet. The body should not be held rigid but an undulating movement should proceed from the feet to the hips to the shoulders. When the swimmer feels that he has learned this fairly well he may attempt it by kicking with the arms at the side and with the face in the water. Next try the *arm movement* with a minimum of leg movement, keeping in mind the direction of the arm pull and executing it slowly. Without breathing, take several strokes in this same unhurried manner. Following this, attempt to kick slightly more, remembering that it is most important to try to place the kicks at the correct sequence with the armstroke. When these two skills have been mastered, attempt to coordinate them with *breathing* and at first attempt to breathe every third or fourth stroke. The breath should come near the end of the push and it should be completed as the arms start over the water on the recovery. Take each step in turn and put them together slowly, trying not to swim too far until you know that you have all phases of the stroke working in perfect coordination.

Helpful hints for dolphin stroke

1. On the kick do not attempt to lift the hips, but allow the kick to raise them.
2. Rotate the hands outward when the arm recovery is started.

3. Avoid excessive bending of the knees on the upward lift.
4. Don't fail to slide the hands forward or outward in order to attain the all-important timing that is needed to get two kicks evenly spaced in the stroke.
5. Inhale quickly and place the face back in the water just as quickly.
6. Do not submerge the head when placing it back in the water after taking a breath.
7. Be sure to press downward to a point beyond straightening the knees.
8. Keep the hands shallow on the pull and push, and finish the push.

Treading water

Treading water is the ability to remain afloat in a vertical or semi-vertical position with a minimum of movement by the arms and legs. It is a valuable water safety skill, especially for those who venture in deep water in any small craft.

DESCRIPTION.   (See Fig. 26-7.) The body should be in a position as near that of riding a bicycle as possible, which means there is a flexion at

FIGURE 26-7.   Treading water

the hips. The arm movement is a sweeping movement of the extended arms near the surface. The arc of this movement should not extend beyond 180 degrees and the hands may cross in front. There should be constant, slight pressure on the water at all times.

Four types of kicks may be used effectively

while treading water. First is the scissors kick which is the simplest and easiest for most swimmers; second, the frog kick which is used and described in the breaststroke; third, the "egg-beater" kick, which is an alternating frog kick and widely used by water polo players; and fourth, the bicycling movement of the legs which most closely resembles the flutter kick used in the crawl stroke. The more buoyant the person is the less effort he needs to expend to remain in this position. Those who are less buoyant will find it better if they assume as nearly as possible the position of a bicyclist.

Helpful hints for treading water

1. Lean over the water with the upper body.
2. Make all movements as slowly as possible in order to relax and so be more buoyant.
3. Develop the kicks and try them all, to find which takes less energy.
4. Keep the lungs well filled in order to give added buoyancy.
5. Practice without the use of the hands.

Surface diving

Surface diving should be learned along with underwater swimming. It is amazing how difficult it may be to get under the water when the same people may find it so difficult to remain on the surface.

DESCRIPTION. The head-first surface dive will be described first. The easiest approach for this dive can be made by breaststroking or using an overarm stroke in order to gain some momentum. At the desired spot for submerging, the arms reach down, the head snaps down and the hips are raised. The legs assume a pike or tuck position first and then are straightened, causing the body to submerge at a better angle and with more speed. If depth is desired, the swimmer can use a breaststroke arm action, which means that the arms are pushing against the surface.

The feet-first entry is done by placing the body in an upright position and then ceasing all leg and arm action. The legs should be straight and together and the arms placed at the sides. If the body is not too buoyant it will sink, but in order to speed up this submersion the palms are turned outward and the arms are held straight and lifted against the surface. When they meet overhead the entire body should be submerged. It is more difficult to reach any depth with this type of dive but the entire body can be submerged faster than with the head-first entry.

Helpful hints for surface dive

1. Level the body as much as possible on the surface before attempting the dive.
2. Gain momentum first.
3. The head must be snapped quickly and the chin kept tucked until the body is moving downward.
4. To reach greater depth, raise the legs overhead with a snap and then stroke against surface.
5. Do not arch the back until ready to come to the surface.

Underwater swimming

There are any number of strokes that may be used for underwater swimming but it is generally agreed that a form of breaststroke is superior. This skill can be learned along with breaststroking and it does help to dispel fear of the water.

DESCRIPTION. A description of the breaststroke version will be given because this is the most accepted stroke. The leg kick is identical with the breaststroke kick and the arm pull is the same, except the arms are pulled all the way to the sides and there is no downward pressure with the hands. The pull and the kick may come together or alternate as in the breaststroke. If the action is together it should be followed by a glide. If they are separate, there can be a glide after each. The reason the timing does not matter too much is that no effort is needed to keep the body on or near the surface.

The breath control is an important phase of the skill. Before attempting an underwater swim, several deep breaths should be taken and just before going under a normal breath will be best. The breath should be held as long as possible without creating tension—then it should be released slowly. The stroke and kick actions should not be hurried but should be relaxed. Everything to reduce tension in the chest muscles should be practiced so that there is not that feeling of "bursting" that so often accompanies this swim. Depth can be regulated by the angle of the head and the direction the hands are pressed against the water.

Many swim under water with a breaststroke arm action and with either a flutter kick or a scissors kick. Others use a sidestroke, with both arms pulling simultaneously. However, better vision, better direction, and more relaxation can be gained through a version of the breaststroke than through any other movement.

Helpful hints for underwater swimming

1. Take only a normal breath before submerging.
2. Keep the eyes open if possible for more relaxation.
3. Do not hurry any stroke.
4. Glide after each stroke to use full momentum and save energy.
5. Learn a good stroke and do not simply condition yourself to a poor one.
6. Practice breath control by sitting on the bottom or hanging on the gutter.

SPRINGBOARD DIVING

The sport of springboard diving is perhaps the most demanding and difficult of all water sports. It is commonly associated with swimming, for diving boards are standard equipment in most pools, and diving has become an integral part of the competitive swimming program. It should be noted that springboard diving does not include platform diving in which the diver performs from a stationary platform and at much greater heights. Diving is a sport that requires much in the way of coordination and "gameness." Certainly not every person is capable of becoming a springboard diver any more than all are capable of becoming gymnasts. This should not keep the average water-sport enthusiast from learning how to manipulate a springboard and to learn the basic, simple dives. In this manner a deeper appreciation for the sport will be developed and a greater respect for those who excel.

It has always seemed unfair that so much of the space at most pools was allocated to diving when so few have actually tried to use the boards for diving. Too often it is used for "cannonballing" and other acts that are entirely uncoordinated and not deserving of that much space and costly equipment. Anyone with a certain amount of patience and practice can attain a degree of proficiency on the board that will be most satisfying and worthwhile.

Diving equipment

Springboards should be either 14 feet or 16 feet long with 16 feet recommended for competitive diving. Wooden boards are now obsolete and today boards are made of aluminum or an alloy, with a few made of fiberglass. The aluminum boards are so constructed that they are almost uniform in spring power, which makes it easier for divers to adjust to boards when away from home. These boards are mounted on standards so that five feet of the board projects over the end of the pool. On the low boards the end of the board projecting over the water is exactly one meter above the water. On the high boards the water is exactly three meters below the end of the board. There is a fulcrum mounted on the standard about midway under the board, and this fulcrum may be adjustable or stationary. If the board is to be used for competitive diving the fulcrum should be adjustable. This means that the fulcrum can be moved forward or backward, thereby changing the "springiness" of the board. When the fulcrum is moved forward (toward the water) the board becomes stiffer and the diver is not able to "ride" the board as long, in which case a fast takeoff must be made, and it is called a "fast" board. If the fulcrum is moved backward the board becomes "slower" and the diver must ride the board longer if maximum benefit is to be derived from the board. With the fulcrum in this position, more height will be attained. These fulcrums can be operated manually (turning a wheel on the side) or they can be operated with hydraulic pressure or electrically. Most fulcrums are operated manually because there are fewer mechanical problems involved with this type.

The depth of the water is important. The standard depth of water recommended under a one-meter board is ten feet and 12 feet for a three-meter board. Anyone diving in a strange pool for the first time should check the depth by jumping in feet first and then proceed to dive carefully until he has adjusted to the depth.

Five groups of dives

All dives are grouped into five classifications. The *forward group* includes all dives done with a forward take-off followed by any number of somersaults, providing they are all done in a forward manner. The *backward group* includes all dives executed backward from a standing position on the board with the back to the water as long as they are all performed backward. The *reverse group* includes all dives that are executed with a running approach and a backward (back toward board) entry into the water, regardless of the number of somersaults performed. The *inward group* includes all dives executed from a standing position on the board with the back to the water and the dive is performed with the body entering the water facing the board. Again, any number of somersaults inward place the dive in the inward group. The fifth and last is the *twist group,* and this group includes all dives executed from a standing or running approach that have a twist or

FIGURE 26-8. Approach for running dive (This and the remaining figures in the chapter are adapted from Anne Ross Fairbanks, *Teaching Springboard Diving*, Englewood Cliffs, N.J.: Prentice-Hall, Inc., 1963, and are reproduced here through the courtesy of the author.)

a combination of a twisting maneuver and a somer-saulting maneuver.

Each dive has been pre-rated and assessed a degree of difficulty depending on the complexity of the dive and the difficulty encountered in executing it properly. Thus, diving judges do not have to decide how difficult a dive is when they judge, they simply decide how near perfection the diver performed the dive announced.

Each group has one dive designated as the basic dive of that group, and mastery of this particular dive will insure the novice a better chance of learning the more difficult dives. It should be noted that in all championship competition each diver is required to perform each of the five basic dives. They are:

Forward group: The running forward dive (pike or layout)

Backward group: Back dive (tuck, pike, or layout)

Reverse group: Reverse dive (tuck, pike, or layout)

Inward group: Inward dive (tuck, pike, or layout)

Twist group: Forward dive half twist (pike or layout)

APPROACH (RUNNING DIVES). The approach for all dives is very important, especially in the running dives. The rules stipulate that the diver must have an approach that has at least three steps and a hurdle (jump). The term *running dives* is misleading, for actually the diver should not run forward on the approach. Instead, the approach should be slow and controlled, which will allow the diver to get a good lift from the end of the board and will not cause him to lose balance. (See Fig. 26-8.)

The diver can get an approximate idea of where to start the approach on the board by reversing an approach, starting at the take-off end of the board and taking three steps and a hurdle (jump) and marking where this ended. Thereupon the diver simply uses this finish mark for a starting mark and proceeds with an approach. This mark may have to be altered somewhat but it does give the diver some approximation of where to start. The steps forward should be controlled and unhurried and there should be no unnecessary arm swinging. The body should be carried upright and the arms should be at the side, elbows straight, with a minimum of swinging. As the diver takes the hurdle the arms are lifted sideways with elbows straight to a point

FIGURE 26-9. Position for backward dive

just above shoulder height. The take-off foot must push from the board and the other leg is lifted with the thigh at right angles to the body and the lower leg at right angles to the thigh. The hurdle may be anywhere from 15 to 30 inches and as the diver lands on the board the legs are together, body is straight with the weight over the feet. The arms are raised and the entire body is stretched as the landing is made on the board. Immediately, the knees bend, the arms come down to the side and the diver rocks down onto his feet as the board is pressed downward with the impact of the diver landing on it. As the board starts to come up the diver rides the board up with the knees straightened, the arms lifted up and slightly forward of the body and a push with the feet downward to gain more lift. This drive should always be upward, regardless of the dive to be performed.

It is best for a novice to practice jumping in feet first using this approach and take-off. An attempt to "ride" the board upward and to use the arms should be made so that they are coordinated with the leg lift until he feels he is balanced and is getting good lift and dropping into the water near the end of the board.

Remember, the purpose of the springboard is to get more spring (height) to enable the diver to perform more difficult dives with ease and grace. There is no way to gain maximum height from a diving board unless the diver is balanced when he completes the hurdle and lands on the end of the board preparatory to take-off. The approach should be practiced often; no diver gets so good that this phase of diving does not have to be practiced. Any diver who is to perform on a strange board should practice the approach diligently until he is sure he has "caught" the board and feels sure of himself on it.

APPROACH (STANDING DIVES). The approach for dives from the backward and inward groups is performed in a standard method. The diver "addresses" the board, which means he takes a position of attention at the spot where the diver normally takes off for running dives. Following this action, the diver walks forward to the end of the board using a careful but firm walk. On the last step (if a turn to the left is planned) the left foot is placed near the right side of the board and to the right of the right foot. Immediately the diver pivots on this foot to the left by swinging the right leg around and raising the arms to a position in front of the body, shoulder width and shoulder height, with the right foot placed on the end of the board and about half of the foot projecting over the end. The left foot is then brought around and placed alongside the right so as to form a V, with the heels touching. The diver is now standing in a position for the dive with the body upright and straight from head to heels.

POSITIONS OF EXECUTION. Most dives can be executed in one of three positions, namely, tuck, pike, or layout. A dive performed in tuck position requires the diver to bend at the waist and knees; there must be a tight tuck with those stipulations. A dive performed in a pike position requires the diver to bend at the waist only with the knees remaining straight. A dive executed in layout position requires the diver to keep the body straight from head to feet. The tuck is generally considered the easiest position, with layout the most difficult.

FORWARD DIVE (LAYOUT). This dive may be executed in either pike or layout position. (See Fig. 26-10.) The running approach has been analyzed earlier so this description will start from the time the diver leaves the board. It is especially important that the diver press the board firmly on the take-off in order that the legs rise and level the body at the peak of the dive. As the diver leaves the board the arms reach forward and upward and the entire body is straightened from head to toes, with the head being held in a firm "at attention" position. In order to insure the diver's feet rising properly the muscles in slowly in the same arc and drops to a position with the heels down and the knees bent. This action presses the board downward and allows the diver to be lifted upward by the board. As the board starts its upward movement the diver straightens the knees and raises the arms in an upward and slightly forward movement. The arms should be slightly bent on this lift. The diver rides the board as high as possible and at the last moment he should push with his feet forcibly against the board. The body starts upward with the head set at "attention" position and the arms reach upward and almost together. The thigh and stomach muscles must be contracted (tightened) at the moment of take-off in order to make the legs rise and level with the upper body. As the body levels the arms are brought to a position at right angles to the body. The "drop" follows and this is initiated by dropping the head backward and pulling the arms together, as is done in all other entries. The body

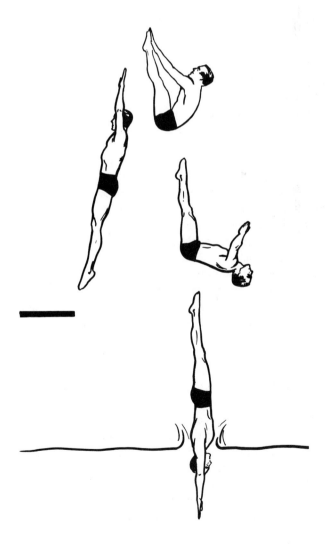

FIGURE 26-11. Back dive in pike position

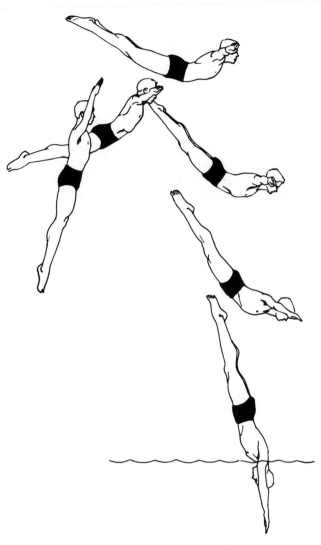

FIGURE 26-10. Forward dive in layout position

the lower back and buttocks must be contracted firmly and this action, along with the press from the board, will cause the body to level at the top. When this point is reached the diver moves the arms to a position at right angles to the body. The "drop" begins when the body has leveled and on the descent the diver brings the arms together and presses them against the ears. The body will swing downward to a vertical position and the entry will follow.

THE BACK DIVE (LAYOUT). This dive may be executed in either pike or layout position. (See Fig. 26-11.) The approach for all standing dives (back to the water) has been analyzed earlier and now the diver is ready to start the lift from the board. The diver starts by raising the arms slowly in an upward and sideward movement and at the same time rising up on the toes. These actions will prepare the diver for the downward press that will follow immediately. On this downward press the diver lowers the arms

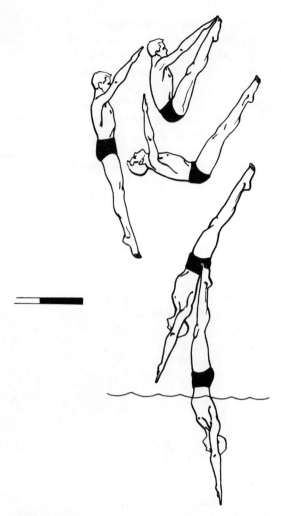

FIGURE 26-12. Reverse dive, pike position

body backward and lowering the arms sideward and downward to a position alongside the head for the entry. During this opening the thigh and stomach muscles must be contracted firmly in order to maintain the legs in the overhead position. The body swings to a vertical position and follows the hands into the water.

THE INWARD DIVE (PIKE). This dive may be executed in a tuck, pike, or layout position. (See Fig. 26-13.) Incidentally, this dive is often called the "cutaway" or back jackknife dive. The approach for this dive has been described; as soon as stability is gained, the arms are lowered sideward alongside the body. The diver starts the dive by raising the arms sideward and upward and rising to a position on the toes, which action prepares the diver for the press to follow. On the downward press, the diver lowers the arms and at the same time lowers the heels and bends the knees. This total action presses the board downward, and the upward rise of the board will come when the diver straightens the knees and raises the arms forward and upward with the

FIGURE 26-13. Inward dive, pike position

should swing to a vertical position and follow the hands into the water.

THE REVERSE DIVE (PIKE). This dive may be executed in layout, tuck, or pike position. (See Fig. 26-12.) This dive is commonly known as the half gainer. Incidentally, this dive should not be attempted until the diver is able to perform a good back dive in pike position and be consistent on the approach. There is a tendency to rush the approach for this dive and this results in a poor take-off. The final press from the board is firm and the arms reach upward as they are placed together above and slightly in front of diver's head. The diver immediately raises the legs upward and during this action the upper body must be maintained in a vertical position until the feet reach the hands. At this point the diver has piked the dive and this pike should be such that the thighs are pressed against the chest of the diver with the knees straight. Now the diver is ready to open the pike and prepare for the entry. This opening is done by dropping the head, shoulders, and upper elbows bent slightly. The diver rides the board as high as possible, and the feet should push from the board forcibly at the last moment of contact. The arms have reached a point overhead, and as the feet leave the board the head is dropped and the hands reach downward for the feet to assume the pike position. As soon as the pike position is gained the legs must be raised backward and upward to a position directly above the body, which places the body in a straight line. The head, arms, and body must remain in the piking position, and as the diver prepares to enter the water the hands should be circled slightly outward and then brought to a position alongside the head. The body should be perfectly vertical on entry into the water.

FORWARD DIVE WITH HALF TWIST (LAYOUT). This dive may be executed in pike or layout position. (See Figs. 26-14 and 26-15.) This dive is extremely difficult to master even though it does not appear to be difficult on first observation. The diver should try to learn a good forward dive in layout position first, as this dive starts in exactly the same

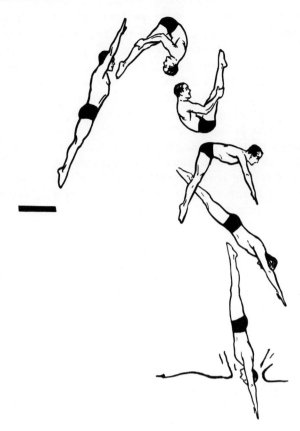

FIGURE 26-14. Forward dive with one-half twist, layout position

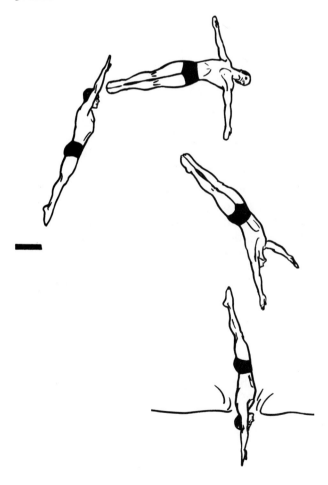

FIGURE 26-15. Forward dive, one and one-half somersaults, pike position

manner. When the diver reaches a point where the feet have risen to the level of the head and shoulders, the diver should drop one shoulder and raise the other upward and backward. The arms are maintained at shoulder level throughout this twisting action, and the head is kept in a position with the chin thrust forward slightly. Since the body is kept rigid, this twisting action of the shoulders will twist the entire body. The twisting must be done with steady pressure and not with a jerky movement. As the body rolls to a position on the back the head is dropped backward and the hands are brought together as in the drop and entry of the back dive. The body and legs will follow the hands into the water.

Diving from poolside

This skill should be treated as a separate activity, for it is really tumbling or acrobatics with the water as a landing place. It is fun for the novice and it may be used to stimulate interest, although care should be exercised that some swimming skills are taught first.

DESCRIPTION. The standing dive is the third

and final step in the progression used in learning to dive. The first step is the sitting dive. The learner sits on the edge of the pool with his feet spread slightly and placed in the gutter. His arms are together and extended over his head. He should lean forward from the hips, his head between his arms and his hands pointing to a spot under water about three to five feet in front of him. He keeps leaning until balance is lost and he enters head first. The feet should not leave the gutter until the hands hit the water. When he is completely under water, the back, head and arms should be arched and he will rise to the surface.

The second step is the kneeling dive. One foot is placed on the deck with the toes hooked over the edge, and the other leg is in a kneeling position. The arms and head are in the same position as in the sitting dive. The diver leans forward until balance is lost and then a slight push is given with the kneeling leg, which makes the angle of entry sharper than in the sitting dive.

The third step is the standing dive. Both feet are hooked over the edge and the arms and head are in the same position. The body is bent slightly at the waist and the diver leans forward again until balance is lost. At that moment, both legs spring and the body enters the water at such an angle that the entire body follows the arms and the head into the same hole. Short practice will enable the learner to abandon raising the arms overhead and crouching, and soon the dive will appear smooth and easy.

Helpful hints for diving

1. Know the depth of the water before attempting any dive.
2. Do not arch the back until the body is well under the water.
3. Spring as soon as the balance is lost.
4. Keep the arms straight and together until the body starts to rise.
5. Do not raise the head before the water is reached.

SAFETY

Safety in swimming may be broken down into two groups—safeguarding from infection and disease, and safeguarding from accidents. Pools present problems different from those encountered in open water swimming.

Safeguarding from infection and disease

1. Never swim while having any type of contagious infection.

2. Soap showers without suits should be taken before entering any pool and after using lavatory.
3. Bathing caps should be worn in all pools by women and men with long hair.
4. Expectorating on the deck should be prohibited.
5. Only those in barefeet or bathing sandals should be allowed on the deck.
6. Animals of all types should be excluded from bathing area.

Safeguarding from accidents

1. Never swim alone.
2. Never dive into any strange body of water head-first without testing for depth by a feet-first entry or a surface dive.
3. Adjust to the water slowly through a cold shower or by rubbing the extremities first.
4. Allow ample time to elapse after eating a heavy meal before entering the water.
5. Never yell for help unless real trouble is present.
6. Never push or throw anyone into the water.
7. Do not bring articles to the area that might cause injury to others.
8. Only one diver should be allowed on any board at a time.
9. The diving area should be cleared of swimmers except those diving.
10. Running on the deck, tag, and horseplay in the water should be prohibited.

CONDUCTING DIVING COMPETITION

Diving has always been a part of dual and championship swimming meets and in recent years there have been many diving meets conducted without swimming competition. When held in conjunction with swimming, diving has afforded a beneficial break for the swimmers, and for a great many of the fans it provides a most interesting and spectacular event. Diving competition can be very "drawn out" and boring if it is not well organized, so each meet director should make certain that this does not occur.

The officials needed for a diving meet consist of the referee, a secretary, either three or five judges and, if possible, at least one scorer who is efficient at computing. The referee is in complete charge of the competition and his duties are many, including checking the entry sheets for individual divers, instructing the judges and placing them in proper position to view the divers, announcing each dive clearly, and verifying that each diver has executed the dive announced before signaling for awards from the judges. He may rule that a diver should have another try if any unusual incident occurs while the diver was performing. The secretary shall record the judges' awards and with the aid of a scorer and computer determine the total awards for each dive. He shall keep a running total of the scores for each diver and be ready to announce the total score at the completion of competition.

The diving judges should be former divers, coaches, or officials who are familiar with diving. In dual meets three judges officiate, while in championship meets five judges should be used, with the top and low awards being cancelled. Recently several college conferences have come up with the idea of using all of the diving coaches as judges, with each coach judging all divers except his own and again with only the middle three awards used in computing the diver's score.

Judging of dives should be based on the following factors: the approach, the take-off, the technique and grace of the dive during passage through the air and finally the entry into the water. The approach should be smooth, controlled, and performed in such a manner that the diver can gain maximum lift from the board. The take-off should be executed from a balanced position without a forward or backward lean, and height is of great importance. On a standing dive, if the diver allows one foot to precede the other on the take-off, one-half to three points should be deducted from his score. The acrobatics in the air must be executed in the position announced and the body should be kept compact and tight during the dive. The entry should be with as little splash as possible and the body should be stretched with the toes pointed. The angle of entry should be as close to the perpendicular as possible. The dive must be completed a safe distance from the board, otherwise points may be deducted. When the referee signals for awards from the judges, the response must be immediate and in unison.

PERFORMANCE	POINTS
Very good	9, 9.5 to 10
Good	7, 7.5 to 8, 8.5
Satisfactory	5, 5.5 to 6, 6.5
Deficient	3, 3.5 to 4, 4.5
Unsatisfactory	0.5, 1.5 to 2, 2.5
Complete Failure	0

Equipment needed to conduct diving competition

1. An adequate public address system.

2. Flash cards for the judges with numbers ranging from 0 to 10 (including ½ for each number).

3. Diving score sheets which have two parts: one for use by the referee in announcing the dives and one for use by the secretary in recording scores.

4. A diving calculator.

5. An adequate supply of pencils.

6. A whistle for the referee.

Additional officials required to conduct a regulation swimming meet are a starter, judges and timers for each lane, and a clerk or secretary to keep the records.

TERMINOLOGY

American crawl A term often used to describe a form of swimming in which the swimmer takes six flutter kicks to each complete stroke of the arms.

Approach and hurdle A term used in diving. The walking steps (approach) must contain a minimum of three steps. The hurdle is the jump made at the end of diving board by lifting one leg until the thigh is parallel to the board, jumping off other foot and landing on both feet at end of board for take-off.

Australian crawl Stroke in which swimmer takes an arm stroke for each flutter kick of opposite leg, hence a two-beat crawl. This form is very effective in distance swimming.

Backstroke (elementary) A less strenuous stroke in which arms move simultaneously under the water with a frog kick employed by the legs.

Backstroke (racing) A stroke on the back in which arms stroke alternately with recovery out of the water, with legs using a flutter kick, usually six beats to an arm cycle; virtually an inverted crawl.

Bobbing Alternately going below the water surface and ascending in vertical position with head up.

Breaststroke Swimming on breast; both hands must move forward and backward together, with shoulders parallel to the water surface and at right angles to forward progress. Legs must be drawn with a distinct bend at the knees, followed by an outward and backward kicking motion, with no up and down movement as in flutter kick.

Butterfly A stroke in which the arms are recovered simultaneously above the water and the legs are moved together symmetrically. The dolphin kick or frog kick or a combination of both may be used.

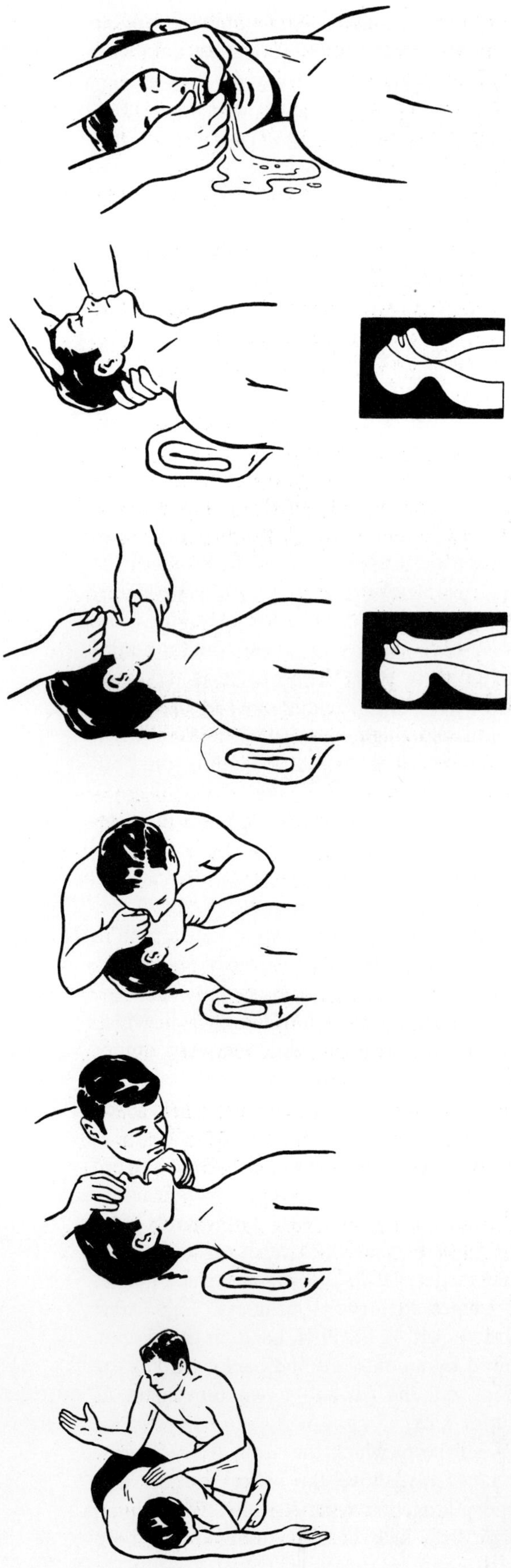

ARTIFICIAL RESPIRATION

How to give mouth-to-mouth resuscitation

Use this method not only on drowning victims but also on persons suffering electrical shock, gas poisoning, and suffocation. To avoid direct contact, a clean handkerchief may be placed over victim's mouth without impeding air flow.

Examine victim's mouth for foreign matter. If there is any, (mucus, food, sand, tobacco, loose dentures, etc.) turn his head to one side and remove it with your fingers or a cloth wrapped around your fingers.

Lift the victim's neck, place a folded coat, blanket, etc. under his shoulders. Tilt his head back as far as possible.

Grasp the jaw with thumb in one side of the mouth and pull it forward. Maintain this position to keep air passage open.

Pinch victim's nostrils shut, take a deep breath and place your mouth over his mouth and your thumb creating a tight seal; or close the victim's mouth, take a deep breath and place your mouth over his nose. Blow into victim's mouth or nose until you see his chest rise. For an infant breathe through both nose and mouth, with thumb in mouth.

Remove your mouth and listen for out-flow of air. For an adult, inflate lungs at rate of about 12 times per minute. For a child, inflate lungs up to 20 times per minute, using relatively shallow breaths.

If first few attempts to inflate the lungs are unsuccessful, turn victim on his side and administer several sharp blows between the shoulders in an attempt to dislodge the obstruction.

NOW REPEAT ENTIRE PROCEDURE.
** FOR INFANTS, SEAL BOTH MOUTH AND NOSE WITH YOUR MOUTH **

FIGURE 26-16.

336

Degree of difficulty A numerical rating given to specific dives in keeping with their relative difficulty. Ratings range from 1.0 for a forward dive tuck on one-meter board to 2.9 points for a three and one-half forward somersault on the three-meter board.

Dog paddle (human stroke) A primitive form of swimming often adopted by beginners in which the arms are extended forward alternately, usually under water with leg kick inconsistent.

Finning A swimming stroke in which the swimmer lies on back, feet together, hands at sides. Propulsion comes from movement of hands pushing towards the feet.

Flutter kick A fast vertical kick, with legs moving alternately and rhythmically in a loose whipping motion, with power for knee and ankle action coming from the hip joints.

Free style Any desired stroke the swimmer may wish to use. Since the crawl is the fastest stroke, it is the one invariably used in competition.

Frog kick A kick used with the breaststroke. The knees are drawn forward and outward slowly with heels fairly close together, and then pressed backward and outward as the feet whip around in an arc. The kick is completed by squeezing the legs together with toes pointed.

Glide Movement of body in water after completion of the propulsion stroke.

Gutter Edge of the pool at water level. Gutter contains drain for disposal of excess water.

High board A term often applied to the three-meter diving board.

Individual medley A four-course swimming event in which a butterfly stroke is used in the first fourth, a backstroke in the second fourth, a breaststroke in the third fourth, and free style in the last fourth.

Inward Diver stands on board with his back to the water, leaps up and out from the board, rotating his body toward the board, head descending toward water.

Jellyfish float Floating position with arms and legs hanging down in water, hands holding ankles, head under water, rounded portion of back showing on surface.

Kick board A buoyant board which may be grasped with the hands and used in developing kicking techniques.

Layout A diving position in which the body is extended with no flexion.

Low board A term often applied to the one-meter diving board.

Pike A diving position in which the body is bent at the hips and the legs are kept straight.

Prone float Floating in water with face down, arms and legs extended.

Scissors kick A kick used in the sidestroke or trudgen. Swimmer starts with legs together, extending them to stride position, with one leg going forward and one backward, both moving in a plane parallel to water's surface. Knees are bent during recovery part of the kick.

Scull Propelling the body in a dorsal position with a rotary motion of the hands and arms.

Sidestroke With body on side, arms alternately reach forward under water, and on the pull they alternately move to the same side of swimmer, while the scissors kick is employed with the legs.

Six-beat crawl A swimming stroke in which there are six beats of the legs in flutter style kick to one full arm stroke. The most common rhythm of the American crawl.

Supine float Floating in water with face up, arms and legs extended.

Tread water A swimming technique that enables the swimmer to remain afloat in a vertical position by kicking the legs and, if necessary, by using the arms extended in a sweeping movement.

Trudgen kick A double overarm stroke using alternate arms, with legs employing a scissors stroke, and with breathing always on the same side.

Tuck A diving position in which the body is bent at the hips and knees.

SELECTED REFERENCES

Ainsworth, Dorothy S., *et al.*, *Individual Sports for Women* (4th ed.). Philadelphia: W. B. Saunders Co., 1963.

American Red Cross, *Life Saving Methods*. Washington, D.C.: American Red Cross, First Aid and Life Saving Service.

Armbruster, D. A., R. H. Allen, and B. Harlan, *Swimming and Diving* (4th ed.). St. Louis: C. V. Mosby Co., 1963.

Clotworthy, R., *The Young Sportsman's Guide to Swimming.* New York: Thomas Nelson & Sons, 1962.

Counsilman, James E., *The Science of Swimming.* Englewood Cliffs, N.J.: Prentice-Hall, Inc., 1968.

Fait, Hollis, John Shaw, and Katherine Ley, *A Manual of Physical Education Activities.* Philadelphia: W. B. Saunders Co., 1967.

Gabrielson, M. A., and B. W. Gabrielson, *Aquatics Handbook.* Englewood Cliffs, N.J.: Prentice-Hall, Inc., 1968.

Harlan, B., *Diving.* New York: Sterling Publishing Co., Inc., 1961.

Higgins, J. F., *et al., Swimming and Diving* (3rd ed.). Annapolis, Md.: United States Naval Institute, 1962.

Juba, B., *Swimming.* New York: Arco Publishing Co., Inc., 1962.

McKenzie, M. M., and B. Spears, *Beginning Swimming.* Belmont, Calif.: Wadsworth Publishing Co., Inc., 1963.

Moriarty, P., *Springboard Diving.* New York: The Ronald Press Company, 1959.

Official AAU Swimming Handbook. New York: Amateur Athletic Union (current edition).

Official N.C.A.A. Swimming Guide. Phoenix, Ariz.: College Athletics Publishing Service, National Collegiate Athletic Association (current edition).

Official N.S.G.W.S. Aquatics Guide. Washington, D.C.: American Association for Health, Physical Education and Recreation (current edition).

Robertson, D. H., and C. W. Russell, *Swimming.* New York: Sterling Publishing Co., Inc., 1962.

Shaw, J. H., C. A. Troester, and M. A. Gabrielson, *Individual Sports for Men* (3rd ed.). Dubuque, Iowa: William C. Brown Company, Publishers, 1964.

Table Tennis

ORIGIN AND DEVELOPMENT

Table tennis probably had its origin during the latter part of the nineteenth century but no one is sure about the identity of the person or persons who actually invented the game. Because of its close similarity to tennis, it is entirely possible that several people could have developed the idea of playing a game fashioned after tennis on a smaller scale than that used in the parent game. The game, in its development, has been called by several names, including indoor tennis, gossima (name given to the game by a British Manufacturing Company), ping pong (a name derived from sound of ball striking paddle and table), and table tennis. The name of "ping pong" was patented by the Parker Brothers, manufacturers of indoor play equipment in the United States, who sold game equipment under this trade name to fans in this country and England. The game enjoyed some popularity in the country when introduced under its name of "ping pong" in 1900 and continued to spread in popularity until 1902. Considered as a new-fangled fad or craze by the fans,

the game lost favor, and it did not become popular again until the late 1920's.

A dispute over the use of the term "ping pong" was instrumental in the adoption of the name "table tennis" in the 1930's. The English Table Tennis Association was formed in 1923, and in 1926 an International Table Tennis Federation was organized. The game is now well past the fad stage and occupies an important place in modern recreational life.

NATURE OF THE GAME

The game may be played by two or four people. Equipment consists of a table equipped with a smooth playing surface, balls, and rackets. (See Fig. 27-1.) Equipment, when well made, is durable and will give long service if reasonable care is exercised. The game may be played with equal enjoyment by the skilled and the unskilled, although the acquisition of a fair degree of proficiency in playing the game usually enhances one's pleasure. The "dub" or beginner has no business competing with a first-rate player, since neither person would enjoy the competition. The game may be played by both old and

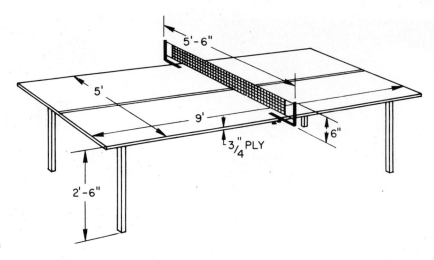

FIGURE 27-1. Table tennis table

young and seems destined to remain as one of our most popular recreational activities.

TECHNIQUE AND FUNDAMENTALS

Because of the close similarity to tennis, the basic fundamentals regarding stroking the ball apply equally well to both sports. Table tennis does not require as much running as tennis and consequently does not require the expenditure of energy demanded of the older game. For this reason table tennis may be played by individuals who do not have the vigor and physical stamina to play tennis, although one will find that skilled players can get plenty of activity in a fast game.

STROKES. There are two basic strokes used in table tennis, the forehand and the backhand. The tennis grip is used by a majority of players and is the recommended grip for beginners. In this grip, the bat is grasped with the thumb and forefinger on the blade, the other fingers around the handle. (See Figs. 27-2 through 27-4.)

For right-handed players, the forehand stroke should be used when the ball approaches from the right, and the backhand when the ball approaches from the left. On the forehand stroke, the left shoulder should face the table while on the backhand, the right shoulder is pointed toward the table. (See Fig. 27-5.) In addition to the forehand and backhand drives, certain variations in arm action and movement of the paddle as it makes contact with the ball will produce different reactions in the bounce of the ball. These variations in ball bounce, which cause the ball to veer sharply from a straight course, are caused by the "English," or spin effect, given the ball by paddle action. Moving the paddle from left to right as it touches the ball will cause the ball to rotate and bounce in the opposite direction.

BASIC RULES [1]

Singles game

PLAYING AREA. The table tennis table is nine feet long and five feet wide, with its horizontal surface 30 inches above the floor.

THE NET AND ITS SUPPORTS. The playing surface shall be divided by a net located in the center of the surface area and parallel to the end lines. The net along its entire top side shall be six inches above the playing surface, its lower side close to the playing surface.

SCORING. The winner of a match shall be the player who first scores 21 points, unless both players have 20 points, in which case the winner must

[1] *Official N.S.G.W.S. Recreational Games and Volleyball Guide,* Washington, D.C.: The American Association for Health, Physical Education and Recreation, latest edition.

FIGURE 27-2. Position of hand in backhand

FIGURE 27-3. Position for forehand play

FIGURE 27-4. Penholder grip; not recommended in fast table tennis

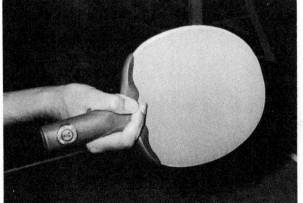

FIGURE 27-5. On backhand, right shoulder faces table

FIGURE 27-6. Preparing to serve

gain a two-point lead in order to win. The choice of ends and service at the start of the game shall be decided by toss.

THE CHANGE OF ENDS AND SERVICE. A game is started with the server making five consecutive services. The receiver follows with five services, each player alternating in this fashion for the duration of the game, unless the score becomes 20–all, in which case the receiver shall make one serve, followed by the original server with one serve, then the receiver, and so on, until a winner is declared. Where the match consists of only one game, or in the deciding game of a match, the players shall change ends at the score of 10. The player who started at one end of the table in one game shall start at the other end in the immediately subsequent game.

THE SERVICE. The service shall be delivered by releasing the ball, without imparting any spin upon release, and striking it with the paddle outside the boundary of the court near server's end. (See Fig. 27-6.) Finger spins and rubbing the ball against the racket face are illegal. Any spin imparted to the ball must come from action of the racket upon impact with the ball. The ball shall be struck so that it first drops into server's court and then into the receiver's court by passing directly over or around the net.

A GOOD RETURN. A ball having been served or returned in play shall be struck by the player so that it passes directly over or around the net and lands in opponent's court; provided that if the ball, during play, returns of its own impetus over or around the net, it may be played the same as a returned ball.

LET BALL. The served ball shall be a let if it touches the net or its supports, and later lands in receiver's court. A let shall also be declared when a serve is made before the receiver is ready, unless the receiver makes an effort to strike the ball. It is a let if either player, because of conditions not under his control, is prevented from making a serve or a return.

Either player shall lose the point:

1. If he fails to make a good service, unless a let is declared.
2. If a good service or a good return is made by his opponent and he fails to make a good return.
3. If racket, or any part of player or clothing, touches the net or its supports while the ball is in play.
4. If the player moves the table in any way while playing the ball.
5. If a player's free hand touches the table while the ball is in play.
6. If, at any time, he volleys the ball. (A volley consists of hitting the ball before it has bounced.)

Doubles game

The rules for singles play shall apply to doubles play in all instances except those indicated below.

THE TABLE. A one-eighth inch white line shall be drawn down the center of the table parallel to the side lines. This shall be called the service line.

A GOOD SERVICE. The service shall be delivered as previously provided and ball must touch first the server's right-half court or the center line on his side of the net, and then, passing directly over or around the net, touch the receiver's right-half court or the center line on his side of the net.

THE CHOICE OF ORDER OF PLAY. The pair who has the right to serve the first five services in any game shall decide which partner shall do so, and the opposing pair shall then decide similarly which shall first be the receiver.

THE ORDER OF SERVICE. Each server shall serve for five points. At the end of each term of service, the one who was receiving becomes the server, and the partner of the previous server becomes the receiver. This sequence of the receiver becoming the server and the partner of the previous server becoming the receiver continues until the end of the game or the score of 20–all. At the score of 20–all, the sequence of serving and receiving shall continue uninterrupted except that each player shall serve only one point in turn, and the serve alternates after each point until the end of the game.

THE ORDER OF PLAY. The server shall first make a good service, the receiver shall then make a good return, the partner of the server shall then make a good return, the partner of the receiver shall then make a good return, the server shall then make a good return, and thereafter each player alternately in that sequence shall make a good return.

PLAYING STRATEGY

Strategic movements in table tennis are similar to those employed in tennis. A change of pace and shifting from the long to the short game, in which an opponent is driven back from the table and then "crossed up" with a short lob or a sharp angle shot, are tactics which all players must employ if they expect to compete on an even basis with good performers. One must learn to impart spin to the ball in order to take advantage of an opponent's position. Some players endeavor to keep the ball in play without resorting to hard drives or smash shots, on the assumption that any opponent will make a mistake if enough opportunities are provided. Such players may not display a spectacular game, but they are tough to defeat because they do not beat themselves by driving the ball off the table or into the net.

A player's best assets are accuracy and control. If he can consistently return all reasonable shots made by an opponent, he will find himself the victor in a majority of his matches.

SAFETY

Accidents occasionally occur in table tennis, but they are very infrequent. One of the greatest hazards involves the possibility of falling on slippery floors; players should always examine for this condition before starting to play. If the table is located in a crowded area where there is a possibility of striking adjacent objects when swinging at the ball, players should note the locations of these hazards and exercise every effort to avoid them. If reasonable precautions are observed, there should be virtually no accident hazard connected with playing the game of table tennis.

HELPFUL HINTS

Observance of the following suggestions should improve one's skill in playing the game:

1. Master the fundamental strokes involved in the forehand and backhand strokes.
2. Develop your footwork and position play so that you are always ready to meet any situation.
3. Concentrate on accuracy—try to make every shot hit its mark.
4. Develop an ability to vary your game by using smashes, drop shots, lob shots, and so forth, in order to throw your opponent off stride. (See Fig. 27-7.)
5. Practice as often as possible and always try to choose an opponent who is better than you are.

PLAYING COURTESIES

Observance of the following courtesies will be appreciated by your opponents:

1. Do not make derogatory remarks during play regarding the ability of your opponent.
2. Always retrieve your share of balls that leave the table.
3. Observe all the playing rules and make no effort to take advantage of an opponent through a technicality.

FIGURE 27-7. The drop shot, secured by placing reverse spin on the ball

4. Compliment an opponent on good plays.
5. Control your temper—remember it is only a game and the attitude you display affects the amount of enjoyment both participants receive from playing.

TERMINOLOGY

Ace   A service which completely eludes the receiver.

Ad   Commonly used as a contraction of "advantage."

Advantage   Next point made after a deuce score. It is "advantage out" if the receiver wins it and "advantage in" if the server wins. The player wins the match who first wins a point after gaining "advantage."

All   Term used to denote an equal score, e.g., 20–all.

Backhand   Stroke frequently used by right-handed player when returning a ball hit to his left, in which the paddle is held so that the back of the hand faces the ball; the ball is usually hit with side of paddle opposite the side used in the forehand.

Backhand flip A half-volley backhand, played as a topspin drive.

Backspin Ball hit so that top of ball rotates toward stroker, bottom moving away.

Ball Constructed of celluloid, hollow, four and one-half inches to four and three-quarter inches in circumference, weighing between 37 and 41 grains.

Block shot A half-volley.

Chop A stroke in which the lower part of the ball is hit with a downward stroke of the paddle, imparting backspin to the ball.

Dead ball Ball is dead if a let is called, when it bounces twice on the table, or at the conclusion of a point or rally.

Deuce When the score is even at 20–all. To win, a player must score two consecutive points.

Drop shot A shot played so softly that it dies before opponent can reach it, or places him at a disadvantage if he does play it.

Finger spin An illegal procedure whereby spin is imparted to the ball by the fingers in serving.

Forehand A stroke or volley made in such a fashion that the palm is the leading part of the movement. Usually hit with the opposite face of the paddle than that used in backhand. In this stroke the left foot of right-handed players is toward the table.

Game Winner is player or team who first scores 21 points, unless each has 20 points, in which case a deuce score results and the winner must score two consecutive points, such as 22–20, or 23–21.

Let Means "play the point over" and occurs when the ball strikes the top of net and falls into correct service court, also if a ball breaks or if a player is interfered with by an official or spectator.

Mixed doubles Doubles game in which each team has one man and one woman player.

Net Table tennis net is of fine meshwork material, mounted six inches above the table and fastened to posts three inches to six inches outside of table, which makes the net five and one-half feet to six feet in length.

Push shot Ball is struck with a pushing motion of the paddle near the top of the bounce so that no spin is placed on the ball.

Service court In singles, the entire table area on the receiver's side, five feet by four and one-half feet. In doubles, the table is divided by a center line so each service court is four and one-half feet by two and one-half feet.

Slice A stroke in which the ball is stroked late so that it tends to spin in a direction away from the paddle.

Topspin Ball is stroked so that the top spins forward in the direction of flight. Is the opposite of backspin or underspin.

Volley Illegal stroking of ball while it is in the air and before it has touched the table.

SELECTED REFERENCES

Barna, Victor, *Table Tennis Today*. London: Sir Isaac Pitman & Sons Ltd., 1962.

Carrington, Jack, *Modern Table Tennis* (revised ed.). London: G. Bell & Sons, Ltd., 1960.

Harrower, Geoffrey, *Table Tennis*. London: English Universities Press, 1966.

Leach, Johnny, *Table Tennis Complete*. New York: Barnes & Noble, Inc., 1960.

Miles, Richard, *The Game of Table Tennis*. Philadelphia: J. B. Lippincott Co., 1967.

Official N.S.G.W.S. Individual Sports Guide. Washington, D.C.: American Association for Health, Physical Education and Recreation (current edition).

Table Tennis for You. Philadelphia: United States Table Tennis Association (current edition).

Vannier, Maryhelen, and Hally Beth Poindexter, *Individual and Team Sports for Girls and Women* (2nd ed.). Philadelphia: W. B. Saunders Co., 1968.

Varner, Margaret, and J. Rufford Harrison, *Table Tennis*. Dubuque, Iowa: William C. Brown Co., Publishers, 1968.

Tennis

28

ORIGIN AND DEVELOPMENT

The game of tennis is most widely held to be derived from handball, which originated in Ireland as early as the tenth century, although some believe tennis dates back 20 or 30 centuries to when royal families were great sports devotees. Handball moved from Ireland to England and Scotland, but did not take hold in either of these countries. The French adopted the game of handball but soon discovered, as did the others, that it was very hard on the hands, so they began to devise methods of protecting the hands by wrapping them with cords, wearing gloves, and eventually by using a paddle.

In 1873, Major Walter Clopton Wingfield, a student of court tennis, introduced tennis, which, as we know it today, is officially called lawn tennis. The game was first intended to be played on a lawn, but eventually the use of hard surfaces grew in popularity. As we know tennis today, it is most often played on clay, asphalt, or cement. However, the annual United States Lawn Tennis Association singles championship matches are played on grass at the West Side Tennis Club located at Forest Hills, Long Island, New York. The terms "grass," "hard," "clay," and "indoor" are used to designate all tournaments sanctioned by the USLTA. The International Lawn Tennis Federation (ILTF) controls the game internationally, in that the association determines and enforces the rules in order that the game be played uniformly in the several countries.

The popularity of the game spread rapidly. A British officer who had observed the game introduced it in Bermuda. Miss Mary Outerbridge, who was vacationing in Bermuda from her home on Staten Island, New York, was attracted to the game. She bought some equipment and learned the rules of the game, and is credited with first introducing it to the United States in 1874. The game spread quickly in the United States and by 1879 it had crossed the continent to California. In 1881, E. H. Outerbridge, the older brother of Mary Outerbridge, called a meeting of the tennis leaders of that day, who organized themselves into the United States Lawn Tennis Association, which is still the governing body of amateur tennis today.

The first National Lawn Tennis Tournament

Championship was played in 1881. Other well-known tournaments are the Wimbledon Tournament in England; the Davis Cup Championship, which is sought by men's teams from various countries of the world; and the Wightman Cup Competition, which is composed of women's teams representing the United States and England. International tennis team competition for women players representing as many as 16 nations was inaugurated by the ILTF in 1963— each team consisting of three players. Two singles and one doubles match are played, with the winners determined on a two-out-of-three basis.

NATURE OF THE GAME

Tennis is a game that has always appealed to both sexes, young and old. It is considered by many to be one of the best forms of corecreational sports. The pace of the game can be set to the individual player's ability, for it may be played merely as a mild form of exercise, or so strenuously that it taxes one's endurance and strength to the very limit. Speed, agility, coordination, and endurance can be developed, and indeed are needed to play a good game of tennis.

Tennis can be played both indoors and outdoors, but we find it most often played in the open air. We usually associate tennis with sunny, dry weather, because the strings of the rackets, which generally are gut or nylon, cannot withstand dampness. The courts have varying surfaces, such as lawn, clay, composition, cement, or dirt.

There are two separate games of tennis. One is the singles game, which has two participants, one individual opposing the other, and the doubles game, which has four participants, two individuals teaming up to compete against another team of two. The doubles court is nine feet wider than the singles court, having a four and one-half foot alley on each side of the singles court. (See Fig. 28-1.)

The basic rules are the same for men's and women's tennis. To start the game, the server stands just behind his baseline to the *right* of his center service line, and puts the ball into play by striking it in the air in such a manner that it lands in his opponent's right service court. The server has two chances to put the ball into play. The ball that does not land in the proper service court is called a "fault" and is not played. A served ball that touches the net during the flight and lands in the proper service court is called a "let"; it is not counted as a fault nor is it played, but is served again.

The receiver should return the serve on its first bounce to the server's court. The rally continues until one of the players fails to return the ball, either on the fly or after first bounce within the boundaries of his court.

When the point has been completed, the server stands just behind his baseline and to the *left* of the center service line and serves to his opponent's left service court, continuing to alternate left and right after each point until the game is completed. Upon completion of the game, the server becomes the receiver.

In doubles, each player serves a game in his turn, first a member of one team, and then a member of the other team, and so on. The same order of serving is kept throughout the set.

Example of scoring

Points in tennis are called Love, 15, 30, 40, Deuce, Advantage, and Game.

0, or nothing, is called Love.

First point won by a player is called 15.

Second point won by a player is called 30.

Third point won by a player is called 40.

Fourth point won by a player gives him Game, provided his opponent does not have more than 30 (2 points).

If each player has won three points (40–all), the score is deuce. The next point won by a player gives him advantage. However, if he loses the next point, the score is again deuce. When either player wins two *consecutive* points following the score of deuce, the game is won by that player. The server's score is always given first. The score should be called loudly and clearly after every point.

IF THE SERVER HAS WON	AND THE RECEIVER HAS WON	THE SCORE IS
1 pt.	0 pts.	15–Love
2 pts.	0 pts.	30–Love
2 pts.	1 pt.	30–15
3 pts.	1 pt.	40–15
3 pts.	2 pts.	40–30
4 pts.	2 pts.	Game for server
1 pt.	1 pt.	15–All
1 pt.	2 pts.	15–30
2 pts.	2 pts.	30–All
2 pts.	3 pts.	30–40
3 pts.	3 pts.	Deuce (40–All)
3 pts.	4 pts.	Receiver's Advantage
3 pts.	5 pts.	Receiver's Game

In scoring, the player who first wins six games wins a *set*, unless both players have won five games; then it take an advantage of two games to win, so the score could be 7–5, or 8–6, or 9–7, and so on.

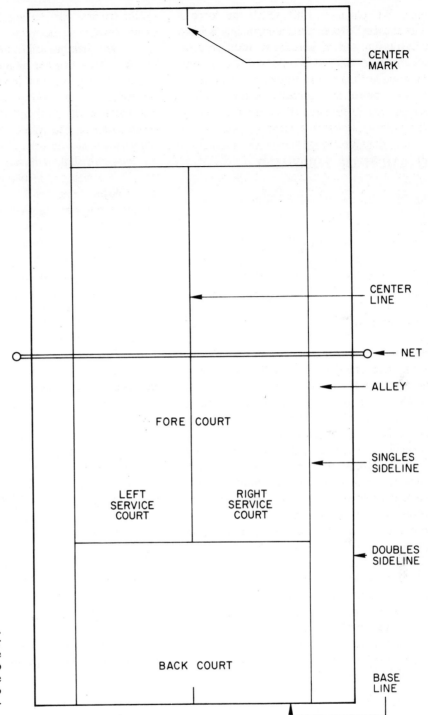

CENTER
MARK

CENTER
LINE

NET

ALLEY

FORE COURT

SINGLES
SIDELINE

LEFT
SERVICE
COURT

RIGHT
SERVICE
COURT

DOUBLES
SIDELINE

BACK COURT

BASE
LINE

FIGURE 28-1. Lawn tennis court. This diagram illustrates the court for the singles and doubles games. The court should lie north and south to give maximum protection from the sun. For specific dimensions, refer to Field and Court Diagrams (see Appendix).

In scoring the *match,* the player first winning two sets is generally declared the winner. In official tennis matches, the winner of three sets is declared the winner of the men's match, while in the women's game, the winner of two sets is declared the winner of the match. For example, match scores could be 6–0, 6–0; 6–3, 6–2; 9–7, 4–6, 10–8; 2–6, 6–4, 6–4; 6–1, 6–1, 6–3; 4–6, 6–4, 6–4, 6–4; 6–0, 5–7, 7–5, 2–6, 8–6. A new scoring system, VASSS (Van Alen Simplified Scoring System) is being used in some tournaments on an optional basis. In this system, 31 points make up a set, provided the winner is ahead by at least two points. Scoring is similar to that in table tennis (1, 2, 3, 4, 5, etc.). A match may be two out of three or three out of five sets. Zero replaces the term "Love." By agreement, a set may be reduced to 21 or 11 points. The service changes every five points. If the score is tied at 30–30, an extra eight-point sequence is played. If the score is tied 4–4 at the end of the first sequence, a second sequence is played and, if necessary, additional sequences are played until one is won by a 5–3 or greater margin. During the sequence(s), servers alternate service courts and contestants change sides every four points.

SELECTION OF EQUIPMENT

The selection of proper equipment is of utmost importance to the beginning tennis player, as well as to the expert player. With good equipment the beginning player can eliminate many handicaps, and thereby get more enjoyment from mastering the fundamental skills.

Racket

The selection of the racket is of primary importance, and the beginning player must give consideration to the weight, the balance, the handle size, the stringing, and the quality of the frame. (See Fig. 28-2.) The weight of the racket will vary with the individual's ability. The beginner wants a racket he can comfortably wield. For younger players, an unstrung frame weighing between 12½ ounces and 13½ ounces is generally the best selection. A frame lighter than 12½ ounces will have a tendency to break down with hard play. Usually women players should not select a racket frame that weighs over

FIGURE 28-2. Parts of the tennis racquet

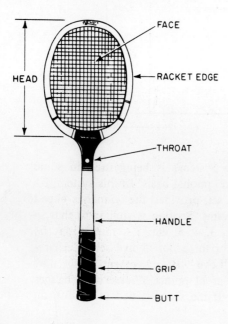

13½ ounces. Men players generally choose racket frames weighing between 13½ and 14½ ounces.

The balance of a racket is one of individual choice. The beginner should swing several different rackets to find the type that suits him best. The point of balance of a racket should fall between 13 and 13¾ inches from the bottom of the racket. Top-heavy rackets are difficult to wield and the beginning player should select an evenly balanced racket, or even one slightly handle-heavy.

The size of the handle will vary with the size of a player's hand. The circumference of the grips varies about one-eighth of an inch, from four and one-half to five inches. Junior and women players usually select racket handles of the lower range, and the average man player will use a handle of four and three-fourths or four and seven-eighths inches in circumference, unless he has a very small hand. The racket handle should be covered with a leather grip of good quality for comfort and to prevent slipping during the strokes.

There are three general types of strings for the racket—gut, nylon, and silk. The best grade of gut comes in different gauges. The beginning player will get much more wear out of the 15-gauge gut stringing than the 16-gauge. The 16-gauge is a light gut used by the better tournament players. Nylon, a newcomer to the field, will play well for the average player, but does not possess the elasticity of gut. It is moisture-proof, and is cheaper than gut. Nylon sells for around $6 to $8, compared to $12 to $20 for good gut. Silk strings are the cheapest of all, but generally are not recommended since they lose life quickly.

The beginning player should keep in mind that, in the long run, the best quality frame will be a better buy than the cheaper one. The better frame can hold up under a greater number of restringings, while the inexpensive racket will spring out of shape and lose its life in a few weeks of play. The best racket frames are made from top-grade ash. Recently, a steel racket has appeared on the market and has been widely accepted by many of the professionals. The shape of the head differs slightly from that of the wood frame.

Balls

The average player will derive greater pleasure from the game and develop a higher level of skill more rapidly if he uses good balls. The better brands of balls on the market meet the specifications of the United States Lawn Tennis Association and sell for about $3.50 to $4.50 a can (three balls). Good balls should provide beginning and average players at least five or six sets of play. When the fuzz and the nap are worn smooth, the balls should be discarded, as the lightened ball has a drifting or floating tendency in flight and is extremely difficult to control.

Nets

The nets vary according to usage. Cheap cotton nets will suffice for use in gymnasiums. For outdoor use, the hemp net treated with tar to resist the weather should be used. In damp climates, the steel net has found favor, as it is entirely weather-proof.

Clothing

Proper tennis shoes are the oxford type of canvas tennis shoe with a smooth rubber sole. Basketball shoes, with the design on the soles, are not to be worn on clay or dirt courts, because they leave an imprint on the court surface.

A lightweight jersey, or T-shirt, and light-weight shorts or slacks are generally worn. White is recommended as the best color, as it reflects the sun's rays and, therefore, is cooler.

In order to keep the feet from getting sore and blistering, the player should wear two pairs of socks, especially when playing on hard courts such as cement, asphalt, composition, or wood.

TECHNIQUES AND FUNDAMENTALS

Grips

The Eastern Grip is the most popular. Place the racket on edge, racket face perpendicular to the ground, and grasp the racket handle as though shaking hands with the racket. Place your hand so the heel is against the leather butt at the end of the handle. Stretch your first finger (index finger) slightly up the handle. The palm of the hand should be directly behind the handle and the V formed by the

FIGURE 28-3. Eastern forehand

FIGURE 28-5. Western

FIGURE 28-4. Eastern backhand

FIGURE 28-6. Continental

FIGURE 28-7. The forehand drive: Frank Sedgman (Photo courtesy *Scholastic Coach*)

thumb and trigger finger should be on the midpoint of the top of the handle. It is necessary to change the grip for the backhand, and this is accomplished by turning the hand about one-quarter of a turn. (See Figs. 28-3 and 28-4.)

THE WESTERN GRIP. This is obtained by laying the racket flat and picking it up, as shown in Fig. 28-5. This grip is not used much, as it does not lend itself well to low balls.

THE CONTINENTAL GRIP. This involves shifting the hand slightly to the left of the position in the Eastern Grip. It isn't a desirable grip as it causes undue strain on the muscles of the forearm and is not effective against a high-bouncing ball. (See Fig. 28-6.)

Strokes

All the strokes are described in terms of a right-handed player's actions. Two important fundamentals in all stroking are: keep the eye on the ball, and strive for accuracy rather than speed.

THE FOREHAND STROKE. This is the fundamental stroke in tennis. The body should be sideways to the net so the shoulders are parallel and facing the right side lines, as illustrated in Fig. 28-7. The feet are set comfortably apart, with the left foot approximately a foot-length in advance of the right. The backswing of your racket should be executed with an extended arm and firm wrist, carrying the racket head at hip level back to a point opposite the right hip. During the backswing, the weight of the body shifts to the right foot, and the upper body is pivoted to the right from the hips. With the forward swing of the racket, the weight of the body is transferred from the right

to the left foot and can be accomplished by stepping slightly forward with the left foot. The knees are bent slightly. The body is pivoted to the left from the hips, bringing the arm movement to the point of impact of the ball when it is opposite the left hip. The arm should be fully extended at the point of impact. The follow-through of the stroke is important. Continue the arm movement forward and let the momentum expend itself in the direction you wish the ball to go.

THE BACKHAND STROKE. This is the second most important stroke in tennis. The grip for the backhand differs from the forehand in that the hand is turned about a quarter circle counterclockwise, so that the heel of the hand rests on top of the handle. (See Fig. 28-8.) This grip is necessary in order to hit the ball with a flat racket face. The grip is changed for the different strokes by holding the throat of the racket with the left hand while the right hand is adjusted to the proper grip. This becomes automatic after much practice.

The mechanics of this stroke are basically the same as those of the forehand stroke. The body should be sideways to the net so the shoulders are parallel and facing the *left* side lines. The feet are set comfortably apart with the *right* foot in advance of the left, approximately one foot-length. The backswing of the racket should be carried back to a point opposite the left hip with the elbow slightly bent. During the backswing, the weight of the body shifts to the left foot and the upper body is pivoted to the left from the hips. With the forward swing of the racket, the weight of the body is transferred from the left to the right foot and the body is pivoted from the hips, bringing the arm and the racket forward.

350

FIGURE 28-8. The backhand drive: Ken Rosewall (Photo courtesy *Scholastic Coach*)

FIGURE 28-9. The service: Lew Hoad (Photo courtesy *Scholastic Coach*)

FIGURE 28-10. The smash

Continue the arm movement to the point of impact of the ball opposite the right hip. The arm is straight and the wrist firm as the ball hits the racket. Continue the arm movement forward and upward until the momentum of the racket expends itself in the direction in which you wish the ball to go.

THE SERVICE STROKE. This has many variations, many of which are excellent strokes, but the beginner should be concerned mainly with getting the ball across the net and into play. After he has mastered the simple fundamental serve, he can then progress to a variation which fits his individual ability.

In hitting the service, the body should be turned slightly sideways in relation to the net, with the left foot forming about a 45 degree angle with the baseline, and the right foot parallel to the baseline. (See Fig. 28-9.) The grip is halfway between the backhand and the forehand grips. The ball is thrown high enough so the arm will be fully extended when the racket hits the ball. To check the toss, re-

frain from hitting the ball and see if it bounces near the left foot. As the ball is thrown into the air, the weight of the body is shifted to the rear foot. The right arm carrying the racket is brought up, then flexed at the elbow permitting the racket to drop down behind the shoulders. The racket is then brought forward as the weight shifts from the right foot to the left foot. The racket is brought to the ball with a slight wrist action to impart speed and a slight spin to the ball. After contact with the ball, the racket should follow through naturally, down across to the left side of the body.

A VOLLEY. This refers to all strokes that are made before the ball hits the ground. The stroke is more like a punching or jabbing stroke in that the backswing is shorter and there is less follow-through than on the ground stroke or the drive. Usually this stroke is executed in the forecourt or when playing the net position. A grip that can be used to receive both the forehand and the backhand shots is one that is halfway between the forehand grip and the

FIGURE 28-11. The lob

backhand grip. A turn of about one-eighth of an inch counterclockwise from the forehand grip eliminates the need for a quick change in grips by using opposite faces of the racket. Try to get a sideways position to the net when executing the stroke since this will give more control and accuracy. However, it often becomes a matter of racket work.

THE SMASH. This requires the same grip as the volley or service strokes. This shot is usually attempted as a "kill" on a ball that has bounced high and close to the net, or on an opponent's short lob. Meet the ball as you would in hitting a service. It is essential to keep your eye on the ball constantly when playing this shot. (Fig. 28-10.)

THE LOB SHOT. This is one that is lifted high into the air above the reach of a net-playing opponent so it lands near the baseline. The forehand grip can be used, but the racket head is tilted back with the racket face toward the net and the knuckles of the hand pointed toward the court. Hit the ball high into the air. As in the volley stroke, the backswing is shorter and there is less follow-through than in the ground stroke or the drive. (Fig. 28-11.)

PLAYING STRATEGY

As soon as a beginning tennis player masters the fundamentals of stroking, he should begin to think of court position and of tactics he can use to maneuver his opponent out of position. Strategy of play is different in the singles games from that of the doubles game, so they will be considered separately.

Singles game

In singles, when rallying from the baseline, a player should try to keep the ball in play, thus forcing his opponent into making the errors. This can be done most effectively by hitting deep to the opponent's backhand consistently, with occasional shots deep to the forehand. Topflight players frequently follow their service to the net. However, this strategy is not recommended until a player has a high level of proficiency in the service and the volley.

A player should not rush the net unless he receives the ball within the baseline and is in position to making a forcing shot that will place his opponent behind his baseline, making it difficult for him to return the ball. The player rushing the net should stop his forward progress and assume a ready position before his opponent hits the ball.

The service position should be near the center mark on the baseline, so immediately after serv-

ing you can take up the center position, waiting for the ball's return. Assume a waiting position, with shoulders paralleling the net and feet spread naturally so you can move equally fast to the left or right. Grasp the throat of the racket with the left hand, which will aid you in securing the right grip within a fraction of a second for whatever stroke is called for. Play to your opponent's weakness.

Doubles game

In the doubles game, each player covers his half of the court from the net to the baseline, from his side line to the center of the court. Each player's position during play should be in relationship to his partner's; they should take up a position parallel to each other and attempt to keep this way during play. Beginners should play near the baseline and rush the net only after one of them has made a shot forcing the opponents out of position. When rushing the net, they should move up together, maintaining their parallel positions, and turn to offensive tactics, utilizing such strokes as the volley and the smash. As the beginner masters these important strokes, he can concern himself more with the prime objective of the doubles game, which is to get to the net and move into attack. When the opponents drive the ball down the center of the court, the teammate who can should return it with his forehand. The position for receiving the service in the doubles game is similar to that for the singles game in that the receiver should stand close to the baseline and quite close to the intersection of the baseline and the singles sideline. The service position in doubles should be at a point on the baseline approximately halfway between the center service line and the sideline. The server should attempt to hit a medium-speed, twist service to his opponent's backhand, thus giving the server time to rush to the net.

RULES FOR TENNIS [1]

1. *Server and receiver.* The players shall stand on opposite sides of the net; the player who first delivers the ball shall be called the server, and the other the receiver.

2. *Delivery of service.* The service shall be delivered in the following manner. Immediately before commencing to serve, the server shall stand with both feet at rest behind the base line, and within the imaginary continuations of the

[1] *Official Tennis Guide and Yearbook* (current issue).

center-mark and sideline. The server shall then toss the ball by hand into the air and before it hits the ground strike it with his racket. The server is not permitted to touch the court inside the baseline until after the racket has made contact with the ball.

3. *From alternate courts.* In delivering the service, the server shall stand alternately behind the right and left courts, beginning from the right in every game. The ball served shall pass over the net and hit the ground within the service-court, which is diagonally opposite.

4. *Faults.* The service is a fault if the server commits any breach of rules 2 or 3; if he misses the ball in attempting to strike it; or if the ball served touches a permanent fixture (other than the net) before it hits the ground. However, if he tosses the ball without making an effort to hit it, there is no fault.

5. *Ball in play till point decided.* A ball is in play from the moment at which it is delivered in service. Unless a fault or a let be called, it remains in play until the point is decided.

6. *Player hinders opponent.* If a player commits any act, either deliberately or involuntarily which, in the opinion of the umpire, hinders his opponent in making a stroke, the umpire shall in the first case award the point to the opponent, and in the second case order the point to be replayed.

7. *Ball falling on line.* A ball falling on a line is regarded as falling in the court bounded by that line. Good ball.

8. *Good return.* It is a good return:
   (a) If the ball touches the net, posts, cord or metal cable, strap or band, provided that it passes over any of them and hits the ground within the court;
   (b) If a player's racket passes over the net after he has returned the ball, provided the ball passes the net before being played and is properly returned;
   (c) If a player succeeds in returning the ball, served or in play, which strikes a ball lying in the court.

9. *When players change sides.* The players shall change sides at the end of the first, third and every subsequent alternate game of each set, and at the end of each set unless the total number of games in such set be even, in which case the change is not made until the end of the first game of the next set.

10. *Doubles, order of service.* Decided at the beginning of each set. The pair who have to serve in the first game of each set shall decide which partner shall do so and the opposing pair shall decide similarly for the second game. The partner of the player who served in the first game shall serve in the third; the partner of the player who served in the second game shall serve in the fourth. The order of serving may be changed following the completion of any set.

11. *Doubles, order of receiving.* Decided at the beginning of each set. The pair who have to receive the first game shall decide which partner shall continue to receive the first service in every odd game throughout that set. The opposing pair shall likewise decide which partner shall receive the first service in the second game and that partner shall continue to receive the first service in every even game throughout that set. The order of receiving may be changed following the completion of any set.

A complete staff of officials for a tennis match includes a referee, an umpire, a net-cord judge, and at least seven linesmen. However, most dual matches are played with only a referee or at most a referee and an umpire.

HELPFUL HINTS

1. Keep your eye on the ball at all times.
2. Strive for accurate placement rather than speed.
3. Always play the game to win, but if you go down in defeat, give your opponent due credit.
4. Play to your opponent's weaknesses.
5. Always give your opponent credit for a well-placed shot.
6. When calling the score always call the server's score first.
7. Keep your weight on the balls of both feet so you can move in any direction with ease and speed.
8. Acquire an understanding of the fundamentals of stroking, and practice faithfully to master these.
9. Notice how your opponent strokes the ball so when he uses the chop or slice stroke you can play the bounce accordingly.

10. Turn the body sideways to the net on all ground strokes.
11. When stroking the ball, avoid stiff leg action by keeping the knees slightly flexed.
12. On the ground strokes, return the ball deep into the opponent's back court near the baseline.
13. On the ground strokes, attempt to hit the ball at waist level and at the top of the bounce.
14. On the ground strokes, the point of contact of the ball and the racket is opposite the hip closer to the net.
15. Hit the ball squarely on the strings of the racket face by hitting "through" the ball instead of chopping under it.
16. The follow-through of the racket is in the direction of the intended flight of the ball.
17. After completing each stroke, assume a waiting position, facing the net and loosely grasping the throat of the racket with the left hand to facilitate change of grip if necessary.
18. Well-placed lobs, which are out of reach of the net rusher, will help keep him away from the net.
19. When serving, attempt to get the first serve in the proper court as often as possible. Stress control and accuracy if a second serve is necessary and concentrate on getting the ball into the proper service area.
20. The server should always have two balls in his possession before starting his service.
21. The receiver should not retrieve or return the ball if the opponent's first serve is a fault. He should remain in his receiving position so the server can immediately follow with his second attempt.

PLAYING COURTESIES

To make the game more enjoyable for yourself and for others, one should follow certain court courtesies or rules of etiquette. If one of your tennis balls rolls into another court, wait until the players on the court have finished their rally before asking for your ball. When you return someone's ball that has rolled into your court, roll the ball back to the player asking for it instead of trying to gain some stroking practice. If they are engaged in playing a point roll the ball back against the screen out of their field of play. If your opponent is interfered with in any way during the play for a point, stop the play, call a "let," and then play the point over. If there is doubt in calling a ball in or out of bounds,

replay the point. When leaving or entering the courts, do not walk behind a player playing a point. Wait until the rally is over, then quickly cross the rear of the court close to the back screen.

SAFETY

1. Warm up sufficiently before starting strenous play.
2. Stop when injured and report injury to the instructor.
3. Remove rings, bracelets, watches, etc., as they may cause bruises and cuts.
4. Check playing surface for glass, nails, stones, slippery spots, etc.
5. Stay in line, on mark, or in own area when swinging or hitting.
6. Control emotions; do not throw the racket or hit a ball in anger.
7. Shout a warning when there is danger of a ball hitting someone.
8. Avoid showing-off and "horseplay."
9. Be aware of the distance(s) between the baselines and walls, fences, screens, etc.

TERMINOLOGY

Ace To score a service ace (a shot which eludes the receiver).

Ad A common contraction of "advantage."

Approach shot A shot used to return a short ball deep to the opponent's weakness after which a player moves to the forward volley position.

Backspin The opposite of topspin.

Baseline The end boundaries of the court.

Bye A term used to denote the fact that a player does not have to play a match in the first round of a tournament and advances automatically to the second round.

Choke To hold the racket at a point nearer its striking surface, shortening the grip.

Continental Grip A forehand grip with the V formed by the thumb joining the hand 45 degrees to the left of the position in the Eastern Grip.

Deuce In general, an even score.

Eastern Grip A forehand grip with the V formed by the thumb joining the hand over the plane of the handle, which is a continuation of the frame.

Fault In general, usually denoting a service failure.

Foot-fault A violation regarding the delivery of service rule.

Handicap An attempt to equalize competition between opponents unequal in ability.

ILTF International Lawn Tennis Federation.

Let A served ball which strikes the top of the net and falls into the proper service court. (The point is replayed.) Also any point which is replayable due to distraction of player, interference with play, etc.

Lob To stroke a ball in a high arc.

Love No score.

Match Two out of three or three out of five sets.

Rally Is a prolonged exchange of strokes.

Seeding The placing of tournament players in certain positions so that they do not meet until late round matches.

Set The first player to win six games wins a set, provided he is at least two games ahead of his opponent (6–3, 6–4, 7–5, 8–6, etc.).

Smash A stroke used to return a lob, similar to that used for service.

Stroke The act of striking the ball with the racket.

Topspin When the ball spins forward in the direction of its flight.

USLTA United States Lawn Tennis Association.

VASSS Van Alen Simplified Scoring System.

Volley A stroke used to return a ball before it has bounced. It is usually made when a player is playing the net position in the forecourt.

SELECTED REFERENCES

Ainsworth, Dorothy, *et al.*, eds., *Individual Sports for Women* (4th ed.). Philadelphia: W. B. Saunders Co., 1963.

American Association for Health, Physical Education and Recreation, *Group Instruction Manual for Tennis*. Washington, D.C.: U.S. Government Printing Office, 1963.

————, Division for Girls' and Women's Sports, *Tennis Handbook*. New York: The Ronald Press Company, 1962.

Barnaby, John M., *Tennis in Brief*. South Lincoln, Mass.: Privately printed, 1963.

Cummings, Parke, *American Tennis*. Boston: Little, Brown and Company, 1957.

Driver, Helen I., *Tennis for Teachers* (Rev. ed.). Madison, Wis.: Monona-Driver Book Co., 1964.

Everett, Peter, and Virginia Dumas, *Beginning Tennis*. Belmont, Calif.: Wadsworth Publishing Co., Inc., 1962.

Hoad, Lew, *The Lew Hoad Story* (as told to Jack Pollard). Englewood Cliffs, N.J.: Prentice-Hall, Inc., 1958.

Jaeger, Eloise M., and Harry Leighton, *Teaching of Tennis for School and Recreational Programs*. Minneapolis, Minn.: Burgess Publishing Co., 1963.

Kenfield, John, *Teaching and Coaching Tennis*. Dubuque, Iowa: William C. Brown Company, Publishers, 1964.

Laver, Rod, *How To Play Championship Tennis*. New York: The Macmillan Company, 1965.

Murphy, Bill, and Chet Murphy, eds., *Tennis Handbook*. New York: The Ronald Press Company, 1962.

Talbert, William F., and Bruce S. Old, *The Game of Singles in Tennis*. Philadelphia: J.B. Lippincott Co., 1962.

————, *The Game of Doubles in Tennis*. New York: Simon and Schuster, Inc., 1957.

Tilden, Bill, *How To Play Better Tennis*. New York: Simon and Schuster, Inc., 1957.

Trengove, Alan, ed., *Tennis the Professional Way*. New York: Simon and Schuster, Inc., 1964.

United States Lawn Tennis Association, *USLTA Official Yearbook*. New York: USLTA, 51 E. 42nd St., New York, N.Y.

USLTA PUBLICATIONS AVAILABLE

United States Lawn Tennis Association

51 East 42nd St., New York, N.Y. 10017

Swim Tennis Clubs and Court Lighting Brochure

Progressions in Teaching Tennis

Plan for Organizing Junior League Tennis Program (Mimeo)

How to Organize Umpires and Linesmen (Mimeo)

Practice and Diet Suggestions—by David L. Freed (Mimeo)

How to Run a Junior Tournament (Mimeo)

Why Tennis Groups Should Join the USLTA

Testing for Tennis—7 Basic Skill Tests—Leighton-Barta

USLTA Silver Certificates—for passing Beginners Test

USLTA Gold Certificates—for passing Advanced Test

USLTA Blue Certificates—for passing Intermediate Test

A Lesson In Net Play—by William F. Talbert (Reprint from *Sports Illustrated*)

How to Serve and Win—by William F. Talbert (Reprint from *Sports Illustrated*)

Tennis Rules Quiz—*50 Questions and Answers* (Mimeo)

The Code—The summarization of procedures and unwritten rules which custom and tradition dictate all players should follow

How to Develop Junior Tennis in Your Club (Mimeo)

Remarks on Drop Shots and Stop Volleys—by Walter L. Pate

How to Build a Practice Board (Mimeo)

How Your Club Can Increase Its Membership (Mimeo)

Shots—by Russell B. Kingman—60 short pithy sayings —suitable for framing (9½ x 12¾ inches)

Rules of Lawn Tennis with Cases and Decisions—16 page booklet

Tennis Group Instruction Manual—by USLTA-AAHPER Joint Committee—63 page book

Tennis Lessons for Young Players (Mimeo)

How to Organize and Conduct a Tennis Clinic—16 page booklet

Tennis Scope

Umpire's Manual and Rules of Lawn Tennis—How to Conduct a Tournament; How to Make a Draw; Supervision of Umpires at Tournaments; Instruction for Tournament Officials; Rules of Lawn Tennis— 48 page booklet

Manual for the School Tennis Coach—Articles describing methods of coaches to develop tennis (Mimeo)

How to Improve Your Tennis—83 page illustrated booklet

A Friend at Court—Tips on tactics, techniques and tennis rules interpretations

Tennis Court Manual (construction, maintenance and equipment)—60 pages

Tennis Workbook—Work-study outline for students and notes for teachers—by Eve Kraft

Tennis U.S.A.—Official magazine of the USLTA— monthly publication

Tennis Clinic Kit—(1) How to Organize and Conduct a Tennis Clinic, (2) How to Improve Your Tennis, (3) Tennis Instructors' Guide, (4) Rules of Lawn Tennis, (5) Your Guide to Good Courtsmanship, (6) Tennis Lessons for Young Players, (7) Tennis Program for Elementary and Secondary Schools, (8) List of Publications

Touch Football and Flag Football

ORIGIN AND DEVELOPMENT

Touch football is an outgrowth of regular football, which was first played in the United States around the middle of the nineteenth century. The first intercollegiate football game was played between Princeton and Rutgers in 1869, and since that time it has experienced a steady growth in this country. Young boys and men who did not have an opportunity to play on organized football teams were interested in the game and began to use many elements of regular football, such as kicking, passing, and running with the ball in informal games on sandlots and playgrounds. Because of the lack of proper equipment and time for the development of highly organized plays, certain changes in regular football were made in these informal approaches to the parent game resulting in the development of a version of football called touch football.

The game has had a steady growth in this country, particularly in public schools and colleges where it is widely played in physical education classes and in intramural contests. There is as yet no stan-dardized set of official rules in general use throughout the country. Variations in rules are found in different parts of the country, but it is usual for interested groups to agree on certain fundamentals, and an official set of rules may be generally adopted before many more years have passed.

NATURE OF THE GAME

Informal games of touch football are often played in areas of any size large enough to give the players running and passing room. In schools and recreation leagues, where the game is played on an organized basis, a regulation football field equipped with goal posts and yard lines is used. A regulation football is used, but players are not required to wear the heavy official football equipment because tackling is not permitted. Runners are stopped by a touch with one or both hands instead of a tackle. The fact that expensive equipment is not needed makes this game appropriate for use in recreational programs and in schools where funds are not available to outfit a regular football team.

The game retains most of the fundamentals

found in regular football, which gives it a popular appeal in the fall of the year when the sport pages are filled with news about forward passes, touchdowns, and long runs. It provides an opportunity for the individual interested in football to duplicate in a relatively safe situation many of the skills utilized by widely publicized members of the gridiron game. Most present-day versions of the game resemble regulation football to the extent that names of positions of players, running and passing plays, punting, placekicking, first downs, and scoring are used in touch football. The tackling element is eliminated in favor of the touch, and in most versions of touch football, certain limitations are placed on blocking. In many cases no limitations are placed on eligibility of pass receivers, making it possible for any player to receive a forward pass. This factor makes the game more interesting to linemen who seldom have an opportunity to score or handle the ball in regulation football. During World War II, many physical education leaders in army camps liberalized the passing rule still further by permitting passing the ball in any direction at any place on the field. This practice produced a wide-open game, which provided plenty of exercise for all team members on both offense and defense, since any player was eligible to catch and pass the ball anywhere on the field. This produced a type of game further removed from football, but it was popular with players who wanted an opportunity to handle the ball.

FLAG FOOTBALL

Flag football is a variation of touch football in which cloth flags are worn by all players. The flag is detached from its place on the ball carrier by the defensive player in lieu of a touch. (See Figs. 29-1 and 29-2.) Flags are usually strips of cloth 12 inches to 18 inches long by two inches to six inches wide, and come equipped from commercial sources with an adhesive substance, or plastic snaps, for attachment to the player. It helps if flags of a different color are used for each team.

The basic rules governing flag football are similar to those used in touch football but again there is no one set of rules generally accepted over the country. In some places players wear only one flag while in other situations players are required to wear two or three flags, which tends to minimize rough contact since the defensive player has greater latitude in reaching a flag if more than one is carried on the person of the ball carrier. Some contend that utilization of the flag tackle in lieu of the one or two hand touch tends to minimize roughness in team play; but the reverse might well be true in that it is more difficult to grab the flag than to touch a person. Officiating is easier in flag than in touch football, since detachment of the flag is readily discernible while there may be arguments regarding a touch. In order to minimize hazardous play in flag football, the following precautionary measures are suggested:

1. Eliminate blocking, tackling, or holding of the ball carrier by a defensive player in attempting to secure the flag.
2. Defensive players must maintain contact with the ground when attempting to secure the flag—no jumping or diving.
3. The ball carrier shall not employ a straight-arm or utilize body contact against a defensive player in order to prevent him from securing the flag.

BASIC RULES

Although rules are not standardized, the rules outlined here have been found satisfactory in many areas and constitute some of the basic deviations from rules of regulation football. Readers should refer to the Official Football Rules for a complete treatment of rules not covered here.

FIGURES 29-1, 29-2. Flag football. Player on left removes the flag from the ball carrier.

EQUIPMENT

PLAYING FIELD. Same as for regulation football, 160 feet wide by 360 feet long.

BALL. Regulation football.

UNIFORM. No special uniform is required, although players will find it advisable to wear soccer or basketball shoes. Since tackling is not permitted, headgear and shoulder pads are not needed.

Length of game

PERIODS. Four ten-minute periods constitute a game, with a three-minute rest between quarters and a five-minute rest between halves.

OVERTIME. Tie games may be decided by one of the following methods.

a. Award the game to the team with the greatest number of penetrations inside the opponent's 20-yard line.

b. Award game to team with greatest number of first downs.

c. Give each team four downs from the 20-yard line and award the game to the team advancing the ball the farthest.

FORFEITS. If a team is not ready to play within ten minutes after scheduled starting time, the opponents are awarded the win on a forfeit. Teams refusing to resume play after an order to do so by the referee forfeit to opponents.

TIME-OUT. Each team is allowed two time-outs per half without penalty. Additional time-outs are penalized five yards. Time-outs are also taken under the following conditions:

a. When ball goes out of bounds.

b. After a score is made.

c. While a penalty is being enforced.

d. At the discretion of the referee.

e. At the end of each period.

Scoring

Scoring is the same as in regulation football.
TOUCHDOWN. Six points.
FIELD GOAL. Three points.
SAFETY. Two points.
POINT AFTER TOUCHDOWN. One point.

Players and substitutes

PLAYERS. A team consists of nine players, although fewer players may be used by mutual con-

sent. The offensive team must have at least five men on the line of scrimmage when the ball is put in play.

SUBSTITUTES. Any number of substitutions may be made at any time during the game. Substitutes must report to the referee.

Playing regulations

STARTING THE GAME. A toss of a coin by the referee determines which team has the choice of kicking-off, receiving, or goals. The loser of the toss has choice of remaining options. Privileges of choice are reversed at the beginning of the third period.

PUTTING THE BALL IN PLAY. The ball is put in play at the start of the game, after a score, and at the beginning of the third period, by a place kick from the 40-yard line. Defensive team members must be ten yards away when the ball is kicked, and members of the kicking team must be behind the ball. If the ball does not go ten yards it must be kicked again. Kick-offs are free balls and may be recovered by either team. If the ball is kicked over the opponent's goal line, it is a touchback, and must be put in play by scrimmage on the 20-yard line.

FUMBLED BALL. A fumbled ball at any time is dead and belongs to the team that fumbled the ball at the point of the fumble, the down and point to be gained remaining the same. A fumbled forward pass is ruled as an incomplete pass.

DOWNED BALL. The ball is dead and the player downed when an opponent touches him with two hands simultaneously.

FIRST DOWNS. If a team does not advance the ball from one zone to the next in four downs, the ball goes to the opponents at that spot.

PASSING. The following regulations govern passing:

a. All players on both teams are eligible to catch passes.

b. Forward passes may be thrown from any point back of the line of scrimmage, and lateral passes may be thrown anywhere on playing field.

c. Any number of passes may be thrown in a series of downs.

Fouls and penalties

It is a foul to push, tackle, shove, trip, hold, or rough another player. The penalty is a 15-yard loss from spot of foul.

BLOCKING. Players may not leave their feet or use their hands in blocking. The penalty is 15 yards from spot of foul.

OFF-SIDE. It is illegal for players to be off-side when ball is snapped. The penalty is five yards from where ball was put in play.

PASS INTERFERENCE. If defensive players interfere illegally with pass receivers, interference shall be called. The penalty is completed pass at spot of foul.

Officials

The officials consist of a referee, an umpire, and linesmen.

TECHNIQUES AND FUNDAMENTALS

The techniques and fundamentals associated with touch football are identical in most instances to regular football. The two areas in which touch football differs from the parent game, as played in most parts of the country, are in tackling and blocking. Since the one-handed or two-handed touch is usually substituted for the regular tackle, it is not necessary to practice the tackling skill. With most touch football rules the blocker must remain on his feet throughout the block in order to minimize the possibility of injury. Players should work on the following fundamentals in the touch game because they will be used by most players regardless of the position played.

Blocking

Since the player is not permitted to leave his feet in executing the block, he must become adept at maintaining his balance while retaining a position between the defensive man and the ball carrier. It is advisable for the blocker to keep contact with the defensive man after his initial charge to prevent the defensive player from slipping away. (See Fig. 29-3.) Since the blocker, in some rule versions, cannot place his hands on the ground, he should assume a semi-crouched position with the hands on the knees when assuming his starting position on the line of scrimmage. The arms must be kept close to the body at all times because it is not permissible to use them in executing the block.

Blockers should not "telegraph" the direction of their charge by leaning or looking toward the direction they intend to go, but always assume the same position on the line of scrimmage and not make a move until the ball is snapped. The initial charge should be made quickly in order that contact may be made with the defensive player before he has a chance to gain an advantage. When blocking for

FIGURE 29-3. Position for blocking

punts, the forward charge is not so pronounced as in the case of running plays; here the blocker attempts to hold his position momentarily after original contact and then rush down the field to cover the return by the punt receiver.

Touching

Defensive men must be continually on the alert to get in a position where they can touch the ball carrier. This requires the maintenance of good balance and body control in order to keep clear of the offensive blockers who will be trying to keep between the defense and the ball carrier. Figs. 29-4 and 29-5 show two-hand and one-hand touch methods.

Ball carrying

Because of the open style of play usually employed in touch football, most players have an opportunity at one time or another to carry the ball, so all should practice this skill. The effective ball carrier is one who can start quickly, change direction sharply, dodge, sidestep, and execute fakes that will throw the defense off stride. The ball should be carried under the outside arm with one end of the ball in the armpit and the other end firmly held in the palm of the hand with fingers spread over the end of the ball, as shown in Fig. 29-6. Ball carriers should learn to follow their interference since it is difficult to elude defensive players without help from teammates.

FIGURE 29-4. Two-hand touch

FIGURE 29-5. One-hand touch

FIGURE 29-6. Ball carrier with ball in proper position

FIGURES 29-7, 29-8. Lateral passing

Passing

Forward and lateral passing usually assume a much more important role in touch football than in regulation football. Passing tends to loosen up the defense for better execution of running plays and provides a more exciting and interesting game for the participants. A fake pass and run is often used with success, and since lateral passes may be made at any time on the field, a trailer behind the ball carrier will increase the effectiveness of this play. (See Figs. 29-7 and 8.)

The ball may be gripped in the hand or held in the palm in a pass. (See Figs. 29-9, 29-10.) Boys with large hands will find it more effective to grip the ball while those with small hands may find it advisable to "palm" the ball. Passing from a standing position is usually more accurate, but since the running pass is usually more effective in keeping the defense spread, players should practice passing

FIGURE 29-11. Watching ball over left shoulder

FIGURE 29-9. Start of a forward pass

FIGURE 29-12. Catching pass

FIGURE 29-10. Pass on its way.

FIGURE 29-13. Completion of pass

from both the standing and running positions. All players enjoy passing the ball, so warm-up drills and pre-game time should be used to practice this skill. Passers should practice hitting their receivers on the run, because they will seldom have a stationary target to shoot at in game situations.

Pass receivers should become adept at eluding their opponents by dodging, faking, and using a change of pace that will enable them to gain a step on the defensive man. The pass should be caught in the hands like a baseball and not against the body where it is more likely to bound away. When catching a pass over the left shoulder, the left arm should be held below the line of vision and the right hand above the eyes. (See Figs. 29-11 through 29-13.) The reverse should be observed on passes caught over the right shoulder. This technique enables the receiver to maintain a clear view of the ball without having an arm obscure his vision as would be likely to occur if the position of the arms were reversed.

Punting

Successful punting depends on the full cooperation of all members of the offensive team. Almost any individual can punt the ball if he has plenty of time and is not interfered with by players rushing at him from the front. When the punt signal is called, all members of the line and backfield must be sure that no defensive player is permitted to break through and interfere with the successful execution of the punt. As soon as the ball is kicked, all linemen and backfield men must rush down the field to cover the punt receiver before he has an opportunity to make a gain on the punt return. Offensive linemen should play shoulder-to-shoulder on defense for the punt and force the opponents to go to the outside, and not permit them to go down the middle for a direct shot at the punter. If any defensive men break through, it is the duty of the blocking backs to protect the inside and keep defensive men away from the line of direction of the kick.

The punter should assume a position far enough back of the line of scrimmage to enable him to get the ball away when he has reasonable protection from his teammates. It is better to be back a yard or two more than necessary than to get too close and have the punt blocked. Distances will usually vary from seven to 12 yards, but practice will be the best guide in determining the exact position the punter will assume. In assuming the position or stance for the kick, the right or kicking foot should be placed about a foot to the rear with the

feet slightly spread. (See Fig. 29-14.) As the ball is received from the center, take a step with the right foot, followed by a natural step with the left foot. The player is now in a position to kick the ball with the right foot. As these steps are being taken, the ball can be adjusted in the hands and held in front of the body about waist high. As the right leg starts its upward swing, the left hand is taken off the ball and the right hand guides the ball to the foot. The flat side of the ball should be placed on the instep of the foot, which is extended and held rigid. The leg is bent at the knee at the start of the

FIGURE 29-14. Initial pass for punt

FIGURE 29-15. Follow-through on punt

swing, but the joint is locked the instant the foot makes contact with the ball. The contact with the ball is made about knee high, but the leg follows through to a point above the head. (See Fig. 29-15.) The ball should not be dropped or thrown from the hands to the kicking foot, but should be kept under control by the hand until just before making contact with the ball.

PLAYING STRATEGY

Touch football permits the use of a wide range of offensive plays ordinarily employed in regular football. In arranging their offensive strategy, a team should plan a signal system that will denote the kind of play to be used—whether run, pass, or punt, who is to carry the ball, and where the play is to go. A starting signal should be agreed on, which may be varied according to the situation. Plays should be kept as simple as possible. Numbers are usually employed to indicate the type of play to be used. Running plays may be numbered from 50 to 59, pass plays from 60 to 69, etc., with a third digit added to indicate direction of play. The backs may be given numbers from one to four and the holes in the line may be numbered from one to six—even numbers to go to the right and odd numbers to the left. Thus, after the ball has been centered (see Fig. 28-16) the signal number 514 would indicate a running play through the number four hole on the right, with the number one back carrying the ball. (See Fig. 29-17.)

Teams should agree on a plan for pass defense, because this offensive weapon is widely used by most teams. Certain linemen should be assigned to rush the passer and others designated to drop

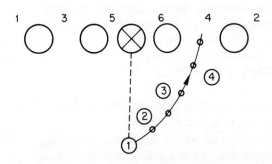

FIGURE 29-17. Numbers for offensive holes

back to help the backs cover possible receivers on plays where it is certain that a pass is to be made. Man-to-man assignments are usually made for pass receivers who go down deep, while a zone type of defense may be employed on short passes close to the line of scrimmage.

SAFETY

Observance of certain safety precautions will tend to minimize the incidence of injuries. Some of these are enumerated below.

1. Do not wear any equipment possessing sharp or projecting surfaces that may injure teammates or opponents.
2. Use rules that prevent leaving the feet in executing the block.
3. Declare the ball dead on all fumbles.
4. See that the playing area is smooth and free from holes and projecting objects that may prove a hazard.
5. Use competent officials who enforce the rules and eliminate rough play.
6. See that adequate treatment is available to players who receive injuries while competing.

HELPFUL HINTS

1. Take every opportunity to practice the fundamentals of passing, kicking, blocking, and ball carrying.
2. Remember that touch football is a team game that requires the full cooperation of every player in the lineup.
3. Watch good players in action on the gridiron and note the characteristics and skills that make them successful there, because these same qualities will increase one's proficiency in touch football.

FIGURE 29-16. Center passing ball to backfield man

4. Warm up thoroughly before engaging in active competition.

PLAYING COURTESIES

1. Refrain from engaging in rough play because it may cause injuries and ill feeling.
2. Refrain from blocking or otherwise interfering with a player after he has gone out of bounds or the ball has been declared dead.
3. Accept decisions of the officials without argument and leave discussion of rule interpretations to your team captain.
4. After a quarterback has been selected, do not question his choice of plays while the game is in progress.

TERMINOLOGY

Backs   Players on the team who ordinarily carry or pass the ball on offense. Stationed back of the linemen.

Backward pass   Play in which the ball is thrown or passed in any direction except toward the opponent's goal. Any player may make a backward pass.

Balanced line   An offensive formation which has an equal number of linemen on each side of the center. Line is unbalanced if more linemen are on one side of center than the other.

Blind pass   A pass in which the passer does not watch the path of the ball; occasionally employed by center.

Block   Action of offensive linemen and backs in which they use their bodies to ward off defensive players from the ball carrier.

Bootleg play   An offensive play in which a back fakes handing the ball to a teammate, conceals it on his hip, and runs in the opposite direction.

Brush blocking   Momentary blocking by an offensive player.

Button hook   A forward pass play in which the receiver runs toward the defender, turns and runs back toward passer to receive the pass.

Clipping   Action by player in which he throws his body across the back of the leg or legs of a player not carrying the ball. This is likely to cause injury and is a personal foul.

Cross-buck   An offensive play in which two backs cross paths in moving toward the line of scrimmage, one faking to receive the ball and the other actually taking the ball.

Cut-back   An offensive maneuver in which the back starts wide and then cuts back toward center of the line.

Diamond defense   A defensive formation often called the 7-1-2-1 defense with seven men in the line, one fullback behind the line, two halfbacks farther back and to the side, and one safety man deeper than the halfbacks.

Double wingback   An offensive formation in which two backs flank the ends by about one yard, the fullback usually behind his strong side guard and tailback about five to six yards behind the center.

End around   An offensive maneuver in which one end wheels around, takes the ball from a teammate, and attempts to run for a gain.

Fair catch   A player may make a fair catch on a kickoff, return kick, or kick from scrimmage by raising his hand clearly above his head before making the catch. He may not be tackled, and must not take more than two steps after receiving the ball. The ball is put in play from the spot of the catch by a free kick or scrimmage.

Flanker   An offensive maneuver in which a player lines up nearer the sideline than a designated opponent.

Flat pass   A forward pass that travels chiefly in a lateral direction and usually thrown with a flat trajectory.

Full spinner   An offensive maneuver in which the man receiving the ball from center makes a half spin, fakes the ball to another back, then completes his turn or spin and attempts to advance the ball.

Hand-off   An offensive play in which one back hands the ball off to another back who attempts to advance the ball.

Lateral pass   An offensive play in which the ball is passed backward or lateral to the line of scrimmage. If ball is thrown toward the line of scrimmage it is a forward pass.

Line of scrimmage   An imaginary line, or vertical plane, passing through the end of the ball nearest a team's goal line and parallel to the goal lines. Thus there is a line of scrimmage for each team, and the area between the two lines is called the neutral zone. Any player of either team is off-side if he encroaches upon the neutral zone before the ball is snapped.

Mousetrap   An offensive maneuver in which an opposing lineman is permitted to charge across the line and then is blocked sideward so the ball carrier may advance through his vacated position.

Naked reverse   An offensive play in which the ball carrier takes the ball from another back and attempts to advance without benefit of backfield blockers.

Off-side   When an offensive player is ahead of the ball before it is snapped. Penalty, five yards.

Safety   A score made when a free ball, or one in possession of a player defending his own goal, becomes dead behind the goal, provided the impetus which caused it to cross the goal was provided by the defending team.

Screen pass   An offensive maneuver in which a wave of eligible receivers converge in area where pass is to be thrown.

Shovel pass   An offensive maneuver in which a pass is thrown, underhand, usually forward to a back behind the line of scrimmage.

Touchback   When the ball becomes dead behind the opponent's goal line legally in possession of a player guarding his own goal, provided the impetus which caused it to cross the goal line was provided by an opponent. No points are scored on the play, and the ball is put in play by a scrimmage at the 20-yard line.

SELECTED REFERENCES

Armbruster, David A., Leslie Erwin, and Frank F. Musker, *Basic Skills in Sports for Men and Women* (3rd ed.). St. Louis: C. V. Mosby Co., 1963.

Daugherty, Duffy, and Clifford B. Wilson, *1st and Ten*. Dubuque, Iowa: William C. Brown Company, Publishers, 1961.

Fait, Hollis, John Shaw, and Katherine Ley, *A Manual of Physical Education Activities* (3rd ed.). Philadelphia: W. B. Saunders Co., 1967.

Miller, Kenneth, ed., *Physical Education Activities for College Men and Women*. Dubuque, Iowa: William C. Brown Company, Publishers, 1963.

Official National College Touch Football Rules. The Athletic Institute, 805 Merchandise Mart, Chicago, Ill. (current edition).

Stanbury, Dean, and Frank DeSantis, *Touch Football*. New York: Sterling Publishing Co., Inc., 1961.

White, Jess R., *Sports Rules Encyclopedia*. Palo Alto, Calif.: The National Press, 1961.

Track and Field

ORIGIN AND DEVELOPMENT

Most of the events of track and field are as old as the history of man. Every race of people has devised and participated in various competitive forms of running, jumping, and throwing. It was the Greeks during their golden age, however, who developed the pattern for the modern events. They held many different track and field games, but the most famous were the Olympic Festivals. They began in 776 B.C., and continued to be held every four years until A.D. 394. The modern Olympic games were revived in 1898 at Athens, and the American men have since dominated the track and field events, except for the distance runs.

Each season finds the college and high school athletes bettering records in the various events until one wonders what the limits of accomplishment are. Most of the seemingly impossible times, distances, and heights of the past have been surpassed during the past decade. The four-minute barrier in the mile run was dramatically crashed by Roger Bannister of England in 1954; in the same year Parry O'Brien

of the United States exceeded the 60-foot mark in shot put; but in 1965 a young giant from Texas A. & M., Randy Matson, shocked the track world by exceeding 70 feet! In 1956, Charles Dumas of the United States cleared the seven-foot mark in the high jump; Ralph Boston leaped beyond the 27-foot barrier in the running broad jump in 1961; Bob Beamon shattered the world record by long jumping over 29 feet; and 1962 brought the downfall of the other "impossibles." John Uelses pole vaulted over 16 feet with the new flexible pole, and Al Oerter tossed the discus more than 200 feet. Then John Pennel vaulted over 17 feet in 1963. During this same time practically every other record, world, collegiate, and high school, has been broken due to more competitors and competition, better coaching, and better facilities and equipment. Many high school track and field records today are much better than the official world records of twenty years ago.

United States women track stars beginning to shine

Women's track and field records have also shown a remarkable development. Just in the last decade have the women and girls of the United States begun to participate in track and field in noticeable numbers. When Wilma Rudolph won the 100 meter dash in the Rome Olympic Games (1960) in 11.3 seconds, and the 200 meter dash in 23.2 seconds, it signified that American women were on the move. She later lowered the world records to 11.2 seconds and 22.9 seconds in 1961. That same year Miss Rudolph anchored the women's 400 meter relay in a world record time of 44.3 seconds. Despite the fact that American women have ever since dominated the sprints, they have not gained international stature in the field events or in endurance races. Recently a number of excellent distance runners have appeared, such as the new queens of the distance runners, Mrs. Vicki Foltz (formerly of Yugoslavia, now of the Falcon Track Club in Seattle), who in 1967 won the national two mile cross-country championship in 11:46.65, and Mrs. Doris Brown of the same club, who was the world champion in this category in 1966 and 1968. The outstanding 880 yd. and 800 meter runners include Francie Kraker of the University of Michigan, Charlotte Cooke, eighteen, of the Los Angeles Mercurettes, and, best of all, Madeline Manning, nineteen, a Clevelander representing Tennessee State University, the home of many track stars, who won the 1968 Olympic 800m. in 2:00.9, a new Olympic and world record. Jane Burnett, a fifteen-year-old

FIGURE 30-1. Francie Kraker, holder of the world's indoor record for 600 yards; time 1:22.4 (University of Michigan)

youngster from Maryland with a 55-second 440 yard race, is another competitor of world stature.

The United States now has two women of world class in the javelin throw, Barbara Friedrich of New Jersey, 198 feet 8 inches (American record), and Ra Nae Bair of San Diego, 196 feet 3 inches.

NATURE OF TRACK AND FIELD

The large variety of track and field events that call for speed, endurance, and skill, including more than thirty different events that are composed of walking, running, jumping, throwing, and climbing activities, offer an opportunity for practically every type of individual to participate successfully. Often one does not realize that he has the native ability to become a track man, especially in such events as distance running, shot putting, and pole vaulting, unless he gives it a try. Many of the great track men have "discovered themselves" in physical education classes or intramural sports, and every young man is urged to try the various events because he usually can find one in which he can succeed or even excel. Over a million high school boys and girls, at least 608,000 college students, and possibly a larger number of elementary school children participate in track and field events each year.

Although track and field events in general are not considered recreational sports that can be practiced in later life, the one basic fundamental, running, is a wholesome exercise that every physically fit person should learn and practice for many years past the accepted retirement-from-sports age. Running is the basic fundamental for practically every sport, and learning to run properly and building up speed and endurance will help anyone who wishes to participate in such active sports as softball, basketball, baseball, soccer, handball, boxing, badminton, and tennis.

The objectives of track and field in general are:

1. To develop speed, agility, and endurance in running, jumping, and throwing.
2. To develop skill in the various events that may lead to successful participation in class, intramural, and varsity participation.
3. To develop an appreciation of the place of track and field in the world of sports.

We shall discuss only those track and field events that are commonly a part of the physical education classwork and that are often used in the testing program, i.e., sprinting, distance running, relays, hurdling, high jumping, broad jumping, shot putting, and relay racing.

TECHNIQUES AND FUNDAMENTALS

Sprinting

Good form in sprinting requires that the toes of the feet be placed straight ahead, that the body lean slightly forward from the ankles, and that the arms be carried akimbo and swung across the body. The head should be in line with the body so that it also is inclined slightly forward. The hands should be open and swung across the chest so that they do not go back of the waist, past the center of the body, or higher than the shoulders. Sprinters usually carry their arms and hands higher than distance runners.

The runner must run naturally. That is, he must not try to lift his knees unusually high, lengthen his stride too much, or keep his feet from kicking behind. It is a common fallacy that these so-called faults can be corrected. He must, however, swing his arms naturally and keep relaxed, especially in the shoulders and neck. He must also keep his knees from wobbling by keeping the toes pointed and the feet placed almost in a straight line. All breathing should be with the mouth open and not "thought about" during the race.

STARTING. There are two general types of starts—the bunch start and the medium or elongated start. The height of the sprinter usually determines which style or variation of styles he should use. Small men usually prefer the bunch start and large men the elongated start. Both require that the runner relax and let the gun "shoot him out of the blocks."

The modified bunch start is most popular at present, so we shall describe it first. The runner sets his blocks so the front foot is 18 to 20 inches from the starting line and the toes of the rear foot back about ten inches or almost even with the heel of the front. The blocks should not be separated sidewise more than a few inches in any type of start, because this has a tendency to throw the man to one side when pushing off.

In the medium start, as shown in Fig. 30-2B, the front foot is placed from eight to 15 inches back and the rear foot is placed so that the knee bisects the front foot and is approximately 32 to 38 inches to the rear. Regardless of the position of the feet, the body and hands are placed about the same as with the bunch start. The hands should be separated about the width of the shoulders, or narrower, and the body bent forward so the shoulders are almost straight above the hands. The head should be down and the eyes focused down the track a few feet. Girls will usually use the shorter spacings.

On "Get set," the runner raises the rump until his back is parallel to the ground, or higher, as preferred, and the body is inclined forward slightly or so that the arms are kept perpendicular, as preferred. Most coaches do not want their men to lean out too far because this may cause a stumbling start. The head should move down as the rump goes up so there is no tension in the neck. The eyes are focused on the ground immediately in front of the starting line.

On the gun the sprinter must drive with both feet, but more with the rear leg, and begin running as smoothly as possible. In other words, he should not jump, nor should he make an effort to take too many small mincing steps. He should not try to run crouched too long but rather get into his running position within about ten to 12 yards. In all sprints the runner must "run on his toes."

THE FINISH. Most coaches believe the sprinter should drive through the tape at the finish line in his regular running form and not try to jump, fall, or

FIGURE 30-2. The sprinter in the set position. (*Left*) Bunch spacing. (*Center*) Medium spacing. (*Right*) Elongated spacing. (From George T. Bresnaban, W.W. Tuttle, and Francis X. Cretzmeyer, *Track and Field Athletics*. St. Louis, Mo.: The C. V. Mosby Co., 1964.)

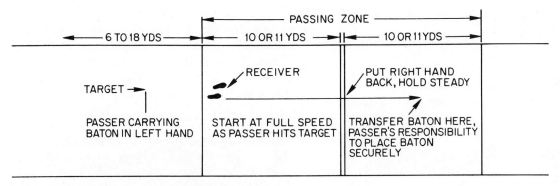

PASSING ZONE

6 TO 18 YDS — 10 OR 11 YDS — 10 OR 11 YDS

TARGET →

PASSER CARRYING
BATON IN LEFT HAND

RECEIVER

START AT FULL SPEED
AS PASSER HITS TARGET

PUT RIGHT HAND
BACK, HOLD STEADY

TRANSFER BATON HERE,
PASSER'S RESPONSIBILITY
TO PLACE BATON
SECURELY

FIGURE 30-3. The blind pass. Used for all sprint relays.

lunge. Above all he should not break stride or pull his chest back by raising his arms over his head.

Middle distance and distance running

The form in running the 440-yard, 880-yard, mile and two-mile distances is about the same as the sprinting form except the longer the distance, the more erect the runner should run, the lower the arms and hands should be carried, the shorter the strides should become, and the more the heels should come down on the track.

In training for these events, the coach usually runs his men considerably over distance early in the season, tapering down to under distance as the season progresses.

INTERVAL TRAINING. The most popular method of training is called interval training. This simply means that the runner runs a number of short distances at a given pace, interspersing them by a few minutes (one to five) of rest or by jogging fixed distances. For example, he may run 220 yards in 30 seconds, jog 220 yards easily, then run again for another 30 seconds. This may be repeated any number of times, depending on his condition. One may either increase the pace or cut down on the minutes of the interval. A typical midseason training schedule may be:

Monday—Run six to eight 440-yard distances in 60–68 seconds with three-minute intervals.

Tuesday—Run six to ten 220-yard distances in 28–34 seconds with three-minute intervals.

Wednesday—Run 660 yards at nine-tenth effort; repeat; sprints.

Thursday—Run one-half of racing distance at racing pace; repeat; starts and sprints.

Friday—Omit practice or warm-up.

Saturday—Compete.

Each of these workouts should be preceded by extensive warm-ups and finished with sprints or jogging as needed.

Relays

There are many types of relays. The common competitive relays are 440 yards, 880 yards, mile, two mile, sprint medley (440 yards, 220 yards, 220 yards, 880 yards), distance medley (440 yards, 880 yards, three-quarter, mile), and the 480-yard shuttle hurdle. Four men compete for a team, each running one-fourth of the distance (except in the medley relays) and passing a baton to the next man. The baton must be exchanged within the 20-meter exchange zone. (The shuttle hurdle relay excepted.) There are two general types of passing (exchanging) the baton, the visual pass and the blind pass.

THE VISUAL PASS. This is used for all of the longer relays in which the incoming runner is tired and uncertain of his coordination. He should extend the baton forward as far as possible with his left hand and the receiver should adjust to his teammate's

FIGURE 30-4. Blind pass. Passer keeps her eyes on the receiver's hand until the pass is completed and she is sure the receiver has a firm grip on the baton. (Adapted from Phebe M. Scott and Virginia R. Crafts, *Track and Field for Girls and Women.* New York: Appleton-Century-Crofts, 1964.)

speed and grasp the baton with his right hand (palm up or down). Sureness of the pass exchange is more important than speed in this type of relay.

THE BLIND PASS is used in relays where the runner is coming in fast and the success of the relay often depends upon a fast exchange. The outgoing runner must judge the speed of the incoming man and take off as he hits a given mark (six to 18 yards back of the pass-zone). They then exchange the baton at a given point without the receiver looking back. (See Fig. 30-4.) The exchange is made by the incoming runner extending the baton forward as far as possible with the left hand and lifting it up to his teammate's right hand, which has been extended backward, palm back and thumb extended. It can also be received with the palm up; the incoming runner places the baton downward into the receiver's hand. The receiver then transfers the baton to his left hand before the next exchange.

Hurdling

The first step in learning to hurdle is to sit on the ground in a hurdling position, as shown in Fig. 30-5. Note that the front leg is nearly straight and the trailing leg has the toe "up" and the knee well forward. Both arms are forward to develop a better stretch. Some coaches think it best to keep both arms forward in hurdling, but it is more common to hurdle with the arm opposite from the lead leg forward and the trailing arm cocked in a running position.

After you have mastered the hurdling position

FIGURE 30-5. Hurdling position (on ground)

(which is often difficult for those who are not supple), it is then necessary to practice taking a hurdle. At first, try to get over any way possible, then learn to assume the ground-hurdling position just practiced. After form and one hurdle have been learned, practice taking two or more and then learn the proper steps. Varsity hurdlers take eight steps to the first high hurdle and three steps between—ten steps to the first low hurdle and seven between.

The only difference between the form in the high and low hurdles is that the hurdler must get down as low as possible over the highs but stay up in a running position over the lows so that he clears them much higher. In both, the hurdler strives to keep his body straight (shoulders square with the hurdle) and takes the hurdle in stride. A good way to learn to control the arms (so they don't fly to the side) is to lock the thumbs, with the arms forward,

FIGURE 30-6. Outdoor hurdle distances and steps.

WOMEN

DISTANCE OF RACE	NO. OF HURDLES	HURDLE HEIGHT	DISTANCE TO 1ST HURDLE	NO. STEPS TO 1ST H	DISTANCE BETWEEN	NO. STEPS BETWEEN	DISTANCE FROM LAST HURDLE TO FINISH
50 yds.	4	2'6"	39'4½" (12 meters)	7–8	26'3"	3	31'10½"
70 yds.	6	2'6"	39'4½"	7–8	26'3"	3	45'9"
80 meters *	8	2'6"	39'4½"	7–8	26'3"	3	39'4½"
100 meters	10	2'6"	13 meters	7–8	8.5 meters	3	10.5 meters
200 meters **	10	2'6"	16 meters	10–11	19 meters	9	13 meters

MEN

DISTANCE OF RACE	NO. OF HURDLES	HURDLE HEIGHT	DISTANCE TO 1ST HURDLE	NO. STEPS TO 1ST H	DISTANCE BETWEEN	NO. STEPS BETWEEN	DISTANCE FROM LAST HURDLE TO FINISH
120 yds.	10	3'6"	15 yds.	7–8	10 yds.	3	15 yds.
120 yds. HS	10	3'3"	15 yds.	8	10 yds.	3	15 yds.
180 yds. HS	10	2'6"	20 yds.	10	20 yds.	7	20 yds.
220 yds.	10	2'6"	20 yds.	10	20 yds.	7	20 yds.
400 meters	10	3'0"	45 meters	24	35 meters	15	40 meters

* Replaced by 100 meter hurdles 2 feet 9 inches high after 1968 Olympics, 12.5 meters to first hurdle, 8.5 meters between and 11 meters to finish.

** Distances between hurdles may return to 28–16–28 meters for international competition.

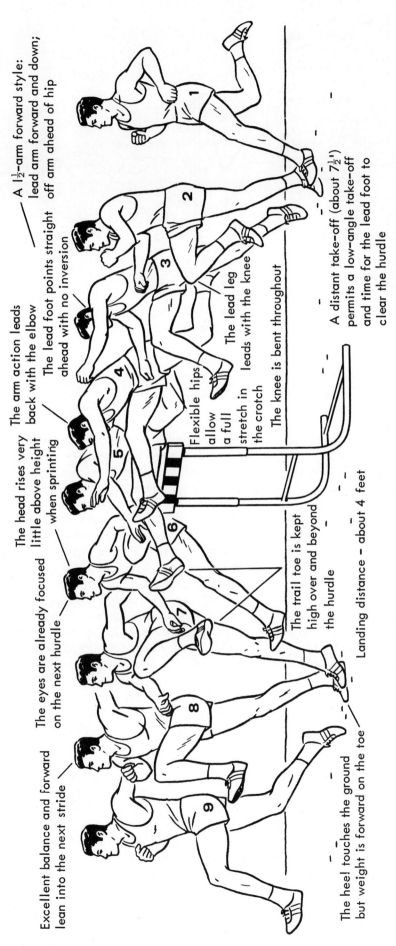

A 1½-arm forward style: lead arm forward and down; off arm ahead of hip

The arm action leads back with the elbow

The lead foot points straight ahead with no inversion

The head rises very little above height when sprinting

The lead leg leads with the knee

The eyes are already focused on the next hurdle

Flexible hips allow a full stretch in the crotch

The knee is bent throughout

A distant take-off (about 7½') permits a low-angle take-off and time for the lead foot to clear the hurdle

Excellent balance and forward lean into the next stride

The trail toe is kept high over and beyond the hurdle

Landing distance – about 4 feet

The heel touches the ground but weight is forward on the toe

FIGURE 30-7. Recommended form in the broad jump, using a modified hitch-kick (From J. Kenneth Doherty, *Modern Track and Field*. Englewood Cliffs, N.J.: Prentice-Hall, Inc., 1953.)

FIGURE 30-8. The final delivery stance

while hurdling until body control is learned. After this is learned, hook the trail hand in the waist band of your trunks while reaching forward and then down over the hurdle with the lead arm (opposite of the lead leg).

By retaining this position (see Figs. 30-5 and 30-7) it becomes easy to take a good-size first step after landing, which is the most difficult phase of attaining the regulation number of steps between the hurdles.

Hurdling for women

Basically, there are no differences in the form used by women to hurdle. However, they do not compete over the high hurdles or the 440 yard (400 meter) intermediates, but compete at the distances specified in Figure 30-6.

Girls are usually quite timid about attempting to hurdle, so it is advisable to begin on heights lower than the low hurdle (2 feet 6 inches) using light bamboo, string, or gauze for the hurdle at about 2 feet. After confidence is gained the low hurdle should be attempted. The top bar may be padded with rubber or other safety devices used to make the clearance less hazardous. Injury is more likely when one balks or slows up to take the hurdle so it is wise to go at them rather fast. The three steps between are most difficult and can be learned only after achieving good form over the hurdle and by making the first step after landing a big one.

High jumping

There are two currently accepted forms of competitive high jumping: the western roll and the belly roll or straddle jump. The easy way to learn the *western* roll is to take a few steps, kick the right leg (assuming you are a left-footed jumper, as most persons are) and, as in punting a football, keep the foot up in the air, then turn the body to the left, touching the hands to the ground. Next do the same thing but this time jump a little into the air off the left and land on the left foot. Continue the exercise, jumping higher each time. Now place the bar at the low height and do the same over the bar. When going over the bar, the left side will be down, the left arm over the bar, the right leg up with the toes pointed, and the left leg bent and tucked in. It is important to take-off with the left foot, roll and land on the left foot, and merely touch the hands to the sand or mat. The *straddle roll* is begun exactly the same as the western roll, but at the top of the jump, the body is turned farther so the body passes over the bar with the abdomen and face down, the right arm leading over (instead of the left as in the western), and the legs straddled so the jumper lands on the right foot (instead of the left as in the western). The jumper should take from six to 12 steps in a firm, springy run starting from a measured check mark. He should approach the bar from about a 45 degree angle in the western but more from the side (about 35 degrees) in the belly roll. (See Fig. 30-8.)

Note: The old-fashioned scissors jump should

not be learned both because one cannot jump very high with it, and because it is too dangerous.

Running broad jump

There are two popular forms of jumping in running broad jump: the *float* and the *hitch kick*. The run is the same for both. It should be about 100 to 120 feet, starting on a check mark and hitting two other check marks with the take-off foot at about six to 14 steps from the board. The run should be fast, with a "gathering" for the take-off; the jump should be as high in the air as possible.

In the float jump, the legs are permitted to hang or to be gathered up, knees to chest, and the arms held over head until just before landing when they are brought down and back to add distance. At the same time the feet are thrown forward to land.

The hitch-kick jump, which is preferred by most track coaches, is executed by sticking out the stomach when taking-off, then running in the air with one and a half steps, while the arms are flung vigorously above the head in opposition to the legs, then pulled down and back just before landing. (See Fig. 30-9.)

The running broad jump is a dangerous event, being particularly hard on the take-off foot and ankle. It must, therefore, not be practiced at top speed too often and the warm-up must be thorough.

Shot putting

The shot is placed in the hand on the fingers, so it does not rest on the palm of the hand, in front of the shoulder fairly close to the neck with the left arm up, bent, and relaxed. All fingers, or two or

FIGURE 30-9. Former World Champion Parry O'Brien's position at the toe-board (From Doherty, *Modern Track and Field.*)

FIGURE 30-10.

FIGURE 30-11.

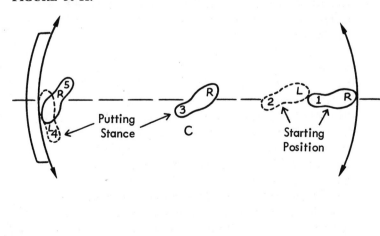

three, may be placed behind the shot. The experts usually place all fingers behind the shot. It is then rested on the shoulder as shown in Fig. 30-10, so the elbow is back and the arm action will result in a put and not in a throw.

Place feet as shown in Fig. 30-11, facing the rear with all weight on the right foot. The left foot is balanced, and then kicked to the front, making possible the hop across the circle. The thrower hops close to the ground. During this time, the body is carried in the same crouched position with the throwing arm and shot unchanged. The shot is then delivered with a powerful heave of the right arm. The body acts with a pumping motion and the hand adds a flip. The head should be kept up. The hand finishes by turning slightly in—not out. It is advisable to practice this delivery from a standing throw before learning the travel across the circle for the complete throw. The shot should land to the right of a line down the center of the arc. Following the throw, the putter may reverse his feet to keep from fouling, or he may simply drag the right foot to the front of the circle without reversing. Some of the champion throwers use the latter, no-reverse method of finishing.

OFFICIATING

Track and field meets require more officials than any other sports contest. Large meets such as the Penn Relays may involve as many as two hundred officials, while a small dual meet may be conducted with as few as six to ten officials. It is impractical to enumerate all of the duties here, but a brief summary of the work of principal officials will give some idea of the tremendous task of staging track meets.

The *referee* enforces all of the rules of competition, including the legality of all implements, supervises the activities of all officials and in general tries to promote fair play, and is responsible for the prompt and efficient handling of the meet. The *clerk of the course* is the official who "runs" the track meet. He assigns heats and lanes and keeps the runners informed of the number qualifying for the event. The *field judge* supervises the field events, keeps to a time schedule, and enforces the rules of competition. Every field event is conducted by a judge and his assistants.

The *starter's* task is to get the track contestants off to an even start and to remove from competition those who jump the gun twice. *Judges of the finish* pick the places at the finish of all races. Small meets

need only three judges, while large meets may need as many as twenty. One acts as *head finish judge* and adjudicates questionable "picks" that the judges make and communicates with the head timer, the starter, clerk of course and the referee. There should be at least four *timers* for a meet, but large meets may use as many as thirty. The *head timer* organizes the timers' assignments, records the results, and communicates with the head finish judge and the referee. The automatic timing devices now used reduce the number of timers needed.

Inspectors are stationed around the track to observe any infraction of the running rules. Each reports such infractions to the *head inspector* who in turn reports to the referee to rule upon the infraction by the offending contestant. The *scorekeeper,* of course, records the results of the various events, and keeps the *announcer* informed so that he can inform the spectators and contestants.

TERMINOLOGY

Anchor The last runner of a four-man relay team.

Baton A hollow cylinder made of wood, metal, plastic, or cardboard, which is carried by one runner to the next in a relay race.

Crossbar A square or triangular bar made of wood, plastic, or metal about 16 feet long, which serves as a transverse obstacle between standards over which the high jumper or pole vaulter must jump or vault.

Dead heat A tie finish between two or more runners.

Exchange zone An area 20 to 22 yards long in which one relay runner must pass the baton to the next runner.

Flight One lane of hurdles. A round of trials for a given number of field event contestants.

Heat Preliminary races in which the winners qualify for the semifinals or finals.

Hurdle A wooden or metal obstacle over which the runners must leap in the hurdle races or steeplechase.

Lane A path marked on the track in which a runner must stay during his race or a specified part of his race.

L-type hurdle An official hurdle whose base forms an L.

Mark The spot where the shot, discus, hammer, javelin, or broad jumper lands.

On the mark A runner's position, directly behind the scratch line, taken at that command prior to "Get set."

	BASIC RULES	SAFETY INSTRUCTION	HELPFUL HINTS
Sprinting	1. Starter cannot touch on or over the line before firing of gun. 2. Must stay in lane. 3. Two false starts disqualify the runner.	1. Warm up thoroughly before starting. 2. Don't jump through the finish tape. 3. Don't practice starts when stiff.	1. Run out of the blocks, don't jump. 2. Get to running position as soon as possible. 3. Relax, don't tighten neck muscles.
Hurdling	1. Must not allow any part of body to get outside own hurdle. 2. May knock any number of official hurdles down.	1. Warm up and stretch well before hurdling. 2. Never take hurdles slowly. 3. Never try to clip the low hurdles too low. 4. Keep lead leg straight.	1. Practice with arms forward. 2. Practice with correct number of steps always. 3. Don't let head rear back.
High Jump	1. Three trials allowed at each height. 2. Must jump from one foot. 3. Displacing bar, passing under it, crossing line of bar extended, or leaving ground shall constitute a trial.	1. Learn to land on a foot or feet, not hands or body. 2. Don't jump when take-off is slippery. 3. Always fix pit or mats for landing safely.	1. Learn to kick the lead leg. 2. Stand up and jump—don't lie down to jump. 3. Run easy and relax for jump.
Running Broad Jump	1. Touching in front of the scratch line or passing line extended shall count as a foul and trial. 2. The jump shall be measured at right angles to the board and point of landing closest to take-off.	1. Warm up gradually—take short, easy jumps at first. 2. Wear jumping shoes or rubber pads in take-off heel. 3. Keep landing pit or mats smooth and soft.	1. Run far enough to get up speed. 2. Work for height. 3. "Throw the belly out" on take-off. 4. Fight for distance just as you go to land.
Shot Put	1. Touching on top or outside the circle or toeboard with any part of body before throw is measured is a foul. 2. Four preliminary throws are allowed and two or three allowed those who qualify for finals.	1. Practice in a secluded place. 2. Never throw when young children are around. 3. Roll the shot back to the circle—don't throw it back.	1. Keep the shot on a straight upward angle line during delivery. 2. Speed across the circle is most important. 3. Deliver with a pumping motion and snap at end with hand and wrist.
Relays	1. Baton must be passed in zone (see Fig. 30-3). 2. Baton must be carried in a hand throughout the race. 3. No competitor shall run more than one leg of the relay. 4. All running rules must be observed.	1. After passing the baton, runner should remain in his lane until all others have passed. 2. In (blind) speed passing keep eyes ahead to avoid collision. 3. If baton is dropped be careful to retrieve safely.	1. In blind passes, responsibility rests with the passer. 2. Responsibility for success in the visual pass rests with the receiver. 3. The receiver in blind passes must not "run away" from passer.

Pace A set speed which the runner desires to run.

Planting box of pit A slot located in front of the pit in which the vaulting pole is placed for vaulting.

Pole The inside edge of the running track. A vaulting pole used to vault over the crossbar.

Preliminaries Four throws in the weight events or four jumps in the running broad jump, to determine those who qualify for the finals.

Qualify To win the right to compete in the finals.

Relay leg One man's race or distance traveled in a relay.

Scratch line A line over which jumpers or throwers must not step during a trial, nor a runner infringe upon before the gun is fired.

Seeded Picking the fastest runners to lead the preliminary heats so that all good men do not compete in the same heat until the finals.

Starting blocks   Devices in which the feet are placed to aid the runner in starting.

Stride   A step in running.

Take-off board   A board from which the running broad jumper takes off.

Throwing sector   The specified arc in which a thrown implement must land.

Toeboard   A board, in the form of an arc, on which or over which the shot-putter must not step.

Trial   An attempt in a field event.

Trial heat   See *Heat.*

SELECTED REFERENCES

Amateur Athletic Union of the United States, *Official Track and Field Handbook.* New York: AAU (current edition).

American Association for Health, Physical Education and Recreation, Division for Girls' and Women's Sports. *Track and Field Guide.* Washington, D.C.: AAHPER (current edition).

The Athletic Institute, *Track and Field Instructor's Guide.* Chicago: Athletic Institute, 1960.

Bresnahan, G. T., and W. W. Tuttle, *Track and Field Athletics.* St. Louis: C. V. Mosby Co., 1964.

Doherty, J. Kenneth, *Modern Track and Field,* Englewood Cliffs, N.J.: Prentice-Hall, Inc., 1963.

Ecker, Tom (ed.), *Championship Track and Field by 12 Great Coaches.* Englewood Cliffs, N.J.: Prentice-Hall, Inc., 1961.

Forman, K., and V. Husted, *Modern Track and Field Techniques for Girls and Women.* Dubuque, Iowa: William C. Brown Company, Publishers, 1965.

————, *Modern Training for Running,* Englewood Cliffs, N.J.: Prentice-Hall, Inc., 1964.

Gordon, James A., *Track and Field: Changing Concepts and Modern Techniques.* Boston. Allyn & Bacon, Inc., 1966.

Jordon, Peyton, and Marshall K. McClelland, *Track and Field for Boys.* Chicago: Follett Publishing Company, 1960.

National Collegiate Athletic Association, *Official Track and Field Guide.* New York: National Collegiate Athletic Bureau (current edition).

National Federation of State High School Athletic Associations, *Track and Field Rules.* Chicago: The Federation, (7 South Dearborn Street) (current edition).

Scott, Phebe M., and Virginia R. Crafts, *Track and Field for Girls and Women.* New York: Appleton-Century-Crofts, 1964.

Wakefield, Frances; Dorothy Harkins, and John M. Cooper, *Track and Field Fundamentals for Girls and Women.* St. Louis: 1966.

Wilt, Fred, *How They Train.* Los Altos, Calif.: The Track and Field News (Box 296), 1959.

Volleyball

GLENVILLE STATE COLLEGE RESIDENCE HALLS

APPLICATION FOR ROOM

NAME: _____
MR.
MRS.
MISS
       LAST   FIRST   MIDDLE

Year of High School Graduation _____ Birthdate _____ DATE _____

Parents Name _____

Home
Address _____
       STREET   CITY   STATE   ZIP CODE
Phone _____ Age _____

COLLEGE CLASSIFICATION:

- ☐ FRESHMAN
- ☐ SOPHOMORE
- ☐ JUNIOR
- ☐ SENIOR
- ☐ SPECIAL

THIS APPLICATION IS FOR THE PERIOD BEGINNING _____

CHOICE OF RESIDENCE HALL: WOMEN: _____ MEN: _____

WOMEN'S HALL ☐
LOUIS BENNETT HALL ☐. VERONA MAPEL ☐.

(FOR COLLEGE USE) _____

(SEE REVERSE SIDE)

ORIGIN AN[D]

Volleyball was fir[st] ...
of the Holyoke, ...
Early rules called ...
the ground and f[or] ...
provided for the ...
any number of p[layers] ...

Two teams ...
strated the game ...
directors, and th[en] ...
their supervision ...
gradually and co[ncerning] ...
the present rules ...

In 1922, th[e cham]pionships were fi[rst] ...
ments have prob[ably] ...
play and compet[ition] ...

The United States Volleyball Association was formed in 1928 with Dr. George J. Fisher as its first president. Under the direction of this organization, the annual tournaments, formerly sponsored by the

... opened to all volleyball teams in the ...

... ball today is played in many foreign ... d is included in most programs of ... eges, recreation centers, playgrounds, ... is now included in the Olympic Games.

[NATU]RE OF THE GAME

... ball for men is played on a court 60 feet ... ivided into two halves, with a net eight ... d two teams of six players each. In ... y, the net is only seven feet four and ... inches high. The six players are desig- ... t, center, and right forwards and left, ... right backs—or they may be numbered ... six, starting with the left forward. When ... s turn to serve, every player rotates one ... ckwise and the right back serves. (See

The object of the game is to keep the ball from striking the floor on your side of the net and to return it so that it strikes the floor on your op-

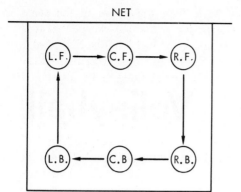

FIGURE 31-1. Rotation in play

ponents' side so they cannot return it. The ball is put in play from behind the rear boundary line by the right back, who serves it across the net into the opponents' court. The ball is then volleyed back and forth until one team or the other fails to return the ball. If the serving team makes the error, it loses the serve. An error by the receiving team gives one point to the servers. A team can score only when it serves and it continues to serve as long as it scores. A ball may be volleyed twice before being played over the net, which makes a total of three hits per side, except, of course, that the serve must go directly from the server to the opponents' court. A match consists of two out of three games. Sides are changed after the first and second games and at the middle (eight points, or four minutes for women) of the third game.

The women's game consists of 15 points or eight minutes, whichever is reached first. If a team is not two points ahead after eight minutes of a play or on reaching a score of 15, play shall continue until there is a two-point difference between scores. Men play 15-point games and, in tournaments, play

FIGURE 31-2. Passing and setting the ball

8 minutes. If the score is tied at 14-all, one team must make two consecutive points to win.

TECHNIQUES AND FUNDAMENTALS

Handling the ball (passing)

HIGH BALL. Most balls are received above the waist, permitting an overhand or chest pass, which is the most effective method of passing with regard to control and power.

To make a chest pass, face the direction to be passed, advance the left foot, bend the knees, arch the back, lift the elbows sideward to a point just below the shoulders, rotate the forearm until palms of the hands are forward, hold hands forehead high with thumbs pointing toward each other, flex and spread the fingers, and bend the wrists back toward the body. (See Fig. 31-2.) The thumbs and forefingers form a triangular pattern through which a player looks while playing the ball.

From this position the ball is played "cleanly" with the inside tips of the fingers and thumbs. The knees are straightened, the arms and wrists are extended in the direction in which it is desired that the ball travel, the back snaps forward, and the shoulders follow the arms. The movement of each part of the body is toward the terminal point of the ball flight with the position of the elbows and degree of back bend determining the direction of this flight. The ball is given a "feathery" touch and passed high into the air. The ball is always passed to the designated set-up player, usually the center forward.

(In championship play the chest pass is seldom used to receive the serve; instead, the underhand bump pass is used.)

LOW BALL. Any ball received waist-high or lower should be returned by hitting the ball on top of the wrists, lower arms, and tops of the thumbs with the hands together as shown in the accompanying illustration (See Fig. 31-3). The arms should be held close together. This method has two advantages. First, it avoids the "throw" prohibited by the rules and second, with it, it is much easier to control the direction of the pass. Women gain control, height, and distance much more easily with this type of "bump."

The feet should be separated slightly and the knees bent. From this position the ball is played by straightening the knees, bringing the hips forward, and lifting the arms in the direction to which it is desired to pass the ball. The ball should be passed high, but it need not be hit hard. For this reason, this method of playing the ball is especially well

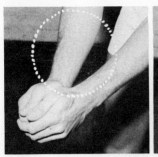

FIGURE 31-3. Two methods of holding the hands on a two-hand underhand pass. The right thumb could also clasp the fingers of the left hand in the open-hand method.

suited for girls and women who normally have difficulty hitting hard enough with the old open-hand lift method.

OVER-THE-HEAD HIT. When necessary to retrieve a high ball that goes over your head, it is best to turn your back to the net and to retreat until

FIGURE 31-4. Method of hitting a ball that goes over one's head. The passer's back is toward the net.

contact can be made with the hands in the same position as described for a low ball except that it is struck at shoulder height or higher. (See Fig. 31-4.) Here, again, care must be taken to hit the ball easily because it strikes the hard surfaces of the arms and thumbs.

THE DIG PASS. The one-hand dig pass is used to return low balls that would be out of reach of the two-hand pass. The fist is closed, and the ball is struck with the heel of the hand and the *second* joint of the fingers; or the fingers are curled, and the ball is struck with the heel of the hand and the *first* joint of the fingers. (See Fig. 31-5.) The ball need not be hit with much force because it rebounds forcefully from the hard fist.

FIGURE 31-5. The one-hand dig pass

SET-UP. The set-up is a special kind of pass made, if at all possible, by a chest pass positioning the ball so that the attack player may spike or kill it. It must be made so the ball will fall in front of the attack player.

There are three kinds of set-ups: (1) a high one, which is passed from eight to ten feet above the net and from six to 18 inches from the net, (2) a low one, which is passed only about three feet above the net and from three to 12 inches back from the net, and (3) when the ball must be passed from ten feet or more from the net, it is sent just above the net but high enough to go over if the attack man does not, or cannot, play the ball.

The player making a set-up should move under the ball fast, and when making the pass he should be facing toward his attack partner, which is in the direction the ball must travel. The spin should be taken off the ball.

Note: Regardless of the position of the ball, it should always be played with both hands if at all possible. Playing the ball with one hand, except in serving, spiking, and dig passing, is considered poor form.

Serving

Although there are many kinds of serves, there are only two basic methods of putting the ball in play—the other serves being, for the most part, variations of the overhand and underhand serves.

UNDERHAND SERVE. This is the simplest, easiest, and safest way to start a play. To make an underhand serve, stand facing the net with the ball resting in the left hand. Increasing the bend of the left knee, swing both arms straight back past the right hip with the ball. Move the right arm to shoulder height and then swing it straight forward, knocking the ball off the left hand with the palm and heel of the right hand. It is necessary to follow through by straightening the left knee at the moment of contact and by letting the right hand follow the path of the ball. An effective "floater" can be hit if the ball is moved backward, then forward, with the left hand as the right hand follows and strikes the ball without spinning it. The ball may also be struck with the palm side of the closed fist or with the thumb and forefinger of a semiclosed fist.

OVERHAND SERVE. This is an advanced serve

FIGURE 31-6. The overhand serve

to be learned only after the underhand serve has been thoroughly mastered. To make the serve, stand facing the net with the left foot advanced and the ball resting on the left hand or on both hands in front of the body. Toss the ball with both hands from three to five feet directly above the head, turn the body to the right, place the weight on the right foot with the right leg bent, raise the right hand up and back with the upper arm parallel to the ground, and arch the back with the hips forward. As the ball falls, cup the hand and hit it with the heel, palm and fingers just above the height of the head. Follow through by letting the hand follow the ball flight, straightening the right leg and turning the body from right to left. The entire movement is quite similar to making an overhand baseball throw. The idea is to hit a hard floater that is difficult to return. (See Fig. 31-6.)

PLACEMENT OF THE SERVE. Every serve should be made so it necessitates either a long pass to the set-up man or a pass moving in the same direction as that in which the set-up man will have to pass to his attack partner. This means that all serves should be made from near the ten-foot mark and to the extreme back corners of the receiving court.

If the set-up player is in the center forward position, the best serve is to the right back, and if the set-up player is in the right forward position, the best serve is to the left back.

Spiking

Spiking is the act of jumping in the air at the net and forcefully hitting the ball down into the opponents' court.

There are two methods of spiking: the standing attack and the running attack. There are two methods of using the spiking hand and each will be described below.

STANDING ATTACK. Before the spring and the actual hitting of the ball is made, the attacker stands with his left side to the net, both arms back, knees bent, body bent somewhat at the waist, and the weight on the balls of the feet. As the spring is made, the right arm is raised with the elbow above and behind the right shoulder. The hand is brought up above the level of the head and behind the right shoulder, the wrist is bent with the palm facing forward and the hand cupped. When the hit is made, the body twists sharply to the left until it is facing the net. The right shoulder is brought down and toward the net, and the arm moves down and the wrist snaps through with the hand hitting down on the top, rear portion of the ball. (See Fig. 31-7.)

FIGURE 31-7. Arm and hand preparation for spike

RUNNING ATTACK. Preparation for the spring is made as follows: the attacker stands five to eight feet from the net, facing half to the right, with the feet on the line and parallel. Three steps are taken directly forward, beginning with the left foot. On the first step, the right arm and shoulder are dropped down and back with the left arm moving forward. A step is then taken with the right foot, and then a short step is taken with the left prior to landing on *both feet,* with the left foot about 12 inches to the left, in front of the right. As the last step is taken, both arms are flexed with the right well back and down, the knees are bent, and the body is tilted forward from the waist. When the spring is made, the knees are straightened and the body projected upward. Care must be taken to leap from both feet so that the body is projected up and not forward or the attacker will foul by landing across the center line or touching the net. Greater stability can often be achieved if the legs are spread as the spring is made. The other style for use of the hand at the time of contact with the ball calls for a relaxed wrist and hand, the hand wraps around the top of the ball. This gives an added whip-like snap that sends the ball with greater force.

Blocking

Blocking is the technique employed by one or more defensive players to counteract the advantage gained by a good spike on the part of the offensive team. Essentially, it is the act of jumping with arms extended straight up and fingers tensed from a position directly in front of the ball at the time it is hit, and returning the ball immediately down into the opponents' court, or deflecting the flight of the ball up and back permitting the blocking team to assume the offense. The spring from the floor is made from both feet with all blockers jumping in unison. The spring should be made at sufficient distance from the net to permit the arms to move forward at the moment of contact with the ball without the danger of touching the net. When one wants to return the ball to the opponents' court from the block, his fingers are held vertical and the hands stiff. If he wants to merely slow the speed at which the ball is moving and still retain control of it, the hands and fingers are tensed but tilted backward. Timing is the key to successful blocking. There is a tendency for inexperienced players to jump too soon. One should be aware that he must delay his jump until the last possible moment. The more advanced the play the larger the number of blockers that are used. Beginners use one or possibly two while advanced team play calls for three or four blockers. International rules permit only two blockers.

Retrieving the ball from the net

To retrieve the ball from the net, stand with one shoulder toward the net, facing the side boundary line, with the knees bent and the left foot in advance of the right and the arms in position to play a low ball. As the ball rebounds from the net, it is played as described under "low ball." If the ball lands in the net near the top, it will drop straight down. If it lands near the bottom of the net, it will rebound two or three feet and the player retrieving the ball must stand near or away from the net accordingly.

Offensive play

For offensive purposes, a team is usually divided into three teams of two men, each team consisting of a set-up man and a spiker. Advanced play calls for four spikers and two set-up men. In the forward position, the set-up always plays on the right side of his attacking partner, provided the partner is right-handed, and on the left side if the attacker is left-handed. The spiker may change position with the set-up after the ball has been served. The players immediately take their defensive positions after the serve.

Generally the first pass should be made to the

set-up who is playing in the center forward or right forward position. He, in turn, passes to his attacking partner. Exceptions to this rule provide that if the set-up receives the first ball, he passes to the right forward, right back or center back, who makes the set-up pass for the attacker. On plays of this type, the first pass is made high but short, and the second passer moves toward the set-up in order to make the set-up pass as nearly as possible from the set-up position.

Once in a great while—for surprise or to catch the other team out of position—the first pass may be the set-up pass.

The spiker should attempt to play the ball into the unguarded portions of the opponents' court. These spots are shown in Fig. 31-9.

If the defensive team blocks, the ball must be cut to one side or lobbed over the players' heads to the back court.

It is a common fault for the front line (forwards) to play too close to the net. Only the set-up should play close.

Defensive play

Defensive play concerns itself primarily with formations best adapted to receiving hard or well-placed drives and with blocking spiked balls. It is too easy to play around a single blocker, so a block is

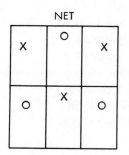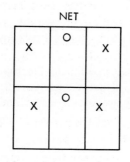

FIGURE 31-8. Player arrangement for 3 spikers and three setters, and for 2 spikers and 4 setters.

X = spiker
O = setter

FIGURE 31-9.

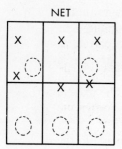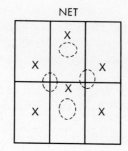

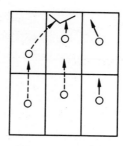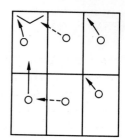

FIGURE 31-10.

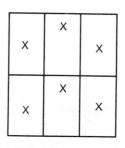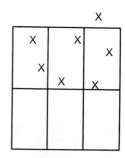

FIGURE 31-11.

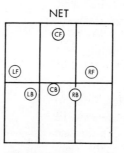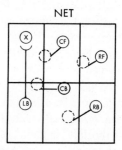

FIGURE 31-12. (*Left*) Receiving the serve

FIGURE 31-13. (*Right*) Covering the offensive spike

generally made by at least two players. When the two blockers converge for the play, the other four men must distribute themselves so as to best cover the court. This movement is indicated in Fig. 31-10.

Two of the better defensive formations for when the block is not utilized are shown in Fig. 31-11.

Receiving the serve

When receiving the serve, the members of the receiving team line up as indicated in Fig. 31-12. The hands should be held up shoulder-high in the "ready" position. They then shift into their offensive position and set for the designated spiker as illustrated in Fig. 31-13.

OFFICIATING

Officials are used primarily in tournament play. They shall be referee, umpire, scorer, time-keeper, and two to four linesmen. The referee is stationed above the net on one side, the umpire on the other side below the net, the linesmen (usually two) sit at diagonal corners, and the timekeeper and scorer sit together opposite the referee.

Their duties are as follows:

The *referee* tosses coin for sides, decides when the ball is in play or dead, when a point is made or side is out, when fouls are committed, when a point is to be replayed, and has the authority to overrule officials and make decisions not covered in the rules. He starts and stops play and time-out by blowing his whistle and uses arm signals to show his decisions.

The *umpire* assists the referee in calling fouls, violations on the center line, conduct, and interference with play, authorizes substitutions, checks on players out of position, and keeps time in men's games.

The *scorer's* responsibilities include operating the scoring devices and recording of scores as determined by the referee. He records the names, numbers, and playing order, including substitutions and time-outs, and notifies the referee of violations.

The *timekeeper* (women use two, one from each team) operates a suitable timing device and keeps a record of time-outs and of the time the ball is in play. The clock begins with each serve and stops when the ball is dead. If no visible device is used he must call out the minutes left to play at four, two, and one minutes.

The *linesmen* (usually each team furnishes one) call balls landing in or out with the hand signals of thumbing "out" and palms down for "good." They assist the referee, especially in regard to foot-faults of the server.

PLAYING STRATEGY

1. Play to the opponents' weaknesses, such as a weak man and the poorest defensive man at the net.
2. Usually serve to your opponents' back right court unless there is a left-handed spiker up. When opponents' spiker is in the center-forward position, it is best to serve to your opponents' back left court.
3. Study the defensive tactics of your opponents and play to their weaknesses.
4. Serve quickly when you are piling up points.
5. Study each spiker and set your defenses to stop his placements.

6. The spiker should not hit the ball straight down the center unless the center forward fails to block.

SIMPLIFIED RULES

Volleyball rules are simple and can be learned quickly by beginners. The simplified rules follow. The penalty for practically every foul is the loss of the ball for the side serving or loss of the point if the receiving side fouls.

1. The ball must be served by the right back *behind* the rear line, right of the 10-foot mark, and may be hit in any manner with the hand.
2. Only one trial serve is allowed per side and it must land within the opponents' court. If it touches the net and continues into the opponents' court, it counts as a serve.
3. It is a foul for players to touch the net, to reach over the net, or under the net and touch an opponent, or to step over the center line.
4. Holding or throwing the ball while it is in play is a foul. The play must be a distinct batting of the ball.
5. A ball landing on a boundary line is "in."
6. A point may be scored only by the side serving.
7. If a ball touches a player or a player touches a ball, he is considered as having played the ball. If the ball hits a player twice, or two or more blockers after being spiked, it is considered as having been played just once.
8. The ball may be played only three times by one team in a volley and a player may not play it twice in succession but may play it twice if it is played by a teammate in between.
9. Players of the serving team must rotate clockwise when receiving the ball to serve, and the right back must serve. Women do not rotate for their first service.
10. Only the front line (forwards) are permitted to spike.
11. When two opponents hit the ball simultaneously out of bounds, the point is played over.
12. Front line players may shift positions after the ball is served.

Suggested rules for co-recreation volleyball [1]

In playing co-recreation volleyball, DGWS rules should be followed with the following exceptions:

[1] *DGWS Official Volley Ball Guide.* Washington, D.C.: American Association for Health, Physical Education and Recreation, Division for Girls' and Women's Sports. July 1965–July 1967.

Rule 2. Net height. For high schools the official net height is seven feet six inches. For junior high schools and younger players the official net height is seven feet. For college and adult players the official net height is eight feet.

Rule 4. The team shall consist of three girls and three boys who shall be placed in alternate positions on the floor.

Rule 7. When a ball is played by more than one player on a team, one of these must be a girl.

Rule 8. Except for the serve the ball may be contacted with any part of the body at the waist or above.

Only players in the front line at the time of the serve may block volleyball. It was deemed advisable to formulate rules that would provide for flexibility in order that they might be adaptable to a great variety of situations and to varying degrees of skill. The simpler forms of play should be used

where necessary to suit the age and ability of the group; experienced players, boys and girls alike, enjoy the game more if it is not too easy.

COMPARISONS OF VOLLEYBALL RULES

Three sets of volleyball rules are currently employed: those of the International Volleyball Federation, those of the United States Volleyball Association, and those of the Division for Girls' and Women's Sports. Although the games are basically similar, minor differences complicate play between groups. Most girls' and women's groups play under DGWS rules, while in the United States most men play under USVBA rules. All international competition, such as that in the Olympics, as well as all play in foreign countries, is under International Volleyball Federation rules. For your interest the three sets of revised current rules are contrasted below:

	DGWS	USVBA	INTERNATIONAL
Number of Players	6	6	6
Court	30' x 60'	30' x 60'	29' x 59'6" (9 x 18 meters)
Net	7'4¼"	8'—men 7'4¼"—women	7'11⅝"—men 7'4⅛"—women
Spiking Line	None	7'6"	10'
Substitution	One player may not enter more than two times in one game. If a player re-enters, he must take his original place in the serving order.	One player may not enter more than three times in one game. If a player re-enters, he must take his original place in the serving order.	Teams allowed only six substitutions in one game, and one player may not enter more than two times in one game. When re-entering must take original position. Only the original player may take the substitute's place. Another substitute may not.
Playing Ball	Only with hands and forearms.	Any part of body above and including the waist.	Any part of body above and including the waist.
Blocking	Permissible, not stated which players may block.	Permissible, not stated which players may block.	Permissible, only two of the three front line players.
Back Line	Not permissible.	Permissible if spiker lands behind 7½-foot line.	Permissible if spiker lands behind 10-foot line.
Rotation	Rotate after 1st service.	Rotate for all services.	Rotate for all services.
Service Receiving Positions	In respective positions until service.	3 front of line and 3 back.	3 front of line and 3 back.
Simultaneous Contacts by Teammates	Permitted, counts as one hit; both may participate in next play.	Permitted, counts as one hit; both may participate in next play.	Permitted, counts as two touches of the ball.
Length of a Game	Two out of three games, 15 points or eight minutes each; winner must be two points ahead.	Two out of three games, 15 points or eight minutes each; winner must be two points ahead.	Three out of five games, 15 points each; winner must be two points ahead.

Courtesy of Joanne Thorpe, *DGWS Volley Ball Guide.*

PLAYING COURTESIES

Volleyball is an unusually sportsmanlike team game. This is true probably because the players are on opposite sides of the net and there is very little occasion for bodily contact with opponents. If one wishes to be a good sport in volleyball, he should:

1. Always return the ball on the floor to the next server.
2. In case of doubt, call the play in favor of the opponents.
3. Compliment the opponents for a good play.
4. Call his own fouls, quickly and honestly.

SAFETY HINTS

The main sources of injury in volleyball are pulled muscles and turned ankles from sudden starts and stops, collision with own players and with objects surrounding the play area, and minor finger injuries caused by improperly playing the ball. To avoid these one should:

1. Be sure to warm up the legs thoroughly by running, jumping, and doing stretching exercises.
2. Keep the space surrounding the play area free from obstacles.
3. Play one's own position.
4. Learn to use the hands properly in blocking, passing, and setting the ball.

HELPFUL HINTS

Volleyball is a great team game that requires more skill and provides an opportunity for more organized effort than is generally thought.

The following hints may help one to become a skilled player:

1. Learn to control the underhand serve so that you can place it "on a dime."
2. Master the skill of receiving a ball on the finger tips but "with the whole body" so that it can be passed or set up as light as a feather.
3. Spike with the hand relaxed so the fingers wrap around the ball.
4. Play the ball underhand with the bump pass.
5. Usually set the ball in the center of the net—this allows the spiker to hit in any direction.

6. To play ball out of the net, squat low and play it straight up.

TERMINOLOGY

Actual playing time The time between contact on the serve and a dead ball.

Add out The team which has scored one point following a tie after any score from 14 on.

Block Defensive play by players (or a player) in the forward positions who place their hands and arms above the net so that a spiked ball rebounds into the opponent's court or back to their own.

Bump pass The forearm bounce pass made on low balls.

Catching or holding the ball The ball must be clearly batted. If it rests momentarily in a player's hands, it is considered illegal.

Dead ball The ball is dead following a point, side-out, or any decision temporarily suspending play.

Delaying the game Any player who, in the opinion of the referee, is unnecessarily slowing down the game.

Deuce When the score is tied at any point from 14 on.

Dig pass A pass made with the hand slightly cupped or with the fist of one hand, usually on a difficult play.

Double foul Infraction of rules by both teams during the same play.

Dribbling When a player touches more than once a ball that has not been touched in between by another player; it is illegal. He may do so, however, in receiving a hard-driven spike.

Game point The last point in a game.

Out of bounds When a ball touches outside a boundary line. If it touches a boundary line it is good.

Playing the ball Any player who is in the act of touching the ball.

Point A point is scored when the receiving team fails to return the ball legally to the opponents' court.

Rotation Shifting of the players, clockwise, just before a "new" person serves.

Service The right back puts the ball in play by batting it over the net to the opponents. His feet must be behind the rear service line.

Side out Side is out when the serving team fails to win a point or plays the ball illegally.

SELECTED REFERENCES

Barnes, Mildred J., *Program in Self-Instruction for Officiating DGWS Volleyball Rules*. Minneapolis: Burgess Publishing Co., 1965.

DGWS Official Volley Ball Guide. Washington, D.C.: The American Association for Health, Physical Education and Recreation (current edition).

Egstrom, Glen, and F. Schaafsma, *Volleyball*. Dubuque, Iowa: William C. Brown Company, Publishers, 1966.

Laveaga, Robert, *Volleyball*. New York: The Ronald Press Company, 1960.

Meyer, Margaret H., and Marguerite M. Schwarz, *Team Sports for Girls and Women* (3rd ed.). Philadelphia: W. B. Saunders Co., 1957.

Odeneal, William T., and Harry Wilson, *Beginning Volleyball*. Belmont, Calif.: Wadsworth Publishing Co., Inc., 1962.

Patterson, Ann, *Team Sports for Girls*. New York: The Ronald Press Company, 1958.

Plotnicki, Ben A., "Brief History of Volleyball," *USVBA Guide*, 1965.

Shaw, John H., *et al.*, *Individual Sports for Men* (3rd ed.). Dubuque, Iowa: William C. Brown Company, Publishers, 1964.

Thigpen, Janet, *Power Volleyball for Girls and Women*. Dubuque, Iowa: William C. Brown Company, Publishers, 1967.

Tom, Marilynn, and Margaret Luckman, *Co-ed Volleyball*. New York: Nation Press Publications, 1966.

Trotter, Betty Jane, *Volleyball for Girls and Women*. New York: The Ronald Press Company, 1965.

U.S. Volleyball Association Guide, *Official Volleyball Guide*. Berne, Indiana: American Sports Publishing.

Vannier, Maryhelen, and Hally Beth Poindexter, *Individual and Team Sports for Girls and Women* (2nd ed.). Philadelphia: W. B. Saunders Co., 1968.

Welch, J. Edmund, ed., *How to Play and Teach Volleyball*. New York: Association Press, 1960.

Weightlifting and Weight Training

Weightlifting

ORIGIN AND DEVELOPMENT

Weightlifting was created out of man's keen desire for continued existence. Primitive man, in order to improve his chances of survival, was forced to push, lift, and throw "weights." However, it took on sporting aspects when in 776 B.C., by will of Ayrominus, young men who desired to compete in the Olympics were required to lift a rough ball of iron before being permitted to participate in the games.

Not only did the sport develop from throwing and displacing weights, which sport practice still exists among youth in certain mountain regions in Switzerland, but weightlifting was said to have had great therapeutic value and was prescribed frequently by such famous ancients as Clelius Aurelianus.

Men such as Duek Christoph of Bavaria and Milus of Crotone (who gained fame by winning six Olympic wrestling titles and in addition managed on an occasion to lap a stadium four times while carrying a four-year-old bull on his shoulders), are but two examples of heroic and memorable figures from the past.

The first attempt to formally organize and regulate weightlifting occurred almost concurrently in France, Germany, and Austria, about 1870. With elementary rules to govern and provide standards, the activity thrived to the extent that professionals soon existed.

With the aid of Hyppolite Trait (1813–1881), the Apostle of Physical Education, who always maintained that weightlifting exercises were the most useful for the preparation of athletes, weightlifting found an especially fertile ground in France.

Germany also, early in the nineteenth century, contributed immensely to the development of weightlifting as a sport, principally through the Turnverein movement. Dr. Friedrich Jahn, who founded the Turnverein, advocated special clubs within its organization that emphasized specific activities. One of these special clubs was for weightlifting. In the middle of the nineteenth century, there was a large German immigration into the United States. Turnvereine were established here, and these gave great impetus to weightlifting in our country.

Dr. Winship, an early pioneer of weightlifting, toured the United States and Canada during the period from 1859 to 1872, in which time he gave exhibitions of weightlifting. By the end of the nineteenth century, weightlifting began to find its way into the athletic clubs and YMCA's. At this time, many strong men were headliners in theaters with their weightlifting exhibitions.

In 1885 a Frenchman, Edmond Dezbennet, established the first series of records and was able to formulate regulations which are still in use today: the two-phase, two-hand clean and jerk, press, etc.

In 1894, the first international championship was held at Mouseron. French, Belgian, and Dutch athletes participated. In 1902, the first world championship was held in London, and in the following year the international championship for professionals and amateurs was organized in Paris.

It was also in Paris in 1914 that the Federation Française des Poids et Haltères was founded and later recognized by the Comité National des Sports.

Weightlifting was a part of the modern Olympic program as early as 1896, but was omitted after 1906. However, in 1920 it made a triumphant return to remain and gain a rightful recognition as one of the "great sports." Competitive weightlifting in the United States is under the jurisdiction of the Amateur Athletic Union. The first national championships were held in 1929.

The United States' weightlifting team made its debut in the Olympic games in 1932. The first Olympic Champion for the United States was Terlazzo, who won the featherweight class in the 1936 Olympics. In 1946, the United States won its first World's Championship in Paris. In the 1947 World's Championship Meet, the United States performed the phenomenal feat of winning first place in every body-

weight class. In the 1948 Olympics in London, the United States won the team championship by winning four of the six classes. In the 1952 Olympics, the United States won four first places and the U.S.S.R. placed second by winning three. In the 1956 Olympics, the United States won four first places and the U.S.S.R. won three first places. In the 1960 Olympics, the United States won only one first place; the U.S.S.R. won five first places; and Poland won one first place. In both the 1956 and 1960 games, C. Vinci of the United States won the bantamweight titles. In 1964, the United States won the silver medal in the featherweight class (Isaac Berger), and the bronze medal in the heavyweight (Norbert Schemansky). Since the United States entered Olympic weightlifting competition, its lifters have won 14 gold medals; the U.S.S.R. has won 15 during the same period.

Description of competitive lifting

There are three lifts that are used universally in competition. These lifts are the *two-hand snatch, two-hand clean and jerk,* and the *two-hand military press.* These are known as the Olympic lifts. There are four other lifts that are recognized and can be used for competition. These lifts are the *one-hand clean and jerk, right and left hand,* and the *one-hand snatch, right and left hand.* The competitor attempts to lift the heaviest weight possible in each lift, and the individual who has the highest total of the contest is declared the winner in his body-weight class.

The beginning competitor must be able to clean and jerk a weight equal to his body weight, to press, and to snatch a weight 80 per cent of his body weight. The competitive beginners must be able to accomplish these exercises before being awarded a weightlifting certificate.

BODYWEIGHTS FOR EACH CLASS OF WEIGHTLIFTERS

AAU COMPETITION
123 lb. class
132 lb. class
148 lb. class
165 lb. class
181 lb. class
198 lb. class
Unlimited class

OLYMPIC COMPETITION

Up to 56 kilograms [1]	Bantamweight
Up to 60 kilograms	Featherweight
Up to 67.5 kilograms	Lightweight
Up to 75 kilograms	Middleweight
Up to 82.5 kilograms	Light-heavyweight
Up to 90 kilograms	Middle-heavyweight
Over 90 kilograms	Heavyweight

[1] A kilogram is equivalent to 2.2046 pounds avoirdupois.

1. Two-hand military press

a. FIRST MOVEMENT. Lay the bar horizontally in front of the feet, grip the bar with both hands, bring the bar with one distinct motion up to the shoulders, and at the same time either lunge or spring on bent legs.[2]

[2] The styles used on the interpretation of "either lunging or springing on bent legs" are the split and squat styles. In the split style, the lifter moves one foot forward about one-third of the total distance of the split, and the other foot backwards about two-thirds the distance simultaneously. In the squat style, the lifter merely squats down under the weight without moving the feet, or may move them both outward slightly. It is necessary to have the knees wide apart, because it is illegal to have the elbows touch the knees when down in the squat. These methods enable the lifter to get down under the weight when it is pulled to the highest point of the lift.

b. SECOND MOVEMENT. After this position is reached, stand still for two seconds, holding the bar motionless. Press the weight overhead to the limit of the arms' length. In pressing the weight overhead, no sudden or jerking motion may be used. Another stop of at least two seconds is required, keeping the arms and legs stiff. The lifter's body and head must remain in constant vertical position during the entire lift.

2. Two-hand snatch

Lay the bar horizontally in front of the feet, grip the bar with both hands, bring the bar up with one continuous motion to arms' length vertically overhead, and at the same time either lunge or spring on bent legs. While the bar is passing with its continuous motion along the body, only the feet may touch or graze the floor.

The weight in this uplifted position must be held motionless for two seconds, with the arms and legs stiff and the feet in line not more than 16 inches apart. The hand position on the bar cannot be changed once the grip has been taken.

It is important in this lift that the action is a single motion. The movement must not be slowed until the wrists turn over, and the wrists shall not be turned over until the bar has reached a higher level than the top of the lifter's head.

3. Two-hand clean and jerk

The bar is laid horizontally at the feet. Then it is gripped with both hands and brought up to the shoulder in one continuous motion, and at the same time the lifter lunges or springs on bent legs.

As the bar travels in its continuous motion to the shoulder, it must not touch the chest. Its final position will be at the shoulders, resting at the chest or on closely flexed arms.

The feet are brought back to the original online position; the legs are bent; then, together with the arms, the legs are straightened with a jerk so as to lift the bar to the overhead position with the arms raised vertically.

The weight in this overhead position must remain motionless for two seconds. The arms and legs must be stiff, and the feet in line and not more than 16 inches apart. To repeat the uplifting would be illegal.

Number of trials

Each participant is allowed three trials for each scheduled event, not to be interpreted as three trials for each weight. The contestant will not be permitted to take any preliminary trials—for either the contest or for record—on or near the platform.

Ten pounds is the minimum increase in weights between trials, with the exception of the last trial, which may be five pounds. As soon as the contestant increases the weight only five pounds it indicates the final attempt. At no time may a contestant make a trial with a weight less than that used in the previous attempt. After the correct shouldering, only one lift is authorized.

OFFICIALS

The officials for competitive weightlifting are a referee, two scorers, two judges, and a weigh master. It is recommended that there also be an announcer and a physician. A meet director is essential when the competition involves a considerable number of entries.

Weight training

NATURE OF THE ACTIVITY

Weightlifting competition has been the forerunner to modern weight training. It became readily apparent that weightlifting produced an increased muscle mass and a high degree of strength. Therefore, it was only to be expected that different groups were stimulated to experiment with weights for their own particular purposes. These groups then came to realize that various systems of weight training not only improved physique, but also contributed beneficially to performance in many sports.

During the past two decades, the effectiveness of carefully planned weight training as a method of improving body development and sports performance has been accepted on the basis of well-controlled studies. The myths of muscle-boundness, reduction in localized muscle endurance, and loss of speed and agility previously thought to result from weightlifting are now considered "old-wives' tales."

Much may be gained through the systematic and intelligent application of modern weight training principles. Movements in sports are highly dynamic; only in a few instances is static contraction necessary. Use of the principle of overload coupled with progressive resistance through dynamic weight training programs appears to be the most efficient and effective means of acquiring dynamic strength. The closer the weight training movement simulates the actions in sports, the greater the transfer of strength to motor performance. Weight training is also an excellent way to develop flexibility, provided the exercise is executed through the entire range of motion. Muscle enlargement (hypertrophy) does not reduce muscle endurance (ability to perform repetitious movements). An increase in capillarization usually accompanies the cross-sectional increase of muscle fibers, and this helps delay local muscular fatigue by (1) making more nutrients available and increasing their efficient use, and (2) speeding up the removal of waste products, the primary cause of muscle fatigue. Increasing the cardiorespiratory endurance also requires specific training; heart and respiratory rates must be intensely increased and maintained at higher than normal resting levels for durations of time. Weight training does not necessarily affect cardiorespiratory function unless movements are executed for this specific purpose; for example, if half or quarter squats are executed with speed. Systematic weight training that applies the principles of progressive resistance, overload, and specificity has positive effects on motor performance parameters and contributes to successful participation in sports.

Most individuals in weight training are interested in body building. In a program that has variety, an individual can develop muscular strength and body symmetry. Weight lifting is frequently taken up to gain or lose body weight. The use of weights is a greater aid to gaining weight than to losing weight, because the lifting of the weights develops the musculature of the body. The overweight individual should concentrate on half squats to bench with light weights and at a fast speed; repetition clean and jerks—50 lbs, 30 reps; side bends—light weight, 50 reps; and sit-ups—10–12 at a fast speed, resting and then repeating. Many centers of rehabilitation find the use of weights valuable in developing weak or injured muscles, strengthening underdeveloped muscles, or rebuilding muscles affected by atrophy following hospitalization.

The weight training program should be so planned that the maximum benefits will result from the exercises involved. To accomplish this, various types of equipment will be needed. One of the principal advantages of weight training is that a strenuous work-out may be had in a small space.

Good results may be obtained with a three-days-a-week schedule. The days should be alternated (one day of work-out, one day of rest) because the body requires time for rebuilding following strenuous exercise. A two-hour work-out is ideal if the time is available; however, a one-hour program will also give excellent results.

EQUIPMENT

The barbells should be five to six feet in length and should be knurled at the handgrip for better control. Easily adjustable collars should be used. Graded weights from one to 25 pounds should be provided. Adjustable dumbbells, which make it easy to select the weight needed, are desirable. Iron boots are valuable for further development of the leg and abdominal muscles. Benches and incline boards are used to vary the body angle and to aid all-around body development. In order to get sufficient poundage for use in the half squat, a stand for holding heavy weights is necessary. Other valuable facilities to aid in securing a well-rounded program are a wrist roller, ceiling and wall pulleys, dipping and chinning bars, leg press apparatus, a head strap, latissimus exerciser, and bench press.

TECHNIQUES AND FUNDAMENTALS

Correct lifting form is essential not only for obtaining quick results, but also for safety. If the weight is brought in close to the body during the performance of a movement, the body leverage is decreased, defeating the purpose of the exercise. Therefore, we can see that if we wish to develop muscles, we should strive for a mechanical disadvantage. (See Fig. 32-1.)

FIGURE 32-1. Correct lifting position. *Note:* the feet are pointed straight ahead and under the bar. The head is erect; the back flat; the knees bent. The overhand grip is used.

When assuming the starting position at the bar, place the toes approximately under the bar with the feet spread about one foot apart. Many beginners have the fault of not starting close enough to the bar; consequently, when they start the lift, the bar swings toward the feet instead of going straight up.

The overhand grip is used in practically all exercises. The thumbs are hooked underneath the bar, placing the knuckles in position above the bar. The width of the grip is a matter of individual adjustment, but it will approximate shoulder width or a little wider. One exception to this is found in the two-hand snatch exercise, where a wide grip is advocated.

The underhand grip, as used in performing the curl, is the exact reverse of the overhand; the thumbs are hooked above with the knuckles under

FIGURE 32-2. Correct overhead position for bar. *Note:* the elbows are locked; eyes and chest are forward; body weight is supported on forward leg. The other leg is extended to rear for balance and is supported on the ball of the foot.

the bar. A third method of grasping the bar is a combination of the overhand and underhand grips accomplished by placing one hand above the bar and one hand below. When performing the Jefferson lift, this reverse grip is used, and it can also be used when performing dead lifts or when holding heavy weights.

Once the hands are gripping the bar correctly, check to see that the weight is equally distributed in both hands. The correct lifting position is then assumed: the legs are semi-flexed, the back is straight above the hips, the head is kept well up, and the eyes are fixed straight ahead. From this position, the lift can be made with full utilization of the legs, back, and arms. (See Fig. 32-2.)

Breathing should come naturally during the course of the exercise, letting the body regulate the demand. Forced gasping and puffing only interfere with proper breathing. The breathing should be done through the mouth because the body demand does increase with the exercise. In most cases inhalation is performed when the body is lifting the weight against the force of gravity, while exhalation takes place during the return movement. Another method of inhalation is to take in the breath when there is a natural lifting of the rib cage caused by the movement of the exercise. Two exercises in which one can utilize this type of breathing are the chest-deepener and the pullover.

Still another type of breathing is the complete inhalation before the movement begins—the breath is then held momentarily during the lift and is expelled upon completion of the movement. This method of breathing is used with heavy weights, since it gives more rigidity to the body and, therefore, aids in the lift. However, in most exercises the breathing remains normal, with the movement of the exercise timed with the rhythmical breathing.

WEIGHT TRAINING SYSTEMS

A characteristic of successful weight training is a dedicated consistency to a systematic plan that enables progressive resistance (ability to handle heavier weights). The selection of a progressive system is dependent upon weight training experience, current level of physical ability, desired rate of progress in muscular strength and muscular endurance, and length of time available for each training session. An excellent beginning system is the "3 x 10" described below, as it provides for an adequate number of repetitions. For faster gains, the working-up system is recommended. However, the fastest gains appear to result from the working-down system; this is logical, as it permits the highest degree of resistance (weight) to be utilized before the muscle experiences a notable degree of fatigue. The heavy-light system appears to be a rather definitive system, and is recommended for the most experienced weight trainer.

The 3 x 10 system (basic system)

This is a system of weight training wherein the individual goes through a routine of various lifts designed for all-round development, doing each exercise ten times and then going on to the next exercise. Once he has gone through the entire group of exercises, he again starts at the top and goes through the entire series again—and then once more.

This type of program is designed for the beginner in weight training.

When the lifter is able to go through the entire series of exercises three times he adds five more pounds of weight to each particular exercise.

This system—which requires many repetitions —results in strength gains. More important, however, it also gives strength to the tendon and muscle origins and insertions, thus enabling an individual to handle heavier weights without fear of injury or strain. The system also increases endurance.

A typical program for the 3 x 10 system would be as follows:

1. Two-arm Curls
2. Military Presses
3. Straight-arm Pullover
4. Flying Exercise
5. Lateral Raises
6. Sit-ups With Weights Behind Head
7. Heel Raises
8. Half Squats
9. Upright Rowing Motion

The working-up system

The lifter begins each lift with a weight with which he can perform 10 to 12 repetitions; then adds to the weight a specific number of pounds that will enable him to do six to eight repetitions; adds more weight and does four to six repetitions; increases the weight and does two to four repetitions; and finally, does one lift of a maximum weight.

The program is generally not repeated as the muscle or muscle group is extensively exerted and the work is quite fatiguing.

A SUGGESTED PROGRAM FOR THE WORKING-UP SYSTEM

1. *Military press*

10–12	presses	100 lbs.
6–8	presses	110 lbs.
4–6	presses	120 lbs.
1	press	140 lbs.

(1 to 2 minutes rest between presses)

2. *Two-arm curls*

10–12	curls	50 lbs.
6–8	curls	60 lbs.
4–6	curls	70 lbs.
2–4	curls	80 lbs.
1	curl	90 lbs.

(1 to 2 minutes rest between curls)

3. *Flying exercise (dumbbells)*

10–12	times	10 lbs.
6–8	times	15 lbs.
4–6	times	20 lbs.
2–4	times	25 lbs.
1	time	30 lbs.

4. *Straight-arm pullover*

10–12	repetitions	20 lbs.
8–10	repetitions	30 lbs.
4–6	repetitions	40 lbs.
2–4	repetitions	50 lbs.
1	repetition	60 lbs.

5. *Half squats*

10–12	repetitions	110 lbs.
6–8	repetitions	120 lbs.
4–6	repetitions	130 lbs.
2–4	repetitions	140 lbs.
1	repetition	150 lbs.

(1 to 2 minutes rest between half squats)

The working-down system

The only count that is made is on the first 10 movements in the exercise.

As an example, 10 curls with 70 lbs., then as many as possible with 60 lbs., then with 50 lbs., and on down until 10 lbs. is difficult to curl. The object of this system is to increase the starting weight as fast as possible. A side benefit of this program is great gains in muscle endurance.

A program for the working-down system

FIGURE 32-3. Bench press. (A) *Note:* the feet are flat on the floor. (B) *Note:* the arms are fully extended when taking the barbell from the spotters. (C) *Note:* wide elbow position.

could be as follows: work down from 10 repetitions with maximum weight in each of the following exercises.

1. Two-arm Curls.
2. Military Presses.
3. Straight-arm Pullover.
4. Lateral Raises.
5. Bent Over Rowing.
6. Flying Exercise.
7. "Good Morning" Exercise.

This program is not repeated as there is maximum use of the muscle until it cannot contract or extend anymore.

It can be followed every day if sufficient sleep and proper diet are maintained.

The heavy-light system

The system is based on three to five movements with a maximum amount of weight and then immediately moving to a weight of lesser poundage that will enable you to do eight more repetitions in the same exercise. The object being to build up the three to five lifts of maximum weight as fast as possible. The eight following repetitions are also increased in weight.

The weight trainer should change from one exercise to another and should try to go through the entire program three times in a training session.

A typical program in a heavy-light system follows.

1. Bench press (wide arm): 4 × maximum weight, 8 × 30 lbs. less

2. Two-arm curls: 4 × maximum weight, 8 × 15 lbs. less

3. Straight-arm pullover: 4 × maximum weight, 8 × 20 lbs. less

4. Upright rowing motion: 4 × maximum weight, 8 × 15 lbs. less

5. Half squats: 4–6 × maximum weight, 8–10 × 50 lbs. less

FIGURE 32-4. Bent over rowing position

EXERCISES

1. *Alternate leg lifts.* Lying in a supine position (with iron boots on both feet), alternately lift each leg (without bending a knee) to a perpendicular position. Lower each leg slowly. Increase weight as progress is made.

2. *Bench press.* From a supine position on a bench with the feet flat on the floor (astride the bench), the barbell is taken from the two spotters in an arms-extended position. Lower the barbell to the chest keeping the elbows parallel to the bar and then raise the bar to the extended position. The spotters must remain at the sides, take the bar following the final repetition, and replace it in the uprights. It is extremely important that the chest cavity be filled with air during the effort to extend the arms upward. The bench should be between 12 and 14 inches wide and approximately 18 inches high and the legs should be braced by attaching 2 x 4's, approximately three feet in length, horizontally to the legs. (See Fig. 32-3.)

3. *Bent over lateral raises.* Holding a dumbbell in each hand, at sides of body, bend forward raising the dumbbells as high as possible—10 repetitions. Return dumbbells to starting position. Increase weight as progress is made.

4. *Bent over rowing.* Bend forward at the waist, keeping the legs and back straight. The weight is at arms' length directly below the neck. Now lift the weight up to the neck, moving the arms only. (See Fig. 32-4.)

5. *Dead lifts.* Stand directly over the barbell. Bend knees and pick up the barbell keeping the back flat. Straighten to a bending position holding the bar with arms fully extended in front of the thighs. Lower the barbell to the floor with bent knees—10 reps. Increase weight as progress is made.

6. *Forward and lateral raise.* Standing erect with the dumbbells hanging at the sides, raise them forward overhead. Return to sides and raise them sidewards overhead.

7. *Flying exercise.* Use dumbbells. Lie on a bench in a supine position. With dumbbell in each hand, extend arms fully to a horizontal position. Raise dumbbells to a position overhead (vertical). Lower dumbbells as slowly as possible to the horizontal position—10 repetitions. Increase weight as progress is made.

8. *French curl.* With dumbbell in hand, place it behind the head so that the elbow is pointing straight up (180 degrees from elbow to shoulder). Raise the dumbbell to an overhead position and return it to position behind the head —10 repetitions. Alternate arms. Increase weight as progress is made.

9. *"Good morning" exercise.* From a standing position with barbell resting on shoulders behind the neck, bend forward slowly keeping the knees locked. The head should be held as high as possible and the back as flat as possible. The hips are extended backward. (See Fig. 32-5.)

10. *Half squat to bench.* With the barbell across the shoulders, behind the head, and with the back toward the bench, squat slowly, keeping the head erect and the back straight, until light contact is made with the bench; then up fast. The bench should be not less than 18 nor more than 20 inches high. (See Fig. 32-6.)

FIGURE 32-5. "Good Morning" exercise. In (B) note that the head is erect and the legs straight.

FIGURE 32-6. Half squat to bench

FIGURE 32-7. Latissimus exercise. On the left, notice that the arms are fully extended at the beginning of the exercise.

11. *Heel raises.* From a standing position with the barbell behind the neck, resting on the shoulders, rise on the toes. May also be performed with the soles of the feet on a block of wood one and one-half to two inches high.

12. *Iron boot exercises.*
    (1) Assume the supine position with the arms out at right angles, bring the right foot over and touch the left hand, return to starting position. Then bring the left foot over to the right hand, return to starting position.
    (2) Lying on the side, raise the leg straight upward as far as possible. Turn over and do the same with opposite leg.
    (3) Lying in a supine position, raise both legs up and touch the toes above the head. Keep the legs straight at all times.
    (4) In the supine position, raise both legs until they are perpendicular to the ground. Now split the legs outward and return.

13. *Latissimus exercise.* Grasp the bar with the hands as far apart as possible. Kneel with the head directly under pulley A and with the arms fully extended. (The weight should be just off the floor at the start of the exercise.) Pull the bar downward behind the neck until it touches the shoulders. Hold this position for one to two seconds. Return the bar slowly to the arms-extended position. This exercise may also be performed in a sitting position. The minimum length of the bar should be 42 inches. (See Fig. 32-7.)

14. *Leg curls.* Lying in a prone position on the machine table with forearms resting on table, place the heels under the upper bar. Raise the legs to a vertical position and return slowly to the starting position—10 repetitions. Increase weight as progress is made. (See Figs. 32-8, 32-9.)

FIGURE 32-8. Leg machine table

15. *Leg machine exercise.* Take an erect sitting position with arms straight and pressing on the machine table, the toes under the lower bar. Raise the legs to a horizontal position. Lower slowly to the starting position—10 repetitions. Increase weight as progress is made. (See Fig. 32-10.)

16. *Leg press.* (With bar contained within a leg press rack.) Lie in a supine position with the hips directly under the bar. Place the arch of each foot under the bar—shoulder width apart —and extend the legs fully (thus lifting the bar). Return slowly to the starting position— 10 repetitions. Increase weight as progress is made.

17. *Posterior raises (dumbbells).* Holding a dumbbell in each hand, lean forward (without bending the knees). Extend the arms to the rear and as high as possible keeping them slightly away from the body. Return slowly to starting position—10 repetitions. Increase weight as progress is made.

18. *Press behind neck.* From a position behind the neck, press the weight to the overhead position and return to behind the neck.

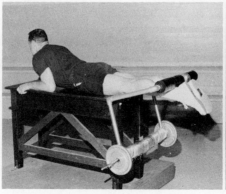
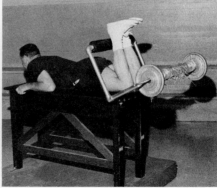

FIGURE 32-9. Leg curls on the machine table

398

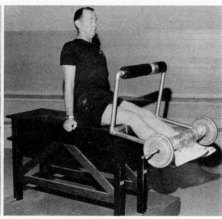

FIGURE 32-10. Leg machine exercise

19. *Reverse curl.* This is done exactly the same as the normal curl, except that an overhand grip is used.

20. *Shoulder shrug.* Stand erect with dumbbell in each hand—arms at sides of body and fully extended. Raise the shoulders as high as is possible without bending the arms.

21. *Side bends.* Stand erect with dumbbells in each hand. With legs and arms straight and dumbbells held at sides, alternately reach down to each side as far as is possible—10 repetitions. Do not lean forward. Increase weight as progress is made.

22. *Sit-ups.* From a supine position with the weight held behind the head, sit up and lean forward to touch an elbow to the opposite knee and return to the supine position. Repeat.

23. *Stiff leg lift.* Stand erect; legs straight on a bench or box which is at least 12 inches high. Hold barbell in front of thighs; lower it to a position as far below the toes as is possible keeping the legs straight—10 repetitions. Use light weight to start. Increase weight as progress is made.

24. *Straight-arm pullover.* Lying in a supine position on the floor or bench, start with the weight overhead at arms' length. Keeping the arms straight at all times, bring the weight in a circular motion to the thighs and return. (See Fig. 32-11.)

25. *Toe raises.* With an iron boot on each foot, sit on a chair. With foot slightly off the floor lift the toes upward toward the shin as far as is possible—10 repetitions. Alternate feet. Increase weight as progress is made.

26. *Torso rotation.* Hold the barbell on the shoulders with the feet pointing straight ahead. Alternately rotate the shoulders as far forward toward center line of body as is possible—10 repetitions. Do not allow the hips to rotate.

27. *Triceps exercise (leaning).* Use light dumbbells. While keeping the legs straight, bend at the waist until the upper part of the body is at right angles to the legs, as shown in Fig. 31-4. The

FIGURE 32-11. Pullover exercise. Notice that the arms are fully extended at the beginning of the exercise.

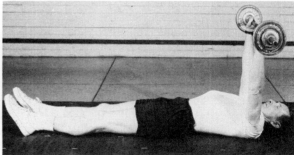

FIGURE 32-12. Two-arm curl. On the left, notice that the arms are completely extended; back flat; chest out; body erect.

upper arms remain stationary along the body, with the elbows at the hips. The forearms are then rotated and extended to limits of range.

FIGURE 32-13. Upright rowing motion

28. *Two-arm curl.* Use the underhand grip. Stand erect with the bar hanging at arms' length. Keeping the elbows at the sides and moving only the forearms, the weight is lifted to the chest and returned. (See Fig. 32-12.)

29. *Upright rowing motion.* Standing erect, with the weight hanging at arms' length, pull the bar up under the chin and return. (See Fig. 32-13.)

30. *Wrist curl.* Assume a sitting position with the forearms on the thighs and the wrists over the knees. Hold a weight (barbell or dumbbell) with the underhand grip and flex and extend hands.

31. *Wrist roller.* Drill a hole in a broomstick and insert a 3 foot rope through the hole and secure it to the broomstick. Tie a weight on the other end of the rope. Holding the broomstick at arms-length "roll" the rope (with palms down) around the broomstick. Increase weight as progress is made.

WEIGHT TRAINING FOR SPORTS

The following programs are recommended for the several sports. Unless otherwise stipulated, the programs are for "off-season" work-outs.

Baseball

1. Warm-up—Clean and Jerk (light weights). These exercises are performed with dumbbells.
2. 3 × 10 Lateral Raises (full range).
3. 3 × 10 Forward Raises (full range).
4. 3 × 10 Posterior Raises (full range).
5. 3 × 10 Behind Neck French Curls.
6. 3 × 10 Straight-arm Pullovers.
7. Side Bends (heavy weights).
8. Wrist Curls (heavy weights).
9. 3 × 10 Flying Exercises.
10. Dead Lifts (heavy weights).
11. Reverse Curls.

In Season

1. French Curls.
2. Lateral, Forward, and Posterior Raises.
3. Wrist Curls.

Basketball

1. Warm-up—Clean and Jerk (light weights).
2. Close-arm Bench Presses, 3 × 10 (increase weights).
3. Wrist Curls, 3 × 10.
4. Forward Raises.
5. Lateral Raises.
6. Half squats (heavy weights).
7. Heel Raises.
8. Dead Lifts.
9. Reverse Curls.
10. Straight-arm Pullovers.

Football

1. Warm-up—Clean and Jerk (light weights).
2. Wide-arm Bench Presses (4 × Max. plus 8 × 30 less than Max.)
   Fast. Total 12 repetitions.
3. Shoulder shrugs (heavy weight), 12 repetitions.
4. Curls—Work down, cheat.
5. Side Bends (heavy dumbbells).
6. Dead Lifts.

7. "Good Morning" Exercises.
8. Heavy Half squats of Leg Presses.
9. Heel Raises.
10. Latissimus Exercises
    (a) Latissimus Machine.
    (b) Bent Over Rowing.
    (c) Straight-arm Pullovers.

Golf

1. Warm-up—Clean and Jerk (light weights).
2. Bent-over Lateral Raises.
3. Forward Raises.
4. Side Bends.
5. Torso Rotations (feet pointed ahead).
6. "Good Morning" Exercises.
7. Wrist Curls.

Gymnastics

1. Two-arm Curls, 6–8 repetitions with maximum. Reduce 10 lbs. and curl as many as possible. Continue down reducing by 10–20 lbs.
2. Military Press, 6–8 repetitions with maximum. Reduce 20 lbs. and work down, doing as many as possible with each weight.
3. Upright Close-hand Rowing Motions—Work down by 10 lbs.
4. Straight-arm Pullovers—Work down by 10 lbs.
5. Wide-arm Bench Presses—Work down from 4–6 maximum reducing 30 lbs. each time. (After maximum effort, do each set as many times as possible.) Work down to 50–60 lbs.
6. Sit-ups (with weights held behind the head).

Hockey

Basically, there are two parts to a training program for ice hockey. First, there is the program for body building purposes and second, there is the program specific to the sport.

Body Building, Off-season

1. Warm-up—Clean and Jerk (light weights).
2. Heavy Curls, 8–10 repetitions (work down).
3. Heavy Wide-arm Bench Presses, 8–10 repetitions (work down).
4. Bent-over Rowings, 8–10 repetitions (work down).
5. Straight-arm Pullovers, 8–10 repetitions (work down).
6. Flying Exercises, 8–10 repetitions (work down).

7. Wrist Curls (very important to hockey players), 8–10 repetitions (work down).
8. Dead Lifts, 8–10 repetitions (work down).
9. Heavy Half squats, 15 repetitions (work down).
10. "Good Morning" Exercises, 8–10 repetitions.

Specific to Hockey (May Be Done During Season)

1. Wrist Curls, 8–10 repetitions (work down).
2. Wrist Rollers (both overhand and underhand). Heavy weight, 15 repetitions.
3. Heavy Slide-bends, 15 repetitions.
4. Heel Raises, heavy, 3 × 20 repetitions.
5. Toe Raises (with weight shoes if possible).
6. Leg Presses, Wide (heavy weight), 3 × 15 repetitions.

Swimming

1. Warm-up—Clean and Jerk (light weights).
2. Bent-over Rowings.
3. Straight-arm Pullovers (full range).
4. Upright Rowings.
5. Wide-arm Bench Presses.
6. "Good Morning" Exercises.
7. Alternate Leg Lifts (iron shoes).
8. Leg Machine.
9. Light Repetition Half squats.

Tennis

1. Warm-up—Clean and Jerk (light weight).
2. Lateral Raises (rotating trunk).
3. Repetition, Light Half squats.
4. Wrist Curls.
5. Wrist Rollers (palms down).
6. Flying Exercises (straight arm).
7. Sit-ups.

Track and field

Distance Runner—440 yds. to 880 yds. and up.
1. Work for endurance (light weights).
2. Half squats, sets of 50 (fast).
3. Military Presses, sets of 20.
4. Two-arm Curls, sets of 20.
5. "Good Morning" Exercises, 50 repetitions.

Sprinters
1. Half squats, 8–10 repetitions (increase weight).
2. Heel Raises (heavy weights).

3. Stiff Leg Lifts from Box.
4. Dead Lifts.
5. Bench Presses.
6. Reverse Curls.
7. Leg Curls.

Jumpers

1. Half squats (heavy weights—down slow, up fast).
2. Heel Raises (heavy weights).
3. "Good Morning" Exercises (heavy weights).
4. Lateral Raises.

Shot Putters and Discus Throwers

1. Wide-arm Bench Presses (heavy weights).
2. Half squats.
3. Dead Lifts.
4. French Curls.
5. Wrist Curls.
6. Side Bends (heavy weights).

Pole Vaulters

Refer to Exercises Listed for Gymnastics.

Wrestling

1. Warm-up—Clean and Jerk (light weight).
2. Two-arm Curls (work down), 8–10 repetitions.
3. Bench Presses (work down), (heavy weights).
4. Bent-over Rowings (work down).
5. Straight-arm Pullovers (work down).
6. Flying Exercises (work down).
7. Wrist Curls.
8. Dead Lifts (work down).
9. Half squats (work down).
10. "Good Morning" Exercises.

EXERCISES FOR SPECIFIC MUSCLE GROUPS

BARBELL ROUTINE	MUSCLE(S) EXERCISED
Military Press; Bench Press	Deltoids; triceps
Upright Rowing; Snatch	Trapezius
Front Raises; Lateral Raises	Deltoids
Bench Press; Pullovers	Pectorals
Bent Over Rowing; Latissimus Exercise; Pullovers	Latissimus
Barbell Curl	Biceps

Reverse Curl
Wrist Curl
Sit-ups
Squats
Rise on Toes

Radial Extensor
Radial Flexor
Rectus Abdominus
Quadriceps
Gastrocnemius

19. Weight training with heavy loads should not be performed by individuals afflicted with cardiac conditions.
20. Individuals with a hernia or weak abdominal wall should avoid heavy lifts.

SAFETY HINTS

1. Warm up sufficiently before beginning to lift.
2. Do not lift near another person or walk close to a person who is lifting.
3. Never lift a bar without collars.
4. Collars should always be secure.
5. Keep poundages minimal until you are familiar with your ability and with the technique of the exercise.
6. Replace worn-out equipment before it breaks.
7. Use spotters when performing bench presses or heavy lifts.
8. In any barbell lift, when the bar is raised overhead with both arms, the arms should not be allowed to pass behind the ears. This will prevent dropping of the barbell and also possible injury to the back.
9. The weight room is not a place for "daydreaming" or "horseplay."
10. In preparing a bar situated on a rack, do not load or unload one side without partially loading or unloading the other side.
11. Do not drop the weights. Weights are made of cast iron and will break easily.
12. Whenever possible, lift weights on mats.
13. Replace all weights after using. Weights carelessly scattered are hazards to other lifters.
14. Know your limitations on how much weight you can safely lift. Remember, it is better to lift a lesser weight more times than to "go all out" once (except for the Olympic lifts).
15. The wearing of gym shoes prevents slippage by enhancing the necessary friction on mat surface. A stable base of support is a must when performing heavy movements.
16. Breath holding can be dangerous; unconsciousness may result from a diminished blood supply to the brain. Do not hold the breath while completing a number of repetitions.
17. Avoid "cooling-off" too rapidly following a work-out.
18. Be careful when swinging loads forward with a ballistic movement and avoid dropping a load under the influence of gravity.

HELPFUL HINTS

1. Follow a well-planned systematic routine.
2. Utilize a varied but well-balanced program.
3. Success depends not on how much work you do, but on how much you do per unit time.
4. Change your program if results are not obtained after a trial period of three months. Remember —you have to be regular.
5. It takes hard work to get results, and generally they are slow in coming; so don't get discouraged easily.
6. Always perform the movement through the entire range of motion.
7. Your head position is the key to keeping the back erect—always look directly forward.
8. A rack for bench presses allows the individual to handle the weights (submaximum) without assistance. The height of the rack should be about two inches shorter than the arm's reach, so that the barbell can be lifted upward and then forward into position.
9. In performing the Olympic lifts, the key to good form is to keep the barbell progressing upward in a straight line from the floor to the overhead position.
10. Include exercises, with or without weights, that increase and maintain a higher than normal breathing and heart rate—this is the key to cardiorespiratory endurance. This factor is frequently neglected in weight training programs.

COURTESY

1. Do not walk in front of or near a person when he is attempting heavy lifts. Even a slight movement or noise is very distracting.
2. Do not talk or interfere with a person doing any exercise.
3. Replace all weights in position for the next man's use.
4. Help a lifter whenever you can by spotting or handing him weights.

TERMINOLOGY

Barbell   A steel bar five to six feet long with disk-shaped weights attached to each end. The weight of the bar varies from 15 to 30 pounds. The Olympic bar weighs 45 pounds.

Cheating   A term used to describe the continuance of repetitions with the action of additional muscle groups. This generally occurs during the last repetitions of the final set.

Class   Group determined by weight of contestants.

Clean   First movement of the clean and jerk; raising the bar to shoulder height before it is jerked overhead.

Disqualification   Denial of lift for a violation of the definition of the various lifts.

Dumbbell   A short barbell—ten to twenty inches in length. There are two types, the non-adjustable fixed-weight, and the adjustable with collars and plates.

Kettle bell   A heavy metal ball with a handle attached.

Odd lifts   One-hand clean and jerk, right and left hand; and the one-hand snatch, right and left hand.

Olympic lifts   The two-hand snatch; the two-hand clean and jerk; and the two-hand military press.

Repetition   Consecutive and identically performed movements within a set. Examples, there are 10 repetitions to each of three sets in the previously described 3×10 system.

Reverse grip   The grip which has the knuckles of one hand above the bar and the knuckles of the other hand under the bar. Used for dead lifts or when holding heavy weights.

Set (or Bout)   A determined number of repetitions constitute one set. Read the above definition for repetition.

Sleeve   A hollow metal device which surrounds the bar between collars; approximately 36 inches in length.

Supine position   A lifting position when the performer is lying on his back.

Weigher   An official whose duty is to weigh the contestants and the weights lifted.

Weight   The implement lifted.

SELECTED REFERENCES

Berger, Richard A., "Effect of Varied Weight Training Programs on Strength," AAHPER *Research Quarterly,* XXXIII (May 1962), 168.

————, "Strength Training for Track and Field," *Athletic Journal,* XLIII, No. 6 (February 1963), 50.

Buehler, Clyde W., "Body Building," *Athletic Journal,* LX, No. 6 (February 1960), 46.

Burnham, Stan, "Better Rebounding Through Weight Training," *Physical Power Magazine,* II (October 1961), 10.

Carnes, Jimmy, "Weight Training for Track and Field." *Scholastic Coach,* XXX (February 1961), 34.

Franz and Melin, *Beginning Weight Training.* Belmont, Calif.: Wadsworth Publishing Co., Inc., 1964.

George, Elvan, and Ralph Evans, *Weight Training for Football.* Englewood Cliffs, N.J.: Prentice-Hall, Inc., 1959.

Goldenberg, Joseph, "Progressive Weight Training Course," *Scholastic Coach,* Part 1, XXXI (October 1961), 40; Part 2, XXXI (November 1961), 60.

————, "Should Athletes Work with Weights?" *Scholastic Coach,* XXX (January 1961), 34.

Gresham, William Linsay, *The Book of Strength.* New York: The John Day Company, Inc., 1961.

Hoffman, Bob, *Weight Training for Athletics.* New York: The Ronald Press Company, 1961.

Hooks, Gene, *Application of Weight Training to Athletics.* Englewood Cliffs, N.J.: Prentice-Hall, Inc., 1962.

Kirkley, George W., *Weight Lifting and Weight Training.* New York: Arco Publishing Co., Inc., 1964.

Krueger, P.C., "Weight Lifting For Football," *Athletic Journal,* XLII, No. 6 (February 1962), 26.

Lazier, Murney M., "Isometrics and Weight Training," *Athletic Journal,* XLIII, No. 8 (April 1963), 58.

Leighton, Jack R., *Progressive Weight Training.* New York: The Ronald Press Company, 1961.

Massey, Benjamin H.; Harold W. Freeman; Frank R. Manson, and Janet A. Wessel. *The Kinesiology of Weight Lifting.* Dubuque, Iowa: William C. Brown Company, Publishers, 1959.

Morehouse, L.E., "Physiological Basis of Strength Developments," *Exercise and Fitness.* Chicago: The Athletic Institute, 1960, 193.

Morehouse, L.E., and Philip J. Rasch, *Scientific Basis of Training*. Philadelphia: W.B. Saunders Co., 1958.

Morgan, Bill, "Weight Training For the Weight Events," *Scholastic Coach*, XXIX (February 1960), 44.

Murray, Jim, "Weight Training and Football," *Physical Power Magazine*, II (October 1961), 6.

Nagle, F.J., and L.W. Irwin, "Effects of Two Systems of Weight Training on the Circulatory-Respiratory Endurance and Related Physiological Factors," *AAHPER Research Quarterly*, XXXI (December 1960), 607.

Nulton, John E., "Breathing for Safety in Weight Training," *Athletic Journal*, XLI, No. 6 (February 1961), 32.

————, "Teaching Tips for Weight Training," *Athletic Journal*, XLII (November 1961), 26.

O'Connor, Robert, "Scientific Weight Training," *Scholastic Coach*, XXXIV, Nos. 1, 2, and 3 (September, October, November 1964).

Peterson, F.B., "Muscle Training by Static, Concentric and Eccentric Contraction," *Acta. Physiologica Scandinavica*, XLVIII (April 1960), 406.

Quigley, Thomas B., ed., *Sports Injuries*. The American Journal of Surgery, Inc., 1959.

Sills, Frank D., *et al., Weight Training in Sports and Physical Education*. Washington, D.C.: American Association for Health, Physical Education and Recreation, 1962.

Stein, Julian, "Weight Training For Track Men," *Athletic Journal*, XLI, No. 3 (1960), 46.

Wrestling

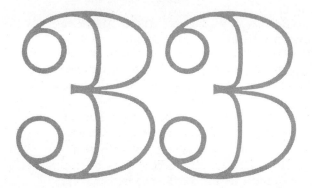

ORIGIN AND DEVELOPMENT

Wrestling is one of the oldest sports. In prehistoric times it was probably a method of learning self-preservation. In early history, wrestling was an accepted method of preparing men for war. The champion wrestlers of ancient Greece were held in high esteem and one has but to read Homer's tales to realize the important and honorable position given the sport during that period of history.

The sport has taken many different forms in the various countries of the world, some of which seem rather ridiculous to those of us who are accustomed to free-style wrestling as practiced in the English-speaking nations. The early history of America is dotted with accounts of wrestling—the most famous of which are Abraham Lincoln's bouts at New Salem, Illinois.

NATURE OF WRESTLING

There are two world-wide styles of wrestling—the *Greco-Roman* and the *free style,* both of which

are represented in the Olympic Games. In this country we use a variation of the free style in which the wrestlers start in an upright position and one attempts to pin the shoulders of the other to the mat for two seconds. This style of wrestling, when practiced in the schools and colleges of the country, is commonly called catch-as-catch-can.

The professional style of wrestling in vogue in the United States can scarcely be classified as wrestling, and has proved very detrimental to the fast, clean, school sport. It gives one a distorted idea of the sport, because the antics of the professionals are merely attempts to entertain. On the other hand, wrestling in school is designed to develop the body and self-confidence, as well as to provide training in fair play.

The greatest harm that can come from competitive school wrestling is "making weight." Wrestlers are warned to reduce weight only under a physician's approval.

Wrestling is primarily a developmental sport, but it is also quite easily adaptable to recreation. It is almost always included in the college intramural program for these purposes, and many "old" wrestlers continue practicing their sport for many years. It is probably the finest of our developmental sports and most young men will benefit greatly if they participate properly.

The purposes of wrestling might be stated as:

1. Developing physical fitness and strength.
2. Developing protective skills.
3. Developing self-confidence.

BASIC RULES

1. To win a fall, the shoulder blades of one's opponent must be held in contact with the mat continuously for two full seconds.

2. Any hold shall be allowed except the hammerlock above the right angle; the twisting hammerlock; front headlock; headlock without the arm; the straight head scissors (even though the arm is included); over-scissors; flying mare with the palm up; full (double) nelson; strangle holds; all body slams; toe holds; twisting knee lock; key lock; overhead double arm bar; the bending, twisting or forcing of the head or any limb beyond its normal limits of movement; locking the hands in a double bar from a neutral position; and any hold used for punishment alone. Contestants may grasp all four fingers in an effort to break a hold, but pulling back the thumb, or one, two or three fingers is illegal. The term "slam" is interpreted as lifting and bringing an opponent to the mat with unnecessary roughness. This infraction may be committed by a contestant in either the top or bottom position on the mat as well as during a takedown. When a contestant lifts his opponent off the mat and brings him forcibly to the mat with the upper half of the body coming in contact with the mat first, a slam will be called. A forceful trip may be considered as unnecessary roughness. Slams shall be called without hesitation following the situation occurring. An intentional drill or forceful fall-back is illegal when the defensive wrestler is in a standing position and the offensive wrestler has a scissor hold or a cross body ride. A leg hooked over the top toe of an opponent's straight body scissors is interpreted as an over-scissor and is therefore illegal. A wrestler applying a legal hold should not be penalized when his opponent turns the legal hold into an illegal hold. The referee shall cause the hold to be released if there is danger of injury. However, the match need not be stopped unless the referee finds it necessary to do so in order to correct the situation. Whenever possible, an illegal hold should be prevented

rather than called. The three-quarter nelson is not to be interpreted as a headlock. Pulling the head over the shoulder with hands locked or overlapped is not to be interpreted as a headlock.

3. Intentional striking, gouging, kicking, hair pulling, butting, elbowing, or any intentional act that endangers life or limb is illegal.

4. If no fall is secured, the referee awards the decision to the contestant who has scored the greater number of points.

5. When a contestant takes his opponent to the mat within the first two minutes, both continue to wrestle until one is thrown or until the time limit is reached. If neither secures a position of advantage before the two minutes have elapsed, the remaining time is divided into two three-minute periods of mat wrestling (two-minute periods in high school). The official flips a coin, and the winner of the "call" chooses the top or bottom for start of the first period of mat wrestling. A fall in this first period terminates that period and the bout. The loser of the coin flip in the first period alternates his starting position for the second. A fall by one wrestler takes precedence over a greater number of points earned by the other prior to the fall.

LENGTH OF PERIODS	
1st period	2 minutes
2nd period	3 minutes
3rd period	3 minutes

6. Wrestlers are considered to leave the mat when they are outside of a 24-foot square that is clearly marked. They are brought back to the center and started again from a starting position on the mat with the top man given the advantage, or if neither has the advantage, they start with both men on their feet from the center of the mat.

Team point system for dual competition (high school and college)

a. A loss either by decision or by fall counts no points for the team.
b. A draw (tie) scores two points for each team.
c. A win by decision scores three points for the team.
d. A win by fall (pin) scores five points for the team.
e. A win by forfeit (failure of opposing team to provide an opponent or failure of the opponent to make weight) counts five points.
f. A win by default (discontinuing match because of

injury or for some other reason) scores five points toward the team score. However, if the match was stopped because of an injury caused by an illegal hold, the injured person's team scores the five points.

Individual scoring system (college)

This system, used to determine the winner when a fall does not occur, is as follows:

a. Two points for the first take-down for each wrestler, and two points for each subsequent take-down.

b. One point for an escape from the position of disadvantage to a neutral position.

c. Two points for a reversal from the position of disadvantage to a position of advantage.

d. Three points for a near fall, which is described as a situation in which the offensive wrestler has control of his opponent with both shoulders or the scapula area held in contact with the mat for less than one full second or when one shoulder of the defensive wrestler is touching the mat, and the other shoulder is held within one inch or less of the mat for two full seconds.

e. Two points for a predicament, which is described as a situation in which the offensive wrestler has control of his opponent and a fall or near-fall is imminent.

   (1) When both shoulders of the defensive wrestler are held momentarily (stopped) within approximately four inches of the mat or less, a predicament shall be scored. A continuous roll-through is not to be considered a predicament.

   (2) When one shoulder of the defensive wrestler is touching the mat, and the other shoulder is held at an angle of 45 degrees or less with the mat, but not sufficiently close to award a near fall, for one second or more, a predicament shall be scored.

A near fall or predicament is ended when the defensive wrestler gets out of the pinning position and into a position in which a fall is no longer imminent.

The referee must not signal the score for a near fall or a predicament until the situation is ended. Only one near fall or one predicament shall be scored in each pinning situation regardless of the number of times the offensive wrestler places the defensive wrestler in a near fall or predicament position during the situation.

Only a wrestler with the advantage who has his opponent in a pinning situation may score a near fall or predicament. Bridgebacks in body scissors or bridgeovers with a wristlock are not considered near fall or predicament situations, although a fall may be scored.

When the defensive wrestler places himself in a precarious situation during an attempted escape or reversal, a near fall or predicament shall not be scored unless the offensive wrestler has control of his opponent in a pinning situation.

f. The offensive wrestler who has control in an advantage position over his opponent is gaining time-advantage. (Control is a situation in which a contestant exercises and maintains restraining power over his opponent.) A timekeeper assigned to each wrestler records his accumulated time-advantage throughout the match or a multiple timer may be permitted to record the time-advantage. At the end of the match the referee subtracts the lesser time-advantage from the greater. If the contestant with the greater time-advantage has less than one minute of net time-advantage, no point is awarded. If he has over one full minute but less than two minutes of net time-advantage, he is awarded one point. If he has two full minutes or more, he is awarded two points. No contestant may be awarded more than two points for time-advantage in any one match. The contestant with the lesser time-advantage receives no points, even though he accumulates over one minute of time in the advantage position.

g. Points may also be scored if an opponent is stalling, commits certain technical violations, or applies an illegal hold. The current rule book should be consulted for details.

h. A fall terminates the match and all points scored up to that point are disregarded.

WEIGHT CLASSIFICATION

HIGH SCHOOL
95 lbs.
103 lbs.
112 lbs.
120 lbs.
127 lbs.
133 lbs.
138 lbs.
145 lbs.
154 lbs.
165 lbs.
180 lbs.
Unlimited.

FIGURE 33-1.

FIGURE 33-2.

FIGURE 33-3.

INTERCOLLEGIATE
115 (by mutual consent)
123
130
137
145
152
160
167
177
191 (by mutual consent)
Unlimited

TECHNIQUES AND FUNDAMENTALS

Orientation

There are several advantages in concentrating on mat wrestling rather than standing wrestling in physical education classes:

1. More pupils can be accommodated, as less space is required for mat wrestling than for take-downs.
2. Fewer injuries are likely. This is true because (a) class members in general will not have attained the level of physical condition enjoyed by varsity competitors, (b) they will have less skill than varsity competitors, and (c) the additional few feet to the mat is enough of a fall to be traumatic until the physical condition and skill have been developed.

Skills are more appropriately referred to as "maneuvers" than as "holds" except for pin holds. The objective in a wrestling match is to dominate physically the opponent, as epitomized by controlling him and holding both his shoulders to the mat simultaneously for two seconds, at the same time

taking all necessary precautions to see that neither participant is endangered.

Take-downs are important in competition for several reasons: they are worth points, an opponent can more easily be worn down and pinned from the position of advantage, and the wrestler who is able to take his opponent down has a distinct psychological advantage.

Take-downs

A tied-up or locked position is not necessary prior to a take-down. The position is one of individual preference. The stance should be one which enables the wrestler to move offensively and at the same time enables him to protect himself against offensive moves of his opponent. General suggestions for the standing position are:

1. Do not tie up unless you can execute a take-down from the tied-up position.
2. Keep your weight distributed on the balls of the feet.
3. Keep the knees slightly bent so as to be able to move quickly.
4. Bend enough at the waist to be able to protect your legs.
5. Never cross the legs.
6. Keep moving and keep trying for the take-down.

There are numerous take-downs, several variations of each one, various means of setting up each one, and counters for all of them.

Approximately 70 per cent of all take-downs, even at the national championship level, have been found to be variations of leg dives, also known as leg tackles and leg pick-ups.

The most basic of the leg dives, the double leg dive, is depicted in Figs. 33-1 through 33-3.

In Fig. 33-1 the wrestler on the left has placed his hands, with thumbs to the outside, below the elbows of his opponent. It must be kept in mind that if this position is attempted only when the wrestler plans a leg dive, it will act as a "telegraph" to his opponent, who will then either prevent such a positioning of the hands or will be alert to the fact that a leg dive will be attempted, and who can then more easily counter it. As stated earlier, the tie-up is not essential, and other means of setting up the leg dive can be used. The leg dive is easier to execute if the aggressor is backing away from his opponent.

As the offensive man drops to one or both knees, he simultaneously lifts his opponent's elbows. The emphasis should be on quickly dropping rather than on lifting the elbows. If the elbows are lifted first, the defensive man has an opportunity to react by throwing his legs backward out of the reach of the aggressor.

Fig. 33-2 emphasizes a number of important points. The offensive man has landed with his right knee as near to his opponent's feet as possible, has encircled his opponent's legs with both arms, and has placed his head to the side. From this position he is able to keep his back straight, to lift with his arms, and to push with his head against his opponent.

In Fig. 33-3 he continues to pivot forward around his opponent, keeping control of his opponent's legs, and finishing in a position of advantage to complete the successful take-down.

The most common counter for this take-down is for the defensive man to quickly throw his legs backward and to spread them. Such a position is usually called a "sprawl."

Mat wrestling

The positions to be assumed at the beginning of the second period, or at any time during the first period if one contestant has a position of advantage over his opponent when they go off the mat, are as follows.

The "bottom" man, man in position of disadvantage, or defensive man assumes a stationary position on his knees facing the official. He must keep both knees on the mat and they shall not be spread more than the width of the shoulders. The legs must be parallel, with the toes turned neither out nor under in an exaggerated way. The heels of both hands must be on the mat not less than 12 inches in front of the knees, and the elbows shall not touch the mat. (As a safety precaution, it is advisable for both wrestlers always to keep the elbows and knees

at least slightly bent, as any pressure on them when they are "locked" could more likely cause a hyperextension injury.)

The "top" wrestler (wrestler in position of advantage or offensive wrestler) assumes a position on his knees on either side of his opponent with his head along the midline of his opponent's back. The arm closer to his opponent shall be wrapped lightly around his opponent's waist, with the palm of the hand lightly against his navel, and with the palm of the "outside" or "far" hand resting lightly on his opponent's "near" elbow. Both of his knees shall be on the mat outside of and not touching the defensive wrestler's near leg. (His knee must not touch the leg of his opponent and must be even with or in front of his opponent's foot.)

Fig. 33-4 illustrates the proper position for both men.

OBJECTIVES. It is the objective of the bottom man to execute a reversal so that he will gain the position of advantage. If he is unable to reverse his opponent, he should try for an escape to the neutral position, after which he must try for a take-down to acquire the position of advantage.

It is the objective for the man in position of advantage to turn his opponent over and hold his shoulders to the mat for one second. The systematic procedure for attaining this objective is to break his opponent down or flatten him out, then to work for the fall.

"Rides" from the top position serve to keep the opponent off balance, to keep him under control, and to wear him down somewhat until a pin hold can be applied.

A standing wrestler who does not try for a take-down, a defensive wrestler who does not try for an escape or reversal, and a wrestler in position of advantage who does not try for a fall can and should be penalized for stalling. As soon as the official is sure that one wrestler is stalling he should issue a warning. At the second warning, one point is awarded the staller's opponent, the next time another point, the fourth time two points, and the fifth time he is disqualified for failure to wrestle. Many officials are hesitant to call stalling, but strictly defensive wrestling defies the objective of the sport, which is to pin the opponent.

If neither wrestler is able to pin his opponent, the wrestler who has gained the greater number of points wins the decision.

Breakdowns, controls, and pin holds

Figs. 33-5 through 33-8 show a progression from the position of advantage to a cross body ride, then a "guillotine," which is an effective pin hold.

FIGURE 33-4.

FIGURE 33-5.

FIGURE 33-6.

FIGURE 33-7.

FIGURE 33-8.

In Fig. 33-5, the top wrestler has slipped his outside leg between the bottom man's legs from in front, and has grapevined the bottom man's near leg. The position which enables the top man to control one leg and the opposite arm is called a cross body ride. He exerts pressure on the bottom man by straightening the grapevining leg, lifting the arm, and pushing downward on the head simultaneously, and shoving his hip into the small of his opponent's back. If enough pressure is thus applied, he is able to flatten his opponent to the mat.

In Fig. 33-6 the top man has flattened his opponent and has gained control of his far arm. He will have better leverage for lifting the arm by grasping it at the wrist, and his lifting power will be greater than the bottom man's power to resist will be.

In Fig. 33-7 he continues his grapevine hold on the leg and continues to lift the arm until he is able to slip his head and near arm under his opponent's arm. Whereas the bottom man originally was faced down, he is now maneuvered so that his back is being turned toward the mat.

In Fig. 33-8 the aggressor has turned his op-

ponent's shoulders to the mat. He is able to hold him there by pulling on the top of his head and shoving forward slightly with the hips. If he feels his grapevine beginning to slip he should hook his grapevining toe behind the knee of his own free leg.

Figs. 33-9 through 33-11 show the progression from a cross face as a control to a double arm tie-up as a pin hold.

In Fig. 33-9 the top man is maintaining some control with the near hand as he reaches in front of his opponent with the far hand and, using a false grip for greater strength, immobilizes his opponent's far arm just above the elbow. Should he not control his opponent's legs his opponent could turn, back away from him, or stand up; if he holds too near the shoulder with his far hand, his opponent can easily pull his arm free; if he holds below the elbow his opponent can simply bend his arm and thus counter the cross face.

In Fig. 33-10 he has shifted the near hand to his opponent's rear ankle and lifted, breaking his opponent down, and beginning to turn his back toward the mat.

In Fig. 33-11 he keeps control of both of his

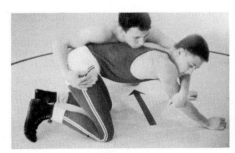

FIGURE 33-9.

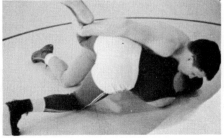

FIGURE 33-10.

FIGURE 33-11.

opponent's arms above the elbow and applies a double arm tie-up pin hold.

Escapes and reversals

Figs. 33-12 through 33-16 illustrate a sit out as an escape.

In Fig. 33-12, the bottom man has moved his far leg out of reach of his opponent. This is the first move to be made for executing numerous escapes or reversals, and prevents the top man from being able to control the legs by means of grasping the far ankle. The far knee has also been lifted off the mat, thus making possible the next move.

In Fig. 33-13, the bottom man has sat out, having brought his near leg under the lifted knee, and has assumed a sitting position. If he hesitates at this point he is vulnerable to being pulled to his back, being followed around, having his near arm controlled, or other counters.

In Fig. 33-14, he has leaned forward and has jerked his near arm free so that it can no longer be used as a handle. He has begun to turn toward his opponent.

In Fig. 33-15, he has turned with so much impetus that the top man is unable to hold him or to counter the move.

In Fig. 33-16, he comes up head-to-head with his opponent. His escape has been completed, and he is now in a position to try for a take-down.

Figs. 33-17 through 33-20 depict a reversal called a "switch."

In Fig. 33-17, the bottom man makes his first move, which is to release his near arm. He reaches in front of himself to move his arm away from his opponent.

Fig. 33-18 is taken from another angle in order to emphasize the important points which will enable the bottom man to reverse. He has sat on his near hip and has reached over his opponent's near arm with his own far arm to his opponent's crotch.

Fig. 33-19 emphasizes a very important step. Instead of driving backward into his opponent, the switcher shifts his hips away from his opponent. This has the effect of magnifying his weight on his opponent's shoulder, thus forcing his opponent's shoulder to the mat.

In Fig. 33-20, only after his opponent's shoulder has been forced to the mat, the switcher pivots to the top position, thus completing his reversal.

Additional maneuvers

Perhaps a dozen additional maneuvers should be included among the fundamentals of wresting.

FIGURE 33-12.

Since this text is for the purpose of introducing students to various activities, a more thorough study of the sport can be made through the texts included in the bibliography. Complete mastery of the foregoing skills, along with a high level of physical conditioning, will enable a wrestler to win against many other wrestlers.

Other fundamentals include:

TAKE-DOWNS
1. Snap down.
2. Fireman's drag.
3. Arm drag.
4. Duck under.

ESCAPES AND REVERSALS
1. Stand up.
2. Wing or side roll.
3. Whizzer.

BREAKDOWNS AND CONTROLS
1. Tight waist.
2. Head lever.
3. Stretcher.

PIN HOLDS
1. Inside crotch and half nelson.
2. Cradle.

Naturally, it would be advantageous for the wrestler to know the counters for each of the maneuvers. Since there are counters for every maneuver, and, in turn, counters for the counters, wrestling is a sport that can be studied endlessly, and the more one knows about it the more intrigued he becomes.

STRATEGY

1. Learn to set up your maneuvers. Your chances of making them work are many times better when you surprise your opponent.
2. The best time to gain an advantage is just as

FIGURE 33-13.

FIGURE 33-14.

FIGURE 33-15.

FIGURE 33-16.

FIGURE 33-17.

FIGURE 33-18.

FIGURE 33-19.

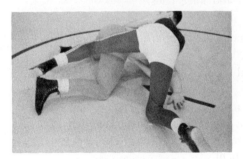

FIGURE 33-20.

your opponent relaxes or is slightly off balance from countering another move.

3. In general, get parallel to escape and perpendicular to pin.
4. Move in the direction in which your opponent has the least support. Sometimes you can control one of his supports, and sometimes you can stabilize one, then drive in that direction.
5. Learn to wrestle in series, that is, if one ma-

neuver does not work, try another immediately, or if it does work, follow through to the pin.

6. Sound knowledge of fundamentals, top physical condition, and a strong desire to win are the ingredients necessary for success in wrestling.
7. Moving before your opponent does gives you a distinct advantage, whether you are standing, on the bottom, or on top.
8. Explosive moves are more effective than slower

ones. Learn not to rely on strength when it can be avoided, as you will tire yourself unnecessarily.

SAFETY HINTS

1. Remember the basic rule: *Anything that endangers life or limb is illegal in amateur wrestling.*
2. Be sure that you are properly conditioned before beginning to compete.
3. Wrestle down on the mat for several weeks before starting on take-downs.
4. Be sure there is adequate room for the workout, as more injuries occur as a result of rolling into or falling over other pairs than from wrestling with opponents.
5. Warm up properly. The neck, especially, should be exercised prior to wrestling, as the muscles in it are ordinarily little-used, and neck soreness is more disabling than other muscles' soreness.
6. Roll when you fall, learn which maneuvers are likely to be most hazardous, and, insofar as possible, know when to resist the opponent's pressure and when not to.
7. Do not compete in an obvious mismatch. This applies both to size and ability.
8. Insist on only qualified officials.
9. See that the mats of the surrounding area are properly padded and that no physical hazards exist in the facilities or equipment.
10. Use the protective equipment needed, such as ear guards and knee pads.
11. Keep mat and clothing as clean as possible.
12. Be sure that all injuries are promptly and properly treated.
13. A physical examination before the season actually gets under way is imperative.
14. Keep the nails short, the hair short and clean, and do not wear rings, neck medals, belt buckles, or other objects that might injure you or your opponent.
15. Do not participate when you have infections or injuries—wait until they are cleared by a competent physician.
16. Do not reduce weight extremely in a short period of time except under the supervision of a physician.

TERMINOLOGY

Arm drag A go-behind or a take-down executed by pulling on the opponent's tricep.

Breakdown In the referee's position, a maneuver in which the wrestler in the position of advantage forces the wrestler in the position of disadvantage flat to the mat.

Bridge A means of supporting weight by using the feet and head and arching the back, thus keeping the shoulders away from the mat.

Counter A block or a movement which prevents the execution of a maneuver by the opponent.

Cradle A pin hold executed by pulling the opponent's head and leg together and holding his shoulders to the mat.

Cross body ride A means of breaking the opponent down and controlling him until a pin hold can be applied; it is executed by grapevining one of his legs, stretching across his back, and holding on to his opposite arm.

Cross face A maneuver used either as a counter or as an offensive breakdown by reaching across the side of the opponent's face and grasping his opposite arm just above the elbow.

Double arm tie-up A pin hold applied by controlling both of the opponent's arms above the elbow.

Double leg dive A take-down performed by gaining control of both of the opponent's legs.

Duck under A take-down secured by ducking under the opponent's arm and taking him to the mat as the act of slipping behind him is completed.

Escape Coming from a position of disadvantage to a neutral position.

Fall Holding both of the opponent's shoulders to the mat simultaneously for two seconds. Same as a *Pin*. This terminates a match.

Fireman's drag Also called a fireman's take-down. A means of taking the opponent to the mat by having the head under his armpit and pulling on that arm above the elbow, and turning in such a direction that the opponent is rolled over the top of the head.

Grapevine A means of entwining a leg around the opponent's leg.

Guillotine A pinhold secured from a cross body ride by slipping under the opponent's arm and pulling on his head.

Half nelson A means of turning the opponent to his back by prying an arm upward, using his head as a fulcrum.

Hammerlock Holding the opponent's arm behind his back. It becomes illegal if his hand is pulled away from his body or if the angle at the elbow is less than 90 degrees.

Head lever A means of breaking the opponent to the mat by exerting pressure on his arm at the armpit with the head, at the same time pulling backward on the corresponding wrist.

Pin See *Fall*.

Referee's Position Position assumed on the mat at the start of the second and third periods or anytime during the first period when one wrestler has control over the other wrestler and they go off the mat.

Reversal A means of scoring by moving from a position of disadvantage to a position of advantage.

Sit out A maneuver executed from the position of disadvantage for the purpose of either escaping or reversing. The wrestler sits, throwing his legs in front of him, and turns quickly.

Snap down A take-down executed by jerking the opponent to his knees, pulling on his neck to force his hands to the mat, and simultaneously spinning around behind him.

Stand up An escape executed by standing up.

Stretcher A means of controlling the opponent by straddling his back, inserting both feet between his legs from the front side, then straightening the legs and arching the back.

Switch A reversal executed by applying leverage near the opponent's shoulder.

Take-down Taking the opponent down to the mat and attaining control over him.

Tight waist A means of controlling the opponent by pulling him off balance onto his near hip, wrapping the arm all the way around his waist, and applying pressure by driving toward his head.

Whizzer A maneuver executed from either neutral or the position of disadvantage by wrapping an arm over the opponent's arm near the armpit and exerting pressure forward. It may be used either as a counter or as an offensive move.

Wing Also called a "side roll." A reversal executed by pulling on the opponent's arm and rolling him under.

SELECTED REFERENCES

Brown, Robert L., and D. Kenneth Ober, *Complete Book of High School Wrestling*. Englewood Cliffs, N.J.: Prentice-Hall, Inc., 1962.

Dratz, John P., Manly Johnson, and Terry McCann, *Winning Wrestling*. Englewood Cliffs, N.J.: Prentice-Hall, Inc., 1966.

Gardner, Frank ("Sprig"), *The Young Sportsman's Guide to Wrestling*. New York: Thomas Nelson & Sons, 1963.

Gianakaris, George, *Action Drilling in Wrestling*. Springfield, Va.: George Gianakaris, 1966.

Hunt, M. Briggs, *Greco-Roman Wrestling*. New York: The Ronald Press Company, 1964.

Kapral, Frank S., *Coach's Illustrated Guide to Championship Wrestling*. Englewood Cliffs, N.J.: Prentice-Hall, Inc., 1964.

Keen, Clifford P., Charles M. Speidel, and Raymond H. Swartz, *Championship Wrestling* (4th ed.). Annapolis, Md.: United States Naval Institute, 1964.

Kenney, Harold E. ("Hek"), and Glenn C. ("Newt") Law, *Wrestling*. New York: McGraw-Hill Book Company, 1952.

Lantz, Everett D., *Wrestling Guide*. Laramie, Wyo.: The Bureau of Educational Research, 1957.

Leeman, Gerald, and T. Ralph Williams, *Learn Wrestling*. Roselle Park, N.J.: T.R. Williams, 1966.

Macias, Rummy, *Learning How—Wrestling*. Mankato, Minn.: Creative Educational Society, Inc., 1965.

Martin, George, *The Mechanics of Wrestling*. University of Wisconsin, Madison, Wis.: George Martin, 1961.

Parker, Charles, ed., *The 1968 Official Collegiate and Scholastic Wrestling Guide*. Phoenix, Ariz.: College Athletics Publishing Service, 1967.

Peery, Rex, and Arnold ("Swede") Umbach, *How to Improve Your Wrestling*. Chicago, Ill.: The Athletic Institute, 1955.

———, *Wrestling Instructor's Guide*. Chicago, Ill.: The Athletic Institute, 1956.

Rasch, Philip J., and Walter Kroll, *What Research Tells the Coach About Wrestling*. Washington, D.C.: The American Association for Health, Physical Education and Recreation, 1964.

Sparks, Raymond E., *Wrestling Syllabus*. Springfield College, Springfield, Mass.: R.E. Sparks, 1956.

Umbach, Arnold W., and Warren R. Johnson, *Successful Wrestling*. St. Louis: The C.V. Mosby Co., 1953.

———, *Wrestling*. Dubuque, Iowa: William C. Brown Company, Publishers, 1966.

Appendixes

A. Sources of official rules

Activity	Source of Rules
Aerial Tennis	Sells Aerial Tennis Co. Box 42, Kansas City, Kan. 66103
Archery (Field)	National Field Archery Assn. Rt. 2, Box 514, Redlands, Calif. 92373
Archery (Target)	National Archery Assn. 23 E. Jackson Blvd., Chicago, Ill. 60604
Archery (Indoor)	American Archery Council 23 E. Jackson Blvd., Chicago, Ill. 60604
Archery (See DGWS listing)	
Badminton	American Badminton Assn. Donald Richardson 20 Wamesit Rd., Waban, Mass. 02168
Badminton	Dayton Racquet Co., 302 S. Albright St. Arcanum, Ohio 43504
Badminton (See DGWS listing)	
Banball (Rules included)	General Sportcraft Co., Ltd. 140 Woodbine St., Bergenfield, N. J.
Baseball (Non-professional) Guide	National Baseball Congress Wichita, Kansas
Baseball (Copyrighted Rules)	National Baseball Congress Wichita, Kansas

Activity	Source of Rules
Baseball (American Legion)	American Legion Box 1055, Indianapolis, Ind. 46206
Baseball, Babe Ruth League	Babe Ruth League, Inc. 524½ Hamilton Ave. Trenton, N. J. 08625
Baseball, Little League	Little League Baseball, Inc. P. O. Box 925, Williamsport, Pa. 17704
Baseball, Little League (Umpire's Handbook)	Little League Baseball, Inc. P. O. Box 925, Williamsport, Pa. 17704
Baseball, Bronco-Pony-Colt	Boys Baseball, Inc. P. O. Box 225, Washington, Pa. 15301
Baseball "Knotty Problems of Baseball" (Professional Rules)	The Sporting News 2018 Washington Ave. St. Louis, Mo. 63166
Baseball (Professional Rules Only)	The Sporting News 2018 Washington Ave. St. Louis, Mo. 63166
Baseball (See NCAA listing)	
Baseball Umpire's Handbook (Does not include actual rules)	American Amateur Baseball Congress P. O. Box 44, Battle Creek, Mich. 49016
Baseball Scorer's Handbook (Does not include actual rules)	American Amateur Baseball Congress P. O. Box 44, Battle Creek, Mich. 49016
Baseball, Rules in Pictures	American Amateur Baseball Congress P. O. Box 44, Battle Creek, Mich. 49016
Baseball, Tournament Manual	American Amateur Baseball Congress P. O. Box 44, Battle Creek, Mich. 49016
Baseball, League Organization	American Amateur Baseball Congress P. O. Box 44, Battle Creek, Mich. 49016
Baseball (See High School listing)	
Basketball Balanced (Height Equalization)	John L. McHale 66 Dale Road, Eastchester, N. Y.
Basketball (See AAU listing)	
Basketball (See High School listing)	
Basketball (See NCAA listing)	
Basketball (See DGWS listing)	
Basketball (Biddy)	Jay Archer 701 Brooks Building, Scranton, Pa. 18501
Bicycling	Bicycle Institute of America 122 E. 42nd St., New York, N. Y. 10017
Billiards (Rules & Records)	Billiard Congress of America 20 N. Wacker Dr., Chicago, Ill. 60606
Bocce	General Sportcraft Co., Ltd. 140 Woodbine St., Bergenfield, N. J.
Bocce	Lignum-Vitae Products Corp., 96 Boyd Ave., Jersey City, N. J.

Activity	Source of Rules
Bowling (Duck Pin)	National Duck Pin Bowling Congress 1420 New York Ave., N. W. Washington, D. C. 20005
Bowling (Ten Pin)	American Bowling Congress 1572 E. Capitol Dr. Milwaukee, Wisc. 53211
Bowling Women (Ten Pin)	Women's International Bowling Congress, Inc. 1225 Dublin Rd., Columbus 12, Ohio
Bowling (See DGWS listing)	
Boxing (See AAU listing)	
Casting (Official Rules for Fly and Bait Casting)	American Casting Education Foundation P. O. Box 51, Nashville, Tenn. 37202
Corkball	Rawlings Sporting Goods Co. 2300 Delmar Blvd., St. Louis Mo. 63166
Croquet	General Sportcraft Co., Ltd. 140 Woodbine St., Bergenfield, N. J.
Dartball	Wisconsin State Dartball Comm. 9333 W. Lincoln Ave.
Darts	West Allis 19, Wisc., c/o E. Dorow, Pres. General Sportcraft Co., Ltd. 140 Woodbine St., Bergenfield, N. J.
Deck Tennis	General Sportcraft Co., Ltd. 140 Woodbine St., Bergenfield, N. J.
Fencing	Amateur Fencer's League of America William Latzko 33—62nd Street, West New York, N. J.
Fencing (See DGWS listing)	
Field Hockey (See DGWS listing)	
Field Hockey	General Sportcraft Co., Ltd. 140 Woodbine St., Bergenfield, N. J.
Floor Tennis	U. S. Floor Tennis Assn. 1580 Sherman Ave., Evanston, Ill.
Football (Junior League)	Pop Warner Football 3664 Richmond St. Philadelphia, Pa. 19134
Football (Six-Man) (See High School listing)	
Football (See High School listing)	
Football (See NCAA listing)	
Golf	U. S. Golf Assn. 40 E. 38th St., New York, N. Y. 10016
Gymnastics (See AAU listing)	
Gymnastics (See NCAA Listing)	
Gymnastics (See DGWS listing)	
Handball (See AAU listing)	

Activity	Source of Rules
Handball	U. S. Handball Assn. 4101 Dempster St., Skokie, Ill.
Horseshoes	General Sportcraft Co., Ltd. 140 Woodbine St., Bergenfield, N. J.
Horseshoes (Professional)	National Horseshoe Pitchers Assn., of America, Elmer Beller, 9725 Palm St., Bellflower, Calif.
Ice Hockey (See NCAA listing)	
Ice Skating	Amateur Skating Union Edward J. Schmitzer, 4135 N. Troy St. Chicago, Ill. 60618
Indoor Hockey	Cosom Corp., 6030 Wayzata Blvd. Minneapolis, Minn. 55416
Lacrosse (See DGWS listing)	
Lawn Bowls	John W. Deist, Secretary, 1525 Ridge Court, Wauwatosa, Wisc. 53213
Marbles Shooting	National Marbles Tournament Cleveland Press Bldg., Cleveland 14, Ohio
Outings (See DGWS listing)	
Paddle Tennis	General Sportcraft Co., Ltd. 140 Woodbine St., Bergenfield, N. J.
Paddleball	Rodney J. Grambeau, Sports Bldg. University of Michigan Ann Arbor, Mich.
Quoits	General Sportcraft Co., Ltd. 140 Woodbine St., Bergenfield, N. J.
Riding (See DGWS listing)	
Roller Hockey	National Roller Hockey Assn., of the U. S., 97 Erie St., Dumont, N. J.
Roque	American Roque League, Inc. 4205 Briar Creek Lane Dallas, Texas 75214
Scoopball (Rules for 26 different games)	Cosom Industries, 6030 Wayzata Blvd. Minneapolis, Minn. 55416
Shooting (See National Rifle Assn. listing)	
Shuffleboard (Deck)	General Sportcraft Co., Ltd. 140 Woodbine St., Bergenfield, N. J.
Shuffleboard (Table)	American Shuffleboard Leagues, Inc. 533 Third St., Union City, N. J. 07087
Skating (Figure)	U. S. Figure Skating Assn. 575 Boylston St., Boston, Mass. 02116
Skating (Roller)	U. S. Amateur Roller Skating Assn. 120 W. 42nd St., New York, N. Y. 10036
Skating (Speed)	Edward J. Schmitzer Amateur Skating Union of the U. S. 4135 N. Troy St., Chicago, Ill. 60618
Skeet Shooting	National Skeet Shooting Assn. 3409 Oak Lawn Ave., Suite 219 Dallas, Tex. 75219

Activity	Source of Rules
Skiing (See NCAA listing)	
Skiing (Downhill, Slalom, Giant Slalom, Jumping & Cross-Country, FIS and USSA Rules)	U. S. Ski Assn. Gloria C. Chadwick, Executive Secretary Broadmoor, Colorado Springs, Colo.
Skindiving (Competitive) (See AAU listing)	
Smash	Smash, 1024 North Blvd., Oak Park, Ill.
Soccer (See NCAA listing)	
Soccer (See DGWS listing)	
Softball (12"—fast and slow pitch)	Amateur Softball Assn., Suite 1300 Skirvin Tower, Oklahoma City, Okla.
Softball (16")	Edw. Weinstein, Chairman Rules Comm. Umpires Protective Assn., of Chicago Apt. 710, 3550 Lake Shore Dr., Chicago, Ill.
Softball (See DGWS listing)	
Speed-A-Way	Marjorie S. Larsen 1754 Middlefield, Stockton, Calif. 95204
Speedball (See DGWS listing)	
Spiral Tennis	General Sportcraft Co., Ltd. 140 Woodbine St., Bergenfield, N. J.
Squash Racquets	U. S. Squash Racquets Assn. 200 E. 66th St., New York, N. Y. 10021
Swimming (See AAU listing)	
Swimming (See NCAA listing)	
Swimming (Synchronized—See AAU listing)	
Table Tennis	General Sportcraft Co., Ltd. 140 Woodbine St., Bergenfield, N. J.
Table Tennis (Instructions)	U. S. Table Tennis Assn. 210 Saturn Dr., North Star, Newark, Del.
Table Tennis (Rules)	U. S. Table Tennis Assn. 210 Saturn Dr., North Star, Newark, Del.
Table Tennis (Instructions & Rules)	Nissen-Sico, 930—27th Ave., S. W. Cedar Rapids, Iowa
Takraw Game	General Sportcraft Co., Ltd. 140 Woodbine St., Bergenfield, N. J.
Tennis (Includes Guide)	U. S. Lawn Tennis Assn. 51 E. 42nd St., New York, N. Y. 10017
Tennis (Rules Only)	U. S. Lawn Tennis Assn. 51 E. 42nd St., New York, N. Y. 10017
Tennis (See DGWS listing)	
Tennis	Dayton Racquet Co., 302 S. Albright St. Arcanum, Ohio 45304
Tennis Umpire's Manual (Includes Rules)	U. S. Lawn Tennis Assn. 51 E. 42nd St., New York, N. Y. 10017

Activity	Source of Rules
Tether Ball (Inflated Ball)	W. J. Voit Rubber Corp. 3801 S. Harbor Blvd. Santa Ana, Calif. 92704
Tether Ball (Inflated Ball)	General Sportcraft Co., Ltd. 140 Woodbine St., Bergenfield, N. J.
Tether Tennis	General Sportcraft Co., Ltd. 140 Woodbine St., Bergenfield, N. J.
Touch Football	The Athletic Institute, 805 Merchandise Mart, Chicago, Ill. 60654
Track & Field (See AAU listing)	
Track & Field (See High School listing)	
Track & Field (See NCAA listing)	
Turf Bowling (Boccie)	Lignum—Vitae Products Corp. 96 Boyd Ave., Jersey City, N. J.
Volleyball (Includes Rules)	U. S. Volleyball Assn., USVBA Printer P. O. Box 109, Berne, Ind. 46711
Volleyball (See DGWS listing)	
Water Polo (See AAU listing)	
Weight Lifting (See AAU listing)	
Winter Sports (See DGWS listing)	
Wrestling (See NCAA listing)	
NCAA Rulebooks and Guides	National Collegiate Athletic Bureau Box 757, Grand Central Station New York, New York 10017
DGWS Official Guides for Women's Sports, Including Rules	Division for Girls' and Women's Sports 1201 Sixteenth St., N.W. Washington, D. C. 20036
High School Activities	National Federation of State High School Athletic Assns. 7 S. Dearborn St., Chicago, Ill. 60603
Official AAU Rule Books and Guides	Amateur Athletic Union of the United States 231 W. 58th St., New York, N. Y. 10019

B. First aid chart

FIRST AID, the immediate and temporary care offered to the stricken athlete until the services of a physician can be obtained, minimizes the aggravation of injury and enhances the earliest possible return of the athlete to peak performance. To this end, it is strongly recommended that:

- ALL ATHLETIC PROGRAMS include prearranged procedures for obtaining emergency first aid, transportation, and medical care.

- ALL COACHES AND TRAINERS be competent in first aid techniques and procedures.

- ALL ATHLETES be properly immunized as medically recommended, especially against tetanus and polio.

Committee on the Medical Aspects of Sports
AMERICAN MEDICAL ASSOCIATION

To protect the athlete at time of injury,

FOLLOW THESE FIRST STEPS FOR FIRST AID:

STOP play immediately at first indication of possible injury or illness.

LOOK for obvious deformity or other deviation from the athlete's normal structure or motion.

LISTEN to the athlete's description of his complaint and how the injury occurred.

ACT, but move the athlete **only** after serious injury is ruled out.

EMERGENCY PHONE NUMBERS

Physician_____ Phone:_____

Physician_____ Phone:_____

Hospital_____ Ambulance_____

Police_____ Fire_____ Other_____

This chart in poster size is available from the AMA

BONES AND JOINTS

Fracture — Never move athlete if fracture of back, neck, or skull is suspected. If athlete **can** be moved, carefully splint any possible fracture. Obtain medical care at once.

Dislocation — Support joint. Apply ice bag or cold cloths to reduce swelling, and refer to physician at once.

Bone Bruise — Apply ice bag or cold cloths and protect from further injury. If severe, refer to physician.

Broken Nose — Apply cold cloths and refer to physician.

HEAT ILLNESSES

Heat Stroke—Collapse WITH DRY WARM SKIN indicates sweating mechanism failure and rising body temperature.
THIS IS AN EMERGENCY; DELAY COULD BE FATAL.
Immediately cool athlete by the most expedient means (immersion in cool water is best method). Obtain medical care at once.

Heat Exhaustion — Weakness WITH PROFUSE SWEATING indicates state of shock due to depletion of salt and water. Place in shade with head level or lower than body. Give sips of dilute salt water. Obtain medical care at once.

Sunburn—If severe, apply sterile gauze dressing; refer to physician.

IMPACT BLOWS

Head—If any period of dizziness, headache, incoordination, or un-consciousness occurs, disallow any further activity and obtain medical care at once. Keep athlete lying down; if unconscious, give nothing by mouth.

Teeth—Save teeth if completely removed from socket. If loosened, do not disturb; cover with sterile gauze and refer to dentist at once.

Solar Plexus — Rest athlete on back and moisten face with cool water. Loosen clothing around waist and chest. Do nothing else except obtain medical care if needed.

Testicular—Rest athlete on back and apply ice bag or cold cloths. Obtain medical care if pain persists.

Eye—If vision is impaired, refer to physician at once. With soft tissue injury, apply ice bag or cold cloths to reduce swelling.

MUSCLES AND LIGAMENTS

Bruise — Apply ice bag or cold cloths, and rest injured muscle. Protect from further aggravation. If severe, refer to physician.

Cramp — Have opposite muscles contracted forcefuly, using firm hand pressure on cramped muscle. If during hot day, give sips of dilute salt water. If recurring, refer to physician.

Strain and Sprain — Elevate injured part and apply ice bag or cold cloths. Apply pressure bandage to reduce swelling. Avoid weight bearing and obtain medical care.

OPEN WOUNDS

Heavy Bleeding — Apply sterile pressure bandage using hand pressure if necessary. Refer to physician at once.

Cut and Abrasion — Hold briefly under cold water. Then cleanse with mild soap and water. Apply sterile pad firmly until bleeding stops, then protect with more loosely applied sterile bandage. If extensive, refer to physician.

Puncture Wound—Handle same as cuts, and refer to physician.

Nosebleed—Keep athlete sitting or standing; cover nose with cold cloths. If bleeding is heavy, pinch nose and place **small** cotton pack in nostrils. If bleeding continues, refer to physician.

OTHER CONCERNS

Blisters — Keep clean with mild soap and water and protect from aggravation. If already broken, trim ragged edges with sterilized equipment. If extensive or infected, refer to physician.

Foreign Body in Eye—Do not rub. Gently touch particle with point of clean, moist cloth and wash with cold water. If unsuccessful or if pain persists, refer to physician.

Lime Burns — Wash thoroughly with water. Apply sterile gauze dressing and refer to physician.

Prepared by the AMA Committee on the Medical Aspects of Sports in cooperation with the National Athletic Trainers Association and the National Federation of State High School Athletic Associations.

Department of Community Health and Health Education

C. How to conduct tournaments

TYPES OF TOURNAMENT DRAWINGS

There are several different kinds of bracket arrangements that may be used in conducting tournament competition and the type of elimination is usually determined by several factors: (1) *The type of activity,* (2) *The number of entries,* (3) *The amount of playing time,* (4) *Playing space and equipment,* (5) *Age of participants,* (6) *Officials available.*

With a large number of entries it is sometimes desirable to run a combination tournament. For example: A double elimination–single elimination tournament. The winners of the double elimination brackets compete in a single elimination tournament to determine the ultimate champion.

NUMBER OF BYES. The first step before making a drawing for the bracket arrangement is to determine the number of entries.

When the number of competitors is 4, 8, 16, 32, 64, or 128, or any higher power of "2," they shall meet in pairs. When the number of competitors is not a power of "2" there shall be byes in the first round. For example: If there are 13 entries, a bracket of 16 with three byes is required. The purpose of having byes is to bring into the second round a number of competitors that is a power of "2." To determine the number of byes subtract the number of competitors from the next higher power of "2"; to determine the number of competitors in the first round subtract the number of byes from the total number of competitors. If the byes are an even number one half of them shall be placed at the top of the draw and one half at the bottom of the draw; if they are unevenly numbered there should be one more bye at the bottom than the top. The byes at the top half shall be the names first drawn. The next names drawn shall be placed in the first round. The byes in the bottom half are drawn last.

SEEDING THE DRAW. It is a common practice to select the best teams or individuals and place them in the bracket so that they will not meet in the early rounds of the play. Two or more entries may be seeded—usually the four best are selected in a sixteen name bracket and eight in a thirty-two name bracket. The seeded entrants are usually placed in the 1st, 5th, 9th, 13th, etc., bracket positions.

The No. 1 and 4 seeded teams are generally placed in the first and fifth positions of the top bracket and the No. 2 and 3 seeded teams in the ninth and thirteenth positions of the lower bracket; or No. 1 and 3 in the upper with No. 2 and 4 seeded teams in the lower half.

Single elimination tournament

If the contestants are of equal strength or their strength is not known, have a drawing for positions in the bracket. If the strength is known, seed the best teams so they will not meet in the early rounds. Place the seeded entries in the 1st, 5th, 9th, 13th, etc., positions.

All byes must occur in the first round of play. The total number of games played is always one less than the number of entries. To determine the number of games that the winner would have to play count the powers of two in the number of entries, e. g., with 32 entries the winner plays 5 games.

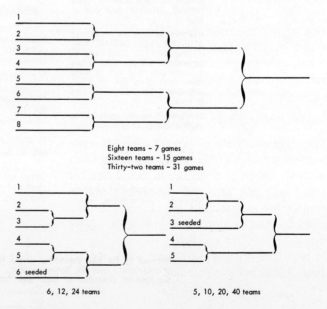

Eight teams – 7 games
Sixteen teams – 15 games
Thirty-two teams – 31 games

6, 12, 24 teams   5, 10, 20, 40 teams

Double elimination tournament

Two defeats eliminate an entry in this tournament. The losers in the first rounds move into the losers' bracket. The teams which advance farthest in either bracket meet each other in the final game.

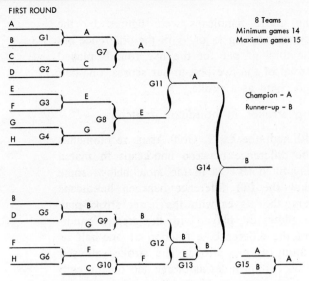

FIRST ROUND

8 Teams
Minimum games 14
Maximum games 15

Champion - A
Runner-up - B

Formula for total number of games, with N representing Number of entries: 2(N-1) = Minimum Games to Play; 2(N-1) + 1 = Maximum Games to Play.

Should the winner of the losers' bracket defeat the winner of the first round bracket, the teams are re-matched for the championship when one team will have lost two games.

Byes are distributed in the first round of the original elimination brackets as in a single elimination tournament, but in the first round of the losers' brackets byes must be arranged to avoid giving a second bye to an entry that has already had a bye. Also, at all stages of the losers' bracket, avoid pairing entries that have met in earlier rounds, if possible.

This type tournament is seldom used unless the entries are eight or less in number. If more than eight entries, double the process and the two winners meet for the title.

Consolation tournament

There are two types of general use: The consolation type tournament is generally used only when the number of entries is 8 or 16. In No. I bracket arrangement only the losers in the first round of play compete for consolation title. In No. II, the losers in all the rounds except the final of the upper bracket compete for 3rd and 4th place.

In both tournaments every team plays at least two games before being eliminated.

Round robin tournament

In this simple but efficient method, each team plays every other team once with the final standing determined on a percentage basis.

The following formula will apply to any number of teams, whether the total is odd or even. With an odd number of teams there is the same number of rounds; with an even number of teams there is one less number of games than teams.

FOR ODD NUMBER OF TEAMS. Assign to each team a number and then use only the figures in drawing the schedule. For example, in a league with 7 teams start with 1, putting down figures in the following order:

7	6	5	4	3	2	1
6-1	5-7	4-6	3-5	2-4	1-3	7-2
5-2	4-1	3-7	2-6	1-5	7-4	6-3
4-3	3-2	2-1	1-7	7-6	6-5	5-4

Note that the figures go down on the right side and up on the left. No. 7 draws a bye in the first round and the others play as indicated. With an odd number of teams, all numbers revolve and the last number each time draws a bye.

FOR EVEN NUMBER OF TEAMS. With an even number of teams the plan is the same except the position of No. 1 remains stationary and the other numbers revolve about it until the original combination is reached. For example, with 8 teams:

1-2	1-8	1-7	1-6	1-5	1-4	1-3
8-3	7-2	6-8	5-7	4-6	3-5	2-4
7-4	6-3	5-2	4-8	3-7	2-6	8-5
6-5	5-4	4-3	3-2	2-8	8-7	7-6

Two things only must be remembered: (1) With an even number of teams, No. 1 remains stationary and the other numbers revolve. (2) With an odd number of teams, all numbers revolve and the last number each time draws a bye.

FIRST ROUND BRACKET - 16 ENTRIES

Champion

TYPE II - CONSOLATION BRACKET

TYPE I - CONSOLATION BRACKET

Consolation winner

3rd place

4th place

Ladder tournament

In a ladder tournament the competition is arranged by challenge and the tournament requires a minimum of supervision. A player may challenge either of the two players above him in the ladder. If the challenger wins, he exchanges places with the loser in the ladder. All challenges must be accepted and played at an agreed time. Players draw for positions in the ladder; a starting and closing date for the tournament must be announced. Each player carries his handicap against all players, in case handicaps are used.

Pyramid tournament

The pyramid tournament is similar to the ladder tournament except the design allows for more participating and challenging. After the original drawings are made any player may challenge any other player in the same horizontal row. If he wins he may then challenge anyone in the row above, the two change places in the pyramid.

```
TABLE TENNIS
1 _____
2 _____
3 _____
4 _____
5 _____
6 _____
7 _____
8 _____
9 _____
10 _____
```

COMPUTING GOLF HANDICAPS

A popular approved system of handicapping is based upon the five best-to-par scores. When the difference between the total of the five best scores and the total of the five pars is 0 through 3, either above or below, the handicap is SCRATCH.

When the difference is:

	HDCP		HDCP		HDCP
4–9	1	35–40	6	66–71	11
10–15	2	41–46	7	72–78	12
16–21	3	47–53	8	79–84	13
22–28	4	54–59	9	85–90	14
29–34	5	60–65	10	91–96	15
				etc.	

The above handicaps were figured by the Short Formula; taking ⅘ of ⅕ of the difference between the total of par for the five rounds played and the total of the five best-to-par scores, one-half or over to count as a stroke.

Adjusting strokes in handicap matches

Although the U. S. Golf Assn. recommends ⅞ of the difference between handicaps in match play (play by holes) as in the table below, some clubs allow the full difference between handicaps and others, the player with the lesser stroke-play handicap allows the player with the greater handicap ¾ of the difference, a fraction of one-half or over counting as one stroke. The strokes allowed are used on certain holes as designated on the club score card.

When the difference between handicaps is:

1 give 1 stroke	11 give 10 strokes	21 give 18 strokes
2 " 2 "	12 " 11 "	22 " 19 "
3 " 3 "	13 " 11 "	23 " 20 "
4 " 4 "	14 " 12 "	24 " 21 "
5 " 4 "	15 " 13 "	25 " 22 "
6 " 5 "	16 " 14 "	26 " 23 "
7 " 6 "	17 " 15 "	27 " 24 "
8 " 7 "	18 " 16 "	28 " 25 "
9 " 8 "	19 " 17 "	29 " 25 "
10 " 9 "	20 " 18 "	30 " 26 "

TOURNAMENT SCHEDULE CALCULATOR

TEAMS ENTERED	BYES TOP	BOTTOM	SINGLE ELIM. NO. GAMES	DOUBLE ELIM. NO. GAMES	ROUND ROBIN NO. GAMES
4	0	0	3	6 or 7	6
5	1	2	4	8 or 9	10
6	1	1	5	10 or 11	15
7	0	1	6	12 or 13	21
8	0	0	7	14 or 15	28
9	3	4	8	16 or 17	36
10	3	3	9	18 or 19	45
11	2	3	10	20 or 21	55
12	2	2	11	22 or 23	66
13	1	2	12	24 or 25	73
14	1	1	13	26 or 27	91
15	0	1	14	28 or 29	105
16	0	0	15	30 or 31	
17	7	8	16	32 or 33	
18	7	7	17	34 or 35	
19	6	7	18	36 or 37	
20	6	6	19	38 or 39	
21	5	6	20	40 or 41	
22	5	5	21	42 or 43	
23	4	5	22	44 or 45	
24	4	4	23	46 or 47	
25	3	4	24	48 or 49	
26	3	3	25	50 or 51	
27	2	3	26	52 or 53	
28	2	2	27	54 or 55	
29	1	2	28	56 or 57	
30	1	1	29	58 or 59	
31	0	1	30	60 or 61	
32	0	0	31	62 or 63	

Diagrams reproduced courtesy of Wilson Sporting Goods Co., Subsidiary of Wilson & Co., Inc., 24th edition, revised, 1968.

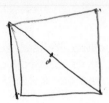

D. Athletic field and court diagrams

SQUASH COURT

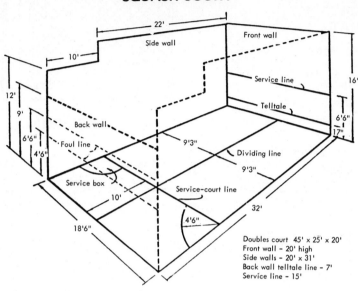

Doubles court 45' x 25' x 20'
Front wall – 20' high
Side walls – 20' x 31'
Back wall telltale line – 7'
Service line – 15'

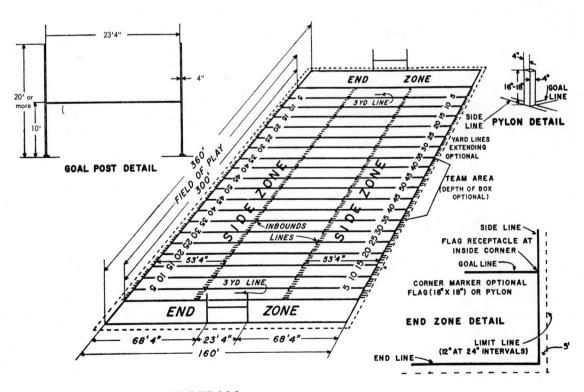

FOOTBALL

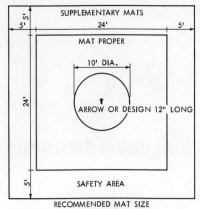

SUPPLEMENTARY MATS

RECOMMENDED MAT SIZE

WRESTLING MAT

CIRCULAR MAT
38' OVER-ALL DIA. 28'
DIA. CIRCLE; 10' DIA
INNER CIRCLE

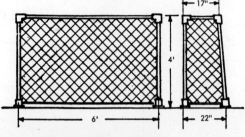

ICE HOCKEY GOAL

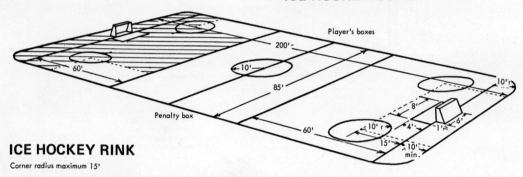

Player's boxes

Penalty box

ICE HOCKEY RINK
Corner radius maximum 15'

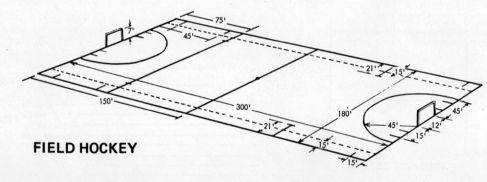

FIELD HOCKEY

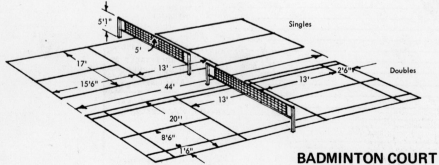

Singles

Doubles

BADMINTON COURT
Measure to outside edge of boundary lines

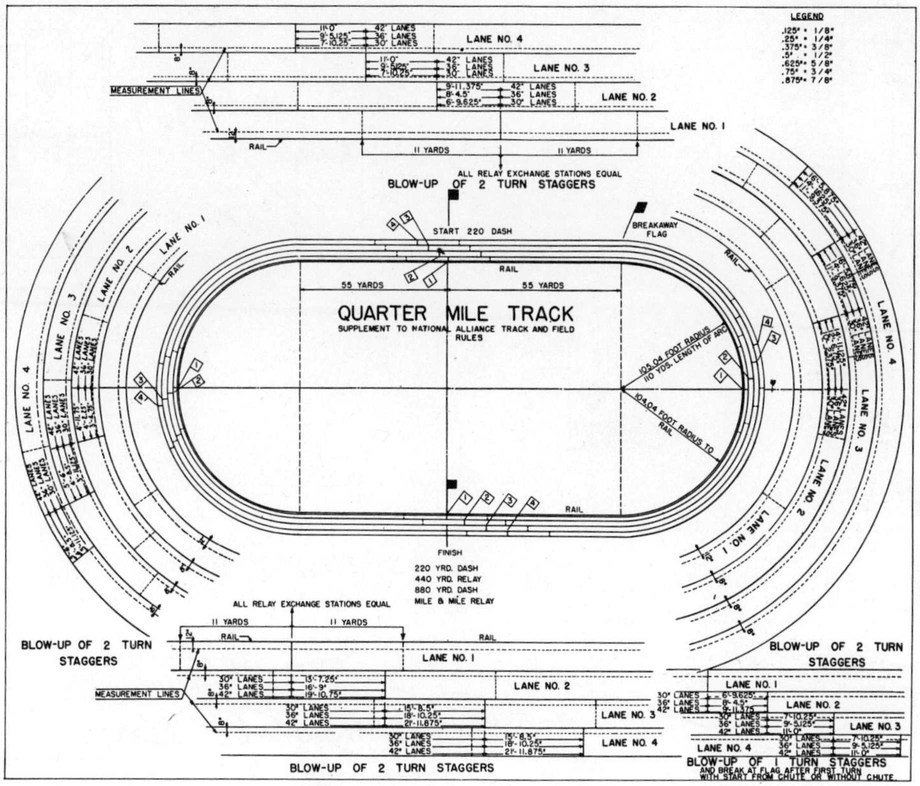
LEGEND
.125" = 1/8"
.25" = 1/4"
.375" = 3/8"
.5" = 1/2"
.625" = 5/8"
.75" = 3/4"
.875" = 7/8"
LANE NO. 4
LANE NO. 3
LANE NO. 2
LANE NO. 1
MEASUREMENT LINES
RAIL
11 YARDS
11 YARDS
ALL RELAY EXCHANGE STATIONS EQUAL
BLOW-UP OF 2 TURN STAGGERS
START 220 DASH
BREAKAWAY FLAG
55 YARDS
55 YARDS
QUARTER MILE TRACK
SUPPLEMENT TO NATIONAL ALLIANCE TRACK AND FIELD RULES
105.04 FOOT RADIUS
110 YDS. LENGTH OF ARC
104.04 FOOT RADIUS TO RAIL
FINISH
220 YRD. DASH
440 YRD. RELAY
880 YRD. DASH
MILE & MILE RELAY
ALL RELAY EXCHANGE STATIONS EQUAL
BLOW-UP OF 2 TURN STAGGERS
BLOW-UP OF 2 TURN STAGGERS
BLOW-UP OF 2 TURN STAGGERS
BLOW-UP OF 1 TURN STAGGERS
AND BREAK AT FLAG AFTER FIRST TURN WITH START FROM CHUTE OR WITHOUT CHUTE

QUARTER-MILE TRACK

Approved by the National Federation of State High School Athletic Associations

HANDICAPS—When races, run in lanes, start on the straightaway and relay exchanges are made on the straightaway, the "staggered" distance may be determined from the following tables. These figures apply to all tracks which are laid out with semi-circular turns, regardless of the number of laps to the mile.

For 30-Inch Lanes

No. of turns to run.....	4	3	2	1
Hdcp., Lane 2 over 1....	27' 2½"	20' 4⅞"	13' 7¼"	6' 9⅝"
Lanes 3, 4, 5, 6, 7 & 8 over next inside lanes..	31' 5"	23' 6¾"	15' 8½"	7' 10¼"

For 36-Inch Lanes

No. of turns to run.....	4	3	2	1
Hdcp., Lane 2 over 1....	33' 6"	25' 1½"	16' 9"	8' 4½"
Lanes 3, 4, 5, 6, 7 & 8 over next inside lanes..	37' 8⅜"	28' 3¼"	18' 10¼"	9' 5⅛"

For 42-Inch Lanes

No. of turns to run.....	4	3	2	1
Hdcp., Lane 2 over 1....	39' 9½"	29' 10⅛"	19' 10¾"	9' 11⅜"
Lanes 3, 4, 5, 6, 7 & 8 over next inside lanes.	43' 11¾"	32' 11⅞"	21' 11⅞"	11'

For 48-Inch Lanes

No. of turns to run.....	4	3	2	1
Hdcp., Lane 2 over 1....	46'	34' 6"	23'	11' 6"
Lanes 3, 4, 5, 6, 7 & 8 over next inside lane..	50'	37' 6"	25'	12' 6"

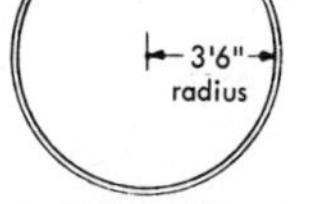
3'6"
radius

SHOT PUT AND HAMMER THROW CIRCLE

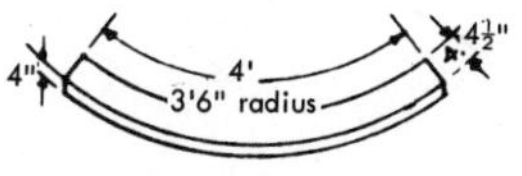
4'
4"
4½"
3'6" radius

SHOT PUT STOP BOARD

POLE VAULT PIT
12' x 16' Min.

HIGH JUMP PIT
12' x 16' Min.

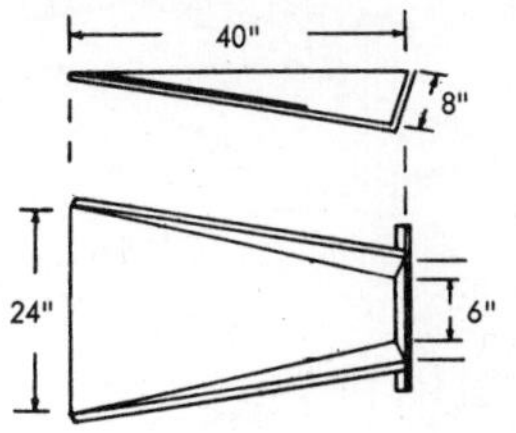
40"
8"
24"
6"

DIAGRAM B. PLANTING PIT FOR POLE VAULT

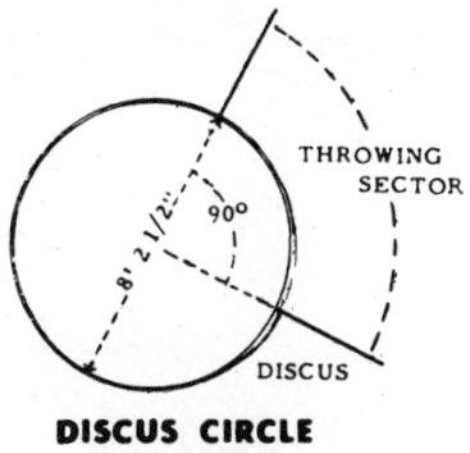
THROWING SECTOR
90°
8' 2 1/2"
DISCUS

DISCUS CIRCLE

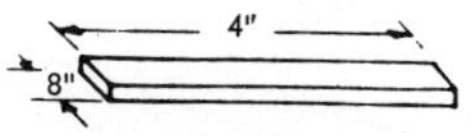
4'
8"

BROAD JUMP TAKE OFF BOARD

BROAD JUMP PIT
9' x 15' Min.

RUNWAY
125' OR LONGER

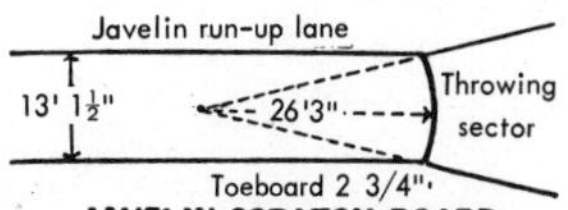
Javelin run-up lane
13' 1½"
26'3"
Throwing sector
Toeboard 2 3/4"

JAVELIN SCRATCH BOARD

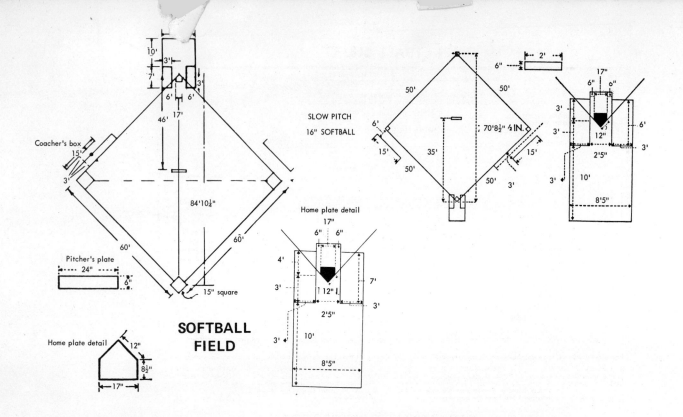

SLOW PITCH
16" SOFTBALL

Coacher's box

Pitcher's plate

24"

6"

15" square

Home plate detail

17"

6" 6"

12"

2'5"

10'

8'5"

**SOFTBALL
FIELD**

Home plate detail

12"

8½"

17"

84'10¼"

70'8½"4 IN.

FOUR-WALL HANDBALL COURT

20'

18"

5'

40' × 20' × 20'

40'

20'

20'

12'

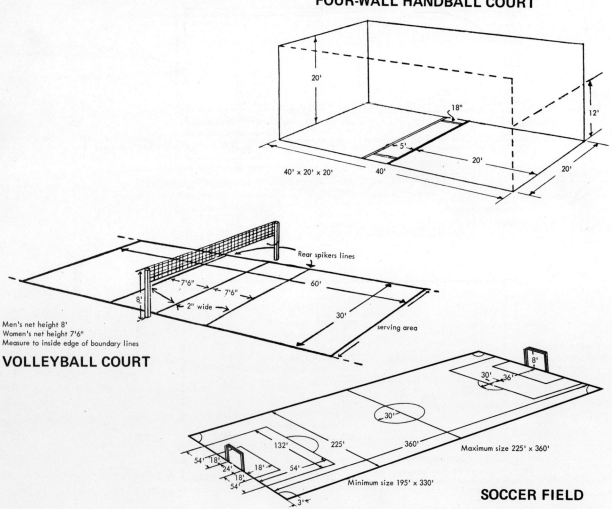

Rear spikers lines

7'6"

7'6"

2" wide

60'

30'

serving area

8'

Men's net height 8'
Women's net height 7'6"
Measure to inside edge of boundary lines

VOLLEYBALL COURT

30'

36'

8'

30'

132'

225'

360'

Maximum size 225' × 360'

54'

18'

24'

18'

18'

54'

Minimum size 195' × 330'

SOCCER FIELD

3'

430